WEST'S ADVANCED TOPICS AND CONTEMPORARY ISSUES

Expanded Coverage for:

**West's Business Law
West's Legal Environment
of Business**

WEST'S ADVANCED TOPICS AND CONTEMPORARY ISSUES

Expanded Coverage for:

West's Business Law
West's Legal Environment of Business

FRANK B. CROSS
Associate Professor of Business Regulation
and
Associate Director, Center for Legal and Regulatory Studies
University of Texas at Austin

WEST PUBLISHING COMPANY
St. Paul   New York   Los Angeles   San Francisco

Composition and Cover: Randy Miyake, Patti Zeman

Index: Lavina Miller

Production, Prepress, Printing and Binding by
    West Publishing Company

WEST'S COMMITMENT TO THE ENVIRONMENT
In 1906, West Publishing Company began recycling materials left over from the production of books. This began a tradition of efficient and responsible use of resources. Today, up to 95 percent of our legal books and 70 percent of our college texts are printed on recycled, acid-free stock. West also recycles nearly 22 million pounds of scrap paper annually—the equivalent of 181,717 trees. Since the 1960s, West has devised ways to capture and recycle waste inks, solvents, oils, and vapors created in the printing process. We also recycle plastics of all kinds, wood, glass, corrugated cardboard, and batteries, and have eliminated the use of styrofoam book packaging. We at West are proud of the longevity and the scope of our commitment to our environment.

Library of Congress Cataloging-in-Publication Data

Cross, Frank B.
    West's Advanced Topics and Contemporary Issues: Expanded Coverage for West's Business
    Law and West's Legal Environment of Business/Frank B. Cross.
        p. cm.
    Includes index.
    ISBN: 0-314-93492-8
    1. Industrial laws and legislation—United States. 2. Trade regulation—United States.
3. Commercial law—United States.
I. Title.
KF1600.C758 1992
346.73'07—dc20   91-43750
[347.3067]   CIP

Contents in Brief

Cross-Reference Chart   x

Preface   xi

1   Business Ethics   1

2   International Business Law   23

3   Individual Employee Rights   43

4   Employment Discrimination Law   63

5   Occupational Safety and Workers' Compensation   83

6   Accounting and the Law   103

7   Securities Law and Regulation   123

8   Mergers and Acquisitions   147

9   Insurance Law   169

10   Real Estate Finance and Liability   187

11   Bank Regulation and Liability   205

12   Unfair Competition   223

13   Advertising Law   243

14   Environmental Liability   265

15   Health Care Law   283

16   Sports and Entertainment Law   301

17   Hospitality Management Law   325

18   Communications Law   345

19   Government Contracts   369

20   Legal Representation of Business   389

Glossary   409

Table of Cases   415

Index   421

Contents

Cross-Reference Chart   x

Preface   xi

1   Business Ethics   1
Key Background,   1
Profit Maximization as Ethical Duty?   1
Obeying the Law as Business Ethics?   2
Sources of Business Ethics,   5
The Requirements of Business Ethics,   6
Does Ethics Pay?   11
Business Beneficence,   12
Putting Business Ethics into Effect,   15
Ethics in the Business Professions,   19
Questions and Case Problems,   21

2   International Business Law   23
Key Background,   23
Performance and Remedies in International
    Contracts,   23
Regulation of Exports,   24
Support of Exports,   28
Customs and Regulation of Imports,   29
Foreign Capital Markets,   35
Foreign Direct Investment,   36
Protection from Investment Risk,   39
Europe 1992,   40
Questions and Case Problems,   41

3   Individual Employee Rights   43
Key Background,   43
Employment at Will,   43
Implied Contract of Employment,   44
Public Policy Exception,   48
Whistle-Blowing,   50
Good Cause,   51
Tortious Discharges,   51
Employee Privacy,   54
Plant Closing Legislation,   58
Additional Employee Rights,   59
Ethical Perspectives: Whistle-Blowing,   60
International Perspectives: Wrongful Discharge in
    Japan,   60
Questions and Case Problems,   62

**4   Employment Discrimination
    Law   63**
Key Background,   63
Title VII,   63
Sexual Harassment,   67
Affirmative Action,   71
Section 1981,   72
Age Discrimination,   72
Americans with Disabilities Act,   75
Ethical Perspectives: Ethics and Comparable
    Worth,   78
International Perspectives: International
    Prohibitions on Employment
    Discrimination,   79
Questions and Case Problems,   80

**5   Occupational Safety and Workers'
    Compensation   83**
Key Background,   83
Occupational Safety Standards,   83
Employer Responsibility,   88
Inspections and Citations,   89
Penalties,   89
Hazard Communication,   90
Record-Keeping Requirements,   91
Workers' Compensation,   91
Benefits,   97
Exclusivity,   97
Ethical Perspectives: The Cost of Occupational
    Safety,   98
International Perspectives: International
    Occupational Safety Protection,   100
Questions and Case Problems,   101

6   Accounting and the Law   103
Key Background,   103
Malpractice Liability to Clients,   103
Liability to Non-Clients,   110
Accountants and Confidentiality,   113
SEC Rules,   114
Management Consulting,   115
Ethical Perspectives: Accounting Conflicts of
    Interest,   118

International Perspectives: International
Accounting Standards, 119
Questions and Case Problems, 120

7. Securities Law and Regulation 123

Key Background, 123
The Securities Act of 1933, 123
Registration and SEC Review, 125
Section 8 Stop Orders, 126
Section 11 Private Actions, 126
Section 12 Private Actions, 127
The Securities Exchange Act of 1934, 129
Insider Trading, 129
Fraudulent Corporate Disclosures, 132
Proxy Regulations, 135
The Williams Act, 135
Regulation of Broker-Dealers, 136
RICO, 139
Ethical Perspectives: Ethics and Insider
Trading, 142
International Perspectives: The International Law
of Insider Trading, 144
Questions and Case Problems, 145

8 Mergers and Acquisitions 147

Key Background, 147
A Factual Scenario for a Takeover, 147
Directors' Duties, 148
Directors' Duties in Mergers and
Acquisitions, 152
State Anti-Takeover Statutes, 160
Greenmail, 160
LBOs, MBOs, and Second-Step Mergers, 161
Federal Regulation of Takeovers, 163
Ethical Perspectives: Stakeholder Rights, 164
International Perspectives: Foreign Takeover
Laws, 165
Questions and Case Problems, 166

9 Insurance Law 169

Key Background, 169
Insurance Coverage Issues, 169
Policy Exclusions, 172
Insurer's Duty to Defend, 173
Wrongful Treatment of Claimants, 175
Wrongful Nonrenewal of Policy, 178
Insurance Company Defenses, 179
Wrongful Issuance of Life Insurance, 183
Ethical Perspectives: Insurance and the AIDS
Crisis, 183
International Perspectives: Insurance and
Europe 1992, 185

Questions and Case Problems, 186

10 Real Estate Finance and Liability 187

Key Background, 187
Real Estate Finance, 187
Commercial Leasing, 193
Real Estate Fraud, 197
Ethical Perspectives: AIDS Disclosure and
Residential Real Estate, 201
International Perspectives: Foreign Investment
in U.S. Real Estate, 202
Questions and Case Problems, 203

11 Bank Regulation and Liability 205

Key Background, 205
Bank Regulation, 205
Lender Liability, 212
Mortgage Lender Liability, 216
Setoff, 217
Ethical Perspectives: An Ethical Duty to
Loan?, 219
International Perspectives: U.S. Banks in
Europe, 220
Questions and Case Problems, 221

12 Unfair Competition 223

Key Background, 223
Wrongful Interference with Business, 223
Trademark Infringement, 227
Disparagement, 234
Robinson-Patman Act, 234
Sections 2(d) and 2(e), 237
State Deceptive Trade Practices Acts, 237
Ethical Perspectives: Opportunistic Behavior
and Business Transactions, 238
International Perspectives: Trademark
Protection and Grey Market Goods, 239
Questions and Case Problems, 240

13 Advertising Law 243

Key Background, 243
First Amendment Rights of
Advertisers, 243
Federal Trade Commission
Regulation, 246
Comparative Advertising, 251
Private Regulation of Advertising, 255
Special Categories of Advertising, 256
Advertising Misappropriation, 258
Advertising Negligence, 259

Ethical Perspectives: Social Responsibility
in Advertising,   260
International Perspectives,   261
Questions and Case Problems,   262

14 Environmental Liability   265

Key Background,   265
CERCLA/Superfund,   265
Environmental Liability in Business
Transactions,   269
Individual Liability for Environmental
Violations,   273
Compliance and Criminal Liability,   275
State Environmental Laws,   279
Ethical Perspectives: Export of Hazardous
Wastes,   280
International Perspectives: Waste Disposal in
Europe,   281
Questions and Case Problems,   282

15 Health Care Law   283

Key Background,   283
Government Regulation of Health Care,   283
Private Regulation,   287
Malpractice,   287
Hospital Direct Liability,   289
Patient "Dumping,"   291
Antitrust Liability,   294
Ethical Perspectives: The Value of Human
Life,   298
International Perspectives: AIDS and
International Health Care,   299
Questions and Case Problems,   300

16 Sports and Entertainment
Law   301

Key Background,   301
Sports Law,   301
Entertainment Law,   309
Ethical Perspectives: Sports Agents and
Ethics,   321
International Perspectives: International
Marketing of Motion Pictures,   322
Questions and Case Problems,   323

17 Hospitality Management
Law   325

Key Background,   325
Guest-Innkeeper Relationship,   325
Responsibility for the Safety of Guests,   326
Responsibility for Guest's Property,   331

Liability for Refusing or Evicting Guests,   336
Reservations,   337
Rights of Guests,   339
Rights of Innkeepers,   339
Licensing and Regulation of Hotels,   340
Licensing and Regulation of Restaurants,   340
Ethical Perspectives: Ethics and
Overbooking,   341
International Perspectives: International
Hospitality Management Law,   342
Questions and Case Problems,   343

18 Communications Law   345

Key Background,   345
Federal Communications Commission
Regulation,   345
New Communications Technologies,   352
Communications Law and the First
Amendment,   355
Mass Media Liability,   357
Ethical Perspectives: Free Press vs. Fair
Trial,   363
International Perspectives: Cross-Border
Broadcasting,   365
Questions and Case Problems,   366

19 Government Contracts   369

Key Background,   369
Types of Contracts,   369
Contract Formation,   370
Contracting Requirements,   371
Collateral Policies,   374
Contract Challenges,   375
Contract Administration,   377
Contract Fraud,   379
Suspension and Debarment,   381
Ethical Perspectives: Government Contracts and
Corporate Codes of Ethics,   385
International Perspectives: International
Government Contracting,   386
Questions and Case Problems,   387

20 Legal Representation of
Business   389

Key Background,   389
Attorney-Client Relationship,   389
Attorney-Client Privilege,   391
Work Product Privilege,   394
Legal Representation of the Corporation,   395
Document Retention and Destruction,   400
Management of Legal Affairs,   400

Ethical Perspectives: Whistle-Blowing and the
Corporate Counsel,   404
International Perspectives: International
Practice for U.S. Attorneys,   405
Questions and Case Problems,   406

Glossary   409

Table of Cases   415

Index   421

Cross-referencing to
West's Business Law, Fifth Edition
by Clarkson, Miller, Jentz, and Cross
and
West's Legal Environment of Business
by Cross and Miller

	Chapter in	Compares with chapter in	
	West's Advanced Topics and Contemporary Issues	West's Business Law, Fifth Edition	West's Legal Environment of Business
1	Business Ethics	2	4
2	International Business Law	24, 56	1, 27
3	Individual Employee Rights	48	16, 17
4	Employment Discrimination Law	48	16, 17
5	Occupational Safety and Workers' Compensation	48	16, 17
6	Accounting and the Law	55	-
7	Securities Law and Regulation	43	22
8	Mergers and Acquisitions	42	25
9	Insurance Law	53	-
10	Real Estate Finance and Liability	51, 52	23
11	Bank Regulation and Liability	29, 30, 34	24
12	Unfair Competition	7, 47	8, 21
13	Advertising Law	45	18
14	Environmental Liability	46	19
15	Health Care Law	-	-
16	Sports and Entertainment Law	-	-
17	Hospitality Management Law	-	-
18	Communications Law	-	-
19	Government Contracts	-	-
20	Legal Representation of Business	55	-

Preface

Even a casual reader of the *Wall Street Journal*, or other business periodicals, quickly becomes aware of the importance of legal requirements in modern business. Detailed government regulations and multimillion-dollar liability actions have become an integral part of conducting businesses of all types. Consequently, a solid understanding of the law and the legal environment is critical in today's business world.

West's Advanced Topics and Contemporary Issues goes into greater detail than the typical business law or legal environment text on some of the most pressing issues confronting business today. It also addresses special legal topics that are not covered in these introductory texts.

The chapters can be used in any order. Students will gain much greater value from the book, however, by using it to build upon knowledge gained from their business law or legal environment of business text. The book can be used in tandem with an introductory text or in a follow-up course.

West's Advanced Topics and Contemporary Issues is keyed to two texts—*West's Business Law, Fifth Edition* and *West's Legal Environment of Business*. There are numerous specific references to these texts. Consequently, this text will be of particular value to students who use or have used *West's Business Law, Fifth Edition* or *West's Legal Environment of Business*.

Coverage

West's Advanced Topics and Contemporary Issues begins by introducing two topics of critical concern today: business ethics and international business law. These first two chapters provide a detailed analysis of these topics, building upon the discussion of business ethics and international business law found in business law and legal environment texts. Ethical concerns are also addressed in each succeeding chapter.

The next twelve chapters offer expanded and more detailed coverage of selected topics covered in business law and legal environment texts. The topics selected involved legal issues which are of particular importance in management, finance, accounting, and marketing. Some of the issues covered in this section are employee rights, mergers and acquisitions, accountant liability, and advertising law.

The remaining six chapters of the text address legal topics of special concern in business. This last section deals with issues that are generally not covered in business law and legal environment texts. Some the topics involve the unique legal problems faced by particular industries, such as the health care industry and the hospitality management industry. Other topics are of general interest, such as the legal representation of business.

Special Features

In addition to the expanded coverage and special topics described above, this text also contains special features to enhance student understanding.

Ethical Perspectives   After Chapter 2, each chapter concludes with an "Ethical Perspective" that relates to the subject matter of the chapter. Ethics has become a critical concern of businesspersons and is an integral part of business law and legal environment courses.

The "Ethical Perspective" for each chapter analyzes an ethical concern that is both current and controversial. Different perspectives of the ethical controversy are presented. The text then attempts to offer some resolution to these ethical dilemmas that confront business.

International Perspectives   In light of the increased importance of international business and applicable legal standards, Chapters 3 through 20 conclude with an "International Perspective." As business becomes more global in scope, managers have a greater need to understand the international legal environment.

The "International Perspective" for each chapter discusses issues that are relevant to that chapter. While it is obviously impossible to detail every international legal requirement for a given issue, the text selects highly relevant and representative international requirements. For example, the text discusses the environmental law controlling hazardous waste in Europe and the law of employer–employee relations in Japan.

Cases   In order to illustrate and amplify important legal principles discussed in the text, excerpted cases are interspersed throughout each chapter. Most of the cases have been decided recently, but some classic cases are included when they stand as landmarks in the law.

Each case presented in *West's Advanced Topics and Contemporary Issues* follows a special format: case title and full case citation, background and facts, case excerpt, and discussion and remedy.

Exhibits   When appropriate, the text contains exhibits to illustrate important legal principles or rules. These exhibits are designed to enhance the material and aid the reader's understanding of the legal concepts discussed.

Questions and Case Problems   Each chapter ends with questions and case problems. Some questions are hypothetical and are intended to help review the understanding of key legal issues in the chapter. Others are actual cases that exemplify the issues discussed in the chapter. The answers to the questions and case problems are available free to professors and can be placed on reserve in the library for students.

Acknowledgments

Many individuals have contributed to this inaugural edition. I wish to thank my editor, Clyde Perlee, Jr., who provided the basic ideas for this text and provided considerable assistance in designing its framework. Jan Lamar, Bette Darwin, and Bridget Neumayr of West also provided substantial assistance. Roger LeRoy Miller performed helpful service in reviewing the chapters for this text and in providing many useful suggestions and comments. Morli Fidler and Bill Stapleton assisted me greatly in researching the issues addressed in this text.

Of course, any errors that may remain are my own responsibility. Please write to me with any ideas about how to improve the usefulness of this work. This is a first edition that doubtless can benefit greatly from the ideas and suggestions of adopters. I welcome your ideas, so that I can incorporate them in subsequent editions.

This is dedicated to Pam.

CHAPTER ONE

Business Ethics

▰ KEY BACKGROUND

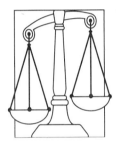

Business ethics seems to some a contradiction in terms. The concept of ethical business took a black eye in the 1980s, with misconduct in the savings and loan industry, insider trading, "junk bonds," Department of Defense supplier overcharges and other scandals. Yet most Americans believe that business should behave ethically. The exact nature of the ethical obligations of business is not so clear. This chapter will set forth the sources of business ethics, the scope of ethical duties, and the interface of ethics and the law.

The nature of ethical behavior has long been debated by philosophers, some of whom argue for universal rules of behavior, while others argue for a utilitarian maximization of human welfare, and still others employ other approaches. The scope of this debate is well beyond our chapter. Rather, the chapter will focus on how the business context influences ethical duties of individuals.

The specific focus of this chapter will be on the ethical duties of the officer or employee of the corporation. The corporate context is not the only scenario for business ethics. For example, the sole proprietor of a business has ethical duties. The problem of business ethics for the corporate officer, though, is the most common situation and also the most difficult to resolve.

▰ Profit Maximization as Ethical Duty?

Cynics about business ethics argue that business is only interested in making a profit. Some authors on business ethics contend, however, that making a profit is *the* ethical requirement for business managers. It is a useful starting point to consider this position, which contends that the only ethical duty of corporate employees is to maximize corporate profits. This position seems contrary to what most persons consider business ethics. A duty to maximize profits could possibly necessitate breaking the law, polluting of water supplies, cheating on contracts, and other acts that seem questionable.

Yet a case can be made for profit maximization as an ethical duty. Milton Friedman, the conservative economist and Nobel prize winner, has declared: "Few trends could so thoroughly undermine the very foundations of our free society as the acceptance by corporate officials of a social responsibility other than to make as much money for their stockholders as possible."[1]

The corporate employee, even a chief executive officer is, after all, managing someone else's money—that of the shareholders. This surely gives the employee some duty to the shareholders. By what authority do such employees have a right to spend their shareholders' money for whatever purpose the employee deems

---

[1] "The Social Responsibility of Business Is To Increase Its Profits," printed in *Ethical Issues in Business* (T. Donaldson and P. Werhane, eds. 1983), p.239.

"ethical"? What makes such employees ethical experts, anyway?

Suppose that Barbara Bookman is a majority shareholder in Tiller, Inc. William Puckett is Tiller's president and chief executive officer. Puckett decides that it would be ethical to make a large contribution to Planned Parenthood for use in promoting birth control. Barbara, however, for religious reasons believes that use of birth control is immoral. Regardless of whether birth control is ethical or not, why should William decide how to spend Barbara's money for what he personally considers ethical?

It seems clear that corporate officers such as William have some ethical duty to shareholders such as Barbara. It is troublesome to have such officers using "others' money" to advance their own ethical agenda. It does not follow, however, that William's only ethical duty is to maximize Barbara's profits.

Consider the implications of an ethical duty only to maximize profits. Under the most extreme form of this theory, the officer should violate the law, even market illegal drugs, at least if the corporation would not be caught and punished. Indeed, the most extreme form of this theory dictates that the employee should lie, cheat and steal whenever such actions would actually increase corporate profits. Something is wrong with such a theory of business ethics. Even Milton Friedman does not adopt this extreme view of profit maximization. He says that corporations have an ethical duty to obey the law as well as to maximize profits. This leads to a second theory of business ethics.

▀ Obeying the Law as Business Ethics?

A more widely held vision of business ethics contends that business should maximize profits within the bounds of legal behavior. The corporate officer acting within the context of this theory would rely on the government to set the bounds of ethical behavior. If an action is illegal, businesspersons should avoid it. If, however, the law permits a certain business action, and if that action is profitable, a company has an ethical right to take the action.

This theory has appeal, for it reflects some duty to shareholders and recognizes the limitations of corporate employees. After all, what qualifies officers to determine ethical behavior? Corporate managers are hired for their ability to make business decisions, not ethical ones. The laws reflect the ethical decisions of society as a whole and perhaps offer a better ethical guide than the instincts of corporate officers.

This theory is frequently invoked by business. For example, the government recently brought an action against Neil Bush, the son of President Bush and a savings and loan official, regarding allegedly unethical loans that he made. The government argued that Bush had a conflict of interest, when he made loans in order to advance his own businesses. An expert witness law professor contended at a hearing that Mr. Bush had not behaved unethically. The witness emphasized that ethical standards varied from state to state and that Mr. Bush should be judged by the laws of Colorado, where the savings and loan institution was located. Because Bush apparently violated no Colorado statute, the expert argued that his behavior was ethical.[2]

This reliance on the law as the only ethical standard, however, is a misuse and misunderstanding of both the law and ethics. The law was never meant to define the full scope of ethical duties. Earl Warren, former Chief Justice of the Supreme Court, wrote that "Society would come to grief without Ethics, which is unenforceable in the Courts and cannot be made part of Law."[3]

There are two reasons why the law cannot define all ethical duties. First, our lawmakers have limited time and cannot write laws to cover every possible ethical problem. Congress is busy with foreign policy, the national budget, and innumerable other issues. Lawmakers cannot consider all of their own ethical problems, let alone every ethical issue in business. Second, Congress cannot deal well with all types of ethical problems. For example, no law could prevent a person from lying to friends or parents. Yet such action would often be unethical. Ethics must go beyond the law.

Indeed, it could be harmful for the law to attempt to enforce business ethics fully. The following opinion emphasizes the difference between law and ethics and contends that the law already has gone too far in attempting to enforce business ethics.

---

[2]*New York Times*, September 27, 1990, p.C2 (National edition).

[3]Speech quoted in *Trends in Business Ethics* (C. van Dam and L. Stallaert, eds. 1978), p.9.

■ Case 1.1
**Oki America, Inc. v.
Microtech International, Inc.**
United States Court of Appeals,
Ninth Circuit, 1989
872 F.2d 312

Background and Facts   *Oki America, Inc., and Microtech International, Inc. were involved in a contract dispute. In connection with this dispute, Oki argued that the parties had no contract. Microtech then brought suit for the tort of "malicious denial of the existence of a contract." The district court granted summary judgment for Oki and Microtech appealed. The appellate court affirmed on the grounds that Microtech had failed to meet its burden of proof. Judge Kozinski wrote an interesting concurring opinion, in which he challenged the basis for such a tort as malicious denial of a contract.*

KOZINSKI, Circuit Judge, concurring:

*   *   *   *

Nowhere but in the Cloud Cuckooland of modern tort theory could a case like this have been concocted. One large corporation is complaining that another obstinately refused to acknowledge they had a contract. For this shocking misconduct it is demanding millions of dollars in punitive damages. I suppose we will next be seeing lawsuits seeking punitive damages for maliciously refusing to return telephone calls or adopting a condescending tone in interoffice memos. Not every slight, nor even every wrong, ought to have a tort remedy. The intrusion of courts into every aspect of life, and particularly into every type of business relationship, generates serious costs and uncertainties, trivializes the law, and denies individuals and businesses the autonomy of adjusting mutual rights and responsibilities through voluntary contractual agreement.

*   *   *   *

It is impossible to draw a principled distinction between a tortious denial of a contract's existence and a permissible denial of liability under the terms of the contract. The test—if one can call it such—seems to be whether the conduct "offends accepted notions of business ethics." *Seaman's*, 36 Cal.3d at 770, 206 Cal.Rptr. 354, 686 P.2d 1158. This gives judges license to rely on their gut feelings in distinguishing between a squabble and a tort. As a result, both the commercial world and the courts are needlessly burdened: The parties are hamstrung in developing binding agreements by the absence of clear legal principles; overburdened courts must adjudicate disputes that are incapable of settlement because no one can predict how—or even by what standard—they will be decided.

*   *   *   *

The eagerness of judges to expand the horizons of tort liability is symptomatic of a more insidious disease: the novel belief that any problem can be ameliorated if only a court gets involved. Not so. Courts are slow, clumsy, heavy-handed institutions, ill-suited to oversee the negotiations between corporations, to determine what compromises a manufacturer and a retailer should make in closing a mutually profitable deal, or to evaluate whether an export-import consortium is developing new markets in accordance with the standards of the business community.

*   *   *   *

Perhaps most troubling, the willingness of courts to subordinate voluntary contractual arrangements to their own sense of public policy and proper business decorum deprives individuals of an important measure of freedom. The right to enter into contracts—to adjust one's legal relationships by mutual agreement with other free individuals—was unknown through much of history and is unknown even today in many parts of the world. Like other aspects of personal autonomy, it is too easily smothered by government officials eager to tell us what's best for us. The recent tendency of judges to insinuate tort causes of action into relationships traditionally governed by contract is just such over-reaching. It must be viewed with no less suspicion because the government officials in question happen to wear robes.

Decision and Remedy   *The court affirmed the dismissal of plaintiff's claim.*

As Judge Kozinski indicated, it can be inefficient to "judicialize" all ethical precepts. This fact makes voluntary private recognition of business ethics all the more important. Indeed, failures of business ethics explain a great deal of government and judicial regulation of business practices.

The law is an important part of ethics, however. The law does reflect societal standards of ethics and provides the context in which business operates. There is considerable overlap between legal and ethical requirements. Legal principles will be used to illustrate ethical duties throughout the remainder of this chapter. Prevailing approaches to business ethics inevitably influence the law as well. The following case indicates how business ethics helps define the law of fraud.

■■Case 1.2
First Federal Savings and Loan Association v. Twin City Savings Bank, FSB
United States Court of Appeals, Fifth Circuit, 1989
868 F.2d 725

Background and Facts   *Twin City Savings Bank sold to the First Federal Savings and Loan Association participation in a multi-million dollar loan to Sea Oats of Juno Beach, Inc., a condominium developer. In negotiating the sale of loan participation, Twin City concealed facts regarding Sea Oats' credit worthiness. Sea Oats ultimately was unable to pay off the loan. First Federal sued Twin City for fraudulent concealment. The district court found that Twin City had indeed fraudulently concealed facts but held for Twin City, because First Federal was negligent in investigating the facts and in failing to detect Twin City's concealment. For example, First Federal had access to Twin City's files on the loan, which revealed that Sea Oats was behind in construction. First Federal appealed the judgment.*

RUBIN, Circuit Judge.

*   *   *   *

To permit the perpetrator of a fraud to escape liability because of the failure of his victim to take precautions to prevent deception imposes on an innocent party a duty of care to avoid the culpable conduct of a miscreant.

*   *   *   *

Prosser and Keeton state in their standard work on Torts:

The last half-century has seen a marked change in the attitude of the courts toward the question of justifiable reliance. Earlier decisions, under the influence of the prevalent doctrine of "caveat emptor," laid great stress upon the plaintiff's "duty" to protect himself and distrust his antagonist, and held that he was not entitled to rely even upon positive assertions of fact made by one with whom he was dealing at arm's length. It was assumed that any one may be expected to overreach another in a bargain if he can, and that only a fool will expect common honesty. Therefore the plaintiff must make a reasonable investigation, and form his own judgment. The recognition of a new standard of business ethics, demanding that statements of fact be at least honestly and carefully made, and in many cases that they be warranted to be true, has led to an almost complete shift in this point of view.

It is now held that assertions of fact as to the quantity or quality of land or goods sold, the financial status of corporations, and similar matters inducing commercial transactions, may justifiably be relied on without investigation, not only where such investigation would be burdensome or difficult, as where land which is sold lies at a distance, but likewise where the falsity of the representation might be discovered with little effort by means easily at hand. The plaintiff is not required, for example, to examine public records to ascertain the true state of the title claimed by the defendant. It is only where, under the circumstances, the facts should be apparent to one of his knowledge and intelligence from a cursory glance, or he has discovered something which should serve as a warning that he is being deceived, that he is required to make an investigation of his own.

Decision and Remedy   *The court reversed the district court's judgment for Twin City and remanded the case for trial.*

▰ Sources of Business Ethics

Assuming that business ethics must be more than maximizing profits and obeying the law, ethical behavior is still difficult to define. While the two preceding theories are incomplete, they make important points. Certainly, corporate officers have some ethical duties to their shareholders. Also, those officers are not necessarily the best judges of ethical behavior. Why and when should these employees go beyond the law and act ethically?

One potential flaw in the first two theories is the assumption that shareholders are only interested in maximizing their profits from a corporation. Ultimately, shareholders are people with their own personal ethics. Shareholders may not want their money used in unethical ways.

In addition, a corporation and its officers may have some duty to society, over and above their duties to shareholders. The ability to form a corporation is granted by government. When the government permits a business to incorporate, it grants important benefits to shareholders. For example, the government limits the potential liability of shareholders in corporations. (This benefit is discussed in Chapter 37 of *West's Business Law, Fifth Edition* and in Chapter 13 of *West's Legal Environment of Business*.) Many philosophers believe that corporations owe a duty to society, in exchange for the benefits provided from incorporation. They argue that corporations have a duty not to act in a way that injures the society at large.

Finally, maximizing profits (even within the law) does not usually conform to our sense of ethical behavior. If a sole proprietor (individual owner) took advantage of every legal loophole to trick customers, suppliers, etc., we would probably not think that he or she was acting ethically. Why should a corporation be judged by a lesser standard?

The Requirements of Business Ethics

The above section explained only the reasons why business may have some ethical duties beyond profit maximization and obeying the law; it did not state what these duties are. Defining ethical obligations is difficult. This is an issue that philosophers have struggled with. The businessperson, who is likely not a philosopher, might simply try to live by several general rules. The following rules are widely accepted by our society. Some refer to these rules as "moral minima" or *prima facie* ethical duties that should always be followed. The requirements of business ethics include: (1) honesty, (2) promise keeping, (3) loyalty, (4) the avoidance of causing harm to others, and (5) fairness.

Honesty

There is widespread agreement that people ordinarily should be honest. Honesty generally means that a person should not intentionally lie to, or deceive, another person. Most people expect some level of honesty from others and should abide by this rule themselves. Telling the truth is expected, unless a person has a good excusing condition. Philosophers dispute the conditions that may excuse dishonesty. St. Augustine considered every lie to be a mortal sin, but Plato supported the "noble lie" as necessary to preserve social harmony.

Many philosophers agree that honesty is not an absolute rule of ethical behavior. It is easy to imagine times when honesty may be inappropriate. One common example suggests that a murderous maniac bursts into your house and confronts you on the first floor. The murderer asks you if anyone else is home. No one would argue that honesty requires you to say that your infant sister is asleep upstairs. These examples are unusual, however. As a general rule, honesty is an appropriate guide to behavior.

Honesty is particularly significant in many business transactions. Suppose that Tom Olsen is the chief financial officer of a large company. The firm needs a major loan from a bank for expansion of the company's operations. The company will be more likely to receive the loan if Tom exaggerates the value of its assets on the loan disclosure form. Honesty dictates that Tom report the true value of the corporate assets, even if that may risk losing the loan.

Honesty is a more difficult rule for other types of business transactions. Suppose that Tom is in charge of marketing his company's products. A rigid standard of honesty could require that Tom objectively describe all of the advantages and disadvantages of the product in its advertising. Such a standard might even say that Tom should tell consumers that his company's product is inferior to that of its competitors. While businesses have some duty of honesty in advertising, they need not necessarily adopt such an extreme position.

Like all ethical duties for business, honesty should be considered in the context of business. Tom is a representative of his company, not of *Consumer Reports*. He has some duty to the company and its shareholders. Moreover, Tom is trying to get customers to engage in an arms-length business transaction. These customers are not wholly dependent on Tom for information, and the customers probably do not expect him to be rigidly honest in his advertising. As customers, we realize that advertisers will promote the benefits of their products. Customers are unlikely to trust advertising completely, and they assume some responsibility to protect their own interests. Nevertheless, Tom still has a duty of honesty and should not claim that his product has certain attributes that it clearly does not possess. If he is selling computers, he should not lie about the objective processing speed of his products.

The American Association of Advertising Agencies has its own ethical code. This code declares that its members "will not knowingly produce advertising which contains:

a. False or misleading statements or exaggerations, visual or verbal.

b. Testimonials which do not reflect the real choice of a competent witness.

c. Price claims which are misleading.

d. Comparisons which unfairly disparage a competitive product or service."[4]

---

[4]American Association of Advertising Agencies, "Standards of Practice," reprinted in *Ethical Issues in the Professions* (1989), p.540.

The code sets additional standards and provides for disciplinary action by the Association if an advertising agency violates the code.

Promise Keeping

An ethical duty related to honesty is that of promise keeping. If a person makes a promise to another, he or she generally should keep that promise. Some promises are explicitly made, but others are implied. An agent makes an implied promise not to engage in conflicts of interest, for example.

Promise keeping is also very important in a business context. Our free enterprise system depends on promise keeping among businesses. Contracts are a form of promise, and businesses depend on contracts being made and kept. If companies could not rely on contracts, the system could degenerate into commercial anarchy.

Like honesty, promise keeping is not a rigid or absolute rule. Sometimes a business cannot keep a contract for reasons beyond its control. The law recognizes this in the doctrine of impossibility of performance (discussed in Chapter 16 of *West's Business Law, Fifth Edition*). Other times, it would be inefficient to keep a contract. Society justifies this situation by permitting a company to breach a contract and pay damages to the injured contractual party. Still other promises may themselves be illegal or unethical to carry out. There is generally no ethical obligation to carry out these contracts.

Nor can businesses expect every promise to be kept. Sometimes, a person or business may make a promise out of excessive generosity and think better of it later. If someone saves your life, you may promise them anything, out of gratitude. While you should always consider your promise and your gratitude, you need not necessarily keep this promise to the letter.

A similar situation arises in the business context. Principles of contract require that you keep promises made in exchange for consideration but need not keep all other promises. (This principle is described in Chapter 11 of *West's Business Law, Fifth Edition*.) If I promise to sell my car to someone for $10,000, I must keep that promise, which would be a contract. Promises to make a gift, however, need not always be carried out. If I promise simply to give my car to a student, I

may not be required to carry out the gift. The ethics of breaking such a promise may depend on specific circumstances.

Even a gratuitous promise to make a gift should be kept if the promise has caused the promisee to rely to her detriment. Suppose Red Owl Stores promises Hoffman a franchise. In reliance on this promise, Hoffman sold his previous business, obtained a loan, and purchased fixtures and inventory necessary to running a Red Owl store. Red Owl then reneged on the promise. Both law and ethics would require Red Owl to go through with its promise to grant Hoffman a franchise.[5]

Loyalty

Another ethical issue is that of loyalty, sometimes called the **duty of fidelity**. This ethical duty is highly dependent on the facts of a situation. The loyalty duty is not the same for all persons. A person has a greater duty of loyalty to his family than to strangers. Usually, certain facts must arise before a strong duty of loyalty is triggered.

The business context creates several circumstances in which loyalty is important. Business creates situations in which one person is given a special position of trust and confidence. If Carol Velarde hires Jesse Mack to manage her investment portfolio, Jesse has some duty of loyalty to Carol's best interests. He should manage her investments in her own interests, not his own. He should not invest Carol's savings into his own business enterprises in order to make more profits for himself. If he thinks that it is in Carol's best interest to invest in Jesse's businesses, he should disclose his potential conflict of interest to Carol, so that she is aware of the potential problem.

The loyalty duty is a source of the duty that corporate officers owe to their shareholders. As discussed above, the loyalty duty is not absolute. While loyalty to shareholders is important to corporate officers, this principle does not give officers the moral right to disregard all other ethical duties, such as honesty and promise keeping.

Many difficult loyalty problems arise in business. One area of considerable dispute is loyalty

---

[5] *See Hoffman v. Red Owl Stores, Inc.*, 133 N.W. 2d 267 (Wis. 1965).

in the employment context. In Japan, employees are extremely loyal to their employer and highly dedicated to the company's success. Many of these employees would not even consider leaving their employer for a higher-paying job with a competitor. Of course, Japanese employers also show a high degree of loyalty to their employees. Japanese companies will go to great lengths to avoid laying off workers, even in an economic downturn.

The situation in the United States is somewhat different. Workers show less loyalty to employers, but this may be because they expect less loyalty in return. This argument has been made by basketball coaches at major universities. Many basketball coaches, such as Rick Pitino of the University of Kentucky, have quit their former jobs in mid-contract in order to take a more prestigious or better-paying job with another team. These coaches often justify their actions by noting that the university would be quick to fire them after a losing season. If the coach receives little loyalty from the school, they ask, why should the coach be loyal to the school? The loyalty duty is highly dependent on context and understandings among the parties.

Employees clearly have some loyalty duties to their employer. For example, if an employer informs an employee of an important trade secret of the company, that employee has a loyalty duty not to disclose the trade secret to competitors. Such a disclosure of trade secrets could also be a violation of the ethical duties of honesty and promise keeping.

Avoid Causing Harm to Others

It seems obvious that persons have some ethical responsibility not to harm others physically. At a most basic level, it is unethical to murder someone. One should also avoid doing emotional or financial harm to others. While this duty seems simple, it is actually quite complex in practice. Often it is impossible to do good without running some risk of causing harm.

Consider the environmental pollution situation. Pollution, almost by definition, causes harm. This harm may be to the natural environment, but often the harm will create some health risk to persons. Under this standard, causing pollution would be unethical. Yet an absolute rule

against polluting would be disastrous. The production of electrical power unavoidably causes some pollution. Emission control devices and other measures can reduce the amount of pollution, but they cannot eliminate it. Eliminating all pollution would require abolishing electrical power production. Surely ethics does not require us to forego electricity, which has offered enormous health benefits to Americans.

As another example, the free enterprise system necessarily involves doing at least some financial harm to others. When one company provides a better service at a better price, that company inevitably does financial harm to its competitors and their employees. Yet providing a better service at a better price is at the heart of our economic system and is something to be encouraged. In our current business context, an ethical duty of never doing any harm would be impossible and unwise.

A better conception of ethical duty would be to avoid doing any unnecessary or unjustified harm to others. This ethical rule could prohibit pollution that could be easily prevented. It would also prohibit unfair competition, aimed only at destroying competitors. This rule would also make it unethical to cause harm recklessly or negligently. The ethical duty could be not to cause harm without sufficient justification. Of course, this raises other difficult ethical questions. What justifications should be considered adequate for causing physical or financial harm in the course of doing business?

Fairness

Another widely accepted ethical responsibility is that of fairness. Fairness, though, is even more vague than the other ethical duties described above. While everyone would agree that fairness is good, individuals might disagree about what is fair.

Fairness arises in a number of business contexts. One component of fairness is acting with good faith and not arbitrarily. If the automobile manufacturing company of Sportsco, Inc., is suffering business setbacks, it may have to lay off workers. Suppose the company decides, for simplicity's sake, to lay off all its workers who are of the Jewish faith. Even if this were legal, which it is not, such an action would be unfair and unethical.

Fairness also means the use of fair procedures. Sportsco is a company that has suffered many employee thefts and that is concerned with the drug problem in society. Suppose that Steve, a Sportsco employee, tells the company president about a rumor that another employee, Janice, is stealing from Sportsco in order to support her drug habit. If Sportsco fires Janice purely because of this rumor, is that fair? Such an action seems unfair to most observers. Janice should have an opportunity to answer the accusation and convince the president that it is false. If Janice agrees to take a drug test and a lie detector test, the employer should give her a chance to prove her innocence.

The Bill of Rights of the United States Constitution requires certain procedures for criminal trials. For example, the Sixth Amendment gives each criminal defendant a right to confront his or her accuser. The Fifth Amendment contains a general requirement of due process, which broadly compels fair procedures. These procedural protections legally apply only to the government's actions and not to those of most private employers. Yet the Constitution's requirements provide some guidance about what procedures are considered fair by our society. These procedures offer help to businesses seeking fair procedures. Because the constitutional rules apply to government prosecution of crimes, they need not always be strictly applied to duties of business ethics. Nevertheless, employers should consider these principles when defining their own rules of fairness. Like other rules, the requirements of fairness depend on circumstances and the understandings of the parties involved.

The above five rules for business ethics—honesty, promise keeping, loyalty, avoiding doing harm to others, and fairness—are not a complete list of ethical concerns for business. Some ethics experts have suggested other duties, including confidentiality, due care, respect for liberty and other responsibilities.[6] The five rules discussed in this chapter provide a good foundation for considering the ethical requirements of business.

Applying Business Ethics to Decision Making

It is easy to acknowledge the importance of ethical duties, such as fairness or honesty. It is much more difficult to apply these rules in business decision making. Often these basic ethical duties may appear to be in conflict. At the beginning of this chapter we discussed how the directions of a duty of loyalty to shareholders could conflict with other duties, such as honesty and promise keeping. This creates a moral dilemma that must be resolved. How should a corporate officer resolve these moral dilemmas?

Most people have some experience in resolving moral dilemmas that arise in everyday living. Often, people make moral decisions based on their "gut instinct" about the right thing to do. This approach may yield the proper result; an ethical person usually has ethical "gut instincts." Reliance on this immediate intuition, however, is inadequate to resolve complex ethical problems. Also, one's "gut instinct" may be subconsciously influenced by selfish interests. In many cases, a decision maker should use a more thoughtful and rigorous methodology for making ethical decisions. Pure logic usually cannot answer ethical questions, but logical thought can help reach a better ethical solution. The following analysis can help make ethical choices, when a person is confronted with a moral dilemma. A business manager should: (1) identify the ethical issues, (2) evaluate the ethical issues, and (3) apply the issues to the business context. The manager can then better resolve the ethical problem.

Identify the Ethical Issues

The first step in ethical analysis is to identify or find the ethical issues in question. It is difficult for a person to make a reasonable ethical decision until all the concerns are recognized. Return to the example in which Sportsco fired Janice because of a rumor of drug use and theft. The president of Sportsco may have acted rashly, due to the company's great concern over drugs and theft. If the president stopped and considered the fairness of his decision toward Janice, he or she would be better prepared to do the right thing.

The very nature of an ethical dilemma suggests that two or more values are in conflict.

[6]Dunfee, "The Case for Professional Norms of Business Ethics," 25 *American Business Law Journal* 385 (1987).

Consideration of these values is necessary to define the existence of such a dilemma. Nor can the dilemma be reasonably settled until all relevant values have been acknowledged.

Evaluate the Ethical Issues

Once the possible ethical issues have been identified, the corporate decision maker should evaluate the significance of all relevant values. Sometimes, value conflicts are more apparent than real. An action that seems to violate an ethical duty may not actually do so.

Consider a corporate president whose company, Multinat, Inc., has substantial investments in the country of South Africa. These investments have been quite lucrative for the company and have yielded great profit for the Multinat shareholders. Individuals outside the corporation have protested these investments, because the government of South Africa denies fundamental rights to native Africans, who form a majority of that country's populace. These individuals argue that the company's investments help prop up a repressive government. The president is concerned about whether the Multinat investments cause harm to South Africans, yet she is also concerned about her duty of loyalty to shareholders. This appears to be a dilemma. It is possible, though, that her shareholders do not want to profit from investments in South Africa. If so, this step in the analysis can provide an easy answer to the apparent ethical dilemma.

Apply the Issues to the Business Context

The next critical step of the analysis is to apply the identified and evaluated ethical concerns to the specific business decision at issue. Philosophers debate ethical issues in the abstract, but the businessperson must make a decision in a specific set of circumstances. This chapter already has described how context and expectations can properly influence ethical choices. The correct decision depends on consideration of all the facts relevant to the perceived dilemma. These relevant facts must be found, and the decision maker should ensure that the perceived facts are accurate.

Applying relevant facts can shed considerable light on the ethics of a business decision.

Return to the case of Multinat's investment in South Africa. Perhaps the Multinat shareholders do wish to maximize profits, even through South African investments. A full review of the facts may show that the South African investments are not as profitable as they seem at first glance. These investments may be quite risky, given the unstable situation in South Africa. Such investment may also give the company a bad name in the marketplace. Multinat may be shunned by potential customers and employees. Such facts should be considered in ethical decision making. Of course, the president of Multinat should also consider the possibility that the South African investments could be used to promote reform of that nation's government.

Full consideration of all relevant facts can improve ethical decision making, but it does not necessarily make decisions easier. Say that Diopaper, Inc., runs an old pulp and paper mill in a small town on a river in the state of Washington. Environmentalists complain that the mill is polluting the river, killing fish, and endangering humans who live near the river. Diopaper's executives determine that the old mill is not very profitable and that closing the mill would appear environmentally responsible and enhance the corporation's goodwill towards the public. Here, the company's responsibility to society seems consistent with its own self-interest. A full consideration of the facts, however, might reveal that the old Washington mill employs hundreds of local workers. Some of these workers may not have alternative job opportunities. The Diopaper mill may even be essential to the entire economy of the small town where it is located. How should the company consider the economic effects of closing the mill on its employees and on the small town? What ethical issues are implicated in this decision?

This step in ethical analysis, full factual investigation and the application of ethical values in the business context, may simplify business decisions. In other cases, such an analysis may make the decisions more complicated. In any event, understanding the facts is essential to ethical judgment.

Problem Resolution

The final step in ethical analysis is problem resolution. The above three steps may filter out some ethical problems and show that apparent dilemmas are actually easy to resolve. Unfortunately, some ethical dilemmas truly are dilemmas in which fundamental values conflict. In these cases, the businessperson faces a more difficult problem in decision making.

When fundamental ethical duties conflict, the businessperson is required to sacrifice some ethical objectives in order to satisfy other duties. Resolving this problem should include two important considerations. First, the businessperson can still attempt to escape from the dilemma through "alternatives analysis" (considering more than one alternative plan). Perhaps some alternative policy can achieve both ethical goals. Second, if the alternatives analysis fails to produce an ideal compromise, the businessperson must make a choice between the conflicting ethical objectives and decide which is the more important.

The first step of alternatives analysis is often critical. Ethical dilemmas are too often perceived as binary or "yes/no" decisions. Few real-world problems actually require a "yes or no" answer. Often, some unconsidered third approach is available to help escape an ethical dilemma. Consider the Diopaper dilemma discussed above. Perhaps the company could upgrade or convert the old mill into a more modern, less polluting facility, while saving the jobs of many (though not all) of their workers.

Each new alternative may raise new ethical issues, however. If Diopaper is to upgrade or convert its old facility, this action will cost money. If the improvement is not the best use of corporate resources, this third alternative could violate some duty of loyalty to shareholders interested in maximizing their profits.

Even after searching for all alternative approaches, the moral dilemma may remain. This is a true dilemma, and the decision maker must choose among imperfect options. The conflicting ethical duties and goals must be compared and weighted. The decision maker must choose which ethical requirement is paramount under the circumstances.

Comparing and balancing conflicting ethical duties is not a simple matter. One cannot simply say, for example, that promise keeping is always more important than fairness. The decision maker also must consider the probability that a course of action will violate an ethical objective and must consider the seriousness of the violation. The seriousness of failure to keep a promise, for example, depends on the significance of the promise to the other party. The seriousness of the duty to avoid doing harm will depend centrally on the type and extent of harm that could be caused.

The resolution of an ethical problem is not a mathematical calculation, but requires thoughtful judgment. Ethical values such as honesty cannot be reduced to equal units that can be traded off. A pure utilitarian (concerned only with maximizing human happiness) may attempt to reduce ethical decision making to a calculation. Since happiness cannot be readily measured, however, even such a utilitarian must employ judgment. There are no easy, all-purpose answers to ethical dilemmas in business. Motivation is important. If the decision maker is sincerely determined to make the ethical choice, ethical results are likely.

Another way to improve ethical decision making is to emphasize the importance of ethics to corporate employees. Employees will find it easier to be ethical in a corporate culture that rewards ethical behavior. Many corporations have developed codes of ethical conduct to guide their actions, as described later in the chapter.

Does Ethics Pay?

Corporate officers often seek to justify ethical behavior on the grounds that "ethics pays." Under this theory, good ethics is good business. If the ethical company succeeds in the marketplace, there is no reason not to act ethically. If ethics pays, there is no dilemma between loyalty to shareholders and other responsibilities to society. Unfortunately, the case that ethics pays is not so clear.

There are logical reasons why ethics pays in some circumstances. For a company that depends on repeat customers, behaving responsibly toward these customers should promote future business opportunities. Behaving ethically toward employees can induce better work habits and can help attract better employees. Ethical companies are less likely to suffer the penalties resulting from violating the law.

There are real-world examples of bad ethics having hurt a company. The leader of the investment firm of E.F. Hutton openly "regarded Hutton's retail customers as sheep waiting to be sheared, and he often said so."[7] Perhaps because of this attitude, Hutton engaged in a series of questionable financial practices. For example, it would write checks simultaneously against accounts in Chemical Bank and Manufacturers Hanover Bank and deposit the checks in the other bank. By so doing, it had a period when the checks were credited to its account (with interest) before their other account was charged for the money. For this and other check-kiting schemes, Hutton pleaded guilty to two thousand counts of fraud. In addition to the legal sanctions, the episode destroyed Hutton's reputation in the business community. E.F. Hutton was once the nation's second largest broker; the ethical scandal all but destroyed the company, and it was eventually taken over by another company.

An example of good and profitable business ethics was the response of Johnson & Johnson after persons were found to be poisoned by contaminated Tylenol, a Johnson & Johnson product. Although the company apparently was not at fault for this tragedy, Johnson & Johnson immediately pulled its product off the market in order to protect its consumers, and then promptly reintroduced the product, this time with tamper-resistant packaging. The after-tax cost of the recall alone was $50 million, but Johnson & Johnson almost immediately recaptured its market share in painkillers and established ample goodwill with consumers.

The E.F. Hutton and Johnson & Johnson examples illustrate that bad ethics can be bad business and good ethics can be good business. Unfortunately, ethical decision making does not always pay. A recent article by two Harvard Business School professors found that "[c]ompared with the few ambiguous tales of treachery punished, we can find numerous stories in which deceit was unquestionably rewarded."[8] Ethical behavior can be expensive, giving less ethical competitors a price advantage. Good ethics and profit maximization are not always correlated.

In addition, the economic benefits of ethical action tend to show up only in the long run.

Cultivating an ethical reputation in business dealings may take years. While good ethics may avoid government regulation and legal penalties, these effects also take years. Today's business climate, however, often demands short-run results, creating pressures to cut corners on ethical duties and show more profit in the next fiscal year.

Sometimes ethical behavior will pay off, and at other times such behavior will require some financial sacrifice. It is easy to be ethical when ethics is profitable. Truly ethical behavior requires sacrifices, however. Ethics is tested when self-interest conflicts with ethical responsibilities.

▄▄ Business Beneficence

The above discussion focussed on the ethical responsibilities of business in making everyday business decisions. Another central ethical issue is that of business beneficence, which means doing acts of kindness and charity. Business beneficence may involve contributing to housing for the homeless or to a local symphony orchestra. How appropriate and necessary is it for business to act with beneficence toward its external society?

Many businesses would argue that they owe no ethical duty of beneficence or philanthropy. Rather, they consider beneficence as going "above and beyond the call of ethics" in order to help the needy and improve the community. This action is usually considered praiseworthy. Beneficence raises significant issues, however. First, it is difficult to decide how much beneficence is appropriate. After a corporation has given a contribution to the symphony orchestra, why shouldn't they also give to the opera, ballet, public television, local educational institutions, poverty aid groups, etc. It is difficult to decide which organizations merit contributions and how much they should receive.

Second, beneficence seems a direct taking of the shareholders' money. When a business gives money to a charity, it is donating its shareholders' profits. Perhaps the corporation should distribute the profits to the shareholders and let them decide whether to give to charities. Corporate contributions are particularly problematic when the shareholder may not agree that the recipient of charity is a worthy cause. This risk was illustrated in the Tiller, Inc., example near the beginning of this chapter.

---

[7]*New York Times Book Review*, October 21, 1990, p.13.

[8]Bhide & Stevenson, "Why Be Honest if Honesty Doesn't Pay," *Harvard Business Review* (September/October 1990), p.122.

Of course, much corporate beneficence returns to help the corporation. A company with a reputation for charitable giving to worthwhile causes may be especially attractive to potential customers. An opera fan may be more likely to purchase gasoline at a Texaco station, because of that company's long-standing sponsorship of Metropolitan Opera broadcasts.

Most corporations see some benefit to philanthropic contributions. The Caterpillar Tractor Company's code of international business conduct has a section called "public responsibility" in which the code provides:

> [Another] category relates to initiatives beyond our operations, such as helping solve community problems. To the extent our resources permit—and if a host country or community wishes—we will participate selectively in such matters, especially where our facilities are located. Each corporate facility is an integral part of the community in which it operates. Like individuals, it benefits from character building, health, welfare, educational, and cultural activities. And like individuals, it also has citizen responsibilities to support such activities.[9]

While there may be some business benefit from corporate contributions, this code seems to treat beneficence as almost a duty to the local community.

Corporate law has itself struggled with the legitimacy of corporate beneficence. Under traditional principles, the directors and officers of a corporation were required to manage the company in the interests of shareholders. Some argued that corporate contributions to charity were contrary to this legal duty. The following case is a landmark in the law of corporate charitable contributions.

---

[9] "A Code of Worldwide Business Conduct," reprinted in Frederick Sturdivant, *The Corporate Social Challenge* (1985), p.167.

■■ Case 1.3
A. P. Smith Manufacturing Company v. Barlow
Supreme Court of New Jersey, 1953
98 A.2d 581

Background and Facts   *The A.P. Smith Manufacturing Company, located in New Jersey, was incorporated in 1896. A.P. Smith manufactured valves and other special equipment for water and gas companies. Over the years, the company had made small contributions to local schools. In 1951, the corporate board of directors resolved to make a $1500 contribution to Princeton University. Some stockholders questioned this action. The company then brought this case to court, seeking a declaratory judgment on the lawfulness of its contribution. The New Jersey Chancery Court found the contribution to be a legal exercise of corporate power, and the stockholders appealed.*

JACOBS, Justice.

*   *   *   *

Mr. Hubert F. O'Brien, the president of the company, testified that he considered the contribution to be a sound investment, that the public expects corporations to aid philanthropic and benevolent institutions, that they obtain good will in the community by so doing, and that their charitable donations create favorable environment for their business operations. In addition, he expressed the thought that in contributing to liberal arts institutions, corporations were furthering their self-interest in assuring the free flow of properly trained personnel for administrative and other corporate employment. Mr. Frank W. Abrams, chairman of the board of the Standard Oil Company of New Jersey, testified that corporations are expected to acknowledge their public responsibilities in support of the essential elements of our free enterprise system. He indicated that it was not "good business" to disappoint "this reasonable and justified public expectation," nor was it good business for corporations "to take substantial benefits from their membership in the economic community while avoiding the normally accepted obligations of citizenship in the social community."

*   *   *   *

When the wealth of the nation was primarily in the hands of individuals they discharged their responsibilities as citizens by donating freely for charitable purposes. With the transfer of most of the wealth to corporate hands and the imposition of heavy burdens of individual taxation, they have been unable to keep pace with increased philanthropic needs. They have therefore, with justification, turned to corporations to assume the modern obligations of good citizenship in the same manner as humans do. Congress and state legislatures have enacted laws which encourage corporate contributions, and much has recently been written to indicate the crying need and adequate legal basis therefor[e]....

During the first world war corporations loaned their personnel and contributed substantial corporate funds in order to insure survival; during the depression of the 1930s they made contributions to alleviate the desperate hardships of the millions of unemployed; and during the Second World War they again contributed to insure survival. They now recognize that we are faced with other, though nonetheless vicious, threats from abroad which must be withstood without impairing the vigor of our democratic institutions at home and that otherwise victory will be pyrrhic indeed. More and more they have come to recognize that their salvation rests upon sound economic and social environment which in turn rests in no insignificant part upon free and vigorous nongovernmental institutions of learning. It seems to us that just as the conditions prevailing when corporations were originally created required that they serve public as well as private interests, modern conditions require that corporations acknowledge and discharge social as well as private responsibilities as members of the communities within which they operate.

*   *   *   *

In the light of all the foregoing we have no hesitancy in sustaining the validity of the donation by the plaintiff. There is no suggestion that it was made indiscriminately or to a pet charity of the corporate directors in furtherance of personal rather than corporate ends. On the contrary, it was made to a preeminent institution of higher learning, was modest in amount and well within the limitations imposed by the statutory enactments, and was voluntarily made in the reasonable belief that it would aid the public welfare and advance the interests of the plaintiff as a private corporation and as part of the community in which it operates.

Decision and Remedy   *The New Jersey Supreme Court affirmed the lower court holding that the contribution was legal.*

A corporate governance project of the American Law Institute has grappled with the law's response to corporate philanthropy. The ALI's corporate governance project has long recognized that the fundamental duty of corporate directors and officers is to enhance corporate profit and shareholder gain. The Institute's influential Principles of Corporate Governance, however, provide that a corporation "may devote a reasonable amount of resources to public welfare, humanitarian, educational and philanthropic purposes."[10]

Some corporate beneficence is regarded as legally and ethically appropriate. It remains difficult to decide how much beneficence is right and where to distribute this beneficence. The following principles can provide some guidance for corporate contributions:

1. The amount of any contributions should be "reasonable" and not threaten the value of the corporation as an ongoing enterprise.

2. The contributions should focus on benefitting the corporation's "community." For some multinational corporations, of course, the relevant community may be the entire world.

3. The contributions should consider need. Rather than giving to the most popular local charity, the corporation should find where its contributions would do the most good.

4. The contributions should consider shareholder opinions. Corporations should avoid contributions that offend the values of a significant proportion of their shareholders.

5. A portion of the contributions should involve areas of interest to the corporation. If a corporation's business activities unavoidably injure the local environment, that corporation should consider making contributions to environmental improvements.

These principles are not meant to be exhaustive, and corporations may reasonably consider other factors. Corporate contributions should not be determined by the "pet charity" of the company's president, however. The beneficence comes from the corporation and should reflect the corporation's position, not that of individual officers.

▰ Putting Business Ethics into Effect

After a corporation affirms the fundamental principles of business ethics, there remains the need to implement these principles in corporate decision making. The company must convince its employees to act responsibly. Three tools for putting business ethics into effect are corporate codes of conduct, social audits, and creation of a positive corporate culture.

Codes of Ethical Conduct

In recent years, many corporations have adopted ethical codes of conduct for their employees. Establishing such a code of conduct can provide guidelines for the actions of employees at all levels in the company. Codes may assure executive officers and managers that a single-minded pursuit of profit should not be their sole objective.

Corporate codes of conduct are especially effective in setting specific rules for situations that can commonly arise. For example, some codes of conduct flatly prohibit payments to government officials, to avoid even the perception of bribery. Another provision might prohibit employees from taking any gifts from suppliers or might limit the value of gifts that could be received. A code can also establish fair procedures for disciplining employees. These specific prohibitions can be enforceable rules for the corporation.

Codes of conduct are less effective for larger and more ambiguous ethical controversies. It is difficult to set clear rules for issues such as product quality or environmental protection. Many corporate codes of ethical conduct contain no provisions for these large issues. One study found that only 20 percent of corporate ethical codes mentioned environmental affairs, and only 35 percent of the codes mentioned civic and community affairs.[11] When codes do address large issues, their provisions are typically quite vague.

Notwithstanding these limitations, writing a code of ethical conduct can be valuable. The simple act of writing such a code "is in itself worthwhile, especially if it forces a large number of people in the firm to think through, in a fresh way, their mission and the important obligations they as a group and as individuals have to the firm, each other, their clients or customers, and society as a whole."[12] The mere presence of such a code can encourage employees to act ethically

---

[10]*Principles of Corporate Governance and Structure: Restatement and Recommendations*, section 2.01(c) (Tent. Draft No. 2, 1984).

[11]Donald Cressey & Charles Moore, "Manager Values and Codes of Ethics," 25 *California Management Review* (Summer 1983), p.56.

[12]Richard T. DeGeorge, *Business Ethics* (1986), pp. 345-346.

Exhibit 1-1

TOPICS COVERED IN CORPORATE ETHICS CODES

Issue	% of companies dealing with this issue in their codes of ethics
Relations with U.S. Government	76.7%
Employee Duties to Corporation	69.0%
Responsibility to Customers and Suppliers	75.0%
Relations with Foreign Governments	42.2%
Community Affairs	34.5%
Environmental Affairs	19.8%
Personal Character Issues	9.5%

Source: Donald Cressey & Charles Moore, "Manager Values and Codes of Ethics," 25 *California Management Review* (Summer 1983), p.56.

---

and reassure customers and the public of the corporation's good intentions. Standing alone, an ethical code has only limited benefit. The principles of the code must be reinforced by supervisors and other corporate officers. The code also should be transmitted directly from the corporate president to employees throughout the company.

A 1986 study by the Center for Ethics at Bentley College found that nearly 80 percent of the companies surveyed were taking steps to implement ethical concerns in daily operations.[13]

[13]Center for Business at Bentley College, "Are Corporations Institutionalizing Ethics?," 5 *Journal of Business Ethics* (1986), p.85.

Of the companies that were implementing ethics policies, 93 percent were using some corporate code of ethics. Nearly every major American corporation has some form of ethical code in effect.

These corporate codes vary considerably and address a range of topics. The issues covered in corporate codes of ethics, as found in one study, are displayed in Exhibit 1-1.

Adoption and enforcement of a corporate code of ethics can have legal benefits for a company. The following decision used a code of ethics as an important factor in ruling for a defendant.

■ Case 1.4
O'Connor v.
CertainTeed Corporation
United States District Court for the
Eastern District of Pennsylvania, 1990
Civil Action No. 87-3866

Background and Facts Glidden O'Connor, employed by CertainTeed Corporation, was promoted to Vice-President. He thus became a participant in CertainTeed's Executive Retirement Plan, which provided deferred compensation. Payments would not be made under the plan if a participant voluntarily resigned or was fired for cause. In 1985, CertainTeed became aware that O'Connor had given corporate contracts to his personally-owned company without disclosing that fact, in violation of the CertainTeed code of ethics. CertainTeed resolved to fire O'Connor but, in recognition of his service, the company offered to allow him to resign. O'Connor agreed to resign.

CertainTeed refused to pay O'Connor benefits under the retirement plan. O'Connor claimed that his resignation was not voluntary and that he was due pension benefits. O'Connor sued to recover these benefits.

SHAPIRO, United States District Judge.

* * * *

Since March, 1974, CertainTeed has had a written Business Code of Ethics and Conduct Policy ("Code of Ethics"). The Code of Ethics lists certain prohibited activities and provides that situations possibly creating conflicts must be disclosed. In the case of a group president, such disclosure must be made to the Chief Executive Officer, who reports to the Board of Directors on the possible conflict. For certain activities, such as an outside directorship, the Code of Ethics requires that employees obtain prior approval of the Board of Directors.

The Code of Ethics also requires annual completion of a "Business Code of Ethics and Conduct Statement and Questionnaire" ("Code of Ethics Statement" or the "Statement") by certain employees including Vice-Presidents. The Code of Ethics Statement requires that the employee set forth activities resulting in possible conflicts of interest, such as CertainTeed employment of any immediate family member or ownership interest in an entity doing business with or competing with CertainTeed or its subsidiaries.

Besson became President and Chief Executive Officer of CertainTeed in July, 1980. As Chief Executive Officer of CertainTeed Besson placed great emphasis on the importance of complying with the Code of Ethics. Besson stressed the importance of the Code of Ethics by sending cover letters in 1982, 1983, and 1984 to employees required to complete the Code of Ethics Statement.

* * * *

If O'Connor's resignation had not been voluntary, the court would find that he had been dismissed for cause. Besson decided to ask for O'Connor's resignation because of his failure to abide by the Code of Ethics. O'Connor was given the option of resigning only because he had worked for the Company for so many years and the issue of his entitlement to Plan benefits was specifically and explicitly reserved. On the facts surrounding his departure as established by the credible testimony, particularly the events of the day his letter of resignation was signed, O'Connor could not have reasonably believed he was resigning voluntarily with Company approval and consequent entitlement to the additional benefits he now seeks. His failure to abide by the Code of Ethics in more than one way on more than one occasion was flagrant and clear cause for dismissal.

Decision and Remedy   The court granted summary judgment for CertainTeed.

Social Audits

Some corporations have begun conducting "social audits" that review corporate policies and actions and inform the public of where they stand on key social issues. There is no defined structure for social audits, which often address and omit a variety of issues.

Social audits are regularly used by European corporations. One very large Swiss corporation, Migros-Genossenschafts-Bund, issued a social audit report conceding that the company underpaid women, provided needlessly boring jobs, and had increased its air pollution emissions over a recent period. Such unusual candor is praiseworthy if the corporation takes steps to correct the problems.

United States companies have not fully employed social audits, but some corporations (e.g., Bank of America, Norton Co. and others) have issued audit reports. It is understandable if American corporations have not been quick to confess wrongdoing. Under U.S. law, such admissions could be used against the company in expensive litigation. Moreover, confessing blame is not as important as correcting ethical shortcomings. Of the companies that conduct social audits, only about half report the results to the public or to their shareholders.

Social audits can be quite beneficial. To be effective, though, audits require a thorough and rigorous consideration of all significant ethical issues. Audits also should be conducted by some independent auditor who has no self-interest in the outcome of the audit. Some corporations have established an office of ombudsman with the charge of conducting ongoing investigations of the ethics of the corporation's activities.

Social audits are not as common as business codes of ethics. The Bentley College survey found that nearly 44 percent of companies had some form of social auditing and reporting. Many of the social auditors, however, came from within the corporation, rather than an independent outsider. Approximately 7 percent of these companies had an ethics ombudsman.

Corporate Ethical Culture

Perhaps the most important method for promoting business ethics is the creation of a corporate culture that rewards ethical behavior. Employees are usually sensitive to the standards and objectives of higher officers. Whether these officers reward or discourage ethical action can have a great effect on ethics throughout the corporation.

In some companies, the prevailing corporate culture can actively discourage ethical action by middle managers. Some corporations have led employees to believe that illegal behavior is practically a job requirement. Many corporations have fired or otherwise punished employees that have "blown the whistle" on illegal corporate actions. Employees caught up in this type of atmosphere will make unethical corporate decisions that they would not consider when acting independently.

Creating an ethical corporate culture should start at the top. Edwin Epstein, a professor of Business Administration at the University of California, stressed that the "ethical sensitivities and proclivities of top management, and, more specifically, the CEO, can and do have a profound impact on the moral ethos of a corporation." The use of codes of ethical conduct and social audits can contribute to a positive ethical culture.

Another measure used to create an ethical corporate culture is ethics training for managers and other employees. In the Bentley College study, 44 percent of responding firms had initiated some program of training in ethics. Most of these programs were addressed to middle managers, but some included everyone from executive officers to administrative staff. While no rigorous studies prove the effectiveness of such training, common sense suggests that the program should have some benefit.

A positive ethical culture has direct benefits for the corporation itself. If employees recognize that the company values ethical behavior, they are more likely to act ethically in many respects. Such employees will be less likely to take corporate supplies for personal use. If employees act ethically toward one another, morale is sure to improve. Companies benefit when employees care about their workplace and their employer.

Of course, even a bad corporate culture cannot excuse unethical actions by employees. Middle managers and other corporate employees can improve the corporate culture from the bottom up. Some such employees have blown the whistle on illegal actions, even at the cost of their jobs. While it is obviously difficult to endanger your own employment, ethics can dictate running such a risk.

Evidence suggests that most companies have a neutral corporate culture with respect to ethics. Business professors have studied advertising and marketing executives to determine whether high ethical standards help or hinder an individual's success in a company. A review of this evidence concluded that executives "appear neither to be penalized nor rewarded based on social responsibility."[14]

▬ Ethics in the Business Professions

The above discussion has focussed on the ethical concerns of the corporate employee, but an increasing number of businesspersons are working as outside professionals, who have their own

[14]Hunt, Kiecker & Chonko, "Social Responsibility and Personal Success: A Research Note," *18 J. of Acad. of Marketing Science* (1990) p.243.

ethical problems. These professionals include accountants, lawyers, investment bankers, consultants, and others who advise and represent corporations. Professionals stand in a different situation from corporate employees.

The typical outside professional works for a company or partnership and represents a client (usually a corporation) who has hired the professional's institution. The professional owes a duty to his or her employer and also owes a duty to the client. Yet the professional also owes duties to the general public, a debt that may be overlooked. The very definition of professional implies a higher standard of duty and care.

Business professionals face a great temptation to cut the corners of ethical obligations. The financial success of outside professionals depends on pleasing their clients. This makes it much more difficult to tell those clients that they cannot take certain unethical or illegal actions. Unfortunately, the weak standards of some professionals contributed to the savings and loan crisis, as illustrated by the following case.

▬ Case 1.5
Lincoln Savings and Loan Association v. Wall

United States District Court for the
District of Columbia, 1990
Consolidated Civil Action
Nos. 89-1318 & 89-1323

Background and Facts   *Lincoln Savings and Loan Association was owned by American Continental Corporation ("ACC"), which in turn was controlled by Charles Keating. In April 1989, the Federal Home Loan Bank Board, which insured deposits in savings and loans, exercised its authority to take over control and management of Lincoln. The Board found that Lincoln was in an unsound financial position, due to the dissipation of its assets by its owners. Lincoln and ACC brought this action to regain control of the savings and loan.*

The case turned on the past practices of Keating and ACC in running Lincoln Savings. The central issue in the case involved a tax-sharing agreement between Lincoln Savings and ACC. The agreement provided that Lincoln would transfer a large amount of its profits to ACC, which had tax deductions to offset the profits. The court found that "the upstreaming of $94 million from Lincoln to ACC on the basis of a contrived tax-sharing agreement was an unsafe and unsound practice that led to a substantial dissipation of Lincoln's assets." In addition, ACC engaged in a series of transactions that produced "paper profits" for Lincoln, thereby causing the transfer of Lincoln's reserves to ACC under the tax-sharing agreement. The court found that the paper profits from these transactions were not actually realized by Lincoln and caused the Savings and Loan Association to become insolvent. The court criticized ACC's manipulation of Lincoln's insured assets and lectured the professionals who were supposedly monitoring the situation.

SPORKIN, Judge.

* * * *

It is abundantly clear that ACC's officials abused their positions with respect to Lincoln. Bluntly speaking, their actions amounted to a looting of Lincoln. This was not done crudely. Indeed, it was done with a great deal of sophistication. The transactions were all made to have an aura of legality about them. They even entered into a so-called formal tax sharing agreement in order to claim they had the approval of the regulatory authorities for this phase of their illicit activities. While it is clear ACC overreached in its relationship with Lincoln, it is not discernible why ACC's officials acted as they did.

There are other unanswered questions presented by this case. Keating testified that he was so bent on doing the "right thing" that he surrounded himself with literally scores of accountants and lawyers to make sure all the transactions were legal. The questions that must be asked are:

Where were these professionals, a number of whom are now asserting their rights under the Fifth Amendment, when these clearly improper transactions were being consummated?

Why didn't any of them speak up or disassociate themselves from the transactions?

Where also were the outside accountants and attorneys when these transactions were effectuated?

What is difficult to understand is that with all the professional talent involved (both accounting and legal), why at least one professional would not have blown the whistle to stop the overreaching that took place in this case.

Decision and Remedy   *The court granted judgment for the government and dismissed Lincoln's complaint.*

In late 1990, the Federal Deposit Insurance Corporation began filing suit against attorneys who represented failed savings and loan institutions, alleging malpractice.

Although professionals may be tempted to behave unethically, the ultimate success of the professions depends upon high ethical standards, which provide credibility and trust. For this reason, many professions have their own strict codes of ethical conduct. For example, the American Institute of Certified Public Accountants (AICPA) has an official Code of Professional Conduct that provides rules for its membership. Article II of the AICPA Code provides in part:

A distinguishing mark of a profession is acceptance of its responsibility to the public. The accounting profession's public consists of clients, credit grantors, governments, employers, investors, the business and financial community, and others who rely on the objectivity and integrity of certified public accountants to maintain the orderly functioning of commerce. This reliance imposes a public interest responsibility on certified public accountants. The public interest is defined as the collective well-being of the community of people and institutions the profession serves.[15]

Other provisions of the code call for integrity, honesty, objectivity, independence, and the exercise of due care in accounting.

---

[15]AICPA, "Code of Professional Conduct," reprinted in *Ethical Issues in the Professions,* p.536.

Questions and Case Problems

1. While still working for Duane Jones Co., an advertising agency, the employees of Jones conspired to start a new firm. After leaving Jones, these employees took along many of their former agency's principal clients as well as many files. Jones Co. filed suit against their former employees. Have the employees who formed the new firm acted unethically? Have they acted illegally? [*Duane Jones Co. v. Burke*, 117 N.E.2d 237 (N.Y.)].

2. Brooks Lee works as a sales assistant at XYZ Co. —a large, publicly held New York corporation. Brooks grew up in a poor family and felt fortunate to get the job. She would rather be an actress but has immediate financial needs that could not be met in an acting career. She has many friends in the theater. At XYZ, Brooks overheard a conversation about a likely merger of the company that would increase its stock price dramatically. Knowing that she could not take advantage of this information as an employee, Brooks tells her acting friends so that they can make enough money to survive in the theater. She saw this as a small correction for society's undervaluation of the arts. The actors buy XYZ shares and profit substantially. Has Brooks behaved unethically?

3. Dale Thomas has worked as an engineer for Perfect Swing Golf Products (PSGP) for many years. The latest product out of PSGP is an attachment for the driver that creates the right "feel" for a perfect stroke. The company developed an expensive marketing campaign for the product and sales have been good. Dale inadvertently discovered that the new product is apt to fly off the driver and injure other golfers. Dale developed a simple safety mechanism to correct the problem. The mechanism will cost little in production but could be quite costly if all the previously sold products had to be recalled. Dale informed his supervisor who told him to "keep quiet" about the problem. How should Dale act?

4. Eddie and Kris received civil engineering degrees from the same university twenty years ago and have maintained their friendship ever since. They still visit at football games and occasionally go on fishing trips together. Eddie is now the president of a large construction company that performs many projects for the state. Kris was recently promoted to the position of construction contract officer at the state highway department and is in charge of reviewing and approving highway contract bids. At a football game, Eddie told Kris that he had the company plane for the weekend and invited Kris on a trip to the Gulf of Mexico for some deep-sea fishing. How should Kris respond to this offer?

5. Bob Maxon works as an account executive at ABC advertising and has made his living in the beauty products area. Bob is currently working on campaigns for a whitening toothpaste and a hardening agent for a nail polish. The toothpaste company is trying to dispel a rumor that their product ruins the finish on nail polish. Bob is wondering whether to provide the toothpaste company with the details of the hardening agent so that they might be able to improve their product. Bob did not sign a non disclosure agreement with the nail polish client, but they did inform him that the product details were a trade secret that should not be disclosed. What action should Bob take?

CHAPTER TWO

International Business Law

▰ KEY BACKGROUND

The essential background for this chapter on international business law is found in Chapters 24 and 56 of *West's Business Law, Fifth Edition* and in Chapter 27 of *West's Legal Environment of Business*. These chapters cover international business transactions and the international legal environment. Among the important points to remember from these chapters are:

- the application and provisions of the Convention on Contracts for the International Sale of Goods

- the provisions for making payments on international transactions

- the United States laws applicable to international transactions

- the laws governing imports and exports.

* * *

Globalization is the watchword for business in the 1990s. International transactions in goods and services threaten to make the concept of a national economic market obsolete. Hundreds of billions of dollars of imports and exports pass through United States ports every year. A new and important development is the globalization of securities markets.

As business becomes increasingly international in scope, legal rules applicable to interna-

tional business must follow. This chapter addresses the key legal issues of international contracting, U.S. regulation of exports and imports, and investments in overseas securities markets and in foreign production facilities. The chapter closes with a discussion of the extremely important economic unification of Western Europe, known as "Europe 1992."

▰ Performance and Remedies in International Contracts

Chapter 24 of *West's Business Law, Fifth Edition*, provides considerable detail on the formation of transnational contracts governed by the United Nations Convention for the International Sale of Goods. This section focuses on requirements imposed after the contract is made. It covers the presence of warranties, performance, discharge, breach of contract and remedies.

The U.N. Convention does not expressly speak of any implied warranties in the goods sold, but certain provisions are similar to warranties. Article 35(2) of the Convention requires that the goods be fit for ordinary use, be properly packaged, and conform to any samples or models provided the purchaser. This Article also requires that goods be fit for any particular use that the purchaser made known to the seller prior to the conclusion of the contract. As under U.S. law, this obligation only arises when the buyer has relied reasonably on the seller's skill in selecting the goods. All these warranties may be disclaimed by agreement of the parties.

Article 41 of the Convention obliges sellers to deliver title to the goods free from any encumbrances and free from any claims by third parties. This goes beyond the Uniform Commercial Code, Section 2-312, which does not require warranty of freedom from third-party claims.

In the event of defective goods, the Convention provides that a seller is not liable for defects of which the buyer was aware or "could not have been unaware" at the time the contract was concluded. For subsequently arising defects, the buyer must inspect the goods "within as short a time as is practicable" and notify the seller of any defects "within a reasonable time" in order to recover damages. The precise meaning of these terms depends on the circumstances of individual cases.

If the seller breaches the contract by providing defective goods, the Convention provides remedies different from those of U.S. law. The purchaser may demand specific performance (the shipment of conforming goods), but only if the defect is so significant as to be a "fundamental breach." A "fundamental breach" is defined as one that "substantially deprive[s] [the buyer] of what he is entitled to expect under the contract." This appears to be a stricter test than under American law. The purchaser may require repair of the defective goods if that is reasonable under "all the circumstances."

The Convention also permits a buyer to avoid payment on the contract if there has been any "fundamental breach" by the seller. The Convention, however, permits a seller the opportunity to cure the defect and hold the buyer to the contract, even in the event of a fundamental breach. This remedy is unavailable, though, when a cure would cause "unreasonable delay" or "inconvenience."

The Convention also enables buyers to sue for damages, both direct and consequential. As under U.S. law, the buyer has a duty to mitigate its damages. Article 50 of the Convention contains an interesting provision permitting buyers who receive defective goods to "reduce the price" paid to the seller. The rules for determining the amount of price reduction are unclear, however, and the buyer must allow the seller to attempt to cure the nonconforming goods before reducing the price paid. Foreseeability of damages is also a condition on recovery.

The Convention's rules for risk of loss are similar to those of U.S. law. Article 67 provides that the buyer bears the risk of loss to the goods once the goods are handed over by the seller to the first carrier, even if that carrier is a local trucker. The parties may change this rule by contract, however, and provide that the seller would bear the risk of loss until the goods reach the buyer's place of business.

If a buyer breaches a contract and refuses to pay for the goods, the Convention provides that the seller may bring a damages action for the price of the goods. The seller may win such damages only if the seller has performed to the extent required by the contract. If the seller is unable to obtain the price, he or she may be able to reclaim the goods that were delivered to the defaulting buyer. Such reclamation is rather difficult under American law but easier under the U.N. Convention.

▬ Regulation of Exports

Although the United States generally encourages the export of products, federal law places controls on certain categories of exports. The United States government restricts exports under the Export Administration Act of 1979, as amended in 1981 and 1985. This law is administered by the Department of Commerce's Office of Export Administration. The Act's coverage is quite broad and prohibits the export of commodities or technical data, unless the exporter obtains a license.

U.S. law is not limited to controlling direct exports from the United States. The law also applies to re-exports of United States-origin commodities and technical data among foreign countries and exports from foreign countries of products with United States-origin parts or technical data.

Suppose that CompuTech exports oil production software containing advanced technical data to Taiwan. A Taiwanese corporation then incorporates this software into computers, to sell to corporations in Indonesia. A United States export license is required in order to ship the U.S.-origin goods from Taiwan to Indonesia.

Some exporters are also subject to the Arms Export Control Act, which applies to exports of defense-related products, services and technical data. Exporters subject to this act must obtain an export license from the State Department, which can deny a license on the grounds that the export is inconsistent with U.S. foreign policy interests.

The Export Administration Act and Arms Export Control Act enable the President to restrict exports as necessary for national interest. The greatest use of the Act has been to restrict exports of military-significant commodities and technology to communist countries. The Act also authorizes restrictions as necessary to "protect the domestic economy from the excessive drain of scarce materials" and "to further significantly the foreign policy of the United States and to fulfill its international responsibilities."[1] When a grain shortage occurred in the 1970s, export controls were placed on soybeans and grains.

The Department of Commerce maintains a Commodity Control List (CCL) that contains all the commodities subject to export regulation. The list is based on factors such as the potential military uses of the goods, how advanced the technology involved is, and the availability of comparable goods from other nations. The CCL is an almost two-hundred-page listing of products and components. Computer equipment has been especially sensitive.

In addition to the commodities list, the Department's Office of Export Administration also regulates export of technical data, which is defined as "information of any kind that can be used, or adopted for use, in the design, production, manufacture, utilization or reconstruction of articles or materials."[2]

Export Licensing

The Commerce Department enforces its export regulations through a process of licensing. Federal regulations prevent the export of any commodities or technical data until a license is obtained. The Export Administration Act provides for two different types of licenses: the **General License** and the Validated License. The **Validated License** is the more restrictive of the two.

A Validated License is required for the export of certain products listed on the Commodity Control List, for certain technical data, and for

exports to certain destination countries. When the Validated License is required, the government scrutinizes specific shipments to consider whether to grant a license.

To obtain a Validated License, a company first needs a customer. The Commerce Department generally requires an "order" from a foreign person or firm for a particular commodity or technical data. The next step is to determine whether a Validated License is required by the export regulations, which can be a complicated determination. The company then applies for a License to fill the order, with full documentation regarding (i) the materials to be exported, (ii) the destination country, (iii) the names and addresses of all parties, and (iv) the proposed utilization of the exported commodity.

The Commerce Department generally approves such license requests within three weeks, when the shipper may go forward with the export. The license typically requires shipment only to the approved destination country and may contain other restrictions, such as the use of the exports by the foreign nation. When shipment is made, the company posts this fact on the reverse of the Validated License form and returns it to the Commerce Department.

In addition to applying for a Validated License, the exporter also generally must submit a Form DIB-629P, a consignee and purchaser statement. This form must be completed by the importer in the foreign country and restates the essential facts of the export transaction as set forth in the application. This is to prevent the unauthorized diversion of exported commodities.

A company may avoid some of the complexity of the Validated License by obtaining a **Distribution License**. This Distribution License permits an exporter to ship even commodities requiring a Validated License to certain destination countries (e.g., any nation in the Western Hemisphere except Cuba). In order to obtain a Distribution License, the exporter must gain advance approval of the Office of Export Administration and must have a written agreement in which the importer agrees to comply with U.S. export control restrictions.

For many commodities, a company can use the more flexible General License, which requires no government documentation for specific exports. There are different types of General Licenses. One

---

[1] 50 U.S.C. Sec. 2402(2).
[2] 15 C.F.R. Sec. 379.1(a).

type authorizes the export of commodities to certain specified countries in a single shipment, up
to a certain total value specified in the license.
Another type of General License authorizes the
export of technical data that is "generally available" or of scientific or educational data to all destinations. Obtaining a General License simplifies
the export process.

An exporter must do some research to determine if it qualifies for a general license. At minimum, the exporter must employ the following
procedure:

1. Check to see if the commodity is on the CCL.
If so, make a note of the Export Commodity
Control Number ("ECCN").

2. Check to see if the destination country is on
the embargo list, which requires a Validated
License for any exports. Embargoed countries
include Libya, North Korea and Cuba.

3. If the country is not embargoed, check to see
of the destination country requires a validated
license for the quantity of the ECCN commodity to be exported.

4. Check to see that the exported commodity does
not contain technical data requiring a Validated
License (e.g., electronic equipment containing
computer software).[3]

The Export Act also places record-keeping
requirements on exporters. These records must
include all correspondence, contracts, financial
records and "other written matter" relating to an
export transaction. These records must be retained
for two years.

---

[3]J. Land & D. Hall, "Overview of the U.S. Export Administration Regulations," 10 *Whittier L. Rev.* 305 (1988).

Enforcement and Penalties

The Export Administration Act makes licensees
strictly liable for compliance with the terms of
their license, and penalties under the Act can be
severe. Whoever knowingly violates the act is
punishable by a fine of up to five times the value
of the exports involved and imprisonment for up
to five years. Willful exports to a prohibited
destination country are subject to potentially
greater sanctions. Even inadvertent violations can
yield fines of up to $100,000. In one case, a com-
pany exported $3 million in equipment to the
Soviet Union for an air traffic control system.
Before obtaining the required Validated License,
the company went forward with the exports.
Although the license was eventually granted (with
many conditions), the company was found criminally liable for violation of the Export
Administration Act and fined $3 million.

In the 1980s, a California company purchased
airplanes, which it routed through West Germany,
France, and Benin, before delivering the planes
to Libya. At least one of the planes became part
of the Libyan air force. This was in violation of
the company's license with the Commerce
Department. The company's owner was given a
fifteen-year jail sentence and a fine in excess of
$6 million.[4]

The penalties under the Export
Administration Act and Arms Control Act are
criminal, so the government must prove the
willfulness of the violation. In the following recent
case, the government failed to meet this burden.

---

[4]*United States v. Elkins*, 885 F.2d 775 (11th Cir. 1989).

■ **Case 2.1**
United States v.
Adames
United States Court of Appeals
Eleventh Circuit, 1989
878 F.2d 1374

Background and Facts   *Ivonne Adames was a vice-consul at the
Panamanian consulate in Miami, Florida. Her brother, Ivan Blasser,
owned a security firm in Panama. Blasser began traveling to Miami
to purchase supplies, including firearms, from a police surplus store
in Miami. Adames obtained letters from the Panamanian consulate
authorizing her brother's purchases and delivered the goods to Air
Panama for shipment to his Panamanian address. She also cosigned
the shipment forms. One of these forms included an "Export Notice,"
which stated that certain products could not be exported without a
license.*

After relations between the U.S. and Panama had deteriorated, Adames refused to sign the export forms. An inexperienced sales clerk released the firearms, however, without her or her brother's signature. Blasser then delivered the guns to Air Panama for shipment, but they were seized by the Customs Department. Adames then issued a back-dated consular letter authorizing the purchase of the firearms. The exports were unlicensed, and the Customs Department prosecuted Adames under the Arms Export Control Act. A jury found her guilty, but the district judge overturned the verdict and entered a judgment of acquittal. The government appealed this decision.

Per Curiam.

* * * *

The commercial export of arms and ammunition from the United States is governed by the Arms Export Control Act (AECA), 22 U.S.C.A. § 2778, and the International Traffic in Arms Regulations, 22 C.F.R. §§ 121-30. Persons desiring to export certain listed munitions must register with the State Department's Office of Munitions Control and obtain an export license for each shipment of arms abroad. 22 C.F.R. §§ 122-23. It is undisputed that Adames twice assisted her brother in exporting controlled firearms without having obtained a license, as alleged in the indictment.

Section 2778(c), however, imposes criminal sanctions only on those persons who "willfully" violate the AECA and the regulations promulgated thereunder. 22 U.S.C.A. § 2778(c) (West Supp.1989). In *United States v. Davis*, 583 F.2d 190 (5th Cir.1978), the court held that this requirement of willfulness connotes a voluntary, intentional violation of a known legal duty. *Id.* at 193 (adopting the Ninth Circuit's analysis in *U.S. v. Lizarraga-Lizarraga*, 541 F.2d 826 (9th Cir.1976)). "Because the items covered by the statute are spelled out in administrative regulations and include items not known generally to be controlled by the government, [we infer] that Congress did not intend to impose criminal penalties on innocent or negligent errors." Davis, 583 F.2d at 193.

The government acknowledges its burden of proving specific intent under each count of the indictment; it concedes that it must prove that Adames knew that it was unlawful to export the unregistered firearms. *See id.* On appeal, the United States asserts, as it did in the court below, that Adames' execution of the Export Notice and her conduct throughout this period of time amply supports the inference that she acted willfully.

Having studied the transcription of the testimony elicited at trial, especially those portions to which the government eludes, we conclude that the government failed to prove that Adames acted willfully. The evidence demonstrates, at most, that Adames was negligent in not investigating the legal prerequisites to the exportation of firearms. It does not prove that she intentionally violated a known legal duty not to export the firearms or purposefully perpetuated her ignorance of the AECA to avoid criminal liability. Though it reasonably could be inferred from Adames' suspicious conduct that she was aware of the generally unlawful nature of her actions, that state of mind is insufficient to sustain a finding of guilt under a statute requiring specific intent. *See United States v. Frade*, 709 F.2d 1387, 1392-93 (11th Cir.1983); *United States v. Hernandez*, 662 F.2d 289, 292 (5th Cir.1981).

Decision and Remedy *The court affirmed the judgment of acquittal.*

In addition to fines and imprisonment, the State Department may revoke or suspend the export privileges of a company. The law creates a presumption of denial of export licenses to those who have been convicted of violations of the Arms Export Control Act.

Whatever the type of license, an exporter generally must file a Shipper's Export Declaration. This Declaration must be presented to customs officials at the point where the exports leave the U.S. The Shipper's Export Declaration must contain the name and address of the parties to the transaction, a description of the exported commodities, and the license number for the exports. For many commodities, the Export Administration Regulations require a "destination control statement" on the invoice or bill of lading. This specifies the intended destination of the exports, in order to prevent their diversion.

In 1988, Congress liberalized somewhat the export controls on computers. While exporters once needed a license merely to export floppy disks, they now can sell computers with an 80286 processor to the Soviet Union. In addition, a new general license permits shipment of many computers to a specified group of about 20 countries (most of the world's industrialized nations). A special license is no longer required to export even mid-range computers to a country such as Germany. This new liberalization does not apply to advanced generation supercomputers, however.

Support of Exports

United States law encourages and supports the export of products not prohibited by the above statutes. The U.S. runs a trade deficit of tens of billions of dollars annually, and increased exports are critical to correct the deficit. Current levels of exports account for approximately 9 percent of our gross national product.

One key piece of legislation in this area is the Export Trading Company Act of 1982. This law enables groups of companies to combine their skills and efforts to promote exports from the United States. When applicable, the Export Trading Company Act grants such combinations an exemption from the prohibitions of United States antitrust laws.

The Export Trading Company Act permits exporters to obtain certificates of review from the Commerce Department to protect their actions. The certificate will be granted unless there is a substantial likelihood that the exporter's activities will have an anticompetitive effect within the United States. Obtaining such a certificate does not guarantee protection from the antitrust laws, as the government may still sue if the export combination threatens clear and irreparable harm in the U.S. The Act does create a presumption that the exporters' actions are legal. The certificate also limits the damages that must be paid, even if the exporter loses an antitrust action.

The National Machine Tool Builders' Association applied for such a certificate of exemption. The member companies of this Association produce metal forming machine tools, woodworking machinery, robotics tools, and other important products. In order to promote U.S. exports of these products, the Association obtained the authority to engage in **joint bidding** for overseas sales and reach agreements regarding to the interface specifications of these products. This type of agreement among competitors is generally proscribed by U.S. antitrust laws but may be permitted to expand exports.

The United States government also provides other incentives to exporters. The International Trade Administration in the Department of Commerce has 48 district offices that provide information on foreign sales opportunities and also provide services to locate foreign buyers for U.S. exporters.

The Export-Import Bank is a government corporation that provides financing to support export activities. To qualify for Eximbank financing support, the exporter must show that the goods to be exported are of United States origin and must agree to use a U.S.-registered ship for carriage.

▀▀ Customs and Regulation of Imports

The law of importing products into the United States is elaborate and potentially confusing. The relevant laws are generally under the auspices of the Customs Service, an agency of the Department of the Treasury.

Most importing is done by licensed customs brokers, who act as agents for importers. Entry documents for imports must be filed within five days and must include the **bill of lading**, the commercial invoice, and certain forms required by the Customs Service. An entry summary must be filed within ten days, including the estimated customs user fees and duties owed on the imported goods.

Duties

Merchandise that is imported into the United States is either duty-free or dutiable. All goods are presumed subject to duty (a tariff charge) unless specifically exempted. When goods are subject to duty, the rates are usually set on an *ad valorem* basis (based on the value of the goods). Such an *ad valorem* rate might be five percent of the estimated value of the imported goods, plus 50 cents per pound of goods brought into the country. These rates are found on tariff schedules published by the government. Value is usually based on the amount actually paid for the imported goods by the importer.

Rates vary depending on the classification of goods as a particular type. Some categories of merchandise must pay a much higher duty than other categories. The tariff schedules contain over 6700 distinct product categories with associated duty rates. When classifying goods, Customs and the courts look to the "common and commercial" meaning of the description of a product category.

In a recent illustrative case, an importer of camping tents alleged that its product was "sporting equipment" (with a 10 percent import duty), and the Customs Service claimed that the tents should be classified as "textile articles not specially provided for (with a duty of 15 percent plus 25 cents per pound). The Court of International Trade held that camping was not a sport, so the higher duty claimed by the Customs Service had to be paid by the importer.[5]

The proper classification of goods under the tariff schedules is a common source of international trade litigation. The following decision represents an example of how these disputes are resolved.

---

[5]*Camel Manufacturing Co. v. United States*, 686 F.Supp. 912 (1988).

▀▀ Case 2.2
Richards Medical Company v. United States
United States Court of Appeals,
Federal Circuit, 1990
910 F.2d 828

Background and Facts *Richards Medical Company imports into the United States three different kinds of hip prosthesis systems (for replacement of hip joints) and medical instruments that are specifically designed to implant the prostheses. A 1982 law provides for duty-free entry of articles that are for the benefit of handicapped persons. Congress specifically excluded, however, devices that are considered "therapeutic." Customs initially classified the prostheses as duty-free under the law but assessed a duty on the medical instruments, ruling that they were therapeutic in nature.*

Richards appealed to the U.S. Court of International Trade ("CIT"), which held that the medical instruments were not therapeutic in nature and should be admitted to the country duty-free. Customs appealed the ruling to this court. Customs now argues that the prostheses themselves are therapeutic and therefore should not be entitled to duty-free status.

RICH, Circuit Judge.

* * * *

The first issue, that of the meaning of "therapeutic," is essentially an issue of statutory construction. As with all questions of statutory construction, we start first with the plain meaning of the statute, and then go to other extrinsic aids such as legislative history if necessary. *Johns-Manville Corp. v. United States*, 855 F.2d 1556, 1559 (Fed.Cir.1988).

Customs' primary argument with respect to the plain or common meaning of the word "therapeutic" is that it is not limited to treatments which are intended to be *curative*, but also encompasses treatments which are *alleviative* or *palliative*. In support of this argument, Customs relies not only on numerous dictionary and encyclopedia definitions, but also on prior case law involving the meaning of "therapeutic" in other statutes. For example, *J.E. Bernard & Co. v. United States*, 262 F.Supp.434, 58 Cust.Ct 23, 28, C.D. 2872 (1967) indicates that "therapeutic qualities embrace the alleviative or palliative, as well as the curative or healing qualities."

However the only conclusion we can reach after reviewing the various definitions from different sources which the parties have provided for us is that the word "therapeutic" has many different meanings and is subject to both broad and narrow interpretations. The question is, which definition best invokes the intent of Congress?

The legislative history is not very helpful on this point. However, one example of an item which is not "therapeutic" is given, and this example definitely cuts against construing this term broadly to include alleviative or palliative treatments, i.e., treatments which help the handicapped person live with his or her handicapped condition.

In particular, the Senate Report accompanying the Act indicates that an automobile fitted with special seats for use by the handicapped or with special attachments to permit a handicapped person to operate the automobile are indicated as being within the scope of the Act. S.Rep. No. 564, 97th Cong., 2d Sess. 20, *reprinted in* 1982 U.S. Code Cong. & Admin. News 4077, 4097. However, such a specially equipped automobile is certainly "alleviative" in the sense that it helps the handicapped person to live with the handicap by helping him or her to ride in or drive a car. Thus, to interpret the word "therapeutic" broadly to include "alleviative" would be inconsistent with the one specific example in the legislative history.

In fact, our impression after reading the legislative history is that the CIT drew a very proper distinction in this case. Congress intended to encourage the importation of that merchandise which is designed to compensate for, or help adapt to, the handicapped condition. At the same time, Congress did not want to allow duty-free importation of merchandise which is used to heal or cure the condition causing the handicap.

Which brings us the second, factual issue: does a hip prosthesis (and consequently the instruments used to implant it) heal or cure a person with a handicap or does it merely allow the handicapped person to better compensate for the handicap? The answer to this question lies heavily in how one defines the underlying condition. Customs argues that a person in need of hip replacement suffers from an inoperative hip. Thus, they conclude, it is "difficult to imagine a better 'cure' for a diseased hip than the insertion of brand new components to replace the area affected by disease." Appellant's Brief at 15. Richards, on the other hand, points out that a person who needs a hip prosthesis because he or she suffers from, for example, severe arthritis still has arthritis after the operation. The prosthesis merely allows the person to better compensate for the arthritis.

In concluding that hip prostheses merely help handicapped persons adapt to their condition, the CIT relied heavily on the parties' stipulation before trial that:

> The Prosthetic Systems are implanted in physically handicapped persons in order to improve their ability to walk or even to allow them to walk when they were severely crippled prior to implantation....

The CIT noted that the implantation of prosthetic hips is performed *because of* the incurable nature of the underlying disease, and that the replacement of the hip joint is a "compensatory remedy of a disability and not a therapy." *Richards Medical*, 720 F.Supp. at 1001.

Decision and Remedy   *The court affirmed the CIT ruling that the medical instruments were not therapeutic and were entitled to duty-free status.*

Rates also vary based upon the country of origin. Most countries are granted most-favored-nation status by the U.S. and their duties are lower than those from less favored nations. The country-of-origin determination can be a difficult one, especially when goods have undergone manufacture, processing or assembly in more than one nation.

Other nations receive duty concessions in a special category for the least-developed developing countries. This is known as the Generalized System of Preferences (GSP). Developing countries are excluded from GSP if they are certified as failing to cooperate in the enforcement of narcotics laws, or aiding international terrorism, or having unlawfully expropriated the property of U.S. citizens, among other categories.

Imports of certain goods from these GSP countries are granted duty-free treatment. Approximately 3000 merchandise categories are eligible for GSP duty-free status, including most agricultural products. Countries lose GSP status when their per capita GNP exceeds $8500. Taiwan, South Korea and other countries have succeeded well enough to lose their GSP protection. Other goods also get duty-free status. Intangibles (such as securities or electricity) are not considered goods and are not subject to import duties.

Partial duty-free status is accorded to firms that ship U.S. component parts to a foreign nation, assemble a final product overseas, and then return this product as a U.S. import. Duties are imposed on the value of the final product minus the value of the U.S. component parts. These imports, including automobile and electronic products, amounted to over $67 billion in a recent year.

In addition, there are "foreign trade zones" in the United States that are statutorily declared to be outside the U.S. and therefore free of import duties. While duties must still be paid when the goods are taken from the foreign trade zone into the U.S., the zones provide savings from repacking or assembly of the goods and from direct sales within the foreign trade zone. Merchandise may be held in a foreign trade zone for any amount of time, perhaps awaiting a reduction in rates of duty for the product.

When duties are owed, the Customs Service may accept the importer's estimate and issue a **liquidation**, which is a final determination of duties. If Customs believes that additional duties are owed, it will send a notice to the importer, who may seek a review of this determination by filing a protest. The protest is heard by the Commissioner of Customs, and the Commissioner's decision may be appealed to the Court of International Trade.

Section 592 of the Tariff Act of 1930 provides strict penalties for violations of importing rules. Violation permits Customs seizure and forfeiture of the imported goods, fines of up to $5000 per violation, and imprisonment for up to two years.

In 1989, a South Korean corporation was fined $34 million for false disclosures to Customs officials regarding steel imports.

Import Relief

United States law provides a number of legal protections for domestic businesses against foreign imports. These provisions are designed to insulate the nation's manufacturers from excessive foreign competition. These include the antidumping laws, countervailing duty provisions, unfair import trade practice actions, and what is known as the "escape clause."

Dumping is the name employed when foreign merchandise is sold in the U.S. at less than its fair market value in the exporting country or less than its production costs. An importer might choose to dump goods in the U.S. at such a low price in order to develop its market share. The Antidumping Act of 1921 proscribes dumping that causes material injury to domestic industry.

Proving dumping may be difficult, because defining fair market value is difficult. Some manufacturers do not sell in their own home market. Others may operate in nonmarket economies without established free market prices. Still others may sell directly to retailers in a home market but to wholesalers in the United States. In these instances, the government may consider sales prices in third party nations or production costs as part of a determination of fair market value.

The Secretary of Commerce or any "interested party" initiates a Customs Service investigation into alleged dumping activity. If dumping is found by the Secretary of the Treasury, the Customs Service assesses **antidumping duties** in an amount equal to the extent to which the foreign market value exceeds the price in the United States. An importer may appeal this assessment in the U.S. Customs Court. A Japanese producer of microwave ovens was found to have violated antidumping rules and directed to pay an additional duty of 13.1 percent.

Countervailing duties apply to offset any competitive advantage held by foreign businesspersons due to export subsidies paid by their home governments. As with dumping laws, material domestic injury is required to invoke countervailing duties. Defining subsidies is also difficult. A U.S. Supreme Court decision held that a Japanese law exempting exports from certain taxes was not a subsidy that warranted countervailing duties.[6]

An interested party also may initiate a countervailing duty investigation. The countervailing duties are imposed in an amount equivalent to the foreign subsidy and in addition to whatever normal duty would be imposed on the goods. Both antidumping action rulings and countervailing duty rulings may be appealed to the Court of International Trade.

The identification of subsidies that warrant a countervailing duty finding is a common subject of dispute. The following decision illustrates some of the difficulties attendant to this determination.

----

[6]*Zenith Radio Corporation v. United States*, 98 S.Ct. 2441 (1978).

■ **Case 2.3**
Ipsco, Inc. v.
United States
United States Court of Appeals
Federal Circuit, 1990
899 F.2d 1192

Background and Facts   *A United States company, Lone Star Steel Company, filed a petition with the International Trade Administration ("ITA") claiming that Canadian manufacturers of oil country tubular goods (OCTG) received an export subsidy that threatened harm to the U.S. OCTG industry. This subsidy took the form of investment tax credits and one-time grants. Lone Star sought a countervailing duty assessment against Canadian exporters of OCTG products. Of the eleven Canadian companies that exported OCTG products, nine either received no government subsidy or a subsidy of less than 0.50 percent (an amount that the ITA considers de minimis and insufficient for a* *countervailing duty assessment). Ipsco, Inc., however, received a net subsidy of 0.72 percent. ITA issued a countervailing duty order in that amount against Ipsco.*

Ipsco appealed to the Court of International Trade, which affirmed the ITA determination. Ipsco then appealed again to this circuit court of appeals. Ipsco argued that the ITA had improperly based its assessment of the countervailing duty on the subsidy received by Ipsco alone. Ipsco argued that the ITA should have averaged the subsidies provided to all OCTG producers in Canada. Because this average would be de minimis, *Ipsco contended that no countervailing duty was appropriate.*

MAYER, Circuit Judge.

*   *   *   *

Section 701 of the Trade Agreements Act of 1979 is the statutory basis for all countervailing duty determinations for countries like Canada that are signatories of the GATT Subsidies Code. Section 701(a) provides in pertinent part:

If-

    (1)   the administering authority determines that-

        (A) a country under the Agreement, or

        (B) a person who is a citizen or national of such a country, or a corporation, association, or other organization organized in such a country, is providing, directly or indirectly, a subsidy with respect to the manufacture, production, or exportation of a class or kind of merchandise imported, or sold (or likely to be sold) for importation, into the United States, and

    (2)   the Commission determines that-

        (A) an industry in the United States-

            (i)   is materially injured, or

            (ii) is threatened with material injury, or

        (B) the establishment of an industry in the United States is materially retarded, by reason of imports of that merchandise or by reason of sales (or the likelihood of sales) of that merchandise for importation, then there shall be imposed upon such merchandise a countervailing duty, in addition to any other duty imposed, equal to the amount of the net subsidy.

19 U.S.C. § 1671(a) (1988). "Subsidy" is defined in subsection 771(5) of the Act:

    (i)   Any export subsidy described in Annex A to the Agreement....

    (ii) The following domestic subsidies, if provided or required by government action to a specific enterprise or industry, or group of enterprises or industries, whether publicly or privately owned, and whether paid or bestowed directly or indirectly on the manufacture, production, or export of any class or kind of merchandise:

        (I)   The provision of capital, loans, or loan guarantees on terms inconsistent with commercial considerations.

        (II) The provision of goods or services at preferential rates.

        (III) The grant of funds or forgiveness of debt to cover operating losses sustained by a specific industry.

        (IV) The assumption of any costs or expenses of manufacture, production, or distribution.

Id. § 1677(5)(A). The next subsection defines "net subsidy," permitting the ITA to offset any gross subsidy by certain fees, taxes, duties, and the like. *Id.* § 1677(6).

Neither the countervailing duty statute nor the applicable regulations promulgated by the Department of Commerce, 19 C.F.R. § 355.0 et seq. (1988), specifically state how a "net subsidy" is calculated. The regulations simply provide: "If the Determination is affirmative, the amount of the net subsidy shall be estimated and stated, and the nature of the subsidy determined. If separate enterprises have received materially different benefits, such differences shall be estimated and stated." *Id.* § 355.33(f).

When the net subsidy is de minimis, the ITA issues a negative countervailing duty determination. For example, in Welded Carbon Steel Line Pipe From Taiwan, 50 Fed.Reg. 53363 (1985) (final negative determination), the benefits received by the two known producers of the subject goods in Taiwan were allocated over the value of their exports during the review period and found to be 0.02 percent ad valorem and therefore de minimis. In Pads for Woodwind Instrument Keys From Italy, 49 Fed.Reg. 17793 (1984) (final negative determination), the only company that received countervailable benefits was found to have been subsidized at a de minimis rate of 0.05 percent of its total sales. The Department of Commerce has memorialized this practice by regulation, 19 C.F.R. § 355.8 (1988): "For purposes of this part, the Secretary will disregard any aggregate net subsidy that the Secretary determines is less that 0.5% ad valorem, or the equivalent specific rate." *See* 52 Fed.Reg. 30660 (August 17, 1987). But Commerce did not define "aggregate net subsidy" or say how it is to be calculated. It only stated that, where the weighted-average country-wide or company-specific rate is de minimis, no countervailing duty will be assessed. *Id.* at 30662.

* * * *

It was inconsistent with the concept of a country-wide rate for the ITA to disregard those companies receiving no benefit or a de minimis benefit when it determined the amount of the net subsidy and whether it was more than de minimis. "Unlike the antidumping law, which is directed to company-specific activity, the countervailing duty law is directed at government or government-sponsored activity." 53 Fed.Reg. 52306, 52325. The purpose of countervailing duties is to discourage foreign subsidization that results in injury to a United States industry because of unfair competition from cheaper imports. To assess a countervailing duty against a single company that was receiving a benefit just above the de minimis level, when many other producers and exporters received no benefit or an insignificant benefit, does not advance this purpose.

There is no evidence that the Canadian government subsidized "the manufacture, production, or exportation of a class or kind of merchandise," 19 U.S.C. § 1671(a) (1988), only that it attempted to aid a single ailing firm. Where the overall level of subsidization provided to a particular industry by a foreign government is de minimis, no countervailing duty should be assessed. And, if there is a non-de minimis subsidy being provided, the countervailing duty should not exceed the weighted-average benefit received by all firms that produce or export the subject goods, including those firms that receive little or no subsidy.

Decision and Remedy *The court reversed the ITA assessment and remanded the case for further proceedings consistent with the opinion.*

Section 337 of the Tariff Act of 1930 prohibits certain unfair trade practices in international commerce. The law does not list the practices to be deemed unfair, but section 337 has been most frequently applied to the infringement of U.S. patents or antitrust violations. These cases are decided by the International Trade Commission. Sanctions for violation of section 337 can be severe, including daily civil penalties of up to the total value of the imported goods and exclusion of articles from entry into the country.

The **escape clause** provides domestic companies some relief from imports even without unfair trade practices. Section 201 of the Trade Act of 1974 provides that a domestic industry may obtain relief when an article is being imported in quantities that will be the substantial cause of at least the threat of serious injury to a domestic industry that produces a competitive product.

Under the escape clause, the affected industry first files a petition with the International Trade Commission ("ITC"). The ITC considers factors such as unemployment in the domestic industry, lost market share, and shutdown of producing capacity, among others. The ITC reports its findings to the president, who may increase duties, establish import quotas, or negotiate agreements with foreign nations to reduce the harm to the domestic industry. The president may also expedite readjustment assistance to workers in the affected domestic industry.

For example, a U.S. manufacturer of motorcycles, the Harley-Davidson Motor Co., petitioned for import relief. The ITC found that imports were up and domestic employment was down 12 percent, production was down 36 percent, and profits were down by 20 percent. Importers claimed that these reductions were actually due to a national economic recession. The ITC disagreed and recommended additional duties on motorcycle imports for the next five years at a declining rate (45 percent in the first year, 10 percent in the fifth year). The president accepted the recommendation and imposed these additional duties over and above the prevailing 4.4 percent *ad valorem* duty that already existed. (A 1980 ruling, however, found that harm to the domestic automobile industry was due primarily to economic conditions rather than due to increased imports.)

Foreign Capital Markets

The financial services industry (including securities, banking, and insurance) is increasingly international in scope. Advanced telecommunications and data processing technologies have made international financial transactions far easier. Companies based in the United States can use foreign markets to raise capital through securities issuances.

The legal and regulatory system has not kept pace with the burgeoning international financial business. There is no global international standard for securities transactions. These transactions are governed by the distinct laws of individual nations. Moreover, any given transaction may be subject to the laws of several different nations.

Japanese Securities Regulation

In spring 1987, the Tokyo Stock Exchange surpassed the New York Stock Exchange as the world's largest. Japanese securities regulation is therefore very important. Trading is governed by the *Shokentorihikiho*, or Securities and Exchange Law. The law is administered by the Securities Bureau, under the national Finance Minister.

The Japanese Securities and Exchange Law was modeled on the United States Securities Act of 1933 and Securities Exchange Act of 1934. In order to issue securities, the issuer must register with the Finance Minister. The law makes exemptions, just as U.S. law does, for private placements and small issuances. As in the United States, the issuer must make full and accurate disclosures.

Japanese securities law also has antifraud provisions. Article 58 of the law prohibits persons from employing "any fraudulent device, scheme or artifice with respect to buying, selling or other transaction of securities," from using documents that contain false statements or omissions of material facts or from using a false quotation of prices.

Foreign companies, including those from the United States, may issue securities in Japan, and foreign stocks are listed on the Tokyo Stock Exchange. Offerings of foreign securities must be registered under Japanese law. Additional information is required of foreign issuers, including a statement on the effect of fluctuations in the exchange rates.

Japan regulates broker-dealers involved in the "securities business." To operate securities companies must obtain a license from the Finance Minister. In 1986, Japan opened Tokyo Stock Exchange membership to foreign brokerage firms. The law imposes minimum capital requirements, and the Minister may revoke licenses as necessary for the protection of investors. A foreign securities firm must deposit in escrow at least 5 percent of its capital (at least 10 million yen) for each of its branch offices in Japan.

Japanese law also restricts practices of securities companies. Article 50, for example, prohibits specific practices, such as "offering a statement of opinion definitively predicting a rise or a drop in the price of certain shares of other securities whose prices fluctuate."

Extraterritorial Application of U.S. Law

United States securities laws will apply to a variety of overseas securities transactions. The details of U.S. laws are set forth in the chapter on Securities Law and Regulation, in Chapter 43 of *West's Business Law, Fifth Edition*, and in Chapter 22 of *West's Legal Environment of Business*. Suppose that PacCorp intends to raise capital by offering their securities on the Japanese market. PacCorp may still be required to comply with the registration provisions of U.S. securities law. If the securities of a foreign corporation are traded in U.S. markets, that company is also subject to United States law and regulations.

In 1985, the Securities and Exchange Commission announced that it would not apply U.S. law to certain foreign offerings of equity securities. The SEC required:

1. An agreement not to offer the shares to North Americans for twelve months following completion of the offering.

2. A conspicuous statement on the cover of the prospectus that the securities were not registered under U.S. law.

3. A restriction on transfer of the securities for twelve months to North Americans.

4. A legend on the stock certificates reflecting the above conditions.

5. Purchaser certification that he agreed to the conditions and was not a North American.

The SEC has also announced that a prospectus meeting the requirements of Japanese law will be generally deemed sufficient for compliance with U.S. law, so long as the offer is not made directly to United States residents.

The antifraud provisions of United States securities law also have extraterritorial application. In the first key case, a Canadian corporation conducting all of its operations in Canada issued shares of stock that were traded on the American Stock Exchange as well as the Toronto Stock Exchange. The company allegedly issued shares to its controlling shareholders for "wholly inadequate consideration," thereby diluting the value of the ownership of other shareholders. The court held that U.S. law applied, because the stock was traded in the U.S. and U.S. citizens were among those allegedly defrauded.[7]

Foreign Direct Investment

Rather than exporting goods produced in the United States, domestic companies may choose to invest in foreign operations that produce overseas. The primary different approaches to such foreign investment are a joint venture, a branch office, a wholly owned subsidiary, or acquisition of an existing foreign corporation. Multinational enterprises, with investments in numerous countries, are responsible for about 15 percent of the gross world product. The rules for foreign investments vary by nation. This section will consider national rules in three different categories of nations: a large, industrialized country (Japan); a country emerging from communist rule (Hungary); and a group of lesser-developed South and Latin American nations (the Andean nations and Mexico).

Japan

Japanese law is best understood by an illustration of foreign investment rules. Hypothesize that Wessex Chemical, a United States company, wants to produce and market a herbicide for rice crops in Japan.

---

[7] *Schoenbaum v. Firstbrook*, 405 F.2d 200 (2d Cir. 1968).

The joint venture approach is the most common one taken for U.S. companies investing in Japan. This approach takes advantage of Japanese corporations' familiarity with that country's laws and business practices, as well as the existence of a preexisting distribution system for products. Wessex thus could seek out a Japanese chemical company to produce and market its product. As with any joint venture, however, the participant loses autonomy in making business decisions, which must be shared with its venture partner. Wessex would also have to share the profits from its operation.

If Wessex decides to go it alone, they might create a branch office in Japan or establish a new Japanese subsidiary company. Creation of Japanese branch offices or wholly owned subsidiaries is much easier now than prior to 1980. In that year, Japan amended its Foreign Exchange and Foreign Trade Control Law, to facilitate foreign investment somewhat. The law still restricts investment in some businesses, including agriculture, forestry, mining, petroleum, leather products, and industries pertaining to the national security of Japan. The law places other, general restrictions on foreign investment in Japan. The foreign investor must give advance notice to the Ministry of Finance and wait at least thirty days before proceeding.

An American company such as Wessex, seeking to create a branch office in Japan, must file a "Report on Establishment of Branch Office, Etc." with the relevant government ministries. If approval is granted, the company then must register and appoint an official branch manager. The branch manager becomes the corporation's official representative in Japan and has broad authority to bind the company under Japanese law. Once established, branch offices are subject to little specific regulation, though of course they must comply with the general laws of Japan.

For Wessex to create a new Japanese subsidiary would also require the filing of a report, called the "Report on Acquisition of Stocks." Once approved, the company must comply with the Japanese Commercial Code in the general legal requirements of incorporation. Most Japanese companies incorporate as a *kabushiki kaisha*, or a stock company. The law requires such stock companies to have seven promoters, or incorporaters, which prepare Articles of Incorporation. Then the company must select at least three directors. The company must be officially registered with a local office and provide information on the name, purpose, capitalization, directors and shares of the corporation. Once this is complete, and if they comply with the Foreign Exchange and Foreign Trade Control Law, Wessex may begin business in Japan.

Doing business in Japan also requires familiarity with its system of administrative guidance. The Bank of Japan receives the documentation required by the foreign investments law and provides the administrative guidance valuable to gaining approval of investment. For example, the Bank informs companies of precisely which ministries must review the investment. The Bank can also inform investors of potential pitfalls to their plans. Under Japanese law, ministries may block transactions under any of the following five criteria:

1. Investments must not harm national security, disturb public order, or hamper public safety.

2. Investments cannot have serious adverse effects on Japanese companies in the same line of business.

3. Investments cannot adversely effect the overall national economy.

4. Reciprocity of investment rights.

5. Investments cannot attempt to evade other restrictions contained in the act.

These criteria are rather vague, and administrative guidance permits U.S. companies to structure their proposals in a way best designed to obtain approval. The Japanese have been particularly protective of their agricultural industry, and a plan such as Wessex's might face obstacles. Administrative guidance can smooth the company's path to entering the Japanese market.

Hungary

Hungary adopted a new business code in the Act on Economic Associations and the Act on Investment of Foreigners in Hungary, effective in 1989. These laws enable domestic or foreign investors to create different forms of enterprises including corporations and partnerships. The most common form is the **limited liability company** (LLC).

To establish an LLC, the company must adopt a "deed of association." This should provide for capital contributions, the number and voting rights of shares, directors and their powers, and other administrative provisions. The LLC has great flexibility under Hungarian law, however, in defining these terms. Hungarian law creates minimum capitalization requirements (one million forints) and requires registration of the LLC.

Government approval is no longer required to establish an LLC. If there will be a foreign majority interest, however, the corporate founders must obtain the permission of the Finance and Trade Ministers. If they do not disapprove the application within ninety days, the law permits the LLC to go forward.

LLC management is not unlike that of a United States corporation. The shareholders' meetings elect directors and can amend the corporate charter, but also arrange for approving any distribution of profits. A simple majority is generally required, though the LLC charter may specify otherwise.

Hungary's Foreign Investment Act guarantees certain protection for foreign investors. Hungary also permits foreign investors to repatriate their dividends and profits and can be exchanged for foreign currency through the Hungarian National Bank. Repatriation of profits is limited by the requirement that the company be able to discharge its obligations to creditors.

Andean Nations and Mexico

Different investment rules govern each country of the world. Investment in poorer, developing countries presents different legal issues. Many of these nations have foreign investment codes in an attempt to capture the benefits of foreign investment. For example, consider the rules of the Andean Common Market, known as ANCOM, which is composed of Bolivia, Venezuela, Colombia, Ecuador and Peru. ANCOM was created by The Cartagena Agreement, which established common rules for foreign investment in member countries, among other joint economic activities.

ANCOM first adopted rules for foreign investment in 1970 in Decision No. 24, which created a Foreign Investment Code. Decision No. 24 created a new set of regulations in addition to the national rules of each member nation. These rules resulted from concern over dependency on foreign investment and technology. The ANCOM rules became a model for nearly every major Latin American country.

Decision No. 24 first prohibited any investment in certain economic sectors. The decision banned investment in sectors including domestic transportation, commercial banking and other financial institutions, the press, and insurance. In addition, members were to exclude direct foreign investment from sectors that they deemed to be "adequately covered by existing enterprises." The Decision also required the "fade-out" of foreign control, such that foreign investment had to be limited to minority ownership in corporations by a certain date and limited the repatriation of money.

The ANCOM rules, along with most other Latin and South American investment codes, had the following characteristics:

1. Screening and approval procedures to be passed by direct foreign investment before the investment is permitted.

2. Performance requirements and maximum ownership percentages for foreign investors.

3. Limitations on the repatriation of capital and profits.

4. Prohibitions or restrictions on direct foreign investment in certain sensitive economic sectors.

5. Restrictions on technology transfer.

The ANCOM nations found that these rules were too restrictive and prevented necessary foreign investment, so they were repealed by Decision 220 of the Quito Protocol of 1987. Individual member states, however, have maintained many of these restrictions. Thus, foreign ownership in all ANCOM countries must still scale back to minority ownership within a certain period (such as thirty years), depending upon the country. Many member states also restrict investment in banking and finance or limit the ability of foreign companies to draw upon local sources of long-term financing.

Other nations also restrict foreign investment based on rules similar to those of ANCOM. For example, Mexico restricts foreign computer manufacturers and investors to 49 percent ownership of most manufacturing facilities and only 40 percent of certain facilities, such as petrochemicals and automobiles. Mexico applies this same 49 percent ceiling to other industries such as mineral extraction. Even those developing countries that do not require a majority of domestic ownership may insist that foreign investment take the form of a joint venture with some domestic participation.

Mexico also strictly regulates the transfer of technology to Mexican firms. The nation seeks to prevent payment of excessive prices for foreign technology and eliminate certain restrictive conditions, including price fixing and limits on technology disclosure. Mexico also could refuse registration of contracts for technology transfer if the investor failed to guarantee the "quality and results" of the licensed technology.

▬ Protection from Investment Risk

Significant economic risks may be involved in direct foreign investment. The investing company is largely at the mercy of the foreign government. That government may, for example, seize and nationalize the property of the investor. There are now devices to help protect against this risk and help encourage foreign investment.

A new organization to help protect foreign investors is the International Centre for Settlement of Investment Disputes, also known as the ICSID. The ICSID Convention provided facilities for arbitration of investment disputes.

Not all nations belong to ICSID, but over seventy countries participate in the Convention. Once a nation has agreed to abide by ICSID, it cannot revoke its consent in a specific case. ICSID arbitration is an exclusive remedy, which means that it is outside the judicial control of any nation.

Suppose that a Latin American country nationalized an Oilco refinery. If the country was a member of ICSID, the two parties would take the dispute to arbitration. If ICSID ruled for Oilco and ordered the country to pay the $10 million value of the refinery, the country would be bound to do so. Nations ordinarily accept the results of arbitration. If the country refused to pay, Oilco

could go to another nation, such as the United States, and sue the country involved for the $10 million arbitration award. The United States would honor the ICSID arbitration and force the country to pay Oilco.

ICSID is of important benefit to foreign investors, but it has its limits. First, the company (such as Oilco) must bear the litigation costs to win the dispute. These costs may be substantial, because the company may be required first to try to recover in the foreign nation's courts, before turning to ICSID. Second, the company will be governed by the law of the foreign country. If that law provides an insufficient remedy, ICSID is of little help.

To further ease the risks of foreign investment, several governments in 1985 created the Multilateral Investment Guarantee Agency, known as MIGA. This agency operates as an insurance fund for investors.

The MIGA Convention covers voluntarily participating countries, which now number over one hundred. A wide range of countries participate, including many lesser developed nations. Eastern European nations, such as Hungary, are also members. MIGA covers actions in these member nations. To be protected, the investor must also be a national of a member country.

MIGA provides insurance against four specific categories of risk:

1. The risk of nationalization or other actions that deprive the investor of ownership or benefits from the investment.

2. Repudiation or breach of government contracts by the foreign nation.

3. The risk of armed conflict damaging to the investment.

4. The risk of government restrictions on currency conversion and transfer.

Other risks may be covered at the discretion of MIGA's governing board. To receive any coverage, investments must be medium or long-term and must contribute to the development of the host country.

If Oilco's property was expropriated by a country, MIGA would pay off Oilco's losses directly. MIGA would then be subrogated to Oilco's claim. This means that MIGA would have the right to take Oilco's claim to court or arbitration and attempt to recover Oilco's loss itself. MIGA is therefore dependent on ultimate recovery and will not guarantee operations in a country until it is satisfied that legal investment protection is available. MIGA's participating countries have agreed to international arbitration as a condition of membership. MIGA's greatest value to the investor is that MIGA both guarantees recovery and assumes the litigation expenses and risks itself.

MIGA was originally capitalized with over $1 billion from participating companies but is intended to be self-funding through premiums charged to investors. Annual premiums range from 0.3 percent to 1.5 percent of the guaranteed amount of investment, depending on the relative risk of the project.

Investors also may obtain private insurance from a company such as Lloyds of London. Private insurance is not restricted to voluntarily participating countries (as under ICSID or MIGA) but also tends to be much more expensive than MIGA and coverage is limited to a short time period, such as three years.

The American government provides special insurance for some investments through the Overseas Private Investment Corporation ("OPIC"). OPIC insurance protects against expropriation, revolution and currency inconvertibility.

OPIC insurance availability has significant limits, however. First, OPIC can be used only if the investor is a U.S. person, which may limit its availability for multinational enterprises. Second, OPIC must give preference to investments in the poorest countries. Third, OPIC will only insure investments that will not hurt the United States balance of payments or employment. Many foreign investments will fail this test, because the investor will desire to sell products in the U.S. market. Fourth, OPIC is limited to nations with which the U.S. has a governmental investment agreement. OPIC insurance has proved to be quite limited in scope.

■ Europe 1992

In February 1986, the twelve member nations of the European Community ("EC") agreed to the Single European Act, which provided for full economic integration of the nations by December 31,

1992. The participating countries are Belgium, France, Germany, Italy, Luxembourg, the Netherlands, Denmark, Ireland, the United Kingdom, Greece, Portugal, and Spain. Europe 1992 provides for the elimination of internal customs and excise taxes, abolition of any obstacles to freedom of movement for persons, services and capital, and adoption of common policies in areas such as agriculture and transportation. Europe 1992 creates a truly common market consisting of 320 million people and an over $4 trillion market.

Some United States companies fear that the Single European Act could result in a "fortress Europe" that restricts imports from America and other nations. One favorable result of 1992 will be the elimination of all quotas established by the individual member states of Europe. If these quotas are not replaced by community-wide quotas, free trade will be enhanced.

The economic integration of Europe will not eliminate all import restrictions by member states, however. Consider the pharmaceutical industry. Individual countries may still regulate pharmaceuticals for safety and effectiveness. Other governments regulate whether a given pharmaceutical drug is eligible for a tax refund. These practices could be used in a protectionist manner. To respond to this problem, the community has adopted a new directive that requires member nations to act within 180 days on requests for the import of new products. Individual member states may still maintain inconsistent laws on such issues as safety, however.

The members of Europe 1992 will also have joint barriers to trade. In the automobile industry, for example, community-wide quotas on car imports are likely to be imposed. In addition, local-content standards will insist that as much as 80 percent of automobiles involve EC-component parts. Even a Nissan plant located in the United Kingdom may face limits on EC sales. Similar local-content rules may apply to television programming in Europe.

The EC may also insist that computer companies increase the scope of their European manufacturing and research operations. A European presence may be essential to market access. In recognition of this concern, The Coca-Cola Company has begun construction of an enormous bottling plant in France and AT&T constructed a semiconductor plant in Spain. Whirlpool Corporation recently entered into a $2 billion joint venture with a Dutch electronics company.

Creation of such a foothold is expected to improve a foreign company's access to European markets.

Questions and Case Problems

1. Europe 1992 is designed to eliminate trade barriers among the continent's nations. Germany has a law requiring alcoholic beverages to contain at least 32 percent alcohol to be labeled as spirits. Rewe, an importer, applied to the Federal Monopoly of Spirits for permission to import Cassis de Dijon from France. The Cassis was only 15 to 20 percent alcohol, so Rewe was unable to import the product. Rewe brought an action against the Federal Monopoly, arguing that the restriction conflicted with the EC treaty. Should Rewe prevail in this action? [*Rewe-Zentral*, AG Bundesmomopol ver Waltung fur Branntwein, Case No. 120/78 (Court of Justice of the European Communities)].

2. Teca-Print A.G. is a small company that manufactures machinery in Switzerland. Teca is a small company that bills foreign sales in Swiss francs and does not want to engage in foreign currency speculation. By November 30, 1983, Amacoil Machinery owed Teca 71,224 Swiss francs. On this date the francs were worth $0.45 U.S. dollars. Amacoil breached the contract, and Teca sued in U.S. court, which can grant awards only in dollars. On December 2, 1986, when Teca won its breach of contract suit, the francs were worth $0.61 U.S. dollars. Teca wants payment based on the higher value of the franc on the date of the court judgment, but Amacoil wants to pay the judgment based on the lower value of the franc at the time of the breach of contract. How should a court resolve this dispute? [*Teca-Print A.G. v. Amacoil Machinery, Inc.*, 525 N.Y.S.2d 535 (1988)].

3. Samuels bought a BMW in Alaska. While he was driving, a transmission problem caused him to lose control of the car and wreck it, injuring himself. He sued Bayerische Motoren Werke, AG and BMW of North America, a wholly owned subsidiary, in Alaska, alleging strict liability. Bayerische disputed the jurisdiction of the Alaska court over the German company. Does Alaska have jurisdiction over Bayerische?

4. Japanese cargo containers were temporarily located in California ports for loading and unloading of goods. The average container spent about three weeks out of a year in the California ports. Los Angeles, California, imposed a personal property tax on the containers, which were also registered and subjected to property tax in Japan. Japan Line, Ltd. sued and claimed that the Los Angeles tax was invalid because it subjected the containers to multiple taxation and thereby discouraged international trade. Should the California law be struck down as unconstitutional? [*Japan Line, Ltd. v. County of Los Angeles*, 441 U.S. 434 (1979)].

5. Smith-Corona is the last remaining manufacturer of portable electric typewriters in the United States. Japanese typewriter companies, Brother and Silver Seiko, export portable electric typewriters to the U.S. Smith-Corona brought an antidumping action, claiming that Brother and Silver Seiko were selling typewriters in the U.S. at a lower price than in Japan. The Japanese companies claimed that the U.S. price only appeared lower, because it provided volume discounts in Japan and because it had additional advertising and other expenses in Japan. They argued that these factors should be considered in the antidumping action. Do the Japanese companies have a good defense to the antidumping action? [*Smith-Corona Group v. United States*, 713 F.2d 1568 (Fed. Cir. 1983)].

CHAPTER THREE

Individual Employee Rights

KEY BACKGROUND

The essential background for this chapter on individual employee rights is found in Chapter 48 of *West's Business Law*, *Fifth Edition* and in Chapter 17 of *West's Legal Environment of Business*. This chapter covers employment and labor relations law. Among the important points to remember from this chapter are:

- individual employment rights under contract

- individual protection from wrongful discharge under public policy

- tort liability for wrongful discharge.

The reader will also benefit from familiarity with the discussion of employer/employee relationships and termination in Chapter 36 of *West's Business Law, Fifth Edition*.

* * *

The law of the workplace has undergone enormous changes in the past decades. Individual employees once had very few rights in their jobs and had to unionize to obtain protection. Now business faces thousands of individual employee rights cases every year, challenging an improper firing of a worker, claiming invasion of privacy, or other issues. Courts have given employees more bases to sue employers, especially over discharge from employment, and the federal and state governments also have passed statutes to protect workers. This chapter discusses the most prominent issues in the area.

Employment at Will

The traditional employment contract would be either for a defined term (e.g., one year) or for an indefinite term. Most employment contracts were for an indefinite term and these were described as **at-will contracts**. This meant that the employer could at any time fire the employee, and the employee could at any time quit the employer. Neither act would represent a breach of contract. Roughly two-thirds of all employment contracts are at-will.

Under the traditional rules of at-will employment, no reason was required for the discharge of an employee. An employer could fire a worker for a purely arbitrary reason or even for a bad reason.

Thus, suppose Hank Kimble worked for Used Motors Cars, and Hank's employer told him to turn back the odometers of their inventory of automobiles. Hank refuses because the act is both illegal and unethical. If Used Motors were to fire Hank, traditional common law would offer him no remedy.

The once-broad scope of at-will employment has been narrowed considerably. Federal statutes provide protection against specific illegal bases for discharge. For example, an employee may not be fired for participating in a union or on the basis of the employee's race, sex, or religion. These laws are discussed in Chapter 48 of *West's Business Law,*

Fifth Edition and in Chapter 17 of *West's Legal Environment of Business*.

The common law has also created exceptions to the pure employment-at-will contract, as discussed below. While employers still may fire workers for a plethora of reasons, the courts now provide greater job security for workers. The leading doctrines in this regard are the **implied contract of employment**, the prohibition on discharges that are contrary to **public policy**, and the development of a **wrongful discharge tort** cause of action.

Wrongful discharge actions are an important concern of management. A recent survey of these cases found that the employee won in approximately 70 percent of wrongful discharge actions and the average award was over $175,000. In a recent unreported jury verdict, Mobil Chemical Company was ordered to pay $1.375 million to an employee whom it fired in an alleged attempt to cover up environmental violations.

▬ Implied Contract of Employment

Some workers have claimed that their discharge violated an implied contract that they had with their employer. Although the actual employment contract may clearly provide for an indefinite term, employer actions or statements may have modified the contract and promised the employee a long-term job.

For there to be an implied contract of employment, the alleged agreement must contain all the elements of a binding contract. Thus, there must be an offer and acceptance, consideration, capacity, legality, and proper form for an agreement (as discussed below, some agreements must be in writing) in order to be enforceable.

Consider the following circumstance. Denise Booth works as an executive for Bell Diamond & Co. Denise receives a job offer from a competitor at a higher salary. Denise goes to her boss at Bell Diamond and discusses her plans to resign. The boss begs her to stay and promises her that she can keep her job at Bell Diamond "for a lifetime" and that she will get a promotion and raise in six months. Denise stays at Bell Diamond. Six months later, with the economy in recession, the company fires Denise. She can sue the company for violation of an implied modification to her at-will employment contract.

Employment Manuals

Many employers publish and distribute an employment manual or handbook that contains a list of their policies. These manuals help establish clear rules for the workplace and help ensure equitable and uniform administration of rules. They also may enhance employee morale by giving security or demonstrating the employer's sense of fairness.

Many courts have held that statements in these employment manuals create binding policies that the employer must follow in dealings with employees. The theory is that employees read the manual and continue working for the employer (do not exercise their legal right to quit) in reliance upon the manual's terms.

Several key provisions in employment manuals have been found to be enforceable implied contracts. These include a guarantee of a certain level of severance pay, a promise that discharge will only be for "good cause," and assurance that certain procedures will be used before an employee is fired.

Not all employment manuals are binding contracts, however. Suppose that the employee did not read the manual or that the manual was not made available to certain employees. Communication of an offer is an essential component of agreement. Nor could the employee have relied on a manual of which he or she was unaware. Most courts hold that an unread manual is not a binding contract.

This principle is illustrated in a Minnesota decision. A discharged employee sued and claimed that his discharge was contrary to an employees' manual that guaranteed certain procedures before he received disciplinary firing and a supervisors' manual that permitted termination for only good cause. The court held that the first claim was good but that the employee could not sue under the supervisors' manual because it was not given to him.[1]

The effect of any employment manual depends on the standard contractual investigation into the intention of the parties. If the language of the handbook appears binding, it will be held binding. Thus, if a manual speaks of the employees' "rights," the manual is likely to be found binding.

---

[1]*Pine River State Bank v. Mettille,* 333 N.W.2d 622 (Minn. 1983).

Employers may be bound by even policies that are not stated in a manual. The following decision involves a famous instance of wrongful discharge.

■ Case 3.1
Rulon-Miller v.
International Business
Machines, Corp.
California Court of Appeals,
First District, 1984
208 Cal.Rptr. 524

Background and Facts   *Virginia Rulon-Miller began work with IBM as a sales person and data processor. She was given the highest employee ratings and steadily promoted within the company. She eventually became a marketing manager, working under Phillip Callahan, her supervisor. Ms. Rulon-Miller had begun dating Matt Blum when he was an account manager for IBM. He eventually left the company and joined QYX, a competitor of IBM's. She dated Mr. Blum while she was working at IBM. IBM was aware of this but gave her a promotion and substantial raise nevertheless.*

Not long thereafter, Mr. Callahan summoned Ms. Rulon-Miller and inquired about her relationship with Mr. Blum. He expressed concern about a conflict of interest and asked her to halt the relationship. After she refused, Callahan first dismissed her and then merely transferred her to another division, removing her from management.

She sued over her demotion, which the court considered a discharge. Among her claims was IBM's breach of an implied contract of employment, based on the company's frequently stated policy of respect for employee privacy. She also sued for intentional infliction of emotional distress. A jury ruled on her behalf and awarded her $100,000 in compensatory damages and $200,000 in punitive damages. IBM appealed the decision.

RUSHING, Associate Justice.

*   *   *   *

When Callahan questioned her relationship with Blum, respondent invoked her right to privacy in her personal life, relying on existing IBM policies. A threshold inquiry is thus presented whether respondent could reasonably rely on those policies for job protection. Any conflicting action by the company would be wrongful in that it would constitute a violation of her contract rights.

*   *   *   *

In this case, there is a close question of whether those rules or regulations permit IBM to inquire into the purely personal life of the employee. If so, an attendant question is whether such a policy was applied consistently, particularly as between men and women. The distinction is important because the right of privacy, a constitutional right in California (*City and County of San Francisco v. Superior Court* (1981) 125 Cal.App.3d 879, 883, 178 Cal.Rptr. 435), could be implicated by the IBM inquiry. Much of the testimony below concerned what those policies were. The evidence was conflicting on the meaning of certain IBM policies. We observe ambiguity in the application but not in the intent. The "Watson Memo" (so called because it was signed by a former chairman of IBM) provided as follows:

"TO ALL IBM MANAGERS:

"The line that separates an individual's on-the-job business life from his other life as a private citizen is at times well-defined and at other times indistinct. But the line does exist, and you and I, as managers in IBM, must be able to recognize that line.

"I have seen instances where managers took disciplinary measures against employees for actions or conduct that are not rightfully the company's concern. These managers usually justified their decisions by citing their personal code of ethics and morals or by quoting some fragment of company policy that seemed to support their position. Both arguments proved unjust on close examination. What we need, in every case, is balanced judgment which weighs the needs of the business and the rights of the individual.

"Our primary objective as IBM managers is to further the business of this company by leading our people properly and measuring quantity and quality of work and effectiveness on the job against clearly set standards of responsibility and compensation. This is performance—and performance is, in the final analysis, the one thing that the company can insist on from everyone.

"We have concern with an employee's off-the-job behavior only when it reduces his ability to perform regular job assignments, interferes with the job performance of other employees, or if his outside behavior affects the reputation of the company in a major way. When on-the-job performance is acceptable, I can think of few situations in which outside activities could result in disciplinary action or dismissal."

* * * *

Callahan based his action against respondent on a "conflict of interest." But the record shows that IBM did not interpret this policy to prohibit a romantic relationship. Callahan admitted that there was no company rule or policy requiring an employee to terminate friendships with fellow employees who leave and join competitors. Gary Nelson, Callahan's superior, also confirmed that IBM had no policy against employees socializing with competitors.

This issue was hotly contested with respondent claiming that the "conflict of interest" claim was a pretext for her unjust termination. Whether it was presented a fact question for the jury. Do the policies reflected in this record give IBM a right to terminate an employee for a conflict of interest? The answer must be yes, but whether respondent's conduct constituted such was for the jury. We observe that while respondent was successful, her primary job did not give her access to sensitive information which could have been useful to competitors. She was, after all, a seller of typewriters and office equipment. Respondent's brief makes much of the concession by IBM that there was no evidence whatever that respondent had given any information or help to IBM's competitor QYX. It really is no concession at all; she did not have the information or help to give. Even so, the question is one of substantial evidence. The evidence is abundant that there was no conflict of interest by respondent.

Decision and Remedy *The court affirmed the judgment and award of damages.*

Courts will also look to other factors to determine the intent of the parties. Extensive litigation in California has produced a list of relevant factors. These factors include the length of the employees' service with the country, oral statements supplementing the manual, industry practice, and whether the employee gave any extra consideration for a manual's benefits.

Employers may protect themselves from the binding effects of an employment handbook or manual by including a disclaimer. In one case, a manual's preface stated that the manual was "informational only" and that its terms "are not conditions of employment and may be modified, revoked or changed at any time with or without notice."[2] The court therefore ruled for the employer on a wrongful discharge claim. Companies such as Montgomery Ward and Sears have effectively used disclaimers.

Even a disclaimer will not always insulate an employer from being bound by its employment manual. Courts have emphasized that any disclaimer must be clear and unambiguous. The disclaimer also must be communicated to the employee. Finally, the disclaimer may be undermined by subsequent oral statements that the employer will abide by the terms of the manual.

If a binding manual exists, can an employer modify its policies through issuance of a new manual? Courts are still divided on this issue. Some hold that a new manual creates a new contract, which the employee accepts through continued work. Others hold that an employer cannot offer a new manual with reduced protection unless the employer offers the employee some additional consideration for the changes.

Oral Assurances

An implied contract of job security may exist even in the absence of a binding employment manual. If a prospective employee is told in a job interview that she can only be fired for good cause, she may have a binding implied contract. To be enforceable, such assurances must be express and specific.

Oral assurances may even override disclaimers or modifications of employment manuals. In one case, an employment manual provided for severance pay in the event of termination, but the employer retained the right to modify this policy. The employer then modified the handbook to eliminate the assurance of severance pay. A supervisor orally assured employees that the original severance pay policy would remain in effect for them. The court upheld a verdict for the employees based on the oral promises.[3]

As with employment manuals, oral promises must meet the requirements of contract law to be enforceable. One common problem for employees is the Statute of Frauds, which is discussed in Chapter 14 of *West's Business Law, Fifth Edition*. A key Statute of Frauds provision states that contracts which require more than a year to perform must be in writing.

Suppose that a Bell Diamond executive orally promises Henry Washington that he will be retained for at least three years and provided with three years of training. This contract is not enforceable because it cannot be performed within one year and must therefore be in writing to be binding.

The Statute of Frauds provision is narrow, however, and many oral promises will remain binding. Suppose that an employer promises Henry Washington he will be guaranteed a job for the rest of his life. Because Henry could possibly die within one year, this promise is not within the Statute of Frauds and would be binding. Courts do not consider the probability of Henry's dying.

For another example, suppose that Bell Diamond and Henry Washington orally agree on a three-year employment contract, unless there is good cause for discharge. Because a good cause could arise within one year, many courts have held that this type of contract can be enforced.

On the other hand, suppose that Bell simply promised Henry that he would have a job until his retirement. Henry is thirty-four years old, and the company's policy does not permit retirement until the age of sixty. This contract could not be peformed in one year and will not be binding unless it is put in writing.

[2]*Crain v. Burroughs Corp.*, 560 F. Supp. 849 (C.D. Cal. 1983).

[3]*Helle v. Landmark, Inc.*, 472 N.E.2d 765 (Ohio App. 1984).

▬ Public Policy Exception

Most states that recognize employment-at-will contracts make an exception for discharges that violate public policy. If the employer's reason for discharge is so objectionable that it violates a fundamental public policy, the employee will have a good case for wrongful discharge.

The public policy exception is a vague one. Governments have innumerable public policies as reflected in thousands of statutes. Most courts have interpreted the public policy exception rather narrowly and limited it to clear violations of fundamental public policies.

The classic case for the exception of public policy occurs when the employer fires a worker for a refusal to violate a law. Examples of discharges under this principle were cases when an employer fired a worker for refusing to participate in a gasoline price-fixing scheme, refusing to perform an illegal medical operation, refusing to fraudulently modify reports on pollutant emissions, and refusing to employ accounting practices that violated state law. The employees prevailed in all these cases.

Another circumstance for the public policy exception occurs when an employer fires an employee for exercising his or her legal rights. One common situation involves a discharge in retaliation for an employee's filing of a legitimate workers' compensation claim. In many states (including Illinois, Florida, Michigan and Oregon), courts prohibit employers from firing workers for filing justifiable workers' compensation claims. Some states, such as North Carolina, have adopted statutes codifying this principle.

Courts are more divided on whether employees are protected for filing other legal claims. New York has held that an employee cannot be fired in order to deprive him of pension benefits, but other courts have disagreed. Courts have recognized a good wrongful discharge claim when workers were discharged for serving on a jury. California has held that an employer cannot fire a worker for suing the employer, as long as the employee had a good claim.

Constitutional principles also may be the basis for the public policy exception. In a Pennsylvania case, an employee was fired for refusing to lobby the state legislature on an issue to which he was opposed. The court held that the discharge violated the employee's political rights of free speech.[4] Other decisions have permitted employers to fire workers over free speech that injured the employer's interests and conflicted with the employee's duty of loyalty.

An employee public policy claim must be closely hinged to a specific law. The following decision explains the limits of the public policy exception.

---

[4]*Novosel v. Nationwide Insurance Co.*, 721 F.2d 894 (3rd Cir. 1983).

▬ Case 3.2
Pierce v.
Ortho Pharmaceutical Corp.
Supreme Court of New Jersey, 1980
417 A.2d 505

Background and Facts *Dr. Grace Pierce was a physician engaged in research by the Ortho Pharmaceutical Corporation. Dr. Pierce was an at-will employee of Ortho. In spring 1975, Dr. Pierce was the only medical doctor on a research team developing loperamide, a drug for treatment of infant diarrhea. The formulation of the drug contained saccharin. Ortho was planning to develop an investigational new drug application ("IND") for filing with the Food and Drug Administration ("FDA") to permit clinical testing of the drug on humans.*

Dr. Pierce objected to the research because of a controversy over the safety of saccharin. She opposed the decision to seek an IND on the grounds that saccharin might be harmful and the formulation would violate her Hippocratic oath as a doctor to do no harm. The company announced that she would not be promoted and would be demoted, so she resigned her position. She then sued for wrongful discharge on public policy grounds. Ortho moved for summary judgment, which the trial court denied. The appellate court affirmed this decision. Ortho then appealed to the New Jersey Supreme Court.

POLLOCK, Justice.

*   *   *   *

In recognizing a cause of action to provide a remedy for employees who are wrongfully discharged, we must balance the interests of the employee, the employer, and the public. Employees have an interest in knowing they will not be discharged for exercising their legal rights. Employers have an interest in knowing they can run their businesses as they see fit as long as their conduct is consistent with public policy. The public has an interest in employment stability and in discouraging frivolous lawsuits by dissatisfied employees. Although the contours of an exception are important to all employees-at-will, this case focuses on the special considerations arising out of the right to fire an employee-at-will who is a member of a recognized profession. One writer has described the predicament that may confront a professional employed by a large corporation:

Consider, for example, the plight of an engineer who is told that he will lose his job unless he falsifies his data or conclusions, or unless he approves a product which does not conform to specifications or meet minimum standards. Consider also the dilemma of a corporate attorney who is told, say in the context of an impending tax audit or antitrust investigation, to draft backdated corporate records concerning events which never took place or to falsify other documents so that adverse legal consequences may be avoided by the corporation; and the predicament of an accountant who is told to falsify his employer's profit and loss statement in order to enable the employer to obtain credit.

*   *   *   *

(2) Employees who are professionals owe a special duty to abide not only by federal and state law, buy also by the recognized codes of ethics of their professions. That duty may oblige them to decline to perform acts required by their employers. However, an employee should not have the right to prevent his or her employer from pursuing its business because the employee perceives that a particular business decision violates the employee's personal morals, as distinguished from the recognized code of ethics of the employee's profession. See Comment, 28 Vand. L. Rev. 805, 832 (1975).

(3) We hold that an employee has a cause of action for wrongful discharge when the discharge is contrary to a clear mandate of public policy. The sources of public policy include legislation; administrative rules, regulations or decisions; and judicial decisions. In certain instances, a professional code of ethics may contain an expression of public policy. However, not all such sources express a clear mandate of public policy. For example, a code of ethics designed to serve only the interests of a profession or an administrative regulation concerned with technical matters probably would not be sufficient.

Absent legislation, the judiciary must define the cause of action in case-by-case determinations. An employer's right to discharge an employee at will carries a correlative duty not to discharge an employee who declines to perform an act that would require a violation of a clear mandate of public policy. However, unless an employee-at-will identifies a specific expression of public policy, he may be discharged with or without cause.

*   *   *   *

Viewing the matter most favorably to Dr. Pierce, the controversy at Ortho involved a difference in medical opinions. Dr. Pierce acknowledged that Dr. Pasquale was entitled to his opinion that the oath did not forbid work on loperamide. Nonetheless, implicit in Dr. Pierce's position is the contention that Dr. Pasquale and Ortho were obliged to accept her opinion. Dr. Pierce contends, in effect, that Ortho should have stopped research on loperamide because of her opinion about the controversial nature of the drug.

Dr. Pierce espouses a doctrine that would lead to disorder in drug research. Under her theory, a professional employee could redetermine the propriety of a research project even if the research did not involve a violation of a clear mandate of public policy. Chaos would result if a single doctor engaged in research were allowed to determine, according to his or her individual conscience, whether a project should continue. Cf. Report of the Ad Hoc Committee on the Principles of Medical Ethics, American Medical Association (1979). An employee does not have a right to continued employment when he or she refuses to conduct research simply because it would contravene his or her personal morals. An employee-at-will who refuses to work for an employer in answer to a call of conscience should recognize that other employees and their employer might heed a different call. However, nothing in this opinion should be construed to restrict the right of an employee-at-will to refuse to work on a project that he or she believes is unethical. In sum, an employer may discharge an employee who refuses to work unless the refusal is based on a clear mandate of public policy.

Decision and Remedy   *The court reversed the denial of summary judgment and remanded the case for entry of judgment for Ortho.*

Whistle-Blowing

"Whistle-blowing" is the term for an employee who protests, publicly or privately, against the company's participating in criminal or unethical behavior. This is a variant of the public policy exception. Some statutes provide direct protection to whistle-blowers. These include civil rights acts and Department of Defense procurement laws.

Even in the absence of specific statutory protection, some courts have protected whistle-blowing employees from termination. A Connecticut decision protected an employee who objected to his employer over mislabeling of foods. A West Virginia case protected an employee who alerted state authorities over the employer's violation of banking laws.

Other state courts have refused to extend protection to whistle-blowers. In a recent California case, an employee claimed that he was discharged because he notified management that his supervisor was being investigated by the FBI over past embezzlements. The court held that the discharge was legal, and the employee had no right to spread rumors (even true ones) about fellow employees.[5]

Courts also have required the employee to have solid evidence of a violation before protecting whistle-blowers. A mere suspicion of illegal activity is not sufficient justification.

One important issue in both the public policy and the whistle-blowing cases is whether the employee's case is in contract or tort. This is important because damages can be larger in tort claims. For example, punitive damages are available in tort but generally unavailable in contract claims. Most, but not all, states have held that these wrongful discharge cases are torts. Some states have specifically approved the application of punitive damages in wrongful discharge cases.

---

[5]*Foley v. Interactive Data Corp.*, 254 Cal.Rptr. 211 (1988).

▬ Good Cause

For any of the above wrongful discharge claims, in contract or tort, the employer has a **good cause defense**. If the employee were fired for good cause, the courts will rule in favor of the employer.

A large number of cases have helped define what constitutes good cause for discharge of an employee. Violation of the employer's rules generally satisfies the good cause requirement. The following is a partial list of conditions that represent good cause for discharge:

- illegal actions
- absenteeism or tardiness
- alcoholism or drug addiction
- incompetence or poor performance
- refusal of work assignment or overtime
- disruption of work
- dishonesty in job applications
- fighting and threats
- profanity or harassment of coworkers
- moonlighting
- appearance or violation of dress code
- reduction in force due to financial problems

Most courts also defer to employers' decisions regarding good cause. The employer need not prove conclusively that the employee engaged in one of the proscribed behaviors. Rather, courts require only that the employer had a good faith belief in the good cause for terminating the employee.

▬ Tortious Discharges

On some occasions, the act of terminating an employee may constitute a separate tort by the employer. The most common torts alleged in discharge cases are fraud, intentional infliction of emotional distress, negligence, and defamation.

For an employee to succeed on a *fraud* claim, he or she must show a representation of a false fact, made with knowledge of its falsity, which produces reasonable reliance by the employee. Suppose that Anna Juarez is offered a job with Artmark, Inc., but is soon fired. She might be able to allege that she was promised three years employment by Artmark and turned down other opportunities to accept the job. But she would have to prove that Artmark knew that her position would be eliminated before the promised three years.

A fraud claim is difficult to win, because the employee must show that a false statement was knowingly made. In a famous case, Christine Kraft sued a Kansas City television station that had fired her, on grounds of appearance. She brought a fraud claim, based on the statement that she was hired on the understanding that no change was required in her appearance. She lost the case because she could not prove that the hiring assurances were falsely made. The station successfully maintained that it simply changed its mind after she was hired.[6]

Some employees have succeeded in fraud claims. In one case, a company's management hired replacement workers while their regular workers were out on strike. The replacements were hired with a promise that they would be retained after the strike was settled. The strike was settled only one week later, and the replacement workers were fired. The employees sued in fraud and won both compensatory and punitive damages.[7]

Another common tort claim in discharge cases is **intentional infliction of emotional distress**. This claim requires proof of an outrageous act, with reckless disregard of its consequences, which actually causes severe emotional distress.

The mere termination of employment will not constitute intentional infliction of emotional distress. The procedures used in termination can constitute the tort, however. Certain facts can give rise to intentional infliction of emotional distress. If the discharge is accompanied by inaccurate assertions of dishonesty or other unethical practice, a court may permit an employee's recovery. Sexual or racial slurs also constitute the tort.

The following case provides some examples of facts that do or do not constitute intentional infliction of mental distress in connection with an employment termination.

---

[6]*Kraft v. Metromedia, Inc.*, 766 F.2d 1205 (8th Cir. 1985).

[7]*Verway v. Blincoe Packing Co.*, 698 P.2d 377 (Idaho App. 1985).

■ Case 3.3
**Mansfield v.
American Telephone &
Telegraph Corporation**
United States District Court,
Western District of Arkansas, 1990
5 IER Cases (BNA) 1383

Background and Facts *Martha Mansfield was a national accounts manager for AT&T. Ms. Mansfield was an at-will employee. AT&T officers wanted to hire Beverly Burns as a political favor to an Arkansas state legislator, B.G. Hendrix. Ms. Mansfield refused to go along with this hire, believing it to be illegal. After her repeatedly stated opposition to the hiring of Ms. Burns, Ms. Mansfield was fired.*

Before firing her, AT&T officials engaged Ms. Mansfield in six hours of intense questioning, some of which involved personal issues. Ms. Mansfield sued AT&T and among her allegations was a claim for intentional infliction of emotional distress. AT&T moved the court for summary judgment, claiming that the alleged facts did not sufficiently make out a claim for this tort.

ARNOLD, District Judge.

*   *   *   *

Finally, the defendants argue that Ms. Mansfield has failed to produce sufficient evidence to create a genuine issue of material fact as to her claim for outrage. The court disagrees.

To establish such a claim, Ms. Mansfield must present evidence of "conduct that is so outrageous in character, and so extreme in degree, as to go beyond all possible bounds of decency, and to be regarded as atrocious and utterly intolerable in a civilized society." See *AMI Civil* 3d, 404. The emotional distress suffered as a result "must be reasonable and justified under the circumstances and must be so severe that no reasonable person could be expected to endure it." Id.

Judgments for outrage have been upheld, grants of summary judgment to a defendant reversed, and dismissals for failure to state a claim reversed in Arkansas cases where an employee alleged that she was fired because she would not agree to her supervisor's demands for sexual favors and that her employer then represented in relation to her unemployment compensation claim that she had been fired for misconduct, see *Lucas v. Brown and Root, Inc.*, 736 F.2d 1202, 1206-07 (8th Cir. 1984); where allegations were made that an employee with an outstanding record was intentionally dismissed on account of her age, see *Smith v. Southern Starr of Arkansas, Inc.*, 700 F.Supp. 1026, 1027-28 (E.D. Ark. 1988); where, over a period of two years, the plaintiff was followed by the defendant and people hired by him, the defendant made repeated unwarranted complaints about how the plaintiff was doing his job, and the defendant made numerous threats to get the plaintiff fired, see *Hess v. Treece*, 286 Ark. 434, 440 (1985), cert. denied, 475 Ark. 1036 (1986); where an employee being questioned about alleged thefts from his employer was repeatedly denied the opportunity to take tranquilizing medication during the questioning even though he was highly agitated at the time, see *Tandy Corp. v. Bone*, 283 Ark. 399, 407-08 (1984); where a construction crew unnecessarily drove heavy equipment over family graves, exposed the burial vaults within, and than told distressed family members not to visit the sites if these events were so upsetting, see *Growth Properties I v. Cannon*, 282 Ark. 472, 475-76 (1984); and where evidence was presented that a fired employee was given reasons for her termination inconsistent with the circumstances and, even after passing a polygraph test, was denied her back pay until the state labor department intervened, see *MBM Company, Inc. v. Counce*, 268 Ark. 269, 271-72, 281 (1980).

Judgments for outrage have been reversed, directed verdicts or summary judgment granted to a defendant, and complaints dismissed on outrage claims in Arkansas cases where evidence was presented that an employee was refused a promotion, denied raises, and given poor performance evaluations in an effort to pressure him to resign after he confronted his employer about alleged kickback schemes, see *Puckett v. Cook*, 864 F.2d 619, 620, 622 (8th Cir. 1989); where a religious sect persuaded one of its members to repudiate his family, see *Orlando v. Alamo*, 646 F.2d 1288, 1289-90 (8th Cir. 1981); where an insurance company disputed the plaintiff's interpretation of policy language and refused to pay a claim, see *Glenn v. Farmers and Merchants Insurance Company*, 649 F.Supp. 1447, 1448-50 (W.D. Ark. 1986); where the plaintiff stopped making payments on a camper trailer that had developed multiple problems, the seller secured a warrant for the plaintiff's arrest after having been unable to locate him, and the plaintiff was subsequently arrested and held for two hours until he posted bond, see *Cordes v. Outdoor Living Center, Inc.*, 301 Ark. 26, 29-30, 34 (1989); where an employer was verbally abusive to the plaintiff and had made derogatory comments about a review process of the employer's work in which the plaintiff was involved.

* * * *

Ms. Mansfield alleges that during six hours of questioning, without notice, by AT&T representatives about an alleged conflict of interest, unauthorized use of company property, and submission of false expense vouchers, she was not given a chance to defend herself, she was repeatedly laughed at and accused of lying whenever she tried to speak, was not permitted to smoke even though she told the AT&T representative that she was a heavy smoker, was not permitted to eat, was implicitly accused of having used sexual favors to get customers' accounts, was implicitly accused of having a lesbian relationship with a coworker, was subjected to questioning while one of the AT&T officials had unzipped pants, and was not permitted to leave until she signed a statement; that the reasons given for the interrogation were pretextual; that after she was fired, AT&T refused to pay various benefits due her; and that AT&T representatives suggested to others that she might be having affairs with customers or a lesbian relationship with a coworker.

Decision and Remedy   *The court denied defendant's summary judgment motion on plaintiff's claim for intentional infliction of emotional distress.*

Some employees have brought a *negligence* claim in connection with their discharge. Ordinarily, negligent discharge is not a tort, because employers' only duties to employees are those set forth in their contract. An employee may succeed in a case based on negligent evaluation, however, if the employment contract provides that the employee can be discharged only for good cause.

Virtually all employers conduct some form of periodic job evaluation for their workers. Some courts have recognized a cause of action for negligent evaluations. This tort must generally be accompanied by some contract right to be discharged only for good cause.

Michigan courts have recognized a claim for negligent evaluation. If the employee can show a legal right to performance evaluations (such as in contract), the employer has a duty to conduct such evaluations fairly and objectively. If a negligently conducted evaluation causes a worker's discharge, the employee can recover damages.

Another common discharge claim is **defamation**. Defamation requires a false statement about a person, communicated to others, that causes harm to the person's reputation. In one case, a newspaper fired a sportswriter and published an article explaining its decision. The explanation suggested that the writer was insufficiently energetic and was "on the downswing." A court found that this explanation could constitute defamation.[8]

The largest barrier to defamation actions is the requirement of communication to third parties. If a GovCorp Co. manager calls in Jim Jones, privately accuses him of embezzlement, and fires him, there is no defamation. Only Jim Jones heard the accusation.

Some courts are creating an important exception to the communication requirement, which is called the **doctrine of compelled self-publication**. When Jim Jones interviews for a new job, the interviewers ask why he left GovCorp. Jim honestly states that he was fired because he was an accused embezzler. Courts have held that this repetition by Jim was foreseeable by the employer, and GovCorp may be liable for defamation if the accusation was false.

Employer comments on employees have a qualified privilege under defamation law. If one employer gives another job reference to another, the qualified privilege protects the first employer from defamation claims. To be protected, however, the employer's reference must meet several requirements. The reference must be communicated in good faith, in a proper manner, to the proper parties (not to the general public), related to job requirements and limited to disclosures that are necessary to performance evaluation.

▬ Employee Privacy

Privacy rights of employees are a major new area of the law. The United States Constitution protects citizens' privacy against the intrusions of the government but generally does not apply to employer "invasions of privacy." Employees generally lack a strong common law basis for privacy protection.

There is a tort of invasion of privacy, but this tort is restricted in the employment context. A leading court case explained that an employer "may seek certain personal information concerning an employee when the importance of the information in assessing the employee's efficacy in his work outweighs the employee's right to keep this information private."[9]

An employer may be liable for invasion of privacy if there is no legitimate or significant employer interest in the matter. In one case, a flight attendant provided her employer with medical information, including the details of planned gynecological surgery. The employer's medical examiner disclosed this information to her supervisor and to her husband. The flight attendant won damages for invasion of privacy, because the employer had no legitimate interest in disclosing this information.[10] This case was relatively unusual, though, and employers typically will have a legitimate basis for their actions.

While common law will often fail to provide privacy protection to employees, the federal and state governments have passed a series of laws that protect certain privacy rights of workers. The primary areas of concern are in polygraph testing, drug testing, AIDS testing, and monitoring of performance.

Lie Detector Tests

Employers have used polygraphs and other lie detectors to screen job applicants and to investigate for employee theft. After thousands of companies began using these tests, states and the federal government adopted legal restrictions on lie detectors in the workplace.

Employer use of lie detector tests is restricted by the Employee Polygraph Protection Act of 1988. This law makes it illegal for employers to "directly or indirectly, require, request, suggest, or cause, any employee or prospective employee to take or submit to any lie detector

---

[8]*Falls v. Sporting News Publishing Co.*, 834 F.2d 611 (6th Cir. 1987).

[9]*Bratt v. International Business Machines Corp.*, 467 N.E.2d 126, 135 (Mass. 1984).

[10]*Lewis v. United Airlines*, 500 N.E. 2d 370 (Ohio App. 1985).

test." The law also restricts inquiries about the results of lie detector tests and any discharge or discipline based upon the results of a test or refusal to take a test.

The Act created significant exceptions when lie detector use is allowed. An exemption exists for government employers in national security, private employers of security personnel, and employers authorized to produce or distribute controlled substances.

A more general statutory exemption applies to "ongoing investigations." This exemption allows an employer to request that an employee submit to a polygraph test if the employer can meet the following requirements:

1. The test is used in an ongoing investigation involving losses that result from intentional wrongdoing.

2. The subject employee had access to the property loss in question.

3. The employer has a reasonable suspicion that the employee was involved in the investigated loss.

4. The employer provides a statement to the employee setting forth the legal rights under the act. This statement also must specify with particularity the incident under investigation.

This exemption permits tests for employee theft but does not allow random employee testing.

The law provides additional protections even when testing is allowed. The employee cannot be required to take the test. The Act prohibits degrading or needlessly intrusive questions. Thus, questions about religious or political beliefs or sexual behavior are expressly prohibited.

The law provides that employees must be informed of the nature and characteristics of the test. Standards for polygrapher qualifications are established. Disclosure of test results is restricted.

Violation of the law is punishable by a civil penalty of up to $10,000. Employees can sue in a private right of action and obtain reinstatement with the company or the payment of lost wages and benefits.

While the federal legislation applies to many types of lie detector tests, it does not apply to "pencil-and-paper" questionnaires of employees or prospective employees. These tests are used

to check for dishonesty and may involve highly personal questions. Note, though, that states have passed laws restricting employee testing, and some state laws may ban these written tests as well. The Massachusetts law expressly bans such pencil-and-paper tests for detecting potential employee dishonesty.

Drug Testing

Recent years have seen an enormous increase in employer testing for drugs or alcohol abuse by employees. Over 80 percent of the Fortune 200 companies and over 30 percent of the total workforce are now subject to such testing.

Many employees have challenged drug and alcohol testing in the workplace. For private employers, drug testing has generally been upheld as an exercise of management discretion.

The U.S. Constitution constrains drug testing of government workers and testing that is required by government action. The Department of Transportation, for example, adopted regulations for drug testing that apply to approximately 4 million private sector employees. These regulations require random testing, periodic testing of some employees, and post-accident testing for transportation workers. Those who test positive must be removed from their duties.

The Supreme Court recently ruled on the constitutionality of these Department of Transportation regulations. The court upheld the rules due to the significant safety concerns in transportation and the protections provided against inaccurate test results.

A federal statute, the Drug-Free Workplace Act of 1988, requires private employers who contract with the federal government to certify their good-faith effort to maintain a drug-free workforce. While this law does not expressly require drug testing, it effectively encourages such testing.

For most private employees, there is no privacy right against drug testing, even intrusive forms such as observed urinalysis. A recent Texas decision upheld an employer's drug testing plan, but emphasized that the plan had safeguards for accuracy and confidentiality and provided rehabilitation programs for those who tested positive. The following recent decision also upheld a corporate drug testing plan but placed some limits on its scope and operation.

Case 3.4
Jevic v.
The Coca Cola Bottling
Company of New York, Inc.
United States District Court,
District of New Jersey, 1990
5 IER Cases (BNA) 765

Background and Facts *Donald Jevic applied for a position as district sales manager with Coca-Cola Bottling. As part of its application process, Coke requires all prospective employees to take a drug test. Jevic consented to this condition of employment. The Redi-Med medical center took a urine sample from Jevic and sent it to be analyzed at MetPath Laboratories. MetPath used two procedures to analyze the sample and both were positive for the presence of marijuana. Coke then informed Jevic that his conditional employment offer was revoked.*

Jevic claimed that the test was erroneous as he had "not smoked marijuana in over a year." He took an independent test that proved negative and informed Coke of these results. He asked permission for a second test at Redi-Med, but Coke refused. Jevic then sued Coca-Cola, which moved for summary judgment in the case.

POLITAN, Judge.

* * * *

Plaintiff's Third Count alleges that defendant "negligently failed to perform another drug test on plaintiff to rule out a false positive." There is no merit to this allegation. The essence of a cause of action in negligence is the breach of a legal duty. *Fortugno Realty Co. v. Schiavone-Bonomo Corp.*, 39 N.J. 382, 393 (1963). That legal duty may be defined by statute or the common law. In certain case the duty may also be found in fundamental concepts of decency and fair play. While there are numerous constitutional and statutory enactments which circumscribe private employers' treatment of employees and prospective applicants, these provisions do not define Coke's relation to Jevic with respect to drug testing. Nor is there a common law doctrine proscribing what duty a prospective employer owes to prospective employees in terms of drug testing procedures. It is, therefore, appropriate to address this issue by first analyzing what duty Coke would have owed Jevic if he were hired.

If hired, Jevic would have been an at-will employee. He thus could have been fired with or without cause so long as his termination did not offend public policy. *Pierce v. Ortho Pharmaceutical Corp.*, 84 N.J. 58, 72 [1 IER Cases 109] (1980); *Erickson v. Marsh & McLennan Co.*, 1990 WL 9492, Feb. 5, 1990 (S.Ct. N.J.). The preemployment statement expressly delineates this and, moreover, specifically states that Jevic could be fired on the basis of a single positive drug test. There is nothing to suggest that these terms of employment were unconscionable or violative of public policy. Logic thus demands that whatever limited rights Jevic had as a prospective employee could not have been any greater than the rights he would have had if hired. While defendant surely could have tested Jevic a second time there is a significant distinction between what one may do and what the law requires one to do. If hired Jevic could have been terminated after a single positive drug test. Coke thus had no legal obligation, in the pre-employment setting, to test Jevic a second time.

Nevertheless, the court declines to accept defendant's assertion that Coke had no legal obligation to assure that the employment decision was not based on an erroneous false-positive test. Coke has a definite obligation, as a matter of public policy, to insure that its drug testing procedures are scientifically sound. This duty is consistent with the concept of an at-will employee. An at-will employee fired on the basis of a false positive, procured through second rate or negligent test procedures, would surely have a cause of action based on public policy for wrongful termination. Similarly, Coke's limited duty to a prospective employee should extend only to insuring that any drug tests are reliable in design and application. A contrary holding would invite the use of suspect procedures and techniques which could easily be skewed to mask other impermissible hiring policies. The evidence is clear, however, that Coke did use the most advanced and accurate scientific procedures available.

*   *   *   *

Plaintiff's Fourth Count alleges that "defendant violated public policy in the wrongful termination of plaintiff's employment." There are a variety of problems with this allegation. First, as stated, no employment relationship ever arose between Coke and Jevic. More importantly, plaintiff has not identified a legitimate public policy offended by a private employer not hiring an individual who tested positive for drug use.

*   *   *   *

Finally, plaintiff's allegation is deficient because Coke's drug testing procedure is in no way offensive to public policy. In fact, it is a manifestation of the overwhelming public understanding of the plague of drugs in the United States and the need to rid all work places of their influence.

The use of marijuana and other illegal narcotics exacts an enormous toll on this country in terms of business productivity and public health costs. Their use deprives the employee of the ability to function at peak efficiency and thus deprives the employer of part of what he bargained for. We should not seek to shield their use by creating amorphous legal rights but should rather sanction policies which reasonably balance the interest of the citizen with that of the country and the employer. In this case Coke's policy was reasonable in design and scope. Plaintiff's argument is thus entirely unpersuasive.

Decision and Remedy   *The court granted Coca-Cola's motion for summary judgment.*

Several states have passed laws that regulate employment drug testing. Typical state laws require licensed testing facilities, an opportunity for confirmation or disproof of positive results, prompt employee notification, limited disclosure of results, and an opportunity for participation in some form of rehabilitation program for first-time offenders.

AIDS Testing

An increasing number of employers are testing their workers for the Acquired Immune Deficiency Syndrome (AIDS). Few public issues are more controversial than this practice.

The primary legal question in AIDS testing was the Rehabilitation Act of 1973. This law applied to companies that received federal grants or contracts. Congress recently passed the Americans with Disabilities Act of 1990 that covers most purely private workforces.

These laws prohibit discrimination against individuals who are handicapped or considered to be handicapped. The term handicapped has been broadly defined to include those who suffer from diseases such as AIDS.

To be protected under the Rehabilitation Act or Americans With Disabilities Act, a handicapped person must demonstrate that he or she is "otherwise qualified." Victims of some communicable diseases will not be otherwise qualified, because they threaten other employees with contagion. Courts have generally held, however, that AIDS is not so contagious as to disqualify employees in most jobs. An exception would exist for certain jobs in which infection (such as blood-to-blood transfer) is more likely.

These laws also require that an employer make reasonable accommodation for its handicapped employees and cannot discriminate against them based on their handicap. Thus, the law may not prohibit AIDS testing but may be interpreted to prohibit the discharge of employees based on AIDS tests or even the disclosure of AIDS test results.

Some state laws more directly restrict AIDS testing. In 1985, Florida adopted a law making it illegal for employers to use AIDS tests in making employment decisions. Wisconsin prohibits employers from requesting or requiring employees or job applicants to take an AIDS test. California prohibits involuntary testing and proscribes negligent or willful disclosure of test results. New York encourages testing that is both voluntary and confidential. Some cities, including Los Angeles, San Francisco, Boston and Philadelphia, prohibit AIDS discrimination. State and local handicapped protection laws also limit testing for AIDS and other diseases.

Enhanced Monitoring

As technology advances, so does the employer's ability to closely monitor its employees' work. Companies have increasingly employed monitoring of telephone calls, closed-circuit television monitoring, and monitoring of computer work stations. Over 15 million employees are now subject to phone monitoring.

The legality of such enhanced monitoring is an important future issue. To date, most courts have permitted electronic monitoring of employees under the common law. Courts have suggested, however, that employees must be notified of the possibility of such monitoring.

The only directly applicable federal legislation on employee monitoring is the Electronic Communications Privacy Act of 1986, which regulates wiretapping. An employer's telephone monitoring might be an illegal interception of oral communication under this act. The act contains significant exemptions, however, including one for monitoring on an extension of the phone line for business purposes. The act also creates an exception where consent is given to monitoring.

Several states have proposed laws to regulate employee monitoring. Relatively few laws have been adopted, but Connecticut, for example, has legislation that would prohibit electronic surveillance of lounges, locker rooms and other nonwork areas. Some additional restrictive legislation can be anticipated in future years.

Plant Closing Legislation

Even during the economic growth of the 1980s, over one million workers lost their jobs every year due to plant closings or relocations. In 1988, Congress passed the Worker Adjustment and Retraining Notification Act ("WARNA") to assist workers in danger of job loss.

WARNA covers companies with one hundred or more employees or with 4000 or more work-hours per week. WARNA requires advance notice to workers in the event of a plant closing or a "mass layoff."

A plant closing is defined as a shutdown of one or more facilities at a single site that results in an employment loss of fifty or more employees during a thirty-day period. A plant closing may also involve a series of related layoffs of over fifty workers during a ninety-day period.

A mass layoff occurs when employment at the site is reduced by laying off at least fifty workers representing at least 33 percent of the employees at a site, within a thirty-day period or related layoffs within a ninety-day period. An exception exists for layoffs of six months or less. The employer can also avoid the legal requirements by offering to transfer an employee to a different site of employment within a reasonable commuting distance.

If a statutorily defined plant closing or mass layoff is to occur, WARNA creates certain advance notice requirements for workers. The employer must serve a written notice of its plans for such action to the union representative for the workers. If the workers are not unionized, the employer must notify each affected employee personally. The employer also must notify certain local government officials.

This notice must be provided at least sixty days prior to the layoff or plant closing. If the notice is not given sixty days in advance, laid off employees may sue to recover their back pay, benefits and attorneys' fees. Back pay and benefits cover the portion of the sixty-day period prior to layoffs that was without notice.

WARNA has certain exemptions from the advance notice requirement. The first is called the **faltering company exception** and applies only to plant closings, not mass layoffs. The employer under this exception can reduce the sixty-day period if it was actively seeking capital or business that would have enabled it to avoid the closing. The employer also must show that giving notice to workers would have precluded obtaining the necessary capital or business.

The second exception is for unforeseeable business circumstances, such as a sudden cutback in work because of the loss of a major customer. A third exception exists when the closing or mass layoff is the direct result of a natural disaster, such as a flood or earthquake. A fourth exception applies when closings or layoffs are caused by worker strikes or layoffs under the National Labor Relations Act, as described in Chapter 48 of *West's Business Law, Fifth Edition* and in Chapter 16 of *West's Legal Environment of Business*.

WARNA was quite controversial when passed, because the law significantly limits the flexibility of many manufacturing businesses. Suppose that King, Inc., borrows money for a leveraged buyout of Parsons & Co. Parsons may desire to fight off the takeover by improving operating efficiencies through plant closures. WARNA effectively forces Parsons to keep the plants open for at least two months (or pay workers two months' worth of wages and benefits). By that time, King may have completed the takeover.

Additional Employee Rights

Various laws provide additional rights to individual employees. The right to unionize is protected by federal law, and discussed in Chapter 48 of *West's Business Law, Fifth Edition*. Rights against certain forms of discrimination are guaranteed by civil rights laws and discussed in Chapter 48 and this book's Chapter 4 "Employment Discrimination Law." Rights of workplace safety are discussed in Chapter 48 and this book's Chapter 5, "Occupational Safety and Workers' Compensation." These topics are also covered in Chapters 16 and 17 of *West's Legal Environment of Business*.

■ Ethical Perspectives

Whistle-Blowing

Whistle-blowing has been the source of considerable ethical debate. The concept of whistle-blowing sets two moral goals in conflict. First, the employee has a duty of loyalty to the employer. Second, the employee has a duty to external society (such as honesty, doing no harm, etc.)

A large number of employees believe that whistle-blowing should be morally prohibited. There is a strong strain of American opinion against "ratting" to the boss. Blowing the whistle directly confronts and accuses the moral behavior of another. In addition, whistle-blowing may give the entire company a black eye and can produce considerable disruption within the company. Whistle-blowing is a bit like calling a foul on one's own basketball teammate.

Others argue that whistle-blowing is morally required. They contend that whistle-blowing is an altruistic action that places the good of others above selfish personal interests. These advocates would always place societal interest above that of the firm. They would indict an employee who does nothing and fails to blow the whistle on unethical corporate acts. They also have argued that employees have no duty of loyalty to their employing corporation.

A middle ground has been put forth, suggesting that whistle-blowing is morally permitted in some instances, but seldom should be prohibited or required. One leading business ethicist has put forth a three-part test for permitted whistle-blowing:

1. The firm, through its product or policy, will do serious and considerable harm to the public, whether in the person of the user of its product, an innocent bystander, or the general public.

2. Once an employee identifies a serious threat to the user of a product or to the general public, he or she should report it to an immediate superior and make his or her moral concern known.

3. If one's immediate superior does nothing effective about the concern or complaint, the employee should exhaust the internal procedures and possibilities within the firm.[11]

In addition to the above three tests, one might add the existence of strong evidence of the risk of the product. Employees should not be too quick to assume the worst and challenge decisions without good proof. It might also be fair to expect that the whistle-blower seek to correct the problem with the minimum possible damage to the employer.

---

[11]R.T. DeGeorge, *Business Ethics* 230-232 (1986).

| **International Perspectives** | ### Wrongful Discharge in Japan |

The United States has a long tradition of at-will employment that provided employers great freedom and flexibility in discharging workers. Many other nations, including much of Europe, provide much less employer flexibility and, therefore, greater job security. Japan, specifically, has relatively elaborate restrictions on discharging employees.

Interestingly, Japanese statutory law is quite close to U.S. law. The relevant statutes state that an employer may discharge an employee at any time and for any reason. The law simply requires two weeks' notice. The reality is far different, however, as the statutory law is influenced by national culture and by other legal requirements.

Japan draws a distinction between regular (permanent) employees and temporary hires. Regular employees are typically recruited directly from universities and secondary schools. While these workers receive indefinite, at-will employment contracts, they are expected to work for the employer until their retirement. Temporary employees are hired from a pool of experienced workers and are the first (and often only) workers to lose their jobs in the event of an economic downturn.

The Japanese Constitution, adopted in 1946, makes it relatively difficult to fire workers. The Constitution declares that work is a fundamental human right and declares that "the promotion of job security [is] a matter of public order." The constitutional provision has been implemented in part by the nation's Labor Standards Law. This law establishes prohibitions on discriminatory treatment, establishes minimum working conditions, and limits the discharge of employees. Violation of the law can produce criminal penalties.

Japanese courts have placed several restrictions on at-will discharges of regular employees. The Labor Standards Law specifically requires thirty days' advance notice of any discharge. Courts require that an employer provide good reasons for dismissing any worker.

A key protection for workers is found in "employment rules" that each employer (of more than ten employees) must establish and file with the government. These rules provide for the terms and conditions of employment. The rules virtually always contain a dismissal clause. The dismissal clause specifies conditions for which workers may be terminated. The conditions are specific, and Japanese courts have held that a discharge for reasons other than the conditions of the employment rules is invalid. The rules of employment are similar to a detailed employment manual in the U.S.

Even discharges within the employment rules have been overturned by the courts of Japan. The nation's Supreme Court has declared that any discharge is wrongful if it is considered unreasonable on the facts of the case. Any discharge contrary to public policy will be unlawful. The courts of Japan review discharges closely and reject those that are deemed an abuse of employer discretion. If a discharge is invalid, the employee is generally reinstated.

Wrongful discharge law illustrates substantial cultural differences between Japan and the United States. Japan's system typically guarantees lifetime employment to regular employees. This cultural feature is reflected in the application of Japan's laws.

Questions and Case Problems

1. Lincoln Life merged its Wisconsin agency into its Chicago agency. The merger was ordered by Steinhaus, who became manager of the expanded agency. Kumpf, the former manager of the Wisconsin agency, was an at-will employee and lost his job. Kumpf argued that he had been wrongfully terminated, and that Steinhaus had engineered the merger simply to increase his authority and his percentage of revenues from Lincoln Life's business. Does Kumpf have a good claim for wrongful termination? [*Kumpf v. Steinhaus*, 779 F.2d 1323 (7th Cir. 1985)].

2. Charles Toussaint was employed in a middle management position at Blue Cross. After being employed for five years, Toussaint was fired without any reason being given. Blue Cross personnel policies stated that it was the "policy" of the company that employees would be fired for "just cause only." In addition, he was told that he would not be fired so long as he was "doing the job." Toussaint sued Blue Cross, arguing that he had an implied contract of employment that the company violated. A jury ruled for Toussaint and awarded him damages in excess of $72,000. Blue Cross appealed this judgment. Should the court of appeals overturn the jury verdict? [*Toussaint v. Blue Cross & Blue Shield of Michigan*, 292 N.W.2d 880 (Mich. 1980)].

3. Flanigan had worked for Prudential Federal for many years and was promoted to branch office bookkeeper and then assistant loan counselor. She performed satisfactorily in all her positions with the bank. The bank suffered an economic downturn and adopted a new policy that eliminated her position but enabled her to take a new job as a teller. One month later, she was fired from her new position. She argued that the bank had dealt unfairly with her and fired her due to the vindictiveness of her supervisor. She sued for wrongful discharge. A jury awarded her nearly $1.5 million in actual and punitive damages, and the bank appealed. Should the court overturn the jury verdict? [*Flanigan v. Prudential Federal Savings & Loan Ass'n*, 720 P.2d 257 (Mon. 1986)].

4. The manager of a brake shop was directed by its owner not to purchase a new lathe and to reduce inventory. He went ahead with the purchase and did not reduce inventory, because of his sincere belief that this was in the company's best interest. The manager then was fired for insubordination. He claimed that he was given the right to manage the shop and make purchasing decisions and sued for wrongful discharge. Should the manager succeed on his claim? [*Thomas v. Bourdette*, 608 P.2d 178 (Ore App. 1980)].

5. Kelley was a barge engineer on an oil platform in the Gulf of Mexico. His employer had a drug testing policy that involved the taking of a urine sample under the observation of a company agent. Kelley's sample tested positive for marijuana. Subsequently, Kelley was discharged from his job. He sued for negligent infliction of emotional distress, and a jury awarded him $125,000 in damages. The employer appealed this verdict. Should an appellate court overturn the jury award? [*Kelley v. Schlumberger Technology Corp.*, 849 F.2d 41 (1st Cir. 1988)].

CHAPTER FOUR

Employment Discrimination Law

▰ KEY BACKGROUND

 The essential background for this chapter on employment discrimination law is found in Chapter 48 of *West's Business Law, Fifth Edition* and in Chapter 17 of *West's Legal Environment of Business*, which cover employment and labor relations law. Among the important points to remember from these chapters are:

- the coverage and application of Title VII

- the procedures and proof requirements for enforcement of Title VII actions

- the defenses available for Title VII actions

- other antidiscrimination laws providing protection based on age and handicapped status.

* * *

Employment discrimination law is one of the most important issues confronting business today. An informal survey of the daily "law" section of the *Wall Street Journal* found that it reported more discrimination cases than any other category of law.

Employment discrimination law is also becoming increasingly complex. The categories of individuals protected from discrimination continue to be expanded. The requirements of discrimination law are also expanded as laws are amended and court cases are decided. Even a "pure

heart" cannot avoid discrimination liability for an employer who is unfamiliar with the details of discrimination law.

▰ Title VII

Title VII litigation continues to grow, as courts extend the section to new forms of discrimination. Different protected classes continue to face different forms of discrimination.

Racial Discrimination

The central protected classes of Title VII are race and color. The primary purpose of the Civil Rights Act was to prevent racial discrimination. Recently, there have been several disputes over what constitutes discrimination based upon race or color.

For example, an Arab university professor alleged that he suffered discrimination based on race. The university defended on the grounds that being Arab is not a distinct race that is protected under Title VII. The United States Supreme Court disagreed and held that race should be interpreted broadly to prohibit discrimination against any subgroup, including "Finns, gypsies, Basques, Hebrews, Swedes," etc.[1]

In a more recent decision, a light-skinned black woman claimed that she had suffered discrimination from darker-skinned black supervisors based on her skin color. A court agreed that this type of discrimination was also prohibited by Title VII.[2]

---

[1]*Francis College v. Al-Khazraji*, 481 U.S. 604, 611 (1987).
[2]*Walker v. IRS*, 713 F. Supp. 403 (N.D. Ga. 1989).

A central form of unlawful discrimination is **disparate treatment**, in which a member of a group is intentionally treated differently. The prima facie case of disparate treatment discrimination is relatively simple, as a plaintiff must first show:

1. The person was a member of a specific protected class under Title VII.

2. The person was qualified for the job in question and undertook other necessary requirements (e.g., applying for the job).

3. The person suffered some loss of employment opportunity (e.g., was fired, not hired, offered lower pay).

4. The employer left the job open or gave the employment opportunity to someone outside the plaintiff's protected class.

Once the plaintiff makes out the prima facie case, the defendant employer need only state a lawful reason why the plaintiff suffered a loss of job opportunity (e.g., was not hired). For example, an employer might state that the plaintiff was not hired because he or she was less qualified than other applicants or was fired due to frequent absences.

While the employer has no burden of proof regarding the stated reason, the employer must state that the legitimate reason was the basis for its action at the time. The employer cannot produce legitimate reasons after the fact.

For example, suppose that a black employee applied for a promotion and was denied as unqualified. Later, a white employee applied and was hired. The black employee sues for unlawful discrimination. The company now concedes that the black employee was qualified but states that the white was more qualified. This is an insufficient reason—the white employee had not applied at the time of the black employee's rejection, so comparative qualifications cannot explain the employer's decision.

Once the employer articulates this reason, the plaintiff has an opportunity to demonstrate that the stated reason is a pretext (a cover-up for discrimination). There are several ways for a plaintiff to show pretext. A plaintiff might show that standards were applied inconsistently. For example, an employer fired a black woman for excessive absences, but white men with an equal number of absences were not fired. Racist or sexist statements by responsible persons also provide some evidence of pretext. If the plaintiff can show pretext, he or she wins the case.

Disparate treatment discrimination involves intentional discrimination but does not require proof of blatant racism or sexism. Any purposeful different treatment, even well-intended, could be a basis for unlawful disparate treatment discrimination. This principle is illustrated by the following decision.

■ **Case 4.1**
Vaughn v.
Edel
United States Court of Appeals,
Fifth Circuit, 1990
918 F.2d 517

Background and Facts   *Emma Vaughn was a black female attorney who worked for Texaco's Land Department. Her supervisors were Robert Edel and Alvin Hatton. In her early years with the company, she received promotions and was the "highest ranked contract analyst" in the department. In 1985, after she returned from a maternity leave, Edel complained to her about her low productivity and excessive visits by other black employees. He was concerned that she was becoming a "black matriarch" for the company and that this hurt her work. Vaughn was offended by these remarks and discussed the matter with another attorney. Concerned about charges of race discrimination, officials told Edel not to criticize Vaughn.*

From 1985 to 1987, neither Edel nor Hatton expressed any criticism of Vaughn's work to her, and her annual evaluations rated her as "satisfactory." There was testimony that the company's satisfaction was overstated. In 1987, to meet cost-reduction goals, Texaco fired its two "poorest performers" in the division, one of whom was Vaughn.

Vaughn filed a discrimination claim with the EEOC, which decided that there was no violation of Title VII. She then sued in court, and a magistrate also found that there was no illegal discrimination. Vaughn appealed.

WIENER, Circuit Judge.

*   *   *   *

Vaughn presented direct evidence of discrimination. Keller testified that to avoid provoking a discrimination suit he had told Vaughn's supervisors not to confront her about her work. His "black matriarch" memorandum details the events that led Keller to initiate this policy. Keller also testified that he had deliberately overstated Vaughn's evaluations in order not to start the process that might eventually lead to termination. This direct evidence clearly shows that Keller acted as he did solely because Vaughn is black. Texaco has never offered any evidence to show that in neither confronting Vaughn about her poor performance nor counselling her it would have acted as it did without regard to her race. Vaughn has, consequently, established that Texaco discriminated against her.

*   *   *   *

Although Vaughn's race may not have directly motivated the 1987 decision to fire her, race did play a part, as the magistrate found, in Vaughn's employment relationship with Texaco from 1985 to 1987. Texaco's treatment of Vaughn was not color-blind during that period. In neither criticizing Vaughn when her work was unsatisfactory nor counselling her how to improve, Texaco treated Vaughn differently than it did its other contract analysts because, as the magistrate found, she was black. As a result, Texaco did not afford Vaughn the same opportunity to improve her performance, and perhaps her relative ranking, as it did its white employees. One of those employees was placed on an improvement program. As for the others, Texaco does not deny that they received, at least, informal counselling. The evidence indicates that Vaughn had the ability to improve. As Texaco acknowledges, she was once its "highest ranked contract analyst."

Had her dissatisfied supervisors simply counselled Vaughn informally, such counselling would inevitably have indicated to Vaughn that her work was deficient. Had Keller given Vaughn the evaluation that he believed she deserved, Texaco's regulations would have required his placing her on a ninety-day work improvement program, just as at least one other employee—a white male —had been placed. A Texaco employee who has not improved by the end of that period is fired. Consequently and employee on an improvement program certainly knows what Texaco thinks of his performance, knows that he is in imminent danger of being fired, and at least has an option to improve, thereby reducing or removing the risk of being fired.

*   *   *   *

Initially, Texaco's decisions not to criticize Vaughn and not to state her correct evaluations may have appeared beneficial, even— had she been aware of them—to Vaughn. She did, for example, receive a merit pay increase in 1986 that she would not have received had Keller given her the evaluation that he believed she deserved. Ultimately, however, whether Texaco's decisions may have damaged Vaughn's employment status at Texaco will never be known. Furthermore, whether Texaco's decisions ultimately benefitted or harmed Vaughn is irrelevant. The decisions not to apply the usual procedures in Vaughn's case were racial decisions. Texaco has never stated any reason other than that she was black for treating Vaughn as it did. Had Texaco treated Vaughn in a color-blind manner from 1985 to 1987, Vaughn might have been fired by April 1987 for unsatisfactory work; on the other hand, she might have sufficiently improved her performance so as not to be one of the two "lowest ranked" employees, thereby avoiding termination in April 1987. Consequently, Texaco must bear the cost of its lost opportunity to determine whether Vaughn might have remained one of the two "lowest ranked" contract analysts had it not made decisions based on race. This circuit will not sterilize a seemingly objective decision to fire an employee when earlier discriminatory decisions have infected it.

Decision and Remedy   *The court reversed the magistrate's ruling, held that Title VII was violated, and remanded the case for calculation of damages.*

Disparate treatment involves intentional discrimination against a single individual and the employer's overall fair practices are no defense. Some employers sought to use a "bottom-line" defense, by arguing that their work force had proportional representation. After a black worker claimed that a test for promotion was discriminatory, the company defended by showing that it had employed a large number of black employees. The Supreme Court held that this was no defense to a claim of discrimination by an individual employee.[3]

Some of the most difficult discrimination cases involve allegations of sex discrimination, of a type known as **sex plus discrimination**. This arises when an employer has different rules for men and women and, for example, disciplines a woman worker for violating the dress code that is specific to women.

Courts have accepted the legality of applying somewhat different standards to men and women. Different rules were upheld in the following circumstances: a rule requiring that male employees wear ties, a rule prohibiting female employees from wearing pants, a ban on male employees wearing beards or long hair. All these practices were found legal.

Under "sex plus" discrimination, the rules cannot be much stricter for one sex than another and must enable most workers to comply. Courts have struck down rules that placed maximum weight requirements on female flight attendants only and that prohibited female flight attendants from wearing glasses.

A second type of unlawful discrimination is **disparate impact** discrimination. This is unintentional discrimination that results when a seemingly neutral hiring practice has discriminatory consequences. A minimum height requirement for a police department, for example, does not directly discriminate but has the effect of ruling out a higher percentage of women and certain nationalities.

The Supreme Court decision in *Wards Cove v. Atonio*, set forth in *West's Business Law, Fifth Edition* and in *West's Legal Environment of Business*, made disparate impact cases somewhat more difficult to win. The plaintiff's prima facie case is to identify a specific employer practice that has the statistical effect of discriminating against a protected class.

For example, suppose Golden Co. used a written test to hire construction employees. A member of a minority group who applied and failed the test might complain that the test had a discriminatory effect. To show this discriminatory effect, the plaintiff must show that a higher percentage of qualified minority applicants than the percentage of other groups failed the test.

The Equal Employment Opportunity Commission (EEOC) has adopted a rule of thumb for guidance in determining whether such a test has an unlawful discriminatory impact. This is

---

[3]*Connecticut v. Teal*, 457 U.S. 440 (1982).

known as the four-fifths or **80 percent rule**. If a test's selection rate for one group is 80 percent or less of the selection rate for another group, there is evidence of a disparate impact.

After a plaintiff makes out a prima facie case of disparate impact discrimination, the employer must give a business justification for its practice. For example, Golden Co. would state that the written test was necessary to ensure that workers had sufficient ability to communicate effectively.

Under *Wards Cove*, the plaintiff then has the burden to show that the asserted business justification for the practice is wrong. For example, the plaintiffs could show that the written test of Golden Co. does not in effect help demonstrate workers' ability to communicate. Alternatively, they might show that the ability to communicate is unimportant or that there is some nondiscriminatory, superior way to test for ability to communicate.

Most commentators argued that the *Wards Cove* decision made it extremely difficult for plaintiffs to win a disparate impact case. They theorized that few plaintiffs will be able to prove that a practice has no business justification.

Some employment practices may still be unlawful, however. Suppose that Golden Co. adopts a policy of refusing to hire anyone who has an arrest record. The EEOC has suggested that this policy will often have an unlawful and unjustifiable disparate impact.

The use of arrest records has a statistically disparate impact for blacks, Hispanics, and other groups. The EEOC has found that members of these groups are arrested at a higher rate than are whites.

There may seldom be a good business justification for refusing to hire anyone with an arrest rate. First, an arrest is not a conviction, so there is a poor correlation between arrests and the sort of actions that Golden Co. wants to avoid. Second, one may be arrested for many different crimes. There may be a business justification for not hiring those arrested for larceny, but there is less justification for rejecting those arrested in, for example, a political protest.

Some employers may consider certain arrest records for certain jobs. For example, a trucking company had a policy of refusing to hire anyone as a driver who had been arrested for theft. A court found that this rule had a business justification, because the drivers would be transporting valuable property.[4]

On other occasions, employers may not use arrest records to screen job applicants. The EEOC provided the following example:

> Lola, a black female, applies to Bus Inc. for a position as a bus driver. In response to an inquiry whether she had ever been arrested, Lola states that she was arrested five years earlier for fraud in unemployment benefits. Lola admits that she committed the crime alleged. She explains that she received unemployment benefits shortly after her husband died and her expenses increased. During this period, she worked part-time for minimum wage because her unemployment check amounted to slightly less than the monthly rent for her meager apartment. She did not report the income to the State Unemployment Board for fear that her payments would be reduced and that she would not be able to feed her three young children. After her arrest, she agreed to, and did, repay the state. Bus Inc. rejected Lola. Lola's rejection violated Title VII. The commission of fraud in the unemployment system does not constitute a justification for the rejection of an applicant for the position of bus driver. The type of crime which Lola committed is totally unrelated to her ability to safely, efficiently and/or courteously drive a bus. Furthermore, the arrest is not recent.[5]

Sexual Harassment

Many recent employment discrimination cases have involved sexual harassment. Such harassment is considered a form of discrimination because it is a burden suffered by only one sex. Two types of sexual harassment concern Title VII —**quid pro quo harassment** and **hostile environment harassment**.

Whatever the form of the action, there are five parts to a prima facie case of sexual harassment:

---

[4]*EEOC v. Carolina Freight*, 723 F. Supp. 734 (S.D. Fla. 1989).

[5]*EEOC Compliance Manual*, No. 915-061 (September 7, 1990).

1. Plaintiff belongs to a protected class.

2. Plaintiff was subject to unwelcome sexual harassment.

3. The harassment was based on sex.

4. The harassment affected a term, condition or privilege of employment.

5. The employer is subject to respondeat superior liability (responsible for the acts of employees).

Quid pro quo sexual harassment is the stereotypical form of harassment. For example, suppose that a supervisor tells an office worker that she must be physically intimate with him or be fired (or lose a promotion, etc.). If she refuses to comply with the supervisor's demands and loses an employment opportunity, she has a good case for quid pro quo harassment.

Hostile environment harassment is more common. In this form of harassment the employee may suffer no direct adverse financial consequences. The employee must continue to work, however, in an environment made uncomfortable by harassment. This is considered discrimination in the terms and conditions of employment.

Courts have struggled with the definition of what constitutes an unlawful, harassing hostile environment. An occasional sexist comment may be inappropriate but is not illegal. To constitute a harassing environment, the harassment must be both significant and pervasive.

Courts have considered several factors in harassing environment cases. Unwanted touching, for example, is significant in establishing a hostile environment. So is direct sexual propositioning or frequent speculation about an employee's private life.

Courts have been somewhat less likely to find sexual harassment when sexism was not directed specifically at an individual. Several courts have held that the presence of sexually explicit posters in the workplace does not in itself constitute unlawful harassment.

A defense in sexual harassment cases is that the alleged harassment was welcomed by the plaintiff. There are romantic relationships that occur between employees that are mutually welcome. Indeed, one study found that 55 percent of executive women were romantically involved with men they met professionally.[6] When such a relationship falls apart, a sexual harassment claim may occur.

Whether given actions were welcome is a factual matter to be judged on the available evidence. Evidence suggests that the majority of sexual harassment claims do not involve welcome advances, but rather involve some sort of pressure to comply.

It is important to recognize that "welcome" is not the same as "voluntary." Courts have recognized that a woman may "voluntarily" agree to sex even when it is unwelcome. A woman may agree out of fear of losing her job, even when this threat is unstated. Men also may be victims of sexual harassment and have equal rights to sue if they are so victimized.

Employer Liability

Title VII makes only employers liable. In sexual harassment cases this seems awkward, because a company does not harass a person; individuals do. The employer can be liable under *respondeat superior*, which makes it responsible for the unlawful acts of its employees.

Employers are not strictly liable for the actions of their employees. When sexual harassment was by a supervisory or high-level official, however, the employer is likely to be found responsible. The knowledge of such upper-level employees is generally imputed to the employer under agency law. This is especially likely if the company lacked an effective sexual harassment policy.

When harassment is by coworkers or clients, the plaintiff must show more evidence to find the employer responsible. The plaintiff first must show that the employer was aware, or should have been aware, of the existence of the sexual harassment. The employer may be aware because the employee filed a grievance. Alternatively, the employer may be liable for failure to provide an effective, protected grievance policy.

Once the employer is made aware of the harassment, it must respond effectively. Firm actions must be taken to prevent recurrence of harassment, and this action must be taken promptly.

---

[6]*Success*, April 1986, pp. 34-35.

Many companies have adopted policies against sexual harassment. These help avoid liability but are insufficient by themselves. Firms must vigorously apply these policies in seeking out sexual harassment problems and correcting them.

Employer liability has been particularly disputed in hostile environment cases. The following decision describes the facts used to make out a case for an illegal hostile environment and the circumstances that produce employer liability for that environment.

■■ **Case 4.2**
Robinson v.
Jacksonville Shipyards, Inc.
United States District Court for the
Middle District of Florida, 1991
Case No. 86-927-Civ-J-12

Background and Facts   *Lois Robinson was employed as a welder at Jacksonville Shipyards, Inc. ("JSI"). While she worked at JSI, "[p]ictures of nude and partially nude women appeared throughout the JSI workplace in the form of magazines, plaques on the wall, photographs torn from magazines and affixed to the wall or attached to calendars supplied by advertising tool supply companies." These posters were pervasive throughout the workplace and some were more offensive and degrading. There were no posters of nude or partially nude men. In addition, male workers made a number of highly suggestive comments to Robinson. Highly offensive graffiti were written on walls of the shop.*

In 1980, JSI had adopted its first sexual harassment policy. Robinson lodged some complaints with supervising employees. They relayed the complaints to higher management levels and took steps to paint over some of the most offensive graffiti. The nude pictures and calendars were not removed, and she was told that the shipyard was a "man's world." When Robinson's complaints became widely known, the workers made a joke of them and sought to increase the number of pinups.

Robinson sued JSI for creating a hostile working environment. At trial, the court heard testimony from professors of psychology to the effect that JSI's practices caused stereotyping of women as sex objects and denigrated their ability as employees. This is especially pronounced when women compose a small fraction of the work force. The professors also testified that such practices cause stress and loss of self-confidence among women.

WALTON, Judge.

*   *   *   *

A reasonable woman would find that the working environment at JSI was abusive. This conclusion reaches the totality of the circumstances, including the sexual remarks, the sexual jokes, the sexually oriented pictures of women, and the nonsexual rejection of women by coworkers. The testimony by Dr. Fiske and Ms. Wagner provides a reliable basis upon which to conclude that the cumulative, corrosive effect of this work environment over time affects the psychological well-being of a reasonable woman placed in these conditions. This corollary conclusion holds true whether the concept of psychological well-being is measured by the impact of the work environment on a reasonable woman's work performance or more broadly by the impact of the stress inflicted on her by the continuing presence of the harassing behavior.

The fact that some female employees did not complain of the work environment or find some behaviors objectionable does not affect this conclusion concerning the objective offensiveness of the work environment as a whole.

* * * *

In this context the effect of pornography on workplace equality is obvious. Pornography on an employer's wall or desk communicates a message about the way he views women, a view strikingly at odds with the way women wish to be viewed in the workplace. Depending upon the material in question, it may communicate that women should be the objects of sexual aggression, that they are submissive slaves to male desires, or that their most salient and desirable attributes are sexual. Any of these images may communicate to male coworkers that it is acceptable to view women in a predominantly sexual way. All of the views to some extent detract from the image most women in the workplace would like to project: that of the professional, credible coworker.

* * * *

Two, JSI cannot stand on an "ostrich defense" that it lacked knowledge of many of the complaints, because its handling of sexual harassment complaints deterred reporting and it did not conduct adequate investigation of the complaints it did receive. JSI received reports at the supervisory level and at the line level (quartermen and leadermen) concerning incidents of sexual harassment. Additionally, many supervisory personnel admitted that they knew of the sexually oriented pictures throughout the workplace. Defendants concede several such reports in a series of tables attached to their post-trial brief; the testimony as recorded in the findings of Fact documents many more reports. These reports should have alerted JSI management to the need to conduct a more thorough investigation of conditions in the shipyards. A duty to conduct further investigation arises when a report or reports of sexual harassment to management suggests that the workplace may be charged in a sexually hostile manner.

* * * *

Not only were the behaviors repeated throughout the workplace and over time, but examples show that the same individuals would repeat sexually harassing misconduct following intervention from management. Moreover, JSI cannot escape the burden or responsibility for many unreported instances of sexual harassment. Although JSI did not receive the opportunity to respond to these instances due to the lack of a formal complaint, the fact that a complaint was not made resulted from the failure to maintain an effective sexual harassment complaint procedure and other circumstances in the work environment that deterred the reporting of episodes of sexual harassment.

Decision and Remedy   *The court granted Robinson injunctive relief that required JSI to adopt, implement and enforce a sexual harassment policy substantially in the form proposed by Robinson and awarded her attorney's fees and nominal damages.*

Paramour Liability

Courts are still divided on the concept of **paramour liability**. This refers to an employer's representative favoring an employee because of a romantic relationship. A more qualified employee who felt more deserving of a promotion may sue the employer under Title VII.

The District of Columbia Circuit Court of Appeals has held that favoring a lover is a violation of Title VII.[7] In this case a female nurse in a jail was denied a promotion and claimed that it was because another nurse had an intimate relationship with the jail's chief medical officer. The court held that if sex was a substantial contributing factor to the employment decision, that decision was unlawful. The court ultimately ordered the jail to promote the plaintiff nurse.

The Second Circuit Court of Appeals held that favoring a lover is not a violation of Title VII.[8] In this case, seven male therapists alleged that they lost an opportunity for promotion because the administrator was involved in a relationship with a female therapist, who was promoted. The court held that voluntary, consensual sexual relationships were outside the scope of Title VII.

Obviously, the law in this circumstance is uncertain. Plaintiffs will have a well-established case, however, if they can show that the presence of workplace relationships created a hostile working environment for those who did not wish to participate.

In one case, a court found that an office of the Securities and Exchange Commission was rife with sexual relationships and inappropriate activity in the office. A court found that the sexual conduct was so pervasive that it created a hostile and offensive work environment for other women who worked at the office.[9]

▬ Affirmative Action

Title VII protects all races, colors, sexes, religions and national origins, including white Anglo-Saxon Protestants. Discrimination against white males, for example, is ordinarily illegal under Title VII.

An exception has been created, however, to permit employers to grant certain preferences for certain minority groups and women. This is known as **affirmative action**. Some, but not all, affirmative action plans are legal. Courts strictly enforce the following standards.

First, there must be some demonstrated need for a voluntary affirmative action program. This may be found when a workforce has statistical disparities in representation that may be the product of past discrimination. For example, suppose that a private bus company in Detroit had only 10 percent black drivers, though the city has a majority black population. This would probably be grounds for an affirmative action program.

The employer who wants to adopt a voluntary affirmative action program need not concede that it has discriminated in the past. Such a concession would open the employer to innumerable lawsuits. The employer need only demonstrate that some group in the workforce, such as women, are underrepresented in certain jobs.

Courts have also suggested that a second requirement of an affirmative action program is that it only benefit qualified individuals. Affirmative action cannot be used to grant token opportunities to unqualified individuals. Affirmative action can be used to choose among qualified applicants and not necessarily take the most qualified applicant.

Third, affirmative action cannot unduly "trammel" the rights of whites, or males, or whichever protected class does not benefit from the program. Suppose that an employer adopted a plan that said that only Hispanic women could be promoted in a given year. This would be unlawful because it denied all opportunity to other protected classes.

To be legal, an affirmative action plan must leave some opportunity for all. A program that established a training system and reserved 40 percent of the slots in the training system for Hispanics might be legal. This would leave a large number of positions for other protected classes.

Courts have been especially concerned about affirmative action plans that force layoffs of a protected class. Courts have tended to strike down plans that caused white males to lose their existing jobs. Indeed, Title VII contains a specific provision that authorizes seniority systems for layoff

---

[7]*King v. Palmer*, 778 F.2d 878 (D.C. Cir. 1985).

[8]*DeCintio v. Westchester County Medical Center*, 807 F.2d 304 (2d Cir. 1986).

[9]*Broderick v. Ruder*, 685 F. Supp. 1269 (D.D.C. 1988).

protection even if they have a disparate impact on minorities.

Fourth, the affirmative action program must be tailored to, and limited to, correcting the evidence of past discrimination. A plan cannot do more than correct the past statistical underrepresentation of women or a minority group. The plan also must be temporary and must cease once the underrepresentation is corrected.

The above discussion has addressed affirmative action programs adopted voluntarily by private employers. In some circumstances, a court may compel an employer to adopt an affirmative action program as part of a remedy for past discrimination.

Section 1981

While Title VII remains the primary tool to prevent discrimination in employment, other laws also protect victims of discrimination. Laws passed shortly after the Civil War prohibited some forms of racial discrimination. The key provision in these laws is known as **Section 1981**,[10] which prohibits discrimination in private contracts.

In some respects Section 1981 offers greater benefits to plaintiffs alleging discrimination. Damages under Title VII are quite limited to direct pecuniary losses resulting from unlawful discrimination (such as back pay awards). Section 1981 also permits a court to order damages for pain and suffering and punitive damages. Section 1981 also provides for jury trials, unlike Title VII.

Section 1981's coverage is more limited than that of Title VII. First, this section only prohibits

race discrimination. Second, Section 1981 only applies to discrimination in the making of contracts and their enforcement. An important Supreme Court decision held that this section did not apply to discrimination in the terms and conditions of employment.[11] Consequently, a worker who suffers racial or sexual harassment on the job has no claim under Section 1981. Nor is it clear whether this section applies to discriminatory firing of employees.

Age Discrimination

The Age Discrimination in Employment Act ("ADEA"), closely parallels Title VII in its protections. The prima facie case for plaintiffs is similar to Title VII as are the employer's defenses. The ADEA prohibits employment discrimination based on age for anyone who is older than forty. Age discrimination against individuals less than forty years old remains lawful. Mandatory retirement is outlawed, with a few exceptions.

The ADEA applies to all employers with twenty or more employees. An exception permits mandatory retirement for employees who are in a "high policy-making position," such as a chief executive officer. The law is enforced by the EEOC but, unlike Title VII, jury trials are available in ADEA actions.

ADEA cases closely parallel Title VII in terms of types of discrimination and burdens of proof. The following decision reflects unlawful behavior by an employer.

---

[10]42 U.S.C. section 1981.

[11]*Patterson v. McLean Credit Union*, 491 U.S. 164 (1989).

Case 4.3
Taggart v.
Time Incorporated
United States Court of Appeals
for the Second Circuit, 1991
Docket No. 90-7318

Background and Facts   *In October 1982, Preview Subscription Television, Inc., a subsidiary of Time, Inc., hired Thomas Taggart as a print production manager. At the time, Taggart was fifty-eight years old. After Preview was dissolved, employees were notified that they would receive special consideration for other positions at Time. Taggart applied for thirty-two positions in various divisions of Time and its subsidiaries. He was turned down for all of these.*

Time said that Taggart was not hired because he was underqualified for some positions, was overqualified for other positions, he was argumentative, and received several unfavorable references. No one ever specifically mentioned his age. Taggart stated that three younger and less qualified persons were hired by Time for positions for which he interviewed. He claimed discrimination based upon his age and especially objects to his rejection for being over qualified.

Taggart filed a charge with the EEOC. After they declined to pursue the case, Taggart sued in federal district court under the ADEA. The district court granted Time's motion for summary judgment, and Taggart appealed.

CARDAMONE, Circuit Judge.

*   *   *   *

Research has unearthed no cases when an overqualified applicant was ruled "unqualified" in the context of age discrimination litigation. Since overqualified is defined as having more education, training or experience than a job calls for, Webster's New Collegiate Dictionary 841 (9th ed. 1983), a ruling that overqualified means unqualified is a non sequitur. Thus, it is not surprising that what case law there is comes to the opposite conclusion.

The record reveals that Michele Rios-Nicosia, the hiring manager at HBO, stated that because Taggart was overqualified, she did not think the position would interest or challenge him. Ms. Rios-Nicosia gave no other reason for not hiring Taggart. Taggart stated he was willing to take any job available simply to continue to earn a decent living, and, as a Time employee with preferred status in obtaining the position, alleges he would have been hired had he not been sixty years old. Time admits that its sole reason for refusing to hire Taggart for this position was because he was overqualified. It did not cite any of Taggart's obviously pestering job search techniques as a basis for not hiring him; nor could it since Taggart's interview with Rios-Nicosia took place before all but one of these incidents occurred. If other nondiscriminatory reasons existed for refusing to hire appellant they should have been stated in Rios-Nicosia's affidavit.

Moreover, characterizing an applicant in an age discrimination case as overqualified has a connotation that defies common sense: How can a person overqualified by experience and training be turned down for a position given to a younger person deemed better qualified? Denying employment to an older job applicant because he or she has too much experience, training or education is simply to employ a euphemism to mask the real reason for refusal, namely, in the eyes of the employer the applicant is too old. See EEOC v. District of Columbia, Dept. of Human Services, 729 F. Supp. 907, 915 (D.D.C. 1990) (overqualified and overspecialized are buzzwords for too old); Vaughn v. Mobil Oil Corp., 708 F. Supp. 595, 601 (S.D.N.Y. 1989) (overqualified supported employee's contention that she was capable of assuming another position).

An employer might reasonably believe that an overqualified candidate—where that term is applied to a younger person—will continue to seek employment more in keeping with his or her background and training. Yet, that rationale does not comfortably fit those in the age group the statute protects; for them loss of employment late in life ordinarily is devastating economically as well as emotionally. Instead, an older applicant that is hired is quite unlikely to continue to seek other mostly nonexistent employment opportunities.

Consequently, refusing to hire Taggart for the sole reason that he was overqualified refutes Time's assertion that it was not discriminating on the basis of age. Taggart met the four prongs for presenting a prima facie case of age discrimination for the HBO position. This constitutes circumstances from which a reasonable juror could infer discriminatory animus on the part of Time based upon a finding that the reason proffered was pretextual and unworthy of credence.

Decision and Remedy   *The court reversed the district court's grant of summary judgment and remanded the case for a trial on the merits.*

Discharging Older Workers

The most common ADEA problem involves a company that fires a group of older workers in a general reduction in force or replaces them with younger workers, who may command a lower salary. This action may or may not be unlawful age discrimination. An employer cannot fire older workers simply because they have high salaries. An employer can fire older workers, however, as long as the decision is based on reasonable factors other than age.

A common ADEA problem involves corporate reductions in the labor force. Corporations may lay off a large number of workers due to an economic downturn or in order to make the company more efficient. If many of the laid-off workers are over forty, they may claim age discrimination.

These workers cannot meet the fourth requirement of the prima facie case, however, because their jobs were abolished and not left open or filled by younger workers. Some courts have therefore modified the prima facie test to require that the laid-off workers produce some evidence showing that the employer intended to discriminate based on age. This might be true if an unusually high proportion of laid-off workers were older.

The business could still state a legitimate reason for the lay-off pattern. For example, it could say that it laid off the least efficient workers. The workers would then be required to prove that this reason was a pretext.

Courts have reached different results in reduction in labor force cases. Some of the factors that courts have considered are:

- Whether the employer had and followed a specific plan for its reduction in force.

- Whether the employer followed seniority policies and considered the plan's impact on older workers.

- Whether the employer gave the fired employees' work to younger employees.

- Whether the employer used objective criteria in determining which jobs were cut.

Voluntary Retirement

Most voluntary retirement programs reflect some age discrimination. Many voluntary retirement programs commence at age sixty-five, thereby discriminating based on age. In addition, many plans provide the greatest incentive for retirement at sixty-five, with declining retirement incentives thereafter for older workers. Nevertheless, the ADEA explicitly permits certain voluntary retirement programs.

The first requirement for a voluntary retirement program is that the employer provide a legitimate business reason for structuring the plan with specific age limitations. Courts have permitted many justifications as legitimate business reasons. For example, if an employer provides a retirement incentive so as to permit replacement by younger workers with lower salaries, courts have found this to be a legitimate business reason for a voluntary retirement program.

The second requirement is that the retirement plan be truly voluntary. Employers cannot compel, or even coerce, employees to accept the retirement offer. In one important case, an employer announced a voluntary retirement program for workers who were sixty and older. The company gave these workers only five days to accept the program, though, and hinted that future layoffs were planned. After accepting the retirement program, the workers sued for age discrimination. A court held that the program was not truly voluntary, because the workers had insufficient time and information to make a free choice.[12]

▆▆ Americans with Disabilities Act

Restrictions on discrimination against the handicapped traditionally fell under the Rehabilitation Act of 1973, which applied to companies that contracted with or received grants from the government. In 1990, Congress passed the Americans with Disabilities Act ("ADA"), which expanded the coverage of handicapped protection to parallel that of other discrimination laws. In July 1992, the ADA takes effect for employers with twenty-five or more employees, and in July 1994, the Act applies to employers with fifteen or more employees.

The prohibitions of ADA are also similar to that of other discrimination laws. Employers are precluded from discrimination in hiring, promotions, firing and benefits. There are some differences in the ADA, however. The law prohibits employers from asking about the existence or nature of a prospective employee's disability. Under other laws, an employer may ask about a job applicant's race, sex, etc., but cannot use this information to discriminate.

The ADA presents unique problems, however. Unlike race, some handicaps will make it more difficult or impossible for workers to do the job. There is also confusion about exactly what constitutes a protected "handicap."

Definition of Handicapped

In many cases, the existence of a handicap or disability will be obvious. The ADA obviously was intended to protect individuals who are blind,

deaf, or reliant on wheelchairs. What about individuals who have a disease, however, or an eating disorder?

The ADA defines the term disability as follows:

- A physical or mental impairment that substantially limits one or more of the major life activities of such an individual.

- A record of such an impairment.

- Being regarded as having such an impairment.

There is some precedent for defining protected handicapped individuals under the Rehabilitation Act. "Major life activities" include walking, seeing, performing manual tasks, and working.

One key controversy was whether an individual with a disease, such as cancer or AIDS, is protected as handicapped. Courts have held that these individuals are regarded as having an impairment and are therefore protected. An exception would exist when the disease was sufficiently contagious to threaten coworkers. Under the Rehabilitation Act, courts were divided on whether hypertension could be considered a protected disability.

Qualified Individuals

The ADA protects those disabled persons who are deemed "otherwise qualified," but for the disability. A qualified handicapped person is one who can perform the essential functions of the job with only reasonable accommodation by the employer.

This provision deals with the following situation. Suppose that Janet Lutz, confined to a wheelchair, applies for a secretarial job at Friendly Cards, Inc. Janet is qualified as a secretary but cannot even enter Friendly Cards' building, which has steps up to the door. Janet is not unqualified simply because she cannot enter the building. The employer could make a reasonable accommodation, by providing a ramp, after which she would be qualified for the job.

To determine whether an individual is otherwise qualified, the court must determine the essential functions of the job. An accountant may occasionally need to lift heavy boxes, but this is hardly an essential function of accountancy.

---

[12]*Paolillo v. Dresser Industries, Inc.*, 821 F.2d 81 (2d Cir. 1987).

A controversial case was decided under a California statute similar to the ADA. A telecommunications equipment installer suffered from asthma that was complicated by certain aspects of her job. A court found that only 12 percent of the work time was spent on the problematic activities and ruled that they were therefore not an essential function of the job.[13]

---

[13]*Ackerman v. Western Electric Company*, 643 F. Supp. 836 (N.D. Cal. 1986), aff'd, 860 F.2d 1514 ((9th Cir. 1988).

The following case illustrates a circumstance when a disabled person was deemed unable to perform the essential functions of a job. Although this was decided under the old Rehabilitation Act, the language of the ADA is the same and the result would probably be similar.

■ **Case 4.4**
Chiari v.
City of League City
United States Court of Appeals,
Fifth Circuit, 1991
920 F.2d 311

Background and Facts *Antonio Chiari was a sixty-six-year-old professional engineer who was hired by League City as a construction inspector, which involved the approval of construction plans presented by private contractors and the inspection of their work. About 50 percent of the job involved on-site inspection, which included "climbing into ditches to inspect pipes and climbing up the structure of uncompleted buildings."*

Chiari was diagnosed with Parkinson's disease. He began having trouble walking and on one occasion fell at a construction site. He visited neurologists at the request of his supervisors. After reviewing the physician's reports, the supervisors concluded that Chiari could no longer safely be a construction inspector and sought an alternative position. They could find no such position, and Chiari was fired.

Chiari filed suit against the city, claiming discrimination. The district court dismissed Chiari's claims, and he appealed.

THORNBERRY, Circuit Judge.

* * * *

1. *Could Chiari still perform the essential functions of his job?*

The unchallenged affidavits from Murphy and Nutting demonstrate that Chiari must be able to visually inspect construction sites to perform the "essential functions" of a construction inspector's job. Chiari presented some evidence that he was still competent to make these inspections. For instance, his intellect was unaffected by the disease. Moreover, his immediate supervisor, David Hegemier, testified that Chiari's job performance was satisfactory at the time he was fired. The City's sole justification for maintaining that Chiari was not capable of doing the job was its concern that his loss of balance would endanger him and others working with him.

The regulation that defines a "qualified handicapped person" under section 504 does not explain whether a court may consider the risk which an individual's handicap may pose to himself or others; it requires only that the person be able to perform "the essential functions of the job in question." *See* 45 C.F.R. § 84.3(k)(1)(1989). But courts which have applied section 504 unanimously have held that a handicapped individual cannot perform the essential functions of a job if his handicap poses a significant safety risk to those around him. *See, e.g., School Bd. of Nassau County v. Arline*, 480 U.S. 273, 287 n. 16, 107 S.Ct. 1123, 1131 n. 16, 94

L.Ed.2d 307 (1987) (noting that"[a] person who poses a significant risk of communicating an infectious disease to others in the workplace will not be otherwise qualified for his or her job if reasonable accommodation will not eliminate the risk"); *Bentivegna v. United States Dep't of Labor*, 694 F.2d 619, 622 (9th Cir.1982) (holding that a job qualification can exclude handicapped individuals if the qualification substantially promotes safe performance). To support its assertion that Chiari's presence would endanger others, the City presented affidavits from two neurosurgeons, Dr. Sinha and Dr. Borne, who stated that Chiari's unsteady "shuffling gait" and muscle rigidity, which caused him to lose his balance, prevented him from performing the job of construction inspector safely.

Chiari maintains that, despite the testimony of the three physicians, a jury still could find that he is capable of performing his job without endangering others. He contends, and the City concedes, that he has never fallen on anyone or injured any one in the past. The risk, he stated, is not that he will hurt others but that he will hurt himself, and he argues that this court cannot consider the risk of personal injury to the handicapped individual as one of the factors in determining whether that individual is qualified to do a job. We disagree.

*   *   *   *

Similarly, a significant risk of personal injury can disqualify a handicapped individual from a job if the employer cannot eliminate the risk. In regulations supplementing section 501 of the Rehabilitation Act, 29 U.S.C.A. § 791 (West Supp. 1990), the Equal Employment Opportunity Commission defines a "qualified handicapped person" as one who "can perform the essential functions of the position in question without endangering the health and safety *of the individual or others....*" See 29 C.F.R. § 1613.702(f) (1990) (emphasis added). Section 501 refers to the duty of federal, rather than federally funded, employers to accommodate the handicapped, but it imposes a greater burden on the employer than section 504 does: federal employers must take affirmative action toward applicants and employees with handicaps. *See* 29 U.S.C.A. § 791(b). In *Mantolete v. Bolger*, 767 F.2d 1416, 1422 (9th Cir.1985), the court applied section 501 and held that the Postal Service could prohibit an applicant with epilepsy from operating a letter sorting machine if the Postal Service could show a reasonable probability that the applicant could suffer substantial injury.

Decision and Remedy   *The court affirmed the district court's dismissal of Chiari's action.*

Reasonable Accommodation

The most significant and controversial provision of the ADA is the obligation on employers to make reasonable accommodations for otherwise handicapped individuals. Testimony before Congress indicated that most accommodations would be inexpensive (about $50), but the law may require employers to undertake more expensive accommodations.

The law itself suggests some examples of accommodations that would be considered reasonable and therefore required. These include making facilities physically accessible, job restructuring through modified-time work schedules, acquisition of equipment or devices, and the provision of readers and interpreters.

The reasonability of accommodations also will vary with the type of business. The law states that courts should consider the overall size of the business and its type of operation in deciding reasonableness.

Perhaps the most difficult issue in reasonable accommodation is the need to hire assistants for some individuals with disabilities. For example, a visually impaired person may be able to perform most office work but may require a person to read memoranda and other papers.

The employer need not hire an assistant who will essentially perform the job of the handicapped individual. For example, a supermarket need not hire someone to operate a cash register so that a visually impaired person could work a check-out stand.

In the case of the office worker, however, the reader would not do the job of the worker and would be much less expensive to hire. The reasonability of this accommodation may depend centrally upon the size of the employer's business and the ability to afford such an accommodation.

Operation and Enforcement

Once the above coverage issues are addressed, the ADA will function much like Title VII or the ADEA. The theories of discrimination developed under Title VII, including disparate treatment and disparate impact discrimination, will apply under the ADA.

The enforcement of the ADA also mirrors Title VII, in the procedures of filing a charge with the EEOC, investigation, and either EEOC or private action against the employer. Remedies of the ADA also parallel those of other antidiscrimination laws.

> ### ■ Ethical Perspectives

Ethics and Comparable Worth

Ethics is central to employment discrimination law. Title VII exists because our society considers discrimination to be unethical. When, if ever, should employers go beyond Title VII to fight discrimination?

One controversial example is the "comparable worth" controversy. Some jobs in our society have traditionally been held by women (nurse, secretary, elementary school teacher, etc.), while other jobs have traditionally been held by men (mechanic, construction worker, etc.). The traditionally male jobs historically have paid higher wages than the traditionally female occupations.

One frequently hears the statistic that the average working woman makes only 65 cents for every dollar made by the average working man. This is not primarily because woman mechanics, say, are paid less than male mechanics. It is primarily because mechanics (most of whom are male) make more than secretaries (most of whom are female).

Some argue that these disparities among jobs are unethical because they resulted from and continue to perpetuate stereotypes about males being "breadwinners" and needing higher pay to support a family. They argue that wage rates in these jobs should be modified to reflect the relative value of these jobs to society. This is called **comparable worth compensation**.

While it may seem ethical to pay individuals based on their "worth" or value to society, this approach raises serious problems. What kind of worth should we compensate? Moral worth? How does one compare the moral worth of a mechanic and a secretary? Perhaps most important, who should be given the authority to decide questions of moral worth?

A free enterprise society does not even try to base wage compensation on the relative moral worth of occupations. Under the market a job is worth whatever someone will pay to have it done. This is said to allocate labor efficiently, because the jobs that are in most demand by prospective employers will offer the highest wages and will thereby draw the necessary employees.

This does not mean that the free market is necessarily immoral. By promoting economic efficiency, it can maximize the wealth of the entire society and indirectly benefit everyone. Also, many individuals who take especially "moral" occupations (e.g., charitable work) do so for compensation other than monetary.

To the extent that the free market allocates wages based on sexism, however, it increases inefficiency as well as being ethically dubious. The main problem with comparable worth is designing a solution to this problem. Most people do not want government assigning wage rates for occupations. One must always make sure that the cure is not worse than the disease.

▬ International Perspectives

International Prohibitions on Employment Discrimination

Many millions of individuals work in countries other than their nation of citizenship. It is estimated that over one million Americans work in foreign countries. Many of these U.S. citizens work for branches of U.S. companies operating abroad. To what extent are these individuals protected from discrimination by Title VII or other international prohibitions on employment discrimination?

In one leading case, the Fifth Circuit Court of Appeals held that Title VII did not protect a U.S. citizen who was working for a foreign subsidiary of an oil company incorporated in the United States. Other cases, however, have held that Title VII does have some extraterritorial application, and the EEOC guidelines call for use of Title VII in cases of U.S. employees working for U.S. firms in foreign countries. The Supreme Court recently held that Title VII does not necessarily apply to protect U.S. employees working overseas for U.S. companies.[14]

Even this Supreme Court decision does not answer all questions about overseas discrimination, however. Such discrimination is clearly legal if the laws of a foreign nation compel such discrimination (e.g., a law stating that only members of certain religions may work in certain holy sites). Such discrimination is likely to be illegal if the discriminatory actions were taken in the United States.

Even if Title VII does not apply, foreign workers may receive some protection from discrimination. The International Labour Organization Employment Policy Convention prohibits

---

[14]EEOC v. Arabian American Oil Co., 111 S.Ct. 1227 (1991).

discrimination based on "race, color, sex, religion, political opinion, national extraction or social origin." This convention lacks enforcement authority, however, unless it is implemented by the laws of member states.

The European Community (EC), an enormous market, has taken steps to implement prohibitions on employment discrimination. In some respects, the EC provisions go beyond Title VII. The EC Treaty prohibits discrimination based on worker nationality or sex but does not prohibit religious discrimination. These provisions are not merely declaratory but impose a duty on the courts of individual nations to prevent discrimination. Individuals suffering prohibited discrimination may sue for compensation.

Questions and Case Problems

1. Marietta Conner was a bus driver for Fort Gordon Bus Company. She made an illegal left turn when the owner of the bus company happened to be behind her bus. The company had recently paid a $35,000 damage judgment after another driver made an illegal left turn. The owner rushed into the bus terminal and asked who was driving the bus. After discovering it was Conner, he fired her. Conner claimed employment discrimination, because male drivers had not been fired for traffic violations, because the company policy did not clearly state that this was a reason for discharge, and because the owner did not discharge the driver until after he discovered her name and sex. Was Conner's firing unlawfully discriminatory? [*Conner v. Fort Gordon Bus Co.*, 761 F.2d 1495 (11th Cir. 1985)].

2. Cash & Thomas was a pipe-laying firm owned by Jack Thomas. His son, Steve, was employed as a supervisor and was married to Savonda. Jeri Platner was a secretary with the firm. After a time, Savonda began to suspect that Steve was having an affair with Platner and became extremely jealous. Platner dressed and behaved appropriately, but Steve may have fueled Savonda's jealousy by flirting with Platner. Savonda became increasingly upset and her marriage to Steve became jeopardized. Out of concern for his son's marriage, Jack Thomas fired Platner and replaced her with a male employee.

She sued the company for employment discrimination. Should Ms. Platner succeed in this action? [*Platner v. Cash & Thomas Contractors, Inc.*, 908 F.2d 902 (11th Cir. 1990)].

3. The owners of a small, closely held corporation made a covenant with God that their business would be a "Christian, faith-oriented business." The company held a devotional service once a week during work hours and required all employees to attend. An employee who was an atheist sought to be excused from the service. The company refused to excuse the employee but told him that he could wear earplugs and read a book or sleep during the service. He still objected and sued for religious discrimination under Title VII. The employer argued that it was simply exercising its own freedom of religion. Should the worker succeed with his discrimination claim? [*Equal Employment Opportunity Commission v. Townley Engineering & Manufacturing Co.*, No. 89-2272 (9th Cir. 1988)].

4. A job applicant placed high enough on a civil service test to be chosen as a clerk but was rejected because of his "heavy Filipino accent." The job involved dealing with 200 to 300 disgruntled people per day regarding their problems with various city services. The job description required that the applicant be able to "deal tactfully and effectively with the public." The city claimed that the accent precluded the applicant, but he claimed that he was subjected to unlawful national origin discrimination. Should the job applicant succeed in a job discrimination claim? [*Fragrante v. City and County of Honolulu*, No. 87-2921 (9th Cir. 1989)].

5. RIA sells publications for tax specialists. Simms Normand, who was hired at age fifty, worked nine years for RIA but then was forced to resign. His sales performance had been excellent for the first seven to eight years but began to decline significantly, and he also missed sales meetings. A supervisor told Normand that he was suffering from the "old salesman burnout syndrome" and suggested that he resign to avoid being fired. On other occasions, RIA workers were referred to as "old geezers" or "old buzzards." Normand resigned, and RIA soon hired a thirty-one-year-old worker for his position. Normand sued and claimed illegal age discrimination by RIA. A jury ruled for Normand and found RIA's action to be willful, enabling him to receive extra damages. The trial court reversed the jury verdict. Normand appealed this reversal. Should an appellate court uphold the trial court decision or reverse and provide Normand with his damages in the jury verdict? [*Normand v. Research Institute of America, Inc.*, 927 F.2d 857 (5th Cir. 1991)].

CHAPTER FIVE

Occupational Safety and Workers' Compensation

KEY BACKGROUND

The essential background for this chapter on occupational safety and workers' compensation is found in Chapter 48 of *West's Business Law, Fifth Edition* and in Chapter 17 of *West's Legal Environment of Business*. These chapters cover employment and labor relations law. Among the important points to remember from this chapter are:

- the powers of the Occupational Safety and Health Administration
- the requirements for compliance and enforcement of occupational safety regulation.
- the basic rules for coverage and recovery under state workers' compensation statutes.

* * *

Each year, thousands of Americans die because of risks found in their workplace. Every eighteen seconds, an employee is injured on the job. A recent study estimated that, in addition to this human tragedy, occupational injury and death costs the nation over $50 billion per year.

The law has responded to this risk in two different manners. First, the law creates occupational safety and health standards to prevent the risks whenever feasible. Second, the law provides a special compensation system for workers who are harmed on the job. This chapter addresses the two approaches in sequence.

Occupational Safety Standards

The most prominent occupational safety standards are set by the Occupational Safety and Health Administration, known as OSHA, and administratively located within the Department of Labor. OSHA was created and empowered by the Occupational Safety and Health Act of 1970 (the "OSH Act"). The OSH Act has very broad coverage, applying to all companies with employees. A few job categories are exempted from the Act (e.g., agricultural workers, professionals, household domestics).

OSHA has adopted many detailed standards that can be quite expensive to obey. In addition, OSHA has created more generalized, nonspecific standards and duties for employers.

General Duty Clause

The Occupational Safety and Health Act requires that each employer furnish a workplace free from recognized hazards that are likely to cause death or serious physical harm to employees. This duty is above and beyond any specific OSHA standards. The **general duty clause** is violated when (1) a recognized hazard is present, that (2) was likely to cause death or serious physical harm, and that (3) could feasibly be remedied.

The key provision in the general duty clause is that the hazard must be a "recognized" one. Recognized means that the hazard is known or foreseeable by the employer. An employer will be liable under this clause if the industry in general recognized a hazard, but the particular employer was unaware of it. Conversely, the employer also will be liable if that employer was aware of the hazard, even if the industry in general was unaware of it.

Nevertheless, some hazards are not recognized and do not subject an employer to liability under the general duty clause. For example, one court held that an employer could not anticipate that an employee would use a cigarette lighter in examining a propane tank for leaks.[1]

If a recognized workplace hazard exists, the employer must take the maximum feasible protective measures for employees. The employer is not expected to eliminate all risk and guarantee safety, however. One court noted that "a demented, suicidal, or willfully reckless employee may on occasion circumvent the best conceived and most vigorously enforced safety regime."[2] This is known as the **unpreventable employee misconduct defense**.

The mere existence of employee negligence, however, is not a defense to violations of the general duty clause. The employer has some responsibility to prevent employee risk-taking, as illustrated in the following case.

---

[1]*William R. Davis & Son, Co.*, 6 O.S.H.C. (ALJ 1978).

[2]*National Realty and Construction Co. Inc. v. OSHRC*, 489 F.2d 1257, 1266 (D.C. Cir. 1973).

■ Case 5.1
CMI South, Inc. v. Occupational Safety and Health Review Commission
Administrative Law Judge, 1990
OSHRC Docket No. 89-1600

Background and Facts *CMI South, Inc., operates a foundry in Alabama. Early one morning, the foundry began to experience a problem with its sand system, which feeds sand from a 200-ton capacity tank onto a conveyer/feeder and on into the plant. Workers speculated that the sand had become wet, which prevented it from flowing as it should. Employees and supervisors gathered and sought to loosen the sand by beating on the outside of the tank, a method that had worked before. After this failed, two employees opened an inspection plate located over the conveyor and crawled inside. Two workers began to loosen the sand with a shovel, and the sand fell fast, burying and killing one employee.*

CMI was cited for a violation of the general duty clause. CMI contested the citation, the secretary of labor prepared a complaint, and the case was tried before an OSHRC administrative law judge.

BRADY, Administrative Law Judge.

*   *   *   *

CMI contends that the record establishes that, since the plant opened in 1977, no one knew of any person who had entered the tank from the bottom (Tr. 25, 63). There was no known reason for anyone to enter the tank, because there was no machinery or other mechanical devices that required maintenance inside the tank.

CMI's argument does not refute the evidence that entry into the tank was a recognized hazard. CMI argues that it is not a hazard to enter the tank, because everyone knows how dangerous it is. This is circuitous. "Recognition of the hazard can be inferred from the obvious nature of the hazard." Litton Systems, Inc., Ingalls Shipbuilding Division, 81 OSAHRC 101/C12, 10 BNA OSHC 1179, 1182, 1981 CCH OSHD P25, 817 (No. 76-900, 1981). In the present case, entry into the bottom of a 200-ton capacity tank to unclog sand in a system that depends on gravity to move the sand is such an obvious hazard that recognition of the hazard is implied.

CMI's second point, that the hazard was not likely to cause death or serious physical harm, is actually an unpreventable employee misconduct defense. CMI states, "The incident that resulted in the death of Leonard Royster was a freak accident. Mr. Royster as the Acting Plant Manager, did something which no reasonably sane person would do— he entered the bottom of a tank containing at least 150 tons of sand over his head and began to dig into the sand, hoping to cause it to fall onto him" (CMI brief, p. 8). CMI is correct in asserting that Royster's behavior is inexplicable.

Hazardous conduct is not preventable if it is so idiosyncratic and implausible in motive or means that conscientious experts, familiar with the industry, would not take it into account in prescribing a safety program. Nor is misconduct preventable if its elimination would require methods of hiring, training, monitoring, or sanctioning workers which are either so untested or so expensive that safety experts would substantially concur in thinking the means infeasible. National Realty and Construction Co., 489 F.2d 1257 (D.C. Cir. 1973).

CMI would perhaps prevail on this argument if the record established that one or two defiant employees had entered the tank without supervision, or even if Royster, as plant manager, had entered the tank unseen, or over the protestations of the other supervisory personnel present. That, however, is not the case. Three supervisors were present at the tank. The supervisor in charge of the entire plant at the time, Royster, was the person who ordered entry into the tank. Another supervisor, Phillips, immediately went into the tank. A third supervisor, Tate, stood by without protest while this occurred. Such conduct by the supervising personnel cannot be excused as idiosyncratic and implausible.

This conduct can also not be explained as a coincidental lapse in the minds of all present as to the danger involved. One man, Earl Hughes (a maintenance employee who should not be expected to be more concerned with safety than his supervisors), did speak up and warn the others not to enter the tank. He was told to shut up by the ranking supervisor. As soon as Phillips and Royster entered the tank, Hughes left to get some rope and two shovels. When asked why, Hughes replied that, in the likely event that the sand would fall, "we would have something to dig them out with and the rope, I was going to tie around his feet" (Tr. 55).

CMI argues that Royster did something "which no reasonably sane person would do," but he was joined in this action by Phillips, and the action was condoned by Tate, both of whom are presumably sane. Under these circumstances, unpreventable employee misconduct cannot be established.

Decision and Remedy   *The administrative law judge affirmed the citation and imposed a $1000 penalty on CMI.*

OSHA has begun to make greater use of the general duty clause, especially when employers of all types have exposed their workers to toxic substances. For example, OSHA has cited several hospitals and clinics for overexposure of female workers to nitrous oxide, based on citations in scientific literature linking such overexposure to miscarriages and birth defects.

Special Duty Clause

OSHA has adopted many precise standards to protect against specific hazards in certain types of workplaces. These regulations typically involve detailed specifications for employers. Compliance with these standards is under the **special duty clause**.

For example, one traditional source of injury was the mechanical power press, a large machine that produced molded plastic products, among other things. Workers would inadvertently get a hand or a limb inside the press, which would then crush the appendage if the machine was turned on. OSHA adopted safety regulations for mechanical power presses that fill many pages of small print.

If the press is operated by foot pedals, OSHA has a number of requirements, including the type of spring on the pedal and a proper nonslip surface. Some machines require that two hands must be on external levers to activate operations, thereby assuring that one of the operator's hands is not caught in the machine. Another provision states in part:

> (c) Safeguarding the point of operation— (i) it shall be the responsibility of the employer to provide and insure the usage of "point of operation guards" or properly applied and adjusted point of operation devices on every operation performed on a mechanical power press. . . .
>
> (3) Point of operation devices. (i) Point of operation devices shall protect the operator by:
>
> (a) Preventing and/or stopping normal stroking of the press if the operator's hands are inadvertently placed in the point of operation; or
>
> (b) Preventing the operator from inadvertently reaching into the point of operation, or withdrawing his hands if they are inadvertently located in the point of operation, as the dies close . . . .[3]

This rule goes on with many more details. The guards required to comply with all provisions of the above rule had a cost of thousands of dollars per machine.

OSHA has similar rules for many different workplace situations. Some of these rules are rather vague and challenging to meet. For example, one rule requires:

> Protective equipment, including personal protective equipment for eyes, face, head, and extremities, protective clothing, respiratory devices and protective shields and barriers, shall be provided, used, and maintained in a sanitary and reliable condition wherever it is necessary by reason of hazards of processes or environment, chemical hazards, radiological hazards, or mechanical irritants encountered in a manner capable of causing injury or impairment in the function of any part of the body through absorption, inhalation or physical contact.[4]

OSHA provides no specific guidance on when "it is necessary" to provide elaborate protective equipment of this type.

An employer may apply to the Secretary of Labor to grant a *variance* from a specific OSHA standard. An employer can get a permanent variance if it can show that its practices are "as safe and healthful" as those prescribed in the standard. For example, OSHA has a standard requiring that fire extinguishers be mounted at a specified height above the floor. OSHA provided a variance for an employer whose fire extinguishers were mounted on retractable boards hung from the ceiling and which were just as accessible as under the agency standard. If OSHA grants such a variance, it will usually attach numerous terms and conditions.

OSHA will also grant a temporary variance when an employer can show an inability to comply by the regulation's deadline. This requires a strong showing that material, equipment, or technical personnel are unavailable or a showing that necessary construction or modification of facilities cannot be completed in time.

Employers are expected to be aware of and comply with all OSHA regulations that are relevant to their workplace unless they have obtained a variance. The company must comply with the regulation precisely; the employer's absence of workplace injuries is no defense.

Unfortunately, many OSHA standards are less than specific. This makes the assurance of compliance more difficult and also may provide employers with a defense, as demonstrated in the following decision.

---

[3] 29 C.F.R. Sec. 1910.217 (1990).

[4] 29 C.F.R. Sec. 1910.132(a).

■ Case 5.2
**Spancrete Northeast, Inc. v.
Occupational Safety and
Health Review Commission**
United States Court of Appeals,
Second Circuit, 1990
905 F.2d 589

Background and Facts   *Spancrete Northeast, Inc. was installing precast concrete slabs and grouting the keyways between the slabs in the second floor of a building under construction. Leonard Drew, an OSHA inspector, visited the site and issued a citation to Spancrete. The citation was for violation of a section requiring a "standard railing or the equivalent" on all platforms that are six feet or more above ground level. The proposed penalty was $200. Spancrete contested the citation.*

At a hearing before an administrative law judge ("ALJ"), Spancrete convinced the judge that a railing was unnecessary and would have been difficult to construct. The ALJ did, however, accept Drew's contention that Spancrete should have provided safety belts for workers, with lanyards connecting the belts to wires from the perimeter steel posts. Safety belts could be required under a different OSHA rule that requires the use of "appropriate" personal protective equipment when hazards exist. The ALJ apparently accepted this contention and imposed liability on Spancrete. Spancrete then petitioned for review in federal court.

VAN GRAAFEILAND, Circuit Judge.

*   *   *   *

During the hearing that followed service of Spancrete's answer, the Secretary produced only one witness, Inspector Drew. Drew proved to have a very limited knowledge of general grouting procedures. He had no prior experience with precast concrete and had only inspected one precast construction job prior to Spancrete's. He did not observe Spancrete's employees while they were grouting, and his testimony concerning the grouting and the construction environment in which it was performed was sparse and in some respects erroneous. The exhibits and testimony introduced by Spancrete, none of which is contradicted, illustrate this very well.

*   *   *   *

Spancrete's other witness, Morgan Wildey, was Spancrete's erection foreman. Wildey testified that he had been employed by Spancrete for twenty-two years, that he had not erected a perimeter guard in all that time, and that no one ever had fallen off a building. In his opinion, there was no danger of this occurring.

*   *   *   *

Mr. Drew, the Secretary's sole witness, lacked the experience to testify as an expert on the grouting of precast concrete and could not speak to the customary practices in the industry. He had inspected only one other precast concrete job, and he had never seen any precast erectors wearing safety belts while grouting. He at no time observed Spancrete's employees in the process of grouting. Under 29 C.F.R. § 1926.104(b) provides that lifelines for safety belts "shall be secured above the point of operation to an anchorage or structural member capable of supporting a minimum dead weight of 5,400 pounds." The ALJ made no finding as to how or where the lifelines could be attached in the instant case, and it may be assumed that he adopted Drew's suggestion that the lifelines could be cables strung between the posts that Drew mistakenly believed were near the floor's perimeter. Not only were the posts in question not near the floor's perimeter and thus "above the point of operation," wires connecting them would not be universally parallel to the perimeter of the octagon-shaped core building. In some cases, the outer edge of the floor would run at an angle of 40-45 degrees to the proposed safety cable. Assuming that the existing posts would not be suitable as anchorages, there was no evidence whatever concerning whether other structural members capable of supporting a dead weight of 5,400 pounds could be attached to the precast concrete slabs for the short period of time that perimeter grouting was going on without causing permanent damage to the slabs. This was a matter of particular significance with respect to the use of safety belts in Wing C where there were no upright posts.

Mr. Wildey, Spancrete's foreman, testified that the use of safety belts would create a hazard of tripping or falling. The ALJ dismissed this testimony as speculation, since Mr. Wildey never had used safety belts while grouting. Having rejected Wildey's testimony as speculative, the ALJ proceeded to speculate on his own to the effect that the use of safety belts would not rise to the level of a greater hazard, an opinion that is not shared universally. *See Ray Evers Welding Co. v. OSHRC, supra, 625 F.2d at 732-33; Eagle Sheet Metal, Inc., 1979 O.S.H.D. 23,598* (May 1, 1979); *Crouch-Walker Corp., 1979 O.S.H.D. 23,227* (November 9, 1978). "Reasonableness is an objective test which must be determined on the basis of evidence in the record." *Ray Evers Welding Co. v. OSHRC, supra, 625 F.2d at 732.* The ALJ's findings should be based on testimony from knowledgeable witnesses experienced in the technical area involved, not upon the ALJ's subjective feelings unsupported by the record.

Decision and Remedy *The court vacated the citation and penalty against Spancrete.*

Employer Responsibility

Employers cannot satisfy their OSHA obligations simply by making structural changes and installing equipment demanded by the agency. Rather, the employer has the duty of oversight in the workplace.

Employers generally must provide safety training to their workers under the general duty clause, and some specific standards require that employees demonstrate a level of competence before they are permitted to use certain equipment.

An employer sometimes will be liable for unsafe conditions or accidents that resulted from the carelessness of their employees. This is especially true when the risk was foreseeable and preventable or when the risk could have been avoided

with better training programs. For example, in one case, an employer instructed employees to keep certain safety doors closed. The employees generally ignored this requirement, and the employer was aware of this fact. The employer was penalized because nothing was done to enforce the safety rules.[5]

Employers are not guarantors of safety. They do have a duty to supervise reasonably but are not expected to anticipate and prevent all accidents. OSHA sought enforcement against one employer after a worker was crushed to death between a logging truck and a crane loading logs onto the bed of the truck. The employer was not liable because it could not be expected to provide

---

[5]*Whaley Engineering Corp.*, 8 O.S.H.C. 1644 (1980).

constant one-on-one supervision.[6] Less supervision is required if workers are experienced and have good safety records.

Inspections and Citations

To ensure compliance with the above clauses, OSHA conducts periodic, unannounced inspections of worksites. OSHA can only inspect about two percent of covered worksites in any given year. Consequently, inspection resources are prioritized to focus on industries and plants with a poor safety record. OSHA also focuses on sites where there have been employee complaints of hazards.

The OSHA inspector is usually prohibited by law from giving any advance warning of the inspection to the employer. Strictly speaking, OSHA requires a search warrant for nonemergency inspections of a plant. These warrants are very easy for OSHA to obtain, and most employers do not insist upon a warrant but consent to an inspection without a warrant.

OSHA inspections follow a fairly standard procedure. The inspector begins by presenting his or her credentials. The OSHA representative has the right to inspect throughout the worksite and to interview workers about potential hazardous conditions.

The law provides "walkaround" rights both to the employer and to employees. This means that each may provide a representative to accompany the inspector on the tour throughout the plant. The employer representative may help the inspector interpret plant conditions and explain why they are legal. The employee representative may help ensure that the inspector does not overlook safety violations.

If the inspection reveals a violation of the law, the Act requires that the inspector issue a written citation to the employer that describes the violation with particularity. This must be done within six months and is generally done while the inspector is still at the worksite.

An OSHA citation will be accompanied with a notice of the proposed penalty. The citation will also contain an abatement period, a time during which the employer must correct the hazard or risk further penalties. An employer may accept the proposed penalty or contest it. In order to challenge the citation and penalty, the employer must file a notice of contest within fifteen working days of receipt of the citation.

After a notice of contest is filed, the government has twenty working days in which to file a complaint against the employer. The complaint sets forth the alleged violations and the standards violated (e.g., general duty or specific duty under standards).

The dispute is tried before an administrative law judge of the Occupational Safety and Health Review Commission ("OSHRC"). OSHA has the burden of proof in this hearing but may rely on circumstantial evidence. The judge's decision may be appealed to the full OSHRC and then to federal court.

Penalties

Penalties under the OSH Act can be quite strict but vary considerably. The amount of penalty depends on the gravity of the violation. OSHA may assess a penalty of up to $1000 for a nonserious violation and must assess a penalty of $1000 for each serious violation.

A serious occupational safety and health violation is one that creates a risk of death or serious physical harm. Nonserious violations vary and some are so trivial as to receive no penalty. An employer violated a standard requiring the availability of a waste receptacle for paper cups at a water cooler but received no penalty.[7] The average penalty for nonserious violations in 1988 was less than $2 per violation.

Penalties are especially strict for willful or repeated violations of the Act. Under recent amendments, employers can be fined up to $70,000 for each willful or repeated violation. This amount is per violation, and USX Corporation was recently fined $7.3 million for violating the OSH Act.

The law also provides for criminal penalties in certain circumstances. A crime is committed if a willful violation causes the death of an employee or if false statements are knowingly made in a required report. Penalties for these crimes include up to six months in prison. Criminal prosecutions have been few, however, and only one person has

---

[6]*Hansen Brothers Logging*, 1 O.S.H.C. 1060 (1972).

[7]*R.H. Bishop Co.*, 1 O.S.H.C. 1767 (1974).

been convicted and incarcerated for a violation of the Occupational Safety and Health Act.

Hazard Communication

The most common OSHA citation is for violations of the **hazard communication standard,** which is sometimes called the "workers' right-to-know rule." This rule requires that workers be informed of the hazards presented by chemicals that they are exposed to on the job. One-fourth of America's 25 million workers are exposed to potentially hazardous substances on the job.

Manufacturers and importers of hazardous chemicals must provide **material safety data sheets** (MSDS) for any hazardous chemicals. The MSDS describe the risks of the chemical. The MSDS is sent to and can be used by other employers to inform their employees, and an employer must have an MSDS for all hazardous chemicals that they use.

Employers must provide training on hazardous chemical exposures to their affected workers. Training describes the risks of the chemicals and the availability of further information. This training must also include methods to detect the release of hazardous chemicals and measures that employees can take to protect themselves from exposure to the chemicals.

The hazard communication standard also requires that employers provide a list of hazardous chemicals known to be present in the workplace and maintain MSDS at a central location providing additional information. The contents of the MSDS are described in Exhibit 5-1. Each container of the hazardous chemical must be labeled with the identity of all hazardous chemicals contained therein. Labeling requirements are also summarized in Exhibit 5-1.

Exhibit 5-1

MSDS Requirements

1. Chemical identity and common name
2. Physical and chemical characteristics
3. Possible physical hazards presented (e.g., flammability)
4. Health hazards and symptoms of exposure
5. Primary routes of entry
6. Information on safe exposure levels
7. Information on whether the chemical causes cancer
8. Any known safety precautions
9. Any known control measures to be taken
10. Any known emergency first aid procedures
11. The date on which the MSDS was prepared
12. The name, address and telephone number of the preparer

Labeling Requirements

1. The identity of the hazardous chemical or chemicals
2. The necessary hazard warnings
3. Name and address of the chemical manufacturer or importer

There are some exceptions to OSHA's hazard communication standard. If a consumer product or a drug containing a hazardous chemical is found in the workplace, it need not be labeled. Another exception exists for "articles," which are manufactured items with their end use in the workplace. An article would include objects such as a chair or a tire.

Disclosure under the hazard communication standard also may be limited by the need to protect trade secrets. A manufacturer or employer need not disclose the chemical identity of trade secrets on an MSDS, so long as the identity is available for use by health professionals and others in an emergency.

Employers are being cited for more than 10,000 violations a year under the hazard communication standard. A nonserious violation can be punished by up to $1000. Willful or repeated violations are punishable by a fine of up to $10,000 per violation. These penalties may continue for each day that the employer fails to correct the violation.

Record-Keeping Requirements

OSHA places extensive record-keeping and reporting requirements on employers. These requirements are not especially costly, but they are extremely technical. OSHA regularly imposes million-dollar fines on employers for violation of the agency's record-keeping and reporting requirements.

Most industries must maintain a log and summary of all occupational injuries and illnesses that cause the loss of at least one workday or that require medical treatment. The summaries must be posted every year, the records must be preserved for five years, and the records must be made available to employees. The employer must record any workdays missed or restricted due to occupational injuries.

Suppose that the UA Steel company employs a welder. The welder takes an accidental fall at work and suffers a muscle pull. The welder continues to work but is restricted from overhead welding for one week due to the muscle pull. The employer must record one week of restricted work due to occupational injury.

Record-keeping violations are punished like other OSHA violations. OSHA has issued citations for failure to record employee injuries and illnesses and has issued penalties. If the violation is based on an employer's good faith misinterpretation of the requirements, however, the Occupational Safety and Health Review Commission has generally vacated the penalties.

Workers' Compensation

Under traditional common law principles, an employee injured on the job could sue the employer under a theory such as negligence. Negligence was difficult to prove, however, and the worker lawsuits took considerable court time and expense. By the early twentieth century, virtually all states had adopted a workers' compensation system to supplant the traditional common law approach.

The workers' compensation system was adopted by state legislatures but was presented as a bargain between employer and employee. The employer gave up common law defenses and virtually guaranteed compensation for work-related injuries of the employee. In return, the employee accepted a lower compensation level and gave up the right to sue in court for additional damages.

The workers' compensation system has generally worked well but is beginning to show serious deficiencies. For many workers the recoveries for certain injuries seem insufficient. For employers, the costs of the system doubled between 1985 and 1990 and reached $60 billion per year.

Although the goal of the system was to avoid court litigation, considerable litigation has arisen over issues of workers' compensation coverage.

Covered Employees

The workers' compensation systems of the various states are limited to employees and do not attempt to cover independent contractors. The key defining differences between employees and independent contractors are described in Chapter 36 of *West's Business Law, Fifth Edition*.

Nor do the workers' compensation laws cover all employees. Very small businesses are not covered, though the typical state law will cover employers that have three or more employees. In most states, agricultural and farm workers are excluded from coverage. Domestic employees are also excluded. Coverage of professionals varies. Nurses, for example, are generally covered by workers' compensation acts.

Administration

A common feature of state workers' compensation systems is the establishment of a nonjudicial system to administer the statute. A government commission establishes the rules and compensates workers.

The workers' compensation system is invoked when an employee informs the employer that an injury has been suffered. This notice must be given promptly to facilitate effective medical treatment and help in the determination of the injury's cause. States have varying statutes of limitations for the filing of workers' compensation claims.

After notice is filed, many statutes have waiting periods applicable to disability claims. This is to permit the full extent of the injury to be discovered and to encourage the employee's prompt return to the work force.

If the employer disputes liability under workers' compensation, the states provide for an administrative hearing. These hearings are somewhat like a court trial but generally are less formal. For example, hearsay evidence is readily admitted in workers' compensation administrative hearings.

Covered Injuries

The determination of the injuries to be covered by workers' compensation is one of the most controversial issues in this area of the law. The standard legal test in most state laws is that of a "personal injury by accident arising out of and in the course of employment."

Many cases have disputed the "arising out of" requirement of workers' compensation coverage. Workers' compensation was originally designed to address the more traditional sources of workplace accidents. Suppose that Joseph Abboud is working on a mechanical power press. He attempts to clear some loose plastic out of the press when it engages and crushes his hand. Workers' compensation will clearly cover this accident.

Modern circumstances have presented nontraditional sources of workplace injuries, however. Suppose that Mr. Abboud is working late one night. While leaving the plant after hours he is mugged and seriously injured. Should this be considered an accident "arising out of" his employment?

Under traditional law, Joseph Abboud's mugging would not be covered, because it would be considered a "common risk." Nonworkers face the risk of mugging just as do workers, so this risk was not peculiar to his employment.

Modern doctrines are broader, however, and might permit Abboud to recover medical expenses related to his injuries under workers' compensation. Some courts use a **doctrine of increased risk**. If the employment subjects the worker to an increased risk of a certain type of harm, the employee is covered. Abboud could contend that the necessity of his working late in a certain part of town subjected him to such an increased risk of mugging.

Other state courts have adopted an even broader view, known as the **doctrine of positional risk**. This doctrine permits recovery if the injury resulted because the employment placed the worker in the particular position resulting in injury. In a well-known early case, an employee recovered under workers' compensation when he was struck by an arrow fired by a youth outside the work site.[8]

A worker will not be covered if the source of the injury is personal and not work related. In one unusual case, a school janitor noticed a child near his automobile and, fearing vandalism, spanked the child and sent him home. The child's grandmother then approached the janitor on the school premises and shot and killed him. A court said the death was not covered under workers' compensation because it arose out of the janitor's non-work actions.[9]

Courts have construed this personal animosity exception narrowly, however. If an injury is connected to the job duties of the worker, coverage will be applied, as demonstrated in the following decision.

---

[8]*Gargiulo v. Gargiulo*, 95 A.2d 646 (N.J. 1953).

[9]*Porter v. Dallas Independent School District*, 759 S.W. 2d 454 (Tex. App. 1988).

▬ Case 5.3
Security Insurance Co. v. Nasser

Court of Appeals of Texas,
Fourteenth District, 1988
755 S.W.2d 186

Background and Facts   *Izzat Nasser was the manager of a Hamburgers by Gourmet outlet. He became acquainted with Marianne Dawes, who worked nearby and visited the restaurant two or three times a day. Nasser and Dawes would sit and talk at the restaurant. "Although [Nasser] and Dawes did go out on one date, they both claimed that there was no romantic involvement between them." Dawes explained that she had a boyfriend, Victor Daryoush, who had suffered a head injury and had been diagnosed as psychotic and schizophrenic.*

Daryoush came to Nasser's restaurant and asked to see him. Nasser suspected trouble and told Daryoush he was busy talking to his girlfriend. Some time later, Nasser was leaving his office, and Daryoush attacked him with a knife. Nasser sought coverage of his injuries under workers' compensation.

At the initial trial, the court granted summary judgment for the workers' compensation insurance agency and against Nasser under the **personal animosity exception.** *This ruling was reversed by the state supreme court and the case was remanded. On remand a jury rendered a verdict for Nasser. The insurance company appealed this verdict.*

DRAUGHN, Judge.

*   *   *   *

The Supreme Court's holding that the injury in this case was incidental to some duty of Nasser's employment and, thereby, precluded the personal animosity exception, merits further explanation. The court, in reaching its conclusion, reasoned that it was part of Nasser's job to talk with and be nice to customers; as a result of performing this aspect of his job, he was stabbed. The court also held that whenever conditions attached to the place of employment are factors in the catastrophic combination, the consequent injury arises out of the employment. 724 S.W.2d at 19. The Court cited as primary support for this holding *Garcia v. Texas Indem.,* 146 Tex. 413, 209 S.W.2d 333, 336 (1948).

Garcia involved a worker, who because of a pre-existing physical condition, epilepsy, fell against a sharp-edged physical object that was a fixed part of his workplace. (For an analogous comparison of such so-called "idiopathic-fall" cases, see A. Larson, The Law of Workman's Compensation, @12.14(b) (1982).) The Supreme Court similarly concluded that the dispute, if any, between Nasser and Daryoush "arouse in the workplace, or was exacerbated by, or in the very least, was incidental to a duty" of Nasser's employment. Id.

This conclusion is apparently based to a large degree on the Court's earlier finding that had it not been for Dawes' visits to the restaurant as a customer, Daryoush would never have seen Nasser talking to her. However, we find no evidence in the record that Daryoush ever saw Dawes talking to Nasser at the restaurant. There is testimony that Nasser and Dawes dated on one occasion away from the restaurant. We assume the Court's conclusion was grounded on the rationale that the jury must have inferred from the evidence that Daryoush saw Nasser and Dawes together at the restaurant. The jury is entitled to make such an inference if it is reasonable and based on the facts proved. *Walters v. American States Ins. Co.,* 654 S.W.2d 423 (Tex. 1983).

We find the jury could, from the evidence, rationally infer that Daryoush must have seen Dawes talking with Nasser at the restaurant.

The evidence shows that for some period of time, between six months and a year and a half, Dawes worked next door to the restaurant and went there as a customer at least twice each day, during which time she would sit and converse with Nasser. The evidence also shows that Dawes never told Daryoush about such meetings or about her one social date with Nasser. This date occurred during the time when Daryoush was in the mental ward of a local hospital. Nasser testified that he did not know Daryoush prior to the assault. Based on this evidence, the jury could reasonably infer that Daryoush must have learned of Nasser's contacts with Dawes by observing them together at the restaurant. This reasonable inference enables the jury to conclude that Nasser's contacts with Dawes at the restaurant were a causal factor in the assault. The Supreme Court has now clearly said that if such causal factors are part of the catastrophic combination of elements which results in injury, it is compensable. The rationale is that Nasser was carrying out a duty of his employment—being friendly with a customer—and this was an important factor in the chain of events that led to the assault and injury.

Decision and Remedy   *The court affirmed the trial court decision that Nasser's injuries were covered.*

Workers also are not covered for what the law considers to be "Acts of God." If a worker is struck by lightning, the workers' compensation system will not cover the injury. If, however, the worker's job itself made him or her more likely to be struck by lightning (e.g., television antenna repairer), the injury will be covered.

Another common controversy involves the **"in the course of"** employment requirement of workers' compensation coverage. Injuries are only covered by workers' compensation if they arise during the time of employment.

A typical "in the course of" employment controversy would be an employee who was injured while commuting to work. The general rule, sometimes called the "going and coming" rule, holds that the employee is *not* in the course of employment when commuting.

Special circumstances may bring a commuting employee within the scope of workers' compensation. If the employer provides a truck for commuting and places the employee "on call" while commuting, the employee will be in the course of employment even while driving home from work.

Another set of cases involves recreational injuries. Suppose an employer has a company picnic and a worker is injured while playing softball. This injury may be covered by workers' compensation if participation at the company picnic was expected and considered a part of employment at the company.

To be covered, the injury need not occur at work, so long as the injury's cause resulted from the course of employment. For example, an employee inhaled chemical fumes at work shortly before his shift ended. His residual intoxication from these fumes caused him to have an automobile accident on his trip home. A court held that this injury was covered by workers' compensation.[10]

Another "in the course of" employment problem involves preexisting worker conditions. Suppose that an employee with epilepsy has a seizure on the job. This probably would not be covered by workers' compensation. But if the epileptic were a construction worker on a new office building, and if the seizure caused the employee to fall several stories to the ground, the injuries suffered would be considered in the course of employment and covered by workers' compensation.

Just because an injury occurs on the worksite does not automatically render it "in the course of" employment. Injuries from fights among employees are generally not covered. If a worker is intoxicated and is injured, statutes often

---

[10]*Technical Tape Corp. v. Industrial Commission*, 317 N.E.2d 515 (Ill. 1974).

exclude coverage. Coverage is frequently denied if the worker's injury was caused by the express disobedience of an employer's safety rules.

Yet another requirement of workers' compensation coverage is a **personal injury by accident**. For a time, courts distinguished injury from disease and denied coverage to workplace diseases. Now, all courts recognize that at least some diseases will be covered under the workers' compensation statutes.

Some states distinguish occupational diseases from common diseases. An *occupational* disease would be one such as mesothelioma, caused by high exposures to asbestos that are found primarily at work. A *common* disease would be one like pneumonia, which is typically caused by factors other than occupational exposures.

Some courts will allow workers' compensation recovery for even common diseases, if the worker can prove that this disease was caused by the job. For example, a deliveryperson may be required to work outdoors in cold, rain, and snow. If there is proof that this exposure caused the deliveryperson to contract pneumonia, the disease could be covered.

The leading workers' compensation controversy today involves claims for injuries resulting from occupational stress. Stress is a major source of modern diseases and injuries, and workers'

compensation claims for stress-related problems have increased dramatically. To be recoverable in some states, the stress must result in a physical injury.

Workplace stress may cause mental illness or even physical illness. For example, stress may cause the onset of a heart attack. In other circumstances, a physical injury may bring on stress. In one case, a court found that a work-related injury caused a deranged mental condition that caused the worker's suicide. The court held that the worker's dependents were entitled to compensation under a workers' compensation statute.[11]

One problem with stress claims is proving that they are caused by the workplace. Numerous sources of stress exist in the personal lives of many workers. Before stress is compensable under workers' compensation, there must be evidence of particular workplace events of mental trauma or generalized causes of stress, such as very long working hours, unusually high responsibility, or the threat of job loss. Ultimately, the causation of stress harms is a factual medical question, as illustrated by the following holding.

---

[11]*Jakco Painting Contractors v. Industrial Commission of the State of Colorado*, 702 P.2d 755 (Colo. App. 1985).

■ Case 5.4

State Accident Insurance Fund Corporation v. McCabe

Court of Appeals of Oregon, 1985

702 P.2d 436

Background and Facts *At the age of twenty-nine, Peter McCabe was the chief executive officer of the Amalgamated Transit Workers Union in 1979. He took on a great deal of work in this position, working six- and seven-day weeks and sometimes as much as sixteen hours a day. He also took work-related telephone calls at home. Shortly after assuming the job he learned of the possibility of financial irregularities within the union and "became obsessed with investigating the matter." During this time, his "personal habits, attitudes, demeanor and personality began to change significantly." He began to smoke and drink heavily and suffered memory loss and bursts of anger.*

In 1980, McCabe was diagnosed as having high blood pressure and placed himself under the care of a physician. In 1981, he was at a convention and became involved in an argument with a government officer. He returned to his room and, while engaged in sexual intercourse, suffered a ruptured cerebral aneurysm, which left him severely disabled. He claimed for benefits, and the compensation board decided that the claim was compensable. The insurance fund appealed this ruling.

RICHARDSON, Judge.

*   *   *   *

We need not address the issue of whether the claim is compensable as an injury, because we hold that it is compensable as an occupational disease. The medical evidence indicates that claimant's aneurysm was congenital. To establish an occupational disease claim relating to a preexisting condition, a claimant must prove that work conditions caused a worsening of the underlying condition producing disability or the need for medical services. *Weller v. Union Carbide*, 288 or 27, 602 P2d 259 (1979). Additionally, he must establish that the work conditions were the major contributing cause of the worsening of the preexisting condition. *Dethlefs v. Hyster Co.*, 295 or 298, 667 P2d 487 (1983); SAIF v. Gygi, 55 Or App 570, 639 P2d 655, rev den 292 Or 825 (1982).

Two doctors, neither of whom examined claimant, testified at the hearing. They disagreed over the cause of the ruptured aneurysm. The parties have devoted a substantial portion of their briefs to a discussion of which doctor was more qualified to express an opinion. We find both well qualified.

Dr. Uhland testified in claimant's behalf. He is a board-certified specialist in internal medicine and has had considerable experience with cardiovascular medicine. His testimony indicates that work stress was the major contributing cause of the disability. He stated that claimant was probably born with the aneurysm and that the enormous amount of work stress and the intermittent rise in blood pressure exhibited in the months preceding the rupture caused a thinning of the walls of the aneurysm. The walls became so thin that small amounts of blood leaked out. That leakage, he testified, would explain the headaches, memory lapses and personality changes that claimant suffered. He agreed that the act of sexual intercourse was the precipitating event causing the rupture but stated that work stress contributed "in a major way" to claimant's disability by weakening the wall of the aneurysm. He testified that, in his opinion, the aneurysm would not have ruptured as soon as it did without the weakening of the arterial wall caused by the work stress induced rise in blood pressure.

Dr. Raaf, board certified in neurosurgery, testified for SAIF. In a report before the hearing, he stated that the aneurysm was the result of a defect in the arterial wall and that claimant's work was not a factor in the cause of the aneurysm or its rupture. At the time he wrote the report he had not read some of the relevant medical reports discussing claimant's personality change and showing his elevated blood pressure. At the hearing, however, he stated in response to a hypothetical question that included claimant's work history that his opinion was unchanged by those additional facts. His opinion was that the aneurysm was a congenital defect which naturally weakened with age and that the sexual intercourse caused an increase in blood pressure, causing the aneurysm to rupture. He stated that the act of sexual intercourse was the major contributing cause of claimant's disability. He testified that he was aware of no scientific information that intermittent rises in blood pressure cause an aneurysm to weaken.

Dr. Mundall was one of the physicians who treated claimant in the emergency room. He stated in a letter to SAIF that claimant's condition "was not likely due to the work he was performing for the Amalgamated Transit Union but was rather a natural progression of a weakening in the wall of his blood vessel that he was probably born with and then precipitated by physical exertion."

We are confronted with two opposing theories. On de novo review, we are free to choose which medical hypothesis is correct, *Coday v. Willamette Tug & Barge*, 250 Or 39, 49, 440 P2d 224 (1968), and we find Dr. Uhland's more persuasive. Unlike Dr. Raaf, he had examined all of the medical reports before the hearing and was therefore apparently better acquainted with claimant's medical history. His testimony was well-reasoned. Dr. Raaf's answers were not as well-explained as Dr. Uhland's. Dr. Mundall's letter supports Dr. Raaf's theory, but it does not explain why work was not a major factor in claimant's disability or whether he was even aware of the amount of stress involved in claimant's work. In short, we find Dr. Uhland's theory more persuasive.

Decision and Remedy   *The court affirmed the finding that the harm suffered by McCabe was compensable under workers' compensation.*

Some states, such as Texas, have limited recovery for stress under workers' compensation. Texas workers can recover only for stress that results from physical injuries and cannot recover for stress resulting from "mental stimuli." A truck driver suffered depression and gastritis resulting from long hours and timetable pressure but was denied recovery because these harms were deemed the product of mental, not physical, trauma.

In states that permit stress claims resulting from mental trauma, such as New York, most use the **average worker test**. That is, a worker can only recover if the stress was greater than could be borne by the ordinary employee.

The average employee test was used by the courts of Wisconsin. A purchasing agent was placed under a new supervisor who was "negative, brusque and belittling, especially to women" and the agent's job became "unusually nerveracking and subjected her to far greater pressures and tensions than those experienced by the average employee."[12]

Benefits

Workers' compensation provides specified recoveries in the event of a covered accident. Death benefits are made available to dependents of the deceased worker. The amount of death benefits is generally computed on the basis of a percentage of the worker's average wage. Burial expenses are also commonly included.

For workplace injuries, the workers' compensation system provides reimbursement of medical expenses and rehabilitation costs. Recovery of medical expenses is generally unlimited, though some states permit the employer to select the doctor to be used. Some states limit benefits to workers who are incapacitated for at least one week.

Workers can also recover for disability. Statutes generally classify disabilities in one of four categories: temporary partial, temporary total, permanent partial, or permanent total. Temporary partial disabilities are compensated for any wages lost as a result of the disability. Temporary total disability is compensated for economic losses during the worker's recovery period.

Permanent partial disability results from an injury such as the loss of a finger. If the employee is able to return to work, compensation for these injuries is generally based upon a recovery schedule established by the state. Permanent total disability is compensated by such a schedule or by a wage loss calculation. California provides disability payments based on medical and rehabilitation costs plus two-thirds of any income loss resulting from the accident.

Exclusivity

As described above, workers' compensation is an *exclusive* system. This means that an employee has a right to recover in workers' compensation

---

[12]*Swiss Colony v. Dep't of ILHR*, 240 N.W.2d 128 (Wis. 1976).

but may not recover in any other forum, such as a negligence claim in court. There are exceptions to exclusivity, which have become more important as court recoveries have become much greater than workers' compensation recoveries in many instances.

The first issue in workers' compensation exclusivity is whether the accident is even within the coverage of a workers' compensation statute. It is not uncommon to find a worker arguing to a court that his or her injury is *not* covered by workers' compensation, so that the worker can bring a lawsuit for damages.

Even covered injuries may permit a lawsuit under certain exceptions to exclusivity. One of these is the **intentional tort exception**. The employee can choose to use either workers' compensation or common law recovery when the workplace injury or death results from the employer's intentional act.

The most common use of the intentional tort exception is when the employer physically assaults an employee. The exception may not apply when coworkers conduct the assault, however. In one case, a waitress was preparing to close a restaurant when she was attacked and raped by her supervisor, an assistant manager. A court held that her exclusive remedy was in workers' compensation.[13]

A number of workers have sought to sue for intentional infliction of emotional stress damages outside of workers' compensation. If the employee claims physical injuries, such as hypertension or a heart attack, courts have generally held that workers' compensation is the exclusive remedy. For purely mental injuries, however, many courts have permitted workers to sue under common law.

Another typical exception to exclusivity is for **fraudulent concealment**. The worker may bring a lawsuit if he or she has suffered a work-related injury and if the employer either aggravates the injury or conceals the presence of the injury from the employee.

In one case, a worker was employed by a company that manufactured and packaged asbestos products. After working for the company for decades, the worker contracted asbestos-related illnesses, including lung cancer. The worker claimed that the company was aware of these risks and fraudulently concealed from him that he suffered the early stages of these diseases. The court agreed and permitted the worker to sue in court.[14]

Another important exception to exclusivity is product liability. Workers' compensation and exclusivity only apply between the employee and the employer. If a workplace injury is caused by a third party, such as a manufacturer of a defective product found in the workplace, the injured worker can go to court and sue that manufacturer. The worker may be limited to workers' compensation, though, if the manufacturer of the product is also the employer.

In most states, the worker also may sue in court if the employer has failed to maintain workers' compensation insurance coverage.

---

[13]*Schatz v. York Steak House*, 444 A.2d 1045 (Md. App. 1982).

[14]*Johns Manville Products v. Contra County Superior Court*, 612 P.2d 948 (Cal. 1980).

■ **Ethical Perspectives**

The Cost of Occupational Safety

Employers have a variety of financial incentives to improve the safety of their workplaces. Workers' compensation insurance will be less expensive if they suffer fewer claims. Economic studies have shown that workers demand higher wages for jobs that have higher risks. The threat of fines for noncompliance with OSHA standards is always present.

Improving the safety of a workplace is not inexpensive, however. The costs of enhancing safety at times may far exceed the financial benefits to employers. If an OSHA standard requires such enhanced safety devices, the employer must implement the devices, regardless of cost. OSHA cannot regulate every workplace risk, though. The ethical question is how far above and beyond OSHA standards an employer should go.

Some might argue that mere compliance with OSHA standards discharges the employer's safety duties to its employees. The law does not define the limits of ethics, however. Moreover, OSHA has found standard-setting to be a slow, costly and difficult task, subject to challenge by both employers and unions. Everyone agrees that OSHA standards are an incomplete guide to occupational safety. This fact is recognized in the act itself, through the general duty clause.

Suggesting that an employer should go beyond minimum OSHA standards does not answer the question of how far beyond the standards the employer should go. To what extent should the employer consider the costs of workplace safety in deciding whether to adopt additional safety protections for employees.

Some argue that costs should not be considered. The idea of balancing costs against human lives seems repugnant. Who can say how many dollars a life or limb is worth? This ethical vision is too simplistic, however it would dictate unlimited spending on safety. Because no workplace can be absolutely safe, this approach would suggest that employment itself is unethical.

The costs of safety improvements inevitably will be considered. Some cost consideration is even in the interest of workers. Higher costs of production mean higher costs of products, which means less demand for products, so the costs of safety improvements will sometimes cost jobs. The more money spent on safety improvements, the less will be available for employee benefits or wage increases. Many workers have made clear that they will accept higher risk in return for a higher wage.

The ethical legitimacy of some cost consideration does not justify a disregard for worker safety, however. Human life and welfare is more than a pure matter of the balance sheet. Ethics does not limit safety improvements to those that are cost-effective for the employer. Interests of the worker and of society are also relevant.

The appropriate extent of safety improvements may depend on the circumstances of the employer. If the employer is flush with profits, it can afford and should institute more workplace safety. If safety enhancement is unaffordable, the employer could at least inform its workers of the risks and help them take their own precautions against injury or disease.

■ **International Perspectives**

International Occupational Safety Protection

Each nation has its own system to protect the health and safety of workers. Some foreign systems may go beyond U.S. protections. Most European nations, for example, required labeling of hazardous workplace chemicals long before the U.S. adopted its hazard communication standard. Great Britain's Health and Safety at Work Act of 1974 is similar to U.S. law. A British company was recently hit with a penalty of over $1.3 million for repeated violations that resulted in three deaths.

A key concern in international trade involves those countries with weak occupational safety and health laws. Some nations offer little legal protection to workers. Even nations with protective laws for workplace safety may do little enforcing of those laws.

Compliance with occupational safety laws and workers' compensation in the United States and other industrialized nations can be quite expensive. Consequently, a number of companies have moved production facilities to less developed nations that lack strict standards. There is considerable concern both for the welfare of the workers in these nations and for the jobs of American workers.

The International Labour Organization (ILO) of the United Nations, created in 1919, has established guidelines for worldwide occupational safety. The ILO has little power, however, for the enforcement of these standards and no real sanction authority. The ILO can only publicize noteworthy violations and encourage their correction.

The United States has taken steps in its trade legislation to encourage occupational safety. U.S. law specifies certain "internationally recognized worker rights." Among these rights are: "taking into account the country's level of economic development, acceptable conditions of work with respect to minimum wages, hours of work, and occupational safety and health."

The Office of the United States Trade Representative (USTR) reviews the practice of trading partners against this standard. If the USTR finds that a country is violating internationally recognized worker rights, the United States may declare an unreasonable trade practice. The USTR is then empowered to suspend trade agreement concessions or impose import fees or other restrictions, at the direction of the President.

The U.S. also may deny other trade opportunities. The USTR may suspend the Generalized System of Preferences that grants duty-free entry to the goods of certain less-developed nations. The U.S. may also cut off Overseas Private Investment Corporation insurance for such nations.

United States trade sanctions have not been widely used to protect worker rights such as health and safety. Sanctioned nations have been few, including Nicaragua, Romania, Chile, Ethiopia and Paraguay. The USTR has rejected numerous petitions to sanction other nations. Application of the law's provisions may depend more on generalized foreign policy objectives than on worker rights.

Questions and Case Problems

1. Manno Equipment was visited by an OSHA inspector. Manno's foreman asked to accompany the inspector on his trip throughout the Manno plant, but the inspector refused. After visiting the plant, the inspector issued a number of citations. Manno refuses to pay and claims that it was wrongfully denied its walkaround rights with the inspector. Manno contends that the evidence in the inspection should be inadmissible. Is Manno correct?

2. Sky Sailmakers runs a plant in which workers stitch sails together. Sky failed to provide guards for sewing machine needles, though workers had to move their hands within inches of the needle. A number of minor puncture wounds had resulted from the failure to provide guards. OSHA cited Sky Sailmakers for a violation and sought a penalty for willful violation of the law. Sky contended that its violation was de minimis and warranted no penalty. Should Sky Sailmakers be subject to a significant fine in this case?

3. An OSHA standard requires that workers wear hard hats for certain jobs. Seattle Stevedoring told its workers that they must wear the hard hats. The workers resisted wearing the hats, however, and Seattle Stevedoring was issued several citations. The company consistently insisted that the workers wear the hard hats, but the workers repeatedly took them off. Finally, OSHA issued a strict citation against Seattle Stevedoring for a

willful violation of the act. Seattle Stevedoring appealed that it should not be blamed for its workers' refusal to wear the hats. Should Seattle Stevedoring be liable for a willful violation? [*Seattle Stevedoring Co.*, 8 O.S.H.C. 1240 (1980)].

4. Richard Lanno was a project engineer for Thermal Equipment Co., which manufactured pressure vessels for the aerospace industry. Lanno was sometimes required to proceed from his home directly to a job site and was on call at home after hours and on weekends. In order to answer these calls, Lanno needed the company truck, in which he carried tools. Thermal provided Lanno with the truck, gasoline money, and permitted him to use the truck for personal purposes. One day, Lanno left work and was driving home. He went out of his way to stop at a store. Before reaching the store, Lanno had an automobile accident. Was Lanno in the scope of employment at the time of the accident? [*Lazar v. Thermal Equipment Corp.*, 195 Cal. Rptr. 890 (1983)].

5. John Jacobs worked at a textile plant and complained to another worker that his back hurt when he performed certain lifting required by the job. The company doctor determined that Jacobs had strained his back muscles. Jacobs continued to work and the problem became worse. Not long thereafter, Jacobs died of cancer. Doctors found that the back strain had caused the cancer to spread more rapidly. Should Jacobs' widow be able to receive workers' compensation benefits in this case?

CHAPTER SIX

Accounting and the Law

KEY BACKGROUND

The essential background for this chapter on accounting and the law is found in Chapter 55 of *West's Business Law, Fifth Edition*. This chapter covers liability of accountants. Among the important points to remember from this chapter are:

- accountants' potential liability for breach of contract and negligence

- accountants' potential liability to non-client third parties

- accountants' potential liability under the federal securities laws

- rules for accountants' work papers and client communications

* * *

As the significance and complexity of financial transactions increases, so too does the role of accountants. Accounting firms are increasingly expanding their services into areas such as management consulting. Recent years also have seen an explosion of potential legal liability of accountants. More lawsuits were filed against accountants in the last fifteen years than in the entire previous history of the profession.

Malpractice Liability to Clients

The most traditional source of liability for accountants is to their clients for accounting malpractice or negligence. If a company hires an accountant to audit the company's financial condition and that accountant does a defective job, the accountant may be liable to the company for damages that it suffered from reliance on the inaccurate audit.

Much litigation results from accountants' performance of financial audits. Auditing typically involves rendering an opinion on the accuracy of a company's financial statements, including its balance sheet, its income statement, and its cash flow statement. The accountant tests these statements against general professional principles.

The most important such principles are **Generally Accepted Auditing Standards** (GAAS) and **Generally Accepted Accounting Principles** (GAAP), a set of accounting methods for recording assets, liabilities, revenues and expenditures. GAAS and GAAP are derived from the principles set forth by a private organization, the American Institute of Certified Public Accountants (AICPA) and the Financial Accounting Standards Board (FASB).[1]

The traditional approach for malpractice liability to a client was under contract law for a violation of GAAS and GAAP. The accountant could be sued for breach of contract, when an audit was negligently performed. The potential damages are relatively low in a contract claim and may be limited to the cost charged for the audit.

---

[1]Those in the field pronounce these initials as "fazbee."

In recent years, courts increasingly have found that accountants could be sued in tort, such as negligence, for malpractice to a client. Damages in tort may be significantly greater and could amount to millions of dollars.

Many tort cases allege simple negligence on the part of an auditor. Some cases go further and claim that the accountant engaged in fraud or gross negligence. For both contract and tort cases, the plaintiff client must prove that the accountant violated a legal duty.

Accountant's Duty

Accountants are not insurers of financial statement accuracy. Mere failure to report accurately a company's financial status, or failure to discover problems, does not automatically result in liability. The accountant will be liable for negligent failure to perform his or her duties.

Even in a tort case, the accountant's contract is a central source of his or her obligations. For example, suppose an accountant was employed to prepare income tax returns for a client. The accountant relied on client records that showed certain income to be taxable. The client later discovered that the income was not taxable

and that they were owed a refund that the accountant failed to file to protect. In this case, the accountant was not liable because the agreement with the client provided that the accountant could rely on data provided by the company.[2]

The terms of contracts are not always clear. The accountant and the client will not always place the same interpretation on a contract term. Moreover, an accountant during the course of work may assume duties beyond those specified in the contract.

In addition, accountants have a generalized duty to fulfill the standards of their profession. Minimum standards are found in GAAS and GAAP. Accountants must also follow other standards set forth by the AICPA, FASB, and the Securities and Exchange Commission (SEC).

In some cases, accountants must go beyond the AICPA and other standards. There are some instances in which GAAP or other AICPA standards do not address a specific problem. In addition, some courts have found the GAAP standards to be inadequate and imposed higher standards on accountants. The following case employed such a higher standard.

---

[2]*Lindner v. Barlow, Davis & Wood*, 27 Cal. Rptr. (Cal. App. 1963).

▬ Case 6.1
Bily v.
Arthur Young & Company
Court of Appeals of California,
Sixth Appellate District, 1990,
271 Cal.Rptr. 470

Background and Facts *Osborne Computer Corporation retained Arthur Young & Co. to audit its financial statements for 1982. The next year, Osborne Computer sold stock to the public and obtained loans from other investors in exchange for warrants to purchase stock at an attractive price. There were significant weaknesses in Osborne Computer's internal accounting procedures, and the 1982 financial statements turned out to be far too optimistic. Late in 1983, Osborne Computer went into bankruptcy. The company's stock was reduced to nominal value and the warrants became worthless.*

The stock purchasers and warrant holders sued Arthur Young and others. After a lengthy jury trial, Arthur Young was found liable in negligence. Arthur Young appealed, complaining that the jury instructions had been improper and held Arthur Young to too high a standard of care.

CAPACCIOLI, Judge

* * * *

With respect to professional negligence the trial court instructed the jury, in part, that "[i]n performing professional services for a client, . . . Arthur Young . . . , as an independent auditor, has the duty to have that degree of learning and skill ordinarily possessed by a reputable certified public accountant practicing in the same or a similar locality and under similar circumstances. It is . . . Arthur Young's. . . further duty to use the care and skill ordinarily used in like cases by reputable members of its profession practicing in the same or similar locality under similar circumstances, and to use reasonable diligence and its best judgment in the exercise of its professional skill and in the application of its learning in an effort to accomplish the purpose for which it was employed."

Arthur Young asked for an instruction that "[t]he standard of ordinary skill and competence for accountants is defined by generally accepted accounting procedures, or GAAP, and generally accepted auditing standards, or GAAS." The trial court refused this instruction, and instead instructed the jury that "[i]n determining whether Arthur Young fulfilled its professional duties, you may consider among other evidence whether or not its work complied with . . . GAAP and . . . GAAS."

Arthur Young argues it was error to permit the jury to consider GAAS and GAAP "merely as evidence along with other unspecified evidence"; it asserts that "[t]he standard of care applicable to the accounting profession is exclusively defined by GAAS and GAAP."

We conclude the jury was properly instructed.

Unquestionable GAAS and GAAP are monumental and commendable codifications of customs and practices within the profession of certified public accountancy. But it is the general rule that adherence to a relevant custom or practice does not necessarily establish the actor has met the standard of care.

* * * *

First, neither GAAS nor GAAP is now, or may ever be, so comprehensive as to afford a predictable and repeatable standard of professional responsibility in all conceivable situations. As one commentator has acknowledged: "In situations that are not specifically addressed by the AICPA Professional Standards, a CPA merely has an obligation to use professional care.

Although this requires a CPA to comply in good faith with GAAP and GAAS, neither of these concepts have been clearly defined."

* * * *

Second, in any event so categorical a rule would inappropriately entrust to the accountancy profession itself the balancing of interest implicit in any determination of duty and breach.

Under the general rule, GAAS and GAAP, as compilations of custom and practice, will be relevant and thus admissible as "evidence to be considered in determining the proper standard of care" (*Bullis v. Security Pac. Nat. Bank, supra*, 21 Cal.3d at p. 809), and in many if not most cases an accountant who has complied with GAAS and found compliance with GAAP will be found, in turn, to have satisfied the applicable standard. But this is not to say that GAAS and GAAP define the standard of care. Certified public accountants, like other professionals, must meet the standards of expertise and diligence common to their profession as proved with respect to the facts of particular cases by the testimony of suitable qualified expert witnesses. The trial court so instructed the jury. There was no error.

* * * *

It is undisputed that Osborne Computer Corporation lacked adequate internal accounting controls. There is substantial evidence to support further conclusions that the deficiencies were so serious as to amount to material weaknesses, and that Arthur Young discovered, or should have discovered, the material weaknesses. It is undisputed that Arthur Young did advise certain Osborne Computer Corporation managers of weaknesses in the company's internal accounting controls, but did not characterize the weaknesses as material weaknesses or communicate its findings to senior management, to the board, or to the board's audit committee.

Decision and Remedy   *The court affirmed the lower court judgment and remanded the case to trial court to settle issues regarding litigation costs.*

An important factor in accountant liability is the presence or absence of qualifying or explanatory statements accompanying the accountants' report. If the accountant did not independently verify records supplied by the client, the accountant should include a qualifying statement to that effect.

An accountant's duties can go beyond the contract, as the accountant may have certain fiduciary duties to the client. An accountant always has the duty to perform with reasonable care and in good faith. An accountant entrusted with a client's funds is held to a high standard of care with respect to those funds.

Sources of Liability

Certain fact situations produce most malpractice lawsuits against accountants. The traditional sources of liability are a report that inaccurately reflects a client's financial condition and a failure to detect the **defalcations** (e.g., fraud, embezzlement) of the client's employees. More recently, accountants may be liable for failure to report on weaknesses in a company's internal control structure against fraud.

False representation of financial condition is a common source of liability. Suppose that a partnership's accountant audits the partnership and fails to note that one partner's contributions to the partnership were substantially overvalued. For example, suppose that a partner contributed used furniture and office equipment to the partnership offices and valued these materials too highly. The accountant may be liable for failure to discover and report this fact. Improper valuation of inventory is another source of liability.

There are now an increasing number of suits filed against accountants in connection with takeovers. When one company acquires another, the acquirer has sued the accountant for misstating the financial condition of the acquired company.

Accountants also are retained to investigate and discover **defalcations by a corporation's employees**. One such act occurs when a client's employee fraudulently falsified inventory valuations for the client. In such a situation, auditors must employ "professional skepticism" and seek out defalcations, though auditors are not expected to discover every conceivable instance of wrongdoing.

In an example case, an accountant failed to discover that well-established commodity prices did not correspond with inventory valuations and that nearly half the freight rates listed were wrong. An employee was manipulating the books. The accountant was held to be liable for failure to discover the problem.[3]

Accountants are increasingly being sued for failure to report on weaknesses in the *client's internal structure to control defalcations* by employees. The internal control structure is the company's system to protect against errors finding their way into the company's financial statements. An internal control system should, among other things, ensure that transactions are reliably recorded in conformity with generally accepted accounting principles and that access to assets is limited by express management authorization. In 1988, the AICPA modified auditing standards to increase an auditor's responsibility for investigating,

---

[3]*Lincoln Grain, Inc. v. Coopers & Lybrand*, 345 N.W.2d 300 (Neb. 1984).

evaluating, and disclosing shortcomings in an internal control system.

In an unreported California case, an audit of a computer company failed to disclose that the company's internal controls were in disarray. Sometime after the audit, management discovered substantial unrecorded liabilities that resulted from the failure of internal controls. The company ultimately declared bankruptcy, and a jury found the accounting firm liable for $4 million.

Another common source of litigation is *tax preparation*. Many accountants are tax specialists, and individuals and companies rely on their accountants for tax preparation. Accountants may be sued for failure to use available deductions. Conversely, accountants may be sued for over-claiming deductions, which resulted in an IRS penalty assessment against the client.

Accountants were found liable in a recent case for failure to discover underpayment of federal taxes, which produced substantial damages causing the client's eventual bankruptcy.[4]

Contributory Negligence

When an accountant is sued for malpractice, the accountant often can claim that the client corporation should be unable to recover because the company was itself negligent. Suppose that a corporate officer was embezzling funds from a corporation. An accountant failed to discover this embezzling in an audit. The accountant would argue that the company was itself negligent in not discovering the embezzlement and should not recover for the accountant's alleged negligence.

Most states use **comparative negligence**. This concept is discussed in Chapter 5 of *West's Business Law, Fifth Edition*. This rule would at least reduce the accounting firm's liability by the percentage of the client's negligence. In a recent case, an accountant was sued for failure to discover embezzlement by a client's employee. A court found that the accountant was liable, but that the client corporation's negligence was itself 80 percent

responsible and reduced the accountant's liability accordingly.[5]

Courts in a majority of states have significantly limited the comparative negligence defense. The mere presence of negligence by the client is not a sufficient defense. Many courts hold that for the accountant to make out a comparative negligence defense, the accountant must show that the client's negligence directly contributed to the accountant's failure to discover and report the truth.

Suppose that Toy's, Incorporated, hired the AB&T accounting firm to conduct a financial audit. An employee of Toy's was diverting inventory for his personal profit and producing false records to cover it up. The AB&T firm did not rely on Toy's records, but conducted its own audit of inventory. AB&T failed to discover the employee's defalcation. While Toy's may have been itself negligent in permitting the employee theft, AB&T could not effectively use this as comparative negligence. Toy's negligence did not cause the accounting firm's erroneous report.

Other states provide for a broader comparative negligence defense. They hold that a client's own sloppiness in bookkeeping may be used by an accountant defendant, even if the accountant did not rely on the client's sloppy records. Florida, Minnesota, and Tennessee have adopted this more liberal approach to comparative negligence.

A successful use of the comparative negligence defense involved an accountant hired to audit a credit union. The auditor failed to discover that an office manager was embezzling from the credit union, and the institution sued the accountant. The accountant was not liable, however, because the credit union officials held out the office manager to the accountant as a trustworthy person whose reports could be relied on.[6]

Accountants also may take advantage of another form of comparative negligence—the client's negligent reliance on an accountant's report. Suppose that an accounting firm submits a financial report and qualifies this report with a statement that it did not verify the underlying data supplied to the auditor. A client's

---

[4]*Greenstein, Logan & Co. v. Burgess Marketing, Inc.*, 744 S.W.2d 170 (Tex. App. 1987).

[5]*Halla Nursery, Inc. v. Baumann-Firrie & Co.*, 438 N.W. 2d 400 (Minn. App. 1989).

[6]*Social Security Administration Baltimore Federal Credit Union v. United States*, 138 F. Supp. 639 (D. Md. 1956).

reliance on the report may be negligent, because the client should have realized the limitations of the audit.

If the client's contributory negligence was foreseeable by the accountant, the defense may fail. For example, an accountant improperly prepared a tax return, which resulted in a penalty for the taxpayer. The accountant argued contributory negligence, because the taxpayer should have discovered the mistake. A court found the accountant liable, because it was foreseeable that the taxpayer would sign the prepared return without reading it and checking for errors.[7]

Unaudited Reports

In order to save costs, many companies hire accountants to perform unaudited reports. This type of investigation is much less thorough than a full financial audit. In an unaudited report,

---

[7]*Bick v. Peat Marwick and Main,* 799 P.2d 94 (Kan. App. 1990).

the accountant merely examines and compiles a company's published financial statements and then applies certain agreed-upon procedures to evaluate the statements.

An unaudited report is far more limited in its representations, but accountants may still be liable for inaccurate unaudited reports. The AICPA has adopted standards for unaudited reports that limit the scope of such reports and specifically states that such a review does not include an evaluation of the client's internal control structure.

The courts have not fully accepted the AICPA position, however, and have held accountants liable for unaudited reports. An accountant may be required to do more than it has contractually promised in the unaudited report. If the accountant happens to discover a defalcation or other problem, the accountant should report that fact, even if such a report is beyond the accountant's contract.

The following decision was a landmark in holding accountants liable for even unaudited reports.

Case 6.2
Robert Wooler Company v. The Fidelity Bank
Superior Court of Pennsylvania, 1984
479 A.2d 1027

Background and Facts *Robert Wooler Company employed a bookkeeper, Dona Raichle, who diverted 94 checks into a personal account of her own. Wooler had employed Touche Ross & Co. as its accounting firm to conduct unaudited services for the company. After this was discovered, Wooler sued the bank and Touche Ross for damages.*

The trial court found that the Touche Ross personnel had "failed to use reasonable care in being alert" and had "failed to make the necessary inquiries in accordance with reasonable professional standards." Nevertheless, that court dismissed the claims against Touche Ross, finding that the accounting firm had been improperly added as a defendant and had no duty to inquire into the client's system of internal controls in such an unaudited engagement.

WEIAND, Judge.

*   *   *   *

Touche Ross' agreement to perform unaudited services was not a shield from liability if it failed to warn its client of known deficiencies in the client's internal operating procedures which enhanced opportunities for employee defalcations. Its agreement, in the absence of specific language relieving it from acts of negligence, did not relieve it from liability for ignoring suspicious circumstances which would have raised a "red flag" for a reasonably skilled and knowledgeable accountant. Thus, in 1136 *Tenants' Corp. v. Max Rothenberg & Co.,* 36 A.D.2d 804, 319 N.Y.S.2d 1007, 1007-1008 (1971), aff'd, 30 N.Y.2d 585, 281 N.E.2d 846,

330 N.Y.S.2d 800 (1972) a New York court held that it was negligence for an accountant engaged to perform unaudited services to ignore suspicious circumstances and fail to inform the client of missing invoices, thereby enabling an employee's defalcations to go unnoticed.

And in *United States v. Natelli*, 527 F.2d 311, 320 (2nd Cir. 1975), cert. denied, 425 U.S. 934, 96 S.Ct. 1663, 48 L.Ed.2d 175 (1976), it was held that auditors preparing an unaudited financial statement in connection with a proxy statement for filing with the Securities Exchange Commission had a duty to investigate suspicious circumstances. Similarly, in *Blakely v. Lisac*, 357 F.Supp. 255, 265-266 (D. Or. 1972), it was held that an accountant preparing an "unaudited write-up" had to undertake at least minimal investigation of figures supplied and was not free to ignore suspicious circumstances. See also: *Ryan v. Kanne*, 170 N.W.2d 395, 404 (Iowa 1969) (accountant liable for negligence in preparing report of accounts payable even though statement unaudited and accountant expressly disclaimed knowledge that information was correct); *Bohhiver v. Graff*, 311 Minn. 111, 248 N.W.2d 291, 297-299 (1976) (accountants having unaudited engagement to bring insurance company's books "up to date" are liable for negligence in failing to examine books made available to them when such an examination would have disclosed the insurance company's insolvency).

When Touche Ross agreed to provide unaudited accounting services for Wooler, it undertook to exercise that degree of accounting skill possessed by other accountants in the community. Touche Ross' obligation required that its personnel be reasonably alert to internal control defects which were patently obvious. Witnesses for the Bank and the accountant agreed that Wooler's internal controls had been defective and had thereby increased the potential for defalcations by a dishonest employee. They agreed that such a danger is inevitably present when the same employee is responsible to post accounts receivable in a sales journal, to handle incoming receivables, and to record daily receipts of moneys received in settlement of accounts receivable. Raichle, it was agreed, performed all these duties for Wooler. There was evidence that on the occasions when Touche Ross sent an accounting employee to examine Wooler's books, that person worked in close proximity to Raichle and observed her perform these several functions. Expert witnesses uniformly expressed the opinion that an accountant possessing reasonable accounting skill would have been aware of the potential for theft inherent in Wooler's internal controls.

Moreover, there was evidence that Touche Ross had supplied to employees who examined Wooler's financial records checklists entitled "Scope of Inquiries." These checklists reminded the accountant's employees to inquire into Wooler's allocation of bookkeeping duties. As a matter of practice, Touche Ross employees were instructed to be "alert for possible improvements in the client's accounting policies and procedures, system of internal control and accounting personnel and the assignment of duties."

Decision and Remedy   *The court reversed the lower court judgment and remanded the case for further proceedings.*

■ Liability to Non-Clients

The most controversial and significant issue in accounting law involves the liability of accountants to parties other than their clients. These third parties may have a greater stake in audit accuracy than does the client itself.

Suppose that Chemco is audited by the AB&T firm. Chemco's financial statements, approved by AB&T, suggest that the firm is financially healthy. Chemco obtains a large loan from CiuBank to expand overseas. CiuBank agrees to make the loan because the audited financial statements appear strong. Then it is discovered that the Chemco financial statements contained substantial errors, and Chemco declares bankruptcy. CiuBank stands to lose much of its money, due to Chemco's bankruptcy. Should CiuBank be able to sue AB&T for accounting malpractice?

Creditors are a common third party that seeks recovery for accounting malpractice. The shareholders in an audited corporation are also third parties who may wish to sue accountants. Another foreseeable third party who might be injured by accounting malpractice is an insurance company.

The traditional rule of **privity**, however, held that only the company could sue for accounting negligence, and third parties had no remedy against an auditor. Chapter 55 of *West's Business Law, Fifth Edition* discusses how the privity rule has been modified and how some third parties can now sue accountants.

The state courts are divided on the circumstances that enable third parties to sue for the simple negligence of accountants. Four different approaches are used: the substantial privity test, the Restatement test, the reasonable foreseeability test, and the balancing test. The applicable test will determine the liability of an accounting firm, such as AB&T, to third parties, such as CiuBank.

Substantial Privity Test

New York, the state that first abandoned the privity test, has adopted the **substantial privity test** to limit accountants' liability to third parties. The nature of this substantial privity defense was set forth in the leading case of *Credit Alliance v. Arthur Andersen & Co.*[8]

---

[8]483 N.E.2d 110 (N.Y. 1985).

Credit Alliance established three tests that must be met before an accountant will be liable to a third party:

1. The accountants must have been aware that the audited reports were to be used for a particular purpose.

2. A known third party relied on the audited report for that purpose.

3. There must be some conduct by the accountants that linked them to the third party and demonstrates the accountants' awareness of the third party's reliance.

This test is highly protective of accountants. The key requirement is the third, linkage criterion. In our opening hypothetical example, AB&T probably would not be liable to CiuBank, unless CiuBank had gone directly to AB&T, mentioned the possible loan to Chemco, and inquired about the audited report. In addition, CiuBank would need to have contacted AB&T before the firm completed the audit.

Restatement Test

The Restatement (Second) of Torts Section 552 states that the accountant will be liable to "a person or a limited class of persons who the auditor can foresee as parties who will and [and who] do rely on the audited financial statements." This is also called the **actually foreseen test**. Many jurisdictions, including Pennsylvania and Ohio, have adopted the Restatement test.

Under the Restatement test, the accountant will be liable to parties whom the accountant knew that the client intended to influence with the audit report. This test has also been applied to unaudited financial statements.

Liability under this test will vary, depending on the nature of the third party. A future lender may well not have been foreseen by the accountant. Courts have suggested that a company's shareholders are by definition a foreseen class of plaintiffs, and accountants therefore will always be potentially liable to shareholders under the Restatement test.

Applying the Restatement test to the hypothetical example, the AB&T might be liable. The accounting firm would only be liable if it was aware that Chemco intended to use the audited financial statements to apply for a loan from CiuBank. AB&T would not be liable if it was unaware that Chemco planned to seek a loan from CiuBank based on the audited financial statements.

While many states have adopted the Restatement test, they have interpreted the rule differently. The following case exemplifies a broad interpretation of the Restatement rule.

■ Case 6.3
**Blue Bell, Inc. v.
Peat, Marwick, Mitchell & Co.**
Court of Appeals of Texas, 1986
715 S.W.2d 408

Background and Facts *In 1972, Blue Bell established an account for and began extending credit to Myers Department Stores, Inc. In 1980, Myers engaged Peat Marwick to audit its financial records. Peat Marwick did so in 1981. Myers provided the financial statements and the accompanying accountants' report to Blue Bell. Blue Bell then extended substantial additional amounts of credit to Myers in 1982. In November 1982, Myers filed for bankruptcy.*

Blue Bell sued Peat Marwick for negligent misrepresentation and fraud in its accounting statement. A trial court granted summary judgment to Peat Marwick, on the grounds that the accounting firm was not liable to such a third party as Blue Bell. Blue Bell appealed.

AKIN, Judge.

*   *   *   *

Section 552 of the Restatement provides, in pertinent part:

(1)   One who, in the course of his business, profession or employment, or in any other transaction in which he has a pecuniary interest, supplies false information for the guidance of others in their business transactions, is subject to liability for pecuniary loss caused to them by their justifiable reliance upon the information, if he fails to exercise reasonable care or competence in obtaining or communicating the information.

(2)   Except as stated in Subsection (3), the liability stated in Subsection (1) is limited to loss suffered:

(a)   by the person or one of a limited group of persons for whose benefit and guidance he intends to supply the information or knows that the recipient intends to supply it; and

(b)   through reliance upon it in a transaction that he intends the information to influence or knows that the recipient so intends or in a substantially similar transaction.

*   *   *   *

* * * we look to section 552 of the Restatement (Second) and decide that, as we construe this section, a fact issue exists as to whether Blue Bell falls within the "limited class" as used in that section. Although we need not go so far today as to adopt the broad standard of foreseeability advocated by some of the commentators, we conclude that the apparent attempt in comment n. under this section to limit the class of third parties who may recover to those actually and specifically known by the defendant is too artificial a distinction.

*   *   *   *

* * * To allow liability to turn on the fortuitous occurrence that the accountant's client specifically mentions a person or class of persons who are to receive the reports, when the accountant may have that same knowledge as a matter of business practice, is too tenuous a distinction for us to adopt as a rule of law. Instead, we hold that if, under current business practices and the circumstances of that case, an accountant preparing audited financial statements knows or should know that such statements will be relied upon by a limited class of persons, the accountant may be liable for injuries to members of that class relying on his certification of the audited reports. *See Note, Accountant's Liability*, 60 Tex. Law Rev. at 776 n.90.

Among the factors relevant to this issue is the fact that Blue Bell was a trade creditor of Myers at the time PMM prepared the financial statements in question and that PMM was, therefore, aware of Blue Bell as one of a limited number of existing trade creditors who would, in all probability, be receiving copies of the financial statements. Furthermore, PMM supplied Myers with seventy copies of the financial statements, indicating knowledge by PMM that third parties would be given the reports. We hold that a current trade creditor is one of a limited class of people contemplated by the language in the Restatement. Consequently, in deciding whether PMM "had a duty to Blue Bell," a fact finder must determine whether PMM knew or should have known that members of such a limited class would receive copies of the audited financial statements it prepared.

Decision and Remedy   *The court reversed the judgment for Peat Marwick and remanded the case for further proceedings.*

Reasonable Foreseeability Test

The reasonable foreseeability test would hold accountants to be liable to any third parties that the auditors could reasonably foresee might rely on their report. This is the broadest test, under which the accountant is most likely to be found liable. California is the leading state in use of the reasonable foreseeability test. New Jersey and Wisconsin also adopted this rule, and a Texas court commented favorably on it.

In the key California case, an accounting firm audited the financial statements of a mortgage company that originated loans to developers and then sold the loans to bankers. A mortgage banking company entered into a contract with the mortgage company. The financial statements were inaccurate and the mortgage banking company suffered over $400,000 in damages. The court held that the bank could sue the accounting firm.[9]

In the hypothetical example, AB&T probably would be liable to CiuBank. It is certainly foreseeable that an audited company would need a bank loan. It is also foreseeable that any bank would rely on audited financial statements in deciding whether to give that loan.

Balancing Test

The balancing test is based on an earlier California decision. Under this test, the accountant's liability to third parties is based on a balancing of: (1) the extent to which the transaction was intended to affect the third party; (2) the foreseeability of harm to the third party; (3) the degree of certainty that the plaintiff suffered injury; (4) the closeness of the connection between the defendant's conduct and the injury suffered; (5) the moral blame attached to the defendant's conduct; and (6) the policy of preventing future harm.

Although California no longer relies on this balancing test, it has been adopted by other courts. In a North Carolina case, a company had

---

[9]*International Mortgage Co. v. John P. Butler Accountancy Corp.*, 223 Cal. Rptr. 218 (Cal. App. 1986).

accountants audit its financial statements and then forwarded them to Dun and Bradstreet for publication. A third party extended over two million dollars in credit to the company, in reliance on the Dun and Bradstreet report. The company went bankrupt, and the audited financial statements had substantially overstated the company's net worth. The court used the balancing test and held the accountants liable.[10]

The outcome of the above hypothetical example is not clear under the balancing test. The foreseeability of CiuBank's reliance, the certainty of its injury, and the closeness of the connection between the audit and the injury all suggest that AB&T could be liable. The first factor, the intent to influence CiuBank, might support AB&T's position.

Fraud or Gross Negligence

Accountant liability to third parties is broader in cases alleging fraud or gross negligence (extreme lack of care). New York courts, for example, have held that third party plaintiffs could not bring a negligence suit due to lack of substantial privity but could bring a fraud case on the same facts, even without substantial privity.

Fraud, of course, is an intentional tort and much more difficult to prove than negligence. Gross negligence is also more difficult to prove than simple negligence. To succeed in fraud, a plaintiff must show that the defendant accountant had actual knowledge of the erroneous records and failed to report it. If fraud is present, courts have suggested that an accountant may be liable to all injured third parties, even unforeseeable ones.

Disclaimers

When accountants issue an audit, they customarily provide a certificate that may include qualifications or other disclaimers. The auditor might state, for example, that certain information is unverified. Such disclaimers have effectively protected accounting firms from liability.

In one case, a firm of public accountants was instructed not to audit the client company's accounts receivable or to adjust those accounts to reflect probable collectibility. The accountant followed these instructions and provided a certificate that reflected these limitations on its audit. When the accountant was sued by a shareholder who relied on its audit, the court held that the disclaimer protected the accounting firm.[11]

Disclaimers may be effective to avert negligence liability but will not protect an accountant from fraud claims. Because fraud is an intentional tort, an accountant could not rely on a disclaimer as a defense.

Although disclaimers can protect accountants from negligence liability, client firms will resist any qualifications on their audit. The presence of disclaimers makes it more difficult for the audited company to obtain financing based on the audit results. A recent study of 1800 audits found that only 9 percent had qualifications for uncertainties in results.

▰ Accountants and Confidentiality

An accountant conducting a full financial audit of a corporation may become aware of significant confidential information about the company. The key legal question is when accountants may be required to divulge confidential information acquired during the audit. Another important question is when accountants may be permitted to disclose such information.

There is no common-law accountant-client privilege comparable to the doctor-patient or attorney-client privilege against disclosure of confidential information. Twenty-four states have adopted statutes providing for some measure of accountant-client privilege. These states include Florida, Illinois, Michigan and Pennsylvania. In addition to state laws, the AICPA ethics rules prohibit disclosure of confidential information obtained from clients.

The coverage of state accountant confidentiality laws varies. In Florida, for example, exceptions exist when the accountant's services were obtained to enable the commission of a fraud or when the information is relevant to an alleged breach of duty by either the client or the accountant. Other states lack these exceptions, although

---

[10]*Raritan River Steel Co. v. Cherry, Beckaert & Holland*, 339 S.E.2d 62 (N.C. App. 1986).

[11]*Stephens Industries, Inc. v. Haskins & Sells*, 438 F.2d 357 (10th Cir. 1971).

most permit disclosure when necessary for the accountant to recover a fee. Suppose that the Acme accounting firm performs services for IntraCo and submits a bill for $200,000. IntraCo claims that it owes only $100,000. Acme may disclose details of its accounting services in order to demonstrate its right to payment.

Even in states with applicable accountant-client privilege laws, the accountant may still be required to disclose confidential information in response to a judicial subpoena. The federal courts have held that the privilege does not excuse disclosure in tax cases, bankruptcy cases or federal investigations.

While an accountant may be compelled to give confidential information in testimony, the accountant still has a duty not to disclose such information unless required. The accountant retains legal title to work records acquired in the audit but generally cannot disclose them to others without the client company's permission. The AICPA has established some limited exceptions to this rule.

In one case, an accounting firm provided bookkeeping services to a company and discovered certain cash flow problems. The firm then advised its other clients not to deal with the company. These other clients cancelled their contracts with the original corporation, which went out of business. The accounting firm was found liable for breach of confidentiality.[12]

Confidentiality problems can arise in a number of circumstances. Suppose that Carolyn Gibson has a long-term successful accounting practice and is planning to retire and sell the practice to Tom Rousseau. Gibson must obtain client permission before giving past working papers to Rousseau.

AICPA provides exceptions to the confidentiality requirement: (1) when necessary to avoid violation of auditing standards and principles; (2) when necessary to comply with a legal command, such as a subpoena; and (3) when in connection with an AICPA inquiry or quality review.

Accountants currently face a disclosure dilemma when it appears that a client has committed fraud or other illegal acts. A new AICPA standard declares that accountants must sometimes breach confidentiality and publicly announce a client's fraud, even if that fraud was unrelated to the audit. The rule is vague, however, on the circumstances compelling disclosure.

This situation places accountants in something of a "Catch-22" position, as they are torn between the duties of confidentiality and those of disclosure. In one case, Fund of Funds purchased properties from John King. Arthur Andersen and Company was the auditor for Fund of Funds but also was the auditor for King. Fund of Funds discovered that the properties were overvalued. Arthur Andersen was found liable because it had not informed Fund of Funds of the information available to it from auditing King. This situation obviously presented a difficult conflict between the duties of confidentiality and disclosure.

▬ SEC Rules

Accurate accounting is critical to the fairness of stock and other transactions governed by the Securities and Exchange Commission. Consequently, Congress has provided the SEC with broad power to regulate the accounting profession. The SEC has not set detailed rules but has largely deferred to the private standard-setting bodies in the profession, such as FASB.

Disciplining Accountants

SEC Rule 2(e) provides that the Commission may punish accountants who practice before the SEC. Any accountant who prepares any filing or opinion filed with the SEC is deemed to practice before the Commission. SEC rules require so many filings by companies that virtually all accountants are deemed to practice before the SEC.

The SEC has stated that Rule 2(e) is not to be used to punish mere mistakes, or even negligence. Sanctions are limited to when the accountant (i) does not "possess the requisite qualifications to represent others, or (ii) [is] lacking in character or integrity or [has] engaged in unethical or improper professional conduct, or (iii) has willfully violated or willfully aided and abetted the violation of any provision of the Federal securities laws."[13]

---

[12]*Wagenheim v. Alexander Grant & Co.*, 482 N.E.2d 955 (Ohio App. 1983).

[13]17 C.F.R. Section 201.2(e)(1).

As a general rule, compliance with GAAS and GAAP will be sufficient for the SEC. The Commission may demand more, however. Moreover, the GAAS centrally calls for "judgment" by the accountant, and the SEC has questioned the judgment of accountants on issues such as how far to investigate a client's claims.

The accused accountant is granted procedural protection before the Commission. He or she has the right to timely notice of charges, representation by counsel, subpoena power, and cross-examination. Trial is generally before an impartial administrative law judge. The losing accountant may appeal to the full Commission.

If an accountant is found liable under 2(e), the Commission may deny, temporarily or permanently, the privilege of practicing before the Commission. During the 1980s, there were more than 50 administrative proceedings against accountants under Rule 2(e). Virtually all ended in consent agreements. In some cases, the accountants were merely censured, but some accountants were suspended from practice before the commission for as long as five years.

The SEC has focused on the accountant's procedures, checking to see if the accountant used engagement letters with the client, a written audit plan and internal control questionnaires. The accountant must also carefully document his or her efforts or risk a disciplinary proceeding.

Opinion Shopping

The SEC is especially concerned with companies' opinion shopping among accountants. **Opinion shopping** occurs when a corporation to be audited retains a series of accountants, in hopes of finding one who will approve of management's position on financial statements.

To control opinion shopping, the SEC adopted item 304 of Regulation S-K. This rule requires certain disclosures whenever a corporation replaces its accountant. A change must be reported within fifteen days. The report must disclose any disagreement between the accountant and the company during the past two years. The discharged accountant must send a letter to the Commission confirming or denying the company's disclosure.

Civil Liability

The Securities Act of 1933 and the Securities Exchange Act of 1934 establish potential civil, or even criminal, liability for accountants. Section 11 prohibits misstatements of financial statements in connection with a securities registration. Section 10(b) generally prohibits any false or misleading statements made in connection with the sale of securities. The scope of these provisions is detailed in Chapter 7 on securities law and regulation. The application of these provisions to accountants is addressed extensively in Chapter 55 of *West's Business Law, Fifth Edition*.

RICO

Accountants have been held liable under the Racketeer Influenced and Corrupt Organizations Act, known as RICO. This law provides for conviction or civil penalties, with treble (triple) damages, whenever a party has engaged in a pattern of racketeering activity (e.g., commission of a series of securities-related crimes). The standards under RICO are set forth and detailed in Chapter 7 on securities law and regulation.

Because the issuance of a faulty audit report may violate the securities laws, plaintiffs may also sue under RICO. Courts are still somewhat divided over whether negligent auditing should qualify as an action that triggers RICO liability. In one case, however, the firm of Laventhol & Horvath paid $15 million to a plaintiff in the settlement of a RICO action involving tax accounting.

▬ Management Consulting

Accounting firms have expanded their services to offer management consulting or management advisory services (MAS) to client corporations. These services now represent as much as a third of the income of major accounting firms. The law of management consulting is still quite unsettled. When accounting firms offer management consulting services, however, they create possible legal problems.

Independence

One of the foremost characteristics of an accountant is independence. Independence is vital to preserve both the reality and the appearance of integrity and honesty on the part of accountants. The U.S. Supreme Court has stressed that an accountant acts as a "disinterested analyst" who "maintain[s] total independence from the client at all times and . . . complete fidelity to the public trust."[14]

The SEC has issued guidelines for independence of accountants practicing before the Commission. These guidelines state that auditors may not engage in bookkeeping services for clients and that auditors cannot undertake jobs when the client owes a material amount of unpaid fees for prior jobs, among other requirements.

The AICPA also has standards for accountant independence. Among AICPA rules are stipulations that accountants cannot have any direct or material indirect financial interest in the client, that the auditor may not charge a contingency fee, and that the auditor should not loan money or accept loans from a client. AICPA Ethics Code Rule 101-B states that the accountant must not assume the role of an employee or of management of the client corporation. The supplementing statement, however, offers no examples of the activities that management consultants should avoid.

The growth of management consulting presents potential independence problems for auditors. Although a management consultant may not actually assume the role of an employee, the consultant will advise on the same decisions as ordinary management. There is a concern that an auditor is unlikely to question management consulting decisions previously made by the same accounting firm.

There is little regulation of the management consulting situation. The SEC adopted rules but then withdrew them and recently held that accounting firms could do consulting work through separate entities within the firm. The AICPA permits management consulting by accounting firms, so long as the consultant only advises and does not undertake final transactions on the part of the client.

Tort Liability

Management consulting may become a source of tort liability for accounting firms. Clients and injured third parties may be expected to sue for negligent or fraudulent management consulting. Few such cases have been brought, so the standards for liability are quite undefined.

Accountants have been sued for giving bad business advice. For example, an accountant recommended to a partnership that it reorganize and liquidate one of the partnership's subsidiary corporations. The accountant was liable for failing to note the adverse effect this had on the partnership's industrial revenue bond financing.[15] One recent case saw a consulting firm sued by a third party (the client's supplier of natural gas) when it advised a client not to pass on refunds that were allegedly due the supplier.

In another recent case, an accountant recommended that its client invest $59,000 with a seafood broker. The accountant was a shareholder, officer and director of the broker and made assurances to the client company. After losing its money, the client successfully sued the accountant. The court held that the accountant had a fiduciary relationship with the client and that the accountant's actions were unconscionable.[16]

None of these cases dealt specifically with management consulting, but they all illustrate how an accountant may be liable for giving business advice. The mixture of accounting and management consulting services creates a still undefined problem of liability. The following decision demonstrates how a combination of auditing and management consulting services may subject an accounting firm to a greater risk of liability.

---

[14]*United States v. Arthur Young & Co.,* 465 U.S. 805, 817-18 (1984).

[15]*The Billings Clinic v. Peat Marwick Main & Co.,* 797 P.2d 899 (Mont. 1990).

[16]*Dominguez v. Brackey Enterprises, Inc.,* 756 S.W.2d 788 (Tex. App. 1988).

■ Case 6.4
**Union Planters Corporation v.
Peat, Marwick, Mitchell & Co.**
Court of Appeals of Tennessee, 1987
733 S.W.2d 509

Background and Facts   *Union Planters Corporation ("UP") retained Peat, Marwick, Mitchell & Co. ("PMM") in 1971 for both auditing and continuous management consulting services. Union Planters' employees were indicted and convicted for engaging in fraudulent and improper banking practices. Union Planters also suffered losses from several million dollars of bad loans attributable to the fraudulent and improper lending practices of its employees.*

Union Planters sued Peat Marwick for breach of contract for both the auditing and the management consulting services. Union Planters contended that Peat Marwick insufficiently tested the company's internal control mechanisms and insufficiently investigated the collectibility of the company's loans. Peat Marwick moved for summary judgment. The trial court granted this motion. Union Planters appealed.

SWEARENGEN, Judge.

*   *   *   *

The contentions of UP are best expressed in the relevant portions of its complaint:

THE BREACH OF CONTRACT   The breach of contract of which Bank complains in this cause, and which is set forth specifically below, generally consisted of a course of conduct followed by PMM whereby, in violation of their contract of employment, it failed to provide an ongoing objective evaluation of the functioning of the Bank's various operating systems, including its systems of internal control as defined herein, in an expert professional manner commensurate with the level of skill, competence, expert knowledge and diligence which had been promised and, by virtue of such failure, failed to call to the attention of the Bank's board of directors certain weaknesses in such operating systems and systems of internal control which required immediate remedial action in order to safeguard the assets of the Bank. Such weaknesses in operating procedures and in internal controls were of such a serious nature that their detection, and reference to the board of directors for appropriate corrective action, by PMM not only was within the contemplation of the parties in entering into the aforesaid contract for auditing and management consulting services but, indeed, was known to the parties, from the outset, to be one of the significant reasons for which PMM was engaged and paid in excess of $1,000,000.00 to perform such services.

*   *   *   *

In its complaint, UP set forth the nature of the services which it contended PMM agreed to provide. In its answer, PMM admitted submitting a detailed written proposal but denied any verbal commitments. Comparative analysis of PMM's written proposal with UP's contention of the verbal promises reveals that they are virtually identical, except for the standard of performance. UP contended that PMM verbally agreed to exercise the highest degree of care. In denying this, PMM contended that "our examination will be made in accordance with generally accepted auditing standards." Nonetheless, PMM emphasized in its written proposal high quality performance based upon specialization within its accounting firm.

In addition, it was disputed by the parties what the terms of the contract meant and what services they involved. PMM's proposal utilizes such terms as "auditing," "management consulting services," and "internal control." The record contains conflicting affidavits as to what a client should expect and what an auditing firm should provide as part of those services. A conclusory analysis shows that PMM contends that Harrison and Merkle, officers of UP, admitted that unsound lending policies and procedures approved by them caused the loan losses. On the other hand, UP contends that these unsound lending policies were brought about by PMM's breach of contract in that it failed to perform many of the functions that it committed itself to when it came on board as UP's independent auditor. There is clearly a dispute as to what or who caused the unsound lending policies.

Decision and Remedy. *The court reversed the grant of summary judgment and remanded the case for trial.*

■ **Ethical Perspectives**

Accounting Conflicts of Interest

As professionals, accountants should comply with a high ethical standard. A common ethical difficulty of accountants is the conflict of interest. A problematic conflict of interest arises whenever a person's ethical obligations conflict with that person's personal interests.

The most basic nature of the accountant's work seems to represent a conflict of interest. An accountant audits a company in order to present an accurate portrayal of its financial health to the public. Yet the company hires, pays, and potentially fires the accountant. A large company may pay between $1 and $6 million for an annual audit. An accounting firm is therefore somewhat beholden to the corporate entity that it should independently and fairly investigate.

The problem has become more pronounced because some accountants seemingly have favored their client's interests over fairness and accuracy. There are numerous cases in which a company received a clean bill of health in a financial audit and then promptly declared bankruptcy. This is especially true in the savings and loan industry.

Accountants have their own rules of ethics, which are intended to hold accountants to strict standards. The codes are necessarily worded vaguely, because so many different situations may arise. While such general codes may help improve the ethical environment, they cannot solve the problem of conflicts of interest.

Accountants are understandably wary about liability to third parties, because this opens firms to the potential for enormous damages. The very point of the accounting profession, though, is to render accurate and independent opinions that third parties can rely on. Liability to third parties may therefore enhance the accountant's concern for ethical obligations and help counterbalance the inevitable concern for the corporate client's opinion.

The growth of management consulting services has created additional conflict of interest concerns. Management consulting business gives an accounting firm a greater stake in the client's business and also necessitates an auditor reviewing and second-guessing the decisions of the firm's own consulting practice.

Suppose a small company producing shoes lacks the knowledge to develop a computerized inventory system and hires a management consultant to do so. If the shoe company is later audited by the same firm, some charge that the auditors are unlikely to criticize their colleague's decisions. The AICPA disputes the existence of a problem, claiming that there is no substantial evidence that management consulting has impaired the independence of accountants. A U.S. Senate Committee, however, has concluded that auditors have subjugated themselves to clients in return for commitments from clients for profitable management consulting business.

Some suggest that a **Chinese Wall** could help ensure independence. This is a set of rules and physical office arrangements that prevent the communication of information within one company. Securities firms and law firms use this approach to guard against conflicts of interest.

While a Chinese Wall will not eliminate conflicts, it may mitigate them. An auditor will be more independent if the consultant is not a close coworker. The wall also could prevent auditors from knowing what the consultant recommended to the client corporation.

A more dramatic resolution would be to prohibit the same accounting firm from providing both auditing and management consulting services to a given company. This approach would largely eliminate any conflict of interest. Accounting firms argue, however, that the combined auditing and management consulting service is more efficient and enables them to offer a more informed service to the client.

■ **International Perspectives**

International Accounting Standards

Major U.S. accounting firms are global enterprises with dozens of foreign offices. The offices are closely tied together and accounting practice is increasingly international in scope. The accounting standards of the world's nations vary considerably, however.

U.S. accounting standards, for example, differ even from those in Canada in some significant respects. This fact has proved to be an obstacle to the full consummation of the United States-Canada free trade pact.[17] Asian standards differ from those in Europe, and there are significant differences among the nations

---

[17]A free trade pact is an agreement between governments that eliminates tariffs and other significant barriers to trade between the countries.

of Europe. Some nations, such as Italy, do not even have a single authority for consistent accounting standards within that nation.

Different accounting standards not only complicate the efforts of accountants, they also have a significant impact on business operations. For example, the General Accounting Office has suggested that British and German companies have an advantage over U.S. companies in corporate acquisitions. U.S. accounting standards require the capitalization of goodwill costs and their amortization against future income. British and German standards permit writing off the costs against shareholder equity and thereby may avoid a decline in future earnings.

Different standards also complicate multinational stock offerings. At the present time, a company that wants to take advantage of such an offering must prepare financial statements according to the home country's accounting rules and must prepare additional statements for all the countries in which the offering will be made. This can be a costly procedure.

The International Accounting Standards Committee (IASC) has worldwide standards but these are voluntary and have had little practical impact. The IASC is attempting to adopt standards by the end of 1992 that will be made binding by governments. These standards apparently would be similar to the United States GAAP and would reduce the alternative accounting treatments permitted in financial statements. The European Community is also attempting to establish uniform community-wide standards and, ironically, this effort could derail the prospects for the IASC worldwide standards.

Questions and Case Problems

1. Arthur, an accountant, prepared the financial statements of the Velveteen Furniture Company. In preparing these statements, Arthur relied on Velveteen's inventory reports in preparation of the financial statements. The inventory report stated that the company's Lawrence warehouse was full of velour furniture. In fact, the warehouse was empty. A bank made a loan to Velveteen based on the collateral in the Lawrence and other warehouses, and the company eventually defaulted on the loan. The bank sues Arthur for negligence. Is Arthur liable to the bank?

2. Maple, an accountant, was employed by his wife to compile financial statements for her corporation and properly did so. His wife's corporation then became the target of an SEC investigation, and the government demanded that Maple provide all his working papers and documents in connection with his wife's business. Maple considers these papers to be confidential and refuses to provide them. Will a court compel Maple to provide the information demanded?

3. Lincoln Grain employed Coopers & Lybrand to audit its financial statements. The firm certified that Lincoln Grain had correctly valued the inventory of its Iowa division at approximately $2 million. In reality, the manager of this division had been embezzling money from the company and the division inventory had a value of only about $140,000. Lincoln Grain sued Coopers & Lybrand, claiming that the audit should have discovered its employee's defalcations and the failure to do so damaged the company. The firm defended on the grounds that Lincoln Grain was itself negligent in failing to discover the embezzlement. Is Coopers & Lybrand liable to Lincoln Grain on these facts? [*Lincoln Grain, Inc. v. Coopers & Lybrand*, 345 N.W.2d 300 (Neb. 1984)].

4. Fidler, the president of Witt corporation, engaged Hanson, an accountant, to examine Witt's financial statements and issue a report for the annual stockholders' meeting, which would be held on March 31. The staff of Witt were slow in providing Hanson with information, however, and sometimes refused information. Hanson did his best and ultimately issued the report on April 4. Fidler refused to accept or pay for the report because it was no longer required. Hanson sued Witt to recover the fee for preparation of the report. Should Hanson be able to recover her fee?

5. A company retained Rothenburg, an accountant, to review its books. Rothenburg prepared a report that failed to discover or disclose very large defalcations by the company's employees. Rothenburg claimed that he was employed only to perform a "write up" of the plaintiffs books and records, and the company claimed that he was employed to conduct a regular audit. Rothenburg's worksheets indicate that he did in fact examine the company's bank statement, invoices and bills. Should Rothenburg be liable to the company for negligent performance of services? [1136 *Tenants' Corp. v. Max Rothenburg & Co.*, 319 N.Y.S. 2d 1007 (1970)].

CHAPTER SEVEN

Securities Law and Regulation

▰ KEY BACKGROUND

The essential background for this chapter on securities law and regulation is found in Chapter 43 of *West's Business Law, Fifth Edition* and in Chapter 22 of *West's Legal Environment of Business*. These chapters cover corporations—financial regulation and investor protection and securities regulation. Among the important points to remember from this chapter are:

- the definition of a security

- the required contents of a registration statement

- the securities that are exempt from registration requirements

- the law restricting insider trading

- the law covering the regulation of investment companies

The reader will also benefit from familiarity with the duties of corporate directors and officers (in Chapter 40 of *West's Business Law, Fifth Edition*) and the Racketeer Influenced and Corrupt Organizations Act (in Chapter 6 of *West's Business Law, Fifth Edition*).

* * *

This chapter expands on the coverage of *West's Business Law* and *West's Legal Environment of Business* by providing additional detail on the definition of securities subject to regulation by the SEC, the requirements of securities' registration, the prohibition on insider trading, and liability under RICO. In addition, the chapter addresses other securities law issues, including liability under sections 11 and 12 of the 1933 Act, corporate liability for false and misleading disclosures, proxy regulations, and regulation of securities broker-dealers.

▰ The Securities Act of 1933

The first substantial law for regulation of securities was the Securities Act of 1933. This law requires that securities be registered with the Securities and Exchange Commission. The registration must be accompanied by extensive disclosure of the nature of the securities being offered.

A threshold issue in securities regulation is the definition of the securities subject to regulation. Most people think of securities as shares of stock in a corporation, but the term is actually much broader and applies to many investment contracts. Creative finance professionals continue to invent new investment approaches. If the approach is not considered a security, considerable regulation and expense can be avoided. Failure to recognize that a new device should be considered a security, however, can have disastrous consequences in both civil and criminal liability. In the past, "many deals have been scuttled, parties held liable, and lawyers sued for failure . . . to recognize that a 'security' was present."[1] Consequently, understanding the definition of a security is of great importance.

The 1933 Act sets the groundwork for securities regulation, including the definition of "security" that may be covered. As discussed in *West's Business Law, Fifth Edition* and *West's Legal Environment of Business*, the basic test for a regulated security is a transaction in which a person:

1. Invests.

2. In a common enterprise.

3. Reasonably expecting profits.

4. Derived primarily or substantially from others' managerial or entrepreneurial efforts.

Courts generally have interpreted this test broadly, to prevent evasion of the securities laws. A wide variety of investment contracts are covered by this definition. A plaintiff may claim that virtually any investment contract should be regulated as a security.

Many limited partnerships are considered securities under federal law. The SEC has said that participation in the sale of condominium units along with an arrangement to manage their rental is a regulated security. In a California case, the court held that the sale of memberships in a country club operated for profit should be considered a security.[2]

Some categories of investments are not covered by the definition of a security. For example, the test of a security requires a common enterprise, which implies a group of investors pooling their funds to share in a success or failure. Courts have found no security when there was only a single investor in a contract. Thus, suppose Kara Nash places her money with the Stevens, Jones investment firm or other brokerage to invest in securities. Is her contract with the brokerage itself a security? Because there is no common enterprise or pooled fund of investors, Kara's contract for placement of her money is not a security under the 1933 Act.

Other investments are not securities because they carry no expectation of profit. After release of the movie "Urban Cowboy," an entrepreneur

marketed certificates representing one-millionth shares of a Texas longhorn steer. The SEC ruled that no security registration was necessary, because the certificates of ownership were mere novelties, and the certificate's purchasers had no expectation of profit from their purchase. While the entrepreneur certainly intended to profit from selling the "longhorn shares," the purchasers did not buy the certificates in hopes of their appreciation and resale for a profit. Also, when an investment is for personal use or consumption, it is not a security under the 1933 Act. Buying a health club membership or shares in a cooperative housing project in which to live is not a securities transaction.

The final test for a security is that the expected profits must derive from the managerial or entrepreneurial efforts of *others*. When an individual personally manages the investment, it is not a security. As a result, a general partner who helps manage the partnership has no security, but a limited partner who cannot participate in management usually does hold a security in a partnership. For the same reason, the holder of a franchise, such as a McDonald's outlet, holds no security, because he intends to profit from his own management efforts.

A 1990 Supreme Court decision slightly broadened the definition of securities regulated by federal law. In that case, an agricultural cooperative sold $10 million in unsecured promissory notes. After the cooperative defaulted on the notes, the purchasers sought to recover for fraud under the securities laws. An appellate court held that the notes were not securities, but the Supreme Court reversed this decision. While these notes were not traded on any exchange, the court found that a note would generally be a security "if the seller's purpose is to raise money for the general use of a business enterprise or to finance substantial investments and the buyer is interested primarily in the profit the note is expected to generate." The Court was careful to hold that other notes, such as mortgages and consumer loans, would not be considered securities.

Some contracts are securities but are exempted from registration under federal law. These include certain small offerings of securities and offerings confined to what the law considers to be accredited investors (who are especially sophisticated). *West's Business Law, Fifth Edition* and

---

[1]Marc Steinberg, *Understanding Securities Law* (1989), p.15.

[2]*Silver Hills Country Club v. Sobieski*, 361 P.2d 906 (1961).

West's Legal Environment of Business contain an excellent and thorough discussion of the exemptions from registration under securities law.

▬ Registration and SEC Review

When securities are issued, the issuer generally must file a registration statement with the SEC that makes certain disclosures about the issuer and the securities, including financial statements. For issuers who must register, the process is a detailed and costly one. The contents of this registration statement are well described in *West's Business Law, Fifth Edition* and in *West's Legal Environment of Business*. This chapter will not repeat the contents but will elaborate the consequences of a defective registration of securities.

An organization planning to issue securities will require some time to prepare the detailed registration materials required by the SEC. The period during which these are being prepared is called the prefiling period. During this time, the issuer may not offer its securities for sale. The issuer cannot even publicize the planned future offering of securities—this is called "gun jumping."

In one well-known case, the owner of land in Florida sought to place it in a new corporation that would be financed through an offering of securities. During the prefiling period, the issuer put out press releases that described the new corporation and spoke of the potential value of the Florida properties. The publicity brought forth numerous purchasers, some of whom were disappointed when it turned out that the land had an undesirable location. The SEC sanctioned the issuer for gun-jumping.[3]

The prefiling period ends when the issuer submits its registration materials to the SEC. The 1933 Act provides twenty days for SEC review before the registration becomes effective. During this time, the SEC scrutinizes the proposed registration for completeness and accuracy. This is called the waiting period. During the waiting period, the issuer may begin to sell the securities through a prospectus. The contents of a prospectus are defined by section 10 of the Act. Most

other written sales materials are prohibited during this period, however.

SEC Rule 134 does permit one special type of written sales material during the waiting period, called the "tombstone ad." Tombstone ads are those with very simple explanatory information, surrounded by a black border, which usually appear in publications such as the *Wall Street Journal*. Tombstone ads are limited to very basic information, such as the name of the issuer, the amount of securities being offered, a brief description of the company's business, the contemplated price of the securities, and the expected date of their issuance.

The number of new securities registrations is so great that the SEC cannot give close scrutiny to each. Registration statements by established companies may not be reviewed and their approval is often accelerated. New issuers generally receive closer examination of registration statements. After review, the SEC may demand more substantiation of claims or seek modifications in the issuer's financial statements. Even SEC acceptance of a registration statement does not constitute a legal finding of the statement's accuracy but simply permits the registration to become effective, allowing the sale of securities to proceed.

After the registration statement becomes effective, the issuer may begin to offer and sell the securities. The offeror can begin to use different forms of written sales literature but must generally still provide purchasers with a prospectus. In some circumstances, the issuer may use a shorter, summary prospectus when making solicitations of sale.

Most major securities issuances are conducted through underwriters—organizations that specialize in placing securities with purchasers. Using underwriters helps guarantee that the offering will succeed. Underwriters usually agree to purchase all the offered securities at a discount and then resell them to investors or securities dealers. On other occasions, underwriters simply act as agents of the issuer, using their best efforts to place the offered securities. Underwriters' activities also are regulated by the SEC.

Exhibit 7-1 summarizes the restrictions on the sale of securities during the various stages of the registration process.

---

[3]*Carl M. Loeb, Rhoades & Co.* 38 S.E.C. 843 (1959).

Exhibit 7-1

Legal Restrictions During Registration Process

Prefiling Period	Waiting Period	Post-Effective Period
Offers to sell and sales prohibited	Oral offers allowed	Offers and sales allowed if prospectus provided
Some publicity of forthcoming offering allowed	Written offers by prospectus allowed	Summary prospectus allowed for solicitation
Negotiations with underwriter allowed	Tombstone Ad allowed	
	Other offers prohibited	
	Sales prohibited	

Section 8 Stop Orders

Section 8 of the 1933 Act empowers the SEC to halt the sale of securities when it deems a registration to be misleading or incomplete. Section 8(d) authorizes the SEC to issue a "stop order" suspending sales even after a registration statement has become effective. While the Commission issues relatively few stop orders, such issuance has serious consequences for the securities in question, preventing their sale. The stop order may even be issued without a hearing, but the SEC must provide such a hearing within ten days of the order. Section 20 of the 1933 Act also permits the SEC to commence criminal proceedings when an issuer has willfully violated a stop order.

In 1989, the SEC used a stop order to suspend the effectiveness of the registration statement of Composite Design, Inc. The SEC found several misleading elements of the registration statement. These included failure to disclose the identity of the controlling shareholder and representing that the proceeds of the offering would be used for the acquisition of business opportunities for Composite Design, when in fact the proceeds were to be sent to another company.

Section 11 Private Actions

If a false and misleading securities registration statement survives SEC review, and if a purchaser is injured by these false and misleading statements, the private purchaser may sue under section 11 of the 1933 Act. To make out a case under section 11, such a private plaintiff must always prove the following elements:

1. The existence of false statements or omissions in a registration statement when it becomes effective.

2. Materiality of those misstatements or omissions.

3. The plaintiff's reliance on the defective registration statement in purchasing the securities.

A plaintiff may sue even if she did not purchase the securities directly from the defendant issuer. For example, assume that Brighttex Corporation issues new securities with a registration statement. Antonio purchases these newly issued securities. Antonio then resells these securities to Margaret. If Margaret can show that the specific securities purchased were issued through a defective registration statement and that she relied on this registration statement when purchasing the securities from Antonio, she can sue Brighttex under section 11.

The issuing corporation, such as Brighttex, is not the only party who may be liable under section 11. The statute lists other potentially liable parties, including the directors of the issuer and principal executive officers of the issuer, as well as every underwriter and certain accountants, appraisers and other experts who prepared or certified a portion of the registration statement. Also potentially liable is anyone who "controls any person liable under section 11."

Defendants are liable only for "material" misstatements or omissions. The materiality of a misstatement or omission is critical to liability under this section of the securities laws, and this concept recurs throughout other sections. Materiality essentially means importance, and the courts will find information to be material if a reasonable investor would consider it important to the decision whether or not to buy a security, considered in the context of the total mix of available information. The determination of materiality is highly fact-specific, depending on close consideration of the disclosures in each disputed case.

The issuer of shares is strictly liable for any material omissions or misstatements in registration, even if the issuer had a good faith belief in the accuracy of the registration statement. Other defendants have the benefit of a due diligence defense. This defense protects those who performed a reasonable investigation and possessed a reasonable belief that the registration statement was complete and accurate. For these defendants, only negligent omissions or misstatements produce liability. Experts and inside directors are subject to a relatively high standard of diligence and accuracy, while outside directors and certain others may be subject to a lower standard of care.

Underwriters are considered experts who are held to high standards of diligence under section 11. Although underwriters may be unaware of the inaccuracies of the registration prepared by the issuer, they usually have access to the necessary information and the leverage required to force full disclosure. Consequently, underwriters must carefully scrutinize registration materials before participating in an offering. The law provides that even an underwriter is protected for "any part of the registration purporting to be made on the authority of an expert" such as a certified public accountant, so long as the underwriter had no reason to believe that the information was misleading.

Section 11 provides money damages to plaintiffs. To measure these damages, the plaintiff first takes the *lower* of the prices at which the security was issued and the price actually paid by the plaintiff. The plaintiff then takes the lower price at which he sold the shares, or, if the shares were not sold, the value of the shares at the time of the litigation. The difference between these figures is the measure of damages. For example, suppose that Gaycorp issues securities at $10/share pursuant to a defective registration. Marie purchases those securities somewhat later at $11/share in reliance on the defective registration. The value declines, and Marie ultimately sells the securities at $8/share. Marie's recoverable damages under section 11 are only $2/share.

Marie need not prove that the false and misleading registration actually caused the decline in share price. Rather, once she proves that the registration statement contained material misstatements or omissions, the law presumes causation. Defendants bear the burden of proving that other factors caused the reduced share price, as a means of minimizing the damages they owe.

Section 12 Private Actions

Section 12(1) of the 1933 Act provides straightforward relief to purchasers for a limited set of circumstances. If anyone offers or sells a security without an effective registration statement, she is liable to the purchaser for rescission or damages. The standard is strict liability, so a plaintiff need not show negligence, nor is there the same type of due diligence defense as under section 11. Defendants include those who offered or sold securities, which may include attorneys, investment bankers and others who were substantially involved in the sale.

Section 12(2) of the 1933 Act provides broad liability against anyone who makes a public offering of securities and makes omissions or misstatements with respect to a material fact. This misstatement or omission need not be made in the registration statement; section 12(2) also covers any other selling documents or even oral statements in connection with the sale of newly offered securities. Indeed, this section covers exempt securities that need not be registered. Potentially responsible defendants under section 12(2) include all "sellers"—those who actually sold the securities and some other parties who actively promoted the sale.

Under section 12(2), a plaintiff purchaser of securities must show a material misstatement or omission in connection with a sale in an initial issuance of securities, just as under section 11. The plaintiff must also allege the defendant seller's awareness of the misstatement, and the burden then shifts to the seller to demonstrate that he did not know of and could not reasonably have known of the inaccuracy.

While section 12 does not contain a specific due diligence defense, the seller normally can avoid liability by proving that it used reasonable care in the sale of securities. Courts have held that reasonable care depends on the circumstances of the offering. Sellers of a small, exempt offering of securities are held to a lower standard of care than those involved in major registered offerings. Section 12 damages are measured in the same manner as damages under section 11.

One controversial issue under section 12 involves which persons, other than the actual seller, are potential defendants. The Supreme Court recently established criteria for liability.

▀▀ Case 7.1
Pinter v. Dahl
United States Supreme Court, 1988
486 U.S. 622

Background and Facts   *Billie J. Pinter sold unregistered securities in oil and gas leases to Maurice Dahl. Dahl then touted the securities to friends, family and business associates and assisted them in subscribing to the securities, though Dahl received no commission. The venture failed, so Dahl and other purchasers sued Pinter for the unlawful sale of unregistered securities. Pinter counterclaimed against Dahl, claiming that he actively solicited the sales of others and should therefore share liability as a "seller" under section 12.*

The trial court granted judgment for plaintiffs and rejected Pinter's counterclaim against Dahl. The court of appeals affirmed, and specifically held that Dahl was not a seller under the terms of section 12 because he received no financial benefit. Pinter appealed to the Supreme Court. One key issue was whether Dahl was a potentially liable seller under section 12.

BLACKMUN, Justice.

* * * *

An interpretation of statutory seller that includes brokers and others who solicit offers to purchase securities furthers the purposes of the Securities Act–to promote full and fair disclosure of information to the public in the sales of securities. In order to effectuate Congress' intent that § 12(1) civil liability be *in terrorem*, see Douglas & Bates, 43 Yale L.J., at 173; Shulman, 43 Yale L.J., at 227, the risk of its invocation should be felt by solicitors of purchases. The solicitation of a buyer is perhaps the most critical stage of the selling transaction. It is the first stage of a traditional securities sale to involve the buyer, and it is directed at producing the sale. In addition, brokers and other solicitors are well positioned to control the flow of information to a potential purchaser, and, in fact, such persons are the participants in selling transaction who most often disseminate material information to investors. Thus, solicitation is the stage at which an investor is most likely to be injured, that is, by being persuaded to purchase securities without full and fair information. Given Congress' overriding goal of preventing this injury, we may infer that Congress intended solicitation to fall under the mantle of § 12(1).

Although we conclude that Congress intended §12(1) liability to extend to those who solicit securities purchases, we share the Court of

Appeals' conclusion that Congress did not intend to impose rescission based on strict liability on a person who urges the purchase but whose motivation is solely to benefit the buyer. When a person who urges another to make a securities purchase acts merely to assist the buyer, not only is it uncommon to say that the buyer "purchased" from him, but it is also strained to describe the giving of gratuitous advice, even strongly or enthusiastically, as "soliciting." Section 2(3) defined an offer as a "solicitation of an offer to buy . . . for value." The person who gratuitously urges another to make a particular investment decision is not, in any meaningful sense, requesting value in exchange for his suggestion or seeking the value the titleholder will obtain in exchange for the ultimate sale. The language and purpose of § 12(1) suggest that liability extends only to the person who successfully solicits the purchase, motivated at least in part by a desire to serve his own financial interests or those of the securities owner. If he had such a motivation, it is fair to say that the buyer "purchased" the security from him and to align him with the owner in a rescission action.

We are unable to determine whether Dahl may be held liable as statutory seller under § 12(1). The District Court explicitly found that "Dahl solicited each of the other plaintiffs (save perhaps Grantham) in connection with the offer, purchase, and receipt of their oil and gas interests." We cannot conclude that this finding was clearly erroneous. It is not clear, however, that Dahl had the kind of interest in the sales that make him liable as a statutory seller. We do know that he received no commission from Pinter in connection with the other sales, but this is not conclusive. Typically, a person who solicits the purchase will have sought or received a personal financial benefit from the sale, such as where he "anticipat[es] a share of the profits," *Lawler v. Gilliam*, 569 F.2d, at 1288, or receives a brokerage commission, *Cady v. Murphy*, 113 F.2d, at 990. But a person who solicits the buyer's purchase in order to serve the financial interests of the owner may properly be liable under §12(1) without showing that he expects to participate in the benefits the owner enjoys.

The Court of Appeals apparently concluded that Dahl was motivated entirely by a gratuitous desire to share an attractive investment opportunity with his friends and associates. See 787 F. 2d, at 991. This conclusion, in our view, was premature. The District Court made no findings that focused on whether Dahl urged the other purchases in order to further some financial interest of his own or of Pinter. Accordingly, further findings are necessary to assess Dahl's liability.

Decision and Remedy   *The Supreme Court vacated the judgment of the court of appeals and remanded the case for a new trial.*

The Securities Exchange Act of 1934

The Securities Exchange Act of 1934 expanded upon the 1933 Act and regulated the markets in which securities are traded. This law initiated regulation of the exchanges where securities are traded and also contained additional disclosure requirements, such as the prohibition on insider trading. Like the 1933 Act, the 1934 law focused upon full and accurate disclosure of material facts in connection with securities transactions.

Insider Trading

Section 10(b) of the 1934 Act, as elaborated by SEC Rule 10b-5, prohibits fraud in connection with securities transactions. One leading form of prohibited fraud is insider trading, in which an individual who has secret inside information about a company uses that information to trade in the corporation's shares and profit from the secret inside information.

The traditional insider trading case was rather straightforward. It involved a true corporate insider, such as a chief executive officer, who became aware of some imminent development regarding his company. If the development were a good one, the insider would buy his company's shares, then the information would become public, increased demand for the shares would drive up their price, and the insider would reap the benefits of the shares' appreciation. If the development were a bad one, the insider would sell his shares in the company before the information became public, thereby avoiding a loss on the stock. This traditional approach is illustrated by the *Texas Gulf Sulphur* case in *West's Business Law, Fifth Edition*.

"Temporary insiders" working on a specific corporate transaction, may also also be liable under section 10(b). Sometimes, a lawyer, accountant or other outsider will receive inside information about a corporation. Courts have held that these temporary insiders owe a duty not to take advantage of this information and profit from insider trading.

Recently, however, courts have grappled with the problem of total "outsiders" who trade on inside information. Occasionally, a person wholly outside a corporation may obtain inside information about the company. There is no absolute rule against outsiders using inside information to profit. Under some circumstances, however, such outsiders may be found in violation of insider trading laws. There are two leading theories whereby outsiders may be liable—the tipper/tippee theory and the misappropriation theory.

The tipper/tippee theory is designed to prevent insiders from indirectly profiting on inside information by "tipping" friendly outsiders with such information before it becomes public. The situation might develop as follows. Baker is an executive vice president of Microwave, Inc. Baker becomes aware that another company is planning to make a lucrative offer for the stock of Microwave at a high price. Baker informs his banker, Prentice, of this still-secret development, in exchange for obtaining a low interest loan. The banker then buys stock in Microwave and profits when the offer is subsequently announced to the public. In this case, both Baker (the tipper) and Prentice (the tippee) are liable under section 10(b).

Not all stock tips are illegal, however. The requirements for tipper/tippee liability are strict. A tipper of information is only liable when the following conditions are met:

1. Disclosure of material inside information.

2. In violation of a legal or fiduciary duty not to disclose the information.

3. In expectation of some benefit in return.

There is no insider trading violation unless the tipper had some duty not to disclose, but most insiders do have such a duty not to disclose inside information about their own companies. Nor is there an insider trading violation if the tipper discloses the information without expectation of benefit in return. These limitations are illustrated in discussions in *West's Business Law, Fifth Edition*. Insider trading is not illegal unless it involves some breach of fiduciary duty.

The tippee may also be liable under section 10(b). Any tippee liability, however, is derivative of the tipper's liability. This means that a tippee can only be liable if the tipper is also liable. One leading case involved Barry Switzer, the former football coach at the University of Oklahoma. Switzer was lying down on the bleachers at a track meet when he inadvertently overheard another observer, G. Platt, mention an impending corporate sale to his wife. Switzer traded on and profited from the information. Switzer was not liable for insider trading, however. Mr. Platt was not an illegal tipper because he did not mean to be informing Switzer of the sale and thus could not have done so with expectation of benefit. Because Platt, the inadvertent tipper, was not liable, neither was Switzer.

If a tipper has violated the insider trading laws, however, the tippee may also be liable. When the tipper is potentially liable, the tippee is also liable whenever the tippee knew or should have known that the information received was material inside information. If the tippee has reason to know that the tip is secret information, she may not trade on the information. Thus, people may come upon nonpublic information and legally trade upon it, so long as they are reasonably unaware that the information is inside information or so long as an unlawful tipper is not involved.

Outsiders trading on inside information may also be liable under the misappropriation theory. This theory is an outgrowth of the *Chiarella* case, discussed in *West's Business Law, Fifth Edition* and in *West's Legal Environment of Business*, in which a financial printer was found not liable for trading on inside information because the printer was not an insider of the corporation whose stock was traded. Use of the misappropriation theory might have convicted Chiarella. Under this theory, a person violates section 10(b) if he or she trades on material inside information

that he or she misappropriated (stole) from another person or corporation. Thus, if an employee of the *Wall Street Journal* buys or sells stock based on inside information acquired through his work at the newspaper, he may be violating insider-trading law. This information is the property of the *Wall Street Journal* and the employee has misappropriated the information when he uses it for private personal gain.

Acceptance of the misappropriation theory has significantly expanded the scope of section 10(b) and Rule 10b-5. Nevertheless, some trading on inside information remains legal. The following case illustrates the potential breadth of the prohibition on insider trading under the misappropriation theory.

■ Case 7.2
United States v. Willis
United States District Court for the Southern District of New York, 1990
737 F. Supp. 269

Background and Facts   *In 1985, Sanford Weill developed an interest in becoming the chief executive officer (CEO) of BankAmerica Corporation. Weill secured a commitment from Shearson Loeb Rhodes and other companies to invest $1 billion in BankAmerica if he became its CEO. At this time, the public information regarding BankAmerica was rather unfavorable, and the company had suffered losses.*

Weill discussed these matters with his wife. Weill's wife was a psychiatric patient of Robert Willis. During the course of their sessions, Mrs. Weill discussed her husband's affairs with Willis. Willis then began purchasing BankAmerica stock. On February 21, 1986, BankAmerica announced that Weill would become its CEO, and BankAmerica share values promptly increased by several points. Willis then sold his shares for a profit of about $27,000. The SEC prosecuted Willis for insider trading, and he moved to dismiss the complaint.

CEDARBAUM, Judge.

* * * *

The Indictment charges that Dr. Willis breached the physician's traditional duty of confidentiality on which his patient was entitled to rely when he misappropriated for his personal profit material, non-public, business information confided to him by his patient for her psychiatric diagnosis and treatment, and that when Dr. Willis purchased BankAmerica securities on the basis of his patient's confidential information, he defrauded his patient in connection with the purchase of securities in violation of Section 10(b) of the Securities Exchange Act of 1934 and Rule 10b-5.

Central to the sufficiency of the Indictment, and central to the misappropriation theory of securities fraud, is a breach of fiduciary or similar duty of trust and confidence. It is difficult to imagine a relationship that requires a higher degree of trust and confidence than the traditional relationship of physician and patient. The "oath" of Hippocrates, which has guided the practice of medicine for more than 2,000 years, concludes with the following words:

Whatsoever things I see or hear concerning the life of men, in my attendance on the sick or even apart therefrom, which ought not be noised abroad, I will keep silence thereon, counting such things to be as sacred secrets.

* * * *

The underlying rationale of the misappropriation theory is that a person who receives secret business information from another because of an established relationship of trust and confidence between them has a duty to keep that information confidential. By breaching that duty and appropriating the confidential information for his own advantage, the fiduciary is defrauding the confider who was entitled to rely on the fiduciary's tacit representation of confidentiality.

* * * *

Willis also contends that the 10b-5 Counts of the Indictment are defective because they do not allege a legally cognizable injury or potential injury to his patient, the victim of the fraud. This argument is unpersuasive. Courts recognize that a patient has a cause of action against a psychiatrist who discloses confidential information learned in the course of treatment. See, e.g., *MacDonald v. Clinger*, 84 A.D.2d 482, 446 N.Y.S.2d 801 (4th Dep't 1982); *Doe v. Roe*, 93 Misc. 2d 201, 400 N.Y.S.2d 668 (Sup. Ct. N.Y. Co. 1977). Cf. *Hammonds v. Aetna Casualty & Surety*, 243 F. Supp. 793 (N.D. Ohio 1965). Furthermore, Mrs. Weill had an economic interest in preserving the confidentiality of the information disclosed because Willis' release of the information might have jeopardized her husband's advancement to CEO of BankAmerica in which she had a financial interest.

The patient also had a property interest in a continuing course of psychiatric treatment. The success of a psychiatrist-patient relationship often depends on the maintenance of the duty of confidentiality.

Decision and Remedy   *The court denied Willis' motion to dismiss the indictment against him. Willis eventually pleaded guilty to the charges.*

▰ Fraudulent Corporate Disclosures

Section 10(b) and Rule 10b-5 do more than simply prohibit insider trading —they outlaw any material fraudulent statements in connection with the purchase or sale of securities. For example, a corporation with publicly marketed shares might manipulate its financial records to conceal a quarterly loss or might artificially inflate its future earnings projections. In these cases, the company has violated section 10(b). Other SEC rules cover fraudulent statements made in certain specific contexts. For example, Rule 13e-3 prohibits deceptive statements made in the purchase of all publicly held shares of a company in a **going-private transaction**. Under these rules, a company is only liable for those misstatements that were made intentionally or recklessly, however.

Knowingly false statements may give rise to section 10(b) liability. In addition, companies may have a duty to speak, and a material omission may violate the section. When a company's officials speak on a topic, they must fully disclose material information or possibly be liable for a material omission. Thus, a company may have a duty to reveal bad news. Section 10(b) imposes potential liability for any of the following actions:

1. A false statement, such as lying about the amount of profits for the past year.

2. A true but misleading statement, such as reporting profits accurately but in a misleading context.

3. An omission, such as failure to disclose the unusual circumstances behind a year's profits.

A key to section 10(b) liability is the concept of materiality. A company is only liable if its false or misleading disclosure or omission is significant enough to be material. The commonly accepted test for materiality is whether the information would have significantly altered the "total mix" of information in the view of the hypothetical "reasonable investor."

There is an ongoing controversy over a company's obligation to disclose "soft" information. "Hard" information is that involving factual, objective information and generally must be disclosed. "Soft" information generally involves future predictions for the company, including corporate plans and forecasts. Generally, soft information need not be disclosed, but courts consider

the issue on a case-by-case basis. Disclosure of soft information may be required, depending on issues such as "the qualifications of those who prepared or compiled it; . . . its relevance to the stockholders' impending decision; . . . and the availability to the investor of other more reliable sources of information."[4] On other occasions, a company may be liable under section 10(b) if it *does* disclose soft information that is not particularly reliable.

Another controversial question is the responsibility of a company to deal with rumors about its stock. One particularly significant rumor would involve a potential merger of the corporation. In the following case, the Supreme Court set forth the standard for how the company can or must respond to rumors of a potential merger.

---

[4]*Flynn v. Bass Brothers Enterprises*, 744 F.2d 978, 988 (3d Cir. 1984).

■ Case 7.3
Basic, Incorporated v. Levinson
United States Supreme Court, 1988
108 S.Ct. 978

Background and Facts   *Basic, Incorporated, was a publicly traded company manufacturing materials for the steel industry. In 1976, representatives of Combustion Engineering, Inc., began meeting with officers of Basic regarding a possible merger. During 1977 and 1978, Basic made three public statements denying that it was engaged in merger negotiations. On December 18, 1978, Basic issued a press release stating that it had been approached regarding a merger. On December 19, Basic's board of directors endorsed Combustion's tender offer to acquire Basic.*

Max Levinson and others were Basic shareholders who held shares after the time of Basic's denial of merger negotiations, but who sold their shares before the merger announcement in December 1978. They contended that they sold their shares for an artificially low price, due to Basic's false and misleading denial of merger negotiations during this time. The shareholders sued for damages under section 10(b). The district court granted summary judgment for defendants, holding that the denials of merger negotiations were not material. The Sixth Circuit Court of Appeals reversed the summary judgment, and the Supreme Court took the case on writ of certiorari.

BLACKMUN, Justice.

*   *   *   *

The application of this materiality standard to preliminary merger discussions is not self-evident. Where the impact of the corporate development on the target's fortune is certain and clear, the *TSC Industries* materiality definition admits straightforward application. Where, on the other hand, the event is contingent or speculative in nature, it is difficult to ascertain whether the "reasonable investor" would have considered the omitted information significant at the time. Merger negotiations, because of the ever-present possibility that the contemplated transaction will not be effectuated, fall into the latter category.

* * * *

Whether merger discussions in any particular case are material therefore depends on the facts. Generally, in order to assess the probability that the event will occur, a factfinder will need to look to indicia of interest in the transaction at the highest corporate levels. Without attempting to catalog all such possible factors, we note by way of example that board resolutions, instructions to investment bankers, and actual negotiations between principals or their intermediaries may serve as indicia of interest. To assess the magnitude of the transaction to the issuer of the securities allegedly manipulated, a factfinder will need to consider such facts as the size of the two corporate entities and of the potential premiums over market value. No particular event or factor short of closing the transaction need be either necessary or sufficient by itself to render merger discussions material.

As we clarify today, materiality depends on the significance the reasonable investor would place on the withheld or misrepresented information. The fact-specific inquiry we endorse here is consistent with the approach a number of courts have taken in assessing the materiality of merger negotiations. Because the standard of materiality we have adopted differs from that used by both courts below, we remand the case for reconsideration of the question whether a grant of summary judgment is appropriate on this record.

Decision and Remedy   *The Court vacated the decision of the court of appeals and remanded the case for further proceedings consistent with this opinion.*

Only a purchaser or seller of securities may bring a section 10(b) action. This requirement significantly restricts the number of potential plaintiffs. Suppose that Cohenco puts out false and misleading information on its future prospects. Because of the information Mr. Shapiro decides *not* to purchase shares of Cohenco. Shapiro has no remedy because he was not a purchaser or seller of shares. Similarly, a shareholder who elects not to sell her shares because of information has no damages remedy under section 10(b).

In addition to the criminal penalties discussed in *West's Business Law, Fifth Edition* and in *West's Legal Environment of Business,* section 10(b) also provides for a private civil action to recover damages from false or misleading disclosures. When a breach of section 10(b) has occurred, a purchaser or seller of securities may sue the responsible party for damages. Suppose Leon buys stock in Keefe & Associates for $50/share, based on unrealistic earnings projections put out by the company. When true information comes out, the price of the shares drops to $40/share. Leon could recover $10/share in a section 10(b) private action. Leon need not even prove that he personally read and relied upon the misstatement, because the law reflects a presumption that the general market has responded to the misinformation. This is generally called the "fraud on the market" theory.

In these cases, there can be an overlap between section 10(b) of the 1934 Act and sections 11 and 12 of the 1933 Act. Section 10(b) is often preferable for plaintiffs, because it is not limited to public offerings of new shares, it offers more potential defendants, and it may provide a longer statute of limitations.

▀ Proxy Regulations

Section 14 of the 1934 Act regulates the solicitation of proxies of companies required to register their securities. The term "proxy" is broadly defined to include any attempt by management to solicit the consent of their shareholders to corporate actions. As described in Chapter 40 of *West's Business Law, Fifth Edition*, shareholders possess certain election rights to select directors, modify corporate articles, and dictate some other corporate policies.

A proxy works as follows. Written proxy statements are sent by management to shareholders to obtain shareholder approval of management policies in an election. Shareholders who approve of management policies return a **proxy card** that authorizes management representatives to vote their shares at a shareholders' meeting. Those who disapprove may give a proxy card to a dissenting group who will vote the shares against management. Companies invariably send proxy solicitations in connection with their annual meeting, and the Act requires that these solicitations contain certain information specified by the SEC in Schedule 14A.

Proxy contests may arise, when some non-management shareholder group seeks to elect a new slate of directors or to adopt some new corporate policy opposed by management. All participants in such an election contest must file a Schedule 14B with the SEC, requiring certain disclosures in proxy materials. The Schedule 14B must disclose the identity of the participants, the amount of their shareholdings, the nature of their involvement in the proxy contest and other relevant facts. The SEC scrutinizes these schedules to ensure that proxy disclosures are not materially false or misleading.

If a material misstatement or omission in a proxy solicitation slips past the SEC review, individual shareholders may sue. SEC Rule 14a-9 prohibits solicitation of proxies with statements that contain materially false or misleading information. Materiality is similar to the standard under section 10(b). In the proxy context, the test for materiality is whether the information has "a significant propensity to affect the voting process." If the shareholders win, they may overturn the results of the shareholder election, which was tainted by proxy materials containing material omissions or false statements.

Rule 14a-8 authorizes shareholders to make their own proposals for corporate governance at annual meetings. If a shareholder presents a proposal that is proper under the relevant state corporations statute, the company's management must include the proposal in the management's proxy statement, along with a brief statement of the shareholder's purpose for the proposal, so long as the proposal is received in adequate time for inclusion (usually 120 days before release of the management's proxy statement).

Shareholders can use this authority to submit proposals for both economic goals and political goals (such as requiring divestment from South African corporations). To be included in proxy materials, shareholder proposals cannot relate to the ordinary conduct of business but must involve some special action. For example, a shareholder proposal that a company should be put up for sale involves an exceptional transaction and must be included. Management may, however, oppose these proposals and present its reasons for opposition.

▀ The Williams Act

In 1968, Congress passed the Williams Act, which amended the Securities Exchange Act of 1934. This Act regulated a newly developed means of taking over a corporation, known as a "tender offer." In a tender offer, some party makes an offer to a target company's shareholders to buy their stock in a company at some set price. For example, Paramount Communications, Inc., tried to take over Time, Incorporated, by making a public offer to all of Time's shareholders to buy their shares at $175/share. Tender offers, by definition, have certain characteristics, such as a public solicitation of public shareholders for a substantial percentage of the target's stock, usually at a significant premium over the prevailing market price.

There are differences among tender offers, however. The offeror may offer to buy all shares or only a percentage, and may offer cash for the shares or new securities. A successful tender offer is usually followed by a merger. The new owner uses majority control of the corporation to approve a merger of the company. Even those shareholders who did not sell in response to the tender offer may thus be compelled to relinquish their shares in a "second-step merger."

Congress passed the Williams Act because some tender offers were considered to be coercive and unfair. For example, some offerors made two-tier, front-end-loaded tender offers. In this type of offer, the acquirer offers a premium price for the first substantial percentage of shares tendered and a lower price for the remaining shares in a subsequent merger. For example, suppose Megacorp makes a tender offer for Minicorp. Megacorp might offer $125 per share in the first tier, for the first 67 percent of shares tendered. Assuming that this percentage of shares was tendered, Megacorp would then use its majority authority to merge the corporation and squeeze out the 33 percent of nontendering shareholders at a lower price in the second tier, such as $75 per share. Such offers tend to stampede shareholders into a quick acceptance of the offer, to avoid falling into the second tier and receiving a lower price. Today, most tender offers are not of this two-tier type, but many commentators still consider them to be coercive of shareholders.

A tender offer is usually preceded by quiet purchases of the target company's stock on the open market. Section 13 of the amended act and SEC Rule 13d-1 require that an individual or group of affiliated individuals must publicly declare when they have obtained more than five percent of the shares of certain corporations. These parties must file a Schedule 13D with the SEC, which requires disclosure of their identity, the number of shares they own, their purpose in buying the shares, and any plans they have for acquiring or altering the corporation's business, among other items. These requirements apply even if the person or group has no intent to make a tender offer.

If the purchaser goes forward and makes a tender offer for the corporation's shares, section 14 requires certain disclosures. Offerors must file a Schedule 14D-1 on the day the offer is commenced, and certain facts must be disclosed either in this Schedule or in the offer itself. Required disclosures include the name and background of the offeror, the source of financing for the tender offer, any plans for changes in the target's management, business or share marketability, and other facts. If disclosures are inadequate or misleading, the SEC and private parties may seek an injunction halting the tender offer.

The SEC recently adopted another regulation of tender offers in Rule 14d-10, known as the "all holders rule." This requires that a tender offer must be open to all a company's shareholders and that all shareholders have the opportunity to receive the same, best price. This rule prevents offerors from playing favorites in their tender offer and excluding certain shareholders from participation.

Section 14 also may require certain disclosures by the target corporation. Neither the target company nor its management can make any recommendation concerning a tender offer unless they file a Schedule 14D-9. Required disclosures are roughly similar to the Schedule 14D-1 and include disclosure of any negotiations with the offeror or a third party for a merger or corporate reorganization.

Rule 14e-2 also requires the management of the target company to respond to the tender offer within ten days by sending its shareholders a statement that recommends acceptance or rejection of the offer or expresses a position of neutrality on the offer. This statement must also provide reasons for management's position.

After a tender offer is commenced, shareholders must decide whether to tender their shares to the offeror or retain them. The Williams Act guarantees that shareholders must be given at least twenty business days to make this decision. Moreover, shareholders who tender their shares retain the right to withdraw their tender during the offering period before the offer closes. The Williams Act also contains a "best price" provision which guarantees all tendering shareholders the same, best price available. Thus, if an offeror raises its offer price during the offering period, the new higher price must be given even to shareholders who tendered prior to the increase. Section 14(e) of the Act also prohibits false and misleading disclosures and certain manipulative devices in connection with a tender offer.

Exhibit 7-2 summarizes the requirements of many of the most important SEC rules.

Regulation of Broker-Dealers

A broker is a "person engaged in the business of effecting transactions in securities for the account of others, but does not include a bank." A dealer is a "person engaged in the business of buying and selling securities for his own account." While broker-dealers are bound by various

---

Exhibit 7-2

Some Important SEC Rules and Schedules

Rule 10b-5
Prohibits deceptive and manipulative practices in sale or purchase of securities

Schedule 13D
Statement of ownership that must be filed when person or group obtains more than 5% of class of company's securities

Rule 13e-3
Prohibits deceptive and manipulative practices in connection with going-private transactions

Rule 14a-9
Prohibits the solicitation of proxies that contain false or misleading statements or omissions

Schedule 14B
Statement that must be filed by all participants in a corporate election contest

Schedule 14D-1
Statement that must be filed by tender offeror, describing identity, financing, purpose of tender offer and plans for subject company

Rule 14d-9
Requires the subject company of a tender offer to disclose certain information

Schedule 14D-9
Statement that must be filed by subject company of tender offer, describing any arrangement or conflicts of interest with offeror, plus company's position on offer

Rule 14d-10
Requires that all shareholders have opportunity to receive the same "best price" in tender offer

Rule 14e-2
Requires that target management respond to shareholders within ten days of tender offer

---

common law agency rules, the 1934 Act subjected them to additional regulation under federal securities law. Section 15(a) of that act requires a broker-dealer for nonexempt securities to register with the SEC. Broker-dealers are also regulated by private organizations, such as the National Association of Securities Dealers (NASD).

One important restriction on broker-dealers is the prohibition on **churning**. When brokers buy or sell stock for the accounts of others, they charge a small commission. The more transactions, the larger the total commission income. Churning is a practice of excessive trading to generate commissions, in which a broker advances his own interests at the expense of his client. In addition to violating the broker-dealer regulations of section 15(c)(1), churning has been held to violate section 10(b) and Rule 10b-5. The SEC may enforce these provisions, as may private plaintiffs injured by churning.

To prove churning, a plaintiff must first show that the broker controlled the client's account. In some accounts, a broker may trade without consulting the client in advance. This establishes the control element. Other factors, such as the client's inexperience with the market and particular trust in the broker, may also be used to establish this control element.

A plaintiff also must show excessive trading, which is a fact-specific, case-by-case determination. In addition to the frequency of trading, courts will consider the relative magnitude of the commissions generated to the size of the client's overall account. Courts may also look for "in and out trading" (selling and repurchasing the same security in a brief time period) and "cross trading" (shifting securities among accounts of different clients). Damages for churning typically include full restitution of all commissions received by the broker.

Another objectionable practice is called **scalping**—in which a broker-dealer purchases a company's securities for its own account and then recommends those shares to its clients, often reselling its own shares for a profit. Scalping can violate section 10(b) of the 1934 Act, because a broker's failure to disclose its purchases and resales to a client can be a material omission.

Broker-dealers may also be liable for recommending stock purchases that are poorly suited to their clients. Brokers are expected to know their clients' needs and to investigate the securities they recommend. Certain high pressure sales tactics and cold-calling for securities sales, often called "boiler room operations," may also violate the duties of broker-dealers. The SEC requires that brokers find out certain minimum information about their client and about the recommended security before entering into a transaction.

In general, securities brokers are considered professionals and held to a high degree of integrity in dealings with clients. The following case demonstrates the potential liability of brokers.

■■ Case 7.4
Securities and Exchange Commission v. Ridenour
United States Circuit Court of Appeals, Eighth District 1990
913 F.2d 515

Background and Facts *Robert Ridenour was a very successful account executive in the institutional bond department of the brokerage firm of Dean Witter. Ridenour participated in over one hundred "matched trades" in which he would buy a security from a client, without informing the client that he was a purchaser. Then Ridenour would resell the same security at a profit to himself of over 90 percent. Sometimes he would resell the securities on the same day that he purchased them.*

The SEC filed a civil action against Ridenour for fraud. The district found that Ridenour had violated federal securities laws and ordered him to disgorge over $470,00 in his profits. Ridenour appealed.

LARSON, Senior District Judge. [sitting by designation]:

* * * *

The SEC acknowledges in its brief on appeal that in the usual bond transaction, a broker-dealer such as Ridenour does not owe a duty to those who are trading in bonds, because the dealer makes no representations about the price the dealer quotes, other than it is what the dealer is willing to pay. The SEC argues, however, that the issue in this case is not what the usual practice is but what Ridenour's relationship with his customers was. The district court agreed, finding that Ridenour was sophisticated and his clients were gullible: they relied on him to quote them the best available market price for the purchase and sale of securities because of the unique relationship of trust and confidence that Ridenour had developed with them over the years. As a result, the court concluded Ridenour had misused his relationship with his clients and had defrauded them in violation of federal securities laws.

* * * *

Ridenour's arguments that he need not register as a broker-dealer pursuant to 15 U.S.C. § 78*o*(a)(1) are equally unavailing. It is undisputed that, during the period from 1979 to 1981, Ridenour engaged in a series of transactions involving municipal and corporate securities. We agree with the government that Ridenour's level of activity during this period made him more than an active investor. Ridenour attempted to obtain and keep a regular clientele for his "private" bond deals, which he negotiated out of his office at Dean Witter, albeit on his own behalf. We find no error in the court's conclusion that Ridenour was a broker-dealer, and that his failure to register as such violated section 15(a)(1) of the Securities Exchange Act, 15 U.S.C.§ 78o(a)(1).

Decision and Remedy *The court affirmed Ridenour's liability but reduced the amount to be disgorged by about $2000, due to an error in calculation by the district court.*

The Insider Trading and Securities Fraud Enforcement Act of 1988 placed additional obligations to detect insider trading on companies and especially upon securities broker-dealers. The law added a new section 15(f) to the 1934 Act, which established a compulsory surveillance system that enlists brokers in the enforcement against insider trading. This system requires each brokerage firm to implement procedures designed to detect insider trading by its employees. While the extensiveness of procedures may vary with the size of brokerages, these organizations generally must establish written policies and procedures to prevent insider trading, control the flow of sensitive information and monitor their employees' trading.

The new Act also establishes liability for any organizations that are deemed "controlling persons." Controlling persons are companies, law firms, accountants and broker-dealers who presumably have control over their employees. The SEC now may bring an action for civil and criminal penalties against these parties who controlled any person who traded on insider information in violation of the law. To succeed in this action, the SEC must show either (1) that the controlling person knew or recklessly disregarded information that the controlled person was engaging in insider trading, or (2) that the controlling broker-dealer failed to maintain the newly required surveillance system and therefore failed to detect the insider trading. A liable control person can be fined up to $1 million or three times the profit from the insider trading, whichever is greater. The SEC may also prohibit a broker-dealer from using national securities exchanges.

RICO

In 1970, Congress passed the Racketeer Influenced and Corrupt Organizations Act (RICO), as discussed in Chapter 6 of *West's Business Law, Fifth Edition*. The primary purpose of this law was to prevent organized crime from further infecting the business world with illegal acts, such as fraud. RICO provided both criminal and civil penalties, and private citizens injured by racketeering activity may bring their own actions and recover triple their actual damages or obtain injunctive relief against responsible racketeers.

RICO was drafted very broadly and is increasingly employed in federal securities litigation. A company that violates section 10(b) will often find itself sued under RICO as well. Under the primary source of private RICO authority, a plaintiff must prove the following elements:

1. Defendant engaged in two or more predicate criminal acts.

2. Constituting a pattern of racketeering activity.

3. Thereby participating in an enterprise affecting interstate or foreign commerce.

4. Causing injury to the plaintiff's business or property.

Nothing in RICO is expressly limited to mobsters or organized crime, as that phrase is generally understood.

The first requirement of RICO liability is proof that a defendant engaged in two or more predicate criminal acts. In the securities context, these predicate acts take the form of violations of section 10(b), 13(d), 14(e) or other provisions of the federal securities laws. Mail and wire fraud are also commonly alleged crimes in securities litigation. While the law requires proof of criminal acts, the Supreme Court has held that the defendant need not have actually been convicted of the alleged acts. Rather, a plaintiff need only allege that the defendant has committed two or more acts that meet the statutory definition of a crime.

A plaintiff also must allege that these acts constituted a "pattern" of racketeering activity. While courts are not entirely agreed on the definition of "pattern," plaintiffs generally must show that the predicate acts involved more than a single illegal scheme. Even a large number of criminal acts will not constitute a pattern of racketeering activity, if they involved only a single scheme over a short period of time. However,

if defendants engage in criminal acts over a longer period of time, such as a year, courts have found a pattern of racketeering even where only a single illegal scheme was involved.

A plaintiff also must show that the defendant, through the pattern of racketeering, invests or otherwise participates in an enterprise. Enterprise is defined broadly as any individual or group of individuals "associated together for the common purpose of engaging in a course of conduct." The key here is proof of a continuing entity engaged in a common purpose. The enterprise must affect interstate or foreign commerce to be illegal, but only a slight effect is required.

RICO is increasingly used in the context of business transactions. The following case illustrates the breadth of RICO's potential application.

▨ Case 7.5
Beauford v. Helmsley
United States Court of Appeals, Second
Circuit, 1989
865 F.2d 1386

Background and Facts   *Harry Helmsley and others converted a New York apartment building, the "Parkchester," into condominium units. Helmsley offered these units for sale to the existing 8286 tenants and others. Some tenants purchased their units. Dissatisfied buyers sued and complained of the offering plan for the units. They alleged that the offering materials concealed the existence of serious structural defects in the building, the presence of asbestos materials, and the need for replacement of plumbing and electrical systems. Plaintiffs sued under RICO, claiming that the misstatements in the offering plan represented numerous independent instances of fraud.*

The district court dismissed plaintiffs' complaint. That court held that the plaintiffs had failed to prove a pattern of racketeering activity. The plaintiffs appealed and a panel of the Second Circuit Court of Appeals affirmed the dismissal. The case was then set for rehearing before the entire en banc panel of the Second Circuit, in order to clarify the scope of RICO law.

KEARSE, Circuit Judge.

* * * *

Within this framework, there is no question that the amended complaint in the present case adequately pleaded the RICO enterprise element. It alleged that there were two such enterprises: the partnership that sponsored the conversion, and all of the defendants in association with one another for the purpose of accomplishing the apartment sales. Each is within the statutory definition of enterprise. The more interesting question is whether the amended complaint adequately alleged a pattern of racketeering activity.

Our *Indelicato* analysis has persuaded us that a RICO pattern may be established without proof of multiple schemes, multiple episodes, or multiple transactions; and that acts that are not widely separated in time or space may nonetheless properly be viewed as separate acts of racketeering activity for purposes of establishing a RICO pattern. Thus, in *Indelicato*, we found that three acts of murder could constitute a RICO pattern even though there was proof of but one scheme, and even though the three murders, carried out virtually simultaneously, could not be viewed as separable episodes or transactions.

*   *   *   *

In the present case, we conclude also that a RICO pattern may be adequately pleaded without an allegation that the scheme pursuant to which the racketeering acts were performed is an ongoing scheme having no demonstrable ending point. We reach this conclusion because nothing in the statute or the legislative history reveals an intent to require such an open-ended scheme. What is required is that the complaint plead a basis from which it could be inferred that the acts of racketeering activity were neither isolated nor sporadic. In *Indelicato*, we found the threat of continuity inherent in the criminal nature of the enterprise at whose behest the three related murders were committed. Were the same type of enterprise alleged here, we would have no difficulty in finding a sufficient allegation of the threat of continuity needed to show a pattern. When, however, there is no indication that the enterprise whose affairs are said to be conducted through racketeering acts is associated with organized crime, the nature of the enterprise does not of itself suggest that racketeering acts will continue, and proof of continuity or the threat of continuity of racketeering activity must thus be found in some factor other than the enterprise itself. We conclude that the amended complaint alleged sufficient other factors with respect to continuity to avoid dismissal for failure to allege a RICO pattern.

*   *   *   *

In assessing the sufficiency of these allegations to show a pattern, we note first that § 1961(1)(B) defines racketeering activity, in pertinent part, as "any act which is indictable under . . . section 1341 (relating to mail fraud)," and that each act of fraudulent mailing is separately indictable, *see Badders v. United States*, 240 U.S. 391, 394, 36 S.Ct. 367, 368, 60 L.Ed. 706 (1916) ("each putting of a letter into the post office a separate offence" under predecessor of § 1341); *United States v. Eskow*, 422 F.2d 1060, 1064 (2d Cir.) (dictum), *cert. denied*, 398 U.S. 959, 90 S.Ct. 2174, 26 L.Ed.2d 544 (1970). Second, there can be no question that the thousands of alleged mail frauds here had the necessary interrelationship to be considered a pattern. All of the mailings were made to groups of persons related by either their tenancy in Parkchester apartments or their potential interest in purchasing such apartments. All of the frauds allegedly had the same goal, i.e., inflating the profits to be made by the defendants in the sale of the Parkchester apartments.

In sum, read with ordinary charity, the amended complaint alleged that on each of several occasions defendants had mailed fraudulent documents to thousands of persons and that there was reason to believe that similarly fraudulent mailings would be made over an additional period of years. These allegations sufficed to set forth acts that cannot be deemed, as a matter of law, isolated or sporadic. We conclude that the relatedness and continuity factors have been adequately revealed in the pleading and that the amended complaint did not fail to satisfy the pattern requirement.

Decision and Remedy   *The Second Circuit vacated the previous circuit court opinion and the district court opinion. The case was remanded to the district court, so that the plaintiffs' case could proceed.*

RICO has been used by management seeking to resist a tender offer. For example, suppose that Megacorp purchases 5 percent of the shares of Minicorp and files a Schedule 13D. Minicorp may allege that Megacorp's Schedule 13D is false and misleading and therefore a violation of federal securities law. If Minicorp can find other instances of similar securities law violations by Megacorp, they can allege two or more predicate criminal acts that constitute a pattern of racketeering in violation of RICO. Minicorp will have a more difficult time, however, proving that a single tender offer would qualify as a pattern of racketeering. If Megacorp had engaged in similar takeovers in the past, this will support the evidence of a pattern.

Another securities law fact pattern invoking RICO could involve insider trading. If a group of individuals has participated in a pattern of insider trading, the victims of this pattern may sue for triple damages, which is more than they could recover under section 10(b) or other securities law provisions. RICO also offers other benefits to securities law plaintiffs. Some laws, such as mail fraud, have no private right of action for individuals' civil recovery of damages. A pattern of mail fraud, however, may enable private recovery under RICO. Other potential securities law plaintiffs may lack standing to challenge insider trading or corporate fraud under section 10(b), perhaps because they did not purchase or sell securities. These individuals may still be able to recover under RICO, which does not have the same requirements for standing.

▬ Ethical Perspectives

Ethics and Insider Trading

Insider trading often is used as a textbook case of unethical behavior. Certainly, the secretive and manipulative use of improperly acquired inside information is ethically indefensible as well as illegal. Some experts argue, however, that insider trading by corporate officers and directors may be ethical.

The ethical analysis of insider trading begins with a consideration of which ethical duties may be violated by such trading. The first issue concerns duties of honesty and promise-keeping toward the insider's employing corporation. Unauthorized use of inside information is considered a breach of fiduciary duty to the corporation and its shareholders. Courts have analogized insider trading as a theft of inside information from the corporation, in order personally to profit.

The second concern with insider trading involves ethical duties toward other investors. Any time that an insider purchases stock, some other person or organization is selling that stock. Use of secret inside information may be considered a breach of an honesty duty toward the other party in the transaction.

The law of insider trading is primarily concerned with the first ethical issue. Insider trading is only illegal if it breaches some fiduciary duty. But what if the corporation authorized its insiders to trade on inside information? Some argue that authorized insider trading would violate no ethical duty and would actually improve the performance of corporations and the economy. They argue that authorized insider trading will provide executives with a greater incentive to increase the stock price of their corporation and will contribute to a more efficient securities market that employs all available information.[5] Others respond that authorized insider trading would corrupt the credibility of the stock market and only encourage executives to produce short-term swings in stock price.[6] Authorized insider trading may be ethical, but it may encourage unethical management by executives, in order to profit themselves. Also, is it ethical for a corporation to authorize its insiders to profit from secret information?

The law is less concerned with the effect of insider trading on third parties who buy or sell stock, but there are still ethical concerns. Suppose Susan is a long-standing shareholder in ChernoCorp and Edward is the president of ChernoCorp. Edward becomes aware of some development that will cause ChernoCorp stock to appreciate dramatically from $10/share to $20/share, once the development is publicly announced. So Edward enters the market and buys ChernoCorp shares from Susan. After the development is announced and the share price increases, Susan may feel cheated. She could argue that her long-term contribution to ChernoCorp's capital base means that she should receive the benefits of the company's success.

There are those who argue that Edward's trading is not at all unfair.[7] People often have special information when they make contracts. The buyer of a house may have information about the local housing market or future rental prospects that the seller lacks. This does not necessarily make the purchase of the house unethical. The free market seeks to encourage and reward parties who obtain information about the value of contracts. One author expressed this issue as follows: "Does morality really require that before I can deal with my indolent neighbor, I should communicate to him all my private plans, my long-sighted views of the future state of the market, my surmises — in short, all the results of that knowledge and address which have been the hard earned acquisitions of my own industry and activity?"[8]

The above theory has its own limitations. Sometimes, it is generally considered unethical to deal on certain forms of special knowledge. The car dealer who sells an automobile, knowing that the auto has a serious latent engine defect, is behaving unethically (and illegally) toward the purchaser. The doctor who uses specialized knowledge and position to recommend an unnecessary operation is also acting unethically toward the patient. The question is whether the specialized information of insider trading is the sort that is ethical to use in market transactions.

---

[5]*See* Carlton & Fischel, "The Regulation of Insider Trading," *35 Stanford L. Rev.* 857 (1983).

[6]*See* Cox, "Insider Trading and Contracting: A Critical Response to the 'Chicago School,'" 1986 Duke L. J. 628.

[7]*See* Lawson, "The Ethics of Insider Trading," 11 *Harvard J. of Law and Pub. Policy* 727 (1988).

[8]*Id.*

International Perspectives

The International Law of Insider Trading

International securities markets have grown dramatically in significance. More investors are diversifying their shareholdings by investments in Tokyo, Hong Kong, London, Paris and other markets. As a consequence, the international law of insider trading is a subject of increasing concern.

United States law on insider trading generally does not apply to foreign transactions. International laws on insider trading vary widely; in many nations there is no prohibition on insider trading. In Europe, for example, only three nations — Denmark, France and the United Kingdom — have meaningful prohibitions on insider trading. Moreover, the United Kingdom's law has strict limitations, lacks specific civil remedies, and is not frequently employed.

The European Community has adopted new rules to ban insider trading, once the Community comes together in 1992. The nations' finance ministers unanimously adopted a directive requiring all twelve member states to adopt and implement a "system aimed at assuring that people with access to confidential information regarding companies cannot use this information in the sale or purchase of securities." The directive also calls for a Community-wide enforcement system to penalize transnational trading. The directive suggests a prohibition on insider trading that is broader than that of U.S. law, but the effectiveness of the directive is dependent on its implementation by the Community's member states.

Japan regulates insider trading under its Securities Exchange Law. While Japanese law on insider trading roughly parallels U.S. law, there is much less enforcement of the law in Japan. By 1987, Japan's Ministry of Finance had brought only one formal proceeding to penalize insider trading. Enforcement has increased recently but is still much less frequent than in the United States.

United States law can affect the enforcement of insider trading prohibitions overseas. The insider trading prohibition has extraterritorial jurisdiction against foreign transactions in a security that is registered in the U.S. or traded on a U.S. exchange, if the conduct has a direct and harmful impact on U.S. citizens. U.S. law also applies to transactions in foreign securities, if the illegal insider-trading conduct occurs within the United States. The Insider Trading and Securities Fraud Enforcement Act, passed in 1988, gave the SEC greater enforcement authority over international transactions by U.S. investors buying foreign stocks. This law gave the SEC authority to conduct investigations in the United States on behalf of a foreign country, to assist in the prosecution of that nation's insider-trading laws.

Questions and Case Problems

1. Patrick has an undergraduate degree in philosophy and then became a lawyer. He calls his friend Mike, a broker, to invest some of his lucrative lawyer salary. Mike realizes that Patrick has no idea how financial markets work and does extensive trading with Patrick's money without informing him of the details, which resulted in substantial commissions for Mike's brokerage firm. Patrick's wife, a finance major, begins to question Mike's decisions and motives. What must she show to successfully challenge Mike's pattern of trading?

2. Alright Company issued $1 million in preferred convertible stock after a long process of registration with the SEC. Upper management and the directors of Alright went out of their way to make sure that the information provided to the SEC was accurate and up-to-date. The stock issuance was a huge success at first but then plummetted. The embezzlement of a lower level employee had seriously undermined Alright's financial position. Upper management was unaware of this embezzlement at the time of the stock issuance, so it was not disclosed. Can a purchaser of Alright shares in the initial issuance recover for the false picture of Alright's financial status?

3. Ira Waldbaum was an insider of Waldbaum, Inc., who told his sister that the corporation was to be sold. She told her daughter, who told her husband, who told a friend, Robert Chestman. Chestman promptly purchased shares of Waldbaum, Inc., and profited enormously when the company was taken over. The SEC prosecuted Chestman for illegal insider trading. Is Chestman guilty of insider trading?

4. Burlington Northern made a hostile tender offer for 25 million shares of El Paso Gas Co. at $24 per share. The El Paso management opposed the offer but the company's shareholders tendered 25 million shares. Burlington, however, rescinded the tender offer under its terms and negotiated a deal with El Paso management. Under the deal, Burlington made another tender offer but for only 21 million shares. As a consequence, shareholders were unable to tender as many shares at the premium $24 per share price. These shareholders sued Burlington and El Paso under section 14(e) for defrauding them. Should the shareholders succeed with this claim? [*Schreiber v. Burlington Northern, Inc.* 472 U.S. 1 (1985)].

5. Nay worked for First Securities and encouraged individuals to invest in "escrow accounts" that were expected to have a high rate of return. In fact, he converted the funds to his own account and later committed suicide. The investors sought to recover their money, but First Securities was effectively bankrupt. The investors therefore sued the accounting firm for failure to conduct proper audits of First Securities. Do the investors have a good claim against the auditing firm under section 10(b)? [*Ernst & Ernst v. Hochfelder*, 425 U.S. 185 (1976)].

CHAPTER EIGHT

Mergers and Acquisitions

▬ KEY BACKGROUND

The essential background for this chapter on mergers and acquisitions is found in Chapters 40 and 41 of *West's Business Law, Fifth Edition*. These chapters cover corporations—rights and duties of directors, managers, and shareholders; and corporations—merger, consolidation, and termination. Valuable background is also provided in Chapter 25 of *West's Legal Environment of Business*, which covers takeovers and mergers. Among the important points to remember from these chapters are:

- the fiduciary duties of corporate directors and officers

- the business judgment rule

- rights of shareholders in the corporation

- procedures for the merger of a corporation

- tender offers and target responses

* * *

The 1980s saw an explosion of activity in corporate takeovers. Many individuals became wealthy by selling their shares in corporations or by purchasing all the shares of a corporation and selling off its assets for a profit. While the 1990s have already seen a decline in takeover activity, multibillion-dollar corporations are still being bought and sold.

The key legal issue on mergers and acquisitions involves the rights of shareholders. These rights are defined by the corporate laws of the states. Because most large U.S. companies are incorporated in Delaware, the Delaware state law is by far the most important and provides the focus for this chapter.

Mergers and acquisitions usually follow the same basic, though sometimes complex, factual scenario. This chapter begins by describing the basic factual setting for takeovers and then discusses how the law applies to these facts.

▬ A Factual Scenario for a Takeover

The following facts represent a fairly typical takeover. Assume that Keggo is a fairly successful oil and mining company. Keggo is listed on the New York Stock Exchange, with two million outstanding shares that trade at about $25 per share. RBM Associates specializes in corporate acquisitions. RBM believes that Keggo's shares are significantly undervalued, because the natural resources owned by Keggo are themselves worth more than $25/share. Keggo becomes a target for takeover by RBM.

RBM would begin its takeover by purchasing Keggo stock on the open market. RBM probably would buy about 5 to 10 percent of Keggo's outstanding shares. RBM would next try to arrange financing (probably a loan) in order to purchase the remainder of Keggo's shares. RBM then would approach the Keggo board of directors and inquire about the possibility of a friendly takeover (with the board's approval). RBM might offer to pay $35/share for all of Keggo's outstanding shares, in cash or securities.

If RBM lacks financial resources to conduct the takeover, it may borrow virtually the entire cost of the takeover, which would make it a highly leveraged takeover. Such borrowing is available because Keggo's assets become **collateral** for the loan, if the takeover succeeds. This is called a **leveraged buyout** or **LBO**. The notes for this borrowing are sometimes called **junk bonds**, because they carry a relatively high risk of nonpayment. Newly acquired companies in LBOs have gone bankrupt and failed to pay off these bonds in full.

The Keggo board would evaluate the RBM offer, with the assistance of an **investment banker** and legal counsel. They might approve the offer as in the best interests of their shareholders. More likely, the board will reject the offer. They might believe that the offer is for an inadequate price or lacks adequate financing or interferes with Keggo's promising future business plans. All of these are legitimate reasons to oppose the RBM offer.

There is a risk, however, that the Keggo board of directors will fight the RBM offer for selfish reasons. The board probably contains several "inside directors," who are also officers of Keggo, such as the chief executive officer (CEO). These directors may fear the loss of their well-paying executive positions in the event of a takeover. To avoid the impression of self-interest, the Keggo board may appoint a special committee of outside directors, who are *not* employees of Keggo.

Once the Keggo board declines the friendly takeover, RBM may proceed in a "hostile" fashion. RBM can make a **tender offer**, which goes directly to all the Keggo shareholders and offers them $35 a share for all their stock. RBM will have to make several filings with the government in connection with the tender offer. The shareholders will have until a designated date to accept or reject this offer.

The Keggo board may recommend that its shareholders reject the offer, but the shareholders are likely to accept an offer that is $10/share over the market price. Therefore, the Keggo board may adopt defensive measures to fight off the takeover. The defensive measures may include the creation of a "poison pill" or a "lock-up" of Keggo's assets.

These defensive measures, which are discussed below, have the effect of making Keggo less attractive to RBM by making the takeover more expensive or less valuable. As a practical matter, they may render the RBM takeover impossible. Typical defensive measures can be eliminated at the board's discretion. Keggo's board may also seek out a **white knight** to take over the company and retain the officers.

RBM and other Keggo shareholders will probably sue Keggo and claim that the defensive measures are illegal. RBM may also raise its tender offer price to $40/share, if Keggo agrees to eliminate its defensive measures. If one of these approaches succeeds, RBM will go through with its tender offer. Perhaps 90 percent of Keggo's outstanding shares accept the tender offer.

Once RBM owns 90 percent of Keggo's shares, RBM runs the company. RBM, as the new majority shareholder of Keggo, will then adopt a **going private merger** plan. In the merger, the remaining 10 percent of Keggo shareholders must sell their Keggo shares, as Keggo is merged into RBM or its subsidiary. This second-step merger will probably be at the same $35-$40/share price as in the tender offer. The remaining minority shareholders will be required to sell their shares, and Keggo will become a wholly owned subsidiary of RBM. RBM can then run Keggo or sell off its assets for a profit, as they choose.

▬ Directors' Duties

One of the key legal questions in mergers and acquisitions law involves the duties of directors. Many cases turn on whether the defensive measures adopted by the directors are legal. The defensive actions are illegal if they violate the directors' state law duties to the company's shareholders. The primary duties are those of loyalty and of due care.

Duty of Loyalty

Corporate directors owe a duty of loyalty to the corporation's shareholders, as fiduciaries of the shareholders' interests. This means that the directors must act in the best interests of the corporation and its shareholders and cannot act as directors in their own personal interests.

The duty of loyalty arises in a number of corporate contexts but is prominent in mergers and acquisitions. As described in the introductory scenario, the Keggo inside directors have a substantial financial self-interest in keeping their jobs. Yet they are charged with making decisions for the corporation. The Keggo directors might decide to reject the RBM offer for legitimate reasons, as not in the best interests of the Keggo shareholders. The Keggo directors might reach this same decision for improper reasons that violate their duty of loyalty, in order to keep their jobs.

Because directors could reach a given decision for either proper or improper reasons, it may be difficult for a court to determine whether the directors violated their duty of loyalty. Courts therefore must investigate the decision closely.

Duty of Due Care

Corporate directors also owe a duty of due care to their shareholders. This demands that the directors make careful, informed decisions for the corporation. In the takeover context, the most significant aspect of the duty of due care is the responsibility to investigate the facts before deciding.

The duty of due care means that directors must fully investigate an acquisition offer before making a decision about the offer. This typically means that the board should consult with investment bankers, attorneys, and other professionals regarding the offer. The duty of care may also compel directors to investigate all reasonable alternatives for the corporation. Directors should keep a full record of their investigation and the bases for their decision.

The directors' duty of care often arises when the directors accept a friendly takeover rather than a hostile one. Although the directors have a right to prefer one offer over another, they have the responsibility to investigate the preferred offer completely, to ensure that it is in the best interests of their shareholders.

The following case has quickly become the classic for alleged breaches of due care.

■■ Case 8.1
Smith v. Van Gorkom
Supreme Court of Delaware, 1985
488 A.2d 858

Background and Facts *Trans Union Corporation's shares were trading at a low level (about $34 per share), and its management sought a merger to improve share value and to take advantage of tax credits that the company had accumulated. The board considered a management leveraged buyout (LBO) and concluded that they could probably borrow enough to offer around $55/share. On September 13, 1980, Jerome Van Gorkom, Trans Union's president, met Jay Pritzker, who was a "takeover specialist." Pritzker was interested in acquiring Trans Union, and Van Gorkom suggested a price of about $55/share.*

Pritzker brought a $55/share offer to Van Gorkom on September 18, who promptly called a board of directors meeting for September 20 but did not disclose its purpose. The directors heard a presentation from Van Gorkom describing the offer and stating that he considered the price fair. No investment banker was retained nor was any valuation effort made. The merger documents were not yet complete, but the directors went forward and approved the merger. Later that night, when the merger documents were ready, Van Gorkom signed them at a benefit for the opera, but he did not read them.

Shareholders of Trans Union sued to rescind the merger agreement, claiming that Van Gorkom and the other directors had breached their duty of due care. The trial court ruled for Van Gorkom, concluding that the board was informed and emphasizing that the merger offer was well in excess of the market price for Trans Union shares. The shareholders appealed.

HORSEY, Justice.

* * * *

The determination of whether a business judgment is an informed one turns on whether the directors have informed themselves "prior to making a business decision, of all material information reasonable available to them." Id.

Application of the [business judgment] rule of necessity depends upon a showing that informed director did in fact make a business judgment authorizing the transaction under review. And, as the plaintiff argues, the difficulty here is that the evidence does not show that this was done. There were director-committee-officer references to the realignment but none of these singly or cumulative showed that the director judgment was brought to bear with specificity on the transactions.

Under the business judgment rule there is no protection for directors who have made "an unintelligent or unadvised judgment." *Mitchell v. Highland-Western Glass*, Del. Ch., 167 A. 831, 833 (1933). A director's duty to inform himself in preparation for a decision derives from the fiduciary capacity in which he serves the corporation and its stockholders. *Lutz v. Boas*, Del. Ch., 171 A.2d 381 (1961). * * * Since a director is vested with the responsibility for the management of the affairs of the corporation, he must execute that duty with the recognition that he acts on behalf of others. Such obligation does not tolerate faithlessness or self-dealing. But fulfillment of the fiduciary function requires more than the mere absence of bad faith or fraud. Representation of the financial interest of others imposes on a director an affirmative duty to protect those interests and to proceed with a critical eye in assessing information of the type and under the circumstances present here.

* * * *

On the record before us, we must conclude that the Board of Directors did not reach an informed business judgment on September 20, 1980 in voting to "sell" the Company for $55 per share pursuant to the Pritzker cash-out merger proposal.

Our reasons, in summary are as follows:

The directors (1) did not adequately inform themselves as to Van Gorkom's role in forcing the "sale" of the Company and in establishing the per share purchase price; (2) were uninformed as to the intrinsic value of the Company; and (3) given these circumstances, at a minimum, were grossly negligent in approving the "sale" of the Company upon two hours' consideration, without prior notice, and without the exigency of a crisis or emergency.

As has been noted, the Board based its September 20 decision to approve the cash-out merger primarily on Van Gorkom's representations. None of the directors, other than Van Gorkom and Chelberg, had any prior knowledge that the purpose of the meeting was to propose a cash-out merger of Trans Union. No members of Senior Management were present, other than Chelberg, Romans and Peterson; and the latter two had only learned of the proposed sale an hour earlier. Both general counsel Moore and former general counsel Browder attended the meeting, but were equally uninformed as to the purpose of the meeting and the documents to be acted upon.

Without any documents before them concerning the proposed transaction, the members of the Board were required to rely entirely upon Van Gorkom's 20-minute oral presentation of the proposal. No written summary of the terms of the merger was presented; the directors were given no documentation to support the adequacy of $55 price per share for sale of the company; and the Board had before it nothing more than Van Gorkom's statement of his understanding of the substance of an agreement which he admittedly had never read, nor which any member of the board had ever seen.

* * * *

A substantial premium may provide one reason to recommend a merger, but in the absence of other sound valuation information, the fact of a premium alone does not provide an adequate basis upon which to assess the fairness of an offering price. Here, the judgment reached as to the adequacy of the premium was based on a comparison between the historically depressed Trans Union market price and the amount of the Pritzker offer. Using market price as a basis for concluding that the premium adequately reflected the true value of the Company was a clearly faulty, indeed fallacious, premise, as the defendants' own evidence demonstrates.

The record is clear that before September 20, Van Gorkom and other members of Trans Union's Board knew that the market had consistently undervalued the worth of Trans Union's stock, despite steady increases in the Company's operating income in the seven years preceding the merger. * * * Van Gorkom testified that he did not believe the market price accurately reflected Trans Union's true worth; and several of the directors testified that, as a general rule, most chief executives think that the market undervalues their companies' stock. Yet, on September 20, Trans Union's Board apparently believed that the market stock price accurately reflected the value of the company for the purpose of determining the adequacy of the premium for its sale.

Decision and Remedy   *The Delaware Supreme Court reversed the lower court and held that the defendants had breached their duty of care. The case was remanded for proceedings to supply the shareholders a remedy for the breach.*

While it might seem obvious for directors to exercise due care and consult with relevant professionals, full investigation can be difficult in the context of mergers and acquisitions. The typical takeover develops very quickly and may demand board action within days, or even hours. Midnight meetings are not uncommon. The need for rapid decision making can create a problem under the duty of due care.

Business Judgment Rule

Directors of major corporations are frequently sued for violating their duties of loyalty and due care. The **business judgment rule** offers considerable legal protection to directors' decisions. This rule states that courts should not second-guess the business judgments of corporate directors, who are experts and better suited to making corporate decisions than are judges.

The business judgment rule usually shelters directors' decisions. If a shareholder sues corporate directors over a program of corporate expansion, for example, courts will defer to the business judgment of the directors. The directors are in the best position to determine whether expansion is in the best interest of the company.

Much takeover litigation centers around the

application of the business judgment rule. If the rule applies, the directors' decision is virtually certain to be upheld. It is therefore critical for the challenger of the board of directors to find an exception to the business judgment rule.

One key exception to the business judgment rule occurs when directors have a personal interest in the decision. The courts will not defer to business decisions that appear to be in the self-interest of directors. If a business director gives a big corporate contract to his or her own company, courts may not apply the business judgment rule. Another important exception to the business judgment rule exists when the directors obviously have failed to investigate an important business decision.

▀▀ Directors' Duties in Mergers and Acquisitions

For some time, courts applied the business judgment rule to directors' decisions regarding potential corporate acquisitions. In recent years, however, courts have recognized the potentially divided loyalties of directors and have limited the application of the business judgment rule in takeovers.

Now, courts in Delaware and elsewhere apply a two-part test to determine whether the business judgment rule should apply when directors seek to fight off a takeover, as Keggo did through the adoption of defensive measures in the opening scenario of this chapter. This is called the *Unocal* test, after the case that adopted the test.[1] This decision recognized the "omnipresent spectre" that defensive actions may be motivated by directors' personal interests.

Unocal first requires that directors show the presence of a *"threat"* to the corporation before defensive measures are authorized. Courts have found that several features of hostile takeovers may constitute such a threat. If a takeover is coercive, thereby denying shareholders a fair choice, a threat is present.

The "two-tier tender offer" is just such a coercive threat. A **two-tier tender offer** occurs when an acquirer, such as RBM, offers one price (e.g., $40/share) for the first group of shares tendered

to the acquirer (such as the first 51 percent of Keggo shares). A different, lower price (e.g., $25/share) is offered for the remaining shares. When a tender offer is structured in this way, shareholders are coerced into accepting quickly, lest they fall into the second tier and receive much less for their shares.

Other features of a tender offer also may represent a threat to a target corporation, such as Keggo. For example, the acquirer might offer to pay for Keggo shares, not with cash but with shares or bonds in RBM or some other corporation. If these shares or bonds are not worth as much as RBM claims, the offer may be deemed to threaten the Keggo shareholders and justify defensive actions.

If a threat exists, the directors also must satisfy the second part of the *Unocal* test. This requires that the defensive action be *proportional* to the threat. The defensive measure may not be greater than the threat presented by the takeover. The larger the threat, the more extensive the defensive measures that will be allowed.

If the directors' action passes both parts of the *Unocal* test, the business judgment rule will protect the directors' decision to adopt the defensive measures. If the *Unocal* test is not met, the court will not use the business judgment rule but will evaluate the directors' decision itself to determine whether it is truly in the best interest of the shareholders.

Courts usually will uphold the initial adoption of defensive measures under the *Unocal* test. This is because defensive measures can buy time for the directors so that the shareholders may find a better deal. Defensive measures can delay a takeover, so that the company's directors can seek out other acquirers. If other companies are interested in acquiring Keggo, the directors can induce a bidding war, or auction, that will yield a higher price for its shareholders.

Even where the initial adoption of the defensive measures is lawful, courts may find that continuation of the defensive measures violates the *Unocal* test. Suppose that Keggo's directors try to induce an auction but no other companies are interested in bidding for Keggo. At this point, the RBM offer may appear to offer the most value to Keggo shareholders, and the directors will have a more difficult time proving a threat that justifies continuation of the defensive measures.

---

[1] *Unocal Corp. v. Mesa Petroleum Co.*, 493 A.2d 946 (Del. 1985).

Specific Defensive Measures

Courts have evaluated the lawfulness of the adoption and continuation of various types of defensive measures. It is important to understand how all of these defensive tactics operate and when they can be used.

One of the most common defensive tactics is a **shareholder rights plan**, often called a **poison pill**. This might involve Keggo's directors giving each of its shareholders one "right" for each share. This right would give the shareholder a valuable bond or cash or stock options at a below-market price. The effect of the rights plan is to give much of the company's wealth directly to its existing shareholders, thereby making the remaining company assets much less valuable to an acquirer.

The typical rights plan is a **flip-in poison pill**. This means that the rights are not actually granted until a person buys a high percentage (e.g., 20 percent) of Keggo's stock. Shareholders therefore do not receive the rights unless a takeover is well on the way to success. In this way, the rights plan does not interfere with the unacquired company. A company could also adopt a **flip-over poison pill**. This is a plan that gives Keggo's shareholders some rights in any acquiring company, such as RBM. This enables Keggo shareholders to receive not only the tender offer price but also shares in RBM at a below-market price.

Poison pills are a relatively common anti-takeover defensive measure, and many have been challenged. The following case is a leading decision on the requirements for validity of poison pills.

■■ Case 8.2
City Capital Associates Limited Partnership v. Interco Incorporated
Court of Chancery of the State of Delaware, 1988
551 A.2d 787

Background and Facts *Steven and Mitchell Rales began acquiring the stock of Interco, Incorporated, through the City Capital Associates Limited Partnership. Once Interco became aware of this pattern, the board of directors adopted a new flip-in and flip-over poison pill. This provided that if anyone obtained 30 percent of Interco's stock, rights would be triggered that had a market value of twice the exercise price. The Rales brothers proposed a friendly merger at $64/share but were rejected by the Interco board.*

The Rales then announced a tender offer at $70/share in cash. The board rejected this as inadequate and adopted a restructuring proposal. This involved the sale of a large quantity of Interco assets, the borrowing of over $2 billion, and the payment of a special dividend of $66/share to shareholders. The Rales brothers increased their bid to $74/share, but the board also rejected this. City Capital then went to court for an order requiring that the poison pill be redeemed and the restructuring canceled.

ALLEN, Chancellor.

*   *   *   *

It is appropriate, therefore, before subjecting the board's decision not to redeem the pill to the form of analysis mandated by *Unocal*, to identify what relevant facts are not contested or contestable, and what relevant facts may appropriately be assumed against the party prevailing on this point. They are as follows:

First. The value of the Interco restructuring is inherently a debatable proposition, most importantly (but not solely) because the future value of a stub share is unknowable with reasonable certainty.

Second.   The board of Interco believes in good faith that the restructuring has a value of "at least" $76 per share.

Third.   The City Capital offer is for $74 per share cash.

Fourth.   The board of Interco has acted prudently to inform itself of the value of the company.

Fifth.   The board believes in good faith that the City Capital offer is for a price that is "inadequate."

Sixth.   City Capital cannot, as a practical matter, close its tender offer while the rights exist; to do so would be to self-inflict an enormous financial injury that no reasonable buyer would do.

Seventh.   Shareholders of Interco have differing liquidity preferences and different expectations about likely future economic events.

Eighth.   A reasonable shareholder could prefer the restructuring to the sale of his stock for $74 in cash now, but a reasonable shareholder could prefer the reverse.

Ninth.   The City Capital tender offer is in no respect coercive. It is for all shares, not for only a portion of shares. It contemplates a prompt follow-up merger, if it succeeds, not an indefinite term as a minority shareholder. It proposes identical consideration in a follow-up merger, not securities or less money.

Tenth.   While the existence of the stock rights has conferred time on the board to consider the City Capital proposals and to arrange the restructuring, the utility of those rights as a defensive technique has, given the time lines for the restructuring and the board's actions to date, now been effectively exhausted except in one respect: the effect of those rights continues to "protect the restructuring."

These facts are sufficient to address the question whether the board's action in electing to leave the defensive stock rights plan in place qualifies for the deference embodied in the business judgment rule.

*   *   *   *

In this instance, there is no threat of shareholder coercion. The threat is to shareholders' economic interests posed by an offer the board has concluded is "inadequate." If this determination is made in good faith * * *, it alone will justify leaving a poison pill in place, even in the setting of a noncoercive offer, for a period while the board exercises its good faith business judgment to take such steps as it deems appropriate to protect and advance shareholder interests in light of the significant development that such an offer doubtless is. That action may entail negotiation on behalf of shareholders with the offeror, the institution of a *Revlon*-style auction for the Company, a recapitalization or restructuring designed as an alternative to the offer, or other action.

Once that period has closed, and it is apparent that the board does not intend to institute a *Revlon*-style auction, or to negotiate for an increase in the unwanted offer, and that it has taken such time as it required in good faith to arrange an alternative value-maximizing transaction, then, in most instances, the legitimate role of the poison pill in the context of a noncoercive offer will have been fully satisfied. The only function then left for the pill at this end-stage is to preclude the shareholders from exercising a judgment about their own interests that differs from the judgment of the directors, who will have some interest in the question. What then is the "threat" in this instance that might justify such a result?

* * * *

Our corporation law exists, not as an isolated body of ruled and principles, but rather in a historical setting and as a part of a larger body of law premised upon shared values. To acknowledge that directors may employ the recent innovation of "poison pills" to deprive shareholders of the ability effectively to choose to accept a noncoercive offer, after the board has had a reasonable opportunity to explore or create alternatives, or attempt to negotiate on the shareholders behalf, would, it seems to me, be so inconsistent with widely shared notions of appropriate corporate governance as to threaten to diminish the legitimacy and authority of our corporation law.

Decision and Remedy   *The court held that the board acted wrongfully in failing to redeem the poison pill but went on to hold that the restructuring was reasonable under Unocal and offered the shareholders a valuable alternative to the sale of the company.*

Roughly similar to a poison pill is a **restructuring**. A corporate restructuring usually involves the target company taking on substantial debt through borrowing and then distributing a substantial cash dividend to its shareholders or repurchasing a significant portion of its shares. This approach makes shareholders happier with the incumbent management and also makes the newly debt-laden company less attractive to the acquirer. A repurchase also removes shares from circulation for potential acquisition by the acquirer.

In 1985, Turner Broadcasting System, Inc., announced a highly leveraged tender offer for CBS for $175/share in junk bonds. CBS responded by offering to repurchase 21 percent of its own stock for $40/share cash and $110/share in bonds. This substantially increased CBS total debt, in order to pay for the repurchase. Turner challenged the restructuring, but a court upheld the CBS actions as offering more value to its shareholders.[2]

Another common defensive tactic is the search for a **white knight**. A white knight is another person or company who would acquire Keggo but leave Keggo's management in place. White knights are often good for shareholders because they may bid up the takeover price but may be bad for shareholders if the board of directors shows favoritism to the white knight and accepts a lower offer from a white knight.

Takeovers are very costly, even to attempt, and the Keggo board in our chapter's opening scenario might have to provide inducements to a potential white knight. One inducement is a **no-shop clause**, in which Keggo promises not to seek out other acquirors to bid against the white knight. Keggo also might offer a **hello fee** (an upfront payment to the white knight to obtain an offer) or a **goodbye fee** or **break-up fee** (an agreement to pay the white knight's expenses if the white knight's efforts to acquire the company fail).

When a white knight is unavailable, a company may use a **white squire**. A white squire lacks the resources to buy the company in its entirety but can purchase a substantial number of the company's shares. Keggo would sell its **treasury shares** (those owned by the company) or issue new shares to a white squire, which would promise not to tender the shares to RBM. This would make it more difficult for RBM to acquire the percentage of shares necessary to take over Keggo. To interest a white squire, Keggo probably will have to sell shares to the white squire at a discount below market price or offer other inducements.

Another defensive tactic is the **lock-up**, which often operates in tandem with the white knight. In a lock-up, the company contracts to sell some

---

[2]*Turner Broadcasting System, Inc. v. CBS, Inc.,* 627 F. Supp. 901 (N.D. Ga. 1985).

asset to a third party (such as the white knight) at a below-market price. Lock-up agreements usually "flip-in," after an acquirer exceeds a certain percentage of shares in the target company.

A lock-up usually involves the company's **crown jewels**. Crown jewels are the especially valuable assets of the target corporation. Consider a diversified consumer products company. One division of this company may be especially profitable, supporting the other divisions. This profitable division is probably the target of the acquirer, who may sell off the less profitable divisions. If the target, such as Keggo, locks up a sale of the profitable division, or crown jewels, in the event of a takeover, Keggo becomes much less attractive to an acquirer such as RBM.

Courts tend to be skeptical of lock-ups, which seem primarily designed to favor some outside party, with little direct benefit to shareholders. The Delaware courts have suggested that a lock-up could be legitimate if it served to attract an outside party into the bidding for the company, thereby driving up share prices.

Another defensive tactic is the creation of an **employee stock option plan**, or **ESOP**. This is where the company issues its own shares to a plan in which its employees can participate in ownership, through stock options. The theory behind an ESOP is that the company's employees will be much less likely to tender their shares to an acquirer such as RBM. Many takeovers have resulted in massive layoffs, as the acquirer strives to make the company more efficient and pay off its debts. For this reason, employees may refuse to sell their shares in order to protect their jobs.

The Delaware courts have been favorable toward the ESOP approach, especially if it does not make a takeover impossible. Polaroid Corporation created a large ESOP in response to a takeover threat. The court upheld the ESOP because: (1) Polaroid had planned for some years to create a smaller ESOP, (2) the ESOP has corporate benefits such as improved employee morale, and (3) the ESOP created only a substantial, but not an insurmountable, barrier to a takeover.[3]

The Keggo directors might also decide to adopt **golden parachutes** for the company's officers and directors. Golden parachutes are lucrative severance arrangements. If the officers are fired after a takeover, they obtain a right to receive a substantial payment, such as two years' salary. If the costs of the golden parachutes are substantial in proportion to the size of the target company, they may deter a takeover. Some argue in favor of golden parachutes, however, noting that they help remove the self-interest of officers in opposing a takeover. Courts have been more skeptical of golden parachutes that were adopted when a takeover was already underway.

Some companies have sought to protect themselves from takeover through amendments to their certificate of incorporation or bylaws, sometimes called **shark repellants**. For example, a company might require a **supermajority vote** of shareholders to approve a merger or other significant corporate action. Keggo might adopt a bylaw requiring an 80 percent shareholder vote before a merger could be approved. This would force acquirers to obtain 80 percent of Keggo's shares (rather than 50 percent) before gaining control of the company.

Another structural provision to frustrate takeovers is the adoption of staggered terms for directors. This provision means that only a fraction of the board of directors is elected annually, and incumbent directors may stay in office and control the corporation for years. Of course, if the acquirer obtains enough shares, it may repeal the rule providing for the staggered terms.

Courts have generally upheld shark repellant structural policies, especially if these policies were approved by a vote of the company's shareholders. This is especially true if the policies are adopted in advance, when no tender offer for the company is pending. Courts are more skeptical if the policies are adopted when a specific acquirer has expressed interest and a takeover seems imminent.

A Delaware court struck down a shark repellant that would have required a sixty-day waiting period before a potential acquirer could have full use of its newly purchased shares. The court emphasized that the bylaw was adopted by the board of directors when a takeover was already proceeding and was adopted without getting the consent of their shareholders.[4]

---

[3]*Shamrock Holding, Inc. v. Polaroid Corp.*, 1 M&A Law Rep. 1250 (1989).

[4]*Datapoint Corp. v. Plaza Securities Co.*, 496 A.2d 1031 (Del. 1985).

One of the most dramatic defensive measures is a **management buyout (MBO)** or **self tender**. This occurs when a group of the directors and officers of the target corporation put together their own offer to buy the corporation. These individuals will usually require some financing assistance from a third party, such as a white knight. Management's self tender then competes with the acquirer's tender offer for control of the target company. The possibility of self-interested dealings is especially obvious in the case of an MBO.

"Just Say No"

Directors can often justify defensive measures as a means to get a higher price for their shareholders. Removable defensive measures can induce an acquirer to raise its tender offer price or attract competing bidders. It may be more difficult to justify defensive measures if the board desires to "just say no"—to fight off any acquisition and continue business as usual.

It can be legal to "just say no." Directors have no duty to sell their corporation or even to maximize the short-run value for their shareholders. Directors can maintain that continuing the business is in the long-run interest of shareholders.

The Delaware courts recently decided a critical "just say no" case, in *Paramount Communications, Inc. v. Time, Inc.*[5] Time and Warner Communications planned a merger, because the two companies fit well together and promised successful operations. Paramount then made a tender offer for Time. Time maintained its poison pill and restructured the merger with Warner. Time took on debt and undertook a friendly takeover of Warner. This made it impossible for Paramount to proceed with its tender offer to acquire Time.

Paramount sued Time, claiming that Time had denied its shareholders a chance to sell their shares. The court agreed that Paramount offered Time's shareholders more immediate cash than did the restructuring and merger. The court nevertheless upheld Time's actions, because the board was furthering a business plan that offered greater long-run benefits to shareholders of the merged Time/Warner corporation.

Auction Duties

Shareholders typically want an auction of their company, because a bidding war promises the best price for their shares. Corporate directors do not have a generalized duty to auction off their company, however, but may choose to attempt to run the company profitably. Once the directors decide that the shares in the corporation should be sold, the directors do assume a duty to get the best possible price for their shareholders, usually through an auction.

The auction duty was defined by the Delaware courts in *Revlon, Inc. v. MacAndrews & Forbes Holdings, Inc.*,[6] and is usually called the *Revlon* duty of directors. Revlon sought to fight off a takeover sponsored in part by MacAndrews & Forbes, by use of a poison pill, a white knight, a lock-up of the crown jewels, and other tactics. The court approved Revlon's initial defensive measures, including the poison pill, as a valuable tool to maximize the value of its shares. After Revlon found a white knight, however, the court held that the company showed improper favoritism for the white knight's offer. *Revlon* stands for the position that, once the directors decide to sell the corporation, they must conduct some sort of auction to obtain the highest bid for their shareholders. The board cannot selectively maintain defensive measures against some but not all bidders.

Delaware courts have applied the *Revlon* duty to any sale of control of a corporation. Suppose that the directors of a corporation want to agree to a friendly takeover by an acquirer. The directors cannot simply accept the friendly takeover but must investigate the possibility of obtaining a higher offer by seeking out competing acquirers.

The courts have not interpreted *Revlon* to always require a formal auction of the company. Thus, directors need not publicly announce the sale of the company and set a date for final and best offers. Rather, a company need only explore the market for possible interested acquirers.

The legal difficulties of conducting an auction and attempting to maximize value for shareholders are illustrated in the following decision. This case was heard in federal court but applied the corporate state law of Delaware.

---

[5]15 *Del. J. Corp.* L. 700 (1990).

[6]506 A.2d 173 (Del. 1986).

■ Case 8.3
**Samjens Partners I v.
Burlington Industries, Inc.**
United States District Court for the
Southern District of New York, 1987
663 F. Supp. 614

Background and Facts   *Samjens Partners I owned about 13 percent of the stock of Burlington Industries, Inc., and on May 6, 1987, made a tender offer for Burlington at $67/share. Burlington's board of directors rejected this offer as inadequate. The Morgan Stanley Group, Inc., subsequently expressed interest in a friendly takeover of Burlington.*

After Burlington threatened a self tender, Samjens increased its price to $72/share on May 15. On May 20, Burlington and Morgan agreed to merge, with Morgan offering $76/share for all shares of Burlington. Burlington agreed to suspend its self tender, if Morgan's tender offer succeeded. Burlington also agreed to a "no shop" clause promising not to seek competing bidders and a $25 million "break-up fee" for Morgan, should its tender offer fail. The board refused to pay Morgan a $7 million "hello fee."

The board recommended that its shareholders accept the Morgan offer. On May 28, Samjens raised its offer price to $77/share. Shortly thereafter, Morgan raised its offer to $78/share. Samjens sued Burlington to obtain a preliminary injunction against any merger between Burlington and Morgan. Among the main claims brought by Samjens, it alleged that the Burlington directors violated their fiduciary duties to shareholders by favoring the Morgan bid and conducting an unfairly biased auction of the company.

KRAM, U.S. District Judge.

* * * *

c. The First Samjens Tender Offer

The Board met five days after the first Samjens offer. After viewing a long, division-by-division presentation about the value of Burlington, the Board reflected the $67 offer as inadequate. The Board then authorized the investment bankers to negotiate with other parties, and authorized the self-tender offer. The self-tender did not foreclose bidding, and in fact seemed to enhance it—Samjens followed soon after by raising its initial bid to $72 per share. At this point, the auction had not yet begun. Although the Board had authorized its investment bankers to negotiate with interested parties, it still preserved the right to seek other alternatives to maximize shareholder value. The Board was still entitled to act in a defensive posture to ward off what it deemed, after due deliberation, to be an inadequate tender offer.

d. The Approval of the Morgan Stanley Merger Agreement

On May 19, the Board was informed that approximately 25 entities had expressed interest in Burlington. Only Morgan, however, was willing to make a bid. When the Board decided to enter into negotiations with Morgan, it was clear that Burlington would be sold, the auction began, and the Board was no longer defending the company, but attempting to get the best bid for it. The evidence indicates the Board fulfilled its duty to do so.

The negotiations with Morgan lasted for two days. The Board members read the merger agreement carefully and went through it with outside counsel. The price the Board secured from Morgan was $76 per share, $4 per share higher than the highest outstanding bid.

The Board negotiated strictly with Morgan about the other terms of the agreement. It rejected the $7 million hello fee. The Board was not happy with the break-up fee, but after investigating it, the Board realized that such a fee was standard, and that the amount of the fee was fair and within the normal range. The Board also realized that Morgan would back out of the deal without the fee, and justifiably decided to agree to it. The Board also insisted on changing the no-shop clause to a "window-shop" clause. The new clause allows the Board to look at other bids, but not solicit them. If the Board sees a higher bid, it can accept it.

The merger agreement is not so onerous as to end the auction or exclude other bidders. The breakup fee and related expenses total approximately 2 percent of the value of the company, leaving other parties free to bid. There is also no auction-ending lock-up agreement. In fact, the merger did not end the auction: in response to the merger, Samjens increased its bid to $77, and Morgan has responded with a bid of $78. Thus, the merger agreement has increased the value to the shareholders by $6 per share, and Samjens has hinted that it might make a higher bid.

The evidence also indicates that the Board reached all of its decisions after thorough consultation with its financial and legal advisors. Its decisions were based on reasonable and thorough investigations, and its conclusions were justifiable and in good faith. The Board did not rush. Its investment bankers solicited bids over an eight-day period. When the Board was assured that Morgan's bid was the best, it pursued its negotiations with Morgan over a two-day period. The Board fulfilled its duty of care in the takeover contest, and its decision is entitled to the protection of the business judgment rule.

In short, if the procedure the Board followed and the merger agreement it approved were not protected by the business judgment rule, the Court doubts that any merger agreements would ever be allowed in the context of takeover contests. This case indicates that this would be detrimental to shareholders. The merger agreement approved in this case has resulted, so far, in an increase of $6 per share in the price that will be paid to shareholders.

Plaintiffs' version of how the auction should have been conducted is unrealistic and ignores a number of important factors. First, the Board was operating under time pressure caused by Samjens. The Samjens offer was to expire on June 3. Thus, when the board met on May 19, it had only two weeks to find an alternative to an inadequate bid. Morgan was the only party ready to make a bid, all the other parties needed additional time. Second, although Morgan might have been Burlington's white knight, it was not Burlington's patron saint. Morgan was involved in negotiations with Burlington because it was an opportunity to make money. Thus, it wanted a response to its bid quickly, it wanted compensation for the risk it was undertaking in tying up its capital, and it did not want to serve as a "stalking horse" and have its bid shopped around. In light of this, however, the Board spent two days negotiating the merger agreement, and bargained vigorously with Morgan.

Decision and Remedy   *The court found that Samjens was unlikely to succeed on the merits of its claim and therefore denied its motion for a preliminary injunction.*

State Anti-Takeover Statutes

State governments have passed a series of laws to make corporate takeovers more difficult. The first set of anti-takeover laws ran into constitutional problems. The primary constitutional problem is in the supremacy clause of the United States Constitution, which preempts state laws that conflict with federal laws.

The federal government adopted the Williams Act to regulate tender offers (discussed in the chapter on securities law and regulation). This act required extensive disclosure on the part of tender offerors and created procedural rules for such offers.

Some early anti-takeover statutes were deemed contrary to the Williams Act, and therefore unconstitutional. Courts held that the Williams Act purposefully allowed for tender offers, when properly regulated. Tender offers gave shareholders the right to sell their shares for a premium price. If the anti-takeover statutes made tender offers virtually impossible, they contradicted the purpose of the Williams Act. Anti-takeover laws could also unconstitutionally interfere with interstate commerce, if they sought to regulate companies incorporated in other states.

States responded by passing a new type of anti-takeover law, called **control-share acquisition statutes**. Delaware passed such a control-share acquisition law. This approach has been found to be constitutional.

Delaware's control-share acquisition law operates as follows. The statute is triggered by an acquirer's purchase of a control share, statutorily defined as 15 percent or more of a company's stock. The statute prohibits the control shareholder from voting its shares to force a second-step merger of the corporation for three years unless certain conditions are met.

A second-step merger can be conducted if the acquirer obtains 85 percent or more of the company's shares or the board of directors and two-thirds of the remaining shareholders authorize the acquirer to do so. This statute makes it more difficult for an acquirer to take control of a corporation. Takeovers are still possible, though, if the acquirer makes a good enough offer to obtain 85 percent of the shares. They are also possible if the acquirer offers a good enough deal in the second-step merger to obtain the approval of two-thirds of the remaining shareholders.

The Delaware statute also provides for a company's directors to decide on its application to their corporation. The directors may decide that they want to facilitate a takeover of their company and make the statute inapplicable. This action may improve the market value of the company's shares.

Greenmail

One controversial issue in mergers and acquisitions is the payment of **greenmail** to a potential acquirer. Greenmail arises in the following situation. Suppose RBM purchases 5 percent of Keggo's shares and threatens a takeover. Instead of adopting defensive measures, Keggo's threatened directors negotiate with RBM. They agree to buy RBM's 5 percent holdings for a substantial premium (such as 20 percent) over the price paid by RBM, thereby eliminating the takeover threat. One study found that American corporations spent over $3 billion a year in this type of greenmail payment.

Greenmail is criticized for entrenching the board, costing most minority shareholders the opportunity for a higher price, and rewarding the greenmailer for merely threatening a takeover. The courts, though, have often upheld greenmail payments.

In one prominent Delaware case, an investment group, known as the Bass Brothers, purchased 20 percent of Texaco, Inc., and proposed what the Texaco board of directors considered to be an unfavorable joint venture. Texaco then repurchased the Bass Brothers Texaco stock for a premium over the market value. A court held that this payment was legal, because the Bass Brothers presented a threat to Texaco, and the greenmail payment eliminated that threat.[7]

The Delaware court appears to treat greenmail as much like other defensive measures, to be evaluated under the business judgment rule or the *Unocal* "threat/proportionality" test described above. Some companies (including Alcoa, Mobil, and Anheuser-Busch) have adopted anti-greenmail provisions in their corporate charters or bylaws to prevent the practice. The Securities and Exchange Commission (SEC) has opposed payment of greenmail and insisted on

---

[7]*Polk v. Good*, 507 A.2d 531 (Del. 1986).

full disclosure of any greenmail payments. Courts in California and New York have overturned greenmail payments, applying a stricter standard than in Delaware.

Although greenmail is widely criticized, it still occurs and can be disguised. After a well-known acquirer purchased five percent of Chesebrough-Ponds, that company repurchased his shares but only at market price. The company also purchased unrelated assets from the acquirer, however, at a price considered to be in excess of their value.[8]

LBOs, MBOs, and Second-Step Mergers

Leveraged buyouts, or LBOs, involve an acquirer's borrowing much of the money necessary to undertake an acquisition. In one recent year, there were over three hundred LBOs with a total acquisition value of more than $40 billion. Federal tax laws actually encourage the use of borrowed money to acquire a corporation.

A substantial number of LBOs are management buyouts, or MBOs. MBOs may be a defensive response to an outside takeover threat or may simply involve a desire by a company's directors and officers to own the company that they manage.

As in most takeovers, the MBO involves a second-step merger, adopted after the acquirer obtains a controlling number of shares. This

[8]*N.Y. Times*, April 10, 1984, at D3.

merger, which eliminates all minority shareholders, takes the company private (under the complete ownership of the acquirer). The success of the second-step merger is often crucial to the acquirer. The merger enables the acquirer to reap all the benefits of the takeover, without sharing these benefits with the remaining minority shareholders.

The key legal problem involves the fairness of the price offered in the second-step merger. As the controlling shareholder can force the merger on minority shareholders, there is a danger that the acquirer will provide an unfairly low price to the minority. Under state law, the controlling shareholder has a duty of fairness to minority shareholders. The duty is especially great in an MBO, given the directors' fiduciary duties to their shareholders.

To help ensure the fairness of the second-step merger consideration, directors usually obtain a valuation of the company from an outside banker, called a **fairness opinion**. The content of this opinion must be fully disclosed to minority shareholders. Simple use of an investment banker may be insufficient, however, and courts have encouraged companies to submit the price to a vote for approval by minority shareholders or to create an independent negotiating committee of directors that are not participating in the MBO.

There is no procedural recipe to guarantee fairness, however. The following case reviewed the fairness of a second-step merger that did obtain a fairness opinion and approval by a majority of minority shareholders.

Case 8.4
Weinberger v. UOP, Inc.
Supreme Court of Delaware, 1983
457 A.2d 701

Background and Facts   *Signal Companies, Inc., was interested in acquiring UOP, Inc., and initiated a 1975 tender offer at $21/share. The tender offer succeeded, and Signal acquired 50.5 percent of UOP's shares. In 1978, Signal decided to acquire the remaining 49.5 percent of UOP shares in a second-step merger. A valuation study for Signal by Arledge-Chitiea concluded that UOP would be a good investment at any price up to $24/share. Signal decided to pay about $20 or $21 per share for the remaining shares of UOP. UOP's chief executive officer, who was recently appointed by Signal, found this price to be fair. The market price of UOP's shares was $14.50/share.*

On February 28, 1978, Signal announced the planned merger. The UOP directors retained Lehman Brothers to provide a fairness opinion on the proposed price. On March 6, Lehman Brothers opined that

$20 or $21/share was fair. The boards of Signal and UOP both met that day and approved the merger. The merger was submitted to a vote of UOP shareholders, who overwhelmingly favored the merger.

Dissenting UOP shareholders filed suit to challenge the fairness of the merger. The trial court held that the terms of the merger were fair and ruled for the defendants. The shareholder plaintiffs appealed.

MOORE, Justice.

* * * *

A public policy, existing through the years, and derived from a profound knowledge of human characteristics and motives, has established a rule that demands of a corporate officer or director, peremptorily and inexorably, the most scrupulous observance of his duty, not only affirmatively to protect the interests of the corporation committed to his charge, but also to refrain from doing anything that would work injury to the corporation, or to deprive it of profit or advantage which his skill and ability might properly bring to it, or to enable it to make in the reasonable and lawful exercise of its powers. The rule that requires an undivided and unselfish loyalty to the corporation demands that there shall be no conflict between duty and self-interest.

Given the absence of any attempt to structure this transaction on an arm's length basis, Signal cannot escape the effects of the conflicts it faced, particularly when its designees on UOP's board did not totally abstain from participation in the matter. There is no "safe harbor" for such divided loyalties in Delaware. When directors of a Delaware corporation are on both sides of a transaction, they are required to demonstrate their utmost good faith and the most scrupulous inherent fairness of the bargain.

* * * *

The structure of the transaction, again, was Signal's doing. So far as negotiations were concerned, it is clear that they were modest at best. Crawford, Signal's man at UOP, never really talked price with Signal, except to accede to its management's statements on the subject, and to convey to Signal the UOP outside directors' view that as between the $20-$21 range under consideration, it would have to be $21. The latter is not a surprising outcome, but hardly arm's length negotiations. Only the protection of benefits for UOP's key employees and the issue of Lehman Brothers' fee approached any concept of bargaining.

As we have noted, the matter of disclosure to the UOP directors was wholly flawed by the conflicts of interest raised by the Arledge-Chitiea report. All of those conflicts were resolved by Signal in its own favor without divulging any aspect of them to UOP.

This cannot but undermine a conclusion that this merger meets any reasonable test of fairness. The outside UOP directors lacked one material piece of information generated by two of their colleagues, but shared only with Signal.

True, the UOP board had the Lehman Brothers' fairness opinion, but that firm has been blamed by the plaintiff for the hurried task it performed, when more properly the responsibility for this lies with Signal. There was no disclosure of the circumstances surrounding the rather cursory preparation of the Lehman Brothers' fairness opinion. Instead, the impression was given UOP's minority that a careful study had been made, when in fact speed was the hallmark, and Mr. Glanville, Lehman's partner in charge of the matter, and also a UOP director, having spent the weekend in Vermont, brought a draft of the "fairness opinion letter" to the UOP directors' meeting on March 6, 1978 with the price left blank. We can only conclude from the record that the rush imposed on Lehman Brothers by Signal's timetable contributed to the difficulties under which this investment banking firm attempted to perform its responsibilities. Yet, none of this was disclosed to UOP's minority.

Finally, the minority stockholders were denied the critical information that Signal considered a price of $24 to be a good investment. Since this would have meant over $17,000,000 more to the minority, we cannot conclude that the shareholder vote was an informed one. Under the circumstances, an approval by a majority of the minority was meaningless.

Decision and Remedy   *The Delaware Supreme court reversed the trial court judgment for defendants and remanded the case for further proceedings to establish a fair price for the plaintiff shareholders.*

Courts have occasionally considered the motive of the majority shareholders in forcing the merger. In one case, the majority shareholders adopted a going-private merger in order to eliminate a lawsuit brought against them by minority shareholders for earlier breaches of duty. The court found that this action violated the duty of fair dealing.[9]

State corporation law also provides shareholders with the right of **appraisal** in these second-step mergers. If a shareholder believes that the consideration offered is unfair, the shareholder can dissent by voting against the merger and then going to court for an appraisal of the fair value of the shares. The appraisal remedy, however, is both costly and risky. The court could value the shares at less than the merger consideration.

▄▄▄ Federal Regulation of Takeovers

While most significant regulation of takeovers occurs under state corporations laws, federal laws also regulate aspects of the process. The 1968 Williams Act establishes rules for tender offers, which require filings with the Securities and Exchange Commission for the disclosure of key information to shareholders. The requirements of the Williams Act are discussed in detail in the preceding chapter on securities law and regulation.

---

[9]*Merritt v. Colonial Foods, Inc.*, 505 A.2d 757 (Del. Ch. 1986).

Federal antitrust laws can also affect mergers and acquisitions. The government through the Federal Trade Commission (FTC) can prohibit mergers that substantially injure competition. Thus, the FTC might sue to halt a takeover of Pepsi-Cola by Coca-Cola, or vice versa. The authority for this regulation is found in the Clayton Act. The restrictions of antitrust law are discussed in detail in Chapter 47 of *West's Business Law, Fifth Edition* and in Chapter 22 of *West's Legal Environment of Business.*

One additional antitrust law, the Hart-Scott-Rodino Antitrust Improvements Act of 1976, is uniquely applicable to takeovers. This law can apply to an acquisition in which one party (either the acquirer or the target) has sales or assets of at least $100 million and in which the other party has sales or assets of at least $10 million. Unless one of the Act's technical exemptions applies, the acquiring party must file information on the acquisition with the Federal Trade Commission.

After the filing, the Hart-Scott-Rodino Act then imposes a waiting period for the acquisition. In the case of a cash tender offer, this waiting period is fifteen days. In other types of acquisitions, the waiting period is thirty days. During this waiting period, the FTC or the Department of Justice considers the potential anticompetitive effects of the takeover. The acquisition cannot proceed until the waiting period elapses or the government expressly authorizes the takeover.

```
■ Ethical
  Perspectives
```

Stakeholder Rights

A current ethical controversy involves the rights of a corporation's **stakeholders** in a takeover. Stakeholders are persons such as the corporation's employees or those holding the company's bonds. Sometimes, the entire community surrounding a major manufacturing plant is considered a stakeholder.

The ethical problem arises in the following situation. Suppose that Keggo, the natural resource company, is trading at about $25/share. RBM makes a takeover offer at $50/share. RBM's offer is highly leveraged, however, and if RBM succeeds in the takeover, Keggo's stakeholders are likely to suffer. RBM may sell off plants and equipment in order to pay off their debt. The new company may go bankrupt. Employees may lose their jobs, and bondholders may lose much of the value of their investments, as the company loses its ability to pay off its debts.

This is not an uncommon situation. A takeover may appear to be an excellent deal for a company's shareholders but a threat to the company's stakeholders. What are the board's ethical duties to the stakeholders?

Corporate law makes the board of directors into fiduciaries for the corporation's shareholders. The directors are legally required to manage the company in the best interest of the shareholders. Traditional corporate law would prohibit the directors from considering the interests of stakeholders and force them to act only in the interests of shareholders.

This traditional approach has received considerable criticism. Some states have amended their corporate laws specifically to authorize directors to consider the interests of stakeholders in their management decisions. This action only permits directors to consider stakeholders, however, and does not dictate the nature of that consideration.

Although the traditional rule may seem somewhat harsh, there is justification for considering only shareholder interests. The shareholder owns the company, after all. The capitalist system generally lets persons sell their property for their own interests. This rule promotes economic efficiency by placing property into the hands of those who value it the most and can best profit from it.

Advocates of takeovers argue that they make corporations more efficient and help the economy overall. While some individual stakeholders may suffer the loss of jobs, a more efficient economy should provide more-than-compensating benefits.

Even such takeover advocates must concede that the system has not worked perfectly. Some takeovers have created enormous profits for a few, while bankrupting companies and throwing thousands out of work. The junk bonds created in LBOs have played a significant role in the collapse of some banks, costing the government billions in bail-out costs for the depositors.

There is a strong ethical argument for considering stakeholder interests. The company has made something of a promise to bondholders. In order to borrow money, the company must assure lenders that they will be repaid. While a company may not have made such a promise to its employees, layoffs cause undeniably severe financial harm to families. While shareholders must retain the right to sell their shares, the board of directors arguably should prefer takeover offers that keep the company running, even at some loss of profit to shareholders.

■ **International Perspectives**

Foreign Takeover Laws

Foreign companies often present promising takeover opportunities. Purchase of a Japanese or European company can provide a United States company with a valuable entry point into a large foreign market. The laws of most foreign nations, however, make mergers and acquisitions somewhat more difficult than in the U.S.

In Japan, there are thousands of corporate acquisitions every year, but the vast majority of these are friendly takeovers. Although Japan allows for hostile takeovers, few are conducted. Part of the difficulty in a Japanese hostile takeover is cultural. The Japanese business culture considers hostile takeovers to be almost unethical and stigmatizes the acquirer. Even should the takeover succeed, the acquirer will suffer in future business relations with other Japanese companies.

Japanese law also affects takeover prospects. Japan's federal law on tender offers is similar to the United States' Williams Act, but contains a provision that requires a ten-day advance notice for a tender offer. This limits the speed and flexibility of the acquirer. In addition, Japanese law does not provide for the second-step merger even after a tender offer succeeds. Many Japanese companies have placed their shares with other companies who act as white squires in most takeover attempts.

The various nations of the European Community (EC) still have differing laws affecting mergers and acquisitions. As a rule, takeovers are more difficult than in the United States. In most European countries, the directors have a wide scope of allowable defensive actions to fend off a hostile takeover. French law restricts defensive measures after a takeover bid has been announced but generally permits such actions in advance of a bid. Italy allows directors a broad range to adopt defensive actions and permits compulsory second-stage mergers only if the acquirer obtains 90 percent of the company's shares. In The Netherlands, the target's employees have the legal power to prevent its acquisition.

The United Kingdom is an exception to the difficulty of European takeovers. Acquisitions, even hostile ones, are relatively common in the U.K. The applicable Code on Take-overs and Mergers was adopted privately by the securities industry and not government legislation. This Code is dedicated to the protection of shareholder interests and limits defensive measures taken without shareholder approval. The Code also regulates takeover offers. Under the Code, any person who acquires 30 percent or more of a company's shares, must offer to acquire all the remaining shares at the highest price paid for the company's shares within the prior twelve months. In some circumstances, the acquirer must offer to pay cash (rather than securities) for minority shares.

There are currently proposals for a new EC Directive to harmonize takeover laws throughout the European Community. This effort is just beginning, however, and its nature is still quite uncertain. In the interim, U.S. corporations are buying companies in Europe. In 1991, the major United States company Philip Morris bought a Swiss producer of candy products, Jacobs Suchard, for $3.8 billion.

Questions and Case Problems

1. Trusts holding 30 percent of the stock in Anderson Clayton were about to expire. Seeing a takeover opportunity, a group of bidders announced an interest in acquiring all the Anderson Clayton stock at $54 per share. The Clayton board of directors then made a two-tiered self tender offer for 65 percent of the company's stock at $60 per share, plus the sale of shares to an ESOP. The group of acquirers argued that the two-tiered self tender was an unlawful defensive measure that prevented shareholders from making a choice between competing acquirers. Should a court enjoin the self tender? [*AC Acquisition Corp. v. Anderson Clayton & Co.*, 519 A.2d 103 (Del. Ch. 1986)].

2. Nuclear Company was a small corporation that had two million shares outstanding. About 20 percent of these shares were held by Nuclear's officers and directors. Armco approached the Nuclear directors and offered to buy the company for $25 per share, based on the report of a financial adviser. Armco made this proposal as a friendly takeover and promised to retain Nuclear's officers in their positions. The Nuclear directors, who were also officers, believed that the takeover would facilitate the company's expansion and

voted to approve a merger agreement with Armco. Minority shareholders in Nuclear sued the directors, claiming that they had breached their fiduciary duty in not seeking other offers. Did the directors breach their fiduciary duty?

3. Grand Metropolitan made a tender offer for all shares of Pillsbury at $63 per share in cash. The Pillsbury board decided that this price was inadequate, based on the report of an independent financial adviser, and adopted defensive measures. This included adoption of a poison pill, the spin-off of the company's Burger King subsidiary, and the sale of some of its other restaurant properties. Grand Metropolitan complained that these defensive measures made its takeover either impossible or unprofitable and sued to enjoin the implementation of these measures. Are the Pillsbury defensive measures a lawful response to a takeover threat? [*Grand Metropolitan PLC v. Pillsbury Co.*, 558 A.2d 1049 (Del. Ch. 1988)].

4. Universal Foods adopted a poison pill. Not long thereafter, Amanda Acquisition made a highly leveraged tender offer for all shares of Universal at $30.50 per share in cash. The Universal board simply rejected the offer and refused to redeem the poison pill, stating that it was in the company's best interest to remain independent. They also claimed that the tender offer contained false and misleading statements about Universal's prospects and the characteristics of the offer. Amanda sued to compel Universal to redeem the poison pill. Should the court require the redemption of the pill? [*Amanda Acquisition Corp. v. Universal Foods Corp.*, 708 F. Supp. 984 (E.D. Wis.), *aff'd on other grounds*, 877 F.2d 496 (7th Cir. 1989)].

5. After observing unusual activity in its stock, the board of directors of TW Services adopted a poison pill. Soon thereafter, SWT Acquisition made a tender offer for 31.5 percent of TW's stock at $29 per share. The offer was subject to a condition that the offer be approved by the TW board of directors. The TW board of directors considered the price to be unfair and refused to take any action. SWT asked a court to enjoin the TW poison pill and reconsider its offer. Should the court provide SWT its requested relief? [*TW Services, Inc. v. SWT Acquisition Corp.*, 14 Del. J. Corp. Law 1169 (Del. Ch. 1989)].

CHAPTER NINE

Insurance Law

KEY BACKGROUND

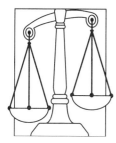

The essential background for this chapter on insurance law is found in Chapter 53 of *West's Business Law, Fifth Edition*. This chapter also covers insurance law. Among the important points to remember from this chapter are:

- the features necessary for a beneficiary to have an enforceable insurable interest

- central features of insurance contracts and their coverage

- the many types of insurance available in the marketplace

* * *

Insurance coverage has enormous importance for modern businesses. Today's companies are subject to enormous liability under a variety of laws involving product liability, employment law, and standard torts such as negligence. An enormous source of future liability is in environmental law.

A judgment under the above laws may amount to millions of dollars, including punitive damages. Such a judgment may bankrupt an otherwise successful company. The ability to insure against the risk of such judgments is therefore important to all industries.

In addition, insurance companies themselves represent an important business sector. Insurance is a multibillion-dollar enterprise, with its own risks.

Insurance law helps balance the interests of insurers and insured, so that effective insurance protection remains available.

Insurance Coverage Issues

Among the most common insurance cases today are disputes over the coverage of insurance policies. When an insured company suffers a loss, it is likely to claim that the insurance policy covers the loss and that insurance should provide compensation. The insurance company may maintain that the loss is outside the policy's coverage. The policy itself may not expressly address the issue.

This section discusses the standards for determining coverage, particularly the "reasonable expectations" doctrine. It also discusses certain exclusions from coverage, and applies the standards to the most significant contemporary issue—insurance coverage of hazardous waste and pollution liabilities.

Reasonable Expectations Doctrine

An insurance policy is a contract, and, like other contracts, its terms are interpreted according to the intent of the parties. Most insurance contracts are considered **contracts of adhesion**, however. This means that the insurance company has written the contract itself and presented it to the insured, with little opportunity for negotiation over contract terms. In this circumstance, the courts focus primarily on the intent of the insured party.

The **reasonable expectations doctrine** was developed to protect the insured. In the United States around 1800 fire insurance companies would issue policies through form contracts that contained unclear provisions. If a fire occurred, the large insurance companies would employ a battery of lawyers to dispute coverage, and individual policyholders had a difficult time recovering. Courts therefore developed the reasonable expectations doctrine.

Courts interpreting insurance contracts emphasize the "reasonable expectations" of the insured party. The court analyzes the insurance contract with an eye to what the insured party thought it was obtaining. A closely related doctrine is called the **ambiguity doctrine**. This states that any ambiguous, or unclear, policy provisions are to be construed against the insurance company and in favor of the insured.

A leading case under the reasonable expectations doctrine involved an Iowa store that purchased a "Mercantile Burglary and Robbery Policy." The policy provided burglary protection for the insured's warehouse, but specifically limited protection to cases in which the burglar left "visible marks" of entry on the outside of the building. The warehouse was robbed by a burglar who entered through a Plexiglass door and left no visible marks. The Iowa Supreme Court held that the insurance company nevertheless was required to compensate for the burglary losses. The court stressed that the limitation to cases of "visible marks" was "buried" in the definitions section of the insurance policy and that a reasonable person would expect the policy to cover this episode.[1]

The reasonable expectations of the insured party often arise from the insurance company itself. Statements by insurance agents may create reasonable expectations in coverage, even if the policy itself is contrary.

A slightly different circumstance concerns a provision in an insurance policy that is somewhat ambiguous in its coverage. If a provision is ambiguous, courts generally will enforce that provision for the benefit of the insured party, under the reasonable expectations doctrine.

Even a perfectly clear term may be ambiguous in its application. For example, a woman was covered by her husband's automobile insurance policy as a "family member." She separated from her husband and continued to drive the car. After she suffered an accident, the insurance company denied coverage, contending that she lived at another site and was no longer a covered family member. A court held that she was covered, under the reasonable expectations doctrine.[2]

The reasonable expectations rule does not mean that the insurance company always loses. Rather, the rule places the burden on the insurance company to inform its policy holder of the true scope of the policy, including its limitations. When unexpected events occur that arguably fall within the policy, the insured will get the benefit of a presumption of coverage.

The key question in coverage is the intention of the parties to the insurance contract. The following recent case illustrates how clear intentions can override even the presence of an ambiguous contract.

[1]*C&J Fertilizer, Inc. v. Allied Mutual Insurance Co.*, 227 N.W.2d 169 (Iowa 1975).

[2]*Gordinier v. Aetna Casualty and Surety Co.*, 742 P.2d 277 (Ariz. 1987).

■ **Case 9.1**
Aromin v.
State Farm Fire &
Casualty Company
United States Court of Appeals,
Eleventh Circuit, 1990
908 F.2d 812

Background and Facts *W.R. Matix was involved in a violent streetside fight with his girlfriend. Thomas Aromin drove up to assist, and Matix and Aromin began to argue after Matix's girlfriend left the scene. Matix then shot Aromin in the groin from six feet away and caused Aromin to become a paraplegic, with damages of approximately $1 million. Matix was insured by State Farm Fire & Casualty Company under a personal liability umbrella policy. Aromin demanded payment of his damages from State Farm, which refused. Aromin then sued to recover. Both sides moved for summary judgment.*

HOEVELER, District Judge.

* * * *

Matix was insured by State Farm under a personal liability umbrella policy at the time of the shooting. The insurance policy provides that it will cover, in its section labeled "personal injury:"

a. bodily injury, sickness, disease, shock, mental anguish or mental injury.

b. false arrest, false imprisonment, wrongful eviction, wrongful detention, malicious prosecution or humiliation.

c. libel, slander, defamation of character or invasion of rights or privacy.

d. assault and battery.

By express terms, therefore, the insurance policy appears to extend coverage for assault and battery, the intentional tort complained of in this case. The policy also proclaims, however, that it will not provide coverage:

[I]f you intended to cause the personal injury or property damage. We will not apply this exclusion if:

a. you were acting in good faith to protect people or property; and

b. your actions were not fraudulent, criminal or malicious.

The state court found that the insured was not acting in good faith to protect people or property and that his actions were not negligent, but were criminal in nature. The parties do not contest this finding.

Discussion   Under Florida law, if the provisions of an insurance contract conflict, the contract must be resolved to afford maximum coverage. *Nu-Air Mfg. Co. v. Frank B. Hall & Co.*, 822 F.2d 987 (11th Cir.1987). If the two provisions in the instant policy–one covering assault and battery, the other excluding coverage for intentional torts–are found to conflict, the court must resolve the question of which provision prevails.

On the other hand, it is a cardinal principle of construction that, if reasonably possible, no part of a contract should be taken as eliminated or stricken by some other part. *Burton v. Travelers Ins. Co.* [341 Mich. 30], 67 N.W.2d 54, 55 (MI 1954). The insurer argues that the terms of its contract do not conflict because coverage extended only to the civil torts of assault and battery, not to criminal conduct. The insurer explains that civil battery—covered under the policy—requires only the general intent to cause a harmful or offensive contact, resulting in a non-consensual contact, whereas the intentional injury exclusion applies to those situations where the actor intended to cause the specific result.

* * * *

While State Farm included coverage for "assault and battery" in its list of covered circumstances, it is equally clear and without ambiguity that it intended to *exclude* coverage where the insured . . ."intended to cause the personal injury . . ." and that the exclusion would *not* apply where the actions were not ". . .criminal or malicious." That the exclusion applies to the circumstances of this case seems quite clear. The question remains, though, what of the coverage for assault and battery. Assistance in finding the answer is provided by reference to the *Appelstein* case. * * * Note also part (a) of the section describing the inapplicability of the exclusion. Where one is acting in "good faith" to protect people or property, the exclusion does not apply. While the apparent conflict in the described provisions seems to create a tension in interpretation that tension is more apparent than real. There can, no doubt, be circumstances where one is charged with an assault (threatened battery) and battery (an uninvited touching or contact) where the insured intended no harm under the circumstances. Clearly, in this case, the act was criminal (the shooting of another at close range) and the injury (or even death) intended. The coverage afforded by the policy should not and does not apply under such circumstances.

Decision and Remedy   *The court granted summary judgment for the defendant insurer.*

Policy Exclusions

Most insurance policies contain some general exclusions of coverage. These include exclusion of damages that the insured expects at the time of the contract and preexisting conditions applicable to the insured.

Expected or Intended Clause

Comprehensive insurance policies generally afford no coverage for damages that the insured party expected to occur or intended to occur. Thus, a company cannot take out a policy to protect against a harm that is almost sure to happen.

For example, a county operated a landfill in which various types of waste were dumped. The landfill was required to pay damages for the release of pollutants and sought insurance coverage for these payments. A court denied coverage, because the landfill company was aware of the pollution problem years before the insurance policy and still continued its dumping practices. Coverage was therefore excluded under the policy's expected or intended clause.[3]

In determining whether a risk was expected or intended, most courts use an objective standard. This means that the court does not look to the actual knowledge of the insured party. Instead, the court considers whether a reasonable person in the position of the insured would have expected this type of damage to occur.

It is important to note that awareness of a possible future harm does not deny insurance coverage. The very act of insurance suggests recognition of the possibility of damages. Courts invoke the expected or intended clause to deny insurance coverage only when there is a "substantial probability" or a "substantial certainty" of the occurrence of damages.

Loss-in-Progress Clause

Insurance policies generally excluded coverage for a preexisting condition or a "loss-in-progress." Thus, suppose Doug Murray visits his doctor, and she diagnoses him as suffering from lung cancer. Doug then runs next door and takes out a cancer insurance policy. The insurance company probably need not make payments on Doug's lung cancer costs, because it was a preexisting condition at the time of insurance.

In one recent case, a company purchased property that contained hazardous waste and purchased a comprehensive insurance policy covering the property. Soon thereafter, the insured was sued for cleanup expenses on the property. Insurance coverage for the lawsuit was denied, because evidence showed that the company had commissioned an investigation of the property that informed it of the exact nature of the pollution problem at the site. The damages, therefore, were part of a known loss-in-progress that was excluded from insurance coverage.

---

[3]*County of Broome v. Aetna Casualty & Surety Co.*, 540 N.Y.S.2d 620 (N.Y. App. Div. 1989).

Environmental Coverage

No insurance law issue is more important than that of coverage for pollution harms and waste cleanup costs. Liability from this source will amount to tens of billions of dollars in coming years, as described in the chapter on environmental regulation and liability. The extent of insurance coverage for these costs is still hotly disputed.

The first important issue in environmental coverage is whether environmental cleanup costs mandated by the Comprehensive Environmental Response, Compensation and Liability Act of 1980 ("CERCLA" or "Superfund") are damages covered by insurance policies. Billions of dollars are spent in these cleanups every year.

Insurance companies argue that the policy term "damages" should be given its precise legal meaning—damages are those paid in response to an action in law. CERCLA cleanups, however, are considered to be in equity rather than in law. Insurers argue that these costs are not damages. A discussion of the differences between equity and damages at law is found in Chapter 1 of *West's Business Law, Fifth Edition* and in Chapter 2 of *West's Legal Environment of Business*.

Some states, such as Maryland and Maine, have agreed that cleanup costs are not damages. More states have found that hazardous waste cleanup costs are damages within insurance policies. In a number of states, the reasonable expectations doctrine was applied to this issue and cleanup costs were deemed to be covered damages. For example, a Michigan court held that the "average person would not engage in a complex comparison of legal and equitable remedies in order to define 'damages,'" but would conclude based on the plain meaning of the words that the cleanup costs imposed on [the insured] under CERCLA would constitute an obligation to pay damages."[4]

Even if cleanup costs are considered to be damages, insurers have sought to deny coverage under a policy's **pollution exclusion**. In the mid-1970s, most standard comprehensive liability policies had provisions that excluded coverage for pollution. These exclusions, however, had their own exception that provided coverage for "sudden and accidental" releases of pollution. A typical pollution exclusion clause would read as follows:

> This Policy does not apply to bodily injury or property damage (1) arising out of pollution or contamination caused by oil or (2) arising out of the discharge, dispersal, release or escape of smoke, vapors, soot, fumes, acids, alkalis, toxic chemicals, liquids or gases, waste materials or other irritants, contaminants or pollutants into or upon land, the atmosphere or any water course or body of water; but this exclusion does not apply if such discharge, dispersal, release or escape is sudden and accidental.

The application of this clause involves the nature of the pollution, not of the resulting damages.

A number of courts have held that this clause precludes coverage for gradual pollution that occurs over an extended period of time. Thus, a hazardous waste site that has been leaking wastes for years or a facility emitting air pollution for years are excluded from coverage from resulting damages.

Most courts have found that the term "sudden" is unambiguous and limits coverage to swift or instantaneous unexpected releases of pollution. A few courts, though, have found that the pollution exclusion is ambiguous and interpreted the policy in favor of the insured company. These courts have broadly defined "sudden" as meaning any unexpected release.

Some insurance companies have responded to uncertainty in judicial interpretation by adopting new provisions. Now, some policies contain absolute pollution exclusions, which deny coverage to even sudden and accidental releases.

▬ Insurer's Duty to Defend

Most liability policies give the insurer both the right and obligation to take over the defense of the case. Suppose that Anna Charnes is involved in an automobile accident with Henry Wong. Henry is injured in the accident and sues Anna,

---

[4]*United States Aviex Co. v. Travelers Insurance Co.*, 336 N.W.2d 838 (Mich. App. 1983).

who has automobile liability insurance coverage. Anna's insurance company would take over the claim against her, to settle or to defend in court.

What if the insurance company refuses to defend Anna in this case, for any reason? Anna will have a case against the insurance company for breach of its duty to defend her. In the case of Henry's action against Anna, the insurance company's duty to defend is rather clear, assuming she had a standard policy. In a pollution case, when the insurer has an argument against coverage, the duty to defend would be less clear.

The general rule is that a duty to defend arises based upon the allegations in the complaint against the insured. If the complaint's allegations fall within the policy's coverage, the insurer has a duty to defend. Courts have tended to resolve doubts in favor of the insured.

Thus, if a complaint contains allegations both inside and outside of coverage, the insurer assumes a duty to defend. Uncertainty about coverage may also establish the duty to defend. Some courts have required the insurer to investigate the complaint to seek out claims that would be covered.

The broad interpretation of the duty to defend can be illustrated by example. Suppose that Richard Glaser has a comprehensive insurance policy for his shop. A customer, Lynne Salbu, enters the shop and is injured by a fall. She sues Glaser and claims assault and battery. Glaser's insurance contract excludes intentional torts, such as assault and battery. The facts alleged by Salbu, however, suggest potential liability in negligence, which *is* covered by the insurance policy. Glaser's insurance company will have a duty to defend, even though the alleged assault and battery is outside the policy's coverage.

The following decision illustrates how an insurance company's duty to defend may be broader than its ultimate responsibility under a policy containing a pollution exclusion clause.

■ Case 9.2
Avondale Industries, Incorporated v. Travelers Indemnity Company
United States Court of Appeals, Second Circuit, 1989
887 F.2d 1989

Background and Facts *Avondale Industries is in the business of building and repairing ships. In the course of this work, it removed certain wastes from the ships, temporarily stored them, and then shipped them to a recycling facility. The recycling facility suffered leaks that necessitated government cleanup. The government sued Avondale for part of the costs of this cleanup. Private parties also sued for damages from the wastes.*

Avondale sought to recover its cleanup cost liability from its insurance company. The insurance policy contained a pollution exclusion that denied coverage for pollution liability unless it resulted from a "sudden and accidental" release. The insurer denied coverage under this exclusion. Avondale sued for a judicial determination that the insurance company had a duty to defend both the government and private claims against the company. A district court ruled for Avondale.

CARDAMONE, Circuit Judge.

* * * *

An insurer's duty to defend and to indemnify are separate and distinct, and the former duty is broader than the latter. * * * The duty to defend rests solely on whether the complaint in the underlying action contains any allegations that arguably or potentially bring the action within the protection purchased. *Technicon*, 74 N.Y.2d at 73, 544 N.Y.S.2d 531, 542 N.E.2d 1048. So long as the claims alleged against the insured rationally may be said to fall within the policy coverage, the insurer must come forward and defend. *Id.*

New York courts have held, in addition, that an insurer seeking to avoid its duty to defend bears a heavy burden. "[B]efore an insurance company is permitted to avoid policy coverage, it must ... establish[] that the exclusions or exemptions apply in the particular case, and that they are subject to no other reasonable interpretation." *Seaboard*, 64 N.Y.2d at 311, 486 N.Y.S.2d 873, 476 N.E.2d 272; *see also Neuwirth v. Blue Cross & Blue Shield*, 62 N.Y.2d 718, 476 N.Y.S.2d 814, 465 N.E.2d 353 (1984) (mem.) (citations omitted). To avoid the duty therefore the insurer must demonstrate that the allegations in the underlying complaints are "solely and entirely" within specific and unambiguous exclusions from the policy's coverage. *See International Paper*, 35 N.Y.2d at 325, 361 N.Y.S.2d 873,320 N.E.2d 619.

Consequently, Travelers can be excused from its duty to defend only if it can be determined as a matter of law that there is no possible basis in law or fact upon which the insurer might be held to indemnify Avondale. *See, e.g., Villa Charlotte Bronte, Inc. v. Commercial Union Ins. Co.*, 64 N.Y.2d 846, 848, 487 N.Y.S.2d 314, 476 N.E.2d 640 (1985) (mem.). A comparison must be made *de novo* between the allegations contained in the complaint or underlying action and the terms of the policy.

* * * *

Examining the allegations of the underlying Louisiana complaints it appears that Avondale is one of 70 named defendants. The allegations charge all the defendants with "insufficient" containment measures; with "generating" hazardous waste; with "knowledge" of the presence of toxins; with culpability for "escape" of hazardous materials. None of these conclusory assertions "clearly negate" the possibility that discharge or escape was "sudden and accidental."

Decision and Remedy   *The court affirmed the ruling that the insurer had a duty to defend both actions.*

If an insurance company breaches its duty to defend, it may be subject to several types of damages. First, the insurer must pay all costs and attorneys' fees incurred by the insured in his or her own defense. Second, the insurer may be required to pay any judgment or settlement by the insured in the case. Third, the insurer may be liable for additional damages caused by its refusal to defend, such as mental anguish on the part of the insured.

Wrongful Treatment of Claimants

Many contemporary cases involve allegations that an insurance company has wrongfully treated the claims made by an insured. These were traditionally called "bad faith actions." Increasingly, though, insurance companies may be found liable even in the absence of real bad faith on their part.

Many jurisdictions consider the wrongful denial of insurance benefits to be a distinct tort cause of action. Other jurisdictions consider the wrongful denial to be a breach of contractual duties to deal in good faith. Even the latter jurisdictions tend to allow punitive damages.

There are several sources of these wrongful treatment actions. These include: (i) failure to investigate claims sufficiently before claims denial; (ii) purposeful and unjustified delay in payment; and (iii) refusal to settle a claim against the insured within the policy limits.

Some of these wrongful treatment claims may be brought by the insured party itself and are called "first party claims." Others may be brought by another party, called "third party claims." Third party claims arise when the third party has a right to recover on insurance. In the automobile accident case discussed above, Henry is a third party seeking to claim against Anna's insurance.

Some first party claims involve improper denial of claims. These usually involve a claim that the insurance company denied a claim after an insufficient investigation of the claim's merits. If a company denies coverage without conducting a thorough and honest investigation of the claim, it may be liable. In some unfortunate cases, an insurance company will deny coverage to get leverage over the claimant for an advantageous settlement of the claim.

In one case, a California woman took out a disability insurance policy and was assured of lifetime benefits should she be permanently disabled. Thereafter, she suffered a stroke that left her permanently disabled. The insurance company made payments for two years. Then, the company discovered that the woman had made trips to church and also made monthly trips to visit her doctor. The company claimed that she was not disabled and discontinued the benefits payments. She sued the company on grounds that she was still disabled and recovered both actual and punitive damages.[5]

Potential damages from wrongful denial of benefits is illustrated by another California action, in which the owner of a laundromat was seriously injured on the job and required extensive medical care. After the insurance company denied payment, the plaintiff sued because he was ejected from two hospitals, denied surgical services, exhausted all his personal assets, lost his business, had his utilities disconnected, had his credit ruined, and had his wheelchair repossessed. He obtained essential surgery only by tricking a third hospital into accepting him on a weekend, before they could check for his coverage.[6] He eventually received $75,000 in actual damages but no punitive damages. In another case, a court awarded $740,000 in punitive damages against an insurance company that sought to exploit the plight of a paralyzed insured.

Refusal to pay a claim, of course, is not necessarily improper. Some claims are uncovered by an insurance policy. The company has an obligation simply to investigate a claim and to pay those that fall within the scope of the insurance policy.

Insurers have also been held liable for unjustified delay in paying claims. For example, an insurer may fail a frivolous appeal of a judgment of its liability to delay payment or coerce settlement from a needy insured. If the delay of payment is without any justification, the insurer may be liable for damages in addition to the liability under the policy.

Another claim against insurance companies is failure to settle claims. The difficulty with settlements can be illustrated by example. In the automobile accident discussed above, suppose that Henry sued Anna for $200,000. Anna had $100,000 worth of automobile liability insurance. After a period of time, Henry approached the insurance company and offered to settle for $100,000. This settlement would be in Anna's interest, because she would have no liability over and above the insurance. The settlement is not in the insurer's interest, however. Because the settlement offer was for the policy limit, the insurer is normally better off taking its chances at trial.

Courts have held that insurers have a responsibility to initiate settlement negotiations. They have also held that the insurer must accept a settlement offer that is reasonable under the circumstances. The company must consider the interests of the insured and not merely its own interests.

The following recent decision illustrates two important points about refusal to settle. First, an insurance company has potential liability for failure to settle. Second, an insurance company is not required to accept any settlement offers but need only deal in good faith.

---

[5] *Wetherbee v. United Insurance Co. of America*, 71 Cal. Rptr. 764 (1968).

[6] *Silberg v. California Life Insurance Co.*, 521 P.2d 1103 (Cal. 1974).

Background and Facts *Duane and Helen Braesch had a family automobile insurance policy with the Union Insurance Company protecting them from damages caused by uninsured drivers. In 1984, their daughter was the driver of an automobile that was involved in a collision with an uninsured driver, in which she died. Union refused to settle the claim or make payments. The Braesches sued to recover. After a 1987 trial, the Braesches won and recovered damages from the accident.*

The Braesches brought a separate action against the insurance company for bad faith refusal to settle and for infliction of emotional distress from forcing them to revisit the circumstances of their daughter's death. They claimed that Union "never entered into serious negotiations and engaged in only a perfunctory investigation and developed no defense." They further alleged that "Union's refusal to settle was part of an effort to put psychological pressure on each of the Braesches to settle the wrongful death claim for sums considerably less than its value." The trial court dismissed the Braesches' claims, and they appealed.

FAHRNBRUCH, Justice.

* * * *

This state recognizes a cause of action for an insurer's bad faith in refusing to settle a claim with a third party. In *Olson v. Union Fire Ins. Co.,* 174 Neb. 375, 118 N.W.2d 318 (1962), the insured collided with a bridge, and one of his passengers sustained injuries resulting in total and permanent disability. In the passenger's suit against the insured, the insurer refused to settle the claim with the passenger despite an offer to settle the claim for $10,000. The jury returned a verdict in the sum of $50,000 against the insured.

Thereafter, the plaintiff, individually and as assignee of the insured, commenced suit against the insurer, asserting negligence and bad faith by the insurer in refusing to settle the passenger's claim for $10,000. This court held: "The liability of an insurer to pay in excess of the face of the policy accrues when the insurer, having exclusive control of settlement, in bad faith refuses to compromise a claim for an amount within the policy limit." Id. at 379, 118 N.W.2d at 320-21. The rationale for the rule is that "[i]n the event the insurer elects to resist a claim of liability, or to effect a settlement thereof on such terms as it can get, there arises an implied agreement that it will exercise due care and good faith where the rights of an insured are concerned." Id. at 379, 118 N.W.2d at 321.

* * * *

We next consider the standard of care required of an insurer in settling concerning the claim, the ground for recovery in this state in this type of case is bad faith.... From the foregoing, it is clear that something more than negligence is required in third-party cases; there must be some level of intentional wrongdoing.

Varying articulations of the standard of care have been announced by the courts which have addressed the issue. The leading case on the standard of care in first-party bad faith actions is *Anderson v. Continental Ins. Co.,* 85 Wis.2d 675, 271 N.W.2d 368 (1978). In Anderson, the court stated: To show a claim for bad faith, a plaintiff must show the absence of a reasonable basis for denying benefits of the [insurance] policy and the defendant's knowledge or reckless disregard of the lack of a reasonable basis for denying the claim. It is apparent, then, that the tort of bad faith is an intentional one. "Bad faith" by definition cannot by unintentional.

*   *   *   *

Based on our existing precedent on the standard of care in the third-party cases, as well as on policy consideration, the standard of care set forth in *Anderson, supra,* is adopted. A requirement of intentional or reckless conduct arises from the commonsense notion that "[t]he insurer ... must be accorded wide latitude in its ability to investigate claims and to resist false or unfounded efforts to obtain funds not available under the contract of insurance." *Travelers Ins. Co. v. Savio,* 706 P.2d 1258, 1274 (Colo.1985).

We conclude that the Anderson standard of care strikes a proper balance between the respective rights of the insurer and the policyholder. Applying the Anderson test to the amended petitions at hand, we conclude that they allege sufficient facts demonstrating the absence of a reasonable basis for denying benefits of the policy and Union's knowledge or reckless disregard of the lack of a reasonable basis for denying the claim. The element of unreasonableness is satisfied by the allegations that Union denied its uninsured motorist coverage to the Braesches despite the fact that the uninsured driver's negligence was the sole and proximate cause of Lori Braesch's death. The allegations of bad faith regarding Union's tactics in refusing to settle meet the second prong of the test.

Decision and Remedy   *The court reversed the dismissal of the bad faith settlement claim and permitted the Braesches to sue for damages, including mental suffering.*

Some courts have granted damages for emotional distress resulting from an insurer's refusal to settle a case, based on the theory that insurance is for the peace of mind of the policyholder. Courts in some states, including California, have limited emotional distress recovery to cases in which the insured suffered some independent harm to person or property. For example, if an insured's car was repossessed or the insured lost a job, she would have suffered independent property harm and be able to recover damages for mental distress.

The results of bad faith claims have depended in part on the type of insurance. Claims are more likely to succeed for medical insurance. Very few states have recognized claims for bad faith handling of workers' compensation insurance claims, however. Even California courts, which pioneered the bad faith insurance claims cases, have refused to recognize such claims under workers' compensation.

▬ Wrongful Nonrenewal of Policy

Insurance policies govern a specific term of time. When the time is up, the insurance policy lapses unless it is renewed. Ordinarily, the insurance company has a right to choose not to renew a policy for a given insured. In some circumstances, though, an insurer may be liable for wrongful nonrenewal even if the insurer has a contract option not to renew. Some state laws require that an insurer have a good reason not to renew certain types of policies.

The presence of a wrongful nonrenewal action depends largely on the type of insurance policy in question. Automobile liability insurance, for example, is of broad public concern because many states require such insurance in order to drive legally. Many states have passed laws that prohibit nonrenewal of automobile insurance policies without good reason.

In one interesting case, a seventy-four-year-old man had a perfect driving record for nearly fifty years. He then received one speeding violation (for driving 54 mph in a 20 mph zone). He then had an accident at an intersection, but no traffic citation was issued. After the insurance policy refused to renew his policy, he sued and won a judgment that the nonrenewal had been unjustified under a state statute.[7]

For fire insurance and other forms of property insurance, however, insurance companies have great discretion in deciding whether to renew a policy. Several insurers have been sued for refusing to renew policies in inner-city areas. Courts generally have upheld this business decision, unless it was racially motivated.

Some states, such as Pennsylvania, have statutes that limit nonrenewal of property insurance to cases of good cause. In one instance, a business policyholder obtained a German Shepherd dog for security, and the insurer cancelled its policy. A court held that this was not good cause, even if the presence of the dog increased the insurance risk slightly.[8]

Policyholders have succeeded in wrongful refusal to renew life insurance contracts, however. Insurance companies may refuse to renew in order to avoid prospective payments. Suppose that Nancy Philpott has had health insurance with National Insurance Company for ten years. In January, Nancy becomes pregnant and will be due in September. Suppose that her insurance expires in July, when she is seven months pregnant. National may refuse to renew the policy to avoid paying the expenses of childbirth. This would probably be considered a wrongful refusal to renew.

Wrongful refusal to renew has also occurred in policies for professional liability insurance. Insurance coverage under a malpractice policy, for example, is usually on a "claims made" basis. Thus, the insurer becomes potentially responsible for claims made during the term of the insurance policy.

In one case, an engineering firm had a malpractice policy. The firm worked on a mine that suffered an explosion during the policy period, but no claims were filed immediately. Fearing that claims eventually would be filed for the explosion, the insurer refused to renew the policy. A court held that this was wrongful to avoid liability for an accident that occurred during the policy term.[9]

In addition to the above common law actions, most states have passed an Unfair Insurance Practices Act or an Unfair Settlement Practices Act. These laws prohibit insurance companies from refusing to settle or taking other unfair actions toward an insured. In most states, these laws do not create a private right of action. Thus, the insured party cannot sue for a violation of the statute. Only the state Commissioner of Insurance can sue to enforce the law in these states.

Under a typical state law, the Commissioner has the authority to investigate alleged unfair practices and hold hearings. If wrongful dealing is found, the Commissioner may assess fines and penalties or even revoke a company's license to sell insurance in the state. State Commissioners have undertaken relatively few enforcement actions, however.

Insurance Company Defenses

The purpose of insurance is to protect insureds from certain consequences, such as fire, for which they pay premiums. As a result, when a fire occurs, the insurance company generally has an obligation to pay the insured. There are some defenses for insurance companies even for risks covered by the policy. If the policyholder sets the fire, for example, the insurance company need not compensate him or her.

Two such defenses are often raised by insurance companies. The first is that the insured party made some misrepresentation to the insurance company in order to obtain coverage. The second is that the insured failed to give timely and proper notice of the problem to the insurance company.

Application Misrepresentations

When individuals or businesses apply for insurance coverage, they will be required to fill out a

---

[7]*Sentry Insurance v. Brown*, 424 So.2d 780 (Fla. App. 1982).

[8]*Lititz Mutual Insurance Co. v. Commonwealth*, 401 A.2d 606 (Pa. 1979).

[9]*Heen & Flint Associates v. Travelers Indem. Co.*, 400 N.Y.S.2d 994 (1977).

questionnaire that includes questions about their past losses. The insurance company will base its decision to enter a contract on the answers to these questions.

If a person has a history of traffic violations, medical problems, or past excessive claims, he or she may be unable to obtain insurance. If the person is aware of this problem, he or she may be tempted to lie on the application in order to obtain coverage. If a person lies on an application for automobile insurance, obtains coverage, and then gets into an accident, the insurance company may attempt to deny coverage for the accident, due to the misrepresentation in the application.

The issue of application misrepresentation is complicated because often a third party is the beneficiary of the insurance coverage. If Robin lies on an automobile liability insurance application and runs over Juan with a car, Juan is the payee on the policy. Juan did not lie to the insurance company and will claim that the company should pay for his damages.

Insurance companies do not want to pay claims resulting from application misrepresentation, and most policies contain language similar to the following:

> We do not provide coverage to an insured who has
>
> **a.** intentionally concealed or misrepresented any material fact or circumstance; or

b. made false statements or engaged in fraudulent conduct relating to this insurance.

Even with this language, the insurance company may be liable to injured third parties.

To avoid coverage, the insurance company must demonstrate that the misrepresentation is material. This means that the company must show that it would have refused coverage if it had known the true facts on an honest application. The insurance company must also show that it actually relied on the application misrepresentations.

Suppose that a chain smoker of cigarettes applied for a health insurance policy. On the application, the person lied and claimed that he never smoked cigarettes. A court would probably find this misrepresentation to be material and deny coverage for the costs of later medical care for emphysema or lung cancer.

If a misrepresentation is material, the insurer may declare the policy void and avoid payments. It is important to realize that the misrepresentation must be material to the issuance of the policy but need not be material to the actual claim made, in order to void the policy. This issue is presented in the following recent case.

■ Case 9.4
New York Life Insurance Company v. Johnson
United States Court of Appeals
Third Circuit, 1991
1991 WL 2064

Background and Facts *In 1986, Kirk Johnson took out a $50,000 life insurance policy on himself and named his father, Lawrence Johnson, as beneficiary. In the application for the policy, Kirk Johnson stated that he had never smoked cigarettes. In fact, he had smoked since 1973 and was then smoking about ten cigarettes per day. Had the insurance company known the true facts, it would have offered a policy but at much higher premiums. In 1988, Kirk Johnson died from an AIDS-related disease unrelated to his cigarette consumption. The insurance company investigated the claim and refused to pay on the life insurance policy, due to misrepresentations in the application. The company offered to refund the premiums paid, but Lawrence Johnson refused this offer.*

Lawrence Johnson sued to recover on the policy. A district court held that the statements about smoking were material misrepresentations but refused to void the policy altogether. The court used the insurance company's rate schedules to determine the additional premiums that Kirk Johnson would have paid if he had honestly disclosed his

*smoking habit. The court then deducted this amount from the policy
value and awarded Lawrence Johnson the difference. The insurer appealed.*

DEBEVOISE, District Judge.

*   *   *   *

In the present case disclosure of the true facts about Kirk Johnson's
smoking practices would have caused New York Life to have demanded higher premiums and thus the misrepresentations were material.

One would have expected that application of this well recognized
Pennsylvania law to the undisputed facts would have required a declaration that the policy was void ab initio [from the beginning]. However,
the district court noted that in Pennsylvania this law typically had been
applied in the context of misrepresentations about the state of one's
medical condition or health background and had never been applied
in the context of a misrepresentation about smoking habits. The additional question was posed, therefore, whether under Pennsylvania
law a material misrepresentation in the smoking context called for the
severe remedy of voiding the policy or whether some lesser remedy
would be appropriate.

*   *   *   *

The logic of the district court's opinion would require abrogating
the void ab initio rule not just in smoking misrepresentation cases but
in all misrepresentation cases where, if the true facts were known, the
insurance company would have issued a policy at a higher precisely
ascertainable rate. There is no suggestion in Pennsylvania law that there
is either a smoking misrepresentation exception or a broader precisely
ascertainable rate exception to the void ab initio rule. The relevant inquiry
is whether the misrepresentation is material. Although not decided in
the smoking context, Pennsylvania cases uniformly hold that a policy
will be void ab initio if issued as a result of a misrepresentation whether
the truth would have resulted in no policy being issued or whether
the truth would have resulted in the policy being issued with a higher
premium.

*   *   *   *

Thus the Courts of Appeals for the Second and Fourth Circuits, the
District for the Southern District of Florida, and the courts of New York
and Oregon have held that a misrepresentation as to smoking habits
in an application for insurance relieves the insurer of liability on the
policy. There is every reason to conclude that the same result would
prevail in Pennsylvania if and when the question is presented.

While a court might sympathize with a beneficiary who does not
receive the proceeds of a policy obtained by the insured's fraud, there
are strong reasons of public policy supporting the rule which we believe
prevails in Pennsylvania. If the only consequence of a fraudulent misrepresentation in a life insurance application is to reduce the amount
paid under the policy, there is every incentive for applicants to lie. If
the lie is undetected during the two-year contestability period, the
insured will have obtained excessive coverage for which he has not
paid. If the lie is detected during the two-year period, the insured will
still obtain what he could have had if he had told the truth. In essence,
the applicant has everything to gain and nothing to lose by lying. The
victims will be the honest applicants who tell the truth and whose premiums will rise over the long run to pay for the excessive insurance

proceeds paid out as a result of undetected misrepresentations in fraudulent applications.

Decision and Remedy *The court reversed and remanded the case for the entry of a judgment that the policy was void.*

An insurance company may also be required to show that the misrepresentation was made knowingly and in bad faith. If the insured party simply misunderstood the application and made an "honest misrepresentation," the insurer would be required to pay.

Even if an insured party made material and intentional misrepresentations, the insurance company may still be liable to make insurance payments to an injured third party. This is under a theory of the insurer's duty to investigate the statements in the application.

In one case, an insured party made numerous significant misrepresentations about his past driving record in an insurance application. An accident victim of the insured sought to recover, but the insurance company refused to pay. A court found the insurance company to be liable because the "quasi-public" character of automobile liability insurance created a duty on the insurance company to "conduct a reasonable investigation of insurability."[10]

Thus, an insurance company cannot simply rely on the truth of the answers in its application questionnaire. The company must make some reasonable investigation of the answers' accuracy, if the insurer wants to rely on material misrepresentations to avoid coverage.

Failure of Notice

Insurance policies typically require that the insured make prompt notice of the existence of facts that create an insurance claim, as well as the claim itself. A typical comprehensive general insurance policy would contain language such as the following:

You must see to it that we are notified as soon as practicable of an "occurrence" which may result in a claim. Notice should include:

1. How, when and where the "occurrence" took place.

2. The names and addresses of any injured persons and witnesses.

3. The nature and location of any injury or damage arising out of the "occurrence."

In addition to requiring notification of such a potential liability-inducing "occurrence," policies also require prompt notification of any claim made against the insured that might trigger insurance coverage. In addition, the insured party must cooperate with the company in investigation of the claim.

Timely notice is important to insurance companies for a variety of reasons. First, it facilitates thorough investigation of potential and actual claims. Second, notice enables the insurer to maintain sufficient reserves to pay losses.

In many cases, an insured party fails to make prompt notice under such policy provisions, especially the notice of the "occurrence" itself. The insurance company may then seek to avoid coverage for lack of timely notice. Failure of notice alone, however, does not absolve the insurer of responsibility to pay.

Many jurisdictions require that the insurer demonstrate that it suffered some prejudice from late notice, before denying coverage. This means that the company must show that the lateness of notice caused it some damage, such as impeding full investigation of the occurrence.

Suppose that a company reached a settlement with the Environmental Protection Agency to pay for environmental cleanup at its facility and only

---

[10]*Barrera v. State Farm Mutual Automobile Insurance Co.,* 79 Cal. Rptr. 106 (1969).

then notified its insurance company. The insurance company could be required to pay for the cleanup costs, unless it could show that the settlement terms were worse than those the insurance company could have negotiated itself.

Some states will deny coverage for lack of timely notice even in the absence of prejudice. Recent decisions in New York and Kentucky denied insurance coverage when an insured waited over two years to notify the insurance company and did not require the insurance company to demonstrate that it suffered some prejudice from late notice.

▬ Wrongful Issuance of Life Insurance

In addition to wrongfully denying insurance renewal, some insurers have been held liable for wrongfully issuing life insurance policies. This problem arises when a person takes out an insurance policy on the life of a second person and then murders that person in order to recover the insurance proceeds. In this circumstance, an insurance company may be liable to the victim's heirs for encouraging the murder.

In order to recover on a wrongful issuance of life insurance claim, the heirs of the murder victim must first show that the company was somehow negligent in issuing the policy. This might be due to the company's failure to investigate the relationship between the parties. The heirs must also show that the murder was foreseeable to the company.

In one case, a company was liable because it had some notice of the beneficiary's murderous intentions, an investigation would have uncovered that the insured was worth much more to the beneficiary dead than alive, the murdered insured's lack of consent to the issuance of the policy, and the financial inability of the beneficiary to make premium payments for any extended period of time.[11]

In an older case, a son took out a $200 life insurance policy on his mother and then killed her for the insurance proceeds. The court held that the company was not liable because it was unforeseeable that he would murder his mother for such a small insurance payment.[12]

The cases of wrongful issuance of life insurance are not frequent, but damages can be great when they arise. More significantly, this doctrine illustrates an important broad principle of insurance law—that insurers have a significant responsibility to investigate facts surrounding a policy and to deal with affected parties in good faith.

---

[11]*Life Insurance Co. v. Lopez*, 443 So.2d 947 (Fla. 1983).

[12]*Holloman v. Life Insurance Co.*, 7 S.E.2d 169 (S.C. 1939).

▬ Ethical Perspectives

Insurance and the AIDS Crisis

Acquired immune deficiency syndrome (AIDS) is an enormous public health problem. The disease currently causes thousands of deaths per year and costs billions of dollars annually. The insurance industry faces a difficult problem in dealing with the AIDS crisis.

To the best of current knowledge, AIDS begins through infection with a human immunodeficiency virus (HIV). For many people infected with HIV, the disease slowly destroys their immune system of resistance to other diseases. The person is then highly susceptible to other fatal diseases. Some HIV-infected individuals, however, may never suffer from advanced stages of AIDS.

The insurance industry has been reluctant to provide insurance for individuals with AIDS or even those with a potential exposure to HIV. These individuals are considered to be relatively likely to make large claims for medical costs.

Insurance companies have been criticized for denying coverage to a group of those who need it most (AIDS patients). The entire point of insurance is to share risks by taking relatively small premium payments from large groups of people and redistributing much of that money to a smaller group of people who are unfortunate enough to suffer an insured occurrence, such as a serious disease requiring extensive medical care. Naturally, though, insurance companies want to take in as much money as possible and pay out as little as possible.

Insurers respond to this criticism by noting that they operate in the free market and must be able to make a profit. Insurance companies typically discriminate against high-risk groups, by charging them more for insurance. The potential costs of AIDS coverage are enormous. The typical AIDS patient requires up to $150,000 a year in medical treatment and total annual medical costs of the disease are approximately $8 billion.

Insurance companies certainly do not have enough profits to enable them single-handedly to pay the costs of the AIDS crisis. Their only alternative, in order to provide AIDS coverage, is to increase insurance premiums substantially. Yet many Americans would object to paying much higher premiums, and some Americans would be unable to pay the premiums.

The insurance companies clearly have a legitimate concern. In general, companies do not have an ethical duty to do business with a particular person. Without insurance, however, AIDS victims are more likely to die sooner for lack of care. AIDS victims need care and at least some insurance practices may be unethical or discriminatory.

Suppose that an insurer denies coverage to individuals who have tested positive for HIV. This policy is likely to discourage voluntary testing for AIDS, thereby frustrating society's ability to respond to the problem. Some companies require a test for HIV before they will issue a policy. This procedure risks public exposure of AIDS sufferers, who may consequently suffer discrimination in housing, employment or even health care.

Still further problems are presented when insurance companies use general categories to avoid insuring potential AIDS victims. For example, a company might refuse to insure homosexuals. Or a company might refuse to insure individuals who live in certain high-risk inner-city areas, many of whom are members of minorities.

In general, insurance companies base their decisions on actuarial information on populations that are likely to suffer covered occurrences. This process is often reasonable, fair and efficient. But there is nothing sacred about this process, which must remain subject to ethical concerns for fairness.

Insurance and Europe 1992

Insurance, like most areas of business, is increasingly becoming global. Insurance also is one of America's advanced service sectors that offer particular promise in international competition. The combined nations of Europe after 1992 may be the world's largest market for insurance products. Consequently, this area is of great interest to insurance companies.

Historically, some European nations have made it difficult for U.S. insurance firms to enter their markets. Greece and Spain had difficult entry barriers in the insurance market. Other countries, including France, had such an elaborate system for foreign insurance companies that direct entry became inefficient. The unification of the European Community in "Europe 1992" promises to break down some of these barriers to American insurance companies.

The Commission of the European Communities has already begun to lay the groundwork for a joint insurance market through a number of directives to member states. The first critical European directive is known as Directive 73/239, which provides for "the coordination of laws, regulations and administrative provisions relating to the taking-up and pursuit of the business of direct insurance other than life insurance."

Directive 73/239 establishes procedures for the formal "authorization" of insurance companies in Europe. Authorization involves a demonstration of solvency, an agreement to keep certain records in the country, a certification of its plan of business, and the designation of an authorized agent within the country. Authorization still must be sought from the appropriate authority of the individual European member state.

Directive 73/239 also contains protections to prevent individual nations from arbitrarily denying or delaying foreign applications for authorization. Denials must contain a statement of precise reasons for that action, and any delay of over six months enables the company to appeal to a court.

Other directives also have been adopted to facilitate the licensing of insurance agents and brokers, giving some credit to the licensing of other nations. Other directives provide coordination for co-insurance operations.

To date, the opening up of European insurance markets has shown substantial progress and continues to advance. Less progress has been made in the life insurance market, however, which remains a problem because a majority of U.S. insurance companies focus in this area. Individual country regulation remains predominant in life insurance. Establishing other insurance operations may provide a toehold for future continent-wide progress in life insurance.

Questions and Case Problems

1. Jim was a homosexual male who had several relationships over the course of a year. He applied for medical insurance, and the form asked if he was a practicing homosexual. Jim was offended by this question and answered it "no." He received the insurance coverage. Subsequently, Jim contracted AIDS and thereafter required extensive medical treatment. The insurance company refused to pay for the treatment, and Jim sued the company for wrongful denial of benefits. The company's defense was Jim's application misrepresentation of his sexual preference. Should the company succeed in its misrepresentation defense to insurance coverage?

2. Ms. Poling was a retired state worker who had group health insurance administered by the Wisconsin Physicians Service. The policy provided reimbursement for skilled care but not for custodial care. She was hospitalized with Parkinson's disease and Alzheimer's disease. The insurance company initially denied coverage on the grounds that her care was custodial. Her physician informed the company that her care was clearly skilled in nature and included occupational therapy. The company continued to refuse to pay, now contending that there was no expectation that the occupational therapy could rehabilitate her. Does Ms. Poling have a good claim against the insurance company? [*Poling v. Wisconsin Physicians Service*, 357 N.W.2d 293 (Wis. Ct. App. 1984)].

3. Wellstone, Inc., was a small corporation owned almost entirely by the Mondale family, but Wellstone had a few outside shareholders. Members of the Mondale family served on the board of directors. Wellstone had an insurance policy covering its directors and officers. One of the outside shareholders brought an action for breach of fiduciary duty against the directors of Wellstone, and the insurance company refused to provide coverage of the lawsuit. The claim sought millions in damages and could bankrupt the company. The directors eventually settled the case for $50,000, and the company then sued their insurance company to recover this sum, plus emotional distress damages. Assuming that the insurance company's coverage denial was wrongful, should the company's stockholders be allowed to recover damages for emotional distress?

4. A man drowned in a municipal swimming pool, and his survivors sued the city for damages. The city was insured, and the city's insurance company defended the action. A jury eventually awarded $350,000 in damages to the survivors. The insurance company first sought a new trial and then appealed this decision to a higher court. The company offered a settlement of less than half the jury verdict. Although the survivors were financially needy, they refused this offer. Some time later, the insurance company and the claimants settled for $300,000. The survivors then brought an additional suit against the insurance company for bringing the appeal and refusing to settle earlier in hopes that financial pressure would force the survivors into a bad settlement. Should the insurance company be liable for delaying the settlement unnecessarily? [*Coleman v. Gulf Insurance Group*, 226 Cal. Rptr. 90 (Cal. 1986)].

5. Mr. Brown was 74 years old. He received a speeding ticket, and his insurance company then notified him that they would not renew his policy. He appealed to them, and they agreed to renew his policy in light of his 49-year tenure with the company. Mr. Brown was then involved in a traffic accident at an intersection, but no citation was issued. Although there was a state law prohibiting nonrenewal of a policy for a single accident for a policyholder of five years or more, the company refused to renew Brown's policy. Brown sued the company for wrongful nonrenewal of his policy. Should he succeed with this claim?

CHAPTER TEN

Real Estate Finance and Liability

▬ KEY BACKGROUND

The essential background for this chapter on real estate finance and liability is found in Chapters 51 and 52 of *West's Business Law, Fifth Edition* and Chapter 23 of *West's Legal Environment of Business*. These chapters cover real property and landlord-tenant relationships. Among the important points to remember from these chapters are:

- the nature of ownership interests in real property

- deeds and other methods of transfer of ownership in real property

- land use controls applicable to real property

- legal rules governing the lease of property

* * *

The ownership of land, generally referred to as **real property** or **real estate**, historically has held great importance, both financially and psychologically. Many of today's largest financial transactions involve real estate. Urban property, such as an office building, periodically sells for many millions of dollars. Individual homes do not sell for so high a price, but the cumulative value of residential sales is enormous.

Real estate business is as closely associated with the law as any business. Detailed legal rules govern most real estate transactions, even relatively small ones. In addition to the common law, states have adopted a significant number of statutes that regulate the real estate business.

This chapter selects three broad categories of the law as it relates to real estate. The first section covers the law and the financing of real estate purchases, a matter of great importance to banks as well as to other businesses. The second section addresses the leasing of real estate for commercial purposes. The final section discusses the growing importance of fraud claims in real estate transactions.

▬ Real Estate Finance

Most real estate developments, ranging from a small single-family home to a multimillion-dollar high-rise office building, require borrowed financing in the form of a **mortgage**. A bank loans the funds necessary to construct a building or to purchase an existing building. The bank retains a security right in the property as **collateral** for this loan. If the borrower fails to make payments, the bank can take steps to assume ownership of the property.

Mortgage loan funds currently come from a variety of sources. Commercial banks and Savings and Loan Associations are traditional sources. Tax laws have encouraged the development of Real Estate Investment Trusts, in which investors pool their money to make real estate loans.

The real estate finance market has become increasingly complex. Once, a home buyer would take out a loan with a local banker and the mortgage would be held by that bank for its 30-year duration. Monthly payments would be made to the local bank.

Today, there is a thriving secondary market in mortgages. The original lending bank will sell the mortgage (the right to receive monthly payments) to another institution. This permits banks to exchange the uncertain rights to future payments for immediate funds.

A wide variety of legal issues arise in mortgage lending, including securities laws, environmental laws, and other seemingly unrelated regulations. This section discusses three important legal issues—government regulation of mortgaging, legal restrictions on mortgage provisions, and rules for foreclosure in the event of mortgage default.

Government Regulation

Several government laws regulate the mortgage process. One important act is the Real Estate Settlement Procedures Act of 1974, also known as "RESPA." An important purpose of this law is to protect prospective homebuyers from paying unanticipated or excessive fees in obtaining a mortgage.

RESPA does not apply to all real estate loans. The Act covers only mortgage loans for the purchase of family residential property that is the first lien on the property (the act does not cover secondary mortgages taken out against accumulated equity in the home). RESPA is also limited to loans by federally supervised lenders.

RESPA mandates certain disclosures to the homebuyer. The lender must make a good faith estimate of all loan closing costs at the time of the borrower's loan application. The lender also must provide the prospective buyer with an informative booklet on settlement costs that was prepared by the Department of Housing and Urban Development.

In addition to these disclosure provisions, RESPA also has provisions regulating the substance of loans. The law prohibits certain fees or "kickbacks" for referring mortgage business.

Another important federal regulation of loans is found in the federal Truth-in-Lending Act, which passed in 1968. This law does not apply to business or commercial real estate loans but does cover consumer real estate loans.

The central requirement of the Truth in Lending Act is the required disclosure of the interest rate on the loan and total finance charges in the loan. The terms of this law are discussed in greater detail in Chapter 45 of *West's Business Law, Fifth Edition*.

Mortgage Terms

Most mortgage terms are set by the lender and are not subject to negotiation. Often borrowers may not understand the full significance of such mortgage terms. Many borrowers have sued under state law, claiming that certain terms of the mortgage are unfair and should be held to be invalid. These challenges have often involved provisions that require the entire mortgage to be paid off ahead of the term, prohibitions on paying off the mortgage early, and penalties for late payment.

A significant legal controversy arose over mortgage clauses that permit the lender to accelerate the debtor's full payment of the principal before the loan term is complete. An important type of loan acceleration provision is the **due-on-sale** clause found in many home mortgages. These clauses accelerate the time for payment of the full mortgage principal when the property is sold.

Suppose that Frank takes out a 30-year home mortgage. After seven years, Frank sells the house to Sharon. Sharon may wish to assume the mortgage payments of Frank. If the mortgage contained a due-on-sale clause, however, she could not do so. The bank would insist that Frank pay off the original mortgage upon the sale of the house, and Sharon would have to obtain a new mortgage.

For a time, some state courts held that such due-on-sale clauses were invalid. In the 1980s, however, federal statutes and judicial decisions clearly established the validity of due-on-sale clauses in home mortgages.

Today, some borrowers still challenge due-on-sale conditions. The main argument is that the due-on-sale clause was not clear in the original mortgage. If the mortgage was ambiguous, it will be construed against the lender and the court may find the clause inapplicable.

In addition, some acceleration clauses may still be challenged as unconscionable in special circumstances. If the clause permits arbitrary acceleration without reason and this right is abused, a court may refuse to enforce an acceleration clause.

Another dispute arose over mortgage clauses with **prepayment prohibitions**. This is the converse of the acceleration clause. A homeowner may find herself with a surplus of cash and may desire to pay off the mortgage ahead of its full term. A lender, though, may refuse to permit such prepayment. Alternatively, the mortgage may impose financial penalties for prepayment.

A lender may have sound financial reasons for opposing prepayment. Banks profit from interest received on loans that they make and their future lending and other practices are based on their expected future income. Prepayment can cost a bank or other lender those expected future profits.

Prepayment restraints may create serious difficulties for a borrower, however. Suppose now that Frank wants to sell his house to Sharon, but she refuses to assume his mortgage terms (perhaps interest rates have dropped significantly). If Frank cannot prepay his original mortgage, he may be unable to sell the house. Frank might sue the lender by claiming that the prepayment prohibition unfairly prevents him from selling the property.

Under some circumstances, courts have struck down prepayment clauses as unfair. In general, most courts have held that prepayment clauses, standing alone, are legal protections of the lender's interests. The following decision presents an illustrative analysis.

■ **Case 10.1**
Trident Center v.
Connecticut General Life
Insurance Company
United States Court of Appeals,
Ninth Circuit
847 F.2d 564

Background and Facts   *In 1983, Security First Life Insurance Company and others formed a limited partnership, named Trident Center, for the purpose of constructing an office building complex. The Center obtained financing from Connecticut General Life Insurance Company. The loan documents provided for a loan of $56.5 million at 12 1/4 percent interest over a 15-year term. The note provided that Trident "shall not have the right to prepay the principal amount hereof in whole or in part" for the first 12 years of the term.*

After interest rates began to drop, Trident sought refinancing, but Connecticut General refused. Trident then sued, seeking a declaration that it was entitled to prepay the loan, subject only to a 10 percent prepayment fee. Connecticut General moved to dismiss. The district court agreed and dismissed Trident's action. Trident appealed.

KOZINSKI, Circuit Judge.

*   *   *   *

The parties to this transaction are, by any standard, highly sophisticated business people: Plaintiff is a partnership consisting of an insurance company and two of Los Angeles' largest and most prestigious law firms; defendant is another insurance company. Dealing at arm's length and from positions of roughly equal bargaining strength, they negotiated a commercial loan amounting to more than $56 million. The contract documents are lengthy and detailed; they squarely address the precise issue that is the subject of this dispute; to all who read English, they appear to resolve the issue fully and conclusively.

*   *   *   *

Trident nevertheless argues that it is entitled to precipitate a default and insist on acceleration by tendering the balance due on the note plus the 10 percent prepayment fee. The contract language, cited above, leaves no room for this construction. It is true, of course, that Trident is free to stop making payments, which may then cause Connecticut General to declare a default and accelerate. But that is not to say that Connecticut General would be required to so respond. The contract quite clearly gives Connecticut General other options: It may choose to waive the default, or to take advantage of some other remedy such as the right to collect "all the income, rents, royalties, revenue, issues, profits, and proceeds of the Property." Deed of Trust ¶ 1.18, at 22. By interpreting the contract as Trident suggests, we would ignore those provisions giving Connecticut General, not Trident, the exclusive right to decide how, when and whether the contract will be terminated upon default during the first 12 years.

In effect, Trident is attempting to obtain judicial sterilization of its intended default. But defaults are messy things; they are supposed to be. Once the maker of a note secured by a deed of trust defaults, its credit rating may deteriorate; attempts at favorable refinancing may be thwarted by the need to meet the trustee's sale schedule; its cash flow may be impaired if the beneficiary takes advantage of the assignment of rents remedy; default provisions in its loan agreements with other lenders may be triggered. Fear of these repercussions is strong medicine that keeps debtors from shirking their obligations when interest rates go down and they become disenchanted with their loans. That Trident is willing to suffer the cost and delay of a lawsuit, rather than simply defaulting, shows far better than anything we might say that these provisions are having their intended effect. We decline Trident's invitation to truncate the lender's remedies and deprive Connecticut General of its bargained-for protection.

Decision and Remedy *The court affirmed the legitimacy of the prepayment clause but remanded the case to permit Trident to present evidence that the contract permitted some prepayment.*

Suppose that a loan contains both an acceleration clause and a prepayment prohibition. The acceleration clause would permit the lender to take advantage of higher interest rates by calling in the loan and requiring refinancing. The prepayment prohibition prevents the borrower from comparably taking advantage of lower interest rates. One court found this combination to be invalid.[1]

State statutes also restrict prepayment prohibitions. New Mexico has a law prohibiting such clauses. More common are state laws that require full disclosure of such clauses to borrowers.

Late Payment Fees

Most mortgages have specific fees charged for late mortgage payments. These fees are often quite significant and more substantial than may seem justified by the lateness of the payment. For example, a borrower who makes a payment three weeks late may be required to pay a late fee that is the equivalent of three months of interest.

Borrowers have challenged these late payment fees in mortgages. Some courts have found these fees to be invalid. Many decisions have characterized the late fees as an attempt at imposing **liquidated damages** for breach of contract. These damages are discussed in Chapter 17 of *West's Business Law, Fifth Edition*. Because the fees seem excessive and because actual interest is readily calculable, some courts have found the late payment fees to represent a **penalty clause** in the contract, which courts will not enforce.

Other courts have struck down late payment charges as a violation of the state usury laws (which set maximum interest rates allowable). The effective interest rate charged on the late

[1]*Wisconsin Ave. Associates, Inc. v. 2720 Wisconsin Ave. Co-operative Assoc.*, 441 A.2d 956 (D.C. App. 1982).

payment may exceed the maximum permitted under state usury laws.

Default and Foreclosure

Recent years have seen an increase in defaults on mortgage payments and resulting **foreclosures** by lenders. This is a procedure in which the lender takes ownership of the property, after the borrower proves unable to keep up the required payments on the loan.

The first important legal issue is whether there has been a default. A single late payment does not qualify as default. After a borrower has repeatedly missed payment deadlines, however, or has failed to pay altogether, the lender will use an acceleration clause to make the full debt come due. Most mortgages permit acceleration if the borrower fails to keep up payments.

If the lender chooses to accelerate the debt payment, it is generally required to notify the borrower of this decision. The borrower may waive this right to notification, however.

Assuming that the borrower cannot pay off the loan, the lender can then institute foreclosure on the property. Many states provide the borrower with a **redemption right**. If the borrower can obtain the money to pay off the mortgage within a certain period of time (usually six months), the foreclosure is canceled.

When foreclosure goes forward, it is governed by the terms of the mortgage deed of trust and by state law. The mortgage deed may provide for power-of-sale foreclosure, which enables the lender to act unilaterally. If the mortgage does not authorize direct sale, the lender must go to court for judicial foreclosure.

In foreclosure, the borrower puts the property up for sale and uses the proceeds to pay off the loan. Both power-of-sale and judicial foreclosure are governed by state statutes. In Texas, for example, the debtor must be notified three weeks before the foreclosure sale and the sale must be by an auction at the local county courthouse during a certain time period.

The foreclosure auction must be conducted impartially, in an attempt to get the highest price for the property. Suppose that Reiner Kutor defaults on a $200,000 loan for a residence. If the property sells for $250,000, more than the loan balance, the $50,000 surplus is paid to the borrower, Kutor. If the property sells for only $150,000 or less than the loan balance, the lender can attempt to get a $50,000 **deficiency judgment** against Kutor to make up the difference.

The foreclosure system and deficiency judgments have a significant problem. Often, the only bidder at a foreclosure auction is the lender. In these circumstances, the lender can obtain the property at auction for a low price (even below fair market value) and obtain a large deficiency judgment against the borrower. The following case reflects this problem.

■ Case 10.2
Savers Federal Savings & Loan Association v. Reetz
United States Court of Appeals, Fifth Circuit, 1989
888 F.2d 1497

Background and Facts   *Horst and Kathleen Reetz obtained a $6.3 million note from Savers Federal Savings & Loan Association. The note was secured by two deeds of trust for two parcels of real estate. The note was payable in monthly installments, but the Reetzes soon fell into default on the note, and Savers accelerated the note. The Reetzes were unable to pay and the property was put up for sale at a judicial foreclosure auction.*

At the foreclosure sale, Savers purchased the parcels of property for $4 million. Savers then sought a deficiency judgment against the Reetzes for the balance of the note. The Reetzes filed a response in which they claimed that the fair market value of the property was $8 million and that they should owe no deficiency judgment. The court found no irregularity in the auction procedures and entered a deficiency judgment for Savers for more than $3 million. The Reetzes appealed.

GARWOOD, Circuit Judge

*   *   *   *

We conclude under controlling and long-established Texas law that where there has previously been a valid nonjudicial deed of trust foreclosure on real property securing a debt, the amount to be credited on the debt for deficiency judgment purposes is the amount received at the foreclosure sale; that inadequacy of the consideration received on the foreclosure sale cannot alone invalidate an otherwise valid deed of trust nonjudicial foreclosure on real estate; that in order for inadequacy of consideration to have that effect, there must also be some irregularity in the foreclosure which caused or contributed to cause the real property to be sold for a grossly inadequate price; and that all these rules are fully applicable where the creditor is the purchaser at the foreclosure.

*   *   *   *

Thus Texas nonjudicial foreclosure sales of real estate under deed of trust powers have for approximately a century been conducted pursuant to a special, structured and formal statutory scheme calling for public sales between 10:00 a.m. and 4:00 p.m. of the first Tuesday in each month preceded by three weeks' public notice. This statutory scheme, by its own terms, applies only to real property sales. The amendments to the statute in 1975, 1983-84, and 1987 preserved the basic scheme, but added specific provisions designed to enhance the fairness of the sale, the likelihood there would be public bidders, and the protection of debtors in respect to deficiency actions. These amendments were made well *after* the Texas Supreme Court's decisions in *Tarrant Savings Ass'n* and *Maupin* (and, except for the 1975 amendments, after *Musick*) which held that gross inadequacy of price (absent and irregularity in the sale contributing thereto) was not a basis on which to set aside a real estate deed of trust foreclosure, even though the creditor was the purchaser, and that if the sale were valid, the foreclosure sales price, rather than the then market price, constituted the proper amount to credit on the debt for deficiency judgment purposes, again even though the creditor was the purchaser at foreclosure. Accordingly, the Texas Legislature may be deemed to have found that the rules applied in those cases were appropriate components of a proper scheme for regulating real estate nonjudicial foreclosures, and consequent deficiency claims, which did not need to be changed except in the specific respects addressed by the amendments. *Cf. Coastal Industrial Water Authority v. Trinity Portland Cement*, 563 S.W.2d 916, 918 (Tex. 1978); *Kennedy v. Hyde*, 682 S.W.2d 525, 529 (Tex. 1984). Subsequent judicial abrogation of the settled rules which furnished the legal context on the basis of which the legislature may be presumed to have acted in amending the statute would constitute an unwarranted upsetting of the overall balance which the legislature struck.

Decision and Remedy   *The court affirmed the district court judgment to Savers.*

A majority of states restrict deficiency judgments in some manner. Most jurisdictions impose strict notice requirements and time limits for deficiency judgments. Other laws are even more restrictive. California prohibits deficiency judgments in power-of-sale foreclosures. Other states also prohibit deficiency judgments when the mortgage was for the purchase of residential real estate.

The above discussion assumes that the bank is the only lender on the property. Foreclosure is more complex when the real property is encumbered with more than one lender. For example, suppose that Kutor had construction workers do extensive building on the property. If he failed to pay the workers, they have a mechanic's lien on the property. They, too, will seek proceeds from the foreclosure sale.

▄▄ Commercial Leasing

Most retail stores and offices do not own the building in which they are located. Instead, they lease the property from a building owner, often a real estate developer, and pay rent on the space. The commercial leasing process is of great economic significance and productive of many legal disputes. The market for commercial leases has been volatile, and parties have often tried to escape the terms of certain leases.

Several legal issues are of recurring importance in commercial leasing. This section discusses the presence of an **implied warranty of suitability** of the commercial lease, the material breaches of a lease that permit a party to avoid the lease, the rules for determining abandonment of lease rights, and the tort of wrongful interference with a commercial lease.

Warranty of Suitability

A tenant in a commercial lease may be disappointed in the quality of the facilities provided. If so, the tenant may attempt to avoid the lease or escape rental payments by contending that the space provided breached the lessor's implied warranty of fitness or suitability.

Traditional common law provided the tenant with no implied warranty of the property's quality, except those expressly stated in the lease contract. Increasingly, courts have adopted an implied warranty of habitability for residential leases (the premises must be in a livable condition). Some courts have extended this implied warranty to commercial leases.

Suppose that a group of doctors leases space in a commercial development for their practice. After moving in, the air conditioning breaks down, the water supply is irregular, the electricity cuts off frequently, and little maintenance or janitorial service is provided. The doctors would try to escape their lease under an implied warranty of suitability.

Some states have refused to imply a warranty of suitability in commercial leases. They rely on a position that commercial tenants have sufficient bargaining power to provide *express* contractual protections for themselves. Recent decisions in Massachusetts, Missouri, Ohio, Iowa and other states have found no implied warranty in commercial leasing.

Other states, however, have found an implied warranty of suitability. Precedents in California, New York, New Jersey and Louisiana recognize at least some such implied warranty of suitability. In one case, a parking and automobile storage garage leased space in a building. The roof of the building was in disrepair, chunks of concrete fell onto the floor, large quantities of rainwater leaked in and damaged cars, and the garage suffered frequent electrical failures. A court found that this was a breach of the lessor's implied warranty.[2] In contrast, courts have found that a leaky bathroom roof in an office does not breach an implied warranty of suitability.

The following recent decision represents an important extension of the implied warranty of suitability in a state that had not previously recognized the warranty.

---

[2]*Reed v. Classified Parking System*, 232 So.2d 103 (La. App. 1970).

▄ Case 10.3
**Davidow v.
Inwood North Professional
Group—Phase I**
Supreme Court of Texas, 1988
747 F.2d 373

Background and Facts *Inwood North Professional Group—Phase I leased commercial space to Joseph F. Davidow, M.D., for use as a medical office. Davidow entered into a five-year lease agreement that required him to pay approximately $880 per month. The lease obligated Inwood to provide air conditioning, electricity, hot water, janitor and maintenance services, light fixtures, and security services.*

After moving in, Dr. Davidow began experiencing problems. The air conditioning did not work properly, causing temperatures to rise above 85 degrees. The roof leaked after a rain, which resulted in stained tiles and mildewed carpets. Pests and rodents often infested the office. Hallway lights were not replaced, so hallways were dark. Cleaning and maintenance and hot water were not provided. The parking lot was constantly filled with trash. Several burglaries and acts of vandalism occurred.

Fourteen months before the lease expired, Dr. Davidow moved out and refused to make further payments. Inwood sued for unpaid rent, and Davidow counterclaimed. After a trial, a jury ruled for Davidow and awarded him $9300 in damages. The court of appeals reversed the trial court judgment, holding that there was no implied warranty of suitability and that Inwood's breaches did not justify Davidow's total breach of the lease contract. That court awarded Inwood damages for unpaid rent and attorney's fees. Davidow appealed.

SPEARS, Justice.

*   *   *   *

In the past, this court has attempted to provide a more equitable and contemporary solution to landlord-tenant problems by easing the burden placed on tenants as a result of the independence of lease covenants and the doctrine of *caveat emptor. See, e.g., Kamarath v. Bennett*, 568 S.W.2d 658 (Tex. 1978); *Humber v. Morton*, 426 S.W.2d 554 (Tex.1968). In *Kamarath v. Bennett*, we reexamined the realities of the landlord-tenant relationship in a modern context and concluded that the agrarian common-law concept is no longer indicative of the contemporary relationship between the tenant and landlord. The land is of minimal importance to the modern tenant; rather, the primary subject of most leases is the structure located on the land and the services which are to be provided to the tenant. The modern residential tenant seeks to lease a dwelling suitable for living purposes. The landlord usually has knowledge of any defects in the premises that may render in uninhabitable. In addition, the landlord, as permanent owner of the premises, should rightfully bear the cost of any necessary repairs. In most instances the landlord is in a much better bargaining position that the tenant. Accordingly, we held in *Kamarath* that the landlord impliedly warrants that the premises are habitable and fit for living. We further implicitly recognized that the residential tenant's obligation to pay rent is dependent upon the landlord's performance under his warranty of habitability. *Kamarath*, 568 S.W.2d at 660-61.

When a commercial tenant such as Dr. Davidow leases office space, many of the same considerations are involved. A significant number of commentators have recognized the similarities between residential and commercial tenants and concluded that residential warranties should be expanded to cover commercial property.

*   *   *   *

It cannot be assumed that a commercial tenant is more knowledgeable about the quality of the structure than a residential tenant. A businessman cannot be expected to possess the expertise necessary to adequately inspect and repair the premises, and many commercial tenants lack the financial resources to hire inspectors and repairmen to assure the suitability of the premises. * * * Additionally, because commercial tenants often enter into short-term leases, the tenants have limited economic incentive to make any extensive repairs to their premises. Consequently, commercial tenants generally rely on their landlords' greater abilities to inspect and repair the premises. Id.

* * * *

There is no valid reason to imply a warranty of habitability in residential leases and not in commercial leases. Although minor distinctions can be drawn between residential and commercial tenants, those differences do not justify limiting the warranty to residential leaseholds. Therefore, we hold there is an implied warranty of suitability by the landlord in a commercial lease that the premises are suitable for their intended commercial purpose. This warranty means that at the inception of the lease there are no latent defects in the facilities that are vital to the use of the premises for their intended commercial purpose and that these essential facilities will remain in a suitable condition. If, however, the parties to a lease expressly agree that the tenant will repair certain defects, then the provisions of the lease will control.

Decision and Remedy   *The court reversed the portion of the appellate court judgment that had denied damages to Davidow.*

Material Breaches of Contract

Commercial tenants should have legal protection even in those states that fail to recognize an implied warranty of suitability. Most commercial lease contracts contain **covenants** in which both parties to the contract make certain promises. For example, the tenant promises to pay rent and the landlord promises to provide quality facilities.

A breach of a lease covenant gives rise to remedies against the breaching party. A breach does not necessarily permit the other party to terminate the lease, however. Rather, only a "material" or "substantial" breach permits rescission of the lease. The tenant or landlord can then avoid its obligations under the lease.

The law of material breaches has been of economic significance. Suppose that a developer leases space in an office building to an accounting firm for 25 years at $30 per square foot. After a few years, rents escalate dramatically. The developer could now get over $75 per square foot for the space. The accounting firm is two weeks late in its rent payment. Does this permit the developer to cancel the lease and find a better-paying tenant?

Section 241 of the Restatement (Second) of Contracts provides a series of standards for determining whether such a breach of lease terms is sufficiently material to terminate the lease. These standards are:

a. The extent to which the injured party was deprived of the benefit reasonably expected.

b. The extent to which the injured party can be adequately compensated for the damages.

c. The extent to which the party failing to perform will suffer from forfeiture.

d. The likelihood that the party failing to perform will cure the failure.

e. The extent to which the behavior of the party failing to perform comports with standards of good faith and fair dealing.

These standards were applied in a recent case. A tenant was using office space to operate a mail-order business but inadvertently failed to obtain a certificate required by the government. The lease had a provision permitting termination if the tenant used the property for any "unlawful purpose." The lessor therefore sought to rescind the lease arrangement.

A court held that the lease could not be rescinded. The court noted that the landlord had failed to act for two years after discovering the problem, that the tenant had not acted wilfully or in bad faith, that the tenant eventually cured the breach, and that the landlord was acting in bad faith, trying to get rid of the tenant for economic reasons.[3]

---

[3]*Entrepreneur, Ltd. v. Yasuna*, 498 A.2d 1151 (D.C. App. 1985).

Some tenants have claimed landlords committed a material breach by "double-leasing." For example, if a lessor leases a small parking lot for the use of one office and then leases the same lot for another office, the first office make seek rescission. This has been found to be material so long as the lot was insufficient for the parking needs of both offices.

Lessees may also avoid a contract due to the landlord's failure to provide services. Lack of heat, air conditioning or electrical power may represent a material breach, unless the problem was infrequent.

Another problem arises over noncompetition covenants. Suppose that a shopping center developer leases space to a drug store. Ivy Drug accepts the lease only after the developer promises not to lease any other space to competing drug stores. Then the developer has trouble leasing space and breaks the covenant, leasing other space to Laurel Drugs. Is this breach sufficiently material that Ivy Drug can break the original lease? A court would probably say yes.

Many cases involve breaches by tenants and attempts by lessors to break a lease. Nonpayment or late payment of rent is a common problem. A court found a material breach when a tenant failed to pay rent three months during one year. Chronic late payment has also been found to be a material breach. If a landlord consistently accepts late payments without protest, however, it may waive the right to terminate the lease.

Late payment of a single month's rent, especially if it is only days late, will generally not be held a material breach. In one case, a court found that even a two-month delay in rent payment was not material in the context of a 15-year lease. The court reasoned that a small interest payment could fully compensate the landlord.[4]

In some cases, such as a shopping center, the landlord takes its rent payments in a percentage of the tenant's profits rather than in a flat fee. In these instances, a landlord may terminate a lease if the tenant fails to take actions necessary to make profits. If a tenant movie theater consistently shows low-profit, unpopular films, for example, the lessor might terminate the lease.

Other material breaches by tenants have been found when the tenant fails to pay taxes or utility bills as required in the lease, when the tenant fails to make repairs or keeps the premises in poor condition, when the tenant makes unauthorized physical modifications to the property, and when a tenant violates a convenant prohibiting subleasing of the property.

Abandonment

The issue of whether a tenant has "abandoned" the leased property has legal significance. If so, the landlord can enter the property and terminate the lease, if it desires. Abandonment by a tenant may be necessary to protect its interests in a **wrongful construction eviction claim**. This occurs when a tenant complains that the landlord made the space uninhabitable and sues the landlord for damages.

A finding of abandonment requires acts by the tenant suggesting abandonment plus other evidence of an intention to abandon the property. The key issue is the intent of the tenant.

Mere breach of the lease is insufficient to constitute abandonment. Suppose that AJ Spirits leases property for a liquor store. AJ cannot get a liquor license and stops making payments on the lease. AJ informs the landlord that it is seeking someone with a license to operate the store. The developer cannot claim that AJ abandoned the lease. The developer's only remedy would be to argue that nonpayment was a material breach justifying rescission.

Nonpayment may be evidence of abandonment, however. If a tenant stopped paying, had no employees or property present on the leased premises, and failed to communicate with the landlord, abandonment may be found. Courts will also consider whether the tenant kept a key to the property, although other facts are also relevant.

When a tenant removes its furniture and other property from the leased space, abandonment is strongly suggested. This would not be abandonment, though, if the tenant were merely freeing up the space for an authorized subtenant.

If abandonment does occur, the landlord may consider the lease terminated or may permit the premises to remain vacated and then seek to recover rent from the tenant. A tenant that abandons leased space can then sue for constructive eviction.

[4]*57 E. 54 Realty Corp. v. Gay Nineties Realty Corp.*, 335 N.Y.S.2d 872 (1972).

In one case, a shopping center entered a ten-year lease with a retail store. At the time of the lease's commencement the store owners did not move in for years and the center leased the space to another store. Mall construction had been delayed, however, and the mall was not fully completed. A court found no abandonment by the original tenant, because the delay in occupying the space was due to the construction delays.[5] The shopping center developer remained liable on the original lease.

Wrongful Interference with Lease

Suppose that Kalbin & Orman, lawyers, have a long-term office space lease in the First Plaza building. Other lawyers may greatly desire this space and try to interfere with Kalbin & Orman's lease commitment. Or the Congress Square office building may be desperate for tenants and try to induce Kalbin & Orman to break the lease and move to their space. These actions may constitute wrongful interference with a lease contract.

Wrongful interference with contracts in general is discussed in Chapter 7 of *West's Business Law, Fifth Edition* and in Chapter 8 of *West's Legal Environment of Business*. In a case for wrongful interference with a commercial lease, a plaintiff must meet five requirements:

1. The existence of a binding lease.

2. The alleged wrongdoer's knowledge of the lease.

3. Its intentional causation of breaking the lease.

4. Without sufficient justification.

5. Resultant damages.

Possible liability also exists for interference with an expected lease that is not yet finalized.

In one case, a tenant had a ten-year oral commercial lease with a lessor. A competing building caused the tenants to breach their contract by making repeated visits to their leased property and offering inducements to move. The lease with the original lessor was unenforceable because it was not in writing. Nevertheless, the court enabled the original lessor to sue the new lessor for wrongful interference with contract.[6]

Competition among commercial lessors is legal. Suppose that the First Central office building advertises for new tenants from existing buildings. The building promises six months' free rent and to pay the last month's rent that the tenant owed its previous lessor. This is considered fair competition and not wrongful interference.

Other cases deal with interference with the tenant's rights in a lease. In one recent case, a small business operated a combination gas station and grocery store in leased property. The gasoline tanks and pumps were independently owned by an oil company. The oil company then locked the gas pumps (even though the store owed it no money) and suggested that the lessor evict the business. The court held that the oil company had wrongfully interfered with the lease contract.[7]

Several additional factors are relevant to the interference cases. First is the issue of fair competition. Both lessors and lessees have a right to seek out the best deal available and advertise for business. Competition becomes tortious when a party singles out a specific lease and seeks to induce a party to break that lease.

Second, where the lease is a prospective one, the relative certainty of the leasing is crucial. If parties are merely negotiating a lease, third parties have a right to jump into the negotiations and offer a better deal.

▬ Real Estate Fraud

As real estate transactions become increasingly important and costly, fraud claims have multiplied. There may be no more actual fraud in real estate transactions than there is in other types of business, but the high stakes make litigation more likely. Courts also have tended to adopt especially strict disclosure requirements for real estate sales, which make fraud claims easier to prove.

The basic requirements for a fraud claim are the same in real estate as in other contracts and include:

---

[5]*Fera v. Village Plaza, Inc.*, 218 N.W.2d 155 (Mich. App. 1974).

[6]*Daugherty v. Kessler*, 286 A.2d 95 (Md. 1972).
[7]*Fossett v. Davis*, 531 So.2d 849 (Ala. 1988).

1. A misstatement of material fact.

2. The misstatement is made intentionally or with reckless disregard for the truth.

3. Reasonable reliance on the part of the other party.

4. Damages caused due to the reliance on the misrepresentation.

Fraud may also result from silence, or the failure to disclose material facts when a party has a duty to disclose them. This is sometimes known as **constructive fraud**.

Fraud arises in many different situations in real estate sales. One frequent issue is whether the allegedly false statement was a fact (which may be fraud) or a mere prediction or opinion (which generally is not fraud).

Suppose that a seller of residential property describes it as "high and dry" on a promotional document. After sale of the property, the buyer discovers that the basement floods every time it rains in the area. The seller may argue that "high and dry" is too nonspecific to represent an assertion of fact. Some courts have held that this type of language is a statement of fact sufficient to constitute fraud, if incorrect.

In another disputed action, the seller's agent informed the purchasers of condominiums that the wooded land behind the building would remain undeveloped. In fact, she was aware that the community planned a playground for this site, which was eventually constructed. The seller argued that the playground was not built at the time of the statement and the statement was a prediction not a fact. The court disagreed and found fraud.[8]

Another common issue is whether a false statement is material enough to constitute fraud. Was the nature of the false statement really significant enough to affect the buyer's decision?

The materiality issue arises in cases where a seller has misrepresented the cost of heating or cooling the property to be sold. In one case, the seller of an apartment building informed the buyer that the electric and heat cost was $4000. The actual cost had been $5400 in the most recent year. The court held that this disparity was material —the difference could cause a temporary net loss that could ruin the buyer's investment plans.[9]

The following case presented an unusual issue of materiality and also presented the question of when silence (failure to disclose facts) could constitute fraud.

---

[8]*Boykin v. Hermitage Realty*, 360 S.E.2d 177 (Va. 1987).
[9]*Levy v. Bendetson*, 379 N.E.2d 1121 (Mass. App. 1978).

▬ Case 10.4
Reed v. King

California Court of Appeals
Third District, 1983,
193 Cal. Rptr. 130

Background and Facts *Dorris Reed purchased a house from Robert King for $76,000. King and his real estate agents were aware that a woman and her four children had been murdered in the house ten years earlier. They did not inform Reed of this fact, however. They did inform Reed that the house was fit for an elderly lady living alone. After the transaction, Reed learned of the house's history from a neighbor. She claims that the house is only worth $65,000 and sued to rescind the sale and for damages. The trial court dismissed Reed's action, and Reed appealed.*

BLEASE, Judge.

* * * *

Accordingly, the critical question is: does the seller have a duty to disclose here? Resolution of this question depends on the materiality of the fact of the murders.

In general, a seller of real property has a duty to disclose: "where the seller knows of facts materially affecting the value or desirability of the property which are known or accessible only to him and also knows that such facts are not known to, or within the reach of the diligent attention and observation of the buyer, the seller is under a duty to disclose them to the buyer." [Italics added; citations omitted.] (*Lingsch v. Savage*, supra, 213 Cal.App.2d at p. 735.) This broad statement of duty has led one commentator to conclude: "The ancient maxim caveat emptor ('let the buyer beware.') has little or no application to California real estate transactions."

*   *   *   *

Whether information is of sufficient materiality to affect the value or desirability of the property... depends on the facts of the particular case." (Lingsch, supra, 213 Cal.App.2d at p. 737.) Materiality "is a question of law, and is part of the concept of right to rely or justifiable reliance." (3 Witkin, Cal. Procedure (2d ed. 1971) Pleading, @ 578, p. 2217.) Accordingly, the term is essentially a label affixed to a normative conclusion. Three considerations bear on this legal conclusion: the gravity of the harm inflicted by nondisclosure; the fairness of imposing a duty of discovery on the buyer as an alternative to compelling disclosure, and its impact on the stability of contracts if rescission is permitted.

*   *   *   *

The murder of innocents is highly unusual in its potential for so disturbing buyers they may be unable to reside in a home where it has occurred. This fact may foreseeably deprive a buyer of the intended use of the purchase. Murder is not such a common occurrence that buyers should be charged with anticipating and discovering this disquieting possibility. Accordingly, the fact is not one for which a duty of inquiry and discovery can sensibly be imposed upon the buyer.

Reputation and history can have a significant effect on the value of realty. "George Washington slept here" is worth something, however physically inconsequential that consideration may be. Ill-repute or "bad will" conversely may depress the value of property. Failure to disclose such a negative fact where it will have a foreseeably depressing effect on income expected to be generated by a business is tortious.

*   *   *   *

Whether Reed will be able to prove her allegation that the decade-old multiple murder has a significant effect on market value we cannot determine. If she is able to do so by competent evidence she is entitled to a favorable ruling on the issues of materiality and duty to disclose. Her demonstration of objective tangible harm would still the concern that permitting her to go forward will open the floodgates to rescission on subjective and idiosyncratic grounds.

Decision and Remedy   *The court reversed the lower court's dismissal of Reed's claim.*

An allegedly fraudulent statement about future profitability was found to be immaterial in a case where a person purchased land with car wash facilities. Evidence showed that the purchaser was only interested in tax advantages of ownership and evidence on an overclaim of taxable income was therefore not material to the purchaser.[10]

[10]*Jackson v. Fontenot Building, Inc.*, 314 So.2d 516 (La. App. 1975).

Silence as Fraud

Still another important issue is whether the seller had a duty to disclose certain facts. This arises where everything said by the seller was perfectly honest, but the seller failed to inform the buyer of some hidden problem in the property. This can be constructive fraud due to the seller's silence in the face of a duty to disclose.

Water problems are relatively common in real estate. Sellers have been found liable in constructive fraud for failing to disclose that the property was in a flood zone, for failing to disclose a known erosion problem, for failing to disclose periodic water leakage problems, for failing to disclose a defective roof over the property, and for failing to disclose foundation or septic tank problems.

To recover for fraud, however, a purchasing plaintiff must show a reasonable reliance on the seller's statement. Suppose that Claire Serice, a home-seller, failed to tell Mike Kirk, a potential buyer, that her basement had water problems. When Mike visits the home during an open house, he is taken to the basement where there is a pool of water in a corner, but he asks no questions about it. On these facts, Mike had no reasonable reliance on Claire's failure to disclose the problem, because it was obvious from reasonable inspection of the property.

Remedies for Fraud

As a general rule, a person defrauded in a contract can choose either to rescind the contract and recover past payments or to affirm the contract and recover damages that resulted from the fraud. The plaintiff must choose between these remedies, however, and cannot recover both.

Many plaintiffs seek to rescind the real estate contract. Damages from fraud are often difficult to prove with the reasonable certainty demanded by the law. For example, what were the money damages in the case in which a playground was built on wooded land behind the purchased property? In other cases, the seller may lack the resources to pay damages.

Some plaintiffs may want to keep the property and recover damages for the fraud. Such plaintiffs may even recover punitive damages. To provide for punitive damages, the fraud must be especially reckless or malicious. Constructive fraud will seldom qualify for punitive damages.

Broker Liability

Purchasers of land increasingly are suing the real estate broker in the sale for fraud, as well as the seller. In many cases, the broker has "deeper pockets" than the seller and is better able to pay a damages judgment.

Over 80 percent of real estate sales involve the use of one or more brokers, who bring the buyer and seller together and help negotiate the contract. As a legal matter, the broker almost always represents the seller, even if the broker was working with the buyer throughout the negotiations. The broker is paid by the seller out of the purchase price. Some buyers are now paying brokers themselves, so that the broker represents their interests, rather than representing those of the seller.

As the seller's agent, the broker's central responsibilities are to the seller. As a result, courts traditionally held that the broker had no fiduciary duty to purchasers. Now, most courts hold that a broker has some fiduciary duties to the purchaser, however, and may certainly be sued for fraud.

Fraud by the broker has been found in a variety of situations, including when the broker inaccurately described zoning restrictions on property, and when the broker misrepresented condominium units as "outstanding investments" and "luxurious" although the broker knew the units to be of substandard quality.[11]

To prove fraud against a broker, the purchaser must meet the same legal standards as for a case against the seller. In the case of brokers, it may be more difficult for a plaintiff to show that the broker was aware that a representation was false, however. Brokers generally get their information on property from the seller and may unwittingly make false representations.

Although an unintentional false statement cannot be fraud, a broker might still have some liability for negligent misrepresentation. If the broker should have known that the information was unreliable, the broker may be liable for negligent misrepresentation. According to one ruling, the real estate broker must "employ a reasonable degree of effort and professional expertise to confirm or refute information from the seller which he knows, or should know, is pivotal to the transaction from the buyer's perspective."[12]

---

[11]*Cooper v. Jevne*, 128 Cal. Rptr. 130 (1976).

[12]*Tennant v. Lawton*, 615 P.2d 1305 (Wash. App. 1980).

A broker may also have liability in constructive fraud for failing to mention latent defects in the property. Some decisions have simply required brokers to disclose those defects that are "reasonably discoverable."

■ Ethical Perspectives

AIDS Disclosure and Residential Real Estate

A current controversy in both law and ethics concerns the extent to which sellers or real estate brokers must disclose that residents of a property for sale were infected with the virus that causes acquired immune deficiency syndrome ("AIDS") and may have died from the complications of the disease. Some argue that brokers have an ethical duty to disclose this fact. Others argue that brokers have an ethical duty *not* to disclose this fact.

The problem arises due to the following facts. First, many people are extremely fearful of contracting AIDS and seek to avoid any contact with the virus. Second, the actual risks of contracting AIDS from a house owned by an AIDS victim are essentially nonexistent.

Those who argue for a duty to disclose emphasize the importance of honesty and the buyer's right to make his or her own decisions. Ordinarily, ethics commands full disclosure of any information that would be material to a buyer. Buyers should not be "tricked" into purchasing property through nondisclosures.

This ordinary rule respects the individual rights of each human being to make his or her own choices. Even if a choice might seem irrational to others, each person has a right to make his or her own decisions and accept the consequences of those decisions. The contrary position is authoritarian.

While there are good reasons for fully informing buyers, there are exceptions to this rule. For example, federal civil rights laws prohibit discrimination in housing and in contracts, and a broker would not be required to disclose that a seller was African-American, even if that fact were significant to a prejudiced potential purchaser.

The AIDS context creates countervailing concerns. An irrational fear of contracting AIDS from a house may seriously harm AIDS sufferers. Such AIDS sufferers may be unable to sell their homes when it becomes financially necessary.

Disclosure of AIDS seems to discriminate against those who have already suffered greatly. Moreover, disclosure may also serve to enable discrimination against homosexuals. The very fact of disclosing the problem may reaffirm the public's inaccurate perceptions about the risks of AIDS and perpetuate unfair and false stereotypes about the disease and its victims.

The law has dealt with this problem by holding that a broker must answer honestly if a buyer asks about whether the previous owner had AIDS. This seems consistent with the ethical requirements of honesty. The law has *not* imposed a duty on brokers to disclose AIDS if unasked, however. This leaves the disclosure choice to ethics, rather than law.

■ **International Perspectives**

Foreign Investment in U.S. Real Estate

Foreign investment in United States real estate remains a controversial issue. When a huge Japanese company bought 51 percent ownership of Rockefeller Center in New York, a hailstorm of concern and criticism resulted. Many oppose foreign purchases of U.S. land.

Foreign investment is important to the real estate industry, however. With the decline of the dollar's value against foreign currencies, foreign investors became attracted to U.S. real estate. Maintenance of this foreign interest may be crucial to finding future buyers and maintaining real estate values. Many foreign investors work with U.S. investors in joint ventures for purchase of real property in this country.

The International Investment Survey Act of 1976 requires reporting of foreign purchases of certain United States assets. When a foreign person acquires a 10 percent or greater interest in a U.S. business enterprise, that enterprise must file a form BE-13 within 45 days of the acquisition transaction. The definition of a business enterprise also encompasses real property. An exception exists for purchases of less than 200 acres.

When filing is required, form BE-13 calls for information on the identity of the parties, the percentage ownership of the parties, and certain financial projections, among other information. In addition, the new owners must make annual periodic reports on the property in a form BE-605.

If these reports are not filed, or if filing is late, the company is subject to a civil penalty of up to $10,000, and individuals may be imprisoned for up to one year. The law is enforced by the Department of Commerce, which has been relatively tolerant of late filings so far.

Purchases are also subject to the Foreign Investment in Real Property Tax Act of 1980. This law also imposes reporting requirements on foreign purchases of land and creates special tax rules requiring immediate withholding of a percentage of profits at the time of the transaction. The federal government places additional reporting requirements on foreign purchases of U.S. farm property under the Agricultural Foreign Investment Disclosure Act of 1978.

Questions and Case Problems

1. A real estate broker told prospective buyers that a home could be heated for "a little over a hundred dollars a year." In fact, a defect in the house's boiler meant that the house could not be heated at all. After purchasing the house and discovering the defective boiler, the buyers sued for misrepresentation by the broker. The broker stated that she was simply speaking of the energy efficiency of the house and was unaware of a defect in the heating system. Should the broker be liable to the buyers? [*Spargnapani v. Wright*, 110 A.2d 82 (D.C. App. 1954)].

2. A property owner placed an advertisement in the paper that read: "Home and income . . . Be sure to see this 8-family on 90 ft. corner lot." A purchaser bought the land with the intent to rent out the eight units in the building. A local zoning ordinance, however, precluded renting out all the units. The purchaser complained that the advertisement was fraudulent by implying that the entire building could be leased. Was the advertisement fraudulent? [*Emily v. Bayne*, 371 S.W.2d 663 (Mo. App. 1963)]

3. The buyers of a building had a mortgage that prohibited them from prepaying more than 10 percent of the mortgage debt in any single year. The buyers later complained that they were unable to refinance the property in order to obtain access to their equity for use in other investments. They argued that the mortgate clause was an invalid restraint on their access to their own equity. The lender resisted prepayment, and the buyers went to court. Should the court order the lender to permit prepayment of the mortgage loan? [*Hartford Life Ins. Co. v. Randall*, 583 P.2d 1126 (Ore. 1978)].

4. A survey of California state-licensed savings and loan associations (S&Ls) found that a majority (113) of the institutions charged between 1 and 10 percent of the monthly payment for delinquent payments on loans. Twenty-one S&Ls charged one percent of the balance, and eleven charged a flat fee of about five dollars. Coast & Southern charged two percent of the total loan balance per year for the period of delinquent payment. A borrower who paid off a loan late complained that this charge was excessive and an unlawful penalty. Should the court uphold the S&L's late fee? [*Garrett v. Coast & Southern Federal Savings and Loan Ass'n*, 108 Cal. Rptr. 845 (1973)].

5. A commercial building rented space in a long-term lease to a pharmacy and granted the pharmacy an exclusive right to engage in this business in the building. Years later, the building owner leased a floor of the building to a medical group that operated its own pharmacy on the premises. The pharmacy sought to get out of the lease for the building. Was the rental of space to the medical group a material breach that enabled the pharmacy to break its lease on the building? [*Medico-Dental Bldg. Co. v. Horton & Converse*, 132 P.2d 457 (Cal. 1942)].

CHAPTER ELEVEN

Bank Regulation and Liability

KEY BACKGROUND

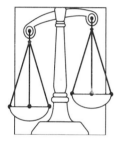

The essential background for this chapter on bank regulation and liability is found in Chapters 29 and 34 of *West's Business Law, Fifth Edition.* These chapters cover checks and banking and lender liability. Among the important points to remember from these chapters are:

- the duties of banks to customers

- federal regulation of banking deposits

- liability of lenders under contract law

- liability of lenders under tort law

* * *

The traditionally technical subject of banking has found its way onto the front pages of today's newspapers. Unfortunately, this reflects the troubles of banking, not its successes. As more and more banks face financial woes, banking has become increasingly intertwined with the legal system.

Legal structures have been important to banking since the first United States bank (the Bank of North America) was incorporated by the Continental Congress in 1781. Nineteenth-century American banks were subject to a variety of laws, but the legal system was broadly restructured during the Great Depression, after thousands of banks failed. The Federal Deposit Insurance Corporation ("FDIC") provided protection for depositors and set regulations for banks. Other laws restricted the types of financial activities in which banks could engage.

Many of the Depression-era laws remain critical to banking regulation. There are over 10,000 commercial banks in the United States, and virtually all of them belong to the FDIC insurance and regulation system. Banks remain subject to detailed regulation under other laws as well. Recent years have seen increased bank liability under various doctrines of lender liability.

Other depositary institutions, such as savings and loan associations (S&Ls), are closely related to banks and have suffered enormous problems in recent years. This chapter will focus on bank regulation and liability, because banks are the most economically significant institutions, but much savings and loan regulation roughly parallels that of banks.

Bank Regulation

Banks are regulated by several agencies. The FDIC regulates practices of all its member banks (which include all nationally chartered banks and most state-chartered banks). The Federal Reserve Board has supervisory authority over these banks and also regulates bank mergers, consumer credit protection laws, bank holding companies, and other issues. The Board also has some authority over nonmember banks to protect industry stability. States also have banking commissions that regulate their own banks. All regulation begins with

205

the decision of the federal government or a state government to grant a banking charter.

Bank Charters

A **charter** is necessary to enter the banking business. One cannot merely start up a new competing bank in the manner that one would start a new restaurant, for example. A new bank must meet state or federal chartering standards.

To obtain a new bank charter, one must first fill out an application with the relevant authority. The application generally must include a plan of operations, describe the management capabilities of the operators, set forth earnings prospects, and demonstrate sufficient initial capitalization to ensure that the bank is sound.

At the federal level, a decision whether to grant a charter is within the control of the Office of the Comptroller of the Currency, which is an agency in the Department of the Treasury. The Comptroller has great discretion in deciding whether to grant the charter. The key considerations are the effect of a new bank on consumer services and on the overall banking industry.

Minimum capital requirements must be met for a new bank charter. Some states will allow banks to be chartered with as little as $100,000 in initial capital. The Comptroller of the Currency, however, generally requires at least $1 million of initial capital to obtain a national charter. The amount of capital required may depend upon the size of the bank's community.

Bank Regulatory Supervision

Once a bank is chartered it becomes subject to a variety of regulations. The bank probably belongs to the FDIC system. This insurance is required for national banks and many state banks to enter the system in order to provide the assurance necessary to attract depositors. The FDIC presently insures deposits of up to $100,000 per account.

Because the FDIC does not want to be liable under this insurance, much of its regulation is directed toward preventing the failure of its member banks. A bank can fail when it makes loans to parties who cannot make payments (called "nonperforming" loans). If losses on nonperforming loans outstrip the bank's capital reserve, the bank may go into bankruptcy.

Every bank has some nonperforming loans. The key to solvency is to minimize the amount of these nonperforming loans and retain sufficient capital reserves to account for such loans. The federal government places specific limitations on banking activities to protect the solvency of banks.

One important regulation involves **lending limits**. Under law, a bank can loan no more than 15 percent of its capital stock and surplus to any single person or entity. Some exceptions to this limit exist, but it is designed to require diversification of lending in order to reduce risks.

Suppose that the Capital Bank has a capital stock and surplus of $100 million. The American Railway Co., a long-standing reliable bank customer, approaches Capital for a loan of $20 million in order to purchase new cars and upgrade their facilities. This would exceed the bank's lending limit. The bank could still make the loan if it could show that the extra 5 percent was secured by readily marketable collateral. The bank would have to demonstrate that railroad cars securing the loan were readily marketable.

The law used to restrict the amount of lending that was secured by real estate. A 1982 law removed much of this restriction, and consequently nonperforming real estate loans have become a major problem for banks.

Other regulations involve **transactions with affiliated banks**. As a rule, a bank cannot loan more than 10 percent of its capital stock and surplus to a single affiliated bank. Banks are prohibited from loaning more than 20 percent of their capital stock and surplus to all their affiliates combined.

Insider lending is also regulated. **Insider lending** is when a bank makes loans to its officers, directors, or to shareholders owning more than 10 percent of its voting stock. Insider lending is not prohibited, but specific approval requirements exist for loans to insiders that exceed a certain amount (e.g., 5 percent of capital surplus).

The FDIC also establishes *minimum capital ratios* for banks. These ratios require that a bank maintain a specific percentage of capital to its total assets. The minimum capital ratio now required is 3 percent. Additional capital requirements exist for banks that have a significant number of riskier loans.

The FDIC can also threaten to terminate deposit insurance coverage for banks that engage in unsafe or unsound practices or violate laws or regulations. To do so, the FDIC must provide the bank with notice of the intent to terminate and allow the bank 120 days to correct the problem. This period may be shortened to twenty days if necessary. If the problem is uncorrected, the bank must be provided with a hearing in order to defend itself.

The FDIC also has control over the ownership of insured banks. The Change in Bank Control Act of 1978 ("CBCA")[1] provides that a federal banking agency can disapprove a bank acquisition or change in control that is considered contrary to the public interest. The following decision illustrates an application of this power.

---

[1] 12 U.S.C. section 730q.

■ **Case 11.1**
Sletteland v.
Federal Deposit Insurance
Corporation
United States Court of Appeals,
District of Columbia Circuit, 1991
924 F.2d 350

Background and Facts   *The Sletteland family has controlled the Pigeon Falls State Bank since the 1920s. In the spring of 1988, George Sletteland, the bank's principal owner and chairman of the board of directors, was removed from his position by an FDIC order. The FDIC forbade him from further involvement in the bank, including the voting of his shares in directors' elections. George Sletteland then signed an agreement with his son, Peter Sletteland, already a bank director, giving Peter control over 41 percent of the bank's stock.*

The FDIC issued a notice disapproving of Peter's acquisition. Peter Sletteland objected, and a three-day trial was held before an administrative law judge ("ALJ"). The ALJ agreed with the FDIC that Peter lacked the competence and experience to warrant approval of the change in control of the bank. The FDIC adopted the ALJ's conclusions, and Peter appealed to federal court.

GINSBURG, Circuit Judge.

*   *   *   *

The FDIC determined that, because of Petitioner's youth, inexperience, and tenuous financial status, the change in control application should be disapproved. The record shows that at the time Petitioner filed for the change in control, he was only twenty-six years old. He had spent a total of three and a half years at three universities but had not earned a degree. He had not studied finance or banking, and his only banking experience consisted of summer employment as a teenager at another Wisconsin bank in which his father had an interest. More recently, Petitioner had worked for one year at a mens-wear boutique, and then had conducted an interior decorating business operating out of a spare bedroom in his apartment.

*   *   *   *

The record also shows that Petitioner had overstated to the FDIC the value of his interest in the interior decorating firm, that he had not disclosed a $5,000 loan from one of his father's business ventures, and that his father had been instrumental in arranging and guaranteeing the financing for the purchase of Petitioner's major asset (a partnership interest in a real estate venture).

*   *   *   *

The CBCA contemplates that financial regulatory agencies have the authority to deny approval of a change in control application when the proposed acquisition shows the potential for future problems. Thus, the Act allows an agency to disapprove an application if "the effect of the proposed acquisition ... may be substantially to lessen competition," or if "the financial condition of any acquiring person is such as might jeopardize the financial stability of the bank." See 12 U.S.C. § 1817 (j)(7)(B), (C) (emphasis added). Similarly, the Act instructs that an agency may disapprove a change in control where "the competence, experience, or integrity of any acquiring person ... indicates that it would not be in the interest of the depositors [or the public]." See 12 U.S.C. § 1817 (j)(7)(D) (emphasis added). This prescription requires the agency to make a predictive judgment, tied to supporting evidence, about problems that might result from the change in control. In light of Petitioner's youth, lack of a college degree or other relevant educational background, and limited work experience, we are satisfied in this case that there is substantial evidence "indicat[ing]" that Petitioner's "competence, experience, or integrity" rendered the proposed acquisition not in the best interest of the Bank's depositors or the public.

Decision and Remedy   *The court affirmed the FDIC's ruling.*

Director Liability

A bank director who fails to comply with statutes or regulations may be held personally liable for this failure. If a director undertakes a "knowing" violation of the law, he or she may be sued by regulatory agencies or by individual bank shareholders who have suffered damages.

For example, if a director assents to loans that exceed the federal lending limits, the director may be liable for resultant losses suffered by the bank. Directors recently received some legal protection in these claims. After an administrative law judge held directors liable for violating lending limits, a court overturned the ruling and found that directors could only be held liable in a court action.[2]

Bank directors may be sued even if they did not directly participate in the violation. A court approved an FDIC action that removed two directors who were aware of, but did not personally engage in, unlawful lending practices made by another director. The court found that the non-participating directors had a duty to prevent such transactions.[3]

Bank directors can also be liable whenever they engage in unsafe and unsound banking practices. Unsafe and unsound practices include failure to maintain an adequate cash reserve, failure to diversify the bank's loans, or making loans without sufficient precautions.

A director may be liable for irresponsible conduct or even the failure properly to monitor bank activities. In one case, a bank director was held personally liable for more than $1.4 million. The court found that the director had invested the bank's funds irresponsibly and continued to do so even after the bank suffered losses.

Bank directors and officers can be liable to make restitution for improperly acquired funds. The following decision demonstrates this authority.

Bank directors may even be criminally liable. Most state laws make it a felony for a bank director to make a false entry in the books or statements of a bank. Directors may be guilty of a misdemeanor for other actions, including a false statement about insurance of a bank's deposits.

Federal regulatory agencies also have power to remove an officer or director of a bank. This authority can be exercised if the director or officer has violated a law or regulation, has breached his or her fiduciary duty, or has engaged in any unsafe or unsound banking practice. Removal requires notice and a hearing for the director.

---

[2]*Larimore v. Comptroller of the Currency*, 789 F.2d 1244 (7th Cir. 1986).

[3]*Brickner v. FDIC*, 747 F.2d 1198 (8th Cir. 1984).

■■ Case 11.2
Hoffman v.
Federal Deposit Insurance
Corporation
United States Court of Appeals,
Ninth Circuit, 1990
912 F.2d 1172

Background and Facts *Alaska Continental Bank ("ACB") began encountering financial difficulties in 1986. Harold Hoffman was the president of the bank. The FDIC and state regulators informed Hoffman in May 1988 that they considered ACB to be technically insolvent and that it should be sold. Hoffman was told to be a caretaker of the bank in the interim and maintain the bank's assets as well as possible.*

Among the actions taken by the ACB board of directors was to buy out the balance of Hoffman's employment contract with the bank, because he declared that he would resign as of June 10, 1988. The cost of this buyout was over $61,000. The FDIC concluded that Hoffman was "bleeding off" the bank's assets and initiated an administrative proceeding. The Administrative Law Judge approved a cease and desist order entered by the FDIC that required Hoffman to make restitution of the buyout of his salary. Hoffman appealed.

FERNANDEZ, Circuit Judge

* * * *

A. *The Authority to Issue the Cease and Desist Order*

Hoffman claims that the FDIC had no authority to order him to make restitution of the $61,796.48 payment he received for his contract. We disagree.

There can be no doubt that the FDIC has authority to issue a cease and desist order if it finds that an institution has engaged in an unsafe or unsound practice. 12 U.S.C. § 1818(b)(1).

It has been said that an unsafe or unsound practice is one "'which is contrary to generally accepted standards of prudent operation, the possible consequences of which, if continued, would be abnormal risk or loss or damage to an institution, its shareholders, or the agencies administering the insurance funds'" and that it is a practice which has a "reasonably direct effect on an association's financial soundness." *Gulf Fed. Sav. & Loan Ass'n v. Federal Home Loan Bank Bd.*, 651 F.2d 259, 264 (5th Cir.1981), *cert. denied*, 458 U.S. 1121, 102 S.Ct. 3509, 73 L.Ed.2d 1383 (1982). Self-dealing has been identified as an unsafe or unsound practice because of the conflict it creates between the interests of the institution and the interests of an individual. *First National Bank of Lamarque v. Smith*, 610 F.2d 1258, 1265 (5th Cir.1980); *Independent Bankers Ass'n of America v. Heimann*, 613 F.2d 1164, 1168 (D.C. Cir. 1979), cert. denied, 449 U.S. 823, 101 S. Ct. 84, 66 L.Ed.2d 26 (1980). Those cases turn on the principle that breaches of fiduciary duty by bank officials are inherently dangerous and cannot be considered safe. Cf. *Federal Sav. & Loan Ins. Corp. v. Molinaro*, 889 F.2d 899, 903-04 (9th Cir. 1989).

As the FDIC board pointed out, during a time when Hoffman and ACB's board knew that they were supposed to be acting as caretakers of a bank that was rapidly declining, they decided to divert some of its assets in a way that could not help but cause detriment to the shareholders and other creditors of the bank. Evidence before the ALJ and the FDIC indicated that Hoffman was cashed out because the bank was about to close. The terms were favorable to Hoffman; they amounted to prepayment of his salary to the end of his contract—December 2, 1988—although it was rather obvious that he would not be working that long. This would raise eyebrows under the best of circumstances; the FDIC properly determined that it was considerably more dubious under the circumstances of this case. Even if there are cases in which the FDIC and the courts should countenance the idea that a breach of fiduciary duty is not an unsafe or unsound practice, this is not one of those cases.

* * * *

B. *Due Process*

Hoffman asserts that he and ACB were deprived of due process at the hearing before the ALJ, because he was not permitted to contest the determination that ACB was, in fact, insolvent. The ALJ did not consider that to be relevant to the cease and desist hearing. We agree.

Hoffman's theory seems to be that if ACB were not really insolvent, he and the Board could not have known that it was insolvent. Thus, the argument goes, their actions could not have been unsafe or unsound and, surely, they could not have had any intention of doing wrong. Therefore, when he was not allowed to prove that ACB was not really insolvent, he was deprived of his right to a fair hearing.

There is some surface appeal to that argument, but it will not withstand and analysis that dips even slightly below the surface. The FDIC has the authority to issue a notice of charges if an insured institution has engaged or is engaging in an "unsafe or unsound" practice. 12 U.S.C. § 1818(b)(1). If the FDIC finds an unsafe or unsound practice, then the FDIC may issue an order to cease and desist, whether the institution is insolvent or not.

Whatever else the Board and Hoffman chose to tell themselves, they could hardly doubt that ACB was in serious financial straits, that the regulators thought ACB's condition so serious that closure was coming in a matter of weeks, and that they had been told to act as caretakers and preserve the bank's assets to the extent possible. Their activities during that period can hardly be viewed as anything but an attempt to preserve their own positions at the expense of the bank. Whether, as it ultimately turned out, the bank was insolvent or not, it was most apparent that its assets must be preserved. Given that, it was hardly prudent to decide that the best thing for ACB and its assets was to buy out Hoffman's contract, because he had decided to abandon a rapidly sinking ship.

In other words, the decision of the ALJ and the Board was quite right and they denied Hoffman no rights by refusing to entertain an attack upon the determination that insolvency actually existed. The FDIC found Hoffman's position to be disingenuous; that is a good characterization.

Decision and Remedy   *The court affirmed the FDIC's order.*

Failing Banks

In addition to the specific regulations described above, federal agencies conduct generalized bank examination and supervision in an attempt to avoid bank failures. This system is intended to prevent bank failures and alleviate the consequences when failure does occur. The FDIC considers a bank's capital adequacy, asset quality, management ability, earnings performance, and liquidity. Then banks are rated on a scale of 1 to 5.

A rating of "1" is best and reflects a very sound bank. A rating of "3" suggests a potential problem bank, and regulators will keep an eye on its practices to prevent further deterioration. A rating of "4" is a serious problem bank that requires immediate action. A rating of "5" is lowest and reflects a bank that is likely to fail even with rescue measures (these banks are sometimes called "zombies").

Suppose that the Second National Bank made a significant number of large real estate loans, whereupon the local real estate values collapsed. Second National may have low capital adequacy (due to nonperforming loans), poor asset quality (its loans may not be paid off), and correspondingly low earnings performance. The above factors may also call into question the bank's management capabilities.

If the FDIC found the bank to be "unsafe or unsound" it could then step in to attempt to save Second National from its management practices. The FDIC has great influence because it can threaten to terminate the bank's insurance unless the bank agrees to certain reform measures. The FDIC may also obtain a cease-and-desist order from an administrative law judge that compels certain corrective actions.

The FDIC might force changes in management practices on Second National, including tougher standards for making loans, cutbacks on bank overhead expenses, seeking additional capital from private sources or the Federal Reserve, and even the suspension and removal of bank officers and directors.

Procedural protections are required for final cease-and-desist orders. The regulatory agency must serve notice on the bank and provide for a hearing after at least a month. Violation of a cease-and-desist order is punishable by a $1000-per-day fine.

Bank Closures

If a bank is insolvent, or failing, the FDIC may seek to shut down the bank before further deterioration occurs. The FDIC lacks authority to close a bank directly. The FDIC can use its authority to terminate insurance coverage to impel the bank to close, however. The Comptroller of the Currency, which charters banks, also has the authority to close them down.

The FDIC takes over as the receiver of a failed bank. As receiver, it manages the bank in order to preserve as much equity as possible. It may also liquidate the assets of the bank and distribute them to creditors. The FDIC pays off depositors from the bank's funds or from its insurance fund. In the past, over 99 percent of bank depositors have been repaid in full.

As receiver, the FDIC also is subrogated to the bank's legal claims against others. The FDIC may attempt to obtain damages from the bank's directors, officers or other parties who contributed to the failure.

The FDIC often tries to save a failed bank through a **purchase and assumption transaction** ("P&A"). In a P&A, a successful bank agrees to assume the liabilities of the failed bank in exchange for the assets of the bank. The FDIC pays cash to the successful bank to make up for any excess of liabilities over assets.

The FDIC's powers over failed banks are complicated by the ability of a company to declare bankruptcy and place itself under the jurisdiction of a bankruptcy court. The complexity of the situation is illustrated by the failure of First RepublicBank Corporation in Texas.

First RepublicBank was a holding company with forty-one subsidiary banks. The FDIC provided $1 million in emergency assistance to the subsidiary banks in order to reassure depositors. The FDIC then sought out a buyer for the subsidiary banks. The FDIC found NCNB Corporation as a purchaser.

The Comptroller of the Currency then shut down First RepublicBank's subsidiary banks and sold them to NCNB. The next day, First RepublicBank itself filed for bankruptcy. The FDIC sought to recover from First RepublicBank itself for allegedly diverting hundreds of millions of dollars from the subsidiary banks (by overextracting dividends and purchasing property at less than fair market value). The bankruptcy filing helped protect First RepublicBank from these claims.

FIRREA

Congress provided bank regulators with broad new powers in the Financial Institutions Reform, Recovery and Enforcement Act of 1989 ("FIRREA"). While much of FIRREA was intended to correct crises in the savings and loan industry, FIRREA's provisions also affect other banking institutions.

FIRREA expanded the enforcement powers of the FDIC and other regulatory agencies. FIRREA makes clear the authority to issue cease-and-desist orders to restrict the growth of the banking institution, rescind agreements or contracts, and force parties to make restitution for losses caused by an officer or director of the bank.

FIRREA also modified the authority of the FDIC to collect monetary penalties. If a bank or officer violates a law, regulation or FDIC agreement, it is subject to a fine of up to $5000 per day of violation. If the violation is part of a pattern of misconduct or causes a significant loss to the institution, the fine may be up to $25,000 per day. Knowing misconduct that causes a substantial loss is punishable by fines of up to $1,000,000 per day.

Other Bank Regulations

There are a myriad of detailed bank regulations. In addition to the broad supervisory authority of the FDIC and other regulatory agencies, specific regulations limit banks in the areas of branch banking, bank holding companies, bank mergers, and depositor privacy.

Branch banking has historically been a regulatory controversy. This is the ability of a bank to establish branches in other geographic areas. Government policy dating back to the nineteenth century has limited the ability of a bank to establish branches in other states, or even in other counties.

Recent years have seen some liberalization of branch banking, with many states permitting branch banks. State laws vary, however. Massachusetts allowed branch banking but only with other New England states. Many states, such as Illinois, permit reciprocal branch banking, i.e., with banks from states that permit Illinois banks also to establish branches.

Bank holding companies also are regulated under the Bank Holding Company Act of 1956. Some corporations sought to evade branch banking restrictions by creating holding companies controlling many different banks in different states. The 1956 Act largely prevents this action.

Bank holding company acquisitions are limited to preserve competition in banking. Banks are also restricted in their ability to participate in insurance, securities and other riskier financial transactions. Bank holding companies are also restricted in these activities.

Bank mergers raise many of the same antitrust concerns as mergers of other corporations but are subject to special legislation in the Bank Merger Act of 1960. This law requires the written consent of the Comptroller of the Currency or other federal supervisory agency whenever an insured bank seeks to acquire another insured bank.

In 1989, the Comptroller refused to permit St. Croix Valley Bancshares, Incorporated, to acquire the Stillwater Bancorporation, Incorporated. Federal officials were concerned that the resulting bank would not be adequately capitalized.

Traditional antitrust concerns are also present in bank mergers. Courts have halted horizontal mergers among competing banks in a given market. Courts have been more willing to permit mergers that extend competition into new geographic areas.

Federal regulations also protect the financial privacy of bank depositors. The Fair Credit Reporting Act of 1970 limits the use and release of credit reports. A bank must have a proper purpose for requesting credit information and must inform the customer if it takes any adverse action based upon the credit report.

▬ Lender Liability

Lender liability is not only one of the most significant issues in banking law, but is among the most significant issues in all business law. In one recent year, six of the ten largest jury verdicts against defendants were in lender liability cases. Several lender liability cases resulted in verdicts in excess of $100 million.

Chapter 34 of *West's Business Law, Fifth Edition* sets forth the foundations of lender liability. This chapter covers potential sources of liability under contract law, under tort law, and under environmental law. This section expands on the coverage of Chapter 34 and extends into other areas of lender liability.

Common Law Sources of Lender Liability

A primary source of lender liability is found in the loan contract. A lender may be liable for breach of contract or for promissory estoppel, even in the absence of a binding contract.

In addition to specific duties created in a contract and by contract law, the lender is subject to a duty of good faith and fair dealing with the borrower. This very general duty requires that the lender deal honestly and fairly with the borrower.

Another source of lender liability is tort law. The lender may be liable for the torts of fraud, duress, interference with business relationships, or an emerging tort of breach of fiduciary duty.

Contexts of Lender Liability

Banks face lender liability in certain recurring contexts that call for caution. These include preliminary loan negotiations, extension of credit, and loan terminations.

Banks may find themselves liable in loan applications and commitments. In the course of negotiating a loan, a bank may make certain promises to a prospective borrower. That borrower may seek to hold the bank to its "gentlemen's agreement" or negotiating promises, even in the absence of a firm binding loan contract. A bank may be liable to provide credit based on its conduct in such negotiations.

In one important case, a company negotiated a loan of $6 million and obtained a commitment letter. In finalizing the loan, the lender added a new condition that the borrower refused to accept. The loan fell through, and the company was forced into bankruptcy. The lender was held liable for a breach of good faith.[4]

Banks can also be liable for negligent handling of loan applications. Where a bank solicits loan applications but fails to process them promptly, the bank is subject to liability. Suppose that Capital Bank negotiates a loan with Hallstrom, Inc. Capital receives a loan application and promises to process the application within two months and lock in a favorable interest rate. If the bank negligently fails to do so, it may be liable.

Banks have also been held liable for the termination of lines of credit extended to regular customers. In one case, a bank terminated a $1 million line of credit with borrowers. The borrower demonstrated that the bank wrongfully terminated the borrower due to inaccurate rumors of organized crime involvement in the borrower's business. A court granted the borrower $15 million in damages, including punitive damages.

Another source of liability is loan termina-

tion. Banks can be found liable for wrongfully accelerating a loan and demanding full payment without sufficient cause. In one case, a borrower was consistently late in payments, but the bank took no action. Finally, after a payment was again late, the bank called in the loan and demanded full payment. This destroyed the borrower's business. The court found the lender liable, because the latest payment was only one day late and because the bank had previously accepted late payments without penalty.[5]

Banks also have been found liable for refusal to release security interest in property. In one significant case, a bank extended two loans to one party, for $1.5 million and for $185,000. The smaller loan was secured by a deed of trust on a piece of land. After the second loan was paid off, the bank refused to release its security interest in the land, hoping to use it as collateral against the larger loan. This prevented the borrower from using the land to obtain further financing and ultimately caused the borrower's bankruptcy. A jury held the bank liable for over $9 million in actual damages and $50 million in punitive damages.[6]

Another source of lender liability arises out of **participation agreements**. This is where two or more banks jointly extend credit to the same borrower. One bank is considered the lead lender and administers the loan.

Suppose that Second State Bank wants to make a loan to a local developer but cannot fund the entire loan itself. Second State then presents the loan to other banks for their participation. If Second State exaggerates the creditworthiness of the borrower, other participating banks may sue Second State, as lead lender, if a problem arises. The lead lender and other participants also may be liable to borrowers.

Banks may also be liable for negligent loan administration. Failure to properly post loan payments to a borrower's account has been the basis for lender liability. Other banks have been held liable for failing to obtain insurance as agreed.

Lenders are more frequently found liable under a combination of the above circumstances. Lenders are not always liable for borrowers' problems, however, as demonstrated by the following decision.

---

[4]*999 v. CIT Corporation*, 776 F.2d 866 (9th Cir. 1985).

[5]*Sahadi v. Continental Illinois National Bank and Trust Company of Chicago*, 706 F.2d 193 (7th Cir. 1983).

[6]*Robinson v. McAllen State Bank*, 48 BNA Banking Rptr. 1004 (Tex. Dist. Ct. 1987).

Case 11.3
The Bank of Shaw v. Posey
Supreme Court of Mississippi, 1990
573 So.2d 1355

Background and Facts   *John Posey and Danny Watkins considered opening a sporting goods store to be called the Delta Outdoorsman. Posey, forty-six years old but unable to read or write, was to arrange the financing, and Watkins, thirty years old and without retail experience, was to manage the store. Posey and Watkins contacted Glenn Sandroni, Vice President of The Bank of Shaw about financing. They alleged that he promised to lend them $125,000 for the first year's start-up costs and later convert the loan to a five-year loan.*

Posey and Watkins began borrowing money in February 1984 and took out a series of loans totaling $134,000 within a month. The president of the bank had ordered Sandroni not to make loans in excess of $100,000, but he went forward with the additional $34,000. The Delta Outdoorsman opened on March 14, 1984. Soon thereafter, Posey and Watkins sought a $115,000 loan from the Small Business Administration ("SBA"), but their application was rejected. They claimed that Sandroni had promised to make the loan, if the SBA refused.

The store never operated at a profit. The bank refused to make additional loans. Posey and Watkins sued the bank alleging fraud, breach of contract, and negligent misrepresentation, due to alleged promises to provide financing. Soon thereafter, the store was foreclosed, and Posey and Watkins filed for bankruptcy. After a trial, a jury returned a verdict against the bank of $240,000 for Watkins and $162,000 for Posey. The bank appealed.

PITTMAN, Judge.

*   *   *   *

Even assuming, for the sake of argument, that Sandroni had made all of the representations which are attributed to him, the evidence is far from clear and convincing that the failure of The Delta Outdoorsman and the resulting financial difficulties of the Posey and Watkins were the result of Sandroni's representations. It is obvious that The Delta Outdoorsman was a losing proposition from the beginning. The evidence raised serious doubt that either partner invested any of his own funds in the business and showed that Posey and Watkins were in default on their accounts before they even opened for business. The business never made a profit, even in its best months, despite the fact that Sandroni disbursed a greater amount of funds than Posey and Watkins allege he promised. The Delta Outdoorsman (Posey and Watkins) failed to pay the rent for seven straight months. Having received all of the first-year loans that they asked for, Posey and Watkins were nevertheless unable to show that the business could or ever would be a profitable venture. There were several stores in Cleveland selling essentially the same merchandise and several of those stores, because of greater volume, could sell at significantly lower prices than could The Delta Outdoorsman. At trial, Posey acknowledged that the business could not have generated the $8,000.00 per month which would have been required to service the debt of $362,373.49 and probably could not have generated the $3,000.00 per month required to service the debt of $157,473.49. Given these facts, it is not possible to say that Posey and Watkins proved, by clear and convincing evidence, that the business's failure and their attendant losses were attributable to any fraudulent representations by Sandroni or any actions by the Bank.

An examination of the alleged fraudulent representations shows that not only did Posey and Watkins fail to prove they were damaged by any such representations, they also failed to prove other essential elements of fraud by clear and convincing evidence.

First, Posey and Watkins claimed that they were damaged by Sandroni's statement, made before they went into business, that he would lend them $125,000.00 and later convert first-year interim loans to a long-term note. Sandroni denied making any promise to lend that amount and any promise of long-term financing. However, the short-term loans were advanced. Prior to any request for converting the debt to long-term debt, there was a failure known to The Bank of Shaw and to the plaintiffs, a failure to pay for inventory, to pay rent, or to conduct The Delta Outdoorsman business in an acceptable business-like manner. This Court will not require a financial institution to lend funds to a failed business in contradiction to good judgment and in detriment to the resources of the Bank, a public institution and a private investment. Even had he made the representations, they both were promises of future conduct which would not undergird recovery unless there were also clear and convincing evidence that the promises were made with a present, undisclosed intention not to perform. Posey and Watkins failed to put on any such proof.

Decision and Remedy *The court reversed the jury verdict and rendered judgment in favor of The Bank of Shaw.*

Statutory Sources of Lender Liability

In addition to general principles of common law, lenders are susceptible to liability under certain federal and state statutes.

A common statutory source of lender liability is under the federal *securities laws*. A lender that buys or sells stock based on nonpublic information acquired from a borrower can be liable for insider trading. The most relevant securities law provisions are those that prevent fraud. A lender may also be liable for securities fraud, when the lender has participated in preparing documents that are misleading or false.

Lenders are usually not directly liable under securities laws, because they do not control the corporation selling the securities. Lenders may be liable, however, for aiding and abetting a securities law violation. Aiding and abetting lender liability has the following three elements:

1. Some person committed a violation of securities laws.

2. The lender was aware of playing a role in an activity that was unlawful.

3. The lender knowingly and substantially assisted the violation.

A lender is not liable for aiding and abetting a securities law violation simply by making a loan to a corporate violator. A lender is subject to liability for taking a more active role. Suppose that the First National Bank's appraisers provided inflated real estate appraisals to DevelopCo., which were published in a prospectus for issuing new securities. First National could be liable for aiding and abetting a securities law violation.

Another statutory source of lender liability is found in the environmental laws, especially the Comprehensive Environmental Response Compensation and Liability Act of 1980 ("CERCLA"), which is discussed in Chapter 14 on environmental liability. This law requires landowners, among others, to pay the costs of cleaning up hazardous waste problems on their property.

Lenders become potentially liable under CERCLA when they take property in a foreclosure proceeding. Lenders can also be liable if they participate in the management of a company that owns a hazardous waste disposal site.

A third source of statutory lender liability is the antitrust laws. Banks are potentially liable under the general antitrust laws for such violations as price fixing, group boycotts, and other anticompetitive activities.

In 1970, Congress passed a specific antitrust law to governing banking practices, in the Bank Holding Company Act Amendments. These amendments contain three major prohibitions on lender actions:

1. A prohibition on a bank's extending credit conditioned on the borrower's willingness to obtain some additional service from the bank.

2. A prohibition on a bank's extending credit conditioned on the borrower's providing some additional credit or service for the bank.

3. A prohibition on a bank's extending credit conditioned on the borrower's not dealing with some competitor of the bank.

The borrower can sue for damages to enforce these provisions. Triple damages are provided under the act.

In a leading case, a bank agreed to loan money to a corporation on the condition that stock in the corporation be transferred to one of the bank's other customers. A court held that this violated the Act's prohibition on demanding additional services in exchange for credit.[7]

▰ Mortgage Lender Liability

Lending for new homes creates different and significant sources of lender liability. Many residential mortgages are held by savings and loan institutions, but banks and life insurance companies also have a significant share of the home lending market.

The special problem of mortgage lenders is illustrated by the following scenario. Paul Barro obtains a loan to build a new house. After the house is built, Paul discovers serious defects in the house that destroy its value. Paul might sue the construction company that built the house, but suppose that the construction company lacks the funds to pay Paul's damages. Paul may sue

the lender to recover the damages from his defective home.

Contract Liability

A contract between a lender and a home purchaser takes the form of a loan agreement that sets forth the basic terms of the mortgage. For its own protection, a bank will usually make provisions for inspections of the property during the construction process and provisions for surveys of the property. Borrowers have used these provisions as a source for lender liability.

Suppose that Paul's construction loan had a provision for periodic inspections by his lender. The bank made these inspections but either did not discover the defect or did not disclose it. Courts may permit Paul to recover from the bank. Paul will lose, however, if the contract or other evidence demonstrates that the inspections were intended only for the benefit of the bank and not of the borrower.

A second mortgage lender liability problem involves claims against the borrower by third parties. In order to protect their collateral, lenders obligate themselves to ensure that no third parties have security interests in the property. For example, construction companies may have a **mechanics' lien security interest** in the house until they are paid.

In one case, a lender agreed to ensure that the property was not encumbered by mechanics' liens. The general contractor who built the house was not paid and recorded a lien against the property. The borrower had to pay off the general contractor and sued the bank for damages. A court found the lender liable because it had assumed a duty to protect the mortgaged real estate from third-party liens.[8]

Lenders may also be liable for assuming a duty to survey property under construction. In one case, a builder had much of the house built, when it was discovered that two feet of the garage were on the property of an adjacent owner. The bank had not procured a survey. The borrowers had to tear down the garage and rebuild it. A court found the lender was not liable, though, because the lender had not promised to obtain a

---

[7]*Swerdloff v. Miami National Bank*, 584 F.2d 54 (5th Cir. 1978).

[8]*Prudential Insurance Co. v. Executive Estates, Inc.*, 309 N.E.2d 1117 (Ind. App. 1978).

survey at any particular time in the construction process.[9]

Negligent Misrepresentation

A borrower may recover from a mortgage lender for negligent misrepresentation, if the lender failed to use reasonable care in informing the borrower of information. Negligent misrepresentation may involve a failure to inform the buyer of construction defects, as well as other material facts.

In one leading case, the borrowers contracted to purchase a home, conditioned on securing a mortgage. A lender conducted a negligent appraisal of the value of the home and approved the mortgage application. After moving into the house and discovering significant structural defects, the buyer sued the lender for negligently misinforming him of the home's value. The court found that the lender negligently performed the appraisal and that the buyer relied on the negligent appraisal in purchasing the property. The lender was liable for the buyer's damages.[10]

Indirect Lender Liability

Under some circumstances, a lender may be liable to a home buyer, even if the lender did not make the loan to purchase the home. This arises when a lender makes a loan to a large developer who builds an entire subdivision. The developer then markets individual houses to buyers. Some dissatisfied buyers have sued the lender, after the developer proved insolvent.

Courts have held lenders to a duty to indirect purchasers, depending upon their involvement in the subdivision development. In the first significant case, which arose in California, buyers of a home suffered serious damages because the house was built on adobe soil that could not support the home's foundation as constructed. After the developer suffered financial problems, the lender was held liable to home purchasers because it retained the right of first refusal on mortgages to home buyers, had the right to inspect and control construction work, and obtained

profits from the development over and above its interest payments.[11]

In a subsequent case, California courts held that a lender was not liable for defective development. The court emphasized that the lender did nothing more than provide funds for development for interest and took no additional profit.[12] Other states are divided over whether lenders may be indirectly liable to home buyers.

Setoff

A common source of banking litigation is known as **setoff.** This problem arises in the following circumstances. Suppose that Nancy Nallor has a large savings account with the Capital Bank. Nancy also takes out a loan from Capital Bank. The note then comes due, but Nancy refuses to pay. Setoff means that Capital Bank can apply Nancy's funds from her savings account to pay off the loan.

There are some limitations on the right of setoff. Some states require that the bank notify the depositor of the setoff. California law precludes a bank from reducing a demand deposit account below $1000, when the debt is from a consumer credit transaction. Setoff is not allowed if the bank has contracted or promised not to do a setoff.

Setoff is also complicated when other creditors have a claim to the depositor's funds. Many setoff questions involve the priority on claims to a depositor's funds. A bank must compete with other creditors for a right to the funds.

If the depositor has granted a security interest in the bank deposit to a third party, and if the institution is aware of this fact, it may not set off the deposit to the detriment of the third party. Banks may not set off funds deposited in a special account with restrictions upon its use.

Banks also are limited in setoff to debts that have come due. A bank generally cannot use its setoff rights in anticipation of a future default. The following case illustrates some of the complexities in assigning setoff rights in a disputed case.

[9]*Mosley v. Perpetual Savings & Loan Association,* 227 S.E.2d 163 (N.C. App. 1976).

[10]*Larsen v. United Federal Savings & Loan Association,* 300 N.W.2d 281 (Iowa 1981).

[11]*Connor v. Great Western Savings & Loan Association,* 447 P.2d 609 (Cal. 1968).

[12]*Bradler v. Craig,* 79 Cal. Rptr. 401 (1969).

■ **Case 11.4**
Carpenters Southern
California Administrative
Corporation v. Manufacturers
National Bank of Detroit
United States Court of Appeals,
Sixth Circuit, 1990
910 F.2d 1339

Background and Facts   *Pheney Construction Company had an*
account with the Manufacturers National Bank of Detroit. In September
1986, Carpenters Southern California Administrative Corporation,
which administers employee benefit plans, obtained a judgment of over
$96,000 against Pheney for unpaid contributions to an employee plan.
In December 1987, Pheney obtained a loan and executed a promisso-
ry note of $140,000 in favor of Manufacturers, and the due date for
this note was in March 1988. The loan contained an acceleration clause
permitting the bank to call the note whenever the bank "deems itself
insecure."

In February 1989, Carpenters served Manufacturers with a
court writ of garnishment in an attempt to levy Pheney's bank accounts
(of $33,000) to pay in part the judgment that Carpenters had received
in court. Manufacturers promptly accelerated Pheney's note and took
his deposits as setoff on the loan. Carpenters sued the bank over the
Pheney deposits, and a federal district court granted summary judg-
ment to Carpenters. Manufacturers appealed.

NORRIS, Circuit Judge.

*   *   *   *

Generally, a bank may set off a depositor's bank accounts against the
depositor's indebtedness to the bank under the following conditions:
(1) the funds used for the setoff are the property of the depositor; (2)
they are deposited in a general account without restriction as to their
use; (3) the existing indebtedness is due and owing at the time of the
setoff; and (4) there is a mutuality of obligation between the depositor
and the bank and between the debt and the funds on deposit. *Hansman*
v. Imlay City State Bank, 121 Mich.App. 424, 430, 328 N.W.2d 653, 656
(1982). Thus, when exercising the right to setoff in the garnishment context, a bank may not set off a judgment-debtor's bank account against
an indebtedness which is not mature at the time of setoff. *See, e.g., Walter*
v. Nat'l City Bank, 42 Ohio St.2d 524, 330 N.E.2d 425 (1975).

The district court concluded that Manufacturers was not entitled
to set off Pheney's accounts because the promissory note did not mature
until after the garnishment writ was served. Manufacturers contends
that the note was mature when it exercised its right of setoff, since it
became due, albeit after service of the writ, when the bank in good faith
deemed itself insecure and invoked the acceleration clause. Accordingly,
the bank argues, it was at that point entitled to set off the funds, even
though under normal circumstances the note would not have fallen due
until March 14, 1988.

A majority of courts have held that a garnishee-bank may exercise its right of setoff against indebtedness which matures after the garnishment writ is served. *See, e.g., State Nat'l Bank v. Towns*, 36 Ala.App.
677, 62 So.2d 606, 607 (1953) (setoff allowed even though bank invoked
acceleration clause after being served with garnishment writ); *Valley*
Nat'l Bank v. Hasper, 6 Ariz.App. 376, 379-80, 432 P.2d 924, 927-28 (1967)
(setoff by bank allowed even though bank accelerated debt due under
conditional sales contract after it was served with garnishment writ);
Messall v. Suburban Trust Co., 244 Md. 502, 224 A.2d 419, 421-23 (1966)
(setoff allowed even though note accelerated after service of garnishment writ); *Brown v. Maquire's Real Estate Agency*, 343 Mo. 336, 121 S.W.2d

754, 759-61 (1938) (setoff allowed even though note accelerated after service of garnishment writ); 6 Am.Jur.2d *Attachment and Garnishment* § 374 (1963).

This seems to us to be the better rule. Although we are unable to find authoritative Michigan case law precisely on point, neither has anything been called to our attention that leads us to believe that the Michigan Supreme Court, if presented with the issue, would adopt a different rule. In a garnishment proceeding, the judgment-creditor garnishor stands in the same position as the judgment-debtor with respect to the garnishee and may not prevail against the garnishee unless the debtor could do so. *See Poelman v. Payne*, 332 Mich. 597, 52 N.W.2d 229, 230 (1952); *State Nat'l Bank v. Towns*, 62 So.2d at 607; *Valley Nat'l Bank v. Hasper*, 432 P.2d at 924; Mich.Ct.R. 3.101(H)(2). Carpenters concedes that, if Pheney had attempted to withdraw funds from his account to pay Carpenters before the note was due, Manufacturers could have invoked the acceleration clause, set off Pheney's account against the note, and refused the withdrawal. A holding that Manufacturers could not accelerate the note and set off the account after Carpenters served the bank with a writ of garnishment would place Carpenters in a better position than Pheney with respect to the funds in Pheney's bank accounts.

Accordingly, so long as Manufacturers acted in good faith in deeming itself insecure and invoking the acceleration clause, it was entitled to set off Pheney's bank accounts against the note.

Decision and Remedy   *The court reversed the district court judgment and remanded for further proceedings consistent with this opinion.*

Ethical Perspectives

An Ethical Duty to Loan?

A general principle of our free enterprise system is that each businessperson has a right to decide which contracts to enter. Like others, a banker has a right to decide which loans to make. The law places only limited restrictions on this right, such as a prohibition on racial discrimination in lending decisions.

Despite the prohibition on racial discrimination, studies have shown that blacks and other minorities are denied loans far more often than are whites. People who want to borrow for construction in minority communities generally have more difficulty obtaining loans than people in more affluent, white communities.

Some bankers explain that this statistical disparity has nothing to do with discrimination. They note that blacks applying for loans may have less income or a poorer credit history. They also note that properties in minority communities are less marketable and therefore riskier for lenders. These are, of course, legitimate and nondiscriminatory reasons for loan denial.

But might bankers have an ethical responsibility to relax their lending rules somewhat for minority communities? Loan denials may create a self-reinforcing spiral of poverty in such communities. If builders cannot obtain loans to renovate these communities, the existing buildings will deteriorate further and more affluent individuals will move to wealthier areas. This will in turn make the minority community worse and make it even more difficult to get future development loans. An inability to obtain financing can damage a community.

A banker might recognize an ethical duty to clients but respond that he or she is not in business to help poor people. The business of a bank is to make a profit, and bad loans will only undermine the bank, endanger its shareholders and depositors and perhaps harm the greater community. The banker would contend that it is the government's responsibility to help poorer or minority communities.

There are no clear-cut ethical duties for a banker's social responsibility to a community. No one would argue that a bank must make a risky loan to an individual simply because he or she wants to build in a minority community. But the bank could take some action to assist these communities.

Most banks, like other corporations, acknowledge some need to benefit their communities. For example, many banks contribute money to local charities, which may include help for the poor or may include donations to the local symphony or art museum. Bankers should carefully consider the nature of their contributions.

A bank might consider making its contribution in the form of loans to minority communities. The bank might even make these loans at low interest rates. Providing development financing is especially suited to banks, which may uniquely possess the ability to facilitate development. Other institutions can donate money to other causes. Furthermore, the bank may discover that these loans prove to be profitable. The bank can find trustworthy minority developers who benefit both their community and the bank, by paying off the loan.

■ International Perspectives

U.S. Banks in Europe

Since the end of World War II, United States banks have been very successful in international markets. After the nations of the European Community (EC) unite in a single economic market on December 31, 1992, the banking opportunities will be enormous. These nations will have a combined population of over 330 million people and a combined gross national product in excess of $4 trillion. U.S. banks will strive to compete for a portion of this market.

To seize the financial opportunities of the emerging European market, U.S. banks must understand the new legal rules for banking in Europe. The EC's first banking directive, in 1977, prohibited discrimination among member European states. The second banking directive established standards for foreign banks seeking to do business in Europe.

The key to banking in Europe is governmental reciprocity. The ability of a U.S. company to establish a bank in Europe, or to purchase an existing bank, is dependent upon the ability of a European bank to undertake similar actions in the United States. While the U.S. generally does not discriminate against the establishment of foreign banks in this country, U.S. law does place significant restrictions on banking activities. There is some concern that U.S. banks operating in Europe may face similar restrictions.

In 1989, EC officials stated that U.S. banks operating in Europe would have all the same rights as European banks, but this assurance was not legally binding. Once a bank obtains a single license, it will be authorized to provide a wide range of products and services in all the member states of the EC. Assuming that U.S. banks are able to establish branches in Europe, the banks then must understand the banking regulations of the EC.

The EC will not abolish all member country regulation of banking practices. The EC has prohibited discrimination against banks outside the country and has also created a uniform system for certain essential supervisory standards.

The second EC banking directive creates a framework for minimum capital standards for banking. Individual member states may apply for even higher minimum capital standards for banking in their country.

The EC will exercise control over major shareholders of banks. A bank must inform the relevant authorities of the identity of any more-than-10-percent shareholders, and the authorities may disapprove such shareholders, whom they believe would not provide safe and sound banking management.

The second directive also provides for community-wide controls on accounting and control mechanisms. This includes the adoption of minimum solvency rations, requiring banks to limit lending to a certain multiple of their capital reserves. Many of these rules will be administered by member states, but the administration must conform to community-wide standards.

Questions and Case Problems

1. The Bank of Edwardsville loans Stapleton Construction Company $60,000 for the purchase of new equipment over a two-year period. The principal will be allotted to Stapleton in $15,000 increments every six months. Under the terms of the agreement, the Bank of Edwardsville is required to advance the funds so long as Stapleton maintains certain carefully specified financial ratios. The contract contains a covenant that obliges both parties to a duty of good faith and fair dealing in the contract's performance. Stapleton fails to meet the financial ratios after the second allotment of money and the bank refuses to lend further. Can Stapleton recover the remaining $30,000 from the original agreement?

2. The Santa Fe Apartments Project was developed and built with financing from the sale of tax exempt bonds issued by the Salt Lake County Housing Authority. Commonwealth Savings facilitated the financing by issuing a Letter of Credit to Zions Bank (the trustee for the bondholders), guaranteeing repayment of the principal and interest on the bond loan to the Housing Authority bondholders. In return, Commonwealth received a Letter of Reimbursement from Santa Fe and a loan fee. In 1986, Santa Fe entered into an agreement to sell the project to Castleglen, in which Castleglen assumed the obligations of the loan documents. Castleglen had trouble servicing this debt and was declared in default. Castleglen sued Commonwealth, claiming that telephone conversations with the officers of Commonwealth promised that it would not be found in default. Commonwealth was then put into receivership due to insolvency. The government sought to recover from Castleglen in default. Can the government recover from Castleglen, in light of the telephone promises by the Commonwealth officers? [*Castleglen, Inc. v. Commonwealth Savings Association*, 728 F. Supp. 656 (D. Utah 1989)].

3. Target Corporation is a longstanding client of MegaBank, as is the Raider Company. One day, the general manager of the Raider Company comes to MegaBank and seeks a loan in order to conduct a hostile takeover of Target Corporation. The bank approves the loan, and the officers and directors of Target become extremely distressed. Target sues MegaBank for violation of the bank's fiduciary duties. Should Target succeed on this claim?

4. Sunshine State Bank is a state-chartered institution located in South Miami, Florida. The Corona family, including Rafael, Ray, and Ricardo, acquired the bank in 1978. Since acquiring control, each of the Coronas has served as an officer and director of Sunshine. In 1983, the FDIC conducted an examination of the bank and reclassified $30 million of the bank's loans to more doubtful recovery categories. About 47 percent of the loans were adversely classified and this amounted to 581 percent of Sunshine's total equity capital and reserves. The FDIC also found numerous violations of law in the bank's procedures. In 1984, the FDIC removed Rafael, Ray, and Ricardo Corona from their roles as bank directors and officers and forbade them from participating in banking activities at FDIC insured institutions. Was the FDIC action lawful? [*Sunshine State Bank v. FDIC*, 783 F.2d 1580 (11th Cir. 1986)].

5. Amidst a deep recession, Gallagher Equipment Company needed to obtain additional capital to retool their outdated machinery. Gallagher negotiated a loan with The Bank of Logan on January 15 for $500,000. On January 15, the prime rate is 9 percent, and Logan promises to process the application within a month to enable Gallagher to obtain a favorable interest rate. The loan processing became delayed, however, and on February 17, the Federal Reserve Board caused interest rates to increase by one percent. When Logan granted the loan on February 22, the interest rate was 10 percent. Gallagher sues Logan for the costs of the extra point of interest. Can Gallagher succeed on this claim?

CHAPTER TWELVE

Unfair Competition

KEY BACKGROUND

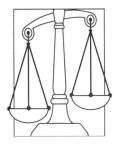

The essential background for this chapter on the law of unfair competition is found in Chapter 7 of *West's Business Law, Fifth Edition* and in Chapter 8 of *West's Legal Environment of Business.* Among the important concepts to remember from this chapter are:

- wrongful interference with a contractual relationship
- wrongful interference with a business relationship
- trademark infringement
- disparagement

The reader will also benefit from familiarity with the requirements of the Robinson-Patman Act, discussed in Chapter 47 of *West's Business Law, Fifth Edition* and in Chapter 21 of *West's Legal Environment of Business.*

* * *

Capitalism relies on competition to function properly and efficiently. Such competition may often be fierce, with competitors vigorously cutting prices to capture a larger market share. Economic theory generally suggests that the fiercer the competition, the better the system works. Some particularly fierce types of competition, however, are considered to be unfair. The law prohibits certain defined types of unfair competition.

There is no clear-cut test for what makes competition unfair. Certain categories of actions, though, are clearly illegal. The unfair trade practices discussed in this chapter include intentional interference with contracts or business expectations, trade disparagement, trademark infringement, and predatory pricing under antitrust law.

Wrongful Interference with Business

It may be unlawful for a company to interfere with the business relations of another business, especially a competitor. The relevant tort claims are wrongful interference with contractual relations and wrongful interference with business expectation.

Suppose that Cherno and Flood are competing to obtain a government contract to produce armored vehicles. To compete for the contract, Cherno requires electronic equipment produced by Shriver, and Cherno contracts to obtain the equipment. Then Flood pays Shriver to break the contract with Cherno, in order to get the government contract for itself. Flood has wrongfully interfered with the Cherno/Shriver contract and is liable for the tort of intentional interference with contract.

The tort of intentional interference with a contract has three essential elements:

1. Plaintiff has a valid contract with another party.

2. Defendant knows that this contract exists.

3. Defendant acts intentionally to cause the third party to breach the contract with plaintiff in order to advance the defendant's own economic interests or with some other wrongful purpose.

The first requirement is that an actual contract exist, before a party may be liable for interference. If the underlying contract is void for *illegality*, there can be no liability for inducing its breach. A defendant may be liable, however, for interfering with a contract that is *unenforceable*. For example, an oral contract for land will not be enforceable due to the Statute of Frauds, which requires a writing. Wrongfully interfering with such an unenforceable oral contract, however, will expose a party to liability.

The second requirement, that the defendant be aware of the contract, is necessary because this is an *intentional* tort. If a defendant is unaware of the contract, it will not be liable. It is not necessary for a plaintiff to prove that a defendant knew all the details of the contract, however. The plaintiff need only prove that the defendant was aware of facts that should put it on notice of the presence of a contract.

Under the third requirement, that the defendant intentionally induce the breach, the plaintiff need not prove that the defendant acted with **malice** toward the plaintiff. The plaintiff must show self-interest or some improper motive or methods, however. The plaintiff also must show that the defendant *caused* the breach of contract.

Consider the following scenario. Michael Nassau has a contract to purchase all the shares of Acomp, Inc., for $15 per share. The chief financial officer of Acomp then approaches Anna Bayardo and asks her to pay $18/share. Anna agrees and acquires Acomp. Michael does not have a good case against Anna because (a) she was unaware of the Nassau/Acomp contract and (b) she did not induce the breach of contract but merely accepted an offer from Acomp.

A company may be liable for intentional interference with contracts even if the actions that it takes are within its legal rights. For example, one company owned a quarry that had only a single access road to market. A railroad company often blocked this access road and prevented the quarry operator from delivering his product on time. Although the railroad had a perfect legal right to park its cars anywhere on its track, a court found the railroad company liable for intentional interference with contract. The court found that the railroad's actions in blocking the road were malicious and had no valid business purpose.[1]

Businesses are increasingly bringing actions for intentional interference with contracts. Not all interferences with contractual relationships are wrongful, however. Some persons have a privilege to interfere with contracts. Corporate officers are generally privileged to cause their company to breach a contract. This is sometimes called the **manager's privilege**.

Manager's privilege means that an officer can lawfully breach a contract, if to do so is in the best interest of the employing company. Suppose that the Glaser Company has a contract to buy a tractor manufacturing plant from Salbu, Inc., for $5 million. Ms. Winslett, a financial officer of Glaser, does some research and discovers that the manufacturing plant is full of hazardous wastes and is worthless. She persuades Glaser to breach the contract. Winslett will not be liable to Salbu, Inc., for intentional interference with contractual relations. Glaser may still be liable to Salbu, however, for breach of contract.

The manager's privilege is not absolute. A manager is only privileged to induce a breach of contract when the manager is acting for the best interests of the employing company. If the manager is acting out of self-interest, he or she can still be liable for intentional interference with contract.

In one recent case, a corporate employee was fired and sued two vice presidents of the company. He alleged that they had him fired because his success was a threat to their position. The court found that the employee had stated a valid claim, because the vice presidents' alleged actions were entirely selfish and not motivated by the general interest of the corporation.[2]

Another important defense is **fair competition**. Some acts may induce a breach of contract, yet be perfectly proper. For example, low prices or effective advertising may attract customers away from competitors. These acts, however, are considered fair competition and are therefore lawful.

Although a valid, underlying contract is necessary for the tort of wrongful interference with

---

[1] *St. Louis S.F.R. Co. v. Wade*, 607 F.2d 126 (5th Cir. 1979).

[2] *Presto v. Sequoia Systems*, 633 F. Supp. 1117 (D. Mass. 1986).

contract, a business could sue for wrongful interference with business expectations, even in the absence of a contract. While a contract is not essential for this tort, there must be some reasonable certainty of business for a defendant to be liable. A plaintiff has the burden to prove a reasonable probability that, but for the wrongful interference, the business relationship would have been realized. Plaintiff need not prove a certainty of such business, however.

Interference with business expectations is also an intentional tort. Consequently, the plaintiff must show that the defendant had knowledge of the plaintiff's business expectancy. A plaintiff also must show that the defendant intentionally interfered with the business expectancy.

The following case shows the facts that give rise to a claim of wrongful interference with business expectancy and the standards applied by courts.

■■ Case 12.1
Leigh Furniture & Carpet Co. v. Isom
Supreme Court of Utah, 1982
657 P.2d 293

Background and Facts *The owner of Leigh Furniture agreed to sell his furniture business to Richard Isom. Leigh also owned the building where the furniture store was located and agreed to provide Isom with a ten-year lease on the first floor store and an option to buy the entire building, once Isom finished paying for the business. Sometime thereafter, Leigh wanted to sell the entire building but was unable to do so because of Isom's lease. Leigh and his wife began making demands on Isom, repeatedly visited the store, disrupted operations, and filed lawsuits against Isom. Isom sought to take on a partner and pay off the purchase price to Leigh, but Leigh refused to approve the partner or accept the purchase price.*

Isom filed a counterclaim in one of Leigh's lawsuits, claiming intentional interference with contract and business expectancy. Soon thereafter, Isom went bankrupt and claimed that this was due to Leigh's harassment. A jury ruled for Isom and awarded him compensatory and punitive damages. Leigh appealed.

OAKS, Justice.

*   *   *   *

Reviewing the record, we conclude that there was sufficient evidence to sustain the jury's verdict against the Leigh Corporation for intentional interference with prospective economic relations that caused injury to Isom.

There was ample evidence that Isom had business relationships with various customers, suppliers, and potential business associates, and that Leigh, the former owner of the business, understood the value of those relationships. There was also substantial competent evidence that the Corporation, through Leigh, his wife, and his bookkeeper, intentionally interfered with and caused a termination of some of those relationships (actual or potential). Their frequent visits to Isom's store during business hours to confront him, question him, and make demands and inquiries regarding the manner in which he was conducting his business repeatedly interrupted sales activities, caused his customers to comment and complain, and more than once caused a customer to leave the store. Driving away an individual's existing or potential customers is the archetypical injury this cause of action was devised to remedy.

Other actions by which the Leigh Corporation imposed heavy demands on Isom's time and financial resources to the detriment of his ability to attract and retain customers and conduct the other activities of his business included: numerous letters of complaint, Leigh's demand for an audit of Isom's books and inventory during the busy holiday season, his continued threats to cancel the contract and sell the building and business to another buyer, his refusal to pay the contracted share of the heating bills or the cost of repairing the furnace and the store's broken window, his refusal of the tendered payment of the balance due under the contract, and his suit for repossession, termination, and injunction. Leigh's refusals also prevented Isom from consummating potentially advantageous business associations with Hunter, with Talbot, and finally with Applegate, all experienced retailers able to contribute expertise and additional capital to Isom's business.

Taken in isolation, each of the foregoing interferences with Isom's business might be justified as an overly zealous attempt to protect the Corporation's interests under its contract of sale. As such, none would establish the intentional interference element of this tort, though some might give rise to a cause of action for breach of specific provisions in the contract or of the duty of good faith performance which inheres in every contractual relation. Even in small groups, these acts might be explained as merely instances of aggressive or abrasive—though not illegal or tortious—tactics, excesses that occur in contractual and commercial relationships. But in total and in cumulative effect, as a course of action extending over a period of three and one-half years and culminating in the failure of Isom's business, the Leigh Corporation's acts cross the threshold beyond what is incidental and justifiable to what is tortious. The Corporation's acts provide sufficient evidence to establish two of the elements in the definition of this tort: an intentional interference with present or prospective economic relations that caused injury to the plaintiff.

* * * *

By forcing Isom to defend what appear to have been two groundless lawsuits, the Leigh Corporation was clearly employing an improper means of interference with Isom's business. Such use of civil litigation as a weapon to damage another's business, besides being an intolerable waste of judicial resources, may give rise to independent causes of action in tort for abuse of process and malicious prosecution.

The jury's verdict can therefore be sustained on the ground that the Leigh Corporation intentionally interfered with Isom's economic relations by improper means.

There is also another basis for affirming that verdict on the basis of improper means.

A deliberate breach of contract, even where employed to secure economic advantage, is not, by itself, an "improper means." Because the law remedies breaches of contract with damages calculated to give the aggrieved party the benefit of the bargain, there is no need for an additional remedy in tort (unless the defendant's conduct would constitute a tort independent of the contract).

Neither a deliberate breach of contract nor an immediate purpose to inflict injury which does not predominate over a legitimate economic end will, by itself, satisfy this element of the tort. However, they may do so in combination. This is so because contract damages provide an insufficient remedy for a breach prompted by an immediate purpose to injure, and that purpose does not enjoy the same legal immunity in the context of contract relations as it does in the competitive market-place. As a result, a breach of contract committed for the immediate purpose of injuring the other contracting party is an improper means that will satisfy this element of the cause of action for intentional interference with economic relations.

Decision and Remedy   *The court affirmed the jury verdict for Isom.*

Courts often focus on the existence of improper motives of business methods in claims for wrongful interference with business expectations. When one business defendant acts with a malicious purpose—only to destroy another business—courts will find the defendant liable. Similarly, the use of force or threats to scare off potential customers of a rival is considered wrongful.

For example, Sportsmen's Boating Corporation ran a fishing charter, called the Mijoy. For potential customers to reach the Mijoy, they had to pass by the dock of a competing charter, called the Blackhawk. The Blackhawk's employees would direct the Mijoy's prospective customers to their own boat and would falsely state that the Mijoy was full that day or was not sailing. A court found that the Blackhawk's owners were liable for wrongful interference with a business expectancy.[3]

An important aspect of the wrongful interference with business torts is the availability of punitive damages, which are unavailable in a standard breach of contract case. Because wrongful interference involves intentional conduct, a plaintiff can obtain punitive damages if the defendant's behavior is especially egregious. In addition to actual damages suffered from a loss of business, a plaintiff may receive thousands or even millions of dollars in punitive damages.

As a general rule, a person will not be liable for negligent interference with business. Suppose that a rock group, called The Hot Shots, is to play a lucrative concert at a local opera house. Then a local citizen, Janet Claire, negligently starts a fire that burns down the opera house. She will not be liable to The Hot Shots for the concert's cancellation (though, of course, she may be liable for damages to the opera house).

▥ Trademark Infringement

A great deal of modern litigation involves the alleged infringement of a company's **trademark**. A legally valid trademark is protected from copying by competitors. The courts also protect "trade dress," which is the distinctive visual appearance of a product. For example, a new soft drink business could not sell its product in a can that used Coca-Cola's distinctive colors and pattern and certainly could not call the product "Coke." Traditional common law protected trademarks, and Congress passed the Lanham Act to provide statutory protection.

The first essential requirement in a trademark action is that the plaintiff possess a **valid trademark**. Some product names cannot be used as valid trademarks, often because they are generic. A **generic trademark** is one that identifies the type of product rather than the producer. Thus, a company cannot trademark "Shampoo" brand shampoo. Miller Brewing was not allowed to trademark "light" or "lite" for their low-calorie beer, because the word simply described the color and other characteristics of the beer.[4]

Even a perfectly good trademark can become generic over time. Long ago, the name aspirin was a defensible trademark for a pain reliever. People began using the name aspirin, however, for any brand of this particular type of pain reliever. The name aspirin became generic and today any company can market this type of pain reliever and call its product aspirin. Loss of a trademark in this way is called "genericide." The trademark "thermos" also became generic for an insulated bottle product.[5]

---

[3]*Sportsmen's Boating Corporation v. Hensley*, 474 A.2d 780 (Conn. 1984).

[4]*Miller Brewing Co. v. G. Heileman Brewing Co., Inc.*, 561 F.2d 75 (7th Cir. 1977).

[5]*King-Seeley Thermos Co. v. Aladdin Industries, Inc.*, 321 F.2d 577 (2d Cir. 1963).

Another requirement for a valid trademark is that it not be misleading. Suppose that a company markets a perfume that it calls "Maid in Paris." If the perfume did not come from Paris, this title would be unprotected in trademark. Seat covers made from manmade artificial components could not obtain a valid trademark in the term "Love Lamb" seat covers. "Durango" tobacco was not protected in trademark because it did not come from the tobacco-producing region of Durango in Mexico.

To be a valid trademark, a mark must be distinctive and not misleading. The most distinctive marks are called "fanciful." These trademarks are often made-up words and have no innate connection to the product. For example, "Kodak" is a fanciful name for cameras and film, because nothing about the word Kodak suggests a connection with those products.

Another category of protected trademarks are those that are "suggestive." These **suggestive trademarks** suggest some of the characteristics of the product. For example, "Coppertone" suntan lotion suggests the benefit of the product. The same would be true of "Penguin" brand refrigerators.

The most difficult area of trademark protection involves "descriptive" marks. This is a name that merely describes the product sold. For example, "Chap Stik" lip balm simply describes a stick for chapped lips. "Newsweek" describes a weekly newsmagazine. Descriptive marks can receive trademark protection but not as easily as for fanciful or suggestive marks. The concern is that descriptive marks can unfairly restrict a competitor's ability to name its product.

A similar analysis applies to trade dress. One cannot get protection in a basic or functional shape, such as a cylinder. Unusual shapes of packaging may be protected. The distinctive bottle of "Pinch" brand Scotch was held to be protectable in trademark. Similarly, in most cases a company cannot get trademark protection in a color. Nutrasweet recently tried to prevent other artificial sweeteners from using a blue package, but lost. Distinctive combinations and designs of colors, though, are certainly protected.

To help ensure that a trademark is protected, a company can register a mark with the U.S. Patent and Trademark Office. Registration is not required—an unregistered trademark is protected to the extent that it was actually used. Registration has some important benefits, though. First, registration protects the mark throughout the entire United States, rather than just the geographic region of use. Second, after a mark has been registered for five years, its validity cannot be challenged.

The government will grant a registration in a trademark if it is considered distinctive, not misleading, and not confusingly similar to trademarks that were previously registered. Competitors may oppose issuance of the registration. A registration lasts for ten years and may be renewed by the user.

If a trademark is registered by the government, it is presumptively valid. Until five years have elapsed, the validity of the trademark may be challenged by a competitor. Even a registered trademark will be unprotected if a court finds it to be generic or misleading.

Even an unregistered trademark is protected by the law, but only to the extent that it is used. Suppose a company markets "Texas Redhot Salsa" in the states of Texas and Louisiana. That company has a protected trademark in those two states, but another company could come along and sell "Texas Salsa" in the other 48 states. Also, unregistered trademarks do not become incontestable after five years.

Protection of a descriptive or unregistered trademark requires proof of **secondary meaning**. Secondary meaning is found when a trademark is associated with a particular maker's product, rather than all products of a type. "Newsweek" has a secondary meaning because it is associated with a particular magazine and not every weekly newsmagazine.

The presence of a secondary meaning is a factual question that may be resolved by surveys asking consumers whether they associate the descriptive trademark with a particular maker's product. Courts also consider other factors. These factors include the length and exclusivity of past use of the mark, the amount of advertising expenditures employed to create the secondary meaning, and unsolicited coverage of the trademark in the media.

Likelihood of Confusion If a company possesses a valid trademark, its competitors cannot use that mark. The company does not have an exclusive right to use the trademark, however. The second key requirement of a trademark infringement action is proof of a *likelihood of confusion*. Trademark law is primarily for the protection of consumers and only prohibits uses that are likely to confuse consumers about a product's origin.

Use by a direct competitor will generally create a likelihood of confusion. When another party takes your valid trademark exactly and puts it on identical goods sold in the same geographic area, proof of likelihood of confusion is easy. Most cases are not quite this easy.

Most competitors will not copy a trademark exactly but will modify it at least slightly. This is not a defense against trademark infringement, however. Marketing the "Cup-O'-Cola" could violate the "Coca-Cola" trademark because the two marks sound very much alike. In one case, a court found that "Tornado" wire fencing violated the established trademark in "Cyclone" wire fencing.[6]

---

[6]*Hancock v. American Steel & Wire Co.*, 203 F.2d 737 (C.C.P.A. 1953).

In making the determination of infringement due to substantial similarity, courts consider the intent of the second user (called the "junior user"). Thus, if the mark is highly descriptive and the junior had good reason for use of a similar mark, the court will find no infringement. Suppose one company had a trademark in "Cool Menthol" cough lozenges. A junior user might be allowed the use of "Soothing Menthol-Flavored" cough lozenges.

On the other hand, if it appears that the junior user is purposefully trying to copy the senior user's mark, courts will find likelihood of infringement. If a company seeks to market "KooKoo Cola," courts are likely to conclude that the company's intent is to confuse customers and take them away from "Coca-Cola."

A junior user may be able to trade on another's mark if it is a parody. By its nature, a parody does not attempt to confuse the customer, as explained in the following decision.

■ Case 12.2
**Jordache Enterprises, Inc. v.
Hogg Wyld, Ltd.**
United States Court of Appeals,
Tenth Circuit, 1987
828 F.2d 1482

Background and Facts   *Jordache is the fourth-largest blue jeans manufacturer in the United States and has a distinctive pocket design. The pocket has "jordache" written in white with a gold horse's head superimposed over the lettering. A New Mexico company, Hogg Wyld, Ltd., began marketing designer blue jeans in large sizes for bigger women. Their jeans were marketed under the name "Lardashe" and had their own distinctive pocket design. Their design had "lardashe" written on the pocket and had a brightly colored pig's head and hooves peering over the pocket.*

Jordache sued Hogg Wyld for trademark infringement. The district court, after a bench trial, found no likelihood of confusion between the two brands of jeans and therefore no trademark infringement. Jordache appealed.

TACHA, Circuit Judge.

* * * *

The similarity between the marks in appearance, pronunciation of the words used, translation of the designs used, and suggestion or meaning is the first factor to consider in determining whether there is a likelihood of confusion. The district court found that the Jordache mark and the Lardashe mark are not confusingly similar. Appellant argues that the court employed an improper legal construction of "suggestion" or "meaning" in reaching this result. Even if we were to reject this argument, appellant would have us hold the finding of no similarity to be clearly erroneous.

Trademarks may be confusingly similar if they suggest the same idea or meaning. For example, this court has held that a trademark consisting of an overflowing stein with the words "Brew Nuts" conveys the same meaning as a trademark consisting of the words "Beer Nuts." *Beer Nuts II*, 805 F.2d at 926. The district court in the present case found that "the two marks suggest dissimilar images or concepts."

* * * *

The "deliberate adoption of a similar mark may lead to an inference of intent to pass off goods as those of another which in turn supports a finding of likelihood of confusion." *Beer Nuts II*, 805 F.2d at 927. "The proper focus is whether defendant had the intent to derive benefit from the reputation or goodwill of plaintiff." *Sicilia Di R. Biebow & Co. v. Cox*, 732 F.2d 417, 431 (5th Cir.1984); *accord* Restatement of Torts § 729 comment f at 594-95 (1938). A conscious choice of a mark similar to a mark already established in the marketplace usually supports a finding of a likelihood of confusion "because the court presumes that [the alleged infringer] 'can accomplish his purpose: that is, that the public will be deceived.'" *Beer Nuts I*, 711 F.2d at 941 (quoting *AMF Inc. v. Sleekcraft Boats*, 599 F.2d 341, 354 (9th Cir.1979)).

Given the unlimited number of possible names and symbols that could serve as a trademark, it is understandable that a court generally presumes one who chooses a mark similar to an existing mark intends to confuse the public. However, where a party chooses a mark as a parody of an existing mark, the intent is not necessarily to confuse the public but rather to amuse.

* * * *

Another factor to be considered in determining whether there is a likelihood of confusion is "the degree of care likely to be exercised by purchasers." *Beer Nuts II*, 805 F.2d at 925. The district court found that customers are likely to exercise a high degree of care in purchasing clothing that costs between fifteen and sixty dollars. 625 F.Supp. at 53. Appellant says that "[o]ne can just as easily surmise" that a lesser degree of care will be used in selecting a pair of blue jeans. Brief of Appellant at 27. Appellant has offered only a guess, not any evidence of the degree of care that would satisfy its burden of proof. The district court's finding a high degree of care is not clearly erroneous.

* * * *

Decision and Remedy *The court affirmed the district court's finding of no likelihood of confusion and therefore no trademark infringement.*

Noncompeting Goods Another common problem involves noncompeting goods. Suppose that a company begins selling "Kodak" toothpaste. There is no likelihood of confusion among customers in this case. Consumers will not confuse toothpaste with cameras. This is why so many companies can have common names, such as "Acme."

A likelihood of confusion may arise when products are different, but similar. This is often called the **related products rule** and recognizes that a trademark holder might want to expand the use of its trademark into related areas. In a classic case, the "Yale" trademark for locks and other hardware was unlawfully infringed by a junior user's attempt to market "Yale" flashlights and batteries.[7]

---

[7] *Yale Electric Corp. v. Robertson*, 26 F.2d 972 (2d Cir. 1928).

Several tests are used by the court to determine the likelihood of confusion. The court considers whether the "ordinary" consumer is likely to be confused but recognizes that purchasers of some products, such as very expensive products, are likely to be more "sophisticated" and are less subject to possible confusion.

Several other factors also are relevant to a finding of likelihood of confusion. These include the strength of the mark (its distinctiveness and fame in the market) and the relative good faith of the junior user. The owners of "Playboy" magazine were able to halt the use of "Playboy" to sell dune buggies, because a court found that the junior user wanted to trade on the magazine's goodwill to promote the sale of its dune buggies.

Courts also consider the degree of similarity (in appearance, sound, etc.) and a concept called "bridging the gap." **Bridging the gap** means the likelihood that a senior user would want to use its trademark to enter the product market of the junior user. In the Yale locks case, it was likely that the senior user would want to bridge the gap and market its own Yale flashlights.

Trademarks are generally unprotected from parodies. As a result, a company might print up a satirical newspaper called the "Off the Wall Street Journal." This parody would be legal under trademark law.

Geography A final element in determining the likelihood of confusion is geography. Under common law, a trademark is only protected in the region where it is used. Thus, a famous New York City restaurant, such as Lutece, could prevent another restaurant from using the same name in the New York area. Lutece would not be protected, though, from a Cincinnati restaurant using its name.

Trademark registration with the federal government provides national protection against competing uses. Anyone previously using the trademark, however, may continue to do so. Suppose that a small Fresno company has been selling chips in Southern California under the name "El Galindo." The company never registered their mark. A large national food products company registers the trademark "El Galindo" for a line of products. The Fresno company may continue to use its "El Galindo" name, but only in the geographic area of Southern California in which it historically used the trademark.

Abandonment A trademark, even a registered one, may be lost through nonuse. If the owner does not use the trademark in selling goods, it will be deemed abandoned. Under the Lanham Act, nonuse for two years is considered evidence of abandonment that enables others to use the trademark for their own goods.

Antidilution Statutes

Trademark law protects consumers against confusion but does little to protect the owners of trademarks against copying for noncompeting uses or parodies. Most states have passed **antidilution statutes** to protect owners from such copying. Even in the absence of possible consumer confusion, these laws protect the reputation of the trademark.

The typical state antidilution law provides protection in the following three circumstances:

1. Actual or potential consumer confusion (this overlaps federal trademark protection).

2. Loss of uniqueness or individuality of the trademark.

3. Tarnishment of the reputation of the trademark.

Consider a company with a unique trademark, such as Polaroid cameras. An antidilution law will protect Polaroid from noncompeting uses of its trademark. If an appliance repair service attempts to call itself Polaroid, the camera company may halt such use, which may hurt the individuality of the camera trademark or damage the reputation of the mark.

Antidilution statutes provide protection when a noncompeting product uses a prestigious trademark in a less-than-wholesome context. For example, a poster company copied the Coca-Cola design for a poster stating "Enjoy Cocaine." A court held that this use tarnished the Coca-Cola trademark and was illegal under the New York antidilution law.[8]

The antidilution laws also provide some protection against parodies of established trademarks. Parody is protected by First Amendment freedom of speech, however, and therefore may be allowed even when they could dilute or tarnish a trademark, as illustrated by the following decision.

---

[8]*Coca-Cola Co. v. Gemini Rising, Inc.*, 346 F. Supp. 1183 (E.D.N.Y. 1972).

■ Case 12.3
**L. L. Bean, Inc. v.
Drake Publishers, Inc.**
United States Court of Appeals,
First Circuit, 1987
811 F.2d 26

Background and Facts   *L. L. Bean, Inc., is the trademark for that company's catalog and other sales of clothing products. Drake Publishers, which owns High Society magazine, published a parody of the catalog in its October 1984 issue. This involved a two-page article called "L. L. Beam's Back-To-School-Sex-Catalog" and featured pictures of nude models in sexually explicit positions using products "that were described in a crudely humorous fashion."*

L. L. Bean sued under the Maine antidilution statute, among other claims. The district court granted Bean summary judgment on the antidilution claim, because the catalog had tarnished the company's reputation. The court entered an injunction prohibiting further publication or distribution of the Sex Catalog parody. Drake Publishers appealed.

BOWNES, Circuit Judge.

*   *   *   *

Parody is a humorous from of social commentary and literary criticism that dates back as far as Greek antiquity. "The rhapsodists who strolled from town to town to chant the poems of Homer," wrote Issac D'Israeli, "were immediately followed by another set of strollers—buffoons who made the audiences merry by the burlesque turn which they gave to the solemn strains." I. D'Israeli, *Curiosities of Literature,* quoted in D. MacDonald, *Parodies: An Anthology from Chaucer to Beerbohm–and After* 562 (1960). The Oxford English Dictionary defines parody as "[a] composition in which the characteristic turns of thought and phrase of an author are mimicked to appear ridiculous, especially by applying them to ludicrously inappropriate subjects." Chaucer, Shakespeare, Pope, Voltaire, Fielding, Hemingway and Faulkner are among the myriad of authors who have written parodies. Since parody seeks to ridicule sacred verities and prevailing mores, it inevitably offends others, as evinced by the shock which Chaucer's *Canterbury Tales* and Voltaire's *Candide* provoked among their contemporaries.

*   *   *   *

* * * the dilution injury stems from an unauthorized effort to market incompatible products or services by trading on another's trademark. The Constitution is not offended when the antidilution statute is applied to prevent a defendant from using a trademark without permission in order to merchandise dissimilar products or services. Any residual effect on first amendment freedoms should be balanced against the need to fulfill the legitimate purpose of the antidilution statute. *See Friedman v. Rogers,* 440 U.S. 1, 15-16, 99 S.Ct. 887, 896-897, 59 L.Ed.2d 100 (1979). The law of trademark dilution has developed to combat an unauthorized and harmful appropriation of a trademark by another for the purpose of identifying, manufacturing, merchandising or promoting dissimilar products or services. The harm occurs when a trademark's identity and integrity–its capacity to command respect in the market–is undermined due to its inappropriate and unauthorized use by other market actors. When presented with such circumstances, courts have found that trademark owners have suffered harm despite the fact that redressing such harm entailed some residual impact on the rights of expression of commercial actors. *See, e.g., Dallas Cowboys Cheerleaders v. Pussycat Cinema, Ltd.,* 604 F.2d 200 (plaintiff's mark damaged by unauthorized use in content and promotion of a pornographic film); *Chemical Corp. of America v. Anheuser-Busch, Inc.*, 306 F.2d 433 (5th Cir.1962), *cert. denied*, 372 U.S. 965, 83 S.Ct. 1089, 10 L.Ed.2d 129 (1963) (floor wax and insecticide maker's slogan, "Where there's life, there's bugs," harmed strength of defendant's slogan, "Where there's life, there's Bud"); *Original Appalachian Artworks, Inc. v. Topps Chewing Gum*, 642 F.Supp. 1031 (N.D.Ga.1986) (merchandiser of "Garbage Pail Kids" stickers and products injured owner of Cabbage Patch Kids mark); *D.C. Comics, Inc. v. Unlimited Monkey Business*, 598 F.Supp. 110 (N.D.Ga.1984) (holder of Superman and Wonder Woman trademarks damaged by unauthorized use of marks by singing telegram franchisor); *General Electric Co. v. Alumpa Coal Co.*, 205 U.S.P.Q. (BNA) 1036 (D.Mass.1979) ("Genital Electric" monogram on underpants and T-shirts harmful to plaintiff's trademark); *Gucci Shops, Inc. v. R.H. Macy & Co.*, 446 F.Supp. 838 (S.D.N.Y.1977) (defendant's diaper bag labelled "Gucchi Goo" held to injure Gucci's mark); *Coca-Cola Co. v. Gemini Rising, Inc.*, 346 F.Supp. 1183 (E.D.N.Y.1972) (enjoining the merchandise of "Enjoy Cocaine" posters bearing logo similar to plaintiff's mark).

While the cases cited above might appear at first glance to be factually analogous to the instant one, they are distinguishable for two reasons. First, they all involved unauthorized commercial uses of another's trademark. Second, none of those cases involved a defendant using a plaintiff's trademark as a vehicle for an editorial or artistic parody. In contrast to the cases cited, the instant defendant used plaintiff's mark solely for noncommercial purposes. Appellant's parody constitutes an editorial or artistic, rather than a commercial, use of plaintiff's mark. The article was labelled as "humor" and "parody" in the magazine's table of contents section, it took up two pages in a one-hundred-page issue; neither the article nor appellant's trademark was featured on the front or back cover of the magazine. Drake did not use Bean's mark to identify or promote goods or services to consumers; it never intended to market the "products" displayed in the parody.

*   *   *   *

Finally, we reject Bean's argument that enjoining the publication of appellant's parody does not violate the first amendment because "there are innumerable alternative ways that Drake could have made a satiric statement concerning 'sex in the outdoors' or 'sex and camping gear' without using plaintiff's name and mark." This argument fails to recognize that appellant is parodying L.L. Bean's catalog, not "sex in the outdoors." The central role which trademarks occupy in public discourse (a role eagerly encouraged by trademark owners), makes them a natural target of parodists. Trademark parodies, even when offensive, do convey a message. The message may be simply that business and product images need not always be taken too seriously; a trademark parody reminds us that we are free to laugh at the images and associations linked with the mark. The message also may be a simple form of entertainment conveyed by juxtaposing the irreverent representation of the trademark with the idealized image created by the mark's owner. *See Note, Trademark Parody*, 72 Va.L.Rev. at 1109. While such a message lacks explicit political content, that is no reason to afford it less protection under the first amendment. *Schad v. Mount Ephraim*, 452 U.S. 61, 65-66, 101 S.Ct. 2176, 2180-2181, 68 L.Ed.2d 671 (1981). Denying parodists the opportunity to poke fun at symbols and names which have become woven into the fabric of our daily life, would constitute a serious curtailment of a protected form of expression.

Decision and Remedy *The court reversed the summary judgment for Bean and remanded the case for district court implementation of the order.*

■ Disparagement

Disparagement is a traditional common law tort involving false statements about a business. Disparagement is similar to defamation of a person's reputation, but disparagement involves a business's reputation or that of its products. Disparagement involves (i) a disparaging statement, (ii) that is false, (iii) that was made with an intent to harm the plaintiff's business; and (iv) causes special damages.

Unlawful disparagement may be done by competitors. Suppose one fast food restaurant chain publishes advertisements stating that a competing chain uses horse meat in its hamburgers. Assuming the claim is untrue, this would be disparagement.

Noncompetitors, such as consumers, may also be liable for disparagement. In a classic case, the entertainer Arthur Godfrey stated that the producers of a cheap ukulele that he disliked "should be jailed." The court ruled that this statement qualified as actionable disparagement.[9]

Some disparaging statements may be protected by the freedom of speech of the First Amendment. A critical movie review, for example, will not be actionable disparagement. In a recent case, the magazine *Consumer Reports* criticized the quality of a company's audio speakers. The company sued for disparagement but lost, because the criticism was protected by the First Amendment.[10]

To recover for disparagement, a plaintiff must show "special damages" in the form of monetary losses resulting from the disparaging comments. Courts generally require a plaintiff to prove a specific amount of sales lost due to the disparagement. This is often difficult. A plaintiff also may obtain an injunction ordering the defendant to cease its disparagement.

In 1989, Congress revised the Lanham Act to provide federal statutory protection from disparagement. The new law prohibits any misrepresentations about the "nature, characteristics, qualities" of "goods, services or commercial activities" in "commercial advertising or promotion."[11] This law does not appear to require proof of special damages or even a defendant's knowledge of falsity.

Under both common law and the revised Lanham Act, a statement must be false to constitute disparagement. A true statement of fact, or an opinion, is thus legal and not disparagement.

■ Robinson-Patman Act

The Robinson-Patman Act addresses **price discrimination**—in which one company sells an identical product at different prices to different customers. Suppose Ranch Produce sold 100 bushels of peaches to May Grocery for $2000. On the same day, in the same city, Ranch sold 100 bushels of identical quality peaches to June Grocery for $1500. This is price discrimination and may be considered a form of unfair competition. The Robinson-Patman Act does not prohibit all price discrimination, but only when the practice injures competition.

Section 2(a)

The basic case of illegal price discrimination under section 2(a) of the Robinson-Patman Act has the following required elements:

1. A person engaged in interstate commerce.

2. Discriminated in price between different purchasers.

3. For commodities of like grade and quality.

4. The effect was substantially to lessen competition.

The first requirement, of **interstate commerce**, will almost always be met. The second require-

---

[9]*The Harmonica Man, Inc. v. Godfrey*, 102 N.Y.S.2d 251 (1951).

[10]*Bose Corp. v. Consumers Union of U.S., Inc.*, 466 U.S. 485 (1984).

[11]15 U.S.C. Sec. 1125(a).

ment, of price discrimination, is also quite straight-forward. This simply requires proof of differing purchase prices between two purchasers. The Act does require a purchase and does not apply to rentals.

The third requirement, that the commodities be of like grade and quality, is more complex. The Act is limited to commodities, or tangible objects, and is generally inapplicable to services. Defining "like grade and quality" can sometimes be difficult. What if identical goods are sold in different packages under different brand names? The Supreme Court has held that such goods are of "like grade and quality" and satisfy the third test.

Most Robinson-Patman Act litigation deals with the fourth requirement, that the price discrimination must substantially lessen competition. One form of lessened competition is in **primary line competition**, between the seller and his competitors.

Price discrimination could lessen primary line competition in the following way. Suppose that Argon computers has a large percentage of the nation's market for large computers. Argon sells its computers for $12,000. A small Florida company, named Xenon, begins selling competing large computers in Florida for $11,000. Argon then sells its large computers in Florida for only $9000 and thereby drives Xenon out of business. This is **predatory pricing** which constitutes an injury to primary line competition.

Price discrimination also is illegal if it lessens **secondary line competition**. This is competition among the buyers of the product. Suppose Argon sells its large computers to ITT Systems for $11,000 and sells the same computers to ITT's competitor, ABS Computing, for $13,000. The price difference may lessen the ability of ABS Computing to compete with ITT. If so, the price discrimination would illegally lessen secondary line competition.

A substantial lessening of competition is necessary for price discrimination to be illegal under the Robinson-Patman Act. Much price discrimination (e.g., different fares for airline seats) does not substantially lessen competition in goods and is therefore legal.

The following Supreme Court decision shows how price discrimination may substantially lessen discrimination at some level down the supply chain and how a primary seller may be legally responsible.

■ Case 12.4
Texaco Inc. v. Hasbrouck
Supreme Court
of the United States, 1990
110 S.Ct. 2535

Background and Facts   *Between 1972 and 1981, Texaco sold gasoline to independent Texaco retailers at "retail tank wagon prices." Texaco also sold gas to intermediary distributors, such as Gull Oil Company and Dompier Oil Company. These distributors transported and then resold the gasoline to service stations. Texaco sold the gas to the distributors at a much lower price than the retail tank wagon price for service station retailers. Texaco also paid the distributors a hauling fee. Eventually, Dompier entered the retail service station market to compete with the Texaco independents.*

The discount enabled distributors to resell the gasoline for a lower price than Texaco charged at the retail tank wagon. In part for this reason, the Texaco independent retailers' share of the market for Texaco gas declined from 76 percent to 49 percent. Some retailers sought to do their own hauling, but Texaco refused. The retailers sued Texaco for illegal price discrimination. A jury ruled against Texaco and awarded the retailers actual damages of nearly $450,000. A court of appeals affirmed this ruling, and Texaco appealed to the U.S. Supreme Court. Texaco claimed that the price to distributors was a lawful "functional discount" and stressed that the distributors were not in direct competition with the retailers.

STEVENS, Justice.

* * * *

Both Gull and Dompier received the full discount on all their purchases even though most of their volume was resold directly to consumers. The extra margin on those sales obviously enabled them to price aggressively in both their retail and their wholesale marketing. To the extent that Dompier and Gull competed with respondents in the retail market, the presumption of adverse effect on competition recognized in the Morton Salt case becomes all the more appropriate. Their competitive advantage in that market also constitutes evidence tending to rebut any presumption of legality that would otherwise apply to their wholesale sales.

The evidence indicates, moreover, that Texaco affirmatively encouraged Dompier to expand its retail business and that Texaco was fully informed about the persistent and marketwide consequences of its own pricing policies.

Indeed, its own executives recognized that the dramatic impact on the market was almost entirely attributable to the magnitude of the distributor discount and the hauling allowance. Yet at the same time that Texaco was encouraging Dompier to integrate downward, and supplying Dompier with a generous discount useful to such integration, Texaco was inhibiting upward integration by the respondents: two of the respondents sought permission from Texaco to haul their own fuel using their own tankwagons, but Texaco refused. The special facts of this case thus make it peculiarly difficult for Texaco to claim that it is being held liable for the independent pricing decisions of Gull or Dompier.

As we recognized in Falls City Industries, "the competitive injury component of a Robinson-Patman Act violation is not limited to the injury to competition between the favored and the disfavored purchaser; it also encompasses the injury to competition between their customers." 460 U.S., at 436. This conclusion is compelled by the statutory language, which specifically encompasses not only the adverse effect of price discrimination on persons who either grant or knowingly receive the benefit of such discrimination, but also on "customers of either of them." Such indirect competitive effects surely may not be presumed automatically in every functional discount setting, and, indeed, one would expect that most functional discounts will be legitimate discounts which do not cause harm to competition. At the least, a functional discount that constitutes a reasonable reimbursement for the purchasers' actual marketing functions will not violate the Act. When a functional discount is legitimate, the inference of injury to competition recognized in the Morton Salt case will simply not arise. Yet it is also true that not every functional discount is entitled to a judgment of legitimacy, and that it will sometimes be possible to produce evidence showing that a particular functional discount caused a price discrimination of the sort the Act prohibits. When such anti-competitive effects are proved—as we believe they were in this case—they are prohibited by the Act.

Decision and Remedy   *The court affirmed the decision against Texaco.*

Defenses

The Robinson-Patman Act contains important defenses to price discrimination claims under section 2(a). The most important defenses are cost justification and meeting competition.

Cost justification enables Argon to sell at a lower price to Customer A than Customer B, if the costs of selling to Customer A are correspondingly less than selling to Customer B. If Argon must bear higher shipping costs for Customer B, Argon may charge Customer A proportionally less to account for those costs. In a similar way, quantity discounts may be justified by lower production costs for large orders.

The meeting competition defense enables a seller to reduce prices selectively to meet lower prices by competitors. In a previous example, Argon sold its computers nationwide for $12,000, and Xenon entered the market in Florida selling a comparable computer for $11,000. The meeting competition defense would enable Argon to lower its prices in Florida to $11,000 to meet the Xenon price. In such a case, Argon may only meet the competitor's price, however, and may not offer a lower price.

Sections 2(d) and 2(e)

Sections 2(d) and 2(e) of the Robinson-Patman Act address a different form of discrimination among customers. These sections prohibit a seller from offering promotional payments, services or facilities to one buyer, without offering comparable opportunities to other competing buyers. The restriction only applies to customers in competition. Significantly, these sections do not require proof of injury to competition, as under section 2(a).

Some examples of illegal promotional discrimination would be a company that grants credit card charge privileges to some but not all buyers, or a company that accepts the return of unsold merchandise from some but not all buyers. If a seller offers some favorable service to one buyer, it must make a similar service available to other competing buyers, on "proportionally equal" terms.

Suppose that Borax, Inc., manufactures and sells a brand of laundry detergent. In Denver, Borax detergent is sold by a chain of grocery stores and another chain of discount department stores. If Borax provides a special service or allowance to the grocery stores (e.g., coupon reimbursement), Borax must provide the same service on proportionately equal terms for the department stores.

The only affirmative defense under these sections is the meeting competition defense. The cost justification defense is not available. The "proportionally equal" language, however, will enable a seller to tailor the promotional services to the amount of goods purchased. Thus, if a seller provides a certain amount of free advertising for large buyers, the seller need not provide the same total amount of free advertising to smaller buyers.

State Deceptive Trade Practices Acts

Every state now has a statute prohibiting deceptive trade practices, often called a "little FTC act." These laws were primarily designed to protect consumers, but most of these laws also permit businesses to recover damages from unlawful business practices. These laws generally prohibit companies from employing unfair business practices.

The state deceptive trade practices acts vary but have certain common elements. First, the definition of "unfair" or "deceptive" conduct proscribed by the laws is generally broad. Therefore, the acts cover many business torts, including interference with business expectations, predatory pricing, disparagement and fraud.

The state laws offer particular benefit to plaintiffs because they typically provide for supracompensatory damages. A successful plaintiff can thus recover two or three times its actual damages (called double or treble damages) under the deceptive trade practices legislation.

The state laws go beyond business torts and may even reach an "opportunistic" or "bad faith" breach of contract. An unfair breach of contract might involve a party's dishonest interpretation of a contract term or strategic refusal to perform the contract in an attempt to extract additional consideration from the other party.

In one modern case, a soft drink distributor had a dispute with its supplier, a bottling company. The distributor refused to pay over $60,000 that it owed, until the bottler provided additional delivery service. A court held that this withholding of due payments was "a form of extortion" to force the bottler to deliver more product, when the bottler had no contractual obligation to do so.

The court therefore found a violation of the deceptive trade practices act and granted the bottler triple damages of over $180,000, plus attorneys' fees.

■ Ethical Perspectives

Opportunistic Behavior and Business Transactions

The law of unfair competition reflects an attempt by government to prohibit certain unethical business practices. In this area, there is considerable overlap between legal requirements and ethical dictates. But is the law alone sufficient to uphold business ethics in competition? Some argue that the law has gone too far in promoting business ethics.

A key contemporary concern of both the law and ethics is "opportunistic" business behavior. Opportunism is "crafty" business behavior that uses every available tool to promote the self-interest of the business.

Consider the following example of opportunistic behavior. Plasco Company makes toys and other items out of plastics. Plasco is a major company that has good relations with the retail outlets that sell its products. Plasco has a long-standing relationship with Petrox Company to supply the raw plastics necessary to make Plasco's toys. Petrox is bound by contract to provide all Plasco's plastic requirements throughout 1990. In August 1990, Petrox refuses to supply more plastic to Plasco, unless Plasco agrees to a 25-percent increase in price for the plastic.

The law would enable Plasco to sue Petrox for breach of contract. Such a lawsuit, however, would be costly and prolonged. Moreover, the lack of plastic could prevent Plasco from making toys for the Christmas season. This could poison Plasco's goodwill with retailers. Plasco may have no economically efficient alternative but to give in to Petrox's demand for a price increase.

To some, the demand by Petrox for a price increase was unfair and tantamount to blackmail. They would argue that Petrox did not use good faith in its business dealings. Reliance on suppliers' good faith is arguably critical to the effective functioning of the free market. Petrox clearly violated the principle of promise-keeping.

To others, including some economists, Petrox did nothing wrong. Petrox simply used its position in the marketplace to make a good deal. Under this view, Plasco has only itself to blame for its predicament, which resulted from *undue reliance* on a single supplier. The free market depends, to a degree at least, on each company's ability to look out for its own interests. Plasco is not a small, uneducated business or consumer and should be expected to protect itself.

The choice between these views says much about one's perspective on business and free enterprise. But the choice is not always so clear-cut. Suppose that Petrox demanded the increase because its raw materials costs had risen unexpectedly and substantially. Without the increase, Petrox might have been required to sell at a loss or even go bankrupt. In such a case, would Plasco have been unethically "opportunistic" in insisting on the price set in the original contract?

The ethical issues in this case may not be easy. This makes it even more difficult for the law to define unfair competition. Some argue that the law should set a few clear-cut rules against fraud and leave the difficult cases for business ethics and the functioning of the market. Otherwise, lawsuits could be used opportunistically. But can we count on businesses to behave ethically in the absence of legal requirements?

▬ International Perspectives

Trademark Protection and Grey Market Goods

The international law of trademarks is "territorial" in nature. This means that a registered trademark only protects a company in the country of registration. If Plasco uses or registers its name as a trademark in the United States, no other company can use the mark in this country. Some other company, however, could market Plasco products in the countries of South America, unless Plasco takes steps to register its trademark in those nations as well.

In addition, registering a trademark in the U.S. may not even provide exclusive control over the trademark in this country, due to grey market goods. The problem is illustrated by the following scenario. Vivimax produces cameras overseas. Americam pays for the exclusive right to market Vivimax cameras in the U.S. and obtains the U.S. trademark rights to Vivimax. Americam maintains a line of retail shops that sell Vivimax cameras. Then ImpoCam begins buying Vivimax cameras overseas, importing them to the U.S., and selling them in U.S. stores. This is known as the "grey market." These cameras are Vivimax-made and identical to the ones sold by Americam. The legal question is whether Americam can use its U.S. trademark rights in Vivimax to prevent ImpoCam from selling Vivimax goods in this country.

The legal rights of a United States trademark holder against grey market importers is of great significance. Studies suggest that one third of all cameras sold in this country are grey market cameras. The grey market is also significant in other product lines and the total grey market sales may exceed $10 billion. Because of currency fluctuations, grey market importers may be able to sell the product for less than the U.S. distributor and trademark holder.

Section 526 of the Tariff Act of 1930 provides some protection to the U.S. trademark owner. This section enables the United States Customs Service to bar the importation of trademarked goods, unless the domestic trademark owner consents. The Customs Service regulations, though, permit third parties to import identically trademarked goods when "the foreign and domestic trademark or trade name owners are parent and subsidiary companies or are otherwise subject to common ownership or control."[12] Section 526 may therefore provide little protection to domestic subsidiaries of foreign manufacturers. In addition, Customs Service enforcement of section 526 is short of perfect.

Section 526(c) provides a private right of action to United States trademark owners against grey market importers. The U.S. owner must prove that the grey market imports cause a likelihood of consumer confusion, however. Some courts have held that if the grey market goods are genuine (the same quality goods from the same manufacturer), there is no possibility of harmful consumer confusion. This interpretation seriously undermines protection for U.S. trademark owners.

[12]19 C.F.R. section 133.21(c)(2).

Questions and Case Problems

1. A very widely known chef, Henri Panglod, fed up with life in the big city, signed a contract in October with a little restaurant in the suburbs called La Vie. La Vie was in the process of renovations and wouldn't be ready for business until April of the next year. In May (with construction still not complete at La Vie), La Vie's chief suburban competitor, The View, solicited Panglod, offering him twice the salary and a quiet apartment nearby. The chef agreed with The View and began cooking for that restaurant. La Vie sued The View, seeking the cost of finding a new chef and their lost profits from losing Panglod. Should La Vie win and be able to recover these damages?

2. A drug company, Ives Laboratories, manufactured the prescription drug cyclandate under the brand name "Cyclospasmol." The company's patent on this drug had expired. Another drug company, Darby Drug, manufactures a generic form of cyclandate and advertises that its drug is similar to Cyclospasmol. Ives produced its Cyclospasmol in red and blue capsules, which were associated with the drug by physicians. Darby Drug also used red and blue capsules for its new generic competitor. Ives sued for trademark infringement. Does Darby's packaging violate the trademark of Ives? [*Ives Laboratories, Inc. v. Darby Drug Co., Inc.,* 455 F. Supp. 939 (E.D.N.Y. 1978); 697 F.2d 291 (2d Cir. 1982)].

3. Warner Brothers produced a television series entitled the "Dukes of Hazard," which featured an automobile called the "General Lee." The car was orange and emblazoned with a confederate flag. Gay Toys manufactured a toy car patterned after the "General Lee." Warner Brothers sued Gay Toys for trademark infringement. Gay Toys defended that the design and appearance of the "General Lee" was functional and therefore unprotectible. Should Warner Brothers succeed against this defense? [*Warner Brothers, Inc. v. Gay Toys, Inc.,* 724 F.2d 327 (2d Cir. 1983)].

4. Benzo gasoline was a company's special product containing a coal derivative. Another company, which was a competitor and sold White Rose gasoline, published a pamphlet stating that Benzo gasoline was harmful to automobiles and urged its readers to buy White Rose, "an honestly made gasoline." The only service station that marketed Benzo gasoline sued the producers of White Rose for disparagement. Should Benzo be able to recover on this claim? [*National Refining Co. v.*

Benzo Gas Motor Fuel Co., 20 F.2d 763, *cert. denied*, 275 U.S. 570 (1927).

5. Borden Co. produced milk under both its own name brand and under other private labels. Milk sold under the Borden label was priced higher than milk sold under the other private labels. The Federal Trade Commission claimed that all the milk produced by Borden was the same, so the different prices constituted illegal price discrimination under the Robinson-Patman Act. Are the milk products of "like grade and quality" so that the price differential would violate the Robinson-Patman Act? [*FTC v. Borden Co.*, 383 U.S. 637 (1966)].

CHAPTER THIRTEEN

Advertising Law

KEY BACKGROUND

The essential background for this chapter on advertising law is found in Chapter 45 of *West's Business Law, Fifth Edition* and Chapter 18 of *West's Legal Environment of Business*. These chapters cover consumer protection law. Among the important points to remember from this chapter are:

- determination of "unfair or deceptive acts"

- remedies for deceptive advertising

- Federal Trade Commission enforcement procedures

The reader will also benefit from familiarity with the adoption of the Federal Trade Commission advertising substantiation rule (discussed in Chapter 44 of *West's Business Law, Fifth Edition* and in Chapter 6 of *West's Legal Environment of Business*).

* * *

Virtually every major company in the United States advertises its goods or services. Moreover, advertising itself is big business. Total billings of advertising agencies in the United States are approximately $50 billion. This sum does not even include the amount spent on advertising by companies that do their own advertising and do not employ specialized agencies.

This chapter focuses on the legal issues dealing with advertising itself. Specifically, the chapter discusses First Amendment rights of advertisers, rules prohibiting deceptive advertising, regulation of comparative advertising, and advertising misappropriation claims. Other advertising issues are discussed in chapters on unfair competition (trademark protection, disparagement) and communications law (tort liability).

First Amendment Rights of Advertisers

The First Amendment to the U.S. Constitution guarantees free speech. For many years, advertising was considered "commercial speech" and was unprotected by the First Amendment's guarantee of freedom of speech. The Supreme Court began to extend some First Amendment protection to advertising in the 1960s and in 1976 the Court held that a purely commercial advertisement had some First Amendment protection from government regulation.

The Court first recognized the First Amendment protection for commercial speech in *Virginia State Board of Pharmacy v. Virginia Citizens Consumer Council*.[1] Virginia had a law that prohibited pharmacists from advertising the prices of prescription drugs for sale. The Supreme Court held that this law was an unconstitutional violation of the First Amendment.

The Court protected commercial speech under the First Amendment in the interest of consumers.

---

[1]425 U.S. 748 (1976).

The rights of the speaker, in this case an advertiser, were not so important as the interest of the listener, or consumer. The Court held that consumers had a strong interest in price comparisons, in order to save money. The consumers' interest justified First Amendment protection for advertisements.

While advertising has some protection under the First Amendment, the free speech rights of advertisers are not as great as those of political speakers, for example. Government may constitutionally prevent false or misleading advertisements. The Supreme Court also has held that Puerto Rico could prohibit advertisements for casino gambling on the grounds that such ads could increase crime and disrupt the island's moral and cultural patterns.[2] The government could not regulate political speakers on these grounds.

Because the government has greater flexibility in regulating commercial speech, it is necessary to define commercial speech and distinguish it from more protected forms of speech. The distinction is especially difficult for "advertorials," which are paid advertisements that take an editorial stand on significant public issues.

In one case, the R.J. Reynolds Tobacco Company took out advertorials claiming that cigarettes were not proven to cause heart disease. The Federal Trade Commission staff tried to halt the Reynolds ads as false and misleading, but Reynolds claimed that the advertorials were political speech protected by the First Amendment.

The Supreme Court has given guidance regarding what speech may be regulated as commercial. Commercial speech usually has the following three characteristics: (a) it is in the form of a paid advertisement; (b) it refers to a specific product; and (c) it is motivated by economic gain. Although the Reynolds ad did not refer to a specific product, the Commission held that it was commercial speech, and Reynolds eventually reached a settlement agreeing not to make such claims in "advertorials".

Commercial speech that is false or misleading has no First Amendment protection. Truthful advertising, however, is protected speech but may still be regulated if necessary. In order to regulate commercial speech, the government must prove three elements:

1. The government must have a substantial legitimate interest that it is protecting.

2. The restriction of speech must directly advance the government interest.

3. The restriction of speech must be reasonably related to achieving the government interest.

On the first test, the courts have recognized many legitimate government interests in restricting speech, as indicated by the Puerto Rico case discussed above. On the second test, the government must show that its advertising restrictions will actually be effective in advancing the government's interest.

The third test requires that the government not restrict advertising more than necessary. Some states have sought to prohibit advertising by lawyers, out of concern that lawyer advertising could deceive potential clients. Courts have held that an absolute prohibition on lawyer advertising is unconstitutional. States can adopt more limited regulation of lawyer advertising in order to prevent deception.

The application of these tests to a government regulation of commercial speech is illustrated in the following case.

---

[2]*Posadas de Puerto Rico Associates v. Tourism Company of Puerto Rico*, 106 S. Ct. 2968 (1986).

■ Case 13.1
National Funeral Services, Inc. v. Rockefeller
United States Court of Appeals,
Fourth Circuit, 1989
870 F.2d 136

Background and Facts *West Virginia passed a law regulating "pre-need funeral contracts," those sold for persons still living. The law required all sellers of such services be licensed by the state. The law also prohibited "in-person and telephonic solicitation of prospective purchasers in nursing homes, hospitals, and private residences, as well as the solicitation of relatives of persons near death."*

National Funeral Services, Inc. ("NFS") argued that the restrictions on solicitation were an unconstitutional interference with its freedom of speech. A district court held that the law was constitutional and NFS appealed.

KISER, District Judge, Sitting by Designation.

*   *   *   *

Turning to the facts of this case, the state has not contended that appellant's solicitations were in any way fraudulent or misleading. Therefore, I must conclude that appellant's speech is legitimate commercial speech, which is protected by the first amendment.

Likewise, I have no difficulty in concluding that the government interests furthered by these restrictions are substantial. The most obvious of these interests is the protection of consumers from overreaching and high pressure sales tactics of this most unique product. *W.Va.Code* § 47-14-10(e)(1983). Directly speaking, the subject of these contracts is funeral arrangement; indirectly speaking, their subject is death–the death of the buyer, or one close to him. This topic is obviously one charged with emotion and one fraught with the potential for overreaching by solicitors. In promulgating the funeral rule, FTC noted that the extremely sensitive nature of this subject in part necessitated its regulation:

While the arrangement of a funeral is clearly an important financial transaction for consumers, it is a unique transaction, one whose characteristics reduce the ability of consumers to make careful, informed purchase decisions.

*   *   *   *

The next inquiry is whether this ban directly advances these interests. The potential for fraudulent overreaching in the sale of these contracts is at its greatest when the consumer is confronted by a salesman:

Unlike a public advertisement, which simply provides information and leaves the recipient free to act upon it or not, in-person solicitation may exert pressure and often demands an immediate response, without providing an opportunity for comparison or reflection. The aim and effort of in-person solicitation may be to provide a one-sided presentation and to encourage speedy and perhaps uninformed decision making....

... And, as the Supreme Court has recently noted, in-person solicitation is "a practice rife with possibilities for overreaching, invasion of privacy, the exercise of undue influence, and out-right fraud." *Shapero v. Kentucky Bar Assoc.*, ... 108 S.Ct. 1916, 1922, 100 L.Ed.2d 475 (1988) (attorney solicitation). Thus, I believe the statute clearly advances both of the state's legitimate interests insofar as it bans door-to-door solicitation. *See May v. People*, 636 P.2d 672 (Colo.1981) (en banc).

*   *   *   *

Unlike direct mail solicitations that can be readily distinguished and easily discarded, a recipient of telephone solicitation must answer the phone to determine who is calling, and must risk an uncomfortable confrontation to rid himself of the solicitor. Further, it is beyond dispute that this most sensitive product makes an uninvited telephone call even more upsetting, especially when it invades the privacy of the home. In the words of one commentator, "[t]he telephone is an instrument with a unique capacity to intrude. Note, *Give Me A Home Where No Salesmen Phone: Telephone Solicitation and the First Amendment*, 7 Hastings Const. L.Q. 129. Thus, like in-person solicitation, telemarketing poses a very real threat to the privacy of a consumer's home. Consequently, because I conclude that telemarketing is in many ways analogous to in-person solicitation, I believe that the state's prohibition of it furthers the state's interests.

I turn to the last step of the analysis, the determination of whether the statute sweeps more broadly than necessary to achieve the state's interests. The Central Hudson Court phrased this inquiry as whether the statute is more extensive than necessary to serve the state interests.

* * * *

In making this determination, a court should view the anti-solicitation statute as a whole. West Virginia has demonstrated that two substantial interests underlie this statute, the protection of its people from fraud and the protection of its people's privacy. To further these interests, the legislature has restricted appellant's speech in a few specific situations that it identified as particularly prone to these problems—when the consumer is in a hospital, in a nursing home, confronted by the death of a loved one, or in the privacy of his own home. *W.Va.Code*, § 47-14-10 (1983). Similarly, the legislature has prohibited only two limited forms of speech that it felt posed special threats to the state's interests–uninvited in-person solicitation and telemarketing. Out of this scheme, appellant challenges only the state's restraint on in-home solicitation. I find it to be constitutional.

In making this finding, I place great weight on the alternatives left open by the statute:

(b) Notwithstanding any other provision of law to the contrary, nothing in this article shall be construed to restrict the right of a person to lawfully advertise, to use direct mail or otherwise communicate in a manner not within the above prohibition of solicitation or to solicit the business of anyone responding to such communication or otherwise initiating discussion of the goods or services being offered.

(c) Nothing herein shall be construed to prohibit general advertising.

W.Va.Code § 47-14-10 (1983).

Thus, the statute does not totally insulate the private residence from appellant's speech. with all of these avenues of communication left open, it would be difficult to conclude that the statute's measures are excessive. Furthermore, the avenues left open confirm that the statute is narrowly drawn, to eliminate no more than the evils it seeks to remedy–fraud and invasion of privacy.

Decision and Remedy   *The court upheld the constitutionality of the West Virginia statute.*

▰ Federal Trade Commission Regulation

In 1938, the FTC was given specific authority to regulate trade practices. The Commission's authority to control "unfair methods of competition" was soon used against deceptive advertising. Since that time, the FTC has adopted rules and undertaken enforcement actions against advertising that the Commission considered to be false or misleading.

Procedures

FTC enforcement begins with an investigation by the Commission's staff. If the FTC believes that advertising is deceptive, the staff draws up a complaint and tries to settle the dispute without a hearing. If settlement proves impossible, the FTC staff prosecutes its complaint in a hearing before an administrative law judge ("ALJ"). This hearing is much like a civil trial, but the ALJ is not a true judge but an employee of the FTC.

If there is a trial, and the advertiser wins the case before the ALJ, the matter is over—the FTC has no authority to appeal the decision. If the FTC wins the administrative hearing, the advertiser can appeal the decision to the Commission and a federal circuit court of appeals.

While deceptive advertising claims may involve a full trial before the ALJ and appeal to federal court, the vast majority of cases are settled by consent decree. This occurs when the FTC and the advertiser reach an agreement on some remedy that usually involves halting the advertisement. A consent order is published for public consideration and does not become final until 60 days after it is signed by the parties.

The FTC has been less active against deceptive advertising in the last decade, but continues to focus on what are sometimes called "outlaw" industries. These include weight-loss promoters, baldness remedies, land speculators, and residential siding companies. The Commission also is especially concerned with safety issues. The Commission enforced the law against a company that advertised a fire mask as effective in helping escape from home fires. This advertisement was deceptive for its failure to disclose that the mask did not protect against carbon monoxide, a common cause of death in fires.[3]

Deceptive Advertising

The FTC has adopted rules and made decisions regarding what sort of advertisements are considered illegally deceptive. When determining whether an advertisement is deceptive, the FTC does not base its judgment on the response of a knowledgeable person. Instead, the Commission decides whether a significant number of consumers, including unsophisticated consumers, actually will be deceived. One court decision emphasized that the law was made for the protection of "that vast multitude which includes the ignorant, the unthinking and the credulous."[4]

A company marketed a product called "Rejuvenescence" and advertised the cosmetic with the claim that it would make skin younger. After the FTC disputed this claim, the company responded that no consumer would reasonably believe that the product actually would reverse the aging process. The court held for the FTC, because the advertisements would be deceptive to naive consumers.

The FTC has a relatively low **burden of proof** in deceptive advertising cases. The Commission does not have to prove that the advertiser intentionally set out to deceive customers. The Commission need not even prove that customers were in fact misled. The Commission need only show that an advertisement is "likely to mislead."

While the FTC may protect the gullible consumer, it only protects those consumers who act reasonably under the circumstances. When a company claimed that its product was "invisible," the Commission held that the claim was not deceptive. No consumer could act reasonably in relying on the claim that the product was literally invisible. Likewise, the Commission has written that pastry need not be actually made in Denmark to be called a "Danish." Advertisers may also claim that their product is "perfect," because no consumer would rely literally on such a claim.

Many different types of advertising claims may be deceptive. The Commission has held specific types of practices to be illegally deceptive. These include clear falsehoods, false testimonials, misleading omissions, and unsubstantiated claims.

First, some advertisements contain claims that are literally false. A company was liable for advertising "antiques" when the products were not old enough to qualify as antiques. Another advertiser was liable for promoting "caffeine free" coffee that actually contained caffeine.

False testimonials are unlawfully deceptive. If a celebrity claims that he or she uses a

---

[3]*In re Emergency Devices, Inc.*, 102 F.T.C. 1713 (1983).

[4]*Charles of the Ritz Dist. Corp. v. FTC*, 143 F.2d 676 (2d Cir. 1944).

product, it must be true. Suppose that Chanel advertises that Tom Selleck uses a new brand of cologne. Chanel must show that Selleck actually used the cologne at the time of his endorsement.

An advertising claim may also be misleading for failing to disclose a material fact. Suppose that a Taiwanese manufacturer of shirts omits to disclose that its product was made overseas. In the past, the Commission has held that goods of foreign origin must disclose that they were not made in the United States.

False implications of expertise are also misleading. The FTC has found advertising deceptive when a company's name included the words "institute" or "laboratories," but the company had no scientific personnel. A company deceptively referred to its salespersons as "trained qualified food consultants" when they had received only one week of training, given by the company.

Good faith honesty is not a defense to a deceptive advertising challenge. Unlike common law fraud, the FTC need not prove an advertiser's knowledge of the falseness of the claim or an intent to deceive. The Commission need only show that the advertising had a tendency to deceive consumers.

The FTC also requires that companies substantiate advertising claims, particularly those claims that are scientific in nature. Advertising statements such as "studies prove" must be supported by substantiation. If a company claims that its muffins help control cholesterol and prevent heart attacks, the company must have good evidence to substantiate the truth of this claim.

Most deceptive advertising claims do not involve an absolute untruth or lack of substantiation. Many claims are true but still deceptive. For example, the Ford Motor Company ran an advertisement claiming that the Ford LTD was quieter than a glider in flight. The FTC complained that the advertisement was unlawfully misleading, because a glider in flight is actually quite a noisy environment. In one interesting case, a bread manufacturer was held to have practiced deceptive advertising. The manufacturer stated that its bread had fewer calories per slice than other brands. While true, the reason was that its bread was sliced thinner.[5]

Remedies

If the FTC finds that a company has engaged in deceptive advertising, the Commission has several remedies that it may enforce. The most typical remedy for the FTC is the cease-and-desist order. This order forbids future use of the deceptive advertisement. A company violating a cease-and-desist order is liable for up to $10,000 per violation.

Every appearance of the illegal advertisement is considered a violation. In one decision, *Reader's Digest* ran a sweepstakes promotion that the FTC prohibited as deceptive. The company still sent out 18 million pieces of mail containing the sweepstakes promotion. The FTC claimed 18 million violations of its order. A court imposed $1.75 million in penalties against *Reader's Digest* (the maximum potential penalty was about $180 billion).

If a cease-and-desist order is considered inadequate, the FTC may require corrective advertising. This means forcing the company to use its own advertising to correct its previous deceptive claim. Warner Lambert Co. advertised the mouthwash Listerine as effective in preventing the common cold. In truth, there was no significant evidence supporting this claim. The Commission ordered Warner Lambert to state in future advertising that: "Listerine will not help prevent colds or sore throats or lessen their severity."

The following case describes a Commission finding that advertising was false and deceptive and an order that a company take some corrective action.

---

[5]*Bakers Franchise Corp. v. Federal Trade Commission*, 302 F.2d 258 (3d Cir. 1962).

■■ Case 13.2
Removatron International
Corporation v.
Federal Trade Commission
United States Court of Appeals,
First Circuit, 1989
884 F.2d 1489

Background and Facts   *Removatron International Corporation sells a product to deal with unwanted hair. Most hair removal mechanisms are either temporary or involve electrolysis, which is painful and can leave scars and pits on the skin. Removatron's project involves tweezers and a machine that emits radio frequency energy that, the company claims, destroys the cells that cause hair to return. Among the* *advertising claims made by Removatron was that it caused permanent hair removal.*

The Federal Trade Commission staff brought a claim against Removatron, and an administrative law judge issued a cease-and-desist order. The judge found that Removatron's claims were insufficiently substantiated and deceptive. The judge also ordered that Removatron include a disclaimer in future advertising. Removatron appealed to the full FTC, but the Commission approved the lower decision in large part. Removatron then appealed to federal court.

BOWNES, Circuit Judge.

*   *   *   *

Petitioners advertise their product mainly in the beauty industry trade magazines. Sales are made after a series of telephone calls, mailings of literature, and meetings. The machine costs about $4,000. During the sales process, the purchasers are told that the machine will not work for everyone and that permanent removal will only be obtained after several treatments. Women who wish to be treated by the machine are given much the same information in written or oral form by the machine owner or operator. The written information is provided by petitioners who also provide purchasers with advertisements to place in local print media. Treatments cost approximately $35 per hour.

Rather than rehash all the evidence about petitioners' advertising, we present only a few typical samples of the types of claims made by petitioners. The petitioners stated that with Removatron treatments, hair removal can be "permanent" and unwanted hair will no longer be a problem; the ads also stated the machine is "effective" and an "alternative to electrolysis." The advertising also included statements that the machine has been "clinically tested and endorsed" and "clinically tested and shown superior." The ads also claimed that the FCC approved petitioners' product.

*   *   *   *

* * * Petitioners defend their advertising claims on three grounds.

First, they argue that they never claimed that their machine would produce permanent hair removal for all people all the time. It is irrelevant that petitioners never claimed 100% efficacy; the common-sense reading of the ads is that the machine will permanently remove hair for most people most of the time.

Second, petitioners contend that their ads and sales pitches qualified their permanency claims in two ways: (1) the machine would not work on everyone, and (2) permanent removal could only be obtained after several treatments. As a part of this argument, they assert that the only relevant audience is the beauty industry since that is to whom they advertised and marketed their product. We reject the contention that the relevant audience is only the beauty industry. While it is true that petitioners placed their ads in trade magazines, it is also true that their sales personnel provided brochures and other information to purchasers who were then instructed to provide these materials to potential clients. Furthermore, petitioners provided advertising to purchasers who would then place it in local print media. The relevant audience thus includes potential purchasers and customers of purchasers * * *.

* * * *

Finally, petitioners argue that the words "clinically tested" do not mean, and would not be taken by a reasonable person as meaning, "supported by rigorous scientific tests." Petitioners claim that "clinical" evidence merely means that a product has been used successfully in a clinical setting, while "scientific" evidence means that actual well-controlled studies had been performed. Regardless of any actual differences there may be between "clinical" and "scientific" evidence, petitioners have offered no basis for us to find that lay people would make such a fine distinction.

* * * *

[The court next considered the portion of the order requiring corrective disclosures.]

* * *   First, the Commission found petitioners' violations to be deliberate and not in good faith. This finding is amply supported by the FDA's Notice to petitioners and the fact they ignored their own expert's advice that they conduct a proper scientific experiment. This factor cuts in favor of a broad remedy. Second, petitioners have not been found liable for any prior violations; this factor cuts in petitioners' favor. Third, the transferability of the unfair practice to other products is irrelevant in deciding whether any such claim, regardless of the product, must be supported by scientific evidence. Fourth, there is no health hazard associated by the product, but there is the possibility of substantial economic harm. Petitioners' machine cost about $4,000. Treatments cost about $35 per hour and clients are told that they will need several treatments in order to obtain permanent removal. This factor points in favor of a broad remedy. Fifth, petitioners have been making permanency claims for years and continue to do so. This factor also points in favor of a broad remedy.

Decision and Remedy   *The court upheld the FTC Order against Removatron and issued an injunction against its violation.*

One remedy that the FTC may lack is an order to pay damages. The Commission has sought to require a company to make restitution to purchasers of products that were deceptively advertised. A federal court held that the FTC had no authority to require such payments, though some companies have obeyed FTC orders to reimburse their customers. The Commission also has required companies to recall products or provide customers with revised product instructions to correct deceptive messages.

FTC Rules

Most of the FTC's regulation of advertising takes place in individual adjudications of deception, as described above. The FTC also possesses the authority to adopt binding rules for advertising where necessary. The Commission has adopted rules to deal with certain specific advertising problems.

One prominent FTC rule involves retail food store advertising and marketing practices.[6] Under this rule, retail food stores that advertise products for sale must have an adequate supply on hand to meet a reasonable demand for the advertised products. This rule prevents stores from advertising very low prices on items not in stock in order to draw customers to the store.

The FTC rule requires that retail stores do one of the following. First, the store can keep sufficient supply on hand to meet reasonable demand. Second, the store can offer a rain check for the unavailable item. Third, the store can offer

---

[6]16 C.F.R. Part 424 (1989).

a substitute for the unavailable item at the advertised price or at a comparable price reduction. A retail food store can avoid the above requirements if its advertising contains a "limited quantity disclaimer," warning consumers that supplies are limited.

▄▄ Comparative Advertising

Comparative advertising is a technique in which a company compares its product with that of a competitor. By comparison, the company tries to demonstrate its superiority and even seize customers of the competitor. The FTC believes that comparative advertising provides valuable information and encourages its use.

Advertisers increasingly employ comparative advertising. Pepsi-Cola and Coca-Cola have engaged in a series of taste tests, each purporting to show that their cola tasted better than that of their rival. Over the past two decades, comparative advertising has increased from 7 percent of all ads to nearly 50 percent.

Comparative advertising is controversial, because so many comparative claims are questionable. Both Pepsi-Cola and Coca-Cola claimed that unbiased taste tests proved that their respective products tasted better. With such directly conflicting claims, one of these advertisements was presumably deceptive.

FTC Action   The FTC may challenge comparative advertising as unlawfully deceptive. Comparative product demonstrations may be misleading. In one case, a company compared its floor wax to rival products in a demonstration. The demonstration did not follow the directions of the rival product, however, and the rival therefore appeared inferior. The FTC found that this comparison was unlawfully deceptive.[7]

Even fair and true comparative advertising has been found deceptive by the FTC. A manufacturer of razor blades ran a commercial showing greatly magnified pictures of its blades and those of its competitor, after five shaves. The pictures showed greater corrosion on the blades of the competitor. The FTC held that this advertisement was unlawfully deceptive, because the greater corrosion had no material effect on shaving effectiveness or safety.[8]

---

[7]*In re American Home Products Corp.*, 83 F.T.C. 579 (1972).
[8]*In re Eversharp, Inc.*, 77 F.T.C. 686 (1970).

Lanham Act Private Remedies

The 1946 Lanham Act enables private companies to sue for false or misleading comparative advertising. Section 43(a) of the Lanham Act permits private parties to sue if they have been somehow injured by deceptive ads. This section permits private actions for "any false or misleading description of fact . . . in commercial advertising or promotion" that "misrepresents . . . goods, services, or commercial activities."

Originally, the Lanham Act only prohibited false statements about the advertiser's own product. The 1988 Trademark Law Revision Act strengthened section 43(a) to prohibit false statements about the competitor's product as well.

Suppose that Federal Airlines runs television commercials claiming "our planes are safer than those of Confederated Airlines." Confederated Airlines believes that this advertisement is false and misleading. Confederated could file a complaint with the FTC, but this action would be time-consuming and would depend on FTC initiative. Confederated could also sue Federal in court under section 43(a) of the Lanham Act.

Courts have held that private section 43(a) actions on comparative advertising have five required elements:

1. The defendant's comparative advertising made false statements about its own product or the plaintiff's product.

2. The comparative advertising actually deceived or had the tendency to deceive a substantial segment of their audience.

3. This deception is material and likely to influence the purchasing decisions of the audience.

4. The defendant put the falsely advertised goods in interstate commerce.

5. Plaintiff was or is likely to be injured by the deceptive comparative advertising.

All these elements must be present for a section 43(a) case to succeed.

In such a Lanham Act case, the plaintiff (Confederated) has the burden of proof to show that the defendant's (Federal) advertising was deceptive. Confederated would have to show that Federal's planes were not safer than the Confederated planes.

The plaintiff also must prove that consumers were deceived by the advertisements or probably would be deceived. If false statements in advertising were made intentionally, some courts will presume deception, so the plaintiff need not prove it. If Federal's statement is false, Confederated probably could show deception.

While a plaintiff such as Confederated must prove deception, it need not prove that all customers are deceived by an advertisement. Courts have been satisfied with evidence that as little as 10 to 15 percent of consumers were deceived.

Confederated next must prove that the deception was so significant, or material, that it would influence consumer decisions. Plane safety is so important that it would surely be material. Confederated also will have an easy time showing that Federal is in interstate commerce. The remaining requirement would be for Confederated to show that it was injured.

An increasing number of companies are suing as plaintiffs under section 43(a), claiming that competitors' comparative ads were deceptive. The comparative advertisement need not expressly name the plaintiff's product to warrant an action.

One leading case was brought by The Coca-Cola Company, which owns Minute Maid orange juice. Coca-Cola sued Tropicana for misleading comparative advertising. Tropicana orange juice ads said that Tropicana juice was "pure, pasteurized juice as it comes from the orange." The ads also showed an actor squeezing orange juice directly into a Tropicana carton. The Tropicana ads did not refer to Minute Maid by name, but implied that competitive products were not so fresh.

The court ruled for Coca-Cola, finding the Tropicana ads unlawfully deceptive. Tropicana orange juice, like most packaged juices, is pasteurized and frozen and does not come straight from fresh oranges. In addition, Coca-Cola presented evidence that surveyed customers were in fact deceived into believing that Tropicana juice came straight from fresh oranges. The court granted an injunction halting future broadcasts of the Tropicana advertisements.[9]

Most plaintiffs seek some sort of injunction against their competitors' deceiving comparative advertisements. A plaintiff ordinarily seeks a prompt preliminary injunction to stop the ads. To obtain such an injunction, the plaintiff need not prove that the public was actually deceived but need only show a likelihood of deception. Deception is presumed if the comparative advertisements are literally false.

In a leading case, the manufacturer of Tylenol sued the manufacturer of Anacin. Anacin ran a television commercial claiming to be superior in pain relief and reduction of inflammation. A court ruled that the two pain relievers were equal, so the Anacin advertisement was misleading. The court enjoined further presentations of Anacin's commercial.[10]

An injunction will compel the defendant to remove the deceptive advertisement as soon as possible. This action may be expensive. For example, a defendant may be required to modify its billboard advertising. In one case, the Noxell Corporation was forced to discontinue shipments of its Clean Lash mascara, because the packaging on the product deceptively claimed that the mascara was uniquely waterproof.[11]

Some competitors now receive money damages under section 43(a) of the Lanham Act. Damages are more difficult to obtain than an injunction. To get damages, a plaintiff must show that customers actually were deceived by the misleading ads. Moreover, a plaintiff may be required to show that it has lost profits as a result. It is difficult to prove the amount of lost profits caused by comparative advertising.

Section 35 of the Lanham Act provides some assistance to plaintiffs in damage actions. That section permits plaintiffs to recover their own lost profits, the wrongfully obtained profits of the deceptive advertiser, and the costs of litigation. In addition, section 35 permits up to triple these damages to punish the deceptive advertiser.

In the leading damages case, U-Haul sued Jartran, claiming that Jartran misleadingly claimed that U-Haul had inferior trucks and was more expensive. These advertisements misstated the cost of U-Haul renting and printed a misleading picture of the two companies' trucks. The court found unlawful deception and awarded U-Haul

---

[9]*Coca-Cola, Inc. v. Tropicana Products, Inc.*, 690 F.2d 312 (2d Cir. 1982).

[10]*American Home Products v. Johnson & Johnson*, 577 F.2d 160 (2d Cir. 1978).

[11]*Maybelline Co. v. Noxell Corp.*, 643 F. Supp. 294 (E.D. Ark. 1986).

$40 million in damages. The court found that it would cost U-Haul $13.6 million in advertising to correct Jartran's misleading ads. The court added $6 million of Jartran's profits and multiplied this amount under section 35, due to Jartran's willful deception.[12]

---

[12]*U-Haul, Int'l v. Jartran, Inc.,* 601 F. Supp. 1140 (D. Ariz. 1984), *aff'd,* 793 F.2d 1034 (9th Cir. 1986). Ironically, Jartran had received a prestigious "Gold Effie" advertising award for the commercial that the court later found deceptive.

On numerous occasions, two competitors will both bring Lanham Act claims against the other's advertising. The following case involves a vigorously fought legal battle between pet food companies and the standards for assessing money damages under the Lanham Act.

■ Case 13.3
ALPO Petfoods, Inc. v. Ralston Purina Company
United States Court of Appeals,
District of Columbia Circuit, 1990
913 F.2d 958

Background and Facts *Ralston Purina Company ran a series of advertisements suggesting that its Puppy Chow product can diminish the harms of canine hip dysplasia, a crippling joint condition. ALPO disputed the scientific basis for this claim and filed suit for false advertising under section 43(a) of the Lanham Act. Ralston counterclaimed, arguing that ALPO's ads were false and misleading. Specifically, Ralston attacked the commercial claim that ALPO Puppy Food contains "the formula preferred by responding vets two to one over the leading puppy food." Ralston argued that this claim was false and misleading about the preferences of veterinarians.*

After a two-month trial, the court found that both advertisements violated the law and issued an injunction prohibiting both parties from making "advertising or other related claims" similar to those found false and ordered both parties to disseminate corrective statements. The court also awarded ALPO $10.4 million in damages, plus costs and attorneys' fees. This sum was based on the amount that Ralston spent on its advertising and then doubling that sum "to capture the full harm that the advertising caused ALPO." Ralston was awarded no damages but only costs and attorneys' fees. The district court refused to award Ralston damages because the "magnitude of the wrongdoing by Ralston in comparison to that of ALPO is so much greater that a damage award would not be justified."

Ralston appealed the judgment against its advertising, the $10 million damage award of the district court, and the lack of damages it received in its claim against ALPO. The D.C. Circuit began by reviewing the record and determining that the advertising was in fact deceptive. The court next turned to the issue of damages.

THOMAS, Circuit Judge.

*   *   *   *

In only one respect do we disturb the district court's analysis of ALPO's section 43(a) claim. As we discuss ... below, the court granted ALPO certain remedies that would be proper only in a case involving actions that evince willfulness or bad faith, such as passing off a product as another seller's product. *See, e.g., W.E. Bassett Co. v. Revlon, Inc.,* 435 F.2d 656, 662 (2d Cir.1970) (affirming award of profits in case involving willful passing off). The district court did not explicitly state that Ralston acted willfully or in bad faith, but its choice of remedies strongly suggests such a finding. *See, e.g., ALPO,* 720 F.Supp. at 215, 216 (awarding attorneys' fees to ALPO); *see also Conservative Digest*, 821 F.2d at 808 (award of attorneys' fees to plaintiff requires a finding of willfulness or bad faith). Moreover, several of the court's findings on Ralston's conduct, taken together, reflect the court's conclusion that Ralston ran advertisements that it knew lacked support. *See, e.g., ALPO*, 720 F.Supp at 213 ("Ralston's claims have "perpetrated a cruel hoax on dog owners"); *id.* at 216 (Ralston persists in its position that its thoroughly inadequate and distorted research permit it to continue to claim its dog food can ameliorate CHD."). In sum, the court found, without stating explicitly, that Ralston had acted willfully or in bad faith. For the reasons that follow, we set that finding aside as clearly erroneous.

None of the district court's observations that amount to a finding of willfulness or bad faith relate to Ralston's intentions at the time that it violated section 43(a). For example, the opinion stresses that Ralston has not recanted its CHD-related claims or shown remorse for having made them. *Id.* at 214-15, 216. Although these considerations can affect the propriety of a permanent injunction by showing whether a defendant is likely to cause future harm, * * * they cannot show that an unrepentant party *has willfully* done its commercial misdeeds. Particularly in a case involving disputes over scientific support for advertising claims, a party's protestations of innocence can reflect an honest difference of scientific opinion, rather than a specific intent to mislead consumers and attack business rivals. Indeed, insisting that a losing party show contrition, especially when an appeal lies ahead, overlooks the nonpenal nature of section 35(a) remedies.

* * * *

Leaving aside whether the *U-Haul* standard or the district court's alternative calculation accurately measures the profits that Ralston derived from its false advertising, we hold that this case does not justify an award of profits. Section 35(a) authorizes courts to award to an aggrieved plaintiff both plaintiff's damages and defendant's profits, but, as this court noted in *Foxtrap*, 671 F.2d at 641, court's discretion to award these remedies has limits. Just as "any award based on plaintiff's damages requires some showing of actual loss," *id.* at 642; see also infra p. 969 (discussing actual damages under section 35(a)), an award based on a defendant's profits requires proof that the defendant acted willfully or in bad faith, *see Foxtrap*, 671 F.2d at 641; *Frisch's Restaurants, Inc. v. Elby's Big Boy*, 849 F.2d 1012, 1015 (6th Cir.1988). Proof of this sort is lacking Ralston's decision to run CHD-related advertising that lacked solid empirical support does not, without more, reflect willfulness or bad faith.

* * * *

In a false-advertising case such as this one, actual damages under section 35(a) can include:

–profits lost by the plaintiff on sales actually diverted to the false advertiser, *see, e.g., Foxtrap*, 671 F.2d at 642 (trademark case);

–profits lost by the plaintiff on sales made at prices reduced as a demonstrated result of the false advertising, *see, e.g., Burndy Corp. v. Teledyne Indus.*, 748 F.2d 767, 773 (2d Cir.1984);

–the costs of any completed advertising that actually and reasonably responds to the defendant's offending ads, *see, e.g., Cuisinarts, Inc. v. Robot–Coupe Int'l Corp.*, 580 F.Supp. 634, 640-41 (S.D.N.Y.1984); and

–quantifiable harm to the plaintiff's good will, to the extent that completed corrective advertising has not repaired that harm, *see, e.g., Engineered*

Mech. Servs., Inc. v. Applied Mech. Technology, Inc., 591 F.Supp. 962, 966 (M.D. La.1984); *see also* Comment, 55 U.Chi. L.Rev. at 650-57 (discussing how courts might directly measure good will).

Decision and Remedy   *The court vacated the $10.4 million award against Ralston, due to the lack of evidence of bad faith. The court remanded the case back to the district court to determine ALPO's actual monetary damages and to permit Ralston another opportunity to prove its monetary damages. The court also modified the injunction against Ralston, to permit the publication of scientific articles on canine hip dysplasia.*

Plaintiffs do not always succeed under section 43(a). In *Mennen Co. v. Gillette Co.*, complaining of misleading comparative shaving ads, the court dismissed the complaint as a "competitive ploy" by the plaintiff.[13] Haagen-Dazs ice cream sued the manufacturers of Frusen Gladje ice cream, alleging that Frusen Gladje's name misled consumers into believing that the ice cream had a Scandinavian origin. The court rejected the complaint because Haagen-Dazs used the same marketing ploy.[14]

Private Regulation of Advertising

Private organizations also regulate deceptive advertising, and much private regulation focuses on comparative advertising. Indeed, until 1972, two national television networks refused to accept comparative advertising. While networks now accept comparative ads, they regulate the content of comparative advertising. Exhibit 13–1 shows the NBC standards for accepting such commercials.

The advertising industry itself employs self-regulation through the National Advertising Division (NAD) and the National Advertising Review Board (NARB). These organizations were created in 1971 to promote truth in advertising. In its first year, the NAD/NARB heard nearly 2000 complaints of unfair advertising. More recently, the NAD has handled about 100 cases per year.

NAD/NARB decision making is much like that of a court. A company or the Better Business Bureau first files a complaint of unfair advertising with the NAD, and the NAD then demands substantiation of the complaint and investigates the facts. If the NAD considers the advertisement unfair, it requests modification or removal of the ad. NAD standards are much like those used by the FTC. Approximately two-thirds of the NAD cases are found to involve deception or lack of substantiation. NAD decisions are officially reported, much like judicial decisions.

One recent NAD decision involved comparative advertising for peanut butter. Bama Peanut Butter ran newspaper ads that stated:

> Peanut butter lovers say "You Can't Beat Bama! Jif Can't! Skippy Can't! In recent taste tests in the South, boys and girls who love peanut butter found Bama Peanut Butter unbeatable!

Bama's taste tests had shown that the product was as good as all its competitors' overall average, but customers preferred the flavor of one of Bama's competitors' products. The NAD ruled against Bama and held that the advertisement was a misleading description of the taste tests.

An NAD decision may be appealed to a five-member panel of the NARB. The NARB decision is final. Although the NAD/NARB process has no legally binding effect, its decisions have always been followed. This process has some limits. The NAD/NARB generally reviews national advertising and often provides no remedy against misleading local commercials. Moreover, no money damages can be awarded.

---

[13]565 F. Supp. 648 (S.D.N.Y. 1983), aff'd, 742 F.2d 1437 (2d Cir. 1984).

[14]*Haagen-Dazs, Inc. v. Frusen Gladje, Ltd.*, 493 F. Supp. 73 (S.D.N.Y. 1980).

Exhibit 13-1

National Broadcasting Co., Inc., Department of Broadcast Standards
Comparative Advertising Guidelines

NBC will accept comparative advertising which identifies directly or by implication, a competing product or service. As with all other advertising, each substantive claim, direct or implied, must be substantiated to NBC's satisfaction and the commercial must satisfy the following guidelines and standards for comparative advertising established by NBC:

1. Competitors shall be fairly and properly identified.

2. Advertisers shall refrain from disparaging or unfairly attacking competitors, competing products, services or other industries through the use of representations or claims, direct or implied, that are false, deceptive, misleading or have the tendency to mislead.

3. The identification must be for comparison purposes and not simply to upgrade by association.

4. The advertising should compare related or similar properties or ingredients of the product, dimension to dimension, feature to feature, or wherever possible be a side-by-side demonstration.

5. The property being compared must be significant in terms of value or usefulness of the product or service to the consumer.

6. The difference in the properties being compared must be measurable and significant.

7. Pricing comparisons may raise special problems that could mislead, rather than enlighten, viewers. For certain classifications of products, retail prices may be extremely volatile, may be fixed by the retailer rather than the product advertiser, and may not only differ from outlet to outlet but from week to week within the same outlet. Where these circumstances might apply, NBC will accept commercials containing price comparisons only on a clear showing that the comparative claims accurately, fairly and substantially reflect the actual price differentials or retail outlets throughout the broadcast area, and that these price differentials are not likely to change during the period the commercial is broadcast.

8. When a commercial claim involves market relationships, other than price, which are also subject to fluctuation (such as but not limited to sales position or exclusivity), the substantiation for the claim will be considered valid only as long as the market conditions on which the claim is based continue to prevail.

9. As with all other advertising, whenever necessary, NBC may require substantiation to be updated from time to time, and may re-examine substantiation, where the need to do so is indicated as the result of a challenge or other developments.

Special Categories of Advertising

The government has created special regulations for specific types of advertising or specific product advertisements. Examples of these special regulations include sweepstakes advertising, advertising aimed at children, and food and drug advertising.

Sweepstakes

Companies may conduct sweepstakes to promote their products. Thus, a publisher may offer a series of prizes in connection with its advertising. Sweepstakes may help draw attention to a product. The government places a number of regulations on sweepstakes, for advertising or other purposes.

First, a sweepstakes may not be a private lottery, which is illegal. An illegal lottery has three elements: prize, chance, and consideration. If a customer must buy a chance to win a prize, there is a lottery. Most sweepstakes avoid being an illegal lottery by eliminating the consideration for participation. Consumers need not pay to participate. For this reason, most advertising sweepstakes have "no purchase required."

The FTC has specific rules governing sweepstakes and other games used in advertising by gasoline and food retailing businesses. This rule requires that contests disclose the odds of winning, the number and value of the prizes available, and the termination date of the game, among other items. The rule also requires random mixing of game cards or their equivalent, to ensure a fair selection of winners. The names of winners of significant prizes also must be disclosed.

Various states also have laws regulating sweepstakes. New York and Florida require advance registration and the posting of a bond to guarantee that prizes are awarded. Other states require that winners be announced or require that prizes actually be awarded within a certain period of time.

Children's Advertising

In the 1970s, the FTC sought to ban all advertising aimed at children, who are more easily deceived than are adults. Congress rejected the FTC's attempted ban. The FTC still reviews children's advertising for potential deception. The FTC also obtained a consent order halting children's advertising for vitamins. Prior to this time, some 30 percent of children's television advertising was for vitamin pills that were required to state on the bottle: "Keep out of the reach of children."

In 1990, Congress passed the Children's Television Act, which limits advertisements during children's television programs to no more than twelve minutes per hour on weekdays and no more than ten and one-half minutes per hour on weekends.

Children's advertising is also regulated by private organizations. The National Association of Broadcasters has a code covering children's advertising that recognizes children's susceptibility to advertising messages. Among the requirements of the NAB code state requirements that advertisements should not use "exhortative language" or certain special effects and should not direct children to ask parents to buy a product for them.

Food and Drug Advertising

The FTC regulates food and drug advertising to prevent deception. Section 12 of the Federal Trade Commission Act specifically prohibits false advertisements for "food, drugs, devices, or cosmetics."[15] In addition, the Food and Drug Administration (FDA) exercises some control over such advertising.

The FDA has rules that require certain nutrition labeling on prepared food products. In 1990, the FDA adopted a tentative final rule setting conditions for companies that want to label their food as "cholesterol free" or "low cholesterol." Such labels may be used only when food contains five grams or less of fat per serving and two grams or less of saturated fat per serving.

In 1990, Congress passed the Nutrition Labeling and Education Act, giving the FDA additional regulatory power. This law mandates that certain nutrition information, such as amount of cholesterol, sodium, sugar and other substances, be contained on food labels. The law also empowers the FDA to establish standards for label use of terms such as "low," "light," "fresh," and "natural."

The FDA also regulates the labels of drugs and restricts the uses that can be recommended. FDA rules also limit advertising for over-the-counter drugs. Advertising can suggest the drug's use only under conditions permitted on the label.

The FTC also monitors food and drug advertising and is concerned about health claims made by companies. The Commission recently prohibited an advertiser of bee pollen products from claiming that the product would be an effective allergy treatment or analgesic. The Commission also reached a recent consent

---

[15]15 U.S.C. section 52 (1988).

agreement against a company that claimed that its corn oil lowered blood cholesterol levels. Advertisements for blueberry juice were held deceptive, because they claimed that their juice contained essential minerals, such as iron, potassium, calcium, and others. In fact, the juice contained only trace amounts of these minerals, too little for any positive effect on health.

Alcohol and Tobacco Advertising

Federal and state governments have adopted specific rules to govern the advertising of alcohol and tobacco products. The Twenty-First Amendment to the U.S. Constitution, which repealed Prohibition, granted the states broad power to regulate alcohol production and consumption. States have used this authority to control advertising of alcoholic beverages.

Most state alcohol advertising laws have withstood challenges that they violated the First Amendment. For example, Ohio law prohibits a seller from advertising the price per bottle or per drink of any alcoholic beverage or any reference to price except within the seller's premises. This restriction was held to be constitutional. The law advanced the state's interest in preventing excessive drinking.

Liquor ads are also subject to voluntary private restrictions imposed by broadcasters. The television networks, for example, do not carry commercials for hard liquor, though they accept beer and wine commercials. In beer and wine commercials, the actors cannot be shown actually consuming the drinks.

Advertising tobacco products is also subject to special regulation. In 1971, Congress prohibited television commercials for cigarettes. Federal law also requires that all cigarette labeling and advertising contain one of several health warnings.

▬ Advertising Misappropriation

An advertiser may be liable for **misappropriation** if it uses the name or picture of a person in advertising without obtaining permission. Misappropriation is sometimes considered a form of invasion of privacy and at other times is simply considered the unauthorized taking of a person or a company's goodwill right to publicity.

For example, a portable toilet company marketed its products under the name "Here's Johnny." Johnny Carson sued the company for misappropriation and won. The court held that a "celebrity's legal right of publicity is invaded whenever his identity is intentionally appropriated for commercial purposes."[16] In another case, a television game show was liable for using the pictures of a past winner in advertisements without permission.

Rules against misappropriation are especially strict for advertising. A newspaper could lawfully use a photograph of Donald Trump in connection with a relevant news story on troubled businesses. But if the same newspaper uses a photograph of Donald Trump in an advertisement for the newspaper, the newspaper may be liable for misappropriation.

A company may unlawfully misappropriate a person's identity, even if it does not physically use the person in an advertisement. The following case involves the practice of "sound-alikes" in commercials.

---

[16]*Carson v. Here's Johnny Portable Toilets, Inc.*, 698 F.2d 831 (6th Cir. 1983).

| ▬ Case 13.4
Midler v.
Ford Motor Company
United States Court of Appeals,
Ninth Circuit, 1988
849 F.2d 460 | **Background and Facts** *Ford Motor Company and its advertising agency, Young & Rubicam, Inc., devised a "Yuppie Campaign" to sell the Ford Lincoln Mercury with commercials that tried to make an emotional appeal to yuppies. The campaign would use songs, including one by Bette Midler. Midler refused to perform the song for Ford. Young & Rubicam then sought out a backup singer for Midler. The backup singer was told to "sound as much as possible like the Bette Midler record."*

The commercial never used the name or picture of Midler, but many people believed that she was singing in the commercial. Midler |

sued for misappropriation. The district court ruled in favor of Ford on a motion for summary judgment. Midler appealed.

NOONAN, Circuit Judge.

* * * *

When Young & Rubicam was preparing the Yuppie Campaign it presented the commercial to its client by playing an edited version of Midler singing "Do You Want To Dance," taken from the 1973 Midler album, "The Divine Miss M." After the client accepted the idea and form of the commercial, the agency contacted Midler's manager, Jerry Edelstein. The conversation went as follows: "Hello, I am Craig Hazen from Young and Rubicam. I am calling you to find out if Bette Midler would be interested in doing . . .? Edelstein: "Is it a commercial?" "Yes." "We are not interested."

* * * *

Why did the defendants ask Midler to sing if her voice was not of value to them? Why did they studiously acquire the services of a sound-alike and instruct her to imitate Midler if Midler's voice was not of value to them? What they sought was an attribute of Midler's identity. Its value was what the market would have paid for Midler to have sung the commercial in person.

A voice is more distinctive and more personal than the automobile accoutrements protected in *Motschenbacher*. A voice is as distinctive and personal as a face. The human voice is one of the most palpable ways identity is manifested. We are all aware that a friend is at once known by a few words on the phone. At a philosophical level it has been observed that with the sound of a voice, "the other stands before me." D. Ihde, *Listening and Voice* 77 (1976). A fortiori, these observations hold true of singing, especially singing by a singer of renown. The singer manifests herself in the song. To impersonate her voice is to pirate her identity. See W. Keeton, D. Dobbs, R. Keeton, D. Owen, *Prosser & Keeton on Torts* 852 (5th ed. 1984).

We need not and do not go so far as to hold that every imitation of a voice to advertise merchandise is actionable. We hold only that when a distinctive voice of a professional singer is widely known and is deliberately imitated in order to sell a product, the sellers have appropriated what is not theirs and have committed a tort in California.

Decision and Remedy *The court reversed the summary judgment against Midler and remanded the case for a trial.*

Incidental use of a person's name or picture is legal, however. Thus, a clothing advertisement might contain a picture of a busy New York street. Individuals who were incidentally present on the street would not have a good case for misappropriation.

In addition, some highly public persons may be unable to sue for misappropriation. For example, a court held that a company could market "Franklin D. Roosevelt cigars" without obtaining permission from the then-President. An All-American football player, who had deliberately sought and received widespread publicity, was denied any recovery for a brewing company's football schedule calendar that contained the name and likeness of the player.[17]

Unlawful misappropriation was found when a women's medical center used a physician's name and picture in the center's annual calendar. The calendar was distributed as a

---

[17]*O'Brien v. Pabst Sales Co.*, 124 F.2d 167 (5th Cir. 1941).

solicitation of patients, and the doctor had not given his permission for use of his likeness.

Advertisers may use pictures of public events. For example a performer at the enormous free rock concert Woodstock complained when a movie producer used a picture of his performance to promote a movie. The court held that the matter was of public interest and legally used in the advertisement. Famous quarterback Joe Namath of the New York Jets complained when *Sports Illustrated* used a picture of him in action as part of their advertising for subscribers. The court held for *Sports Illustrated*, because pictures of a football game could be used in advertising.

Even legitimate use of public pictures may be wrongful misappropriation, when the advertiser falsely suggests that the pictured individuals endorse their product. If *Sports Illustrated* had used a picture of Joe Namath *and* had also suggested that he recommended that fans subscribe to the magazine, the unauthorized endorsement could constitute misappropriation.

▰ Advertising Negligence

If a person is injured by an advertised product, he or she may sue the product manufacturer for negligent advertising. Some smokers, who suffer from lung disease, now are suing tobacco companies, claiming that the advertising for cigarettes suggested that the product was safe.

A negligent advertising claim must meet the traditional requirements of negligence. Thus, a plaintiff must show that the advertiser breached a duty of due care. A careless misrepresentation of product safety would breach the advertiser's duty of due care. One child's parents bought a toy pistol that was advertised as "totally harmless." Later, the pistol emitted flames that set fire to a Santa Claus costume that the child was wearing. A court held that the manufacturer could be liable for negligent advertising.

In another case, a detergent manufacturer claimed that its product was safe enough to put in your eye. A purchaser accidentally rubbed her eyes with detergent and eventually became blind. The detergent contained a chemical that was known to be dangerous to eyes. A federal court held that the injured purchaser could recover for advertising negligence.[18] The false claim breached the defendant's duty of due care.

If advertising is unlawfully false and deceptive under the FTC Act, the plaintiff can use **negligence *per se*** (a legal presumption of negligence). Violation of a statute is considered automatically to be a violation of a duty of due care. A deodorant producer claimed in ads that the product could not cause an allergic skin reaction. This advertisement was found deceptive under a Massachusetts statute, and a plaintiff succeeded in an advertising negligence claim.

A plaintiff in an advertising negligence case also must show that the negligence was the **proximate cause** of the plaintiff's injuries. In one proximate cause case, a victim of a mugging sued the manufacturer of mace. She had purchased mace, based on a statement that it would cause "instantaneous incapacitation." The plaintiff was able to recover for advertising negligence because she bought the mace in reliance on this claim and because she used the mace, without the desired effect.

Suppose that an auto manufacturer advertises a car with the claim that it is inexpensive, gets excellent gas mileage, and has unbreakable safety glass. A woman buys the car because it gets excellent gas mileage. Then she is in an accident, in which the car's glass shatters and injures her. She will be unable to recover because she did not purchase the car in reliance on the advertising claim of unbreakable safety glass.

In addition to negligence, an advertiser may be liable for fraud. This would occur when false advertising claims are made knowingly and with an intent to deceive consumers. In one recent case, a medical clinic that performed abortions sued a pro-life organization that ran a "Help Clinic" that counseled pregnant women. The medical clinic argued that "the Help Clinic, through false and deceptive advertising and related activity, misleads persons into believing that abortions are conducted at the clinic with the intent of deceptively luring those persons to the clinic to unwittingly receive anti-abortion propaganda." The court agreed and awarded the medical clinic $23,500 in compensatory damages and $5500 in punitive damages.[19]

---

[18]*Hardy v. Procter & Gamble Mfg. Co.*, 289 F.2d 124 (5th Cir. 1954).
[19]*Fargo Women's Health Organization, Inc. v. FM Women's Help and Caring Connection*, 444 N.W.2d 683 (N.D. 1989).

Social Responsibility in Advertising

Most advertising is intended to persuade large groups of people to purchase a product. Some argue that this intent is unavoidably manipulative and dishonest toward its audience. For these advocates, advertisers always try to trick the public into buying products that they don't need.

Others, including economists, see great social value in advertising. They contend that advertising provides essential information to potential customers. Because of advertising, consumers can make a more informed choice of products.

The existence of advertising is, of course, a fact of life. Even its advocates concede, however, that some advertising is unethically misleading. Historically, the focus was on truth in advertising, and the government regulates the content of commercials to ensure that it is not misleading.

Recently, an ethical controversy has arisen over advertising's effects on society, regardless of whether it is true. This controversy has been most pronounced in the advertising of "sneakers," or athletic shoes. Several advertising companies have mounted very successful campaigns for sneakers, such as Nike's "Just Do It" campaign using the famous athlete, Bo Jackson.

The sneaker ads may have been too successful. Some allege that these advertisements were targeted at poor minority males in the nation's central cities. The ads have in fact made certain expensive brands of sneakers into status symbols in many inner cities. This, in turn, has spawned violence over the sneakers. *Sports Illustrated* ran a story entitled "Your Sneakers or Your Life" that chronicled a series of fatalities in fights over the possession of sneakers.

At first glance, it seems difficult to blame the sneaker advertisers for these deaths. The critics argue, however, that the advertisers improperly targeted "young black males as buyers, through the use of seductive, macho-loaded sales pitches presented by black stars."[20] Many of these youths, of course, cannot afford to pay for a pair of $100 sneakers. They also argue that the phrase "Just Do It" has a special meaning in the inner city—do whatever is necessary, without moral qualms.

To what extent should an advertiser anticipate and consider the social consequences of its advertising? And is it proper to target advertising to a group that does not need or cannot afford a product? Nike expressed concern over the misinterpretation of its advertisements but continued to run them.

---

[20]"They Know Bo," *N.Y. Times Magazine,* November 11, 1990, p.48.

<table>
<tr><td>

■ **International Perspectives**

</td></tr>
</table>

International Advertising

International advertising is difficult because of language and cultural differences among nations. The cross-national regulation of advertising further complicates global promotion efforts. There is no uniform international code for advertising. Instead, advertising content is regulated by individual nations, and these regulations vary considerably.

Consider advertising in the People's Republic of China. The Chinese require that advertising be "true, wholesome, clear and understandable." This highly subjective standard is enforced by a series of penalties ranging from criticism to monetary fines to the revocation of a license to do business.

In Great Britain, there is no national agency such as the United States FTC to regulate advertising. Rather, advertising is primarily regulated in a voluntary private system, through the British Code of Advertising Practice. This Code requires that advertising be "legal, clean, honest, and truthful" and specifically regulates testimonials, scientific claims, and comparative claims.

The regulation of comparative advertising is particularly controversial and inconsistent, even within Europe. Comparative advertising is essentially prohibited in Switzerland and Finland, allowed with substantiation in Italy, and prohibited if considered denigrating in Austria, Belgium and Sweden. In Spain, advertisers can compare their brands only against other brands that they own. As a consequence, some companies register fictitious brand names and then favorably compare their product with the fictitious brand.

In Germany, comparative advertising must be universally true. Thus, a potato chip marketer was prohibited from advertising its brand as having 40 percent less fat, because this claim was not true as opposed to every other brand of potato chip on the market. The chip may have had 40 percent less fat than average but did not have 40 percent less fat than all other brands. The European Economic Community has been attempting to develop a uniform advertising code but thus far has been unable to do so.

Questions and Case Problems

1. Both Thrill and Dynamics manufacture electric tools designed for the home consumer market. Thrill complains that Dynamics conducted a multimedia promotional campaign in which it explicitly named and showed Thrill products. These advertisements made certain factual statements in comparative and absolute terms concerning the qualities and relative performance of its own products and those of Thrill. These statements asserted that Dynamics products had greater durability than those of Thrill, but used older, now obsolete Thrill products for the comparison. Thrill complains that the statements have caused loss of customers, decreased goodwill and dilution of its trademark. Can Thrill recover under the Lanham Act?

2. Ms. Hanberry purchased a pair of shoes that were advertised as containing the "Good Housekeeping Consumers' Guaranty Seal." Later, she was crossing her kitchen's vinyl floor, and the soles of the shoes became slick, causing her to slip and fall. She sued the producer of the "Good Housekeeping Seal" for negligently advertising that the products carrying the seal were "good ones." Should Ms. Hanberry recover?

3. A well-known packaged goods company started a new advertising campaign for one of its shampoo products. The campaign claimed that its shampoos gave people's hair more body and bounce than a competing product. The competitor sued over the advertisement, claiming that the ad was false and misleading. The parties disputed whether claims about the "body and bounce" of hair were really factual and whether they could be misleading. Who should prevail in this action? [*Vidal Sassoon, Inc. v. Bristol Myers Co.,* 661 F.2d 272 (2d Cir. 1981)]

4. A manufacturer of a consumer pain relief product ran the following advertisement:

"New Un-Burn actually anesthetizes nerves in sensitive sunburned skin.

Un-Burn relieves pain fast. Actually anesthetizes nerves in sensitive sunburned skin.

* * * New Un-Burn contains the same local anesthetic doctors often use * * * I'll tell you what I like about Un-Burn. It's the best friend a blonde ever had! * * * It stops sunburn pain in * * * less time than it takes me to slip out of my bikini. That's awfully nice to know when you're the sensitive type."

The Federal Trade Commission brought an action claiming that this advertisement was false and misleading. What must the company show to defend its ad? [*In re Pfizer, Inc.* 81 F.T.C. 23 (1972)]

5. Absolut Vodka developed a unique and effective advertising campaign. The campaign focused on the name Absolut as evidence of purity and substantially increased the company's share of the vodka market. A new vodka, imported from the Soviet Union, called itself Icy Vodka. This company began running an advertising campaign that was based on the slogan, "Try Icy, It's Absolutely Vodka." Is this advertising campaign lawful?

CHAPTER FOURTEEN

Environmental Liability

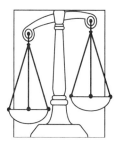 KEY BACKGROUND

The essential background for this chapter on environmental liability is found in Chapter 46 of *West's Business Law, Fifth Edition* and in Chapter 19 of *West's Legal Environment of Business*. These chapters cover environmental protection. Among the important points to remember from this chapter are:

- leading federal environmental statutes, including the Clean Air Act, Clean Water Act, Superfund, and others

- liability for damages under common law

- liability for damages under federal statutes

- the costs of compliance with or violation of environmental law

*   *   *

In the 1990s, business will spend tens of billions of dollars annually on environmental protection. This new item on the balance sheet deserves careful attention. Avoidance of environmental liabilities and efficient compliance may become critical to the success of many businesses.

Businesspersons in most industries must respond to the requirements of a long list of environmental laws. One particular law, the Comprehensive Environmental Response, Compensation and Liability Act of 1980 (known as "CERCLA" or "Superfund") creates the liability of greatest concern to businesses.

This chapter begins by outlining the details of CERCLA's operation. The chapter then goes on to analyze the application of CERCLA and other environmental laws to business transactions and business operations. It also considers the increasing application of criminal liability to corporate officers and directors, for violations of environmental laws.

CERCLA/Superfund

Government and industry in the United States are spending billions of dollars to clean up hazardous wastes under the authority of CERCLA. Knowledge of CERCLA is important because of its potentially enormous liability and because this liability is not limited to the obvious "guilty" parties who unsafely dumped hazardous wastes.

CERCLA liability may apply to businesses who did not participate in hazardous waste production or disposal and who may be wholly unaware of the presence of hazardous wastes on their properties. The act also applies to any disposal of hazardous wastes, not just large dumps.

Suppose Ervin Computer Company takes its leftover bottles of solvents to Consolidated Wastes for disposal. Consolidated then buries them in a very small pile on vacant property. In this circumstance, Ervin could be liable for substantial costs of cleanup.

Application of CERCLA

CERCLA is triggered any time there is a "reasonable basis to believe there may be a release or threat of release of a hazardous substance" or any other pollutant that may endanger public health. Courts have interpreted these terms very liberally, making the law's application quite broad.

Most responses involve hazardous substances. The law defines "hazardous substance" as any substance regulated under certain sections of the Clean Air Act, the Federal Water Pollution Control Act, and other federal environmental lists. Hundreds of substances are deemed hazardous substances. Although the term hazardous waste implies heavy industry to many individuals, even "white collar" office jobs use hazardous substances (for cleaning, in office machines, etc.).

A recent article by environmental attorneys recently noted the breadth of Superfund:

> While it may be a slight overstatement to declare that everything is a hazardous substance, the exceptions are narrow and few. And it is perhaps only slightly more of an overstatement to say that any site in the United States is a potential CERCLA site.[1]

A release means any escape of a hazardous substance into the environment. This can include leakage on the disposal site itself; there is no requirement of potential human exposure. A threatened release is even broader and requires no actual escape of hazardous substances. The court in one case found a threatened release simply because the wastes were not in proper containers and the region's annual rainfall created a potential for leaching of wastes into the groundwater.[2]

Once a release or threatened release triggers the application of CERCLA, the government may enter a site and remove the hazardous substances and clean up the surrounding area. The government may then sue various responsible parties to recover its cleanup costs. CERCLA also authorizes the government to order private parties to clean up the hazardous conditions themselves. In addition to cleanup costs, CERCLA allows the government to sue private parties for any damages to natural resources (e.g., fish kills) that result from hazardous waste releases.

Private parties also may choose to clean up a hazardous waste site. For example, the current owner of land may need to eliminate hazards before developing the property. In such a case, the private landowner may clean up the site and then sue other responsible parties to recover at least a portion of its cleanup costs.

These cleanup costs are usually quite substantial. Hazardous substances must be carefully handled and removed to a well-run disposal site. The average cleanup cost for a disposal site is $25 million, and costs for even a relatively small disposal site will run into the millions of dollars. The government has claimed for billions of dollars in cleanup costs for a single large waste site. The Office of Technology Assessment has estimated that total cleanup costs for all sites may exceed $600 billion or fully 10 percent of the total annual output of the United States.

Responsible Parties

Under CERCLA, several different parties may be liable. The law's liability extends to: (1) the current owner and operator of the site; (2) anyone who formerly owned the site at the time of hazardous substance disposal; (3) the generators of the wastes who arranged for its disposal; and (4) the transporters of the wastes.

The generators of hazardous wastes, such as Ervin Computer, can be liable under virtually any circumstances. In one case, the owners of waste PCB oil (oil contaminated with a highly toxic substance) arranged with a transporter for disposal. Rather than safely disposing of the contaminated oil, the transporter sprayed and thereby contaminated over two hundred miles of rural roadsides in North Carolina. The waste generator was held liable for the costs of correcting this contamination.[3]

In addition, once a generator's waste is taken to a given site, the generator may be liable for any and all cleanup costs at that site. Many leaking hazardous waste sites have produced a "toxic soup," in which it is impossible to identify the source of the leaking substances. As a consequence, CERCLA requires only proof that the generator's hazardous wastes were sent to a site.

---

[1]Anderson & Taylor, "Representing Buyers," *3 Nat. Resources and Env't* 3 (1988).

[2]*Con-Tech Sales Defined Benefit Trust v. Cockerham*, 698 F. Supp. 1249 (E.D. Pa. 1988).

[3]*United States v. Ward*, 618 F. Supp. 884 (E.D.N.C. 1985).

Owner and operator liability is also broad. The current owner of land including a CERCLA site will be liable, even if the owner were entirely blameless or even unaware of the presence of a hazardous waste problem. This application is evidenced in the following decision.

■ Case 14.1
**Tanglewood East
Homeowners v.
Charles-Thomas, Inc.**
United States Court of Appeals,
Fifth Circuit, 1988
849 F.2d 1568

Background and Facts *A residential subdivision was built upon a site formerly owned by the United Creosoting Company. That company operated a wood-treatment facility and deposited toxic creosote waste in pools on the property. The property was later acquired by real estate developers. After the wastes were discovered, the homeowners complained about the wastes and further development ceased.*

The homeowners sued the developer, the bank lender for the development, construction companies, and real estate agents, seeking to compel cleanup of the site and pay their costs. The cleanup would cost millions of dollars. The defendants filed a motion to dismiss, claiming that they were not responsible parties under CERCLA. The district court denied the motion, and the lender brought this appeal of that ruling.

POLITZ, Circuit Judge.

* * * *

Appellant maintains that under § 9607(a)(1), the only owner and operator who discharged hazardous materials was the United Creosoting Company, who abandoned the site in 1972. We find nothing in the wording of § 9607(a) to exclude present owners of properties previously contaminated. We join our colleagues of the Second Circuit in concluding that the structure of the statute removes any doubt. Section 9607(a)(2) expressly applies to past owners and operators who contaminate their surroundings; it is therefore manifest that § 9607(a)(1) applies to current owners of adulterated sites. *See New York v. Shore Realty Corp.*, 759 F.2d 1032 (2nd Cir. 1985). We hold that § 9607(a)(1) imposes strict liability on the current owners of any facility which releases or threatens to release toxic substance.

* * * *

The *Shore* court held the developer-owners liable for the cleanup costs of their facility even though no construction or development had been undertaken. A lending institution was found to be a current owner and operator under § 9607(a)(1) in *United States v. Maryland Bank & Trust Co.*, 632 F.Supp. 573 (D.Md.1986). In that case, a bank which acquired a contaminated site by foreclosure was held accountable under CERCLA. And courts addressing the issue have rejected the argument implicit in appellant's position, that liability may be imposed upon only those persons who both own and operate polluted property.

* * * *

Finally, appellant maintains that CERCLA was intended to cover only persons actually engaged in the chemical/hazardous materials industry and those engaged in businesses which generated such materials. It vigorously contends that the legislation was not meant to impose chilling liability on the defendants' businesses: banking, real estate, construction, and development.

* * * *

We are persuaded beyond peradventure that a determination of the specific businesses and activities covered by CERCLA is beyond the pale of a 12(b)(6) motion. That remains for another day.

Decision and Remedy *The Court affirmed the district court judgment refusing to dismiss the complaint.*

A former owner of property is also liable if the ownership occurred at the time that the wastes were disposed. The former owner need not have participated in or known of the disposal to be liable.

Suppose that Robert Serota has large landholdings in Louisiana and leased this land to a variety of tenants, including an oil company. During the lease, the oil company disposed of hazardous wastes on the land. Serota then sold the land to the oil company. If the government later cleans up the land, the government may recover their cleanup costs from Serota. This is true even if Serota was not involved in the operations of the tenant oil company and exercised no managerial control over the property at the time of disposal.

Owner and operator liability extends even further. The bank who loaned money for a real estate purchase may become liable under CERCLA, especially if the purchaser defaults on the loan and the bank takes over the property. This is called lender liability, a subject that is treated in detail in Chapter 34 of *West's Business Law, Fifth Edition*.

In addition, a parent corporation may be liable for land owned or operated by a subsidiary corporation. Gulf, a large conglomerate, owned Bunker Hill Company, among many other subsidiaries. Bunker Hill owned a hazardous waste facility that became liable for CERCLA cleanup costs. A court held that Gulf could itself be liable for these costs because it controlled and monitored Bunker Hill's management. The court also noted that Bunker Hill was undercapitalized and probably unable to pay the cleanup costs itself.[4]

Liability Standards

The liability standards under CERCLA are quite strict. The act provides for strict liability, which requires no showing of negligence or other culpability. Indeed, the government need not even show that the defendant's actions caused the need for cleanup. The government need only link the defendant with the site (e.g., the defendant sent wastes to the site at some time in the past).

Liability under CERCLA is often joint and several. This means that each responsible party is potentially liable for all the costs at a given site. Suppose that Ervin Computer Company had its wastes taken to a specific hazardous waste site. Ervin's wastes represented 1 percent of all the hazardous wastes at the site. After cleanup, Ervin may be liable for 100 percent of cleanup costs.

In the above example, Ervin may sue the site owner and the generators of the other 99 percent of wastes for contribution to these costs. If these other generators are unidentifiable or bankrupt, however, Ervin may be required to pay the full cleanup bill.

Moreover, Superfund is *retroactive*, applying to wastes disposed long before the act was passed in 1980. As a consequence, a company may be liable in 1991 for wastes disposed in the 1950s, even if those wastes were disposed according to state-of-the-art disposal techniques of the time.

Defenses

Defenses to CERCLA liability are few and narrow. Statutory defenses are available for releases due to what the law considers an act of war or an act of God (such as a massive flood). These defenses are of little use in most cases.

CERCLA also provides a defense for releases that are due to the actions of third parties, but even this defense is very narrow. The defense

---

[4]*Idaho v. Bunker Hill Co.*, 24 Env't Rep. (BNA) 1160 (N.D. Cal. 1986).

applies only if the release was caused solely by a third party and if the defendant had no contractual relationship with that third party. The defendant also must show that it took precautions to prevent the foreseeable acts of third parties.

The third party defense might be available if the owner of a hazardous waste site took great care, but vandals broke into the site and spilled the wastes. Even in this circumstance, the owner would be required to show that it took appropriate precautions against such vandalism. The most common application of this defense is known as the **innocent purchaser defense**, which is discussed in the following section.

▀▀ Environmental Liability in Business Transactions

Virtually every business transaction carries a risk of environmental liability. Suppose that Amco Lines purchases a fleet of trucks from CrossCountry Co. for $500,000. In connection with the truck purchase, CrossCountry agrees to throw in its trucking terminal and garage, with an appraised value of $300,000. This may seem like a good deal, but suppose that the terminal building contains soil contaminated from waste oil or underground petroleum storage tanks. Perhaps the building contains asbestos materials. Amco may have set itself up for multimillion-dollar liability by taking possession of the terminal.

The nature and extent of liability will depend on the type of acquisition. A purchase of assets results in possible liability under CERCLA and other environmental statutes. A purchase of the stock of a company may cause even greater environmental liability.

CERCLA Liability

In today's legal environment, no one should purchase land without first checking for the presence of hazardous wastes. As noted above, an innocent landowner may bear substantial liability for past actions on the site. A 1986 survey found that environmental liability in real estate transactions was the foremost concern of corporate facility planners.

The purchaser of real estate may attempt to protect itself from future CERCLA liability with contractual provisions. The purchaser may demand that the seller provide a warranty that there are no hazardous wastes on the site. Alternatively, the sale may contain a "hold harmless" clause in which the seller agrees to indemnify the buyer for any future hazardous waste cleanup costs. Such an indemnification provision should be as specific as possible.

Contractual protection is of limited value, however. A party cannot contract away its responsibilities to the government. Therefore, the government can still recover all its cleanup costs from the purchaser of land. The contract merely enables the purchaser to sue the seller for these costs. This remedy is only good if the seller is still in existence and sufficiently solvent to afford the costs.

A more promising opportunity for buyers of land is CERCLA's **innocent purchaser defense**. Congress recognized the potential unfairness of CERCLA liability and in 1986 created a defense for innocent purchasers. The defense is limited, though, and ignorance of a problem is not sufficient for "innocence" under CERCLA.

To take advantage of the innocent purchaser defense, the buyer of land must show that it "did not know and had no reason to know" that hazardous substances were on the property. To have "no reason to know" the buyer must show that it conducted "all appropriate inquiry into the previous ownership and uses of the property consistent with good commercial or customary practice in an effort to minimize liability."[5]

Suppose that Kaplan, Inc., wishes to purchase manufacturing facilities, including a refinery, that might contain hazardous wastes. To take advantage of the innocent purchaser defense, Kaplan, Inc., must conduct "environmental due diligence." Government mortgage authorities (such as "Fannie Mae") have established guidelines for what this due diligence should include. At minimum, the buyer should conduct a title search to identify all past owners. The buyer also should search government records for past environmental violations at the site, inspect the site carefully, and interview employees at the site. If any of these steps suggest problems, the buyer probably should undertake chemical testing of suspect areas.

If Kaplan conducts this environmental due diligence and uncovers no problems, it can take advantage of the innocent purchaser defense. This

---

[5] 42 U.S.C. Sec. 4601(f)(35)(B).

means that Kaplan will not be liable for cleanup costs. If a problem arises, however, Kaplan will be required to allow EPA onto its land to clean up the site. This cleanup activity could still cost Kaplan profits from the use of its land.

The innocent purchaser defense has so far been of little assistance to defendants. The following decision involves a case in which the defense was rejected.

■ **Case 14.2**
Washington v.
Time Oil Co.
United States District Court,
Western District of Washington, 1988
27 Env't Rep. Cas. (BNA) 2076

Background and Facts *Time Oil Company purchased land in the state of Washington. This land apparently had been the site of previous hazardous waste disposal operations at a previous time. The site subsequently has begun leaking hazardous wastes. Time Oil leased the site for operations by Drexler. Drexler also disposed of some wastes at the site, although the parties dispute whether these wastes were hazardous.*

Time Oil sought to employ the innocent purchaser defense in an action brought against it to pay for cleanup costs at the site. The government filed for partial summary judgment ruling that the defense was unavailable to Time Oil on the facts of the case.

BRYAN, Judge.

* * * *

42 U.S.C. §9601(35) is a new section of CERCLA that was enacted in 1986 for the purpose of protecting innocent landowners from liability. It supplements the definition of "contractual relationship" found in 42 U.S.C. §9607(b)(3), and provides in relevant part:

(35)(A) The term "contractual relationship," for the purpose of section 9607(b)(3) of this title includes, but is not limited to, land contracts, deeds or other instruments transferring title or possession, unless the real property on which the facility concerned is located was acquired by the defendant after the disposal or placement of the hazardous substance on, in, or at the facility, and one or more of the circumstances described in clauses (i), (ii), or (iii) is also established by the defendant by a preponderance of the evidence:

(i) At the time the defendant acquired the facility the defendant did not know and had no reason to know that any hazardous substance which is the subject of the release or threatened release was disposed of on, in, or at the facility. . . .

In addition to establishing the foregoing, the defendant must establish that he has satisfied the requirements of section 9607(b)(3)(a) and (b) of this title.

In the case at bar, Time Oil, in asserting this defense pursuant to subsection (i) has a burden of prudent inquiry in that it . . . must have undertaken, at the time of acquisition, all appropriate inquiry into the previous ownership and uses of the property consistent with good commercial or customary practice in an effort to minimize liability. For purposes of the preceding sentence the court shall take into account any specialized knowledge or experience on the part of the defendant, the relationship of the purchase price to the value of the property if uncontaminated, commonly known or reasonably ascertainable information about the property, the obviousness of the presence or likely presence of contamination at the property, and ability to detect such contamination by appropriate inspection.

* * * *

The last operator on the property was Time Oil's sublessee, Drexler. As mentioned above, the Court is satisfied Drexler was in an indirect contractual relationship with Time Oil. There is substantial evidence to indicate Drexler ran a sloppy operation, even to the point of prompting Time Oil to seek a preliminary injunction to prevent Time Oil from suffering "immediate and irreparable injury to its premises from the draining of heavy black oil onto the ground at plaintiffs' railroad spur and from defendants allowing plaintiffs' premises to remain in a constant state of disrepair." * * * It is clear that if the Court concludes that the waste oil and other substances handled by Drexler contained the hazardous substances later found on the property, Time Oil will be liable for the harm caused by Drexler's operation. At this time, because of the above-mentioned concerns about expert testimony, the Court is not prepared to make an absolute finding that Drexler's waste oil contained those hazardous substances. On this motion, however, the Governments are still entitled to judgment as a matter of law when Time of Oil fails to carry its burden of bringing out specific facts to show that some third party was solely responsible for the release.

* * * *

The final elements Time Oil must show in order to assert the innocent landowner defense are that it exercised due care and took precautions with respect to the hazardous substances concerned, taking into consideration the characteristics of the hazardous substances in light of all relevant facts and circumstances. This is a burden Time Oil has failed to meet. Although the Court is not prepared at this time to say that all the releases of hazardous substances on the property can be directly linked to the waste oil operations of National Oil, Time Oil, or Drexler, it is clear Time Oil allowed Drexler to run a sloppy operation. Time Oil did not exercise due care to prevent the property from becoming contaminated by this sublessee.

Decision and Remedy *The court granted the government's partial summary judgment motion, ruling that the innocent purchaser defense was inapplicable.*

Other Environmental Laws

The purchaser of land must also be concerned with other environmental statutes. If a purchaser such as Kaplan is acquiring a refinery for its own use, Kaplan will need to be concerned with the environmental compliance of these facilities. A refinery must obtain pollutant discharge permits under the Clean Water Act, hazardous waste permits under the Resource Conservation and Recovery Act, and air pollution permits under the newly amended Clean Air Act. These are only a few of the many environmental permits that may be required.

If Kaplan's newly acquired facility lacks these permits, the refinery may be unable to operate. A refinery that cannot operate is obviously of dubious value. If it does operate, Kaplan will become subject to civil fines and possibly criminal penalties. Kaplan may upgrade the refinery with pollution control devices necessary to obtain permits, but these improvements could cost hundreds of thousands of dollars. The permit may also limit a facility's hours of operation and production rate.

Even if a purchaser obtains land for future industrial development of new facilities, the buyer still has environmental law concerns. Many environmental laws restrict the use of land and prevent its profitable development. If property contains wetlands (similar to swamps), it is strictly regulated. In many circumstances, all development is prohibited on wetlands. This could render the property virtually worthless to the purchaser.

Both federal and state authorities also protect groundwater resources by restricting development. Many types of building programs may be outlawed under these restrictions. Regulations under the Clean Air Act can prohibit new construction in geographic regions that already have excessive air pollution levels.

If land contains the habitat for a plant or animal in danger of extinction, the Endangered Species Act may prohibit development. The golden-cheeked warbler was recently declared an endangered species. This listing will prevent landowners in certain areas of Texas from cutting down trees on their land.

Purchase of Securities

The above discussion has assumed that the purchaser bought only assets. If a purchaser buys an entire existing company (such as in a hostile takeover), the purchaser has even greater potential environmental liability.

In an asset acquisition, the purchaser's liability will be limited to future government actions specific to the on-site assets acquired. In a securities acquisition, the purchaser will succeed to all the liabilities of the acquired company, including past liabilities. The purchaser may also be liable for disposal of wastes off-site.

Suppose Kaplan buys all the stock of Chin Associates. Thirty years ago Chin may have sent asbestos wastes to a disposal site thousands of miles away. If the waste site is cleaned up in 1992, Chin would be liable as a generator, and Kaplan would succeed to this liability. This is true even though Kaplan had nothing to do with the asbestos wastes and never assumed ownership of the disposal site.

The existence of **successor liability** is dependent on corporation law principles discussed in Chapter 42 of *West's Business Law, Fifth Edition*. A complete stock purchase or merger will invoke successor liability. Even a purchase of assets may invoke the broader successor liability if the purchaser continues the seller's business and retains the same personnel.

Seller's Liabilities

The above discussion has been concerned with the liability of purchasers, but sellers have a different set of concerns. The sale of assets can produce later environmental liability, as illustrated by the following example.

Suppose that Kaplan produces some hazardous wastes at its manufacturing facility and disposes them on-site. Kaplan is very careful to comply with the best waste management practices available at the time and the wastes are carefully contained. Then the Zepp Corporation makes a lucrative offer to purchase the land.

Kaplan may desire to sell the land, but it cannot escape the potential liability. Even if Kaplan sells the land, it is potentially responsible for future CERCLA cleanup costs. Kaplan owned and operated the land at the time of hazardous waste disposal. If Zepp is an irresponsible manager, the well-maintained Kaplan waste disposal site may degenerate and leak hazardous substances. Kaplan will be liable for cleanup costs in this case.

Kaplan therefore has a strong incentive to ensure that any purchaser, such as Zepp, will maintain the land carefully. There is no guarantee, however, that Zepp will not resell the land to another party, who may be irresponsible. Kaplan's only guarantee of protection is to keep the land itself and maintain it carefully and indefinitely.

A seller of land may obtain contractual protection against future liability. The contract of sale could require the buyer to indemnify the seller for later liability that is the fault of the buyer. These provisions do not protect the seller from liability to the government, but they enable the seller to sue the buyer to recover its liabilities to the government. The seller is dependent on the buyer's solvency in order to recover, however.

A seller of land may be directly liable to the buyer in tort or contract law. If a seller conveys hazardous waste-contaminated property and fails to disclose that fact, the buyer may sue for fraud. This could enable the buyer to rescind the contract and recover its purchase price. To avoid this risk, the seller should conduct its own environmental due diligence and make full disclosure of risks to the purchaser.

Individual Liability for Environmental Violations

Traditionally, a violation of an environmental statute imposed penalties on the responsible corporation. This approach was criticized, because some corporations would simply violate the laws and pay the resulting fines or might even declare bankruptcy. There is a trend toward holding corporate officers, directors, and even shareholders liable for a company's environmental violations.

In some cases, an individual businessperson may become personally liable for cleanup costs under CERCLA. Individual liability is particularly likely for closely held nonpublic corporations.

In a key case, the president and principal shareholder of a closely held corporation was individually liable under CERCLA. The court emphasized that the president was "responsible for the entire operation" and involved in "basically every facet" of its activities. The president was therefore liable as an owner and operator of the site.[6]

Such total control is not necessary for liability. The following recent decision distinguishes the sorts of executive actions that can produce individual liability under CERCLA.

[6]*United States v. Mottolo*, 605 F. Supp. 898 (D.N.H. 1984).

Case 14.3
Riverside Market
Development Corp. v.
International Building
Products

United States District Court,
Eastern District of Louisiana, 1990
Civ. A. No. 88-5317; 1990 WL 72249

Background and Facts *International Building Products, Inc. ("IBP"), purchased a National Gypsum Company plant in 1981 and continued to manufacture asbestos cement products. A shopping center development wanted to purchase the site for $3.4 million. The site required cleanup, which was undertaken by the purchaser.*

The purchaser then sought to recover cleanup costs from IBP and two individual officers of the corporation, Gerard von Dohlen and T. Gene Prescott. Prescott and von Dohlen moved to dismiss the complaint against them, arguing that they were not responsible parties under CERCLA.

WICKER, District Judge.

* * * *

When IBP purchased the National Gypsum plant, Prescott and von Dohlen were the sole shareholders: Prescott held eighty-five percent (85%) of the stock and served as Chairman of the Board; von Dohlen held fifteen percent (15%) of the stock and served as President. From March 1981 through December 1983, von Dohlen also served as Chief Executive Officer. In 1984, other shareholders invested in IBP. Prescott lived in New York and visited the New Orleans facility only on one to three occasions per year during the time that IBP owned the plant: (1) annual Christmas Party; (2) attendance at a meeting for an Erectors' Association, some of whose members used products from the plant and (3) brief visit with executive personnel.

* * * Von Dohlen testified that Prescott was principally the source of money.

* * * Von Dohlen further explained that as an IBP officer, Prescott reviewed financial statements regularly. "During meeting of officers, he consulted with me or other people but that's about it."

* * * The Court finds no evidence that Prescott was an operator of the asbestos manufacturing facility within the meaning of CERCLA.

As to von Dohlen, however, the Court finds that a genuine issue of material fact exists as to whether or not he was an "operator" under CERCLA.

Unlike Prescott, von Dohlen spent forty percent (40%) of his time in New Orleans. He testified that from March 1981 through December, 1984, he spent ten percent (10%) of his time each month at the New Orleans factory.

* * * Although he states in his affidavit that his major duties involved sales, he testified earlier that he was occasionally involved in the actual day-to-day operations of the factory, that he may have operated some of the machines himself from time to time in order to solve problems in manufacturing processes, and that he was actually out on the plant floor supervising at other times.

* * * Ray Plauche confirmed that through 1984, von Dohlen had an office at the plant, and was at the plant "almost every week–for all practical purposes, three weeks out of the month."

* * * In a later deposition, von Dohlen testified that from December, 1983 until the plant was sold, he visited it twice: once to meet with the buyer while operations were either still going on or had just ceased [April or May of 1985] and once for the auction/sale.

* * * As to his role in the sale of asbestos products and the disposal of hazardous wastes, von Dohlen testified that he ordered asbestos fiber from various companies and negotiated contracts with various fiber suppliers to supply raw asbestos to the plant.

* * * He also explained that he participated in altering the formulations of products previously produced by National Gypsum and participated in decisions as to which formulations were to be used in those products. Despite his assertions that he was not involved in decisions about compliance with environmental regulations except for getting the required by the Environmental Protection Agency ["EPA"] permit (Id. at p. 34), von Dohlen admitted that during his tenure, "We disposed of asbestos pursuant to licenses in the regular course of business in the plant. And we were familiar with those." Von Dohlen was not sure whether there were different regulations for removing asbestos when the plant was demolished. (Von Dohlen deposition, August 21, 1987, p. 43.)

Other evidence shows that when IBP bought the plant from National Gypsum, von Dohlen wrote the cover letter and signed IBP's application for an identification number from the Louisiana Hazardous Waste Management Program for Tchoupitoulas facility. (Plaintiffs' Exhibits 6 and 7.) Also on March 15, 1983, the State of Louisiana sent a warning letter to von Dohlen, as president of IBP, stating that an inspection revealed that a "container of hazardous waste was not marked with required information" and giving IBP thirty (30) days to correct the violation.

Decision and Remedy *The Court granted Prescott's motion to be dismissed from the case but permitted the claims against von Dohlen to go forward to trial.*

Even the officers of large publicly held corporations are possibly liable under CERCLA. A person can be liable as a generator if he or she arranged for the disposal of hazardous substances. An officer directly involved in decision making for waste disposal was found personally liable under this provision.[7] The court emphasized that the officer personally participated in the wrongful conduct.

Compliance and Criminal Liability

In 1981, the Environmental Protection Agency formed the Office of Criminal Enforcement, and the Department of Justice created their Environmental Crimes Unit. Since that time, there have been over 600 environmental criminal indictments and over 450 guilty pleas or convictions. These have resulted in over $25 million in fines and about 300 years of jail sentences. The average guilty defendant was sentenced to slightly over one year.

Most major environmental statutes contain criminal liability provisions. After the massive Alaskan oil spill from their tanker, the *Exxon Valdez*, Exxon was charged with criminal violations of five different federal statutes. Individual officers have also been charged.

RCRA

Perhaps the most common source of environmental criminal liability is the Resource Conservation and Recovery Act, known as RCRA. RCRA governs present and future disposals of hazardous waste by regulating disposal facilities, transporters, and generators of wastes.

The primary tool of RCRA is the creation of a "cradle-to-grave" manifest system. This system requires that records must be maintained for all hazardous wastes from their creation ("the cradle") to their disposal ("the grave"). The generator of the wastes must identify and label them and furnish information about their contents to those who transport, store or dispose of the wastes. The manifest system permits the wastes to be identified and tracked throughout their existence.

RCRA also creates detailed regulations for the ongoing disposal and treatment of hazardous wastes. Government regulations establish detailed technical requirements for treatment or disposal. Permits must be obtained from EPA for disposal. Some especially hazardous wastes may not be disposed on land.

RCRA's first set of criminal sanctions apply to anyone who knowingly causes disposal at an unpermitted facility, makes false representations to the EPA, transports wastes without a manifest, or fails to file records required by the Act. A conviction under any of these provisions is a felony punishable by a fine of up to $50,000 per violation and imprisonment for between two and five years.

RCRA's second set of criminal penalties applies to anyone who knowingly violates the above standards and "knows at the time that he . . . places another person in imminent danger of death or serious bodily injury."[8] An individual violator of this "knowing endangerment" provision is subject to a fine of up to $250,000 and up to fifteen years in prison. A corporation may be fined up to $1 million for violating this provision.

A company was convicted under the "knowing endangerment" provision when it exposed its employees to toxic chemicals without sufficient protection. Some of the employees became seriously ill and all had an increased risk of cancer. The court ordered the defendant to establish a $950,000 trust fund for the employees, ordered the company to pay $440,000 in fines, and placed the company on probation. Probation conditions included the payment of over $2 million in waste cleanup costs.[9]

To obtain a conviction under the key section of RCRA, the government must show that a person or corporation: (1) knowingly; (2) transports or disposes or treats or stores; (3) a hazardous waste; (4) without a permit or in violation of a permit. The key issue in most cases is whether the violation was "knowing."

The term "knowing" does not necessarily mean that the defendant was aware that a crime was committed, however. The following decision involved criminal liability on the part of a supervisor who may have been unaware of potential liability.

---

[7]*United States v. Northeastern Pharmaceutical and Chemical Co., Inc.,* 810 F.2d 726 (8th Cir. 1986).

[8]42 U.S.C. Sec. 6928(e).

[9]*United States v. Protex Industries, Inc.,* 874 F.2d 740 (10th Cir. 1989).

■ Case 14.4
United States v. Hoflin
United States Court of Appeals,
Ninth Circuit, 1989
880 F.2d 1033

Background and Facts *Douglas Hoflin was the director of the Public Works Department for Ocean Shores, Washington. In this position he was in charge of waste paint left over from road maintenance and sludge removed from the kitchen of the city golf course. He instructed an employee to haul the paint drums to the sewage treatment plant and to bury them. Some of the drums were crushed in the process of disposal, and the waste was then covered with sand.*

Neither the sewage treatment plant nor the city had a permit for the disposal of hazardous wastes. EPA became aware of the leaking paint drums and had him indicted for disposing of hazardous waste without a permit. A jury found Hoflin to be guilty. Hoflin appealed, claiming that he believed that the city had a permit to dispose of waste and that he was not "knowing" in his disposal without a permit.

THOMPSON, Circuit Judge.

* * * *

Hoflin's challenge to his conviction on Count II focuses on subsection (2)(A) of 42 U.S.C. § 6928(d) (1982). Section 6928(d) provides in pertinent part:

(d) Criminal penalties

Any person who–

....

(2) *knowingly* treats, stores or disposes of any hazardous waste identified or listed under this subchapter either–

(A) without having obtained a permit under section 6925 of this title....; or

(B) in *knowing* violation of any material condition or requirement of such permit;

....

shall, upon conviction, be subject to [fines, imprisonment or both]. (emphasis added).

42 U.S.C. § 6928(d)(2)(A) and (B).

It is Hoflin's position that "knowingly" in subsection (2) modifies both subsections (A) and (B). Under this interpretation, knowledge becomes an essential element of the crime defined by section 6928(d)(2)(A), and Hoflin could not be convicted on Count II without proof that he knew no permit had been obtained. He correctly points out that the jury was not given an instruction to this effect. This argument requires us to interpret section 6928(d)(2)(A) and decide whether knowledge of lack of a permit is an essential element of the crime the statute defines.

* * * *

Had Congress intended knowledge of the lack of a permit to be an element under subsection(A) it easily could have said so. It specifically inserted a knowledge element in subsection (B), and it did so notwithstanding the "knowingly" modifier which introduces subsection (2). In the face of such obvious congressional action we will not write something into the statute which Congress so plainly left out.

Finally, our conclusion is consistent with RCRA's goals and the treatment Congress gave "knowledge" in 42 U.S.C. § 6928(d)(2)(A) and (B) to achieve these goals. The statute requires knowledge of violation of the terms of a permit under subsection (B) but omits knowledge that a permit is lacking as an element of disposing of hazardous waste without a permit under subsection (A). There is nothing illogical about this. Knowledge of the location of hazardous waste, from its generation through its disposal, is a major concern of RCRA. *See* 1976 U.S.Code Cong. & Admin.News 6264. Those who handle such waste are, therefore, affirmatively required to provide information to the EPA in order to secure permits. Placing this burden on those handling hazardous waste materials makes it possible for the EPA to know who is handling hazardous waste, monitor their activities and enforce compliance with the statute. On the other hand, persons who handle hazardous waste materials without telling the EPA what they are doing shield their activity from the eyes of the regulatory agency, and thus inhibit the agency from performing its assigned tasks. We hold that knowledge of the absence of a permit is not an element of the offense defined by 42 U.S.C. § 6928(d)(2)(A).

Decision and Remedy   *The court affirmed Hoflin's conviction.*

In another case, a defendant claimed that he was unaware that the disposed waste was hazardous. The court rejected this defense, holding that the defendant should have known that waste containing paints was potentially hazardous and should have investigated proper disposal.[10]

CERCLA

In addition to substantial civil liability for cleanup costs, CERCLA contains criminal sanctions. CERCLA creates an obligation on site owners to notify federal and state authorities whenever there has been a release of a "reportable quantity" of a hazardous substance. Notification must be performed by the person "in charge" of the facility. Reportable quantities for various substances are set by regulation, so that owners need not notify for miniscule releases.

This criminal provision of CERCLA contains no requirement of knowledge by the defendant. Simple failure to notify itself can result in conviction and penalties of up to $250,000 per individual and $500,000 per organization.

A separate provision provides criminal sanctions for failure to report by the person "in charge." This provision does contain a requirement that the defendant know of the release. Penalties under this provision include imprisonment for up to one year. Still stricter penalties apply to the knowing destruction or concealment of information that should be reported to EPA.

In a CERCLA case, a maintenance foreman was informed that cans of waste paint were leaking. He said to continue disposal of the cans and later ordered them covered with earth. His supervisory authority was sufficient for him to be convicted and sentenced to one year probation.[11]

The 1986 amendments to CERCLA added provisions to address the problem of hazardous releases from manufacturing facilities, such as occurred with the deadly release of toxic chemicals in Bhopal, India. These amendments are also known as the Emergency Planning and Community Right-to-Know Act (EPCRA). A knowing failure to report a release of certain listed chemicals can result in a fine of up to $25,000 and imprisonment of up to two years under EPCRA.

---

[10]*United States v. Hayes Int'l Corp.*, 786 F.2d 1499 (11th Cir. 1986).

[11]*United States v. Carr*, 880 F.2d 1550 (2d Cir. 1989).

Clean Water Act

The Federal Water Pollution Control Act, frequently known as the Clean Water Act, also contains criminal sanctions. This law sets maximum standards for the discharge of pollutants into the water. While EPA has not yet adopted standards for every industry, all polluters must obtain a permit that regulates their discharges. Some companies discharge pollution into publicly owned treatment works (such as a sewer system), which clean water for household use. EPA has set pretreatment standards for these dischargers, which require them to clean up their discharges somewhat.

The Clean Water Act makes it a crime to discharge any pollutant into a publicly owned treatment work in violation of a pretreatment standard or to discharge any pollutant into the waters of the U.S. without a permit. This is not a strict liability standard, but the government must show that the defendant was at least negligent in violating the standard.

A conviction for a negligent violation of the Clean Water Act can result in a misdemeanor fine of up to $25,000 per day of violation and imprisonment for up to one year. If the law is violated knowingly, the resulting conviction would be a felony punishable by a fine of up to $50,000 per day and/or imprisonment of up to three years. The Clean Water Act also has a "knowing endangerment" provision, like RCRA's, that provides for a fine of up to $250,000 and imprisonment for up to fifteen years for discharges of pollutants into the water.

Clean Water Act liability is not limited to large industries discharging highly toxic chemicals. In one recent prosecution, a fruit juice company pleaded guilty to twenty-one counts of violating the Clean Water Act for unlawfully disposing of cranberry peelings and acidic waste water.[12]

Clean Air Act

The Clean Air Act was broadly amended in 1990 to expand the restrictions on air pollution and also expand the penalties for violation of these restrictions. A key change in the 1990 amendments was to require permits for tens of thousands of "major sources" that discharge hazardous pollutants into the air. The law also calls for strict new regulations on these emissions.

The new permit program requires the states to adopt programs to grant these permits. To obtain a permit, a source must have a compliance plan to ensure that the source will abide by all federal regulations. The source also must periodically certify that it is complying with the rules.

The 1990 amendments also changed criminal penalties for violating the Clean Air Act from misdemeanors to felonies. A knowing violation of the permit provision can mean imprisonment for up to five years. Negligent emissions of hazardous air pollutants in excess of standards can be punished by imprisonment for up to a year, and the new Clean Air Act also contains a knowing endangerment provision that parallels those of RCRA and the Clean Water Act.

An asbestos removal company violated EPA regulations and dropped asbestos-containing materials to the ground, causing a cloud of released asbestos. The company was ordered to pay $50,000 in fines. The foreman in charge was sentenced to 90 days in jail and three years probation.[13]

Other Laws

Many other federal laws also impose strict burdens on business and contain criminal penalties for their violation. The Federal Insecticide, Fungicide and Rodenticide Act regulates pesticides through labelling requirements and other means and contains criminal liability for businesspersons, even if the individuals lack direct knowledge of the violation. Wildlife protection statutes, such as the Endangered Species Act, the Marine Mammal Protection Act, and the Migratory Bird Treaty Act also contain criminal sanctions for knowing and unlawful destruction of protected animals or plants.

In 1990, EPA collected over $40 million in fines under environmental laws. Exhibit 14-1 provides a measure of the penalties imposed on business under a selected group of environmental statutes.

---

[12]*United States v. Ocean Spray Cranberries, Inc.*, 19 Env't Rep. (BNA) 1781 (D. Mass. 1988).

[13]*United States v. DAR Construction, Inc.*, 20 Env't Rep. (BNA) 21 (S.D.N.Y. 1989).

Exhibit 14-1

Penalties Imposed on Businesses that Violate Federal Environmental Laws

Statute	Highest Penalty	Average Penalty
CERCLA	$15,550	$7,295
Clean Air Act (stationary sources)	$600,000	$69,000
Clean Water Act	$1,540,000	$57,000
Resource Conservation and Recovery Act	$2,778,000	$43,300
Safe Drinking Water Act	$125,000	$11,500
Toxic Substances Control Act	$615,650	$13,563

State Environmental Laws

State governments are increasingly active in environmental protection. Many states have passed laws that surpass federal legislation in their requirements. Compliance with state environmental statutes has become a critical concern for businesspersons.

California is a leader in environmental protection and has passed numerous laws that go beyond federal requirements. A key California law was adopted through citizen referendum and is known as Proposition 65. Proposition 65 prohibits any business with ten or more employees from intentionally exposing a person to certain listed hazardous chemicals without a clear and reasonable warning of the hazards.

Hundreds of substances are designated by California as hazardous and within Proposition 65. Many department stores, restaurants, gas stations, supermarkets, and offices therefore must post notices of warning. A typical notice might state: "WARNING: This building contains a chemical known to the State of California to cause cancer." Failure to post the warning subjects the defendant to fines of up to $2500 per day of violation. An exception exists for exposures that present "no significant risk," but the employer bears the burden of proving the absence of a significant risk.

Over twenty states have adopted their own mini-Superfund statutes. Probably the best-known state law is the New Jersey Environmental Clean-Up Responsibility Act (ECRA). ECRA applies any time that real estate is sold or whenever industrial operations cease on a section of property.

When either of these triggering acts occur, the New Jersey ECRA requires the seller or owner to submit a detailed report on the property, including a complete history of actions at the site. This must include an inventory of all hazardous substances present and disclosure of any potentially suspect industrial operations that occurred there.

If cleanup of the site is deemed necessary, ECRA requires that the party develop a cleanup plan and demonstrate its financial ability to complete the plan. The law also creates a **superlien**. This provision creates a lien against the property of the seller or owner to ensure that money is available to conduct the cleanup, and the superlien takes precedence over virtually all other claims against the owner.

Cleanup of a hazardous waste site is a complicated and expensive action. In some cases, precautions can be taken at the site to ensure against future release. In most cases, however, the wastes must be removed to a new waste disposal site that uses modern containment technologies.

States also have adopted numerous controls on emission of pollutants, and many of these laws provide for criminal penalties against responsible parties. Texas, for example, has a Solid Waste Disposal Act with broader coverage than that of

RCRA. The Texas Solid Waste Disposal Act also contains criminal penalties equal in strength of those in RCRA and creates strict criminal liability in some circumstances (meaning that there is no requirement of a knowing or intentional violation). The Texas Water Code also provides strict liability for unlawful discharges, punishable by a fine of up to $10,000 per day.

■ Ethical Perspectives

Export of Hazardous Wastes

As expensive requirements for waste disposal mount in the United States, more companies are seeking to export their hazardous wastes to other nations. American companies now export 160,000 tons of hazardous waste per year. Most of these exports go to poorer nations with less regulation, often in Africa.

There is little legal limitation on hazardous waste exports. RCRA does require that a company file an "acknowledgement of consent" with EPA for hazardous waste exports. This is to ensure that the foreign nation is knowingly accepting the wastes.

Many argue that the export of hazardous wastes is unethical. These wastes may cause great harm to the environment and to humans if they are improperly disposed. Critics contend that the wastes are exported specifically because the disposal requirements of many foreign nations are weak and insufficient to protect the environment.

The export of hazardous waste is sometimes justified by reference to the responsibility to shareholders to make a profit. Some argue that U.S. rules are too strict and unduly restrict our businesses. This justification has not been especially persuasive, because the responsibility not to do significant harm should outweigh profits in circumstances such as this.

Another justification focuses on the consent of the foreign nation. In the typical circumstance, the exporter pays the foreign nation to accept the wastes. As a consequence, some argue that any attempt to restrict the waste exports, on ethical grounds or otherwise, is paternalistic and insulting to other nations. They contend that the governments of these countries need the money and should be given the right to decide whether to take the wastes.

A shortcoming in this argument involves the limitations of foreign governments. Some of these governments are undemocratic and insufficiently concerned about the welfare of their citizens. Other governments lack the resources and expertise to appreciate the danger of the wastes and to ensure their safe disposal. Exporters may use their greater knowledge and influence to trick these governments into unwise decisions.

Critics contend that many foreign governments are simply incapable of protecting their own interests. In one circumstance, however, the government of Sierra Leone dramatically rejected a payment of $25 million to accept the wastes from a U.S.

company. It is noteworthy that this rejection occurred only after the deal became public and the government faced extensive adverse publicity.

There is undeniable ethical merit in allowing sovereign foreign nations to make decisions for themselves about accepting hazardous wastes. Before this becomes a justification for export, however, the foreign consent must be fully informed. The exporter may therefore have an ethical duty to ensure that the foreign nation fully understands the nature of the hazardous wastes and the risks that they present. The company also should assist the nation in providing for the safe disposal of the wastes.

■ **International Perspectives**

Waste Disposal in Europe

As more American companies operate in the nations of the European Community (EC), to take advantage of the 1992 unification, these companies need an awareness of European regulatory laws. The nations of Europe are developing uniform rules for hazardous waste liability under the proposed Directive on Civil Liability for Damage Caused by Waste through the European Commission.

The Directive begins by making producers of waste liable for damage and injury for damage to the environment, under a strict liability standard as under CERCLA. The Directive applies to nearly all forms of waste, except air pollution, nuclear wastes, and some agricultural and mining wastes.

Liability can attach for "restoration" costs, which are like cleanup under CERCLA, but liability may be more limited. Europe would apply a cost/benefit test to cleanups and would not conduct cleanups that are considered unreasonably costly. The European Directive also goes beyond CERCLA and extends to human health harms from waste releases.

The European Directive differs from CERCLA and other U.S. laws in several important respects. First, the Directive focuses on **possessory liability**, which limits responsibility to the person in possession of the waste at the time any harm results from it. Although the producer of the wastes is initially responsible for damages, the producer may avoid long-run liability by arranging for waste disposal at a licensed waste facility.

Joint and several liability, which is the norm in the United States, is quite limited under the European Directive. The Directive also contains strict causation requirements, demanding proof that the defendant's wastes actually caused harm. The plaintiff must show an "overwhelming probability" of a causal relationship. Nor does the Directive apply retroactive liability. These terms significantly limit the liability exposure of waste generators.

The Directive also falls short of U.S. law in other areas. While disposal facilities must be licensed, they need not comply with all the demands of RCRA. No "cradle-to-grave" manifest system is imposed. Liability for hazardous wastes is likely to be less onerous in Europe. The uniform Directive is enforced by member nations, and each nation has "the choice of forms and methods" of its enforcement. Consequently, the enforcement of these rules will vary among European nations, and some may adopt stricter compliance requirements than others.

Questions and Case Problems

1. EPA cleaned up a spill of trichloroethylene at the site of a textile plant, Stamina Mills, that was a subsidiary of Kayser-Roth Corporation. Soon thereafter, Stamina was dissolved. Kayser-Roth had owned a majority of the shares in Stamina Mills, and EPA sought to recover its cleanup costs from Kayser-Roth, as an owner and operator of the site. Kayser-Roth controlled the operations of Stamina Mills, including many budgetary details. For example, Kayser-Roth had to approve any capital expenditure greater than $5000 by Stamina. Kayser-Roth claimed that Stamina was the owner and operator of the site and that Kayser should not be liable. Should Kayser-Roth be held liable for cleanup costs? [*United States v. Kayser-Roth Corp.*, 910 F.2d 24 (1st Cir. 1990)].

2. A bank loaned funds to Swainsboro Print Works, secured by the company's accounts receivable and its plant and equipment. Swainsboro's financial condition deteriorated, and the bank foreclosed on some of the company's equipment. The bank also took a role in managing Swainsboro in an attempt to protect its interest. EPA subsequently found toxic chemicals on the site of Swainsboro's plant and spent $400,000 in cleanup costs to remove them. Given Swainsboro's fragile economic condition, EPA also sued the bank for cleanup costs. Should the bank be liable for these cleanup costs? [*United States v. Fleet Factors Corp.*, 901 F.2d 1550 (11th Cir. 1990)].

3. A worker for Ortho Pharmaceutical claimed that while working for the corporation he was exposed to chemicals that caused him to suffer a reduced sperm count and loss of sexual appetite, among other injuries. He sued the company and its officers and directors in tort for personal injury damages. He claimed that the company and its officers improperly failed to warn him of the risks of work. An officer sought to dismiss the claim. Should the officer be individually liable for the worker's injuries? [*Cruz v. Ortho Pharmaceutical Corp.*, 691 F.2d 902 (1st Cir. 1980)].

4. Friendly Chemical Corp. is intent on "green marketing." The company believes that it can reduce costs and increase revenues by being scrupulous in protecting the environment. Every corporate policy is dedicated in part to environmentalism. Friendly sought to expand to a new site. Before doing so, Friendly hired an expert to examine the site for any sign of hazardous substances. The expert reported that the site was "clean," so Friendly purchased the site. Later, hazardous wastes were discovered, EPA cleaned up the site, and the agency charged Friendly with cleanup costs. Friendly resisted payment, fearing damage to its reputation, as well as to its pocketbook. Should Friendly be liable for cleanup costs at this site?

5. John Stimkorb was the manager of a hazardous waste disposal facility. After an extremely heavy rainfall, Stimkorb ordered his employees to pump rainwater that had accumulated in the site and direct it into a ditch. Because the rainwater had come into contact with hazardous wastes, EPA prosecuted Stimkorb criminally under RCRA. Stimkorb argued that the rainwater was not a hazardous substance and that no harm was done to the environment. Is Stimkorb guilty?

CHAPTER FIFTEEN

Health Care Law

Health care is at the center of many of today's greatest legal and moral controversies, including abortion, the right to die, the epidemic of drug abuse, and AIDS. Health care administrators and providers are daily confronted with these difficult "life-and-death" questions and subject to potential legal liability for their decisions.

Health care is also a large and rapidly growing sector of the economy. The health care industry accounts for well over 10 percent of the nation's gross national product and employs over 8 million persons. Many of the most important legal issues in health care are much more mundane than the above controversies. These less prominent issues, however, may be economically, medically, and legally more important.

This chapter focuses on the everyday issues of health care, such as government regulation of the health care industry. The chapter also concentrates on the perspectives of the hospital, rather than of the individual doctor, though hospitals and doctors share many of the same legal concerns.

▃▃ Government Regulation of Health Care

For most of this century, only state governments actively regulated health care professionals. States maintained boards charged with licensing and disciplining physicians to ensure quality care. These boards have been overwhelmed with their workload and their effectiveness has been criticized.

The federal government's involvement in health care regulation began in 1965 with the enactment of Medicare and Medicaid. These laws funded health care for the poor and the elderly and reimbursed health care professionals for their reasonable costs of care. The costs of Medicare and Medicaid quickly got out of hand.

A portion of the high costs of Medicare and Medicaid was due to advanced technology and increased demand for medical services. Another portion of the cost, estimated at over $1 billion per year, was estimated to be due to physician abuse of the process and overcharging the government.

Suppose that a person covered by Medicare came to a doctor for treatment. The doctor was aware that the individual was backed by unlimited resources. If the doctor undertook procedures that were medically unnecessary, he or she would be compensated, and there was no institution to check the process. Some doctors would even bill the government for care that was not rendered. Over 50 million Americans have some coverage under Medicare and Medicaid, and these programs have tens of billions of dollars of federal funding. The potential for abuse was enormous.

PROs

Congress took steps to control the costs of Medicare and Medicaid. In 1982, Congress passed the Peer Review Improvement Act, which established a **peer review organization** (PRO) system. Under this program, a board of peer physicians reviews health care services to determine if they are "reasonably and medically necessary,"[1] and of proper quality.

Suppose that a PRO decides that a doctor's treatment decisions are incorrect or unnecessary. The PRO cannot take direct enforcement action against the doctor but can recommend that payment be denied under Medicare or Medicaid. The care recipient may then become personally liable for the costs, but most beneficiaries of the government programs lack the funds or private insurance to pay.

The PRO can also recommend that the Office of the Inspector General (OIG) of the Department of Health and Human Services (HHS) take enforcement action against the doctor. The OIG can issue fines or suspend the doctor from participation in Medicare and Medicaid.

A doctor may appeal the PRO decision and is entitled to due process in review of the appeal. The doctor is entitled to be represented by counsel, cross-examine witnesses, and present his or her own expert witnesses at a hearing. The hearing is conducted before an arbitrator or panel of disinterested experts.

Some doctors have even sued the physicians serving on the PRO over their decisions. In one case, a doctor serving on a PRO participated in revoking the hospital surgical privileges of another physician. The sanctioned doctor sued the PRO physician under antitrust law and received a multimillion-dollar verdict.[2] The court found that the PRO was used to enable the physician to monopolize the local market for surgery.

Health Care Quality Improvement Act

Congress sought to correct some of the problems with PROs in 1986, under the Health Care Quality Improvement Act (HCQIA). This law was

intended to encourage physicians to identify and discipline other doctors who were incompetent or dishonest.

One important provision of HCQIA is its provision of partial legal immunity for peer review. If peer review is conducted in compliance with government standards, the reviewing physician, the hospital, and other participants in the process are immunized from liability. Immunity protects these participants from many actions but does not extend to civil rights cases or cases brought by the U.S. Attorney General.

Another key provision of HCQIA is its creation of a national databank on possible malpractice. Hospitals are required to report certain information to the databank. First, a hospital must report any payment made in court or in settlement of a medical malpractice claim. Second, a hospital must report any episode in which a physician is sanctioned for improper practice. Failure to report is subject to a $10,000 fine per instance.

HCQIA also requires hospitals to request information from the databank. Any time that a hospital considers granting clinical privileges to a new physician, dentist or licensed health care practitioner, it must request reported information from the databank. The hospital also must request such information every two years for individuals who maintain privileges at the hospital's facilities.

If a hospital fails to request information, it becomes subject to greater malpractice liability in any future cases. The hospital is much more likely to be liable for failure to investigate the quality of its physicians. This source of liability is discussed below.

Reimbursement Controls

HCQIA and other federal statutes also changed the system of physician reimbursement in the 1980s. Traditionally, the system had reimbursed doctors for their reasonable costs of care, based on the actual costs incurred. Under the new system, there are predetermined reimbursement rates for care of many common medical problems.

This change significantly altered the incentive structure of doctors. Under the old system, doctors had an incentive to provide an excess of care, in order to obtain added reimbursement. Under the new system, doctors have an

---

[1]42 U.S.C. Sec. 1320c-3(a)(1)(A).

[2]*Patrick v. Burget*, 108 S.Ct. 1658 (1988).

incentive to provide an insufficiency of care. Doctors can profit only to the extent that their actual costs of care are less than the predetermined reimbursable amount.

Reimbursement is typically set through **Diagnosis-Related Groups** (DRGs). DRGs break down common medical needs into over 460 separate categories and the care required for treatment of each category of medical need. Reimbursement schedules are then established for the categories of care.

The schedules for reimbursement proved to be extraordinarily complex. One court characterized them as something that "only legislators and accountants can appreciate."[3] For some categories, the reimbursable amount set by the government seems too low and discourages the provision of even necessary medical care.

The new structure puts some physicians and hospitals in a difficult situation. They retain a duty to provide proper care to patients or face malpractice liability. The actual costs of such care, however, may exceed the reimbursement obtainable from the government. This means that the care provider may effectively have a legal duty to lose money. Physicians remain ultimately responsible, however, for their patients and cannot put the burden off on insurers, as illustrated by the following case.

---

[3] *American Medical Association v. Bowen*, 857 F.2d 267, 269 (5th Cir. 1988).

■ Case 15.1
Wickline v. State
California Court of Appeals, 1986
228 Cal. Rptr. 661

Background and Facts   *Lois Wickline, a married woman in her mid-forties, received physical therapy treatment for problems with her back and legs. She was admitted to Van Nuys Community Hospital and treated by a specialist on peripheral vascular surgery, Dr. Gerald E. Polonsky. Polonsky diagnosed her condition as a form of arteriosclerosis that required surgery. Ms. Wickline was covered by the state insurance system, known as Medi-Cal. Medi-Cal authorized the surgery and ten days of hospitalization for treatment.*

On January 7, 1977, Polonsky undertook surgery and replaced part of Ms. Wickline's central artery with a synthetic graft. Later that day, she required additional surgery to remove a blood clot. During her recovery from these operations she suffered a great deal of pain and experienced hallucinating episodes. Five days later, Dr. Polonsky performed further surgery to relieve spasms in her blood vessels. Wickline was scheduled to be released on January 16, but Dr. Polonsky concluded that she would require eight days of additional hospitalization. This required submitting an additional form to Medi-Cal. Medi-Cal rejected reimbursement for this extension but authorized an additional four days of hospitalization.

Wickline's condition remained stable in the four additional days of hospitalization, until January 21. While recognizing that she still faced some danger, Dr. Polonsky discharged her from the hospital on January 21, when Medi-Cal funding expired. After several days at home, Wickline began experiencing great pain in her leg, which also became discolored. On January 30, she was readmitted to the hospital as an emergency patient. Her circulation problems could not be surgically corrected, so her leg was amputated above the knee. Had she remained in the hospital, amputation might not have been necessary.

Wickline sued several defendants for damages, including Medi-Cal. After a jury ruled for Wickline, Medi-Cal appealed.

ROWEN, Associate Justice.

* * * *

Title 22 of the California Administrative Code section 51110, provided, in pertinent part, at the relevant time in issue here, that: "The determination of need for acute care shall be made in accordance with the usual standards of medical practice in the community."

The patient who requires treatment and who is harmed when care which should have been provided is not provided should recover for the injuries suffered from all those responsible for the deprivation of such care, including, when appropriate, health care payors. Third party payors of health care services can be held legally accountable when medically inappropriate decisions result from defects in the design or implementation of cost containment mechanisms as, for example, when appeals made on a patient's behalf for medical or hospital care are arbitrarily ignored or unreasonably disregarded or overridden. However, the physician who complies without protest with the limitations imposed by a third party payor, when his medical judgment dictates otherwise, cannot avoid his ultimate responsibility for his patient's care. He cannot point to the health care payor as the liability scapegoat when the consequences of his own determinative medical decisions go sour.

There is little doubt that Dr. Polonsky was intimidated by the Medi-Cal program but he was not paralyzed by Dr. Glassman's response nor rendered powerless to act appropriately if other action was required under the circumstances. If, in his medical judgment, it was in his patient's best interest that she remain in the acute care hospital setting for an additional four days beyond the extended time period originally authorized by Medi-Cal, Dr. Polonsky should have made some effort to keep Wickline there. He himself acknowledged that responsibility to his patient. It was his medical judgment, however, that Wickline could be discharged when she was. All the plaintiff's treating physicians concurred and all the doctors who testified at trial, for either plaintiff or defendant, agreed that Dr. Polonsky's medical decision to discharge Wickline met the standard of care applicable at the time. Medi-Cal was not a party to that medical decision and therefore cannot be held to share in the harm resulting if such decision was negligently made.

In addition thereto, while Medi-Cal played a part in the scenario before us in that it was the resource for the funds to pay for the treatment sought, and its input regarding the nature and length of hospital care to be provided was of paramount importance, Medi-Cal did not override the medical judgment of Wickline's treating physicians at the time of her discharge. It was given no opportunity to do so. Therefore, there can be no viable cause of action against it for the consequences of that discharge decision.

* * * *

This court appreciates that what is at issue here is the effect of cost containment programs upon the professional judgment of physicians to prescribe hospital treatment for patients requiring the same. While we recognize, realistically, that cost consciousness has become a permanent feature of the health care system, it is essential that cost limitation programs not be permitted to corrupt medical judgment. We have concluded, from the facts in issue here, that in this case it did not.

Decision and Remedy   *The court reversed the judgment against Medi-Cal.*

The new reimbursement system of DRGs apparently has significantly reduced the costs of federally insured medical care. Some observers fear, however, that the system has caused some patients to be refused and others to receive insufficient medical attention.

The government also maintains enforcement mechanisms under Medicare and Medicaid. Medicare fraud is a crime. In addition, the government may discontinue the payment of benefits to facilities that fail to comply with federal requirements.

▰ Private Regulation

In addition to the above government regulations of health care, there is also extensive private regulation. The American Medical Association (AMA), for example, regulates doctors for competence. Most hospitals have their own professional review committees.

Insurance companies increasingly monitor health care activities. Blue Cross/Blue Shield has adopted "Medical Necessity Guidelines" that set forth indications for certain tests, such as x-rays. These guidelines are used to control reimbursement decisions. Insurance companies also maintain databanks on insurance claims for care by specific physicians or hospitals.

▰ Malpractice

More and more individuals are suing physicians for malpractice, to the point that one may consider the system to be in "crisis." The costs of malpractice insurance have skyrocketed and, sometimes, insurance is wholly unavailable. Reducing malpractice liability is a central concern for health care providers.

Standards of Malpractice Liability

Primary malpractice liability usually lies with the treating doctor. It is well-established that physicians owe a very high level of care, described as a fiduciary duty, to their patients. If a physician breaches that standard of care, he or she may be liable in malpractice.

A leading source of malpractice liability is failure to diagnose or treat. Suppose that Patrick Kelly has a skin discoloration on his leg and consults a dermatologist. The doctor examines the skin, diagnoses the problem as a rash, and prescribes an ointment. Patrick later discovers that the problem is skin cancer. The delay in diagnosis may cause Patrick to suffer painful treatment or even death. In this case the dermatologist may be liable for malpractice.

Another source of liability is inappropriate treatment. Suppose that the physician accurately diagnoses the problem but provides some treatment recently found to be ineffective. Or the physician may prescribe a treatment to which the patient is allergic, causing greater medical problems.

The above categories are the most common sources of malpractice liability, but many other potential problems exist. For example, doctors have been found liable for failing to disclose their findings to patients, for breaching the patient's right of confidentiality, or for failing to provide adequate treatment facilities and support staff. A recent decision found a doctor potentially liable for failure to inform a rape victim of the availability of a "morning-after pill" that could avert pregnancy.

A key issue in malpractice litigation is the standard of care to which doctors are held. Historically, the standard of care was a local one. A Montana physician, for example, would have a different standard of care than a doctor in Los Angeles. Today, the standard of care is considered to be uniform nationwide, and all doctors are held to the same high standard.

The standard of care is usually that recommended in expert treatises on medical care and in medical journals. Each case is unique, however, and the malpractice case often comes down to a "battle of experts." Each side in the case will present medical experts attacking or defending the quality of care provided. The jury is left with the decision.

In one case, a plastic surgeon performed silicone implantation for breast enhancement. After the surgery, the patient suffered a series of complications, including soreness, inflammation, hematomas (collections of blood under the skin) and physical disfigurements. She sued the doctor for malpractice. Evidence demonstrated that the doctor's surgical technique was taught to him at a prestigious college of medicine and was used by many plastic surgeons in the area. Other evidence showed, however, that the technique was no longer recognized or accepted by experts. The court held that the doctor had violated the "reasonable and prudent" physician standard, even though many other doctors continued to use this practice.[4]

One defense for physicians is the "honest error in judgment" rule. Physicians typically do not guarantee the success of a treatment regime. If a physician made a good faith treatment judgment that turned out badly, courts are reluctant to second-guess the decision.

Another possible defense is a "good samaritan" statute. Physicians who are responding to an emergency situation without a fee arrangement are freed from liability under good samaritan statutes in most states.

The patient's informed consent may also be a defense under malpractice. Suppose that a certain diagnostic procedure presents a 1 in 100,000 chance of a serious allergic reaction in patients. The doctor should inform the patient of this risk and obtain written consent from the patient to conduct the procedure. If the patient is fully and fairly informed of the risks, the patient normally cannot win a malpractice claim in the event that he or she suffers the allergic reaction.

To recover under malpractice, patients also must show that they were damaged by the improper treatment. Even use of an unwise and negligent treatment does not produce liability unless damages can be traced to that treatment. This is a particular problem in cases of advanced cancer. In these cases, the patient might well have died even with optimal medical treatment.

A doctor may also escape liability if the damages are due to the contributory fault of the patient. If a patient violates a doctor's orders, this may represent contributory negligence. Patient's fault may also be present when the patient incorrectly discloses information to the doctor. A doctor considering a prescription may ask if the patient is taking any nonprescription medication, and the patient may erroneously answer no. A doctor should not be liable for an adverse drug reaction that results from the combination of prescription and nonprescription drugs.

Many states have passed laws to limit malpractice liability. Some states limit punitive damages and noneconomic damages (mental anguish), while others restrict attorneys' fees. Total malpractice liability remains enormous, however.

Hospital Liability

An important legal question is the extent to which a hospital should be liable for the malpractice of doctors who practice within the hospital. This issue has great practical significance. Seventy-five to 80 percent of malpractice actions arise out of treatment in hospitals. Malpractice recoveries may exceed the insurance coverage of individual physicians and therefore plaintiffs seek recovery from hospitals.

Under traditional common law, most hospitals were exempt from liability in these circumstances. Nonprofit hospitals received **charitable immunity**, which meant that they could not be vicariously liable for the acts of even their employees.

Now, charitable immunity seldom protects hospitals. The potential **vicarious liability** of hospitals for malpractice of doctors is generally governed by principles of agency law, as set forth in Chapter 36 of *West's Business Law, Fifth Edition.*

Under these agency law principles, hospitals will generally be liable for the acts of physicians who are employees of the hospital. Most doctors who practice in hospitals, however, are not employees. Instead, the doctors are **independent contractors** who make arrangements for use of the hospital's facilities.

As a general rule, a hospital will not be liable for the torts of an independent contractor. In certain circumstances, though, the hospital will be liable. Courts increasingly apply **ostensible agency liability**, on the theory that hospitals hold themselves out to patients as providers of care through the services of a doctor.

Determination of hospital liability under ostensible agency is highly fact-specific. Consider the following decision. A patient was treated by radiologists at a hospital and suffered damages from overexposure to radiation. She sued the hospital for damages. An appellate court reversed summary judgment for the hospital and held that the hospital was potentially liable.[5] In reaching

---

[4]*Henderson v. Heyer-Schulte Corp.*, 600 S.W.2d 844 (Tex. App. 1980).

[5]*Sztorc v. Northwest Hospital*, 496 N.E.2d 1200 (Ill. App. 1986).

this result, the court considered the fact that the radiologists were located on the main floor of the hospital, and that patients had to enter through the hospital's main entrance and pass through doors labeled "X-ray department." The court also stressed that there was no dress code to distinguish the independent contractor doctors from hospital personnel. The hospital was potentially liable even though the doctors provided all their own equipment and the hospital received no payments for radiation treatments provided.

Other courts have been somewhat less strict in holding hospitals liable. A recent Montana case held that a hospital was not liable for the malpractice of a resident radiologist.[6] That case stressed the rural nature of the area, where virtually all radiologists practiced in hospitals. The issue of vicarious liability is of great concern to hospitals, especially because hospitals have little control over the independent contractor doctors who practice on their premises.

The key question in assessing hospital liability is whether the patient considered himself or herself a patient of the hospital or recognized that the hospital was merely the site of treatment by a doctor. Courts have considered the following factors in deciding whether to assign liability to a hospital:

- Whether the physician had a private practice outside the hospital.

- Whether the patient came to the physician through the hospital or through an outside practice.

- The extent to which the physician received compensation or supplies from the hospital.

- The nature of the physician's staff privileges at the hospital.

- Whether the physician was an administrator or stockholder of the hospital.

None of these factors alone is crucial; they are simply considered by courts, along with other evidence. To help insulate themselves from liability, hospitals can insist that independent contractor physicians wear distinguishing badges or dress and post notices that alert patients that the doctor is not an employee.

---

[6]*Milliron v. Francke,* 793 P.2d 824 (Mont. 1990).

Hospitals are even more likely to be found liable for malpractice by nurses. Nurses are hospital employees. Nurses also have a professional standard of care. Nurses must effectively carry out the orders of physicians.

Suppose that a nurse employee of a hospital is directed to check a patient's vital signs every thirty minutes and notify the physician if the patient's condition appeared to deteriorate. The nurse fails to do so, and the patient dies. The hospital will be liable as the employer of the nurse who committed malpractice.

Nurses must also exercise their own medical judgment. A nurse may have a duty to violate a physician's orders, if he or she knows those orders to be unsafe. Suppose a physician erroneously orders medication that a nurse knows would harm a patient. If the nurse gives the medication, the injured plaintiff would have a strong malpractice case. Nurses have a general duty to supervise patients and inform physicians of any material change in the condition of patients. The hospital may be liable under any of these circumstances of nursing malpractice.

▬ Hospital Direct Liability

Hospitals may also be directly liable to patients of independent contractor physicians under a theory of corporate negligence. Such negligence may exist when a hospital negligently permitted an unqualified doctor to practice. This is especially likely if the hospital failed to avail itself of the HCQIA databank in investigating the physician's qualifications.

Hospital liability may be predicated on violation of some recognized standard. Many hospitals have bylaws to govern physicians who practice at the hospital. A violation of these bylaws may produce liability. In addition, the Joint Commission on Accreditation of Hospitals ("JCAH") sets minimum standards for hospital review of physician actions. Violation of these standards may be considered negligence. For example, the JCAH demands that hospitals provide drug monitoring services to avoid adverse drug interactions.

Hospital liability is not limited to negligent hiring. If a hospital has notice of a physician's incompetence, it should deny the use of its facilities to that physician. Otherwise, the hospital may be liable for negligence.

In one case, a patient in a hospital underwent surgery that was improperly conducted and caused the patient serious harm, including the loss of a kidney. The patient recovered damages from the hospital, which knew or should have known of the surgeon's incompetence and still provided operating room facilities. In this case, the hospital had been sued in two prior cases when the physician conducted the same type of surgery.[7]

---

[7]*Purcell v. Zimbalman*, 500 P.2d 335 (Ariz. App. 1972).

Hospitals may also be liable for failure to supervise and monitor doctors who practice at the hospital. Although the hospital may have no direct control over treatment in individual cases, the hospital can monitor the general quality of the physician. The JCAH standards require that a hospital have an ongoing quality assurance program to monitor and evaluate the quality of patient care provided by doctors.

A hospital is not liable for all instances of medical malpractice that occur, however. This principle is demonstrated in the following decision.

■ Case 15.2
Mele v. Sherman Hospital
United States Court of Appeals,
Seventh Circuit, 1988
838 F.2d 923

Background and Facts *Sheila Mele entered Sherman Hospital for a laparoscopy and tubal ligation to be performed by Dr. Jae Han. In a laparoscopy, a surgeon makes a tiny incision in the patient's navel in order to cut her tubes. This is distinct from a laparotomy, in which the patient's abdomen is opened with a larger incision.*

The hospital's bylaws required that surgery be performed only if the patient had signed a form authorizing the treatment and stating that she was aware of alternative treatments. Dr. Han was not an employee of the hospital but used the hospital's own consent form. Mele signed a form authorizing Dr. Han to perform a laparoscopy.

During the operation, Han nicked a membrane inside Mele's abdomen (a risk that he had not warned her of). He subsequently noticed bleeding and performed a laparotomy to discover the source of the bleeding. After determining that the bleeding had stopped. Han finished the operation by cutting Mele's tubes. The surgery left her with an abdominal scar.

Mele first sued Dr. Han and claimed malpractice, but a jury returned a verdict for Dr. Han. She then sued the hospital for failing to obtain her informed consent to the surgery. The hospital moved to dismiss, and the district court granted the motion. Mele appealed.

MANION, Circuit Judge.

* * * *

B. The Hospital's Standard of Care

Mele did not establish that the standard of care the Hospital had to meet included warning a patient of possible bad results from surgery to be performed by an independent treating physician. At most, she established that the standard of care included requiring such a physician to warn his patients of the risks of surgery.

"It is established that a hospital's duty to its patients requires it to conform to the legal standard of reasonable conduct in light of the apparent risk.... The standard of care to which a hospital must adhere in order to meet its duty is a factual question capable of proof through a wide variety of evidence including expert testimony, hospital bylaws, statutes, accreditation standards, customs and community practice." *Magana v.*

Elie, 108 Ill.App.3d 1028, 64 Ill.Dec. 511, 513, 439 N.E.2d 1319, 1321 (1982) (citations omitted). We agree with the district court that the Hospital's bylaw—which allows surgery only with a patient's informed consent—does not obligate the Hospital to guarantee that a patient has tendered informed consent. The bylaw, which binds independent doctors, is the Hospital's directive to doctors that there be informed consent, not an undertaking by the Hospital to insure that each patient is informed properly. As the district court correctly stated from the bench,

> The bylaw does not say that the hospital has a duty to inform patients about risks. It says nothing of the sort. It is hard for me to believe that a reasonable jury could even find that the bylaw imposes, self-imposes on the hospital a duty to disclose risks or conditions of every particular surgery. As I said before, I don't know how a hospital could assume such a duty.

We further agree with the district court that the preprinted consent form prepared by the Hospital–in which a patient must affirm that she has "been informed that there are risks"–also does not force the Hospital to guarantee that a doctor has fully informed his patient. Mele's expert witness, Dr. Hassan, testified that the filled-in form Mele signed was "incomplete" because it did not disclose the possibility of a laparotomy. That might have been useful to Mele in a suit against her doctor (which she lost). But Mele's expert candidly acknowledged that he did not believe that it was the Hospital's responsibility to place upon the form that Mele might need a laparotomy.

* * * *

The only standard of care derivable from Mele's evidence is that of putting in place a system to facilitate a doctor's obtaining consent. By enacting its bylaw and drafting a consent form, the Hospital sought to increase the likelihood that *doctors* would warn patients. Every doctor who used hospital facilities had to agree to abide by the Hospital's bylaws, and each patient was required to sign the consent form. Until the patient signed that form, surgery would be delayed or postponed.

Decision and Remedy   *The court affirmed the dismissal of the claim against the hospital.*

Hospitals can also be liable for products they supply. Hospitals typically provide medical devices and drugs for patients of doctors that practice in the hospital. Devices must be properly maintained, and a hospital may be strictly liable if they are defective. Hospitals have also been liable for failure to have necessary equipment (e.g., portable oxygen supply) available. With respect to drugs, hospitals may have their own duty to warn patients of potential side effects, in addition to the duty of the prescribing doctor.

▬ Patient "Dumping"

According to a subcommittee of the House of Representatives, William Jenness suffered a serious automobile accident and was rushed to a nearby hospital. Though facilities were available, the hospital asked for a $1000 advance deposit, which he could not provide. He was therefore transferred to a public hospital, where he had to wait four hours for an operating time. During this time, he bled to death.[8]

This example illustrates a pressing health concern, known as "patient dumping" or medical nonpractice. The example is by no means an unusual one. Approximately 250,000 patients

---

[8]*Equal Access to Health Care: Patient Dumping: Subcomm. on Human Resources and Intergovernmental Relations to the House Comm. on Government Operations*, H.R. Rep. No. 531, 100th Cong., 2d Sess. at 6-7 (1988).

every year are refused emergency treatment by hospitals, according to congressional estimates. A study in Chicago found that nearly 10 percent of patients transferred away by emergency rooms died, as opposed to 4 percent among those treated promptly.

When a patient is turned away from a hospital, there usually is some alternative. The patient typically is taken to a public hospital that accepts all patients, regardless of ability to pay. These hospitals are often overburdened, however, and unable to provide prompt quality care.

There are several causes of the patient dumping problem. Eighty-seven percent of the time, dumping is due to the patient's lack of insurance. Over 30 million Americans lack private health insurance. Budget cuts during the 1980s removed millions from coverage under Medicare and Medicaid. Changes in federal reimbursement reduced hospital profits that previously were used to cover care for the uninsured.

When a hospital turns away a desperately needy patient, it seems cruel. But hospitals must receive payments for the expensive care they provide or the hospitals may risk bankruptcy. One hospital administrator bluntly noted: "We don't expect Safeway or A&P to give away free food for people who can't afford it."[9] In some circumstances, however, the law may compel hospitals to provide medical care to the uninsured.

Common Law

Under traditional principles of common law, a hospital or doctor owed no duty of treatment. Historic negligence law imposed no duty of rescue, and this principle extended to health care providers.

Courts in a number of states, however, have created some duty to render care. In some states, courts have held hospitals liable for providing full care, once they initiate any care. If a hospital emergency room admits a person as a patient, the hospital may have assumed a duty of care and can no longer turn away that person.

A Delaware court suggested that a hospital may have a duty to provide care when a patient relies upon the hospital's custom of furnishing emergency services. A few states have gone further and held that hospitals have a duty to provide care in cases of emergency.

About half the states have passed statutes that impose some obligation on hospitals to provide emergency care. Even in these states, the laws may provide no private damages remedy for persons who are turned away from emergency rooms. In addition, most of the laws are rather vague regarding the circumstances and extent of the hospital's duty.

Comprehensive Omnibus Budget Reconciliation Act

In 1986, Congress passed the Comprehensive Omnibus Budget Reconciliation Act (COBRA). Although this legislation was primarily concerned with the federal government's budget, it also contained a small provision that requires hospitals to provide care in emergency rooms.

COBRA applies to all hospitals that both have emergency care departments and that participate in the Medicare reimbursement program. This includes the majority of hospitals.

Under COBRA, the hospital must provide a medical examination for any person who requests one. This examination is used to determine whether the person is suffering from an "emergency medical condition" or is in "active labor" in pregnancy. If so, the hospital must provide the person with necessary treatment (called "stabilization") or transfer the person within the requirements of COBRA. The following case reflects the scope and application of COBRA.

---

[9]*Washington Post*, June 30, 1985, at A14.

■ Case 15.3
**Cleland v. Bronson Health
Care Group, Inc.**
United States Court of Appeals,
Sixth Circuit, 1990
917 F.2d 266

Background and Facts   *The Clelands took their fifteen-year-old son to the Bronson Methodist Hospital emergency room, complaining of cramps and vomiting. He was examined by a doctor, who diagnosed the problem as influenza and discharged the boy. Cleland was actually suffering from intussusception, a serious intestinal disease. Less than twenty-four hours later, he suffered cardiac arrest and died.*

The parents brought this suit under COBRA, claiming that their son had been improperly dismissed from the emergency room. The district court dismissed their claim, and the parents appealed.

BOGGS, Circuit Judge.

*   *   *   *

[The court first held that COBRA was not limited to discharges based upon the patient's inability to pay.]

However, Congress did limit the cause of action provided by the Act to only those who did not receive an "appropriate" screening or who were not "stabilized" before being transferred or discharged. In attempting to interpret those ambiguous phrases, we can look to legislative history, along with other aids to construction.

"Appropriate" is one of the most wonderful weasel words in the dictionary, and a great aid to the resolution of disputed issues in the drafting of legislation. Who, after all, can be found to stand up for "inappropriate" treatment or actions of any sort? Under the circumstances of the act, "appropriate" can be taken to mean care similar to care that would have been provided to any other patient, or at least not known by the providers to be insufficient or below their own standards. Plaintiffs essentially contend that "appropriate" denotes, at a minimum, the full panoply of state malpractice law, and at a maximum, includes a guarantee of successful result.

In one sense, in hindsight, the screening provided in this case could scarcely be called appropriate. The patient came in, he had a condition that was at least conceivably ascertainable by medical science, the condition was not ascertained, and he died within twenty-four hours. At the same time, there is not the slightest indication that this outcome would have been any different for a patient of any other characteristics. Had his sex, race, national origin, financial condition, politics, social status, etc., been anything whatsoever, as far as can be gleaned from the complaint, the outcome would have been the same. Under these circumstances, we hold that the complaint simply fails to allege any inappropriateness in the medical screening in the sense required by the Act.

The same reasoning applies to stabilization, though with even greater force. To all appearances, the plaintiff's condition was stable. He was not in acute distress, neither the doctors nor the patient or his parents made the slightest indication that the condition was worsening in any way, or that it presented any risk that might become life-threatening, or that it would worsen markedly by the next day.

Again, in hindsight, any stability was quite short-run. The patient died. However, neither the normal meaning of stabilization, nor any of the attendant legislative history or apparatus, indicates that Congress intended to provide a guarantee of the result of emergency room treatment and discharge.

* * * *

We can think of many reasons other than indigency that might lead a hospital to give less than standard attention to a person who arrives at the emergency room. These might include: prejudice against the race, sex, or ethnic group of the patient; distaste for the patient's condition (e.g., AIDS patients); personal dislike or antagonism between the medical personnel and the patient; disapproval of the patient's occupation; or political or cultural opposition.

If a hospital refused treatment to persons for any of these reasons, or gave cursory treatment, the evil inflicted would be quite akin to that discussed by Congress in the legislative history, and the patient would fall squarely within the statutory language. On the other hand, if, as appears to be the case here (and as is not contradicted in the pleading), a hospital provides care to the plaintiff that is no different than would have been offered to any patient, and, from all that appears, is "within its capability" (that is, constitutes a good faith application of the hospital's resources), then the words "appropriate medical screening" in the statute should not be interpreted to go beyond what was provided here.

Decision and Remedy.   *The court affirmed the district court's dismissal of this claim.*

After determining that emergency treatment is necessary, COBRA permits a hospital to transfer a patient under some circumstances. Transfer is allowed only when (1) the receiving facility has adequate space and qualified personnel for treatment; (2) the receiving facility agrees to accept and treat the patient; (3) the transferring hospital provides all necessary medical records; (4) the transfer is performed by qualified personnel with appropriate equipment; and (5) the transfer meets other requirements necessary for patient safety.

COBRA is violated whenever a hospital refuses treatment to an emergency patient or transfers the patient without compliance with all federal requirements. If COBRA is violated, hospitals (but not physicians) are strictly liable for damages to the patient or others harmed by the violation. Hospitals who receive patients dumped in violation of COBRA may also sue the transferring hospital for their costs.

In addition to private damages, COBRA provides for civil monetary penalties of up to $50,000 per violation. The government also may suspend Medicare payments for hospitals that willfully or negligently violate the statute.

▇ Antitrust Liability

In addition to all the legal issues specific to the health care industry, hospitals and other providers are subject to more general requirements. For example, the health care industry must abide by federal labor laws, if employees seek to unionize, and must abide by federal antidiscrimination laws in employment decisions. For the health care industry, probably the most important of these general requirements is antitrust law. The basic provisions of antitrust law are set forth in Chapter 47 of *West's Business Law, Fifth Edition* and in Chapters 20 and 21 of *West's Legal Environment of Business*.

Health care professionals are part of a very large and lucrative industry. As in any business, some individuals or hospitals may abuse their position to seek excess profits. In some circumstances, a hospital or other care provider may even attain a monopoly over a segment of the health care market. The medical profession is subject to antitrust laws, just like other industries.

Many antitrust cases are brought under Section 1 of the Sherman Act. This section proscribes contracts, combinations or conspiracies in restraint of trade. Many hospital actions may be subject to Section 1 challenges.

Staff Privileges

Approximately half of all antitrust litigation in health care involves the denial of staff privileges. A doctor who is refused an opportunity to practice at a hospital may sue and claim that the denial violates antitrust laws.

Suppose that York Hospital is the largest hospital in town. Jane Forsythe has a contract to provide radiological services for hospital patients, and she is also a stockholder in the hospital. Jim Walcz seeks permission to offer radiological services in the hospital. After consulting with Jane Forsythe, the hospital rejects Walcz's request. This may violate antitrust laws by permitting Jane to control the largest local market for radiological services.

Exclusive staff arrangements are not always illegal. In a recent decision, a local hospital had an exclusive contract with one physician to perform all pathological tissue analysis. The court rejected an antitrust challenge to this arrangement, because the hospital had no financial interest in the pathologist's practice and because the hospital did not have sufficient local market power to restrain competition in pathology.[10] The following decision further analyzes this situation.

---

[10]*Steuer v. National Medical Enterprises*, 672 F. Supp. 1489 (D.S.C. 1987).

■ Case 15.4
Todorov v. DCH Health Care Authority
United States Court of Appeals, Eleventh Circuit, 1991.
921 F.2d 1438

Background and Facts   *DCH is the largest general hospital in the Tuscaloosa, Alabama area. Alexandre Todorov is a member of the DCH medical staff with privileges to practice neurology. He then applied for the privilege to perform radiological services in the form of CT scans of the head to detect neurological damage. CT scans were currently performed by the hospital's radiology staff.*

DCH denied Todorov's request to perform CT scans on his patients. This was based on the judgment of the hospital's credentials committee. Two physicians advised the hospital that Todorov lacked the competence to administer CT scans. Both physicians were current DCH radiologists. Todorov appealed the denial to the hospital Hearing Panel. This panel concluded that Todorov was competent to perform CT scans but made no recommendation on his application.

The hospital's executive committee heard presentations from Todorov and the credentials committee. The executive committee then denied his application because it did not want to establish a precedent of granting radiology provileges to nonradiologists. It feared that this could make organization and scheduling of radiology chaotic and would drive staff radiologists away from the hospital. The committee also expressed concern that Todorov might have difficulty complying with hospital reporting requirements.

Todorov brought this action against the hospital and its radiologists. He made a number of antitrust claims, including that the hospital and radiologists conspired to deny him privileges, in violation of Section 1 of the Sherman Act. The district court granted the defendants' motions for summary judgment. Todorov appealed.

TJOFLAT, Chief Judge.

* * * *

As we have shown, DCH has an incentive to foster competition among the radiologists in its radiology department: competition might lower the total price of CT scans to consumers (by reducing the portion of that price attributable to the radiologist's fee), attract more outpatients to DCH for CT scans (patients who might otherwise go to West Alabama General), and increase DCH's revenues and profits. Absent competition among the radiologists, however, DCH cannot attract more outpatients and increase its revenue and profits unless it reduces its portion of the total price of CT scans by producing the CT scan films more efficiently.

DCH could have fostered competition among the radiologists–and thus its potential for further profits–by granting Dr. Todorov, and, eventually, other nonradiologists, privileges to practice in its radiology department, but it chose not to do so. At first blush, DCH's decision appears to be anticompetitive and against its own self-interest–and therefore supportive of Dr. Todorov's argument that the hospital conspired to help the radiologists maintain their supercompetitive profits. Dr. Todorov, however, does not explain why the hospital would want to act this way; he simply concludes that it did.

We have searched the record for a possible, and reasonable, explanation as to why DCH would deliberately act against its own economic interest, and find none. What we find, instead, is that DCH denied Dr. Todorov's application for privileges to foster competition and to serve its own economic interest.

The principal reason DCH's board of directors gave for rejecting Dr. Todorov's application for privileges was to preserve the efficient operation of the hospital's radiology department. The board thought that if it granted Dr. Todorov privileges it would invite a flood of similar applications from nonradiologists, and as more of these physicians performed their own radiological procedures, the radiology department would become unmanageable—experiencing scheduling delays, increased operation and upkeep costs, and an overall decrease in the quality of service. This, in turn, would impair the department's ability to turn a profit. DCH thus claims, in effect, that its board decided that the competitive benefits the hospital's radiology department would gain—from greater efficiency—by denying Dr. Todorov privileges outweighed the additional revenue the department might generate–from a greater volume of business—by granting Dr. Todorov privileges.

Dr. Todorov claims that this procompetitive reason for denying him privileges is a mere pretext. According to Dr. Todorov, the board was not seeking to maintain a competitive edge in the market for the provision of CT scans, but acted only to further the radiologists' economic interest in preserving their supercompetitive profits.

Dr. Todorov bears the burden of proving that DCH's board of directors was willing to act against the hospital's economic interest simply to further the goals of the radiologists. He has failed to meet this burden.

*   *   *   *

To infer a conspiracy solely from the radiologists' anticompetitive conduct and the board's denial of privileges would be, in effect, to criminalize perfectly legitimate conduct. Under state law, and the medical staff bylaws, DCH's board of directors is specifically empowered to make the final decision as to whether to grant or deny privileges to an applicant. The application process at DCH is designed to elicit recommendations from medical staff members who may be more qualified to evaluate the competency of applicants than the hospital's board members. The board considers these various recommendations and other relevant information and makes its decision. Dr. Todorov's complaint is simply that the board, in this case, acted consistently with the recommendations it received.

Decision and Remedy   *The Court affirmed the dismissal of Todorov's complaint.*

Antitrust regulation of staff privileges creates problems for doctors. As discussed above, hospitals have a duty to ensure that staff privileges are only granted to capable doctors or they risk negligence liability. Rejection of requests for staff privileges may produce antitrust liability, however. The HCQIA immunized peer review actions from antitrust liability to help alleviate this conflict.

Health care providers have some quality-of-patient-care defense to antitrust challenges. Denial of staff privileges to unqualified physicians will be legal even if it restricts competition. To use the patient care defense, a defendant must show that concern for patients' welfare was their dominant concern, that the concern was objectively reasonable, and that the disputed practices were necessary to protect the quality of patient care.

Conspiracies and Boycotts

Section 1 of the Sherman Act outlaws groups organizing to boycott competitors and groups conspiring to control the market for certain goods and services. One group of physicians or hospitals may combine to drive competing doctors or hospitals out of business. In some circumstances, physicians have conspired to injure competing types of health care providers.

For example, midwives compete with hospitals in providing services to expectant mothers. Hospitals have been held liable for refusing nurse midwives staff privileges and by requiring that in-hospital maternity patients use the services of physicians.

Chiropractors sued the American Medical Association over rules that limited their access to hospitals and prevented them from combining in business with physicians. Indeed, the AMA described chiropractors as an "unscientific cult." The Association sought to use a quality-of-patient-care defense, but the court held that less restrictive approaches, such as public education, should have been used.[11]

Mergers

Hospital mergers are increasingly common. A record number of hospitals are closing down in current financially difficult times, ninety-six in one recent year. New Medicare payment systems endanger providers. Surviving hospitals have increasingly sought to combine to strengthen themselves financially. Mergers are a concern because hospital service markets are often highly concentrated. Many locales have only a few hospitals.

In addition to Section 1 of the Sherman Act, hospital mergers can be challenged under Section 7 of the Clayton Act. This law makes mergers illegal if they produce an overly concentrated market with a substantial impact on interstate commerce. These laws apply to nonprofit hospitals as well.

Hospital mergers present unique circumstances for the law. In defense of mergers, they may improve patient care. In contrast, hospitals may find it especially easy to collude and raise charges, because most patients do not pay for hospital services themselves.

One defense to antitrust attack is the **failing company defense**. This permits mergers when one company is about to go out of business. The theory is that a merger will not cause increased market concentration if one company was failing anyway.

---

[11] *Wilk v. AMA*, 671 F. Supp. 1465 (N.D. Ill. 1987).

| ▆ **Ethical** |
| **Perspectives** |

The Value of Human Life

Many health care cases present serious ethical problems. A majority of the most central problems regard the value of human life. The very idea of placing a financial value on human life is ethically controversial.

Some argue that human life is sacred and therefore priceless. It is difficult for anyone to say that someone else should die because it is not worth the cost of saving his or her life. Health care has traditionally operated under this sort of assumption. Medical knowledge and technology have advanced enormously over recent decades. Much of this innovation is extremely costly to use. Nevertheless, hospitals will spend enormous amounts of money to save a single life.

In the future, hospitals increasingly must confront the issue of whether such large expenditures are ethically (or legally) required. In fact, there are ethical reasons for limiting the expenditures employed to save lives.

Inevitably, lifesaving resources are limited. When a hospital devotes millions of dollars to some highly advanced cardiac-care technology, those dollars are unavailable for other health care facilities. Hospitals could save many more lives by devoting increased resources to prenatal care and emergency rooms and fewer resources to *life-extending* technologies.

In this circumstance, there may be an ethical duty not to spend money to save lives in certain ways. Arguably, some hospitals are now behaving unethically. Hospitals have spent huge resources on advanced technology to care for patients with insurance that will compensate the hospitals. Many poor mothers in need of prenatal care, however, lack insurance. When hospitals spend large amounts of money on advanced technology, this may reflect concern for profit as much as concern for human life.

This issue has arisen in the area of "right to die." When a patient is in a permanent vegetative state, the patient's family may prefer that life-sustaining technology be turned off. Some hospitals have gone to court and argued that their ethics commanded that the patient be kept alive.

In the future, we may confront even more difficult questions. There is already one case in which a hospital is seeking to disconnect life-sustaining technology, when the patient's family wants the patient to be kept alive. In this case, the hospital was not being reimbursed for its expenses. This may seem callous of the hospital, but remember that its resources might be transferred to uses that will save other lives.

As technology advances, the problem will only get worse. We may soon be able to keep many persons alive indefinitely. To resolve these questions, we must consider the meaning of life itself. There is more to life than just its prolongation. Ethics may not demand that we always preserve life as long as technically possible.

AIDS and International Health Care

The health care industry is less international than many other businesses. One cannot export medical services in the same manner as cars. Nevertheless, health care services are increasingly crossing national boundaries. The high level of U.S. health care technology makes this area a promising one for export.

The international health care community has begun to deal with the global epidemic of acquired immune deficiency syndrome ("AIDS") and its relationship with health care workers. The World Health Organization ("WHO") of the United Nations has begun to set forth regulations and recommendations in this area. Individual nations are also adopting policies in this area.

Health care workers are at risk of contracting AIDS from their patients due to the potential transference of blood during surgery and other health care operations. Regardless of how they contracted AIDS, these health care workers present some risk of communicating the disease to their patients. Health care workers also are at the front line of society's AIDS protection policies.

WHO has adopted standards for testing patients for AIDS and for counseling those who have tested positive for the disease. The Organization has adopted general recommendations for the protection against AIDS in the course of the care of patients. WHO generally lacks the authority, however, to impose rules on member nations. WHO does maintain a clearinghouse on important AIDS information for the benefit of physicians in all countries.

Many nations have rules that protect the confidentiality of those suffering from AIDS. The Council of Europe has adopted recommendations to this effect. Statutes in many countries, including Australia, China, Spain, Sweden, and Panama, also protect this confidentiality interest. Numerous other nations also provide confidentiality protection for patients who test positive. These may prevent doctors from informing other health care providers that a prospective patient has AIDS.

Some physicians have refused treatment for patients with AIDS infection. The American Medical Association, the General Medical Council of the United Kingdom and the French National Council of the Association of Physicians have adopted policies against this practice, directing doctors to provide treatment. Other nations have no limitations on denial of treatment.

Another issue of concern is AIDS-infected health care workers. To date, nations have not demanded AIDS testing of health care workers and have not demanded that patients be informed that their care provider has AIDS. There is increasing public pressure, however, to adopt such requirements.

Questions and Case Problems

1. Blue Shield Insurance had substantial market power in private health insurance, possessing about 60 to 80 percent of the market. Ocean State Insurance was a small company competing with Blue Shield in Rhode Island. Blue Shield adopted a policy under which they would not pay participating physicians any more than the lowest amount that they had accepted from Blue Shield's competitors. As a rule, Ocean State payed its participating physicians less for a given act. The Blue Shield policy caused many physicians to drop out of the Ocean State coverage, in order to obtain the higher average reimbursement rates provided by Blue Cross. Ocean State sued Blue Shield under both Sections 1 and 2 of the Sherman Act. Should Ocean State win? [*Ocean State Physicians Health Plan, Inc. v. Blue Cross & Blue Shield of Rhode Island*, 1988-2 Trade Cas (CCH) P68,161 (D.R.I. 1988)].

2. A doctor attending an infant patient left orders that she be given Lanoxin. The nurse felt that the order was unclear about the administration of the drug and contacted two doctors, who told her that there was no concern. She did not contact the attending physician and went ahead and administered the drug by injection. The dosage, when given by injection, was lethal, and the patient subsequently died. The infant's survivors sued the hospital for malpractice. Should the hospital (the nurse's employer) be liable? [*Norton v. Argonaut Insurance Company*, 144 So.2d 249 (La. App. 1962)]

3. An independent physician took biopsy samples from both breasts of a woman, in order to check for breast cancer. Before sending the samples for pathological analysis, the physician directed the nurse to place samples from both breasts in a single container. The nurse questioned this direction, but the physician told her to proceed as directed, so the nurse did so. The pathologist found one of the samples to be malignant. Because the samples had been mixed together, both of the woman's breasts were removed in mastectomy, though only one was malignant. Later, after she discovered the above facts, she sued the hospital for malpractice. Should the hospital (the nurse's employer) be liable in this case? [*Variety Children's Hospital v. Osle*, 292 So.2d 382 (Fla. App. 1974)].

4. Maria Pedroza was pregnant and under the care of Ben Bryant, who was on the staff of Skagit Valley Hospital. She visited Dr. Bryant at his private office, however, and not at the hospital. In her eighth month of pregnancy she began developing complications and became comatose. She was admitted to the hospital, where she was under the care of another doctor. Her child was successfully delivered by emergency cesarean section, but Maria Pedroza died. Her survivors sued the hospital claiming that Dr. Bryant had been negligent in his care of Maria and that the hospital had been negligent in granting staff privileges to Dr. Bryant. The hospital defended that Dr. Bryant was an independent contractor and that she did not even visit him in the hospital. Should the hospital be liable in this case? [*Pedroza v. Bryant*, 677 P.2d 166 (Wash. 1984)].

5. A hospital had a policy of referring patients only to doctors who had been members of the hospital's medical staff for at least five years. A doctor, who had no patients referred to him, sued the hospital, claiming that this practice violated Section 1 of the Sherman Act. The hospital defended that it had a right to establish rules on patient referrals, and that the hospital allowed the plaintiff doctor to use its facilities when necessary. Did the hospital violate Section 1? [*Cooper v. Amster*, 645 F. Supp. 46 (E.D. Pa. 1986)].

CHAPTER SIXTEEN

Sports and Entertainment Law

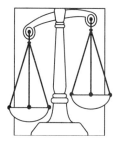

Sports and other forms of public entertainment, such as motion pictures and sound recordings, have become a large part of our nation's economy. As this economic sector has grown, so have legal disputes. The legal issues raised in sports and entertainment law are often common problems of contracts, antitrust, intellectual property, etc. The sports and entertainment context of a dispute, however, can have a significant effect on its resolution. Special rules may apply in sports and entertainment law.

Sports Law

The law of sports covers a broad range of issues and situations, ranging from professional basketball (where the average salary exceeds $600,000) to amateur high school soccer. Sports has become big business—the four major team sports (baseball, basketball, football and hockey) have over a billion dollars a year in gross revenues. Over $1.3 billion is spent by all types of companies in promoting sports events. An increasing number of lawsuits have accompanied this business. As any reader of the sports pages is aware, legal controversies are prevalent in the sporting world.

Private Regulatory Bodies

A rather unusual circumstance of sports law is the presence of private regulatory bodies that set rules for events. In *amateur* sports, at the university level, the best-known body is the National Collegiate Athletic Association (NCAA). Smaller schools are governed by the National Association of Intercollegiate Athletics (NAIA) and other groups of schools, such as junior colleges, have other ruling organizations.

These private organizations have their own governance structures in which member schools participate. The NCAA adopts rules governing recruiting, admissions, financial aid, and eligibility for participating schools. Basic policies are set at a national convention of all member schools and then administered by a governing council and committees.

Most NCAA rules are aimed at protecting the amateur status of its "student-athletes." Detailed recruiting rules prohibit offering gifts to prospective athletes, arranging loans and providing reduced cost services or housing. Other, more technical, rules limit the number of campus visits and off-campus contacts that a recruit may take. The rules also prohibit a recruit from being interviewed on a university coach's radio or television program.

The NCAA recently adopted a Draconian "death penalty" rule. The death penalty applies if the school has twice committed major rules violations within a single five-year period. The

NCAA can then ban participation in the sport subject to the latest violation for up to two years. The death penalty also eliminates athletic scholarships and recruiting activities in that sport. Southern Methodist University twice committed recruiting violations and received the death penalty, which temporarily abolished its football program.

Some NCAA rules are quite controversial and have been challenged in court. The primary legal basis for challenging an NCAA rule is found in the antitrust laws. Antitrust laws are discussed in Chapter 47 of *West's Business Law, Fifth Edition,* and prohibit monopolies and certain combinations of competitors.

The NCAA rules may be challenged under the Sherman Act. Section 1 of the Sherman Act prohibits anticompetitive combinations, such as price fixing. Section 2 of the Sherman Act prohibits monopolization of a product market. Because the NCAA is a combination of competing schools and has a monopoly on a large segment of the sports market, potential antitrust problems are obvious.

Although the NCAA is itself a nonprofit organization, courts have found it subject to the antitrust laws. In so holding, courts have distinguished between "commercial" and "noncommercial" actions of the NCAA. The NCAA rules that limited television coverage of college football were considered a commercial action. The Supreme Court struck down these NCAA restrictions as an unlawful combination in restraint of trade.[1] NCAA regulations to protect amateurism, however, are usually considered noncommercial. A hockey player, who had been paid for hockey in the past, challenged an NCAA rule prohibiting him from playing college hockey. The court ruled for the NCAA because the rule was noncommercial in nature.[2] Courts are reluctant to apply antitrust law to noncommercial rules of the Association. Cheerleaders and alumni of Southern Methodist University sued the NCAA to challenge the death penalty for their football program but lost.

Even noncommercial rules can have a significant effect on individuals. The following case involves a recent challenge to NCAA eligibility rules.

[1]*NCAA v. Board of Regents of the University of Oklahoma,* 468 U.S. 85 (1984).

[2]*Jones v. NCAA,* 392 F. Supp. 295 (Mass. 1975).

■ Case 16.1
Banks v. National Collegiate Athletic Association
United States District Court for the Northern District of Indiana, 1990
Cause No. S90–394

Background and Facts *Braxton Banks entered the University of Notre Dame in 1986 on a football scholarship worth approximately $16,000 per year. Banks played three years as a fullback for Notre Dame and missed one season because of injury. As a consequence, he was eligible for the professional draft but also had a year of collegiate eligibility remaining. An NCAA rule stated that any player who entered the professional draft would no longer be eligible for collegiate football. Banks decided to enter the draft and signed a required form that included the statement: "I HEREBY IRREVOCABLY RENOUNCE ANY AND ALL REMAINING COLLEGE ELIGIBILITY I MAY HAVE." After performing poorly in tryouts, Banks was not chosen in the draft. He sought to return and play for his final year at Notre Dame but was barred by the NCAA rule. Banks filed suit against the NCAA and Notre Dame, claiming that the NCAA rule violated section 1 of the Sherman Act. He moved for a preliminary injunction ordering the defendants to allow him to compete for Notre Dame.*

MILLER, United States District Judge.

* * * *

The NCAA is a private, voluntary, unincorporated association of approximately 1,017 members, consisting of colleges and universities (including Notre Dame), conferences and associations, and other education institutions. According to the NCAA constitution, the NCAA's purpose is to promote intercollegiate athletics in the United States and to maintain amateur intercollegiate athletics "as an integral part of the educational program and the athlete as an integral part of the student body and by so doing, retain a clear line of demarcation between intercollegiate athletics and professional sports." Approximately 187 colleges that play intercollegiate football are members of the NCAA. It is the dominant association of colleges and universities that engage in intercollegiate athletics.

*   *   *   *

In its memorandum, the NCAA first argues that because the NCAA Bylaws challenged here regulate the noncommercial activities of an organization dedicated to fostering amateurism in college sports, the challenged regulations are not subject to the Sherman Act.

Mr. Banks cites a single case in support of his contention that the NCAA is subject to antitrust laws; the NCAA argues that that case may not support so broad a statement of law. In *NCAA v. Board of Regents of the University of Oklahoma*, 468 U.S. 85 (1984), the United States Supreme Court held that the NCAA's efforts to restrict the televising of college football games was subject to, and violated, the Sherman Act. The Court only found an anticompetitive effect in the NCAA television plan. The Court noted that much of the NCAA's activities have a procompetitive effect:

What the NCAA and its member institutions market in this case is competition itself—contests between competing institutions. Of course, this would be completely ineffective if there were no rules on which the competitors agreed to create and define the competition to be marketed. A myriad of rules affecting such matters as the size of the field, the number of players on a team, and the extent to which physical violence is to be encouraged or proscribed, all must be agreed on, and all restrain the manner in which institutions compete. Moreover, the NCAA seeks to market a particular brand of football—college football. The identification of this "product" with an academic tradition differentiates college football from and makes it more popular than professional sports to which it might otherwise be comparable, such as, for example, minor league baseball. In order to preserve the character and quality of the "product", athletes must not be paid, must be required to attend class, and the like. And the integrity of the "product" cannot be preserved except by mutual agreement; its effectiveness as a competitor on the playing field might soon be destroyed. Thus, the NCAA plays a vital role in enabling college football to preserve its character, and as a result enables a product to be marketed which might otherwise be unavailable. In performing this role, its actions widen consumer choice—not only the choices available to sports fans but also those available to athletes—and hence can be viewed as procompetitive.

*   *   *   *

In sum, it is clear that the NCAA is not engaged in two distinct kinds of rulemaking activity. One type . . . is rooted in the NCAA's concern for the protection of amateurism; the other type is increasingly accompanied by a discernible economic purpose. . . . The NCAA sanctions at issue here are clearly of the former variety. Because the sanctions evince no anticompetitive purpose, are reasonably related to the association's central objectives, and are not overbroad, the NCAA's action does not constitute an unreasonable restraint under the Sherman Act.

Decision and Remedy *The court denied the preliminary injunction sought by Banks, because he had little likelihood of success in his case.*

Another legal controversy surrounds the methods of enforcement of NCAA rules. Enforcement is run by the NCAA Committee on Infractions, which is made up of college faculty members. The Committee investigates alleged violations, makes factual determinations, and when appropriate penalizes the member institution in violation of NCAA rules.

Several cases have been brought claiming that the NCAA enforcement procedure violates due process of law (the guarantee of procedural fairness contained in the United States Constitution). Jerry Tarkanian, head men's basketball coach at the University of Nevada at Las Vegas, brought a due process action challenging his suspension for recruiting violations. The due process clause only protects individuals against government action, however. Tarkanian lost his case because the Supreme Court considered the NCAA to be a private organization to which the due process clause does not apply.[3]

The NCAA is subject to government rules for private organizations. The NCAA adopted a random drug testing program for college athletes to detect use of illegal drugs and performance-enhancing drugs, such as steroids. A 1990 California state court decision held that this drug testing program violated the state constitution of California, which guarantees a right of privacy from even nongovernment organizations. Although the binding legal effect of this decision is limited to California, the ruling may force the NCAA to restructure its entire drug testing program.

Professional sports also are governed by private regulatory organizations, such as the National Basketball Association (NBA) and the National Football League (NFL). These professional groups of teams are more clearly commercial, and the antitrust laws are more frequently applied to their actions than to the NCAA.

One key sports antitrust issue involves the concept of free agency. Most sports leagues had some rule that binds players to their existing teams (sometimes known as a **reserve clause**) and that prohibits players from selling their services to the highest bidder (known as **free agency**). Player demands and lawsuits have eliminated the *absolute* reserve clause. Most professional leagues now permit partial free agency to players but place some restrictions on their rights to switch teams.

Suppose that Jose Canseco of the Oakland Athletics baseball team has an excellent year. He may believe that he can substantially increase his salary by creating a bidding war for his services. Perhaps he believes that he could make more money if he played in New York or Los Angeles. Largely because of the antitrust laws, Major League Baseball permits Canseco some opportunity to shop his services. This opportunity is restricted, however, by detailed rules that define limited times in their career when players can seek free agency.

Even baseball players' limited free agency rights have been undermined by the owners. The owners allegedly conspired not to seek other teams' free agents, in order to avoid bidding up player salaries. As a result, many free agents received no offers and had to re-sign with their existing team. After the players challenged the owners' collusion, an arbitrator ruled that the league owed over $100 million in damages to the free agent players.

Several types of professional sports league rules have been found to violate the antitrust laws. When the Oakland Raiders sought to move their franchise to Los Angeles, they were prohibited by a vote of the National Football League. The Raiders ignored this vote and eventually won an antitrust case against the NFL, permitting them to move the franchise.[4] Other courts have struck down a league's reserve clause that prevents

---

[3]*National Collegiate Athletic Association v. Tarkanian*, 488 U.S. 179 (1988).

[4]*Los Angeles Memorial Coliseum v. National Football League*, 726 F.2d 1381 (9th Cir. 1984).

players from being free agents and offering their services to other teams. Major league baseball, however, is partially exempt from the antitrust laws under a 1922 U.S. Supreme Court decision.

In one dramatic case, the United States Football League (USFL) successfully proved that the National Football League was an unlawful monopoly, but the USFL received only $1.00 in actual damages. The jury theorized that the USFL would have gone out of business anyway, regardless of the NFL's monopolistic practices.

Antitrust laws apply to more than just sports leagues. The U.S. Supreme Court has found that boxing promoters violated the antitrust prohibition on monopolization. A small group of promoters acquired exclusive rights to the fights of all four leading contenders for the heavyweight title, and exclusive promotion rights for title bouts in many classes. They used this power to sign up all leading contenders. The Court held that the promoters violated sections 1 and 2 of the Sherman Act.[5]

Many rules of professional sports leagues are questionable under the antitrust laws. Courts have suggested that the annual player **draft**, which brings new players into the leagues, may violate the antitrust laws. The best defense in this and many other cases is the labor exemption to the antitrust laws.

Most professional players are represented by a union. The players' unions bargain with the team owners over pay and other league policies. If a policy, such as the draft, is subject to collective bargaining between the league's owners and a players' union, the courts will respect the labor agreement. This is the labor exemption to the antitrust laws. When players' unions recognize and provide for practices such as the draft or restrictions on free agency in labor agreements, the antitrust laws will not be used to prohibit the agreements.

Other than the antitrust laws, there is little government control over the practices of professional sports organizations. Sports organizations are not government bodies but are voluntary groups. As a result, the government generally lets the leagues make their own rules for the game.

This principle is illustrated by the Pete Rose case, when the Commissioner of Baseball, A. Barlett Giamatti, disciplined Rose for gambling on major league games. Rose claimed that the Commissioner was biased against him and sued. A federal court rejected Rose's case, noting that the Major League Agreement gave the Commissioner extraordinary power to take whatever action was necessary "in the best interests of baseball."[6]

Sports Agents

Not long ago, most professional athletes negotiated their own contracts with a team's general manager. Now, these athletes are virtually all represented by an agent for contract negotiations. Agents are usually lawyers or business professionals who may also represent the athlete in all his or her business dealings, such as advertising and promotions.

A good sports agent can evaluate the value of the client, based on comparable contracts awarded others. The agent also should consider the needs of the client with respect to deferred compensation, injury protection, taxation, education and other contract features. If agreement cannot be reached with the client's team, the agent must decide whether the player should "hold out" and refuse to play until a contract is reached.

Sports agents have suffered a number of scandals in recent years. Some agents paid money to excellent collegiate athletes in hopes of obtaining lucrative representation when the athlete becomes a professional. This arrangement made several players ineligible for further college competition. Other agents have been criticized for conflicts of interest in representing players.

The following case exemplifies the problem of a conflict of interest by a sports agent, the duties of agents to their clients, and the effect of a breach of those duties on resulting contracts.

---

[5]*International Boxing Club, Inc. v. United States*, 358 U.S. 242 (1959).

[6]*Rose v. Giammati*, 721 F. Supp. 906 (S.D. Ohio 1989).

■■ Case 16.2
**The Detroit Lions v.
Argovitz**
United States District Court for the
Eastern District of Michigan, 1984
580 F. Supp. 542

Background and Facts *Billy Sims was an excellent running back for the Detroit Lions of the National Football League. Sims had hired Jerry Argovitz as his agent for negotiations. Argovitz told Sims that he participated in ownership of the Houston Gamblers of the newly formed United States Football League, though Sims did not know the extent of Argovitz's investment. Argovitz sought to negotiate a new contract with the Lions but the parties could not agree on a salary. Argovitz obtained a contract offer from the Gamblers for an amount somewhat more than the Lions offered. Sims had suffered "wounded pride" from the negotiations with the Lions and was amenable to accepting the Gamblers' offer.*

Argovitz did not present the Gamblers' offer to the Lions to try to obtain a better offer from them. Expert witnesses testified that this was contrary to good practice for sports agents. Sims signed with the Gamblers and also signed a waiver agreeing not to sue Argovitz for any breach of duty.

Sims later decided that he wanted to play for the Lions. Both the Lions and Sims filed this suit to invalidate the contract with the Gamblers because Argovitz had breached his duty as an agent of Sims.

DeMASCIO, Judge.

* * * *

10.   Once it has been shown that an agent had an interest in a transaction involving his principal antagonistic to the principal's interest, fraud on the part of the agent is presumed. The burden of proof then rests upon the agent to show that his principal had full knowledge, not only of the facts that the agent was interested, but also of every material fact known to the agent which might affect the principal and that having such knowledge, the principal freely consented to the transaction.

11.   It is not sufficient for the agent merely to inform the principal that he has an interest that conflicts with the principal's interest. Rather, he must inform the principal "of all facts that come to his knowledge that are or may be material or which might affect his principal's rights or interests or influence the action he takes." *Anderson v. Griffith*, 501 S.W. 2d 695, 700 (Tex. Civ. App. 1973).

12.   Argovitz clearly had a personal interest in signing Sims with the Gamblers that was adverse to Sims' interest—he had an ownership interest in the Gamblers and thus would profit if the Gamblers were profitable, and would incur substantial personal liabilities should the Gamblers not be financially successful. Since this showing has been made, fraud on Argovitz's part is presumed, and the Gamblers' contract must be rescinded unless Argovitz has shown by a preponderance of the evidence that he informed Sims of every material fact that might have influenced Sims' decision whether or not to sign the Gamblers' contract.

13.   We conclude that Argovitz had failed to show by a preponderance of the evidence either: 1) that he informed Sims of the following facts, or 2) that these facts would not have influenced Sims' decision whether to sign the Gamblers' contract:

　　　a.   The relative values of the Gamblers' contract and the Lions' offer that Argovitz knew could be obtained.

b. That there was significant financial differences between the USFL and the NFL not only in terms of the relative financial stability of the Leagues, but also in terms of the fringe benefits available to Sims.

c. Argovitz's 29 percent ownership in the Gamblers; Argovitz's $275,000 annual salary with the Gamblers; Argovitz's five percent interest in the cash flow of the Gamblers.

d. That both Argovitz and Burrough failed to even attempt to obtain for Sims valuable contract clauses which they had given to Kelly on behalf of the Gamblers.

e. That Sims had great leverage, and Argovitz was not encouraging a bidding war that could have advantageous results for Sims.

* * * *

17. As a court sitting in equity, we conclude that recision is the appropriate remedy. We are dismayed by Argovitz's egregious conduct. The careless fashion in which Argovitz went about ascertaining the highest price for Sims' service convinces us of the wisdom of the maxim: no man can faithfully serve two masters whose interests are in conflict.

Decision and Remedy *The court entered a judgment rescinding Sims' contract with the Gamblers.*

One of the most remarkable scandals involved sports agents Norby Walters and Lloyd Bloom, who operated as World Sports & Entertainment, Inc. Walters and Bloom paid hundreds of thousands of dollars to sign up college athletes for future representation. Among these athletes were two basketball players from the University of Alabama. When this professional representation was discovered, the NCAA required Alabama to return over $250,000 to the NCAA that the university had received from a post-season tournament appearance.

The University of Alabama sued Walters and Bloom for over $3 million for the tort of intentional interference with a contractual relationship. In addition, Alabama indicted Walters and Bloom for criminal violations of the state Deceptive Trade Practices Act. Both cases were ultimately settled when Walters agreed to pay the University of Alabama $200,000.

Seventeen states now have specific laws regulating sports agents. The most prominent and comprehensive law is the California Athlete Agent Statute. This law requires all sports agents to register with the state's labor commissioner. The agent also must place a $25,000 bond with the labor commissioner to cover potential liability.

The agent must retain all records of transactions with and for the athlete represented. The California law also regulates the content of contracts between agents and athletes for fairness and prohibits certain conflicts of interest. This law provides both civil and criminal penalties for its violation.

In addition to new state laws, sports agents are bound by all the traditional common law rules of agency, as illustrated by the *Sims* case above. The most important of these is the command that the agent always act in the interest of the principal (the athlete), and not for selfish motives. Several athletes have sued their agents for damages but with only limited success. The agents have often lacked the assets to pay off even a meritorious claim. Several NFL players alleged that Probus Management, Inc., defrauded them of $150,000, but the company had no assets to attach.

Agents have also sued athletes for breach of contract. If the contract is legitimate, this is a standard contract claim as judged by traditional common law rules. Walters and Bloom sued a professional football player who took their money while in college in exchange for future representation. The player later hired another agent to represent him as a professional. The court rejected Walters and Bloom's breach of contract case, however, on the grounds that both parties knew their original agreement to be "fraudulent and wrong."[7]

Sports Torts

More and more cases are being brought for tort damages that arise out of a sporting event. Most of these cases involve injury to spectators, and a high proportion of spectator injury cases involve spectators who were hit by baseballs while watching a game. What is the duty of a team owner to protect spectators from injury in such a case?

Spectator cases   Team owners do have a legal duty to provide a protective screen for the baseball spectators in seats most at risk of harm (those behind home plate). With this exception, the traditional rule held that most spectators have assumed the risk of being injured by a ball. Courts have found that most spectators are aware of the risk of being struck by a baseball and accept that risk when they attend a game and sit in unscreened seats. One recent case held that the New York Mets were not liable to a spectator, sitting behind the first base dugout, who was struck by a foul ball.

In some cases, spectators have had more success in recovering damages for their injuries. A baseball spectator was allowed to proceed with his case against the Atlanta Braves, after being injured by a foul ball tipped over the screen. The court reasoned that the screen may have been negligently defective. Another court found that the Pittsburgh Pirates could be liable to a spectator who was struck during batting practice while she was standing on a stadium walkway. The court in that case noted that the walkway was unprotected and forced spectators to turn their attention away from the field.

Professional teams are also potentially liable to spectators for other sources of harm. The Milwaukee Braves were held liable to a sixty-nine-year-old fan who was trampled by other spectators scrambling for a foul ball.[8] The court reasoned that a stadium usher might have protected the fan but was absent from his assigned station at the time.

Another case was brought by a Notre Dame football spectator who was injured by two drunk men while she was on her way to her car in the stadium parking lot. She sued Notre Dame for failure to provide security protection for fans. The appellate court permitted her case to proceed because Notre Dame was well aware of the drinking that went on at "tailgate" parties in the area and should have taken action to protect their fans.

The Los Angeles Dodgers were found potentially liable for providing inadequate medical care to an injured fan. A spectator was struck unconscious by a foul ball. The doctor employed at the Dodgers' emergency medical station advised the fan that he was not seriously injured and should return to his seat. Four days later, the spectator died of a brain hemorrhage. The court held that if the doctor were guilty of malpractice, the Dodgers could be guilty as the doctor's employer.[9]

A sports organization may also be liable to an injured passerby. In one instance, a golf course used a public waterway as a water hazard. When a wayward golf ball struck a boater in the eye, the course owners were held liable for the injuries.[10]

Athlete cases   Sometimes even the participants in sporting events will sue for their injuries. Usually, a court will find that a participant has consented to the risk of injury. For example, a football quarterback can hardly sue a linebacker for a hard tackle.

Players cannot recover for injuries suffered within the rules of the game. Nor can players recover for negligent actions by other players. A player may be able to recover for injuries from intentional actions of other players that were outside the legal rules of the game.

Probably the most-publicized case involved Rudy Tomjanovich of the basketball Houston Rockets. His face was shattered by an unprovoked punch delivered by an opposing player during a game. A jury awarded Tomjanovich over $3 million in damages. The fight in this case was wholly unrelated to the game.

A more controversial case involved Dale Hackbart, a defensive back for the NFL's Denver

---

[7]*Walters v. Fullwood*, 675 F. Supp. 155, 164 (S.D.N.Y. 1987).

[8]*Lee v. National League Baseball Club*, 89 N.W.2d 811 (Wis. 1958).

[9]*Fish v. Los Angeles Dodgers Baseball Club*, 128 Cal. Rptr. 807 (1976).

[10]*Kirchoffner v. Quam*, 264 N.W.2d 203 (N.D. 1978).

Broncos, who sued the Cincinnati Bengals and one of that team's players. While Hackbart was down on the field, Charles "Booby" Clark struck him in the back of the head with a forearm. No penalty was called. Hackbart suffered a serious neck fracture injury. The district court ruled for the Bengals, but an appellate court reversed. The Tenth Circuit Court of Appeals ruled that a football player does not consent to violence that is not within the rules of football. That court held that Clark's actions could constitute assault and battery.[11]

Mere negligence by another athlete will not support liability, however. There are several horse racing cases in which jockeys have sued on the basis that careless riding by other jockeys caused injury. In these cases, courts have held for defendants and found that a jockey assumes the risk of careless riding or "jockey error" by other participants in the race.

Jockeys and race car drivers have recovered on occasion against the owner of a racetrack, when the track itself created a danger. The owner of a sports facility has a duty to exercise reasonable care to prevent foreseeable injury to the sports participants. Many facility owners now require race car drivers to sign a waiver and release assuming the risk of injury and promising not to sue the owner. Thus, when a stock driver was injured due to a defect in the track, he could not recover because he signed a release in which he agreed not to sue.[12]

Several athletes have sued their teams for providing inadequate medical care. Most sports teams maintain their own trainers and team doctors to care for injured players. There have been several scandals when a team and its doctor unsafely urged an athlete back into a game and aggravated an athlete's injury. A pitcher for the baseball Philadelphia Phillies sued when the team physician gave him massive doses of pain-killing drugs so that he could continue pitching. He argued that the high doses caused his subsequent mental illness.[13] Players also have successfully sued the manufacturers of sports equipment (such as football helmets) for defective products that contributed to an injury.

Entertainment Law

Entertainment law primarily involves motion pictures and television, though it may also include popular books, artistic works, and other forms of art or popular entertainment. Entertainment law presents important issues of contracts and copyright protection. Unique issues of artists' rights are also present in the entertainment business.

Entertainment Contracts

Entertainment contracts are governed by traditional rules of contract law, as set forth in Chapters 9 through 17 of *West's Business Law, Fifth Edition*. The unique context of the entertainment industry, however, presents special contract problems. This is true for several reasons. When an actor or a musician first signs a contract, he or she is typically unknown to the public. Consequently, the artist may receive relatively little compensation. Such unknown artists may become "overnight successes." This situation enables record and film companies to make enormous profits from an artist's work, yet pay the artist little. Moreover, many artists are not well informed about their legal rights.

To help protect themselves in transactions, most artists hire an agent or management company. The artist must make a contract with the agent. Normal practice in the music business provides an agent with a commission of 10 percent to 25 percent of the artist's gross receipts from recordings, plus expenses. The agent also generally receives exclusive rights to represent the artist.

Unfortunately, agents also may take advantage of performers. Courts are willing to protect performers from unfair contracts with their agents as well as production companies. The following case illustrates this principle.

---

[11]*Hackbart v. Cincinnati Bengals*, 601 F.2d 516 (10th Cir. 1979).

[12]*Lee v. Beauchene*, 337 N.W. 2d 827 (S.D. 1983).

[13]*Bayless v. Philadelphia National League Club*, 579 F.2d 37 (3d Cir. 1978).

Background and Facts   *Maxim Gershunoff and his wife were well-known Russian ballet artists who emigrated to Israel in 1974. They were described as a "hot property" in the United States and elsewhere, and their services were in great demand. Valery Panov was a manager of entertainers who signed the Gershunoffs to a management contract. Panov was also an "impresario" who personally produced entertainment events. This contract provided for a 20 percent commission to be paid Panov on all bookings for the Gershunoffs.*

After they "became wiser in the world of free private enterprise," the Gershunoffs became dissatisfied with their contract with Panov. Panov (the named plaintiff) sued for alleged breach of contract, and the Gershunoffs (defendants) counterclaimed for breach of fiduciary duties. After a trial, the judge dismissed Panov's claim and ordered relief for the Gershunoffs to recover damages for the breach of fiduciary duties.

Opinion

*   *   *   *

Defendants knew only the Russian language; plaintiff was fluent in Russian, his native tongue, and well schooled in English. He was expert in the ways of the Western world, particularly with the ins and outs of show business deals; defendants, fresh from a mile where everything, inclusive of the performing arts, is operated by the State, were untaught babes in a world where freedom exists as well for the blandisher and trimmer as for others.

*   *   *   *

Evidence was adduced at trial, by those with impressive credentials, experience and repute in the field, that a manager of an artist undertakes to promote the artist and obtain engagements for him for a commission which ranges customarily from 10% to 20%. An impresario, however, occupies a different status akin to a producer of events, and undertakes to pay the artist an agreed-upon fee, produce the event at his risk, and retain as his compensation whatever profits are engendered. The credible proof adduced indicates that plaintiff sought to obtain the benefits accruing to both positions, while not being burdened with their risks. Thus in November, 1974, at plaintiff's behest, the Panovs agreed in writing to perform in Philadelphia and Washington on certain dates for a fee of $10,000 for each performance, and to pay plaintiff a 20% commission on their earnings from each engagement. Plaintiff failed to inform them that he had entered into an agreement with Spectrum, the Philadelphia producer, whereby $25,000 was to be paid for this their premier performance. This contract was signed by the plaintiff as manager. He even received and advance of $12,500 for this Philadelphia engagement. While plaintiff has argued that he bore the risks of an impresario with respect to the expenses of the productions, examination of these two contracts reveals that the exposure of plaintiff was minimal at best, and nonexistent, in all likelihood. By seeking to obtain both the impresario's profit and the manager's commission, without full and fair disclosure, plaintiff has forfeited the right to both. It is unnecessary, for the purpose of this decision, to consider whether plaintiff's obligations to the Panovs were greater than normal by reason of their unique status as recent emigres, their inability to speak and read English, their unfamiliarity with business and the language of the agreement, their lack of independent legal representation, and plaintiff's contrasting expertise in these areas. Considering only the facts established, and specifically the non-disclosure of plaintiff's arrangements for the Philadelphia and Washington engagements, his having been paid in advance a sum greater than that which he would pay the Panovs, plaintiff's failure to abide by the requirements of his own contract in not discussing all fees when he was to act as impresario, his failure to disclose these arrangements even when disclosure was demanded, all evidence clear violation by plaintiff of the most minimal obligations imposed upon an agent who acts for his principal.

Decision and Remedy   *The court affirmed the dismissal of Panov's claim and the award to the Gershunoffs of over $235,000.*

While agents are hired to represent and protect the artist, it is not uncommon for artists to sue their agents. In one case, the widow of Jim Croce, a singer and songwriter, sued their agent for negotiating a bad contract on their behalf. She complained because their agent was also an officer of the publisher and production company with whom the Croces signed. As a result, she claimed an improper conflict of interest. The court found that the contract was not unconscionable (unlawfully unfair), because the Croces were aware of the agent's representation of both sides in the contract. Mrs. Croce did receive some damages. The court held that the agent breached his duty to the Croces when he failed to advise them to hire another independent counsel to evaluate the contracts.

Many performing artists are represented by a union, the American Federation of Television and Radio Artists (AFTRA) which regulates the relationship between the agency and the performer. AFTRA has developed standard agency contracts that are regularly used. Exhibit 16-1 contains some key portions of the AFTRA agency contract for performers working under AFTRA's jurisdiction, including singers.

The artist or agent negotiates a contract with the production company. For a musician, the contract provides a royalty for sales of the record to be produced. The usual royalty rate for a new artist is about 8 percent. This rate often increases for sales above a specified number, such as 500,000 records. Musicians with a record of success often can negotiate a better royalty rate, as high as 17 percent.

Contracts with production companies often limit royalties in other ways. A certain percentage of the receipts from record sales is deducted for packaging. In addition, royalties may be paid on only 90 percent of records sold to stores (to account for returned records). Suppose that a musician sells 1 million records at $8.98 apiece. The basis for royalty calculation could be reduced 10 percent for packaging costs and another 10 percent under the 90 percent rule. The actual royalties would be about 65 cents per album and total royalties would come to $650,000. This total is not all profit. Many contracts provide that the performer must bear the costs of producing the recording. The performer's agent may also take a percentage of the royalties.

Another provision in the typical recording contract permits the company to renew the contract at its option. In this way, the company can benefit for many years. If the performer's record fails to sell, the company does not renew the contract. If the performer's record is a success, the company renews the contract and keeps the rights to produce the artist in the future under the terms of the original contract.

It is not uncommon for performers to be dissatisfied with their contract rights, especially after an initial success. The performer has a binding contract, however, and cannot market his or her services to other record companies. The performer may simply refuse to produce additional records.

If a performer refuses to perform, the company's remedies are somewhat limited. The company usually cannot collect damages, because there is no way of knowing the success of the potential future records that the artist refuses to produce. The company also cannot compel the performer to record. This would be specific performance, which normally is not granted in

---

Exhibit 16-1

American Federation of Television and Radio Artists
Standard AFTRA Exclusive Agency Contract under Rule 12-B

THIS AGREEMENT, made and entered into at _____, by and between _____, hereinafter called the "AGENT," and _____, hereinafter called the "ARTIST."

Witnesseth:

1.   The Artist employs the Agent as his sole and exclusive Agent in the transcription, radio broadcasting and television industries (hereinafter referred to as the "broadcasting industries") within the scope of the regulations (Rule 12-B) of the American Federation of Television and Radio Artists (hereinafter called AFTRA), and agrees not to employ any other person or persons to act for him in like capacity during the term hereof, and the Agent accepts such employment. This contract is limited to the broadcasting industries and to contracts of the Artist as an artist in such fields and any reference hereinafter to contracts or employment whereby the Artist renders his services, refers to contracts or employment in the broadcasting industries, except as otherwise provided herein.

2.   The Artist agrees that prior to any engagement or employment in the broadcasting industries, he will become a member of AFTRA in good standing and remain such a member for the duration of such engagement or employment. The Artist warrants that he has the right to make this contract and that he is not under any other agency contract in the broadcasting fields. The Agent warrants that he is and will remain a duly franchised agent of AFTRA for the duration of this contract. This paragraph is for the benefit of AFTRA and AFTRA members as well as for the benefit of the parties to this agreement.

3.   The term of this contract shall be for a period of _____, commencing the _____ day of _____ 19 _____ (Note—The term may not be in excess of three years.)

4.   (a) The Artist agrees to pay to the Agent a sum equal to _____ per cent (not more than 10%) of all moneys or other consideration received by the Artist, directly or indirectly, under contracts of employment entered into during the term specified herein as provided in the Regulations. Commissions shall be payable when and as such moneys or other consideration are received by the Artist or by anyone else for or on the Artist's behalf.

(b) Any moneys or other consideration received by the Artist or by anyone for or on his behalf, in connection with any termination of any contract of the Artist on which the Agent would otherwise be entitled to receive commission, or in connection with the settlement of any such contract, or any litigation arising out of such contract, shall also be moneys in connection with which the Agent is entitled to the aforesaid commissions; provided, however, that in such event the Artist shall be entitled to deduct arbitration fees, attorney's fees, expenses and court costs before computing the amount upon which the Agent is entitled to his commissions.

This exhibit represents only a portion of the complete document. Printed with permission from AFTRA.

---

personal service contracts. No person can use contract law to require personal service performance. Often, the company's best available remedy is to get an injunction. This injunction would prohibit the artist from performing for any other company.

Suppose that a new performing group, called Caress, signs an exclusive contract with CBS

Records for a low royalty rate. The first album produced by Caress is an enormous success. CBS probably has an option to renew the contract for many years and to keep selling future Caress records, under the original royalty agreement. Caress discovers that MCA Records will offer the group a much better royalty rate for future albums. Caress then refuses to produce more records for CBS in order to get out of the contract. CBS cannot force Caress to record. CBS can probably get an injunction preventing Caress from recording for MCA or any other company.

Such an injunction can be a powerful weapon for recording companies. If Caress wants to make records, it will have to abide by its contract with CBS. If Caress wants to make money from its music and collect royalties, it will be bound to the deal that it made with CBS.

California law provides some protection for artists such as Caress. The law contains a "minimum compensation" requirement for such injunctions. The minimum compensation requirement provides that CBS must guarantee Caress a minimum of $6000 per year, in order to utilize its right to an injunction. If this guarantee is not present, CBS cannot get an injunction, and Caress can sign with MCA or some other recording company that offers a better royalty rate than in the original contract.

California's minimum compensation law was successfully used by Redd Foxx, a comedian. Mr. Foxx was a struggling comedian performing in nightclubs when he signed a contract to produce comedy records at a royalty rate of only 2 to 3 percent. When his records were a success, Foxx sought to get out of his contract and refused to perform. The company sought an injunction, preventing Foxx from making records for anyone else. The court denied the injunction, because Foxx's contract did not entitle him to a minimum guarantee of $6000 per year. This was true even though Foxx actually had received more than $6000 per year in royalties.[14]

In another case, the singer Teena Marie signed a contract with Motown to produce her first record. After producing four successful records, Teena Marie wanted out of her contract. After learning of her intent to perform for another com-

pany, Motown invoked a contract clause providing her with $6000 per year and sought an injunction prohibiting her performance for a competitor. The court ruled for Teena Marie, holding that the company must guarantee her $6000 per year in the *original* contract and could not simply retain the option to pay her that sum at some later date.[15]

California law provides a second route for artists to escape production contracts. The law states that a personal service contract cannot be enforced after seven years from the date that service began. This prevents production companies from extending their renewal option on performers' contracts beyond seven years.

Copyright

The most significant legal benefit available to successful artists, directors, writers, and other creative individuals is the law of copyright. The owner of an entertainment product's copyright has control over the use of that product and can sell the rights to that product. The details of copyright law are set forth in Chapter 8 of *West's Business Law, Fifth Edition* and in Chapter 26 of *West's Legal Environment of Business.*

Most entertainment vehicles can be copyrighted. The law permits copyright of original expressions that are fixed in some medium (e.g., written down, tape recorded, filmed). Literary works, musical works, films, photographs and most forms of art can be copyrighted. An author also can receive a copyright in a particular compilation, such as a collection of essays or songs (e.g., a "Best of . . . " compilation).

Copyright law provides great control to the owner of a copyright. The owner, however, is not necessarily the creative artist. Many entertainment products are in the category of "work for hire." In this system, the directors, screenwriters, and other participants in producing a movie assign all their rights to the production or distribution company, in exchange for compensation (a flat fee or a percentage of profits). The copyright of a work for hire belongs to the employer of the creative artist. The production or distribution company reaps the financial benefits of copyright

---

[14]*Foxx v. Williams*, 244 Cal. App. 2d 223 (1966).

[15]*Motown Record Corporation v. Brockert*, 160 Cal. App. 3d 123 (1984).

ownership and the artist receives whatever the employment agreement provides.

In many cases, the production contract will specify that any product is a work for hire, belonging to the employer. If the contract does not specify these rights, the employer's ownership depends on whether the work is prepared by an employee in the scope of employment or is specially commissioned for the employer. To qualify as a work for hire, the company must actively supervise production or at least retain control over those who produce the work. Otherwise, the creative artist controls the copyright in the product.[16]

Gilbert is a free-lance photographer and writer who prepares travel articles for magazines. Gilbert prepares an article on Barbados and sells the article to *Travel & Leisure* magazine. Because Gilbert is a free-lancer, he retains the copyright in this article, unless the copyright is transferred to the magazine in a written contract. If he were a staffwriter, however, the copyright would belong to the magazine.

The owner of a copyright in an entertainment work has broad power over the use of that work. The owner has exclusive rights to publish, sell, and rent the work. The owner also has exclusive rights to performance and display of the work. The owner controls the right to make derivative works (such as making a movie from a copyrighted book). The owner also has the right to control and prevent copying of the entertainment work by others.

The copyright protects the owner against unauthorized copying and sale of the work. Thus, if a counterfeiter makes unauthorized copies of videotapes and sells them to the public, the owner's copyright has been violated, and the owner can sue for damages. In addition to actual damages from lost sales, the Act provides for statutory damages (like punitive damages) of $50,000 per violation.

In a recent case, a company made unauthorized recordings of several record albums, including "Breezin" by George Benson and "Bat Out of Hell" by Meatloaf. The plaintiff record company had difficulty proving damages, because it could not determine the number of counterfeit records sold by the defendants. The court awarded the plaintiff all the defendants' profits from the illegal sale, which exceeded $42,000. In the alternative, plaintiffs could accept statutory damages under the Copyright Act of $50,000 for each record that was unlawfully copied, totalling in excess of $1.4 million.[17] Obviously, plaintiffs chose the greater sum.

Unlawful copying of copyrighted works is not limited to underground counterfeiters. For example, Joseph Schlitz Brewing Company was found liable for using "The Theme from Shaft" in a beer commercial, without obtaining permission from the copyright holder.

Most copyright problems do not involve literal copying of an entire work of entertainment, however. More typically, the owner of a copyright in a work of entertainment sues for a work that is very similar to the copyrighted original. The copyright is violated only if the new work by the defendant is "substantially similar" to the plaintiff's original.

The "substantially similar" test is used to determine whether the second work was copied from the first. If the works are extremely similar, a court will infer that the second work must have been copied. Courts also consider proof that the defendant had access to the original work before producing the second work.

The copyright owners of the song "He's So Fine" sued George Harrison for his best-selling song, "My Sweet Lord." The court ruled for the original copyright owners, because Harrison's song was "strikingly similar."[18] The court did not hold that George Harrison intentionally copied the earlier song. Unintentional or "subconscious" copying also produces copyright liability.

Given the limited number of melodies and common lyrics, songwriters are often subject to copyright infringement claims. The following case illustrates the scrutiny that a court must give to such claims.

---

[16]*Community for Creative Non-Violence v. Reid*, 490 U.S. 730 (1989).

[17]*RSO Records, Inc. v. Peri*, 596 F. Supp. 849 (S.D.N.Y. 1984).

[18]*Abkco Music, Inc. v. Harrisongs Music, Ltd.*, 722 F.2d 988 (2d Cir. 1983).

■ Case 16.4
Siskind v. Newton-John
United States District Court for the
Southern District of New York, 1987
No. 84 Civ. 2634

Background and Facts   *In 1980, Laura Taylor Siskind wrote a song entitled "Take Another Chance on Love." She registered a copyright at that time. Siskind produced several songs, including "Take Another Chance on Love" to submit to The Entertainment Company ("TEC"). Steve Lukather played guitar on a different song, entitled "Paradise." In 1983, Lukather, singer Olivia Newton-John, and other artists composed the song "Take a Chance" for performance by Newton-John and John Travolta. "Take a Chance" was used in a motion picture. Siskind filed suit against Newton-John, Lukather, the record company, and others, claiming that "Take a Chance" infringed her copyright in "Take Another Chance on Love."*

To show access, Siskind alleged that Lukather may have heard "Take Another Chance on Love" after it was submitted to TEC on the tape on which he had performed "Paradise." Lukather stated that he never heard this tape. Defendants moved for summary judgment to dismiss Siskind's complaint. Given the weak evidence of access, the court focused on the similarity of the two songs.

GRIESA, Judge.

* * * *

Plaintiff's claim relates to the chorus of her song, which she alleges was copied in the chorus of defendants' song. The choruses are only portions of the songs, and they are the only portions about which there is any claimed similarity or copying.

In plaintiff's song the chorus appears for the first time after Verse 1. The lyrics of the chorus are:

> Take a chance, take a chance; Take another chance on love. Take
> a chance, take a chance; Take another chance on love.

This is followed by Verse 2, after which there is a repetition of the chorus. Then comes Verse 3. The song concludes with the chorus repeated twice and a fade.

Defendants' song commences with Verses 1 and 2, followed by the chorus:

> Take a chance, take a chance. Shall I take another chance on
> love? Take a chance, take a chance. Shall I take another chance
> on love? When it feels so right; When I'm safe and warm inside?
> Take [a] chance and fall tonight.

After this comes Verse 3. The song concludes with the chorus repeated twice and then a fade.

The verses of the two songs are entirely different. However, as the quoted material indicates, the lyrics of the first four lines of defendants' chorus are the same as the lyrics of plaintiff's chorus, except that the words "Shall I" appear at the beginning of the second and fourth lines of defendants' chorus. Defendants argue that the words and phrases in these choruses are commonplace, and as such have appeared in various popular songs other than those of the parties to this action. Defendants cite songs with the titles "Take a Chance," "Take a Chance on Love," and "Take Another Chance." However, no other song has been found with the precise arrangement of the phrases as contained in the songs in the present case.

* * * *

On the issue of similarity, basically all the facts are before the court which could be presented at a trial. Plaintiff has not made out a case of similarity of the kind which could raise an inference of copying, particularly in view of the lack of access. The lyrics in both choruses are a series of commonplace phrases. The commonplace phrases in defendants' song fit quite naturally into the theme of the movie for which the song was written. All this is consistent with independent creation rather than copying.

As to the music, the melodies are entirely different. The limited rhythmic similarities relate to the rhythm of the words and do not indicate copying of plaintiff's rhythm. To the extent that there are similarities in harmonic progressions, it is a matter of standard or usual harmonic progressions, something which does not indicate copying. In any event, it is the melody which is the most important feature of the music, and the melodies in plaintiff's and defendants' works are quite different.

Decision and Remedy   *The court granted summary judgment for defendants and dismissed Siskind's complaint.*

In one case, an underground comic book used characters created by Walt Disney, including Mickey Mouse. In the underground comic, the Disney characters took drugs and engaged in "bawdy" behavior. Defendants argued that their comic should be legal, as a parody. The court held that defendants had substantially infringed Walt Disney's copyright in the characters because of the great similarity of the drawing of the characters and their names.[19]

Not all copying is illegal. The copyright act permits individuals to make "fair use" of a copyrighted work. Courts consider four factors in deciding whether the use of a copyrighted work is fair:

1. The purpose of the use (educational use is broader, commercial use is more restricted).

2. The nature of the copyrighted work (entertainment works of great creativity are especially protected).

3. The amount and substantiality of the portion of the copyrighted work used.

4. The effect of the use on the market for the copyrighted work (if the use does not hurt sales of the work, the use is more likely to be considered fair).

These standards are applied on a case-by-case basis to determine whether copying is fair use. Copying a small portion of a use for personal or educational purposes will be legal. Copying larger amounts for commercial use is more problematic.

There is currently a dispute over fair use in rap recordings. Rap musicians often "sample" previous records for use in new music recordings. Sampling involves the copying and modifying of portions of previously recorded works. The rap group De La Soul sampled several seconds of a previous recording by the Turtles in a new song. The Turtles sued for copyright infringement, and the case was settled for an undisclosed amount.

Compulsory Licensing

In general, copyright law permits the copyright owner to license the use of the work at its discretion. Thus, the owner of a novel, such as *Gone with the Wind*, can license a movie studio to make a film of the book for an agreed-upon fee. Or an author will enable a book company to produce and sell a copyrighted work, in exchange for royalty payments.

Although most copyright holders can refuse to license their works to others, the Copyright Act creates compulsory licensing for musical

---

[19] *Walt Disney Productions v. Air Pirates*, 581 F.2d 751 (9th Cir. 1978).

recordings that have been distributed. This means that a record can be played on the radio, or on a jukebox, without requiring specific permission from the copyright holder. The law provides a specific royalty payment for these uses. The present royalty rate is five cents per recording or 0.95 cents per minute of playing time, whichever is greater.

Trademark, Misappropriation, and Unfair Competition

In addition to copyright, the producer or owner of an entertainment work has protection under the law of trademark, misappropriation, and unfair competition. These issues are discussed in more detail in Chapters 11 and 12 of this book. Some expressions, such as the title of a movie or the name of a group, are too short to obtain full copyright protection. While titles are not protected in copyright, they may be protected under other sources of law.

The law of trademark protects against copying of trademarked names and figures, such as Superman. The law of misappropriation prevents persons from profiting from the unauthorized use of the name and identity of others, such as celebrities. The tort of unfair competition generally protects against unfair trade practices. The requirements of these actions are discussed in more detail in Chapter 11 of this book.

DC Comics, Inc., claimed trademark protection in the comic book character Aquaman, an underwater hero, who fights the forces of evil with his female companion, Mera, and his loyal, walrus-like companion Tusky. CBS showed a cartoon television series featuring Manta, an underwater hero, accompanied by Moray, his female companion, and Whiskers, a walrus-like companion. DC Comics sued for infringement of trademark and misappropriation of their characters, and a jury awarded nearly $400,000 in damages. The appellate court overturned the damages award, because DC Comics had not proved that the television show had caused financial loss to DC Comics. The court found some damages resulted from a television cartoon on "Superstretch" that copied the comic books' "Plastic Man" character.[20]

Movie companies have also sued to protect the titles of their films from use in the movies of others. George Romero produced "Night of the Living Dead" and "Dawn of the Dead." He sued another movie company that produced a film entitled "Return of the Living Dead." The court found that Romero's titles were protected and granted an injunction against the use of the title "Return of the Living Dead" for a competing movie.[21] A famous 1950s musical group, called "The Platters," also won an injunction preventing another group from calling itself the "New Century Platters."[22]

Misappropriation can involve using the name or likeness of a celebrity to promote a product, without the celebrity's authorization. Cher gave a journalist from *Us* magazine an exclusive interview but then obtained the magazine's agreement not to use the interview. The journalist sold the interview to *Forum* magazine and others. *Forum* ran the interview and engaged in substantial advertising, which used Cher's name and picture and which stated that Cher endorsed *Forum* (a *Penthouse* magazine). Cher sued for misappropriation and won $269,000 in damages. While *Forum* had a legal right to publish the interview, they improperly implied that Cher endorsed their magazine.[23]

Artists' Rights

The laws of copyright, trademark, etc., provide strong rights for those artists who have retained the ownership rights in their works of entertainment. Most significant entertainment works, however, are works for hire, in which the artist has given over copyright and other protection to an employing company. What, if any, rights does the creative artist retain in the entertainment product?

The law of some European countries, such as France, provides artists with "moral rights" over the creative product, even after the economic rights have been assigned to a corporation. These moral rights enable an artist to prevent others from modifying his or her work, for example. The

---

[20]*DC Comics, Inc. v. Filmation Associates*, 486 F. Supp. 1273 (S.D.N.Y. 1980).

[21]*Dawn Associates v. Links*, 23 U.S.P.Q. 831 (N.D. Ill. 1978).

[22]*The Five Platters, Inc. v. Purdie*, 419 F. Supp. 372 (D. Md. 1976).

[23]*Cher v. Forum International, Ltd.*, 692 F.2d 634 (9th Cir. 1982)

United States generally does not recognize moral rights for artists.

U.S. law does grant some limited rights to even those artists who have lost copyright control over their creative works. The Directors Guild of America has a labor agreement that permits directors to consult in the final editing of their movies. Other rights are provided by law. California law requires that a movie give proper credit to actors and other participants in a motion picture. California law also protects works of fine art (painting, sculpture, etc.) from mutilation, destruction, negligent framing, and other damage by even the owner of the art.

Giving proper credit is critical to motion picture performers and other artists and this issue has been the subject of much litigation. Actors have even sued over the size of the type in their credit on a movie poster. Credit requirements are often included in contracts with performers. One actor won nearly $2 million in damages when he was promised "fourth-star billing" on a movie but received only alphabetical billing, which placed his name much lower than fourth.

United States law generally provides the artist little control over the final product of a work for hire. This issue became controversial with the development of "colorization." The colorization process enables the owner of a black-and-white film to add color and display the film in color. While directors have complained that colorization improperly altered their films, the law generally permits colorization or other alterations by the copyright owner.

Some limited measure of artists' rights may be found in United States law. The following case involves a comedy group that successfully sued over the modification of its work.

■ Case 16.5
Gilliam v. American Broadcasting Companies, Inc.
United States Court of Appeals,
Second Circuit, 1976
538 F.2d 14

Background and Facts   *The comedy troupe known as Monty Python produced a series of thirty-minute programs telecast by the British Broadcasting System (BBC). The BBC's agreement gave it the right to rebroadcast Monty Python's programs overseas. ABC reached an agreement to do two ninety-minute specials on American television. ABC significantly edited the British programs to make time for commercials and to eliminate skits that were considered to be offensive.*

After the first ABC special, Monty Python sued to halt the edited broadcast of their skits. They claimed that ABC's editing violated its contract with the BBC and mutilated their programs. A district court agreed with Monty Python on the substance of their claims but refused to enjoin ABC's broadcast of the second special, because ABC could suffer a great financial loss from an injunction issued just a week before the broadcast was planned. The district court judge did require ABC to broadcast a disclaimer stating that Monty Python disassociated itself from the special. Monty Python appealed.

LUMBARD, Circuit Judge.

*   *   *   *

Since its formation in 1969, the Monty Python group has gained popularity primarily through its thirty-minute television programs created for BBC as part of a comedy series entitled "Monty Python's Flying Circus." In accordance with an agreement between Monty Python and BBC, the group writes and delivers to BBC scripts for use in the television series. This scriptwriters' agreement recites in great detail the procedure to be followed when any alterations are to be made in the script prior to recording of the program. The essence of this section of the agreement is that, while BBC retains final authority to make changes, appellants or their representatives exercise optimum control over the scripts consistent with BBC's authority and only minor changes may be made without prior consultation with the writers. Nothing in the scriptwriters' agreement entitles BBC to alter a program once it has been recorded. The agreement further provides that, subject to the terms therein, the group retains all rights in the script.

* * * *

It also seems likely that appellants will succeed on the theory that, regardless of the right ABC had to broadcast an edited program, the cuts made constituted an actionable mutilation of Monty Python's work. This cause of action, which seeks redress for deformation of an artist's work, finds its roots in the continental concept of droit moral, or moral right, which may generally be summarized as including the right of the artist to have his work attributed to him in the form in which he created it.

American copyright law, as presently written, does not recognize moral rights or provide a cause of action for their violation, since the law seeks to vindicate the economic, rather than the personal, rights of authors. Nevertheless, the economic incentive for artistic and intellectual creation that serves as the foundation for American copyright law, cannot be reconciled with the inability of artists to obtain relief for mutilation or misrepresentation of their work to the public on which the artists are financially dependent. Thus courts have long granted relief for misrepresentation of an artist's work by relying on theories outside the statutory law of copyright, such as contract law, *Granz v. Harris*, 198 F.2d 585 (2d Cir.1952) (substantial cutting of original work constitutes misrepresentation), or the tort of unfair competition, *Prouty v. National Broadcasting Co.*, 26 F.Supp. 265, 40 U.S.P.Q. 331 (D.C. Mass.1939). Although such decisions are clothed in terms of proprietary right in one's creation, they also properly vindicate the author's personal right to prevent the presentation of his work to the public in a distorted form.

* * * *

These cases cannot be distinguished from the situation in which a television network broadcasts a program properly designated as having been written and performed by a group, but which has been edited, without the writer's consent, into a form that departs substantially from the original work. "To deform his work is to present him to the public as the creator of a work not his own, and thus makes him subject to criticism for work he has not done." *Roeder, supra*, at 569. In such a case, it is the writer or performer, rather than the network, who suffers the consequences of the mutilation, for the public will have only the final product by which to evaluate the work. Thus, an allegation that a defendant has presented to the public a "garbled," distorted version of plaintiff's work seeks to redress the very rights sought to be protected by the Lanham Act, 15 U.S.C.A. § 1125(a), and should be recognized as stating a cause of action under that statute. See *Autry v. Republic Productions, Inc.*, 213 F.2d 667, 101 U.S.P.Q. 478 (9th Cir.1954); *Jaeger v. American Int'l Pictures, Inc.*, 330 F.Supp. 274, 169 U.S.P.Q. 668 (S.D.N.Y.1971), which suggests the violation of such a right if mutilation could be proven.

During the hearing on the preliminary injunction, Judge Lasker viewed the edited version of the Monty Python program broadcast on December 26 and the original, unedited version. After hearing argument of this appeal, this panel also viewed and compared the two versions. We find that the truncated version at times omitted the climax of the skits to which appellants' rare brand of humor was leading and at other times deleted essential elements in the schematic development of a story line. We therefore agree with Judge Lasker's conclusion that the edited version broadcast by ABC impaired the integrity of appellants' work and represented to the public as the product of appellants what was actually a mere caricature of their talents. We believe that a valid cause of action for such distortion exists and that therefore a preliminary injunction may issue to prevent repetition of the broadcast prior to final determination of the issues.

A single example will illustrate the extent of distortion engendered by the editing. In one skit, an upper class English family is engaged in a discussion of the tonal quality of certain words as "woody" or "tinny." The father soon begins to suggest certain words with sexual connotations as either "woody" or "tinny," whereupon the mother fetches a bucket of water and pours it over his head. The skit continues from this point. The ABC edit eliminates this middle sequence so that the father is comfortably dressed at one moment and, in the next moment, is shown in a soaken condition without any explanation for the change in his appearance.

Decision and Remedy *The Second Circuit also found that ABC had violated copyrights retained by Monty Python. The court ordered the district court to enter an injunction barring ABC's broadcast of the second special.*

Tort of Incitement

Some victims of violent attacks have sought to sue television or motion picture producers for their injuries. These plaintiffs sue under a theory that the on-screen violent actions of actors incited real world persons to reenact the program or movie, causing harm to the victim.

In the first important incitement case, a Florida couple sued CBS, ABC and NBC, claiming that their son had become addicted to television violence. They alleged that "TV intoxication" caused their son to murder an eighty-three-year-old woman. The parents referred to no particular program but complained of television violence in general. The court ruled against the parents, because they could not cite specific programs that incited their son to violence.[24]

Since the Florida case, numerous incitement claims have been brought against television stations, motion picture producers, rock-and-roll groups, and others. While these claims have generally failed, the decisions suggest that future plaintiffs could possibly recover for incitement. In a California case, a young girl was horribly raped in a unique manner similar to that shown on a television program the previous night. She sued NBC and an appellate court held that the plaintiff had stated a legitimate claim.[25] The jury ultimately ruled for NBC, finding no incitement to violence, but the court opened the door for potential future liability for entertainment programming.

---

[24]*Zamora v. Columbia Broadcasting System*, 480 F. Supp. 199 (S.D. Fla. 1979).

[25]*Olivia N. v. National Broadcasting Co.*, 74 Cal. App. 3d 383 (1977).

☰ Ethical Perspectives

Sports Agents and Ethics

In hearings before the United States Congress, sports agents were described as "sleazoid" and "slime." These agents have been at the center of legal and ethical scandals, some of which are described above. One additional controversy involved Paul Palmer, once an All-America running back at Temple University. While a senior at Temple University in 1986, Palmer received a $5000 loan and monthly cash payments from sports agents Norby Walters and Lloyd Bloom. After Palmer became a professional player, this arrangement was disclosed. Temple forfeited its 1986 victories and erased all the records that Palmer had achieved while at the school. Walters and Bloom represented Palmer in his professional contract and persuaded Palmer to invest nearly a third of his $450,000 signing bonus in a "credit repair" business. Bloom did not actually invest this money but instead used it to cover his personal expenses, including the lease on a Rolls-Royce, his personal credit cards, and his ex-wife's rent. Palmer saw no benefit from this money.

Examples such as Paul Palmer's, which involve blatant disregard of duties of honesty, loyalty, and promise keeping, clearly involve unethical conduct on the part of sports agents. Recognizing that these examples of dishonesty and corruption were tarnishing the image of some good and honest sports agents, a group of agents formed the Association of Representatives of Professional Athletes (ARPA). The ARPA then adopted a code of ethics for its members.

Membership in ARPA and its ethical code is voluntary. Some athletes have begun insisting that their representation contract specify that the agent will conform to the ARPA code of ethics. Other athletes use screening committees of trusted friends to interview agents and help select an honest representative for the athlete.

While the ARPA ethical code is a step forward, it does not settle ethical problems. The code prohibits representation by an agent who lacks "competence . . . in a particular area." This provision is important, because in the past anyone could be a sports agent. As a consequence, athletes have been represented by a dry-cleaning manager, a caterer, and a dentist. The ARPA code does not define "competence," however, so its benefits are not certain. The code also prohibits excessive fees, conflicts of interest by the agent, and the disclosure of the client's confidential information.

Although the code is a step forward and might prevent the worst excesses of past sports agents, it fails to deal with some important ethical questions confronting sports agents. A common problem involves the ethical duties of agents when negotiating a representation deal with a college or high school athlete. Ordinarily, we expect each party to a contract to look out for his or her own interests.

In a perfect free market, an agent would have a right to make his own best deal with an athlete. It would be the athlete's own fault if the deal were an unfair one. Many of today's young athletes, though, are naive or undereducated. Tragically, even some athletes who graduated from college may be unable to read the English language. Is it realistic to expect such athletes to be able to protect their own interests when dealing with an agent?

The way that sports agents have structured their contracts creates a recurring problem. Suppose that a rookie signs an initial professional contract for $25,000 a year for two years, with a $10,000 bonus. The agent will take $6000, or 10 percent of $60,000, which is the total contract value. Then, the rookie doesn't make the squad and never receives the two years of $25,000 salary. The only money received by the athlete was the $10,000 signing bonus, and the agent took 60 percent of that money, leaving the athlete with only $4000.

The above situation is often legal, because the contract provides for its distribution of revenues, but is the agent's action ethical? Of course, the athlete is the one who signed the contract and failed to make the professional team. But the agent may still have some ethical duty of fairness in negotiating the contract. Perhaps the contract itself is inherently unfair, or perhaps the agent should at least disclose the future financial risk to the athlete. What ethical duties should an agent have in negotiating contracts? Will the acceptance of high ethical standards hurt an agent's financial success?

International Perspectives

International Marketing of Motion Pictures

Foreign distribution of U.S. motion pictures has become big business. The motion picture industry contributes over $1 billion per year to a positive trade balance for this nation. Nearly half of all profits in the motion picture industry derive from foreign distribution of films.

While international film distribution is clearly a success, substantial legal problems interfere with even greater profits. One major problem is the copyright protection provided by foreign nations. A United States copyright directly protects the owner only for U.S. distribution. In foreign distribution, a producer may be required to acquire a special copyright for a foreign nation.

To ease the problem of establishing international copyright protection, over fifty nations, including the United States, have joined in the Universal Copyright Convention (the Berne Convention). Under this Convention, member nations must recognize a United States copyright as protecting the owner of the copyright. The extent of protection, though, is determined by each country. Suppose that a United States producer gets a U.S. copyright and distributes a film in France. The French will recognize the U.S. copyright but will provide only that protection afforded to a French copyright. The U.S. company is still dependent on the strength of foreign copyright protection. The Convention does have a provision requiring that member states provide for "adequate and effective" protection of copyrights.

Other international conventions and agreements also protect copyrights in international law. This international law, including the Universal Copyright Convention, does not provide fully effective protection for motion picture rights. Virtually all nations (even those not members of the Convention) provide for copyright protection, but in practice these laws may not be enforced. Some nations provide insufficient penalties for copyright infringement.

U.S. motion picture companies have lost substantial potential profits from unauthorized performances and even piracy of films, such as from unauthorized reproduction and sale of videocassettes. The film industry estimates that 50 percent of potential videotape revenues in Japan is pirated, resulting in an annual loss of over $250,000 in producers' receipts.

While piracy may never be totally eliminated, U.S. companies can take legal steps to reduce the financial impact of such piracy. Producers and distributors should ensure that they understand the specifics of foreign copyright laws. This can help the U.S. company structure its contracts and distribution arrangements to better protect its copyrights. One company, for example, will not grant a foreign company theatrical exhibition rights for its motion pictures unless the company also agrees to buy the videocassette rights as well.

Joint industry action can also help. A trade association of motion picture companies sent representatives to nations in South America and Latin America to work with their governments in preventing film piracy. While some foreign governments were uncooperative, others actively enforced the laws by raiding the pirates' production facilities. An industry source estimates that this program reduced piracy by 50 percent in Brazil and Mexico and by lesser percentages in other nations.

Questions and Case Problems

1. A grade school gym teacher at a private school took her class of thirty-five students out to the playground for a game of "dodgeball." Kaye Fidler, who was very bright, had skipped several grades and was much smaller and less coordinated than the other students. She was unable to avoid a ball thrown at her head and suffered a severe concussion during the game. Fidler sues the teacher and the school for these injuries. Should Fidler be allowed to recover?

2. A new female singer, Latomma, grew up on the music of Madonna and believes that she is the most talented musician and performer around. Latomma therefore decides that she must dress and act like Madonna. Therefore, she patterned her personal dress and style very closely after Madonna's. Latomma, who is a performer of heavy metal music, signed a five-year record contract and went out on tour. Madonna sued Latomma for misappropriation. Should Madonna succeed in this action?

3. On May 23, 1979, a young boy was watching "The Tonight Show" when a stunt man was performing. The stunt man did a simulated hanging of Johnny Carson on the show, and Carson survived without any injury. Before the simulated hanging, the guest stated: "Believe me, it's not something that you want to go and try. . . . I happen to know somebody who did something similar to it, just fooling around, and almost broke his neck." After watching the show, the young boy, who was a regular viewer of the show, apparently tried the stunt and hanged himself to death. The boy's parents sued NBC. Should they be able to recover for the death of their son? [*DeFillippo v. National Broadcasting Co.*, 446 A.2d 1036 (R.I. 1982)].

4. Margaret Landon entered into an agreement with a study to sell the motion picture rights to her book entitled *Anna and the King of Siam*. The agreement was that the studio would give her credit appropriate to "her contribution to the literary material upon which such motion pictures shall have been based." The study had full editorial control in using Landon's book. The studio produced a series of thirteen films for television, and the film credits stated that they were based on Landon's work. Landon sued the studio, claiming that the films abandoned the theme of her work and that the credit injured her privacy and literary reputation by making a serious work appear frivolous. If she is correct about suffering damages, should she succeed in this lawsuit? [*Landon v. Twentieth Century-Fox Film Corp.*, 384 F. Supp. 450 (S.D.N.Y. 1974)].

5. The Kingsmen were formed in 1962 and recorded a demo tape of the song entitled "Louie, Louie." The lead vocalist on this tape was Jack Ely, who left the group in 1964, before the song became popular. The entire group disbanded in 1967. Sometime later, a record company hired Ely to rerecord "Louie, Louie" for a collection of songs, and the record jacket stated that it included rerecording by the original artists, and mentioned the name, The Kingsmen. The Kingsmen sued the record company, because Ely was the only one of the original Kingsmen to rerecord the song. Should The Kingsmen succeed in this case? [*Kingsmen v. K-Tel International, Ltd.*, 557 F. Supp. 178 (S.D.N.Y. 1983)].

CHAPTER SEVENTEEN

Hospitality Management Law

KEY BACKGROUND

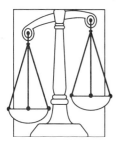

The most important legal issues in hospitality management involve some of the most basic legal principles. One important issue is negligence, which may occur when a hotel is liable for carelessly allowing its guests to be injured. Agency law is also involved when an employer hotel is liable for the acts of its employees. Standard contract law controls several legal issues, such as reservations.

While the basic legal standards of these negligence and contract cases are straightforward, their application in hospitality management may be different because of the special guest-innkeeper relationship. This chapter goes through each of these issues in turn, highlighting the potential liability of hotel and restaurant owners.

Guest-Innkeeper Relationship

The laws governing hotels and similar establishments evolved through the common law. The common law developed rules that placed particular legal burdens on what were then called "innkeepers." The law generally required that innkeepers were required to provide accommodations to all travelers who were able and willing to pay for them. The common law also provided that the innkeeper would be strictly liable for the loss of guests' property brought into the inn.

Since the adoption of these traditional common law rules, the federal and state governments have passed a number of statutes affecting the legal responsibilities of innkeepers. While some of these statutes imposed additional responsibilities on innkeepers, many of the laws have limited the potential common law liability faced by innkeepers.

These special rules only apply when there is a **guest-innkeeper relationship**. Finding this special relationship is therefore an essential threshold matter. The term "inn" or "hotel" is defined very broadly by the law to cover those who provide temporary, furnished lodging facilities for the general public and usually provide food service.

The guest-innkeeper relationship is a contractual one, dependent on the intent of the parties. If a person enters a hotel merely to dine at the restaurant, she will not be subject to the rules of the guest-innkeeper relationship. If she intends to spend the night after finishing her dinner, however, she becomes a guest.

Most controversies arise over when the guest-innkeeper relationship commences and terminates. Suppose that a guest gives his luggage to a doorman upon entering the hotel lobby. His luggage is then lost. The claim is made that the person had not yet registered and was not yet a guest subject to the special guest-innkeeper relationship. A court disagreed, saying that the acceptance of luggage was an ordinary incident to the guest-innkeeper relationship and fell within it.[1]

---

[1]*Korr v. Thomas Emery's Sons, Inc.*, 93 N.E.2d 781 (Ohio 1949).

In another case, a women asked a hotel bell-boy to take her bags to the taxicab area after she checked out. When she came to the cab area, the bag and the bellboy were both missing. One court held that she was no longer within the guest-innkeeper relationship.[2] Some courts have dis-agreed with this latter case.

Responsibility for the Safety of Guests

A key legal issue in hospital management is the hotel's responsibility to protect the personal safe-ty of its guests. The general rule is that a hotel is not an insurer of its guests' safety. As a result, hotels will be liable for injuries only when they (or their employees) are negligent in causing the injury. The special guest-innkeeper relation-ship, though, may mean that a hotel is held to a higher standard of care than under ordinary neg-ligence law.

Liability under negligence, detailed in Chapter 5 of *West's Business Law, Fifth Edition* and Chapter 7 of *West's Legal Environment of Business*, has stan-dard requirements. To win under negligence, a person must show that the defendant had a duty of due care, negligently breached that duty, and that the negligence was the proximate cause of the person's injuries.

Some cases fit the standard pattern of negli-gence. For example, suppose that a hotel has a

[2]*Spiller v. Barclay Hotel*, 327 N.Y.S.2d 426 (1972).

swimming pool that is outfitted with a diving board. Because the diving board was poorly main-tained and the water was too shallow, a guest seriously injures herself. The hotel will be liable in negligence for the guest's injuries.

Rooms

A hotel generally has a responsibility to provide safe premises for its guests. This means that bath-rooms should be functioning and safe. Lighting should be adequate. Furniture, such as beds and chairs, must be safe for ordinary, foreseeable uses. In one case, a hotel was liable after a boxer injured his hand before a fight when a venetian blind collapsed on it.[3]

A hotel may also be liable in negligence for the preventable acts of others. In one famous case, the entertainer Connie Francis was raped while staying at a hotel. The rapist had entered the room through a sliding glass door that could not be effectively locked. Ms. Francis was awarded $2.5 million, because the hotel negligently failed to provide safe lodgings.[4] After appeal, the parties settled for a payment of $1.475 million.

The Connie Francis case shows how hotels can be liable for criminal acts that occur on their premises. The following decision is a more recent analysis of this cause of action.

[3]*Messina v. Sheraton Corporation of America*, 291 So.2d 829 (La. 1974).

[4]*Garzilli v. Howard Johnson's Motor Lodges, Inc.*, 419 F. Supp. 1210 (E.D.N.Y. 1976).

Case 17.1
Crinkley v.
Holiday Inns, Inc.
United States Court of Appeals,
Fourth Circuit, 1988
844 F.2d 156

Background and Facts *Sarah and James Crinkley were guests at the Holiday Inn in Concord, North Carolina. In the two weeks pre-ceding their stay, guests at several area motels had been robbed by a group called the "Motel Bandits." The motel decided not to hire addi-tional security guards but continued its program to encourage law enforcement personnel to frequent the premises by "offering a free snack tray and discount meals in the restaurant."*

Shortly after the Crinkleys checked into their room, an armed man burst inside and beat, bound and gagged James Crinkley. Sarah was threatened, bound and gagged. The robbers took their property, includ-ing her engagement ring. Eventually, Sarah Crinkley escaped her bonds and called the front desk for help.

After the police arrived, the Crinkleys were rushed to an area hospital. Mr. Crinkley suffered a broken jaw and multiple bruises.

Ms. Crinkley suffered a personality change after the assault, becoming "fearful, anxious and withdrawn." A psychiatrist diagnosed her as a victim of post-traumatic stress order. Some fourteen months after the assault, she suffered a heart attack.

The Crinkleys sued the Holiday Inn-Concord, alleging that the hotel was negligent for failing to provide adequate security, which was the proximate cause of their injuries. The jury returned a verdict awarding Sarah Crinkley $400,000 in damages and James Crinkley $100,000. The Holiday Inn appealed.

PHILLIPS, Circuit Judge.

* * * *

To prove that the special duty of care created by the circumstances was breached, the Crinkleys relied primarily on the testimony of an expert in hotel-motel security, Kenneth Prestia.

Prestia testified that security at the Holiday Inn-Concord was inadequate in several respects. The motel had widespread access from several directions, a security problem exacerbated by the fact that the front desk did not provide employees with a view of all points of access. Existing fencing was of inadequate height adequately to deter access to the premises and there were no "no trespassing" signs around the perimeter. He opined that these obvious physical measures have a deterrent effect on crime by conveying the impression that the motel maintained a heightened security posture, and that their absence therefore increased the risk of criminal activity on the premises.

Prestia also opined that there were inadequacies apart from these physical measures. The motel had not instituted a formal security plan specifically tailored to the premises and did not employ security patrols. Prestia testified that security patrols are again particularly important where there is widespread access to the motel and limited observation from the employees. On this same point, he noted that more security patrols could be added during a period of higher crime activity or an increased threat of crime, a measure that could be taken by hiring off-duty law enforcement personnel.

The defendants did not introduce any expert evidence of their own to counter Prestia's assessment of lax security at the motel. Through cross-examination, they attempted to impeach Prestia's contention that security at the motel was lax and that many of the measures he suggested would have the effect of increasing security. The defendants also attempted to portray the Holiday Inn-Concord as a quiet, safe motel that did not require the extreme security measures urged by Prestia.

Considering Prestia's testimony and the fact that Holiday Inn's own Loss Prevention Manual suggests some of the same security measures whose absence he emphasized, we think there was enough evidence for the jury reasonably to conclude that the defendants breached their duty to provide adequate security to protect their guests against the specific, known foreseeable risk created by the circumstances.

The defendants contend that, even if they breached any special duty of care owed their guests by reason of the circumstances their negligence in doing so was not the proximate cause of the assault on the Crinkleys. They make several arguments in support. First, focussing on some of the proposed security improvements—such as "no trespassing" signs and additional fencing that still left open entranceways onto the property—they argue that there is no reasonable probability that these measures would have deterred the specific assault. They point out that the Crinkleys proved no specific facts about the method of the assault that show that any of the proposed security measures might have made a difference. Finally they argue that the specific facts of this case—particularly Sarah Crinkley's admission that the first assailant did not appear suspicious and the fact that McRorie looked about the premises throughout the day of the assault, including sometime between 8:00 and 8:30 p.m.—belie the claim that added security measures, specifically patrol guards, might have detected the assailants and prevented the assault.

Defendants' argument would be persuasive if the stringent rule of proximate causation in cases of this type necessarily implied by their arguments were the rule in North Carolina. Under the rule they suggest, proximate causation between a landowner's failure to provide particular protective measures and an invitee's injury could only be established by proof that the particular measures *would* have prevented the particular injury. Such a rule has indeed been espoused by some able judges concerned that the alternative is effectively to convert landowners into insurers of their guests' safety from all criminal assaults.

* * * *

Under the less stringent test which we understand the North Carolina cases to apply, there was sufficient evidence to support the jury finding of proximate causation. The jury was entitled to accept the expert Prestia's opinions that criminals typically assess the risk of apprehension presented by the security measures in place, frequently by on-site surveillance of practices; and that the measures taken on the premises here in issue would not have acted as an effective deterrent. Having accepted this conclusion, the jury could reasonably have inferred—though surely it need not have—that the Crinkleys' assailants were indeed emboldened by the lax security measures to come on the premises, size up the situation, and plan their assault. The fact that it took some time to get the Crinkleys into their room supports the inference that the assailants were aware that security patrols were not in place.

Decision and Remedy   *The court affirmed the trial court judgment and award for the plaintiffs.*

Hotels also may be liable for failing to accommodate the needs of children as guests. In one case, an eight-month-old infant fell from a standard adult bed against hot radiator pipes and injured himself. The hotel was found liable for failure to furnish a baby crib, and the family was awarded $56,000.[5]

Common Areas

In addition to providing safe rooms, hotels also must make common areas safe. There is a long line of cases in which hotels were liable for malfunctioning elevators or hazardously maintained stairways. Restaurants are another source of potential liability. In one case, a careless waiter preparing cherries jubilee sprayed rum on a diner's shirt and then accidentally ignited it. A court awarded $80,000 for the plaintiff's burns.[6] Swimming pools are another common source of injury and liability for hotels.

A somewhat more difficult question involves guests who are injured while entering or leaving

---

[5]*Seelbach, Inc. v. Cadick*, 405 S.W.2d 745 (Ky. 1966).

[6]*Young v. Caribbean Associates, Inc.*, 358 F. Supp. 1220 (V.I. 1973).

a hotel. The general rule is that a hotel is not obligated to provide a porter or doorman to assist the guests. If such a doorman is provided, however, the hotel will be liable for his negligent actions. If a doorman injures a plaintiff trying to leave a car, the hotel may be liable.

Other cases involve guests who were assaulted and injured while in a hotel parking lot. A hotel is not necessarily liable in these cases because it is not really the cause of the injuries. If, however, the parking lot were especially dangerous (e.g., without sufficient lighting) and if previous guests had been recently assaulted in the same parking lot, the hotel may be found liable for negligent failure to protect its guests.

An important doctrine is *per se* **negligence**. This doctrine states that if the defendant hotel violates a law, it will automatically be deemed to be negligent for injuries that result. In one recent case, a hotel pool attendant sought to adjust the PH balance of the pool. Because the feeder system was inoperative, the attendant simply dumped soda ash into the pool, which made it quite cloudy. This violated state rules for pool maintenance. After a guest drowned, unseen because of the pool's cloudiness, the hotel was found to be negligent *per se*.[7]

Defenses

Hotels may take advantage of the traditional defenses to a negligence action. One important defense is **comparative negligence** (when the plaintiff was negligent in his or her actions, contributing to the injury). Suppose that a 300-pound man stands on a tiny stool in order to adjust the room's thermostat temperature. The stool collapses and and the man is injured. Comparative negligence would be a good defense for the hotel.

Another defense is **assumption of risk**. If the injured guest sees a risky course of action and still voluntarily takes it, the guest cannot recover. A guest was staying at a hotel in the French Quarter of New Orleans during Mardi Gras. Spurred on by the raucous crowd below, the guest climbed on a balcony railing and "mooned" the crowd. The guest then fell to the street and was seriously injured. The court directed a verdict for the hotel, because the plaintiff had assumed the risk.[8]

Suppose that a hotel posts a sign at its pool stating: "No Lifeguard on Duty. Swim at Your Own Risk." A poor swimmer enters the water and drowns. The guest will probably be found to have assumed the risk. There might be a different result, however, if the pool were unusually and unforeseeably hazardous or if some state law required hotels to provide lifeguards at pools when they are open to hotel guests.

Duty of Rescue

As a general rule of negligence law, a person has no duty to rescue another and cannot be liable for failure to rescue. A duty of rescue may arise, however, when the persons are in a special relationship with one another. The guest-innkeeper relationship creates at least some duty to rescue guests in danger.

Suppose that a guest enters the hotel's bar and drinks for an hour or two. Then, on the way to the bathroom, the guest falls down a stairway and seriously injures himself. The bartenders laugh at this event and fail to call for medical assistance. The bar, and the hotel that owns it, may be liable for failure to rescue the guest.

The following case illustrates the special nature of a hotel's responsibility to come to the assistance of its guests.

---

[7]*First Overseas Inv. Corp. v. Cotton*, 491 So.2d 293 (Fla. 1986).

[8]*Eldridge v. Downtowner Hotel*, 492 So.2d 64 (La. 1986).

◼ Case 17.2
Boles v.
La Quinta Motor Inns
United States Court of Appeals,
Fifth Circuit, 1982
680 F.2d 1077

Background and Facts *Jackie Boles was a guest at the La Quinta Motor Hotel in Laredo, Texas. As she opened her motel door one evening, an attacker pushed in and raped her. He then bound and gagged her and left with a threat to return and kill her. Although it was dark and she was bound, Ms. Boles managed to kick the telephone receiver off the hook and contact the front desk of the motel.*

She informed the desk clerk of her situation, after which there was a "long period of silence." Another person came to the phone and she repeated her story. She spoke to three more persons before the police were called. She then asked if someone could come down to her room and assist her. The clerk said no and asked her to hang up the telephone. She said that it was dark and she could not even find the phone. The desk clerk "sarcastically" replied: "Well, Mrs. Boles, if you don't know where the telephone is, how did you call us?"

The hotel managers then waited outside Ms. Boles room until the police arrived. She had been inside screaming for over twenty minutes, but the managers made no attempt to help, nor did they even inform her that they were outside.

Boles sued La Quinta for negligence in permitting the rape to occur and negligence in responding to her distress. The jury held that the motel was not responsible for the rape's occurrence but was liable for slowness in responding. The jury awarded Ms. Boles mental distress damages of $35,000 from the date of the attack to the date of trial, and $43,000 for future psychic damages. La Quinta appealed, challenging its liability and the damage award.

GEE, Circuit Judge.

* * * *

Under Texas law, a duty of ordinary care is owed by a hotel to its guests. *Cain v. George*, 411 F.2d 572, 573 (5th Cir. 1969); *Burrour v. Knotts*, 482 S.W. 2d 358, 360 (Tex.Civ.App.—Tyler 1972, no writ). The case of *Texas Hotel Co. v. Cosby*, 131 S.W.2d 261, 262 (Tex.Civ.App.—Texarkana 1939, writ dism'd, judgment correct), is illustrative of the theory that an innkeeper can be held liable for the manner in which he responds to a guest's peril. In the Cosby case, the plaintiff sued for personal injuries sustained in jumping from a third-story window of the defendant's building during the progress of a fire.

Among the ground for which the jury found in favor of the plaintiff was that the defendant hotel was negligent in failing to warn the plaintiff of the fire after it had been discovered and that this failure to warn was negligence and the proximate cause of the injuries. Thus, whether the defendant's employees used reasonable care in the present case is a question for the jury. It is also clear that under Texas law a restaurant or motel owner owes his invitees the duty of reasonable care to protect them from assaults by third persons while on the premises. *Eastep v. Jack-in-the-Box*, 546 S.W.2d 116, 118 (Tex. Civ.App.—Houston 1977, writ ref'd n.r.e.).

La Quinta argues, however, that the duty of ordinary care is discharged by promptly notifying the police and cites mostly barroom brawl-type cases to this effect. La Quinta argues that a reasonably prudent person would not have gone to Mrs. Boles' room and that La Quinta employees were motivated by reasonable fears for their own personal safety in refusing to do so. The problem is that there is no evidence that the hotel employees ever feared that the rapist was still in Mrs. Boles' room. In fact, the desk clerk testified that she told Mrs. Boles that she would not go to her room because she had to attend to her front desk duties, and Mrs. Boles testified that she informed the desk clerk that the rapist had left and that she was afraid that he would return. Under the Boeing standard of viewing the evidence in the light most favorable to the jury verdict, we cannot overturn the jury finding of negligent delay by La Quinta employees. The fact that three hotel employees stood outside of Mrs. Boles' room listening to her screams and moans without even calling to reassure her, combined with the callous manner in which she was treated by the desk clerk, is adequate evidence to support a finding that the motel did not use ordinary care in protecting Mrs. Boles.

La Quinta further urges that it should not be held liable because Mrs. Boles' injuries were not foreseeable to the employees. Mrs. Boles testified that the delay in getting anyone to come to her room aggravated both her physical injuries (the chafing caused by the bindings) as well as her mental anguish. La Quinta argues that its employees were not required to anticipate these "improbable" consequences. This argument is not convincing. The motel employees knew that Mrs. Boles was alone, bound in her room, fearing for her life. A reasonably prudent person would have anticipated mental anxiety and possible bodily injury resulting from the delay.

Decision and Remedy   *The court affirmed trial court award for Ms. Boles.*

Responsibility for Guest's Property

The common law made a hotel strictly liable for any loss of a guest's property through theft, loss, or otherwise. The hotel's defenses were limited to unusual circumstances, such as what the law considers an act of war or an act of God (e.g., tornado, flood). Today, all states have passed laws that limit the strict liability of hotel owners.

The state laws significantly limit the liability of the hotel industry for lost or stolen property. Exhibit 17-1 lists the maximum liability of hotels that comply with state laws. Although the limits vary by state, most are rather low.

The state statutes preserve some strict liability for the loss of clothing and necessary travel items, but limit liability for jewelry, large sums of money, and other items considered to be valuables. All states also place an absolute monetary limit on the hotel's liability, usually at a rather

low level. A hotel must meet certain statutory requirements, however, before it can take advantage of these limits on liability. If the hotel fails to meet these requirements, it will remain strictly liable for guests' losses of property.

Posting

The **posting** requirement means that guests must be made aware of their inability to recover for the loss of their valuables. This is customarily done through a card placed in the guest's room. The law requires that such posting be sufficiently conspicuous that a guest should reasonably be aware of the limits. Placing the notification of limited liability on the guest's registration statement on a very small card on the dresser is insufficiently conspicuous.

The contents of the posting also must accurately state the limitations on the hotel's liability. Posting an accurate description of the law on a

---

Exhibit 17-1

State Limits on Liability in Hotels

Alabama	$300	Montana	$500
Alaska	$300	Nebraska	$300
Arizona	$500	Nevada	$750
Arkansas	$300	New Hampshire	$1000
California	$500	New Jersey	$500
Colorado	$5000	New Mexico	$1000
Connecticut	$500	New York	$500
Delaware	Total	North Carolina	$500
Florida	$1000	North Dakota	$300
Georgia	$100	Ohio	$500
Hawaii	$500	Oklahoma	$300
Idaho	$500	Oregon	$300
Illinois	$500	Pennsylvania	none given
Indiana	$600	Rhode Island	$500
Iowa	$100	South Carolina	$300
Kansas	$250	South Dakota	$300
Kentucky	$300	Tennessee	$300
Louisiana	$100	Texas	$50
Maine	$300	Utah	$250
Maryland	$300	Vermont	$300
Massachusetts	$1000	Virginia	$500
Michigan	$250	Washington	$1000
Minnesota	$300	West Virginia	$250
Mississippi	$500	Wisconsin	$300
Missouri	none given	Wyoming	none given

---

guest room door, on a normal-sized piece of paper, has been found to be sufficient. Some laws, such as that of New York, also require posting in common areas.

Providing a Safe

Most of the state laws that limit the innkeeper's strict liability require that the hotel must provide a safe for their guests' valuables. The safe must be available to guests at all reasonable times. Some states require that the safe be available for twenty-four hours a day. The law generally protects the hotel, even if the valuables are stolen from the safe.

There are no clear-cut rules on the type of safe that is required for hotels. Some statutes specify that the safe must be fireproof. In a New York case, guests at a Manhattan luxury hotel had in their possession an extensive jewelry collection worth $1,000,000. The guests delivered their jewelry to management for deposit in safe-deposit boxes provided by the hotel. The safe-deposit boxes were contained in an ordinary room. After thieves broke in and stole the jewels, the guests sued. The court held that the hotel's safe may have been insufficient as a matter of law.[9] Had the safe been found sufficient, the guests could have recovered only $500.

Hotels may contractually agree to provide greater protection to their guests for valuables deposited in their safe. Under this procedure, guests first must declare the value of the property they place in the safe. Some hotels will refuse to insure or even accept valuables that exceed a certain value.

In addition, hotels may waive the protection of the liability limitation statute. Charging guests to insure their valuables is one example of such a waiver. Courts also may find a waiver when a hotel employee simply promises guests that the hotel will be responsible for their valuables. Consequently, it is crucial to inform employees of the hotel's practices.

Defining Valuables

Because the hotel's liability for valuables is limited, the definition of a valuable becomes important in many cases. Large amounts of money, very costly jewelry, negotiable instruments, and precious stones clearly qualify as valuables.

Disputes arise over how much money a guest should keep in his or her room and over whether functional jewelry must be deposited in a safe. Most courts have held that watches are utilitarian and are not valuables. As a consequence, the hotel will be liable for watches stolen from guest rooms. In a Washington decision, however, a court held that a watch worth $3685 was a valuable, and the guest was unable to recover for its theft from his room.

Property in Transit

A recurring problem in hospitality management law is the responsibility of hotels for valuables and other property during the time shortly before check-in or during and after check-out. As described above, the hotel's potential liability begins as soon as the parties have formed an intent to establish a guest-innkeeper relationship.

Guests at a New York hotel paid their bill and checked their luggage with a bellhop for a few hours. Unknown to the hotel, the bags contained jewelry worth over $60,000. When the guest returned, the valuable jewels were missing. The court held that the hotel's liability was limited because the retention of the luggage was a service provided for its guests, even though they had checked out.[10]

Automobiles

Eighty-five percent of all guests arrive at a hotel driving an automobile. The automobile is considered neither a "valuable" with limited liability nor "personal property" for which the hotel remains strictly liable. If a guest's automobile is stolen, the hotel's liability will depend on circumstances.

The liability of hotels for guests' loss of automobiles is usually determined under the law of **bailment**. An excellent background discussion on the general law of bailments can be found in Chapter 50 of *West's Business Law, Fifth Edition*.

There are three different legal types of bailment. A gratuitous bailment is one in which the bailee (the person taking control of the car) does so without any benefit. In a gratuitous bailment, the bailee is held to a low standard of only slight diligence. An exceptional bailment is one by which the hotel takes possession of the car solely for the hotel's benefit. In this case, the hotel will be held to a standard of very high diligence.

Most automobile cases will involve mutual-benefit bailments. The guest benefits from the ability to garage the car, and the hotel benefits by providing a service to attract guests and for which they may charge. In such a mutual-benefit bailment, the bailee is held to a standard of ordinary diligence. All bailments contain a promise to return the property to the guest on demand and to no one else.

In a Tennessee case, a guest turned his car over to a hotel bellboy to park in the hotel's lot. Later in the day, the bellboy returned to the lot, took the car for a joyride, and smashed it. Although the hotel may not have been directly negligent in this case, it was liable for permitting the car to be taken by someone other than the bailor (guest).

---

[9]*Goncalves v. Regent International Hotels*, Ltd., 460 N.Y.S. 2d 750 (1983).

[10]*Salisbury v. St. Regis-Sheraton Hotel*, 490 F. Supp. 449 (1980).

A bailment may also exist for the personal property that guests leave in the automobiles turned over to the hotel. To avoid this situation, many hotels state that they have no responsibility for any goods left in the automobile. The hotel may still be liable if its employees knowingly and explicitly accept responsibility for the goods.

A bailment exists when the hotel's employees take custody of the car and park it themselves. A bailment may also exist when the guest parks the car in a garage and receives a ticket from an attendant. A bailment will not exist, if the guest parks the car on the street outside the hotel.

Checkrooms

Hotels and restaurants typically maintain checkrooms for personal property brought into the restaurant or bar. The checkroom is a classic bailment situation and will generally be considered a mutual-benefit bailment.

Some states have laws that limit liability for checkroom losses as well. New York law provides that checkrooms can be liable for no more than $75, if the checkroom does not charge for its services. Restaurants may also post their own limitations of liability, as long as the posting is likely to be seen by patrons. Such a limitation will also fail if employees insist that a patron check a coat, for example.

Owners of checkrooms have been liable in a number of cases. On some occasions, the checkroom attendant was found to be negligent for allowing property to be stolen. More frequently, a checkroom is liable for delivering property to the incorrect patron.

What if the hotel restaurant's patron is also a guest at the hotel? Some courts have held that the statutory limitations on liability for valuables applies to checkrooms as well. This protection may require conspicuous posting in the checkroom area and may not apply if the checkroom is run by an independent contractor concessionaire rather than by the hotel itself.

Negligence and Intentional Torts

State laws clearly limit the liability of hotelkeepers sued for the traditional common law of strict liability. States are divided, however, on whether the limitations on liability protect the hotel from damages based on negligence. Many major jurisdictions, including California, New York, Florida, and Illinois apply the limited liability even to negligence.

It seems clear that the liability-limiting statutes will not apply to intentional torts by the hotel or its employees. The following case illustrates how a hotel may be liable for the intentional tort of conversion.

■ Case 17.3
Bhattal v.
Grand Hyatt-New York
United States District Court,
Southern District of New York, 1983
563 F. Supp. 277

Background and Facts   *Upon arriving at the Grand Hyatt in New York, the Bhattals turned their luggage, including valuables, over to the hotel bell captain. The luggage included pearls and other valuables worth $250,000. After checking into their room, the Bhattals went out to visit the city. On returning to their room that evening, they found their luggage missing.*

Apparently, the hotel computer erroneously instructed hotel employees to take the Bhattals' luggage from their room to JFK International Airport, along with the luggage of an aircraft crew who had been staying in the Bhattals' room at the hotel. The luggage was then placed on an airplane to Saudi Arabia. The Bhattals' bags were never recovered.

The Bhattals sued the hotel for the loss of their property worth $250,000 and for emotional distress damages. The hotel defended by using the New York statute limiting innkeeper liability for valuables.

BRIEANT, Judge.

* * * *

Here, defendant's employees entered plaintiffs' locked room, without plaintiffs' permission or knowledge, and removed their luggage, commingled it with the luggage of the Saudi Arabian aircraft crew members and placed it on a bus headed for Kennedy Airport. The Court infers that if the luggage was not stolen at Kennedy Airport, it arrived in Saudi Arabia and was eventually stolen by a Saudi thief who still had the use of at least one good hand. In this instance, the intentional acts of the defendant clearly constituted conversion under New York law.

Sections 200 and 201 of the New York General Business Law were adopted in the middle of the nineteenth century to relieve an innkeeper from his liability at common law as an insurer of property of a guest lost by theft, caused without negligence or fault of the guest. *Millhiser v. Beau Site Co.*, 251 N.Y. 290 (1929). These statutes and the cases cited thereunder by the defendant extend to the situation where there is a mysterious disappearance of valuable property, either as a result of a theft by an employee of the hotel—or a trespass or theft by an unrelated party, for whose acts the innkeeper is not responsible. The statutes are also intended to protect the innkeeper from the danger of fraud on the part of a guest in a situation where the property said to have disappeared never existed at all, or was taken or stolen by or with the privity of the guest.

* * * *

The reason for providing a hotel safe in compliance with [Section] 200 and the reason for limiting a hotel's liability under [Section] 201 is to protect against just such situations. When a hotel room is let to a guest, the innkeeper has lost a large measure of control and supervision over the hotel room and its contents. While housekeeping and security staff can enter the room at reasonable hours and on notice to any persons present therein, essentially, for most of the time at least, property of a guest which is present in a hotel room can be said to be under the exclusive dominion and control of the hotel guest, rather than the innkeeper.

We have been cited to no case extending the limited immunity provided by statute against the common law liability of innkeepers, where the liability sought to be founded on the innkeeper was based on the exercise of unlawful dominion and control by the innkeeper himself, or his agents and employees acting in the course of their employment; as contrasted with mysterious disappearances due to causes unknown, or criminal acts of third parties or employees acting for themselves rather than for the employer. As noted above, it was only for the latter class of cases that the statutes granted immunity.

* * * *

Plaintiff Mohinder Kaur Bhattal, in addition to asserting loss of valuables of the highest value, alleges extreme emotional distress. She claims (Answer to Interrogatory No. 20) that she "was visibly upset and cried for long periods of time during the week of July 19, 1981 and periodically thereafter. When plaintiff Mohinder thinks of the loss of her jewels she still becomes visibly upset and subject to crying spells. The memory of her lost jewels is a recurring trauma."

All of us who have enjoyed the benefits of civilization have memories of lost jewels of one sort or another. Plaintiff Sukhminder Singh

Bhattal alleges that he was so emotionally upset by the loss of his business effects and luggage that he had to cancel business appointments in New York and Chicago, and because the health certificates in the luggage were also lost. As a result, plaintiffs and their child were required to be vaccinated again for yellow fever and smallpox.

However, under New York law, applicable here, absent proof of malicious intent on the part of the defendant, a party cannot recover damages for mental anguish, humiliation or emotional distress caused by conversion of a chattel. *Cauverien v. DeMetz*, 188 N.Y.S.2d 627 (Sup.Ct., N.Y. Co., 1959). There is no evidence to suggest that the defendant acted maliciously or willfully in converting the luggage of the plaintiffs. The employees of the defendant acted in good faith, in reliance upon the instructions of a computer. Although the propriety of placing such blind faith in a mere piece of unthinking machinery is questionable, it is clear that the conversion of the plaintiffs' luggage was not the result of malice. Therefore, damages for mental anguish or consequential damages arising from re-vaccination, etc., allegedly suffered as a result of the conversion are not recoverable. Absent malicious conduct, the proper measure of damages for conversion is the fair market value of the converted property at the time and place of the conversion, plus interest. *Citizens National Bank v. Osetek*, 353 F.Supp. 958 (S.D.N.Y. 1973).

Decision and Remedy   *The court ruled for plaintiffs on their property claim and scheduled a hearing to determine its value..*

▰ Liability for Refusing or Evicting Guests

Under the traditional common law, innkeepers were required to accept all guests. Limited exceptions existed for circumstances such as the unavailability of rooms. The hotel might also refuse a person who is seriously intoxicated, suffering from a contagious disease, or disorderly. The hotel could also refuse a guest who was unable or unwilling to pay for the room. A restaurant could also deny service to customers for these reasons.

Federal law expressly prohibits rejecting guests on the basis of their race or sex. State laws may go further. For example, New York law prohibits hotel discrimination on the basis of handicap, marital status, and other conditions.

A refused guest may sue the hotel for wrongful refusal. The guest would be required to show that the hotel lacked a reasonable basis to refuse lodging. If the guest wins, the damages may be quite limited, such as the cab fare to another hotel. Some guests have sued for embarrassment and mental anguish resulting from the hotel's refusal, but most states do not recognize these damages in a wrongful refusal case.

In unusual circumstances, damages may be greater. If alternative hotel accommodations are unavailable, and the guests were compelled to sleep in their automobiles, a court could find more substantial actual damages and even punitive damages.

The innkeeper also has the right to evict guests with sufficient reason. Eviction for failing to pay a hotel bill is authorized. If the guest agreement provides for a specific period of stay, the hotel may also evict guests who overstay that period. A hotel also may evict those who have contagious diseases, or who are committing crimes or being disorderly, or who violate hotel regulations.

A guest can also sue for wrongful eviction, much like wrongful refusal. Some courts have awarded mental distress damages in wrongful eviction cases. Cases have even awarded punitive damages against the hotelkeeper for **wrongful eviction** when the plaintiff can show (1) a wrongful act that was (2) performed intentionally, (3) with malice or gross disregard of rights, and (4) with willfulness.

The method of eviction is also important. Hotels customarily lock the guests out of their rooms and may deny them access to their baggage. This is ordinarily a lawful means but its reasonability depends on the circumstances. A hotel could not prevent a guest from obtaining necessary medication contained in his or her luggage. Hotels may even use some force to evict guests but should take care not to employ unreasonable, excessive force.

▰ Reservations

Many hospitality management conflicts involve a guest's reservations. The traditional common law rules did not provide for reservations. Today, most experienced travelers make reservations in advance. Yet many of these travelers either cancel their reservations or never show up at the hotel. As a consequence, many hotels overbook their rooms, taking more reservations than they can accommodate. Problems arise when a hotel cannot honor its reservations.

The legal status of reservations depends in part on whether they may be considered a contract. There will generally be an offer and an acceptance when a guest makes reservations, and a number of courts have held that reservations represent a binding contract. The law allows few excuses for breach of this contract, though impossibility (e.g., a fire destroying the hotel) would be an excuse.

A guest with a reservation who is refused a room may thus sue for breach of contract. A guest may also sue if he or she receives a room that is inferior to the quality of the room reserved.

Some states also have passed statutes regulating overbooking. In Florida, for example, when a guest makes a deposit with the reservation, the hotel must provide a room. If space is unavailable, the hotel must make every effort to find alternate accommodations for the guest, must refund the deposit, and is liable of a fine of up to $500 per guest.

Most guests denied rooms do not sue the hotel. This may be due to the availability of alternative hotels and the high costs of litigation. Some guests have sued, however, and have claimed substantial damages for emotional distress. Punitive damages are generally unavailable in breach of contract claims. The following decision analyzes the damages available for failure to honor reservations.

▰ Case 17.4
Dold v. Outrigger Hotel
Supreme Court of Hawaii, 1972
501 P.2d 368

Background and Facts   *Mr. and Mrs. Dold made a confirmed reservation with the Outrigger Hotel in Hawaii. The reservation was confirmed with the Dolds' American Express Card and a guarantee to pay for one night. When the Dolds arrived, the Outrigger was overbooked, and the hotel referred them to the less expensive Pagoda Hotel. These referrals were common and the Outrigger made a profit on them.*

The Dolds sued the Outrigger for breach of contract and for breach of innkeepers' duty. The Dolds sought damages for mental distress and punitive damages. The trial judge held that the Dolds could recover for mental distress but not for punitive damages. The jury awarded the Dolds $600. They appealed the denial of the possibility of punitive damages.

KOBAYASHI, Justice.

*   *   *   *

The question of whether punitive damages are properly recoverable in an action for breach of contract has not been resolved in this jurisdiction.

In the instant case, on the evidence adduced, the trial court refused to allow an instruction on the issue of punitive damages but permitted an instruction on the issue of emotional distress and disappointment.

In a case involving a similar pattern of overbooking of reservations the court in *Wills v. Trans World Airlines, Inc.*, 200 F.Supp.360 (S.D.Cal. 1961), stated that the substantial overselling of confirmed reservations for the period in question was a strong indication that the defendant airline had wantonly precipitated the very circumstances which compelled the removal of excess confirmed passengers from its flights.

* * * *

We are of the opinion that the facts of this case do not warrant punitive damages. However, the plaintiffs are not limited to the narrow traditional contractual remedy of out-of-pocket losses alone. We have recognized the fact that certain situations are so disposed as to present a fusion of the doctrines of tort and contract. Goo, supra, 52 Haw. at 241, 473 P.2d at 567. Though some courts have strained the traditional concept of compensatory damages in contract to include damages for emotional distress and disappointment (*Kellogg v. Commodore Hotel*, 64 N.Y.S.2d 131 (Sup.Ct. 1946), we are of the opinion that where a contract is breached in a wanton or reckless manner as to result in a tortious injury, the aggrieved person is entitled to recover in tort. Thus, in addition to damages for out-of-pocket losses, the jury was properly instructed on the issue of damages for emotional distress and disappointment.

Decision and Remedy   *The court affirmed the judgment of the trial court.*

Larger damages, including punitive damage awards, can result if the hotel has willfully insulted or abused the guest. This action could involve intentional infliction of emotional distress or defamation.

A New York doctor and his wife, who was recovering from surgery, made reservations for a three-week stay at a Caribbean hotel. They missed the first night because of a snowstorm that prevented plane travel. When they arrived, the hotel denied them a room for more than two nights. The doctor and his wife were unable to find alternative accommodations and were unable even to get on a plane flight back to New York. Eventually, they had to fly to another island and book a ship back home. A jury awarded them $15,000 in damages, though they eventually settled for $6000.[11]

Damages may be much greater in the circumstance of a convention or group travel. A travel agent promoted a group tour of Hawaii and featured a specific hotel for its customers. Although the hotel had confirmed reservations, it refused to honor them. In an unreported decision, a jury awarded the travel agent over $150,000 in damages for harm to their reputation. Another decision awarded approximately $70,000 in damages when a Las Vegas hotel failed to honor a tour group reservation.[12]

When reservations are a contract, they also bind the guest. If the guest fails to arrive, or checks out before the assigned date, the guest may be liable to the hotel. A traveler unable to abide by a reservation should promptly inform the hotel of this fact. Under contract rules, the hotel is bound to attempt to rent the room to another. If the hotel is successful, it has suffered no damages and must refund any deposit to the traveler.

If the guest does not honor the reservation and makes no effort to inform the hotel, the

---

[11]*Scher v. Liberty Travel Service*, 328 N.Y.S. 2d 386 (1971).

[12]*Cardinal Consulting Co. v. Circo Resorts, Inc.*, 297 N.W. 2d 260 (Minn. 1980).

hotel could treat the deposit as its damages. If there was no deposit, the hotel will have to sue the guest for nonperformance. The small amount in question generally makes such litigation pointless. For conventions or group bookings, however, the hotel may benefit from suing over the failure to honor reservations.

In practice, most reservations are made over the telephone and guaranteed by giving the hotel a credit card number. The hotel usually tells the guest a deadline by which to cancel the reservation (usually the day before). If the guest fails to show up and did not inform the hotel by the stated deadline, the hotel may charge the guest's credit card for the cost of one night's stay.

Rights of Guests

In addition to the above rights to sue for dishonor of reservations, property loss, and personal injury, guests have some specific common law rights in hotels. Two such traditional rights are those of courtesy and privacy.

Longstanding precedent requires that an innkeeper treat a guest in a respectful and courteous manner. A guest may sue if subjected to uncivil and abusive treatment at the hands of the hotel employees. Such behavior may give rise to damages for mental distress or loss of reputation.

A guest also has some right of privacy in a hotel room. As a consequence of this rule, the hotel has a duty not to allow third parties access to its guests' rooms. The right is not absolute, however, and the innkeeper retains a right of access to the room. Occasional entries are allowed as necessary for the discharge of the duties of maids, etc.

The hotelkeeper also may enter a guest's room due to a suspicion of criminal activity. The hotelkeeper is not a government agent and is not bound by the requirements of a warrant prior to a search. In addition, the hotelkeeper may request police accompaniment on such an entry to investigate possible criminal behavior, but any police search is limited in the absence of a warrant.

If the entry is instigated by the police, however, the guest retains constitutional protection against warrantless search and seizure. Although the hotelkeeper may use a master key to provide the police access to a guest room, the hotel cannot consent to the search on behalf of the guest. The police must abide by constitutional limits that prohibit unreasonable searches and most warrantless searches. Once the person is no longer a guest of the hotel (e.g., his reserved stay is over), the person may lose these privacy protections.

Rights of Innkeepers

Much of this chapter has focused on the rights of guests, but hotels have rights as well. The paramount right of the innkeeper is the right to be compensated.

The right of compensation is essentially one of contract law. The hotelkeeper has a legal right to whatever price the parties agreed upon. Many hotels use standard rates, and there may be some confusion about the agreed-upon price for the rooms. To avoid this problem many states have enacted laws that require innkeepers to post their rates and charges in every guest room and in certain common areas. The hotel may also charge for extra services (such as telephone calls) but must inform the guest of this charge in advance.

Because hotels deal with travelers from many distant points, the hotels may have an especially difficult time enforcing the duty of compensation. To help ameliorate this problem, state law has created the *innkeeper's lien*.

The innkeeper's lien essentially provides that the hotel has a right to all the goods that the guest brings into the hotel, up to the value of the charges due the hotel. The lien covers virtually all kinds of property (including automobiles and securities left in a safe-deposit box) and enables the innkeeper to take possession of a guest's luggage, for example, pending payment of the guest's bill.

The lien arises as soon as the guest arrives and any charges are incurred. The hotel loses its lien as soon as it voluntarily delivers these goods to the guest. The guest's payment of the bill also ends the lien.

In addition to the hotel's civil remedies, every state has passed a law that makes it a crime to defraud an innkeeper. As an example, Massachusetts law provides for a maximum of two years in prison for defrauding an innkeeper of more than $100 in goods and services and also allows an innkeeper to detain persons that they reasonably believe to have committed such a fraud. Because fraud is a criminal act, a conviction under these laws requires proof of intent to defraud on the part of the guest.

The hotel also has the right to establish reasonable rules for the establishment. The most controversial hotel rules involve those that bar non-guests from the premises. A hotel may exclude "undesirables," such as known criminals. Hotels may also exclude solicitors, even including religious groups that are soliciting members or contributions.

Licensing and Regulation of Hotels

Most cities and states require a license to operate a hotel. State and local building codes also generally require permits or certificates of occupancy before a hotel may operate. Hotels may also require licenses for specific activities such as food and liquor service. Failure to obtain the proper license will prevent the hotel from charging guests. In addition, a license may be revoked if the hotel operates unlawfully.

Many state and local hotel regulation statutes require the hotels to maintain guest registers and keep them for up to three years. The register may be used as an investigatory tool for law enforcement. Private persons may also want to examine the register, but the hotel should obtain the guest's consent before permitting such an examination.

Hotels are also affected by credit regulations. The federal Truth-in-Lending Act requires that hotels provide credit card customers with information on the procedures for disputing billing charges of the hotel. State laws can prevent a hotel from doing a credit check on a guest without first informing the guest and later informing the guest of any adverse outcome of the check.

Various public health and safety laws also govern hotels. Building codes regulate the manner in which buildings may be constructed and operated. Rules applicable to hotels may be especially strict with respect to maximum capacity regulations and required exits.

Hotels also are subject to many federal, state and local fire safety requirements. After the disastrous MGM Grand Hotel fire in Las Vegas in 1981, the county adopted a stringent code for high-rise hotels that required that sprinkler systems be installed in every room and in all exit corridors. Many states and localities require smoke detectors throughout hotels. Violation of these codes can invoke criminal penalties against the hotel or its owner.

Public health laws further regulate other aspects of hotel management. State laws set cleanliness standards for hotel linens and towels and may even prescribe the number of these items that must be provided guests. Hotel swimming pools are highly regulated in many jurisdictions.

Licensing and Regulation of Restaurants

Food and alcohol service is extensively regulated by states and municipalities. Federal and state rules attempt to prevent service of unwholesome food. Civil law also applies to these cases. A woman at a Bermuda hotel sued when she ate a croissant that contained slivers of glass, which caused bleeding when she swallowed it.

Alcohol service is licensed by the states. These licensing laws generally restrict the hours of sale, require maintenance of certain books and records, and prohibit service of alcoholic beverages to intoxicated persons or minors.

Many states also have **dram shop laws**, which statutorily authorize a suit against a server of alcohol. Under these laws, if a person is injured by a drunken person, the injured individual may sue the bar or restaurant that caused the drunkenness. The dram shop laws do not make the bar strictly liable. Most of these dram shop laws limit liability to injuries resulting from the sale of alcohol to a person who is visibly intoxicated or known to be a habitual drunkard.

A new generation of laws imposes additional requirements on restaurants. Many states and localities now require restaurants to maintain a nonsmoking section. Some states require owners to post diagrams or instructions on how to aid a choking victim. A number of states have **truth-in-menu laws** prohibiting the misrepresentation of the identity of food items offered.

Hotel and restaurant owners also must comply with a myriad of more general government regulations. Significant examples of these include employment laws, antitrust laws, consumer protection laws, trademark laws, tax laws and others. These laws are discussed elsewhere in this book, in *West's Business Law, Fifth Edition*, and in *West's Legal Environment of Business*.

Ethics and Overbooking

Overbooking occurs when the hotel makes more reservations than it has rooms available. At first glance, overbooking seems unethical. If a guest with a reservation must be turned away, the hotel has violated an obligation of promise keeping. The hotel may also greatly inconvenience the guest, because alternative accommodations may be unavailable, inferior, too costly, or in an inconvenient location.

A case can be made for overbooking. Consider the Concord Resort Hotel in the Caribbean. The Concord may know from experience that only 80 percent of the guests who make reservations actually arrive at the hotel. While in theory the Concord might sue the remaining 20 percent for breach of contract, it is too costly to pursue the responsible parties in courts all over the world.

Suppose that the Concord does not overbook and never reserves more than 100 percent of its rooms. This means that, on average, the Concord will be 20 percent unoccupied. The lowered occupancy rate will mean that the Concord will have to charge guests a higher rate in order to make a profit. If the Concord overbooked, the hotel could maintain a higher occupancy rate and charge less or offer better services. Everyone, including the average guest, would be better off with overbooking.

In a situation such as that of the Concord, the mere act of overbooking should not be considered unethical. This is especially true if the Concord is careful in its overbooking, and does not exceed 115 percent of capacity. If so, very few, if any, reserved guests should be denied a room. The overbooking simply compensates for the guests who fail to keep their reservation.

There remains an ethical problem, however, on those occasions when a greater-than-expected number of reserved guests arrive and some must be turned away for lack of rooms. The Concord has broken its promise to these potential guests and may have caused them harm.

Perhaps the Concord should adopt a policy of providing extensive assistance to reserved guests who cannot be accommodated. The Concord could itself arrange alternate rooms of equal or superior quality. The Concord might itself make up any difference in cost or provide special services to these individuals. In addition to helping fulfill the hotel's ethical responsibilities, these practices should breed good will.

The hotel probably has one other ethical obligation. It should inform potential guests of its practice of overbooking at the time that they make a reservation. In this way, the guests better understand the risks they take, even after reserving a room.

International Hospitality Management Law

International travel is a multibillion-dollar business. Hospitality management law largely depends on the law of the nation in which the hotel is located. For example, if a British tourist brings securities worth $100,000 and has them stolen from his or her hotel room, New York law will limit the guest's recovery to $500. If a New York tourist loses $100,000 in securities at a London hotel, however, the hotelkeeper will be strictly liable for *all* of his or her damages. There are some common themes in international hospitality management law, however.

As to guests' loss of property, the common law nations of the British Commonwealth make the hotel strictly liable for the losses. European civil law nations (such as Germany, France and Italy) also provide for strict innkeeper liability, but these nations have adopted liability limitations similar to those in the United States.

With respect to personal injuries, most nations (including the United States, the United Kingdom, and Italy) adopt a negligence standard for innkeeper liability. Some countries, such as Germany, hold the innkeeper strictly liable for injuries to guests caused by defects on the premises.

On the issue of reservations, hotels in popular destinations (such as the Caribbean and Europe) typically require significant advance deposits and therefore tend to do less overbooking. When overbooking does occur and a reserved guest is turned away, these nations provide little recourse for the guest. Germany is an exception, making overbooking illegal and subject to significant monetary penalties.

The International Institute for the Unification of Private Law (UNIDROIT) has adopted a Draft Convention on the Hotelkeeper's Contract in an attempt to make international hospitality management law consistent. Although this Convention has not yet been adopted, its terms offer some guidance on a possible future international law of hospitality management.

The UNIDROIT Convention would impose strict liability on the hotelkeeper for property losses but would limit liability for valuables to an amount within the range of 500 to 1000 times the daily room rate, if the hotel posts this limit and provides a safe. The Convention makes the hotel liable for injuries caused by its negligence but permits the hotel to limit its liability in other circumstances. The Draft Convention would also make the hotelkeeper liable for any damage that a guest may suffer because of the hotel's failure to honor reservations.

Questions and Case Problems

1. The assistant manager of the Hyatt Regency was given a briefcase (closed but unlocked) that was found in the main lobby. He opened the briefcase to search for identification and found a wallet plus large bundles of money. When a person came to claim the briefcase, the manager demanded identification, and the individual said that his identification was in his wallet. The conversation became agitated, and the manager paged the hotel's security personnel, who were off-duty police officers. The security personnel opened the briefcase to get out the wallet and discovered a bag of marijuana. The guest was arrested and claims that the discovery of the marijuana was the result of an illegal search. Should the court exclude the marijuana as the result of an illegal search? [*Berger v. State*, 257 S.E.2d 8 (Ga. 1979)].

2. The Roosevelt Motor Lodge had forty rooms on the ground level. After showering, a woman guest of the lodge left the window open, covered only by a screen that could not be locked. An intruder broke into her room through the open window, raped her, and stole some of her property. She sued the motor lodge for damages from her injuries. Should she recover from the lodge? [*Brewer v. Roosevelt Motor Lodge*, 295 A.2d 647 (Me. 1972)].

3. Robert, a business student seeking a job, was running late for a hiring reception being given by a company. He gave his car keys to the valet for parking after taking off his class ring and putting it into the glove compartment. Rushing into the reception room, Robert tossed his new cashmere overcoat on top of a rack that the hiring company had placed outside the reception room. After the reception, Robert returned to the coat rack to discover that his coat was missing. When he obtained his car from valet parking, he found that his ring was missing. Robert sued the hotel for the loss of his coat and his ring. Should he be able to recover from the hotel?

4. Andrea, a sales representative, was running late for her plane to her next sales destination. Running off the elevator, she flagged a bellboy to take her bag, which contained her presentation and samples. When she came out to the taxi stand, she discovered that her bag was missing. She sued the hotel for the loss of her bag. Should the hotel be held responsible for Andrea's damages?

5. Members of the Jehovah's Witnesses religion entered the Endicott Hotel and went down the hotel's corridors, knocking on doors. They sought to give hotel guests literature on their religion. Contributions were not actively solicited but were encouraged and accepted. They conducted this activity as quietly as possible. The hotel manager had received no complaints but nevertheless asked the Jehovah's Witnesses to cease their activities. They invoked their constitutional rights and refused to leave the hotel. The hotel then called the police, which forcibly evicted the Jehovah's Witnesses. After they attempted to re-enter the hotel, they were arrested and prosecuted for disorderly conduct. Was the eviction proper and are the Jehovah's Witnesses guilty? [*People v. Thorpe*, 101 N.Y.S.2d 986 (1950)].

CHAPTER EIGHTEEN

Communications Law

KEY BACKGROUND

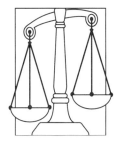

Mass communications form a substantial portion of the modern United States economy. Newspapers, television, radio and other media do a growing, multibillion-dollar business. Moreover, the effects of these media influence political campaigns and individual lives. A special area of law has grown up around mass communications. Television and radio broadcasts are regulated by the Federal Communications Commission (FCC). In addition, all media are affected by potential liability arising from their entertainment and news reports.

Federal Communications Commission Regulation

The federal government's regulation of mass communications began early in the twentieth century with rules for the use of wireless radio by ships at sea. The need for broader regulation became clear with the first commercial radio broadcast, on November 2, 1920. The government's limited authority was unable to avoid chaotic interference on radio airwaves. Some rule was necessary to allocate frequencies for broadcasters.

Congress responded to this need by passing the Federal Communications Act of 1934. This law created and empowered the Federal Communications Commission. Originally, the Commission allocated frequencies for the exclusive use of licensed broadcasters but concerned itself little with broadcast content. In 1939, however, the World Series was broadcast by the Mutual Broadcasting System. Communities that lacked an affiliate of Mutual were denied any radio coverage of the series. The resultant outcry prodded the Commission to expand its regulation into issues of market power and broadcast content.

The modern FCC is organized into a number of bureaus. The two most significant bureaus are:

1. Mass media—dealing with commercial broadcasting and cable radio and television.

2. Common carrier—dealing with telephone, telegraph, facsimile and related communications.

Other bureaus deal with other communications applications, such as the private radio, which regulates police and industrial band transmissions. Each bureau has unique powers over its own special type of communications.

In general, the FCC has a very broad grant of regulatory authority. The preamble to the 1934 Act states that the Commission shall regulate communications "as public convenience, interest, or necessity requires." This has been interpreted to permit regulation when the "public interest" so dictates.

Spectrum Allocation

One of the most important powers of the FCC is the allocation of broadcast spectrum among the various types of communication. Television or radio stations broadcast at a given frequency (actually a number of electromagnetic oscillations per second). There is a continuum, or spectrum, of possible frequencies for communications. Because the length of the spectrum is limited, the FCC must apportion the spectrum among the various types of communications.

Under its "block" allocation system, the Commission estimates the amount of spectrum required for a particular communications service and accordingly devotes a portion of the spectrum for that service. Thus, the Commission allocates a certain portion of the spectrum for AM radio, FM radio, VHF television, UHF television, private radio services, and other uses. This allocation is to respond to the public's need for these varied types of communications.

The FCC has been criticized for being slow to respond to public needs for new communications services. In response, the Commission increasingly uses "flexible use" allocation. For example, the Commission has taken a portion of the UHF television band and permitted its use for land mobile communications (e.g., cellular car phones). The use of this spectrum in any given locality will depend in part upon the market demand for the competing services.

Licensing

Another critical role for the FCC is in the licensing of stations to broadcast at a given frequency.

An FCC license is a legal requirement for broadcasting. License holders also must have their license renewed periodically (seven years for a radio license, five years for a television license). Most broadcast licenses are quite lucrative and there is often intense competition for this right to broadcast. The FCC conducts a hearing among competitors and uses a defined list of criteria to select which applicant will receive the desired license. These criteria are listed in Exhibit 18-1 and summarized below.

Licensing standards   Some of the standards for licensing a broadcast station are straightforward. For example, a licensee must be a *citizen* of the United States. If the licensee is a corporation, no more than 25 percent of its ownership may be foreign. Another standard is that the applicant make a *technical showing* of qualifications. The applicant thus must show that it intends to broadcast with equipment approved by the Commission and operate within the FCC's technical rules for broadcasting. A third standard is *financial qualifications*. An applicant must have the capital necessary to construct and operate the proposed station or to continue its operations if a renewal is being requested.

Other licensing standards are less clear and subject to greater dispute among applicants. For example, the applicant must have **good character**; a license applicant is likely to be denied if he or she has been convicted of a felony, especially if that conviction involved fraud. This is

---

Exhibit 18-1

Criteria for Broadcast Licenses

- Citizenship
- Showing of technical qualifications
- Showing of financial qualifications
- Good character
- Diversity of ownership
- Minority ownership
- Ascertainment of community needs
- Programming quality

not an absolute bar to ownership, however. One applicant was granted a license even though he had a past conviction for running guns to Israel.[1] The FCC also considers the applicant's candor and honesty in the application process.

Diversity of media ownership is also a standard used in broadcast licensing decisions. The Commission has rules to prevent any single entity from dominating media outlets in a community. These rules impose three restrictions:

1. No single entity can own more than one station in the same service (e.g., television) in one single community.

2. No single entity can own more than twelve AM radio stations, twelve FM radio stations, and twelve television stations (a total of thirty-six) within the United States.

3. The owners of daily newspapers may not own AM radio, FM radio, or television stations in the community served by the newspaper.

Even if these rules are met, the Commission will still make comparative judgments of diversity among competing applicants in choosing which applicant should receive the license.

The Commission also considers **minority ownership** in granting broadcast licenses. Minority-owned applicants get some preference in licensing. Minority owners receive an "enhancement." If Station A and Station B are otherwise equal, but Station A is owned by African-Americans, A is likely to receive the license. In addition, all stations must undertake affirmative action programs so as better to represent minority groups among the station's officers and managers, technicians and salespersons.

The final criteria for choosing a licensee are **community ascertainment** and **programming**. Potential broadcasters must familiarize themselves with the needs and problems of the community they seek to serve. Then, the applicant must propose programming that is responsive to the local needs. While programming standards were greatly relaxed during the 1980s, the broadcaster still must demonstrate that its programming will be in the "public interest." The FCC has denied a license renewal due to defamatory and racist programming.

Hearings The FCC will hold a contested hearing and seek to determine which applicant best meets the above criteria. In such a hearing, the parties can present the case for their application, as opposed to the other applications. No one standard is clearly more important than others. The Commission's choice is based on which applicant will provide the "best practicable service" to the public.[2]

A station that is up for license renewal is often awarded **renewal expectancy**. This is a bonus for existing stations and may enable them to keep their station, even as against challengers with somewhat better applications. Renewal expectancy was adopted to encourage stations to invest more in quality service and because incumbents have a proven track record.

Renewal expectancy is not automatically granted for an incumbent station, however. The station must demonstrate that it has engaged in quality programming. The following case discusses the requirements of license renewal.

---

[1]*Las Vegas Television, Inc.,* 14 R.R. 1273 (1957).

[2]1 F.C.C.2d 393 (1965).

■■ Case 18.1
Monroe Communications Corporation v. Federal Communications Commission
District of Columbia Circuit Court of Appeals, 1990
900 F.2d 351

Background and Facts *Video 44 sought a renewal of its license to operate station WSNS-TV in Chicago, Illinois. Monroe Communications Corporation challenged for the right to the license. Video 44 had converted the traditional television station to a subscription television service. Video 44 transmitted various nationally syndicated programs, including a substantial number of adult films that contained nudity and offensive language.*

An Administrative Law Judge at the FCC ruled that the license should be awarded to Monroe. On appeal, the FCC overturned the judge

and ruled that Video 44 was entitled to the renewal expectancy bene-
fit. The Commission also held that the renewal expectancy was suffi-
cient to outweigh any advantages of Monroe's application. The
Commission refused to consider allegations that Video 44 had obscene
and indecent programming. Monroe appealed this FCC ruling to fed-
eral court.

SENTELLE, Circuit Judge.

* * * *

An incumbent applicant may be entitled to a renewal expectancy if its performance during the preceding license term has been "substantial," meaning "sound, favorable and substantially above a level of mediocre service which might just minimally warrant renewal." *Cowles II*, 86 F.C.C.2d at 1006 (quoting *Cowles Florida Broadcasting, Inc.*, 62 F.C.C.2d 953, 955-56 (1977). In deciding whether to award a renewal expectancy, the Commission focuses on non-entertainment programming broadcast by the station, including news, public affairs, and public service announcements. *See, e.g., Radio Station WABZ, Inc.*, 90 F.C.C.2d 818, 840-42 (1982), *aff'd sub nom. Victor Broadcasting, Inc. v. FCC*, 722 F.2d 756 (D.C.Cir. 1983). A licensee is expected to ascertain and respond to community needs and problems in its non-entertainment programming in order to earn a renewal expectancy.

* * * *

Had the Commission properly weighted the station's performance following its conversion to STV format, it may well not have awarded Video 44 a renewal expectancy. The Commission found that through the full final year of its license term Video 44 offered .08 percent news, 2.57 percent public affairs, and only 5.84 percent other non-entertainment programming. *Video 44 III*, 4 F.C.C. Rcd. at 1210. These figures place Video 44 near the bottom of the pack, relative to other Chicago stations, in terms of news, public affairs, and other non-entertainment programming. By the very end of its license period, Video 44 had scaled back its non-entertainment programming to five hours per week and had discontinued local production. Given that the license expectancy analysis focuses on the incumbent licensee's responsiveness to the ascertained problems and needs of its community, *Simon Geller*, 90 F.C.C.2d at 271, the Commission was arbitrary in awarding Video 44 a renewal expectancy in light of record evidence of a strong downward trend in Video 44's responsiveness to community needs in the form of news and non-entertainment programming.

* * * *

We agree that the Commission should not be required to investigate every generalized complaint alleging that a broadcaster offers obscene programming. However, to require ordinary citizens to, in the first instance, set forth allegations constituting a prima facie case of obscenity, as defined in *Miller v. California*, 413 U.S. at 24, 93 S.Ct. at 2615, is arbitrary. For instance, among the complaints the Commission declined to consider in its renewal expectancy analysis was a timely letter from a Chicago resident who reported being shocked to see a broadcast by Video 44 clearly depicting adults engaged in sexual acts.

* * * *

To ignore this citizen complaint in the license renewal proceedings, without at least learning more about the broadcast, because the complaint did not make out a legally sufficient claim of obscenity was arbitrary.

Decision and Remedy *The court remanded the case to the FCC and directed the Commission to consider the downward trend in Video 44's non-entertainment programming and the evidence of obscene broadcasts.*

Sometimes, a party may argue that no applicant should be licensed for a new station. For example, in *Federal Communications Commission v. Sanders Bros. Radio Station,*[3] a station owner opposed a new broadcast station in a city by arguing that local advertising could not support more stations. The Supreme Court held that the Commission could consider the community's ability to support another station but emphasized that the Act was intended to protect the public, not the revenues of incumbent licensees.

The public also may participate in licensing proceedings and petition for the denial of a license to a particular broadcaster. In 1966, a federal court ruled that African-Americans in Mississippi had a right to challenge the license renewal of a station in Jackson for biased and unfair programming.

The FCC has considerable discretion in the licensing process and has been criticized for arbitrariness. One interesting case involved a non-commercial FM radio station in Seattle that was up for license renewal. The station devoted some programming to the 1960's "counterculture" including programs by Lenny Bruce, William Kunstler and others. The FCC criticized the station's broadcast of occasional obscene words. The FCC granted only an abbreviated one-year license renewal. Unsurprisingly, the station eliminated its unconventional programming and eventually obtained a standard seven-year renewal.

In 1971, the FCC became concerned about the lyrics of popular songs that allegedly glorified the use of drugs. The Commissioner provided stations with a "do-not-play" list of objectionable songs, including "Lucy in the Sky with Diamonds" by the Beatles and "Mr. Tambourine Man" by Bob Dylan. The Commission soon revoked this list in response to public outcry.

Broadcasting Regulations

The FCC has adopted a series of rules to regulate broadcasting programs. Regulation of mass media program content obviously raises First Amendment issues. The Supreme Court has granted the FCC considerable constitutional authority over programming, however. This is based on the theory that the broadcast spectrum is limited, or scarce, and the government has a right to control its use.

Equal time One broadcasting programming rule is the equal time rule. This provides that a station that permits a candidate for office to use the station must also provide an equal opportunity for all other candidates for that office.

The equal time rule applies only when a candidate personally appears on a program. The use also must be significant. For example, suppose that Martha Sobel, a candidate for attorney general, makes a three-second introduction to a program on which her supporters appear and urge her election. Because Ms. Sobel herself appeared for such a brief time, the equal time rule would not be invoked for her competitors.

The FCC has several exceptions for its equal time rule. The rule does not apply when a candidate appears in a bona fide newscast or in live coverage of bona fide news events, including political conventions. Under the latter rule, a station can broadcast a privately sponsored debate between candidates as a news event, without having to give equal time to candidates who did not participate in the debate.

The exemptions to the equal time rule have provoked litigation at the FCC and in court over the type of programs exempt. The following case involves a debate over the definition of an exempted "bona fide newscast."

---

[3]309 U.S. 470 (1940).

■ **Case 18.2**
In Re Request of Oliver Productions, Inc.
Federal Communications
Commission, 1989
4 F.C.C. Rcd 5953

Background and Facts *Oliver Productions, Inc. is the producer of a show called "The McLaughlin Group." This show involves a debate among a panel of political commentators. A typical program consists of four to six issues discussed by the panel. Each issue is usually introduced by a videotaped newsclip. These newsclips occasionally contain an interview with or speech by a candidate for political office. Oliver Productions sought a Commission ruling that the program was a "bona fide newscast" and exempt from the equal time requirements of the Communications Act. In November 1988, the FCC's Mass Media Bureau ruled that the program was a bona fide newscast.*

In December 1988, the Telecommunications Research and Action Center ("TRAC") filed a petition for review with the full Federal Communications Commission. TRAC argued that the McLaughlin Group was not a bona fide newscast that could be exempted from the equal time provisions of the Communications Act.

By the Commission.

* * * *

Although the legislative history is vague as to the meaning of "newscast," it does emphasize a congressional intent to increase news coverage of political campaigns, to give broadcasters great deference in making reasonable news programming judgments, and to give the Commission flexibility and discretion in interpreting the exemptions and in applying them to particular program formats in order to further the basic purpose of increased political information to the public. As the court stated in affirming the Commission decision to exempt debates and press conferences:

> In creating a broad exemption to the equal time requirements in order to facilitate broadcast coverage of political news, Congress knowingly faced risks of political favoritism by broadcasters, and opted in favor of broader coverage and increased broadcaster discretion. Rather than enumerate specific exempt and nonexempt uses, Congress opted in favor of legislative generality preferring to assign that task to the Commission.

Chisholm v. FCC, 538 F.2d 349, 366 (1976).

* * * *

9.   We believe the Bureau was correct in its finding that the "news reporting segments" of "The McLaughlin Group" satisfy the criteria necessary for the newscast exemption under Section 315 (a) (1). Regarding the "bona fide" requirement, there is no information before the Commission to indicate that the "news reporting segments" are selected for reasons other than their genuine news value or are designed to advance or harm any particular candidacy. Further, in terms of format, the segments in question are presented to inform the public of major national and world events and the news reports are presented in a conventional newscast manner. The Bureau also noted that the Commission and the Bureau have, on several occasions, granted news interview exemptions to segments of programs which contain bona fide news interviews. See *Multimedia Entertainment, Inc.*, 56 RR 2d 143, 148 (1984) ("Donahue"); *CBS, Inc.*, 2 FCC Rcd 4377 (M.M. Bur. 1987) ("The Morning Program"); *CBS, Inc.*, 55 RR 2d 864 (M.M. Bur. 1984) ("The American

Parade"). While the Commission has not, to date, exempted newscast segments of otherwise nonexempt programs, the Commission has recognized in applying Section 315 that programs may include various segments, including exempt news segments. See *ABC, Inc.*, 46 RR 2d 1205 (1980) ("Good Morning America"); *Lar Daly*, 40 FCC 314 (1960) ("Today"). Thus, the Bureau correctly stated that as long as the brief reports of current news stories on "The McLaughlin Group" are distinct segments and the purpose is not to advance or harm any candidacies, those segments should be accorded the bona fide newscast exemption. We also agree with the Bureau that its ruling was consistent with the statutory objective of increasing the news coverage of political campaign activity.

Decision and Remedy   *The Federal Communications Commission held that the Bureau's decision was correct and denied TRAC's petition.*

While stations may be compelled to provide equal time for candidates, they are not allowed to censor or even regulate what candidates say. Some Georgia stations sought to withhold spot announcements by a local candidate who proclaimed himself a "white racist" and spoke demeaningly of African-Americans. The Commission ruled that the stations could not boycott the material.[4]

FCC rules also require stations to provide political candidates with "reasonable access" to their stations' broadcasts. While stations have some flexibility regarding what access is reasonable, the Commission requires that time be offered on a basis comparable to that offered commercial advertisers. Suppose that station WRES decides that short ten-second political advertisements are misleading to voters and refuses to carry them. This restriction is unlawful if WRES permits ten-second advertisements for commercial products. Stations cannot impose significantly stricter rules for political ads.

For many years, the FCC also used the "Fairness Doctrine" to regulate broadcasting. This required that broadcasters provide balanced coverage of controversial public issues and campaigns. In 1987, the Commission abolished this rule on the grounds that it conflicted with the First Amendment. Congress has sought to reinstitute the Fairness Doctrine but has not yet succeeded.

A final broadcast programming standard prohibits "obscene" or "indecent" programs. The definition of obscenity or indecency depends in part on whether children are likely to be part of the program's audience. Even if children are not expected to be part of the audience, questionable programming must be preceded by a warning to listeners.

Except for the above circumstances, the FCC generally avoids control over programming. For example, the Commission generally does not concern itself with a station's format. In the 1970s, the owner of a Chicago station wanted to change its format from classical music to rock-and-roll. A citizen group petitioned the FCC to halt this change, but the Commission refused to intervene in this type of dispute.

Common Carrier Regulation

A second major form of FCC communications regulations involves common carriers. The Supreme Court has defined a common carrier as one that "makes a public offering to provide [communications facilities] whereby all members of the public who choose to employ such facilities may communicate or transmit intelligence of their own design and choosing."[5] The best known common carriers are the telephone and telegraph systems.

---

[4]*Letter to Lonnie King*, 36 F.C.C.2d 635 (1972).

[5]*Federal Communications Commission v. Midwest Video Corp.*, 440 U.S. 689, 701 (1979).

The key legal principle of a common carrier is that it provides service to everyone on an equal basis. Accordingly, a common carrier exercises no control over the content of the messages that it transmits. Thus, the phone company does not regulate the content of telephone conversations.

The Federal Communications Commission exercises very little content control over messages transmitted over common carriers. The Commission does prohibit the advertising of cigarettes over any common carrier. The Commission also has regulated "dial-a-porn" services to prevent their access to minors. Obscene or fraudulent telephone calls are also illegal.

The primary FCC regulation involves the duties and liabilities of common carriers. The Communications Act imposes a duty on common carriers to provide service to any party "upon reasonable request."[6] The common carrier also must provide this service at rates that are "just and reasonable" and without "unreasonable preference or advantage" to any party using the carrier.[7] The FCC regulates common carriers by requiring them to submit "tariffs" to the Commission for approval. Tariffs are schedules of rates and rules for offering service. The Commission also regulates mergers and prohibits foreign ownership of common carriers in the United States.

---

[6]47 U.S.C. Section 201(a) (1982).
[7]42 U.S.C. Section 201(b), 202(a) (1982).

▬ New Communications Technologies

In recent decades, entrepreneurs have developed many new and innovative communications technologies. The most prominent of these, cable television, is now regulated closely by the FCC. The Commission is still developing its response to other innovative technologies.

Cable Television

The first cable television transmission occurred in 1950, when the industry was intended to provide broadcast services to rural areas. Before long, the industry realized the potential of providing multichannel service in urban areas. More than 80 percent of U.S. households have access to cable service and over 50 percent actually use cable. Cable television advertising revenues have surpassed 1 billion dollars and operating revenues exceed 11 billion dollars.

After hesitating for years, the FCC adopted regulations for cable television service, treating it as something of a hybrid of broadcast and common carrier. The most significant feature of cable television is that the television signal enters the home on a cable (like a telephone line) and does not use the broadcast spectrum.

The FCC initially treated cable television as a hybrid service and sought to impose some content restrictions inapplicable to broadcasters. The following decision was a landmark in defining the type of regulation for cable service and the rights of cable operators.

▬ Case 18.3
Federal Communications Commission v. Midwest Video Corporation
United States Supreme Court, 1979
440 U.S. 689, 99 S.Ct. 1435

Background and Facts   *In May 1976, the Federal Communications Commission adopted a new set of minimum rules for cable systems. These rules included a requirement that the operator provide access channels sufficient so that any member of the public could use the cable system to transmit programs. Cable operators had no control over the content of access programming. Operators were required to accept access programs on a first-come, nondiscriminatory basis.*

Midwest Video Corporation and others challenged the FCC access rules. They argued that the rules improperly transformed cable into a common carrier. The Eighth Circuit Court of Appeals struck down the access rules as contrary to the Communications Act and a possible violation of the First Amendment. The FCC appealed to the Supreme Court.

WHITE, Justice.

* * * *

Because its access and capacity rules promote the long established regulatory goals of maximization of outlets for local expression and diversification of programming—the objectives promoted by the rule sustained in Midwest Video—the Commission maintains that it plainly had jurisdiction to promulgate them. Respondents, in opposition, view the access regulations as an intrusion on cable system operations that is qualitatively different from the impact of the rule upheld in Midwest Video. Specifically, it is urged that by requiring the allocation of access channels to categories of users specified by the regulations and by depriving the cable operator of the power to select individual users or to control the programming on such channels, the regulations wrest a considerable degree of editorial control from the cable operator and in effect compel the cable system to provide a kind of common-carrier service.

* * * *

With its access rules, however, the Commission has transferred control of the content of access cable channels from cable operators to members of the public who wish to communicate by the cable medium. Effectively, the Commission has relegated cable systems, pro tanto, to common-carrier status. A common-carrier service in the communications context is one that "makes a public offering to provide [communications facilities] whereby all members of the public who choose to employ such facilities may communicate or transmit intelligence of their own design and choosing...." The language of [section] 3 (h) [of the Communications Act] is unequivocal; it stipulates that broadcasters shall not be treated as common carriers. As we see it, [section] 3 (h) consistently with the policy of the Act to preserve editorial control of programming in the licensee, forecloses any discretion in the Commission to impose access requirements amounting to common-carrier obligations on broadcast systems. The provision's background manifests a congressional belief that the intrusion worked by such regulation on the journalistic integrity of broadcasters would overshadow any benefits associated with the resulting public access.

Decision and Remedy   *The Supreme Court affirmed the Eighth Circuit decision invalidating the FCC's 1976 access rules.*

Comment   *Although the Court invalidated the initial rules, the FCC repromulgated its access requirements in a legally acceptable form. Cable operators must make channels available for public access but retain some editorial control over this programming.*

In 1984, Congress adopted the Cable Communications Policy Act to provide a comprehensive regulatory system of cable television. This law gave the FCC specific power to regulate cable and treated the technology much like a broadcasting service. The regulatory system for cable differs from that for broadcast services, however.

Franchising First, a local cable television system does not require an FCC license but must obtain a franchise. These franchises are granted by a state or local government, not the FCC. A franchise is somewhat like a broadcast license and typically lasts between ten and twenty years, depending on local rules. The 1984 Act limits the franchising powers of the local government, however.

The 1984 Act established specific standards and procedures for local governments to use in franchise renewals, to protect existing franchise holders. In a franchise renewal hearing, the local agency can consider only four factors—(1) how the cable operator has complied with the terms of the franchise; (2) the quality of cable service provided; (3) the operator's financial and technical ability to provide future services; and (4) the operator's proposal for meeting future community needs and interests.

Rate regulation   Historically, local governments regulated the rates that cable operators could charge their subscribers. The 1984 Act limited rate regulation. No rate regulation is allowed for cable systems that are subject to "effective competition." Effective competition is defined as the presence of "at least three unduplicated television signals" in the community served by the cable operator.[8] If a community is served by broadcast affiliates of CBS, NBC and ABC, there would be effective competition. In such a community, cable rates are set by market forces.

Access channels   The Cable Act permits franchise authorities to require cable operators to provide channels for public access. These channels must be reserved for "public, educational or governmental use." This permits members of the local public to produce programming that is carried on the cable system via the access channels. A typical access program might broadcast the local city council meeting. States also require an opportunity for locally produced programming. Rhode Island, for example, requires each cable system to provide at least seven separate channels for public access. Cable systems also must provide facilities for people to produce this programming.

The 1984 law also required that channels be leased for commercial access. Any cable system with more than thirty-five channels must set aside at least 10 percent of its channels for lease. A common use of these channels is the video shopping program. These leased channels are not like common carriers, however. The cable operator can consider the use of the channel in rate setting and can exercise some content control over the leased channels.

Obscenity and indecency   The Cable Act made it illegal to transmit obscenity over a cable system. Guilty parties can be jailed for up to two years and fined up to $10,000. Cable operators also are required to market "lockboxes" to subscribers, which enable them to prevent certain channels from being used, unless a code is entered.

Subscriber privacy   Another provision of the 1984 Cable Act concerns the privacy rights of cable subscribers. The law prohibits cable operators from collecting personally identifiable information about its subscribers, without consent. An exception was made to this rule when necessary to provide cable service or to detect unauthorized use of cable. Cable subscribers have a right of access to all personally identifiable information collected. Cable privacy laws also have been passed by a number of states, including California, New York, Illinois, and Wisconsin.

Equal employment opportunity   The Cable Act established policies to ensure equal employment opportunity in cable companies. The Act not only prohibits discrimination but also requires that operators establish a program to ensure equal opportunity. The law also requires cable operators to file an annual statistical report with the FCC indicating their success in assuring equal opportunity. Employees who believe that they have suffered discrimination at the hands of a cable operator may file a complaint with the FCC for investigation.

Multipoint Distribution Service

Multipoint Distribution Service (MDS) is primarily useful to rural citizens who have no cable service and who can receive few broadcast transmissions. Approximately one million households have no access to television and millions more can receive only one or two broadcast channels in their home (without a satellite dish antenna). The FCC made channels available for MDS transmission to these citizens.

MDS consists of a microwave transmitter broadcasting on a microwave frequency. The signal is picked up by an antenna and then converted to a frequency compatible with an individual television set. MDS is sometimes called "wireless cable." MDS transmission is on a common carrier basis. As a result MDS services

[8]47 C.F.R. Section 76.33(a) (1987).

are not subject to content regulation, such as the equal time requirement.

MDS is a direct competitor with cable, in urban as well as rural areas. MDS has advantages over cable because it is less regulated and not subject to local franchising requirements. MDS can carry no more than thirty channels, however, and has not expanded as fast as cable television.

Direct Broadcast Satellites

Many television signals are transmitted by satellites to cable operators or others, who then pass the signals on to individual homes. Technology has advanced to the point at which homes can directly receive satellite transmissions, even without the bulky satellite dish that is often seen. This technology would use direct broadcast satellites ("DBS"). DBS may be a broadcast service, in which the satellite owner prepares its own programming. The FCC has suggested that DBS could choose to operate as a common carrier, leasing its frequencies to any party.

Teletext/Videotext

Teletext and videotext, sometimes called electronic publishing, is an especially promising new communications technology. Teletext signals are sent through an unused part of the television picture and show up as words (text) on the television screen. Videotext is teletext with some graphics capability. Teletext already has some prominent uses in connection with normal broadcasting. Closed captioning for deaf viewers and weather information are two examples.

Some entrepreneurs are planning entire channels of teletext service. They view this as an electronic newspaper. Subscribers would have a decoder that would permit them to call up information on news, weather, sports, public events, airline schedules, etc.

The FCC has established some rules for teletext. The first important decision was that teletext would be regulated as a broadcast service, rather than as a common carrier. The second important decision was to exempt teletext from most content rules, such as the equal time provision.

▄▄ Communications Law and the First Amendment

All communications services have some protection from the First Amendment's guarantee of freedom of speech and of the press. The extent of this First Amendment protection depends on the type of communications service.

Print communications, such as newspapers and magazines, receive the highest level of First Amendment protection. Virtually no content regulation of print media is constitutional. For example, newspapers need not provide the public with access to space in the paper. The government may, however, prevent obscene materials even in the print medium.

Broadcast radio and television receive less First Amendment protection than does the print medium. This is because the spectrum for radio and television signals is scarce and controlled by the government. Consequently, the government may consider broadcast content in licensing space on the spectrum. The Supreme Court has held that the rights of listeners take precedence over the First Amendment rights of broadcasters.[9]

The extent of First Amendment protection for cable television is still uncertain. It seems clear that cable operators have First Amendment rights at least as strong as those of broadcasters and perhaps as strong as that of newspapers. Several content regulations on cable television have been struck down in court as contrary to the First Amendment.

One significant decision was *Quincy Cable TV, Inc. v. FCC.*[10] The FCC had adopted "must-carry" rules for cable television that required cable operators to carry the signals of all local broadcast channels. A local cable operator challenged the constitutionality of these rules. The court held that cable television should enjoy greater First Amendment protection than broadcast television, because cable channels were not so scarce. The court struck down the must-carry rules, because they unconstitutionally favored broadcasters and infringed the cable operators' right to choose what to carry.

---

[9]*Red Lion Broadcasting Co. v. FCC*, 395 U.S. 367, 390 (1969).
[10]768 F.2d 1434 (D.C. Cir. 1985).

Some First Amendment issues are common to all forms of mass media. The most significant First Amendment issues relate to news broadcasting or publication. Prominent controversies include reporter's privilege and newsgathering rights.

Reporter's Privilege

When obtaining news, many reporters promise their sources confidentiality. Reporters believe that keeping sources secret is essential to getting controversial information out of the sources. When the news involves a criminal case or civil litigation, however, a court may subpoena the reporter and demand the identity of the source.

Even in the face of a subpoena, many reporters have refused to disclose their source. One Los Angeles reporter wrote an article regarding the 1970 Charles Manson multiple murder trial and reported that one defendant had confessed. The government subpoenaed the reporter, but he refused to disclose his source, and he was jailed for forty-six days.

Reporters argued that source confidentiality was a fundamental part of the freedom of the press protected by the First Amendment. This issue reached the Supreme Court in a series of cases. The Court recognized that there was a First Amendment interest at stake but refused to recognize an absolute privilege for reporters not to reveal their sources.

Courts are more willing to recognize a reporter's privilege in the context of civil litigation. For example, a reporter for the *Saturday Evening Post* published a major article on racial discrimination in the sale of houses in Chicago. A group of citizens sued for damages from this discrimination and sought the reporter's source. While the reporter was sympathetic to their cause, he refused to disclose the identity of his source. A federal court held that he need not reveal his source, to avoid a "chilling effect" on the willingness of sources to come forward.[11]

Reporters have received less protection in criminal cases. Many courts use a three-part test and hold that a reporter must disclose a source if:

1. There is reason to believe that a reporter has information relevant to a specific violation of the law.

2. There is no preferable alternative way to obtain this information.

3. The prosecutor or defense has a "compelling and overriding interest" in the information.

When these three facts are present, a reporter normally will be legally compelled to disclose the identity of a source. Many reporters still will refuse to identify their sources and go to jail for contempt of court.

In addition to First Amendment protection for reporters, at least twenty-six states have passed "shield laws" that protect reporters from a requirement to disclose their sources. Few of these shield statutes are absolute, however. For example, some laws protect only sources of information that are actually broadcast or published. Other statutes protect only the reporter, personally. If the source's identity is known to the station owner, the owner may be required to disclose the source.

Newsgathering Rights

The mass media often claim that they have a First Amendment right to gather news, as well as to broadcast news. Reporters may demand access to government meetings or facilities in order to report on them. The courts have recognized a First Amendment right of newsgathering, but it is not an absolute right.

The government generally may not provide discriminatory access to information. A federal court in Iowa has ruled that the police department cannot show its records to one newspaper and deny them to others. A federal court in Hawaii held that a mayor could not deny access to his press conferences to a reporter whom the mayor disliked.

Federal and state laws provide journalists with broad access to government records and meetings. Laws may not permit such broad access to other government facilities or operations, however. The government may seek to deny reporters access to a prison or to a judicial trial, for example.

Many cases have considered the rights of the press to cover trials. In general, the press and the public both have a right to attend criminal or civil

---

[11]*Baker v. F & F Investment*, 470 F.2d 778 (2d Cir. 1972).

trials. The state of Massachusetts had a law that prohibited access to rape trials in which the victim was a minor, to protect the minor's privacy. The Supreme Court held that this law was unconstitutional, because the First Amendment right outweighed the state's interest in protecting the victim.[12]

Another case that reached the Supreme Court involved a television station seeking access to a county jail. The county provided only monthly guided tours of the jail and prohibited private access to individual inmates. The Supreme Court ruled in favor of the government and held that the press had no special right of access to prisoners.[13] An Oklahoma decision also denied the press a right of access to a nuclear power plant.

Another controversial issue involves the right of press access to accident scenes. In the leading case, a photographer of the *Newark Star-Ledger* took dramatic pictures of the victims of an automobile accident. The police arrived and told the photographer and other members of the public to withdraw from the scene. The photographer refused to leave, was arrested, and was eventually convicted. He argued that the conviction violated his First Amendment rights, but the New Jersey Supreme Court upheld the conviction.

▬ Mass Media Liability

Potential civil liability is a major concern of broadcasters, newspaper publishers and others involved in mass communications. Traditionally, the media have been subject to liability for the torts of defamation and invasion of privacy. More recently, the media were made subject to suit for a general doctrine of media malpractice for negligent and inaccurate reporting.

Defamation

Defamation is a tort consisting of a false communication that injures a person's reputation. The basic elements of a defamation case are set forth in Chapter 5 of *West's Business Law, Fifth Edition*. Defamation law is a particular concern of the mass communications industry.

A controversial recent case involved CBS and its 1982 documentary on the Vietnam War. This documentary suggested that General Westmoreland was involved in a conspiracy to underestimate enemy strength in the war. Westmoreland sued for over $100 million in defamation damages, and the case received enormous publicity. Ultimately, the parties settled and CBS paid no money damages.

The first requirement of a defamation case is that the defendant make a **defamatory statement**, something that would injure the plaintiff's reputation. If the mass media inaccurately report that a person was a criminal, the report would be defamatory. The media must use great precision in reporting on crimes. Suppose that a local politician is stopped for drunk driving. The press report that the politician was charged with drunk driving. If the politician was not actually arrested, but only warned, the press have reported inaccurately and committed defamation.

One common misunderstanding is that the word "alleged" protects the press from defamation. Thus, a television news broadcast may refer to a source alleging that a person is a murderer. This may still be defamatory if the defendant is innocent. The television station is reporting some source that alleges the defendant to be guilty. If the source is wrong, the station is also potentially liable for defamation.

Simple carelessness can produce defamation liability. In the 1970s, *TV Guide* took an item submitted from a talk show that included the question "From Party Girl to Call Girl?" *TV Guide* changed the question mark to a period. For this and other reasons, a jury found that the magazine had misleadingly implied that a guest was a prostitute and awarded over $250,000 in damages.[14]

Photographs also may be defamatory. A magazine of the trucking industry ran an article on bankruptcy in the industry. The article was accompanied with a picture of a trucking firm named Drotzmann's. Drotzmann sued, claiming that the photo misleadingly implied that his successful firm was going out of business. A jury awarded Drotzmann $245,000 in damages, though an appellate court reversed on procedural grounds.[15]

[12]*Globe Newspaper Co. v. Superior Court*, 457 U.S. 596 (1982).

[13]*Houchins v. KQED*, 438 U.S. 1 (1978).

[14]*Montandon v. Triangle Publications, Inc.*, 45 Cal. App. 3d 938 (1975).

[15]*Drotzmann's, Inc. v. McGraw-Hill, Inc.*, 500 F.2d 830 (8th Cir. 1974).

A second requirement of a defamation action is *publication*. Because defamation protects reputation, a successful action requires that the defamatory statement be communicated, heard, and believed. Damages will be in part proportional to the size of the audience. For this reason, the mass media, which reach millions, are particularly at risk from defamation actions.

Defamation also permits actions for republication of defamatory statements. Suppose a politician accuses a rival of theft of government funds. If a radio station reports on this accusation, the radio station may be liable for republishing a defamatory statement.

Truth is a defense to defamation. If a communications outlet publishes true facts that injure a person's reputation, the outlet will not be liable. A true but misleading story may produce liability, however. A Memphis newspaper reported that a Ms. Newton shot a Ms. Nichols when she found Ms. Nichols together with Mr. Newton in the Nichols' home. The paper did not report that three others also were present. The newspaper was found liable because it created a misleading impression of an adulterous affair between Ms. Nichols and Mr. Newton.[16]

In addition, the press has a broader defense of qualified privilege when the plaintiff is a public figure. In these circumstances, the plaintiff must show that the untrue statement was published with malice or with reckless disregard for the truth. An innocent falsehood is protected.

The media have the qualified privilege only when the allegedly defamed plaintiff is a public figure. A publicly elected official, such as a governor or representative, is clearly a public figure. Most celebrities are public figures. Courts have held Johnny Carson, Carol Burnett and William F. Buckley, Jr., to be public figures in all contexts. A former University of Georgia football coach also was held to be a public figure.

Individuals who themselves have created a public controversy are also considered public figures. Say that an environmental activist calls a press conference to report on hazardous conditions at a nuclear power plant. The media report on the press conference but also on the activist's allegedly fraudulent past behavior. The activist will be considered a public figure for purposes of this controversy.

If the plaintiff is a public figure, even some false and defamatory statements are protected. The plaintiff must show that the defendant was unusually careless in checking the facts of the story or intentionally committed defamation. The mass media get some special consideration under this standard. For example, the courts realize that newspapers and television stations have pressure from short deadlines and may not be able thoroughly to check out every story. If a story is from an apparently reliable source, the press usually will not be liable even if the story proves to be false.

The defenses provided the press may be overcome if actual malice can be shown. In such a case, the media are subject to multimillion-dollar liability. The following case reveals the risks of running a controversial news story.

---

[16]*Memphis Publishing Co. v. Nichols*, 569 S.W. 2d 420 (Tenn. 1978).

■ **Case 18.4**
Brown & Williamson Tobacco Corporation v. Jacobson
United States Court of Appeals, Seventh Circuit, 1987
827 F.2d 1119

Background and Facts *Walter Jacobson, a prominent newscaster in the Chicago area, delivers a nightly feature known as "Walter Jacobson's Perspective." One evening's broadcast focused on tobacco industry advertising practices. The program was prepared by Michael Radutzky, a researcher. Jacobson said that a "confidential" federal report indicated that Viceroy cigarettes were targeting their ads at the youth. The federal report actually discussed a marketing proposal by Marketing and Research Counselors, Inc. ("MARC"). Although MARC's report did discuss a campaign aimed at young potential smokers, Viceroy explicitly rejected this approach.*

Viceroy's parent company sued Jacobson and his employer, CBS, Inc., for defamation. A jury found the defendants liable and entered *an award of $3 million in compensatory damages and $2.05 million in punitive damages. The district court judge then reduced the compensatory award to $1.00 but upheld the punitive damages. Both sides appealed this ruling.*

BAUER, Chief Justice.

* * * *

The attitude of most knowledgeable and disinterested persons toward the tobacco industry is certainly negative; at least it has been negative for the past decade. In such an atmosphere, it becomes difficult to imagine how the tobacco people can be libeled. The bashing of the industry by government and private groups has become a virtual cottage industry. This case, however, demonstrates that general bum raps against the whole tobacco industry are different from a specific accusations of skulduggery by a specific company or person. And this case involves some very specific statements against a very specific company in the tobacco industry.

* * * *

Jacobson then reached the portion of his Perspective that the jury and the district court found libeled Brown & Williamson:

The cigarette business insists, in fact, it will swear up and down in public, it is not selling cigarettes to children; that if children are smoking (which they are, more than ever before), it's not the fault of the cigarette business. Who knows whose fault it is, says the cigarette business.

That's what Viceroy is saying. Who knows whose fault it is that children are smoking? It's not ours. Well, there is a confidential report on cigarette advertising in the files of the federal government right now, a Viceroy advertising [sic]. The Viceroy strategy for attracting young people (starters, they are called) to smoking.

"For the young smoker a cigarette falls into the same category with wine, beer, shaving, or wearing a bra," says the Viceroy strategy. "A declaration of independence and striving for self-identity. Therefore, an attempt should be made," says Viceroy, "to present the cigarette as an initiation into the adult world, to present the cigarette as an illicit pleasure, a basic symbol of the growing-up maturity process. An attempt should be made," says the Viceroy slicksters, "to relate the cigarette to pot, wine, beer, and sex. Do not communicate health or health-related points."

Brown & Williamson put forth evidence that it adhered vigorously to the Cigarette Advertising Code, which bars advertising to persons under 21. In addition to adhering to the Code, Brown & Williamson took the additional step of establishing a detailed procedure to ensure that its advertising agencies did not use models who either were or appeared to be younger than 25. When undertaking advertising campaigns that involved the distribution of samples, Brown & Williamson required the individuals distributing the samples to sign statements promising not to distribute cigarettes to people under 21.

* * * *

CBS contends that three advertisements, which were run as part of a six month test market campaign in three cities, were the implementation of the "pot," wine, beer, and sex strategy recommended in the MARC report. These advertisements, according to CBS, were the "more refined and acceptable expression of the MARC strategy" to present the cigarette as part of the illicit pleasure category of products and activities. Responsive Brief at 2. The ads, as described by CBS, show "a well-dressed young woman wading in a public fountain while her date looks on, a young man poised to throw a cream pie at the camera, and a young woman dousing her head under a water pump." At the top of the ads is the slogan "If it feels good, do it. If it feels good, smoke it." According to CBS, the first sentence is "a common slogan of the sexual revolution" while the second sentence is "a thinly veiled reference to marijuana." At the bottom of each advertisement is a picture of a package of Viceroy cigarettes. Under the package is the slogan "Viceroy. It feels good."

We agree with trial counsel that these ads cannot be fairly characterized as "refined" versions of "pot," wine, beer, and sex ads. In the fountain ad, the woman is fully clothed in a dress and a shirt jacket. The water in the fountain is coming up to her knees and her dress appears to be about five inches above her knee on the right leg and eleven inches above the knee on her left leg, which is extended forward. The man in the ad is fully clothed and about ten feet away from the woman. She appears from the picture to be having a good time even though she is not involved in any sexual adventure. The ad seems to imply that this is a woman who has done something (wade in the fountain) because "it feels good." The ad also implies that this woman, who is holding a cigarette in her hand, is smoking that cigarette because it feels good. ("If it feels good, smoke it.") The connection to Viceroy is at the bottom of the ad where it states "Viceroy. It feels good." As we read the ad in context, the full message is that an individual should do things that feel good and that because Viceroy (not marijuana) feels good when one smokes it, the American consumer should choose Viceroy. The other two ads convey essentially the same message. The age range of the models in the advertisements appears to be from the mid to late twenties to the mid thirties. We conclude that these ads are not, even in somewhat refined form, "pot," wine, beer, and sex ads.

* * * *

Brown & Williamson also points to Walter Jacobson's testimony as evidence of actual malice. Jacobson's testimony revealed that he had received and reviewed Radutzky's sample script prior to delivering the broadcast. In addition, he knew that Radutzky's search for "pot," wine, beer, and sex ads had been unsuccessful. Jacobson had also read the FTC report and was aware that the "pot," wine, beer, and sex language in the report was not from a document prepared by Brown & Williamson but was actually from a document prepared by MARC. Nonetheless, his testimony indicated that he had intended to create the impression that the "pot," wine, beer, and sex comment had been made by Viceroy itself. ("I even said that, 'Viceroys says.'") His assertion that he intended to create the impression that the "pot," wine, beer, and sex statement was made by Viceroy indicates that Jacobson acted with actual malice since he admitted that he knew that the statement was made by MARC rather than Viceroy.

Decision and Remedy   *The court affirmed the jury's finding of liability. The court also affirmed the punitive damages award and held that Brown & Williamson should receive $1 million in actual compensatory damages.*

The media may also have a **privilege** against defamation actions in limited circumstances. Broadcast stations have an absolute privilege for broadcasts by politicians. The press also has an absolute privilege when reporting the proceedings of many government bodies, including the courts, the United States Congress, state legislatures, and even local councils. This privilege can be lost, however, if the reportage is inaccurate or malicious.

The press is also privileged for reports of **opinion** or **parody**. Defamation only extends to a false report of facts. When an author called William F. Buckley, Jr., a "fascist," the court found that this term was an opinion, not a fact. A parody, such as a political cartoon, is also protected against defamation challenge.

Defamation cases are of great concern to the media, even if they ultimately win the cases. The cost of litigation can be substantial. A widely publicized defamation can also hurt the public reputation of a broadcaster. In the Westmoreland case described above, CBS spent over a million dollars in legal expenses, and the network's reputation suffered from publicity surrounding the case.

Invasion of Privacy

A second tort of concern to the communications industry is invasion of privacy. News and entertainment stories may cover facts that the stories' subjects consider to be private. The nature of an invasion of privacy claim is discussed in Chapter 5 of *West's Business Law, Fifth Edition.*

One type of invasion of privacy claim involves the public disclosure of embarrassing private facts. *Time* magazine ran an article on a woman with a rare disease that caused her to lose weight, no matter how much she ate. They also printed a picture of her in the hospital and referred to her as a "starving glutton." The court found the magazine liable for invasion of privacy.[17]

An important defense to this type of invasion of privacy claim is **newsworthiness**. The media have a privilege to public information of legitimate news interest to the public. Moreover, courts often defer to the media's judgment that an item is newsworthy.

Events involving crimes or fires are usually considered newsworthy. Unusual skills or actions are also newsworthy. *Sports Illustrated* published an article about a surfer, describing how he would purposefully injure himself, in order to collect insurance, so he could spend time surfing. The article also reported that he ate insects and dived down flights of stairs. The court rejected the surfer's invasion of privacy claim, holding that the unusual practices were legitimately newsworthy.[18]

The newsworthiness defense has no clear-cut dimensions. Public interest alone is not enough to make an item newsworthy, but such interest is relevant. The following case illustrates the complex of factors affecting the determination of newsworthiness.

---

[17]*Barber v. Time, Inc.,* 159 S.W. 2d 291 (Mo. 1942).

[18]*Virgil v. Sports Illustrated, Inc.,* 424 F. Supp. 1286 (S.D. Cal. 1976).

■ **Case 18.5**
Sipple v. Chronicle Publishing Company
California Court of Appeals, First District, 1984
154 Cal. App. 3d 1040; 201 Cal.Rptr. 665

Background and Facts   *In September 1975, Sara Jane Moore attempted to assassinate President Gerald Ford. Oliver Sipple, an ex-Marine, was in the surrounding crowd and grabbed Moore's arm as she was firing a gun. Sipple was hailed as a hero for his protective action. Many news articles about the episode mentioned that Sipple was a prominent member of the San Francisco gay community.*

Sipple filed an action for invasion of privacy against the newspapers that reported his sexual preference. He claimed that the articles caused his family to learn for the first time of his homosexual orientation. The trial court granted summary judgment for the defendants. Sipple appealed.

CALDECOTT, P.J.

* * * *

As referred to above, our courts have recognized a broad privilege cloaking the truthful publication of all newsworthy matters. Thus * * * our Supreme Court stated that a truthful publication is protected if (1) it is newsworthy and (2) it does not reveal facts so offensive as to shock the community notions of decency. While it has been said that the general criteria for determining newsworthiness are (a) the social value of the facts published; (b) the depth of the article's intrusion into ostensibly private affairs; and (c) the extent to which the individual voluntarily acceded to a position of public notoriety. The cases and authorities further explain that the paramount test of newsworthiness is whether the matter is of legitimate public interest which in turn must be determined according to the community mores. As pointed out in *Virgil v. Time, Inc.,* supra, 527 F.2d at page 1129: " 'In determining what is a matter of legitimate public interest, account must be taken of the customs and conventions of the community; and in the last analysis what is proper becomes a matter of the community mores. The line is to be drawn when the publicity ceases to be the giving of information to which the public is entitled, and becomes a morbid and sensational prying into private lives for its own sake, with which a reasonable member of the public, with decent standards, would say that he had no concern.' "

* * * *

In the case at bench the publication of appellant's homosexual orientation which had already been widely known by many people in a number of communities was not so offensive even at the time of the publication as to shock the community notions of decency. Moreover, and perhaps even more to the point, the record shows that the publications were not motivated by a morbid and sensational prying into appellant's private life but rather were prompted by legitimate political considerations, i.e., to dispel the false public opinion that gays were timid, weak and unheroic figures and to raise the equally important political question whether the President of the United States entertained a discriminatory attitude or bias against a minority group such as homosexuals. Thus appellant's case squarely falls within the language of Kapellas in which the California Supreme Court emphasized that "when, [as here] the legitimate public interest in the published information is substantial, a much greater intrusion into an individual's private life will be sanctioned."

* * * *

Appellant's contention that by saving the President's life he did not intend to enter into the limelight and become a public figure, can be easily answered. In elaborating on involuntary public figures, Restatement Second of Torts section 652D, comment f, sets out in part as follows: "There are other individuals who have not sought publicity or consented to it, but through their own conduct or otherwise have become a legitimate subject of public interest. They have, in other words, become 'news.' . . . These persons are regarded as properly subject to the public interest, and publishers are permitted to satisfy the curiosity of the public as to its heroes, leaders, villains and victims, and those who are closely associated with them. As in the case of the voluntary public figure, the authorized publicity is not limited to the event that itself arouses the public interest, and to some reasonable extent includes publicity given to facts about the individual that would otherwise be purely private."

Decision and Remedy *The court affirmed the lower court's grant of summary judgment.*

Another form of invasion of privacy is intrusion into areas in which a person has a reasonable expectation of privacy. If the press uses electronic snooping devices or secret recording devices, this may represent unlawful intrusion. Overzealous harassment may also be unlawful. Jacqueline Onassis successfully sued a photographer for constantly following her and taking pictures.

Still another form of invasion of privacy is misappropriation. This occurs when the press uses a picture of a person for commercial purposes. If *Playboy* magazine takes a newsphoto of a man reading *Playboy* and uses it for promotion, the magazine may be liable for misappropriation of the subject's likeness. To be safe, a magazine should always obtain permission for republication of pictures in advertising materials.

Media Malpractice

Individuals are increasingly bringing actions against the media for inaccurate or negligent reporting of the facts. These claims are lumped under the heading, "media malpractice."

Some plaintiffs have sued the press for inaccurate reporting, even if it is not defamatory. One investor sued over an inaccurate description of corporate bonds in which he then invested. The court dismissed this claim for fear of "chilling" or deterring reporting. Courts have permitted a plaintiff to sue the government for a negligent

weather forecast, though, and some fear that the press could be subject to similar liability.

Other individuals have sued the media for failure to investigate statements, especially those made in advertisements. In one case, *Soldier of Fortune* magazine published an ambiguous advertisement that turned out to be a solicitation by a "hit man" who would kill under contract. The family of a murder victim sued the magazine for failure to investigate the advertisement. A jury returned a verdict of $9.4 million against the magazine. Courts have yet to award liability for nondefamatory news articles under this duty to investigate.

Still another source of potential media liability is the infliction of emotional distress, as discussed in Chapter 5 of *West's Business Law, Fifth Edition*. *Cinema X* magazine described Terry Clifford as an "aspiring erotic actress" and placed her name under a nude photograph of someone else. Clifford received a number of "loathsome and horrifying calls" that interrupted her work and gave her nightmares. She sued the magazine and received $10,000 in damages.[19]

The press also has been found liable to its sources. One campaign worker gave the press information about a rival candidate under a promise of confidentiality. The newspaper later revealed the source. The source sued the paper and initially received a $700,000 judgment.

[19]*Clifford v. Hollander*, 6 Med. L. Rptr. 2201 (N.Y. Civ. Ct. 1980).

<table>
<tr><td>■ **Ethical Perspectives**</td></tr>
</table>

Free Press vs. Fair Trial

Several ethical controversies arise out of the media's coverage of criminal investigations and prosecutions. The media generally recognize an ethical obligation to their viewership or readership and to society as a whole. This obligation takes the form of investigating and publicizing the true facts on matters of great public interest. But what should the media's ethical responsibility be toward the subjects of their reporting, e.g., a criminal defendant? The duties here are not so clearly recognized.

A problem arises when media coverage may prejudice a defendant's right to a fair trial. The classic case arose in Ohio in the 1950s, when a relatively prominent doctor, named Sam Sheppard, was accused of murdering his wife. Newspapers headlined the story. A front page editorial questioned: "Why Isn't Sam Sheppard in Jail?" He was arrested the next day.[20] All but one of the jurors had heard about the case in the media, and two had heard a radio story that Sheppard had fathered an illegitimate child. The judge accepted the jurors' word that they would be uninfluenced by the press reports. Dr. Sheppard was convicted. He spent twelve years in jail and went through a series of appeals before the United States Supreme Court reversed his conviction. The Court found that the extensive publicity had denied Sheppard's right to a fair trial before an impartial jury.[21]

Press coverage of criminal trials also raises privacy questions. The press may have a legal right to publish the names of crime victims, but is it ethical to do so? A Florida court dismissed a rape victim's privacy case against a television station but admonished the station for its "insensitivity" in publishing her name.[22]

These cases involve a balancing of the public's need or right to know information against a lone individual's right to a fair trial or personal privacy. A major criminal trial is surely newsworthy, but the media may have some ethical duty of fair coverage. In the case of crime victims, one can reasonably question whether the public's right to know the victim's identity is particularly newsworthy. This is a situation in which a privacy interest might outweigh the public right to know facts.

Some maintain that the media should not make these ethical judgments, because their only responsibility is to their readers or viewers. This attitude has provoked a backlash against the press, however, and may even yield more government regulation of the news media. In some states, journalists have entered into voluntary agreements with judges and prosecutors regarding the nature of pretrial publicity in criminal cases.

The communications industry increasingly is adopting its own ethical codes of conduct. A landmark 1947 report by the Commission on Freedom of the Press declared that press freedom "can only continue as an accountable freedom" and that the constitutional rights "will stand unaltered [only] as its moral duty is performed."[23] This report provoked considerable reflection by the media.

---

[20]Kent Middleton & Bill Chamberlin, *The Law of Public Communication* 386 (1988).

[21]*Sheppard v. Maxwell*, 384 U.S. 333 (1966).

[22]*Doe v. Sarasota-Bradenton Television Co.*, 436 So. 2d 328 (Fla. App. 1983).

[23]Commission on Freedom of the Press, *A Free and Responsible Press* (1947), p.18-19.

The Society of Professional Journalists adopted a code of ethics that declares its "overriding mission" as protecting the "public's right to know of events of public importance and interest." The code criticizes journalists who use their position "for selfish or other unworthy motives." The code goes on to recognize an obligation to report with "intelligence, objectivity, accuracy, and fairness." Other press organizations have comparable codes of conduct.

The journalists' codes recognize ethical duties in media coverage, but the true significance of the codes is unclear. Most codes emphasize the public's right to know, rather than the rights of individuals covered in the press. The temptation to sensational coverage remains great. After all, dramatic and controversial headlines sell newspapers.

▬ International Perspectives

Cross-Border Broadcasting

Television and radio signals are unaffected by national borders. A signal broadcast from one nation may be received by citizens of a neighboring nation. This is sometimes called a spillover signal. Sometimes, cross-border broadcasting is intentional, as has been the case with Radio Free Europe's broadcasts into communist nations. Such spillover broadcasting has on occasion become politically controversial.

The significance of cross-border broadcasting from traditional television and radio stations was a limited and localized problem. These broadcasts can travel only within a line of sight from the transmitter. The advent of new technologies, however, will increase the conflict of spillover broadcast signals. A single DBS satellite, for example, could theoretically broadcast to 40 percent of the world's surface.

Governments have a variety of reasons for concern with spillover signals. Some governments fear that foreign transmissions could destabilize their governments. Others are concerned that foreign broadcasts will undermine the national culture or moral sensibility. Still other governments are concerned for the integrity of their nation's language.

International controversies over DBS have already begun. A Japanese DBS station recently began broadcasting and its signals were picked up by individuals in South Korea. The South Korean government vehemently protested to the Japanese government, but the protests were essentially ignored.

An individual nation can itself do little about its citizens' reception of spillover broadcast signals. A government could ban individuals from owning satellite dishes, but many governments are developing their own DBS systems. If satellite dishes are allowed, it is practically impossible to prevent reception of signals originating in foreign nations. As a result, any regulation of spillover broadcasting will largely be a matter of international law.

In 1982, the United Nations General Assembly adopted a resolution that required nations to consult with each other about the effects of DBS spillover. The resolution has little legally enforceable effect, however. Moreover, most nations with DBS broadcast capability voted against the resolution.

DBS spillover is particularly significant in Europe, where many economically and technologically advanced nations are in relatively close geographic proximity. Within the twelve-nation European Community, the Single European Act protects DBS transmissions. This law prevents any member nation from discriminating against services that originate in another member nation. Television and radio broadcasts qualify as protected services under the act. Many European nations are not part of the official European Community, however. Switzerland, for example, is located in the midst of the Community's nations, but is not itself a member nation.

There is no globally applicable, clear-cut international law to apply to spillover broadcasting. Some argue that these broadcasts are a form of pollution that should be subject to international environmental law.

Regional organizations may regulate DBS transmissions. In Europe, for example, the European Human Rights Convention recognizes freedom of speech as a right. However, the Convention recognizes limitations on this right where necessary for national security, territorial integrity, public safety, the prevention of disorder and crime, the protection of health and morals, the protection of the reputation and rights of others, the prevention of the disclosure of information received in confidence, and maintaining the authority and impartiality of the judiciary. Obviously, free speech will not receive complete legal protection under these potentially broad exceptions.

Broadcasters also must beware potential liability from cross-border signal transmissions. Beaming a signal into a foreign country may subject the broadcaster to the jurisdiction of a foreign court and the application of foreign laws. Foreign liability for defamation generally tends to be stricter than in the United States. Spillover broadcasting can subject the communications industry to new sources of international liability.

Questions and Case Problems

1. A Utah state statute made criminal the distribution of pornographic or indecent materials by wire or cable. Indecency was defined as including nude figures. A national cable broadcaster challenged the constitutionality of the statute. Utah defended by noting its rights to regulate cable transmissions and its concern for minors viewing cable programs. Is the state statute constitutional? [*Home Box Office, Inc. v. Wilkinson*, 531 F. Supp. 987 (D. Utah 1982)].

2. Preferred Communication, Inc., was organized to operate a cable television system in Los Angeles. Preferred sought to obtain leases allowing it to install cables on utility poles owned by the city utilities. The utilities refused to grant leases until Preferred had a cable franchise from the city. Los Angeles would not grant Preferred a franchise but required the company to go through its competitive franchising process. The city effectively limited access to a given area of the city to a single cable operator, even though utilities are capable of accommodating multiple operators. Preferred claimed that this system was unconstitutional. Does the Los Angeles policy violate the First Amendment rights of Preferred? [*City of Los Angeles v. Preferred Communications, Inc.*, 106 S.Ct. 2034 (1986)].

3. Dale Barshak was caught selling cocaine and heroin to grade school children in the small town of Bellington, Illinois. Dale was charged with selling illegal drugs and held in the county jail to await trial. The law enforcement officials have kept all details about the case, including Dale's identity, a secret. The press increasingly is hounding the police for details about the case, however, and Barshak's defense attorney is nervous that publication of the details of the case could compromise his client's right to a fair trial. The press go to court seeking an order compelling the police to disclose the facts of the case, and Barshak's attorney responds with a motion to prevent any out-of-court statements about the case. What should the court do?

4. Hutchinson was a research scientist who received over $500,000 in federal grants to research aggression in animals. U.S. Senator William Proxmire gives a "Golden Fleece" award for wasteful government spending. Proxmire selected Hutchinson for this "award" and issued a press release and newsletters publishing the details of Hutchinson's allegedly wasteful research. Hutchinson sued Proxmire, claiming that the senator had distorted the substance of his research and defamed him. Hutchinson's research had received little publicity prior to Proxmire's announcement. Is Hutchinson a public figure who must prove actual malice to succeed in his defamation claim? [*Hutchinson v. Proxmire*, 443 U.S. 111 (1979)].

5. *Hustler* magazine published a parody about the Reverend Jerry Falwell entitled "Jerry Falwell talks about his first time." The parody involved incest and portrayed both Falwell and his mother as drunk and immoral. The parody contained a small disclaimer of truth at the bottom of the page. Falwell is widely known throughout the nation and is considered a public figure for defamation purposes. Falwell could not succeed for defamation, however, because no one would have believed the parody. Falwell sued and won for intentional infliction of emotional distress. *Hustler* appealed, claiming that recovery for emotional distress in this case violated their First Amendment rights. Should a court overturn Falwell's damages for emotional distress? [*Hustler Magazine, Inc. v. Falwell*, 485 U.S. 46 (1988)].

CHAPTER NINETEEN

Government Contracts

KEY BACKGROUND

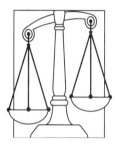

Many government functions are carried out through contracts with private companies. If the Department of Defense wants to procure a new fighter jet, the Department will contract with some private defense company to produce the jet. Government contracts are responsible for many billions of dollars of business.

Every significant agency of the federal government awards private contracts, which can range from the most complex missile system to the most mundane catering operation. The procedures for awarding contracts can be rather complex, with numerous legal requirements. The most important requirements are discussed below.

This chapter also addresses the substantial problem of government contract fraud and its punishment. The chapter deals with the uniform, national law of federal government contracts and not with state and local government contracts that are governed by the law of the appropriate jurisdiction. State and local government contract law tends to be quite similar to federal laws.

Types of Contracts

Many federal agencies award contracts for many different services, but there is great commonality in the basic types of contracts granted. The government awards two basic types of contracts, called fixed price contracts and cost reimbursement contracts.

Fixed Price Contracts

In a **fixed price contract**, the total amount due to the contractor is set in advance. The contractor must first complete the contract and then will be paid the fixed price provided in the contract. The actual cost of performing the contract is irrelevant. The fixed price contract (when adhered to) protects the government from cost overruns and enables the private contractor to increase profits by increasing efficiency.

Many private contractors have insisted on a modified fixed price contract, however, to avoid risk. This is the **fixed price contract with economic price adjustment**. A typical fixed price contract with economic price adjustment would permit the contractor to recover payments in excess of the fixed price, if the costs of labor or material increase during the time of contract performance.

The nature of the adjustment depends on what is provided in the contract with the government. For example, a contract could provide for price adjustment based on some market index. Suppose Norco has a contract with the government to produce tanks. Norco might offer a fixed price, plus an adjustment based on fluctuations in the price of steel or other raw materials.

Cost Reimbursement Contracts

The **cost reimbursement contract** provides payment to the contractor of all costs of contracting plus an added fee. In these contracts, the contractor must provide an estimate of costs, called target costs. If costs exceed the predicted estimate, however, the government must pay for the cost overrun. The contractor is obliged to notify the government of cost overruns in order to recover.

The standard cost reimbursement contract provides little incentive for private parties to be efficient in carrying out the contract and has the potential for defrauding the government. As a consequence, the government has tried to develop incentive clauses in cost reimbursement contracts.

The **cost plus incentive fee contract** offers greater profits for private parties that can keep costs low. Payments are based on a comparison of actual costs with the initial target costs estimated in the proposal. If actual costs exceed the target costs significantly, the contractor receives a smaller additional percentage fee for profit. If actual costs remain low, below even the target cost, the contractor receives a larger additional percentage fee. The incentive fee also may be based on the quality of the contractor's performance.

Incentive contracts may reduce the problems of fraud on the government, but a risk remains. One concern is that contractors will artificially inflate their target cost estimate, as well as actual costs. For example, a company could intentionally overestimate labor costs in its original proposal. Incentive contracts do not protect against this type of fraud.

▄▄ Contract Formation

The legal rules for making a binding contract with the government are much like the rules for purely private contracts, as set forth in Unit Two of *West's Business Law, Fifth Edition* and Chapter 9 of *West's Legal Environment of Business*. The contract requires an agreement with mutual assent, consideration and other requirements of contract. The procedures for government contracts are slightly different.

The government usually initiates the process by publicizing its interest in contracting and issues a solicitation for offers. The solicitation sets forth the specifications of the items to be bid on. The content of the solicitation is very important—the government can select a contractor based only on the criteria set forth in the solicitation.

In response to the solicitation, interested private parties then must make an offer, typically using a required government form. For some procurement, companies submit sealed bids which are to be opened at a specified date. In other procurement, the government negotiates the terms and attempts to obtain a better deal. Offers become irrevocable once the government opens the sealed bids or awards a contract.

The government accepts the preferred bid by signing the offer form submitted by the private party. The standard offer form gives the government sixty days from bid-opening or receipt of proposals to accept. In other cases, the government has a "reasonable time" in which to accept an offer. As in private contracts, the government's acceptance must be unambiguous. In one case, government notification that an offer was "selected as the lowest responsive bid" did not qualify as an acceptance.[1] The intention to accept the contract must be absolutely clear.

The government may give a conditional acceptance. Here, the government would accept the offer with some condition, such as the future availability of funds to pay for the contract. The government may have a good faith duty to attempt to provide funds. If the condition fails, however, neither side would be bound to the contract.

The government also may be bound by an **implied-in-fact contract**. A contract may be implied-in-fact from the actions of the parties. In one case, the government awarded a contract for the production of armor-plated gun carriage parts. The government was to furnish the basic armor plate which was manufactured into the parts in the contract. After the contract was completed, the company asked the government to remove the surplus armor plate, but the government failed to do so. After eleven years, the contractor billed the government for storage costs. A court found that the government was required to pay these costs, due to an implied-in-fact contract.[2]

In private transactions, a party may also be liable in **quasi-contract**. A quasi-contract may

---

[1]*DeMatteo Construction Co. v. United States*, 600 F.2d 1384 (1979).

[2]*Algonac Manufacturing Co. v. United States*, 428 F.2d 1241 (1970).

arise when one party confers a benefit upon another and justice requires compensation. Courts have consistently held that the government cannot be liable in quasi-contract. In such a case, a party is dependent on the good will of the government to provide a benefit.

▬ Contracting Requirements

The government has a series of requirements that must be met before it will grant a contract. First, the contractor must demonstrate to the government that it is qualified to fulfill the contract. Second, the government has rules for competition in contracting.

Contractor Qualifications

Before giving any contract, the government must determine that the prospective contractor is qualified. The government first considers the contractor's *responsibility*. This includes an evaluation of the contractor's ability to perform the contract, which involves the following factors:

1. Adequacy of financial resources to perform.

2. Ability to comply with the government's delivery schedule.

3. Possession of necessary production, construction and technical equipment and facilities.

4. Possession of necessary management, accounting and other technical skills.

5. A historic record of satisfactory performance.

In addition to the responsibility qualification, potential contractors also must demonstrate a satisfactory record of *integrity and business ethics*. Submission of false documents, for example, may disqualify a prospective government contractor. Irresponsible contractors may be barred from all federal contracts, as discussed below.

Competition

The government has several procedures for selecting contractors. The Competition in Contracting Act requires "full and open" competition for government contracts and provides two primary methods for granting contracts: (i) the sealed bid procedure or (ii) negotiated procurement, which is sometimes called competitive proposals.

Sealed bid procedures are best used for contracts where price competition is paramount. In this procedure, the government solicits offers and sets a deadline by which time bids must be submitted. Once the deadline passes, the government conducts a public opening of all the bids.

To select the winning bid, the government first must make a finding of responsiveness. The bid must conform to the solicited specifications sought by the government. If a nonresponsive defect is minor, the bid will be considered as long as the contractor is deemed responsible. If the bid contains a material nonconformity with the solicitation, the bid must be rejected. This is true even if the bidder expresses a willingness to correct the bid.

A material nonconformity might be the offer of a significantly different product or service from that solicited. Thus, the government rejected an offer to furnish a drill with a torque capacity of 6000 ft-lbs at 27 rpm instead of the solicited capacity of 5800 ft-lbs at 50 rpm.[3] Material nonconformity could also be a failure to agree to the government's desired delivery schedule or presentation of a bid that is indefinite and ambiguous regarding the cost or quality of the products to be provided.

The government then evaluates the responsive bids in order to award the contract. The key evaluation involves price, and the government is to select the lowest-cost bid. Because bids may provide for differing payment schedules, the determination of the lowest-cost bid may require financial analysis. Once this determination is made, the government publicly announces the award.

Negotiated procurement may be used where non-price factors are significant in awarding a contract. The negotiated procurement procedure is often controversial and the source of most claims of fraud.

Under negotiated procurement, the government solicits offers but usually with less detail than under sealed bidding. Contractors then submit proposals that must include cost and pricing

---

[3]*Mobile Drilling Co.*, Comp. Gen. Dec. B-216989 (1985).

data. The government must seek out proposals from the maximum number of qualified sources. Then, government representatives conduct written or oral discussions with the contractors. In the course of these discussions, proposals are often modified. The government awards the contract based on price and on non-price factors, such as technical capability.

Negotiated procurement leaves government officials with discretion in awarding the contract. The government official must use the following evaluation factors:

1. Technical and management ability (such as experience, facilities, and quality of proposal design).

2. Contract amount (the compensation sought by the contractor).

3. Other costs to the government (for example, if the government must bear certain transportation costs under the proposal).

4. Responsibility factors (as discussed above).

The government uses varying procedures to evaluate the above factors and weight them against one another.

The government's solicitation should provide contractors some description of its weighting process. In one recent case, the government granted a contract to a bidder whose offer was 27 percent higher than that of another bidder. This resulted because the government gave 91 percent weighting to technical ability and only 9 percent weighting to contract amount. The award was reversed under protest, because the government insufficiently weighted cost and because the government did not disclose its unequal weighting of factors in its initial solicitation.[4]

The Competition in Contracting Act directs the choice of the proposal with the lowest overall cost to the government but permits consideration of other factors. Moreover, it may sometimes be difficult to determine the lowest cost proposal. In pure fixed-price contracts the lowest cost proposal will be clear, but in a cost reimbursement contract, costs can only be known after they are already incurred by the contractor and billed to the government. The relative importance of price and quality should be set forth in the government's solicitation.

The negotiated procurement process has been controversial and is the source of hundreds of protests every year. The government is permitted to conduct discussions with competing contractors but must be careful not to show favoritism in the bidding process. When the government has given only one of the bidders valuable inside information, courts have overturned a contract award to the favored bidder.

When the government improperly conducts a negotiated procurement, the contract may be cancelled and the government may be liable for the costs of the private parties engaged in the bidding. This principle is illustrated by the following decision.

---

[4]*Video Ventures, Inc.*, B-240016 (1990).

■ Case 19.1
Xerox Corporation v.
United States
United States Claims Court, 1990
21 Cl. Ct. 278

Background and Facts *In 1984, the Government Printing Office issued a Request for Proposals for a worldwide electronic publishing system for the U.S. Army. Bidders were invited to demonstrate their own capabilities and prepare draft specifications for the proposed system, to help inform the Army about the current state of the art. Five offerors, including the Xerox Corporation and Electronic Data Systems (EDS) submitted proposals. The government held discussions with the proposing parties.*

EDS apparently received favoritism in the discussions. The government changed the requirements of the system to meet EDS's needs. EDS representatives met secretly with procurement officials after final offers had been submitted. EDS was then allowed to lower its price by $25 million, or about 28 percent of its previous, "final" offer. This made EDS the low bidder.

The contract was initially awarded to EDS. After complaints by Xerox and congressional hearings, the contract was cancelled. Xerox then filed suit to recover its bid and proposal preparation costs because the government breached its implied contractual duty to fairly and honestly evaluate the bids.

MARGOLIS, Judge.

* * * *

The government argues that, in order to recover, Xerox must prove that the government's actions were the result of bad faith or fraud, and that Xerox is unable to make such a showing. Given the record of the government's performance in conducting this solicitation, and the government's admissions that the contract was improperly and illegally wired in favor of EDS, this court is surprised that the government should now contend that the procurement was not conducted in bad faith.

The proper standard to determine if a disappointed bidder is eligible to recover bid and proposal costs is whether the government's conduct was arbitrary and capricious toward the bidder-claimant. *Keco Industries, Inc. v. United States,* 203 Ct. Cl. 566, 574, 492 F.2d 1200, 1203 (1974) (*Keco II*). In Keco II, the Court of Claims set forth four general criteria by which to judge whether the government has acted arbitrarily and capriciously.

The Keco factors can be summarized as follows:

1)   subjective bad faith on the part of the procuring officials which deprives a bidder of the fair and honest consideration of its proposal;

2)   proof that the administrative decision denying the award lacked a reasonable basis;

3)   the degree of proof of error necessary to recover is ordinarily related to the amount of discretion vested in the procurement officials by applicable statutes and regulations; and

4)   proven violation of pertinent statutes or regulations may also be a ground for recovery.

* * * *

By altering EDS's benchmark tests and allowing EDS to lower substantially its bid price after all offerors' BAFOs had been submitted, the government clearly evinced bad faith towards Xerox. The government's actions deliberately prejudiced Xerox, the bidder with the highest score, in favor of EDS, the favored bidder. These actions also satisfy the other three Keco criteria. The government cannot and does not argue that its award to EDS rested on a "reasonable basis." See, e.g., *Rockwell International Corp. v. United States,* 8 Cl. Ct. 662, 663-64 (1985). In addition, the award was found to have been based on violations of pertinent procurement regulations. Finally, there is no amount of discretion (the third criterion) which could justify the actions taken by the government to alter EDS's scores and permit the post-BAFO adjustment of EDS's bid.

Decision and Remedy   *The court granted summary judgment for Xerox to recover its bid and proposal preparation costs. Xerox was directed to submit an estimate of these costs.*

Other practices also are forbidden in negotiated procurement discussions. The government may not use "auction techniques," such as informing one bidder of the price bid by other bidders. Nor can the government help a bidder by pointing out weaknesses resulting from the bidder's lack of diligence in preparing the bid.

Other than competitive bidding is statutorily limited to defined circumstances when a competitive bidding process is unfeasible. This is sometimes called **sole source contracting**, because the government negotiates with only one source. For example, no competitive bidding is required when only one contractor can fulfill the government's needs. In one case, the government needed a certain quality of scanning microscope, and only one company made a microscope of the necessary quality.

Other than competitive bidding also may be used when there is an unusual and compelling urgency to accept a bid imminently. In other cases, sole source contracting was allowed to ensure that new supplies would be compatible and interchangeable with existing supplies. Whatever the reason, the agency must provide a detailed justification for use of less than competitive bidding.

▀ Collateral Policies

Government contracts are not always given to the lowest bidder or the most qualified potential contractor. Congress has adopted a series of collateral policies to be considered in grant awards. These include a small business preference, a domestic preference, and an affirmative action preference.

Small Business Preference

Congress has authorized several programs to encourage the award of government contracts to small businesses. The definition of a "small" business depends on a company's number of employees or average annual receipts. The standards for a small business vary, however, for different classes of business and are set by the Small Business Administration.

Congress has directed that small businesses receive a "fair proportion" of government contracts but has declined to set a percentage quota for what proportion would be fair. Some agencies use "set asides," where the agency reserves a portion of contract awards for only small businesses. Contracts for less than $10,000 are presumptively reserved for small business. Larger proposals may be set aside for small business only if there is a reasonable expectation that at least two responsible small businesses will present competitive offers for the contract.

While small business cannot perform many large government contracts, the government encourages a large prime contractor to subcontract with small business when possible. For contracts in excess of $500,000 the large contractor's proposal must include a plan for granting subcontracts to small business.

Another small business preference occurs in the case of equally low bids in a sealed bidding process. To "break the tie" in bidding, the agency must award priority to small businesses that operate in areas where there is a labor surplus. The second tie-breaker is for small businesses in any area.

Domestic Preference

The Buy American Act established a general preference for acquisition of domestic products whenever possible. For unmanufactured articles in government contracts, the law requires generally that they be "mined" or "produced" in the United States. For manufactured articles supplied in government contracts, the article must be manufactured in the United States and more than 50 percent of its component parts must have been mined, produced, or manufactured in the United States.

The Buy American Act contains certain exceptions enabling the purchase of foreign items. If the cost of United States-produced items is "unreasonable," the contractor may use foreign-produced items. Under federal regulations, domestic cost is unreasonably high if it is more than 6 percent higher than foreign cost. If, however, the U.S. manufacturer is a small business, its costs are considered unreasonable only if they exceed foreign cost by 12 percent or more.

Another exception to the Buy American Act permits purchase of foreign-made articles, if the article is not available in satisfactory quantity or quality from U.S. producers. The Act also exempts purchases that are intended "for use abroad," purchases for which the "public interest" dictates the purchase of foreign products, and certain purchases under U.S. trade agreements.

Affirmative Action Preference

The government also grants a contract preference to businesses owned and controlled by socially and economically disadvantaged persons. This preference primarily extends to businesses that are more than 51 percent owned by members of minority groups.

This preference is under the Small Business Administration, which seeks to identify qualified minority businesses and match them with available contracts. Contracts may be awarded to a minority-owned business, even if that company is not the lowest bidder. In addition, for contracts exceeding $500,000, the potential contractor must include a plan describing its intent to subcontract with minority-owned businesses.

▬ Contract Challenges

The losing bidder in a government contract award has the ability to challenge the government's decision, if the bidder believes that it was treated unfairly. There are a variety of procedures and forums to make such a protest. The vast majority of these protests fail, however.

The losing bidder may protest the award to the government officer who decided the contracting or to the officer's superiors within the agency. The agencies have broad discretion regarding the procedures that they may use to evaluate such protests and the responses they choose.

If the losing bidder wants to take a formal protest outside the agency, the primary method used is to file the protest with the Comptroller General of the General Accounting Office (GAO) or with the General Services Board of Contract Appeals (GSBCA). Any losing bidder is an interested party and has **standing** to file such a protest.

Both the GAO and the GSBCA review the contract award to determine if it violated any statute or regulation. The General Services Board conducts a full evidentiary trial with opportunity for discovery and reverses those decisions that are unreasonable. By contrast, the GAO has a greater presumption of the agency's correctness and decides based on the submission of written reports by the protesting party and the agency. The GAO also provides much less opportunity for **prehearing discovery**, such as taking **depositions** of government officials. The costs of protesting to the GAO may be less, but the prospects for success are somewhat greater in the GSBCA.

Both the GAO and the GSBCA consider the same specific grounds for granting a protest, such as simple arbitrariness or unreasonability. In one case, International Business Machines Corporation and ViON Corporation both bid on a contract for supply of direct access storage devices. IBM's bid was lower, but the contract was awarded to ViON, which had a lower failure rate for the devices. IBM presented statistical evidence to the GSBCA, proving that there was no statistically significant difference in failure rates, so the board granted IBM's protest.[5]

Another ground for protest exists when the agency evaluates the bids on bases different from those set forth in the solicitation. In one recent case, the government solicitation said that certain subfactors (cost, experience, etc.) were to be weighted equally. When granting the award, the government gave one subfactor three times greater weight, and the GSBCA overturned the contract award for inconsistency with the solicitation.[6] The following decision describes a protest on these grounds.

---

[5]*International Business Machines Corp.*, GSBCA No. 8959-P (1987).

[6]*Severn Companies, Inc.*, GSBCA No. 9344-P (1988).

▰ Case 19.2
Protest of DALFI, Inc.
General Services Administration Board
of Contract Appeals, 1986
GSBCA No. 8755-P

Background and Facts   *The Naval Aviation Logistics Center (NALC) sought bids for engineering and technical support services. DALFI, Inc., had the past contract from NALC and bid for this new contract, as did System Dynamics, Inc., (SDI). The NALC source selection plan detailed the evaluation procedures to be used, the specific evaluation criteria, and the application of weighting factors to these criteria. The highest weighted factor was "understanding the requirements and technical approach." The agency also considered experience, qualifications, and other factors. The proposal stated that cost was not as important as technical qualifications.*

DALFI and SDI's bids were technically evaluated and scored according to the weighting criteria. DALFI's score exceeded SDI's on every individual criterion, and DALFI's total score was 91.44, while SDI's was 80.99. The total costs of the parties' Best and Final Offers (BAFOs) were $17,015,174 for SDI and $20,956,668 for DALFI. The contract was awarded to SDI. DALFI protested to the General Services Board, claiming that NALC overestimated the cost factor in awarding the contract.

La BELLA, Judge.

* * * *

The plain language of the solicitation does not mandate that NALC notify offerors if price has become the determinative factor and request a round of BAFOs in such an instance. However, directly at issue is the extent to which NALC was permitted under the solicitation, and hence statute and regulations, to make trade-offs between technical capability and cost/price.

NALC and the offerors are constrained by the evaluation and selection criteria contained in the solicitation. 10 U.S.C. @ 2305 (b) (1) ("The head of an agency shall evaluate . . . competitive proposals based solely on the factors specified in the solicitation."). In particular, the statute provides as follows:

Except as provided in paragraph (2) [involving rejection of all responses], the head of the agency shall award a contract with reasonable promptness to the responsible source whose proposal is most advantageous to the United States, considering only price and the other factors included in the solicitation.

* * * *

While the Board recognizes that contracting officers and source selection authorities may exercise discretion in the areas of selection and award of a contract, that discretion is not unfettered and is within this Board's authority to review when in the exercise of that authority a statute, regulation, or delegation of procurement authority may have been violated. A congressionally recognized and mandated assumption underlying the federal procurement system is that "full and open competitive procedures shall be used by the Department of Defense in accordance with the requirements of this chapter [chapter 137, title 10, United States Code]." 10 U.S.C. @ 2301 (a) (1) (Supp. III 1985), and that the Department of the Navy, among various groups, must promote full and open competition through its procurement policies and procedures, 10 U.S.C. @ 2301 (b) (1) (Supp. III 1985). Part and parcel of requiring that all responsible sources be permitted to submit sealed bids or competitive proposals on a procurement, is the notice that those who participate will be treated fairly and equally.

* * * *

* * * The failures in the reviews tainted all recommendations and determinations of the selection officials. Additionally, based on the information before them, the selection officials violated statutes and regulations when they, in essence, converted the procurement from one for the highest technically rated proposal representing the best buy to the Government into one for the lowest price for a technically acceptable proposal. To the extent that this conversion reflected NALC's intended basis for selection, award could not be so made under the terms and conditions of the solicitation as it read. The result is that NALC violated the solicitation itself, and hence statutes and regulations, in the conduct and award of the procurement.

Decision and Remedy   *The Board granted the bid protest and directed NALC to reevaluate the bids according to the solicitation provisions.*

Another basis for protest is that the solicitation contains unnecessary requirements. In another recent case, a protester claimed that a government solicitation for disk drives had minimum conditions on failure frequency that exceeded the government's needs and thereby restricted competition in bidding. The Board agreed, granting the protest because the performance requirement in the solicitation was not justified by the agency's needs. The agency could consider the criterion as a factor but should not have set such a high minimum for acceptability.[7]

If a protest succeeds, the GAO lacks authority to reverse the agency's contract award. The GAO *can* compel the agency to suspend the award temporarily and can recommend that the agency terminate the contract and reconsider competing proposals. The General Services Board has the power to revoke a contract award but has substantial discretion in making this decision. The Board could find that a contract award was contrary to law but still permit it to take effect.

In addition to the administrative remedies described above, a protesting bidder may also file a complaint in federal district court. A district court will only reverse a contract award when the award has no rational basis or involves a clear violation of a statute or regulation. The district court has broad remedial power and can enjoin, or prohibit, the protested contract award.

A disappointed bidder also could file a complaint in the U.S. Court of Claims. This tribunal is very limited, however, and can only hear cases filed before the contract is awarded. This means that the plaintiff must have some advance reason to believe that it will not receive the contract award. The Court of Claims reverses only those awards that it finds to be "arbitrary and capricious" or clearly contrary to law. This court also has broad remedial powers, similar to a federal district court.

Contract Administration

Once a contract is awarded, the contractor begins performing the contract, and the government monitors this performance. This is to ensure that performance is timely and up to specifications. The government may also monitor the costs of performance in order to avoid overcharges in cost reimbursement contracts.

In general, the interpretation of government contracts and rules for discharge of government contracts roughly parallel the rules for private contracts. Thus, if performance is inadequate, the government need not pay out on the contract. As in private contracts, the contractor must be given some opportunity to cure defective performance and recover on the contract. The contractor also

---

[7]*Memorex Corp.*, GSBCA No. 7297-P (1985).

will be able to obtain at least a partial payment if it has substantially performed the contract.

One important characteristic of government contracts that differs from most private contracts is the **changes clause**. This gives the government the right to insist on changes in contract work during the course of performance of the contract. The government may change characteristics of the goods or services under the contract and may also change the quantity demanded or the time of performance. The changes clause also enables the private contractor to propose changes to the government, which may permit more efficient performance.

The change clauses require that government change orders must be in writing. Many government-ordered changes impose extra costs on the contractor. In this event, the contractor can make a claim for an "equitable adjustment" in the negotiated contract price. This claim must be filed with a court or the relevant agency within thirty days of the time of the change order. The tribunal then adjusts the contract price to provide the contractor with fair compensation for the change required by the government.

There is another important provision that is special to government contracts, called **termina-tion for convenience**. This unique authority, contained as a condition in government contracts, permits the government to terminate the contract at any time. After a termination for convenience, the contractor can recover only costs incurred and profits attributable to work that is *already* done.

The government may terminate for convenience any time that termination is "in the Government's interest." Termination for convenience is most commonly used when the government no longer needs the goods or services under contract. A contractor can avoid a termination for convenience, only if the termination is arbitrary, in bad faith, or independently violates some law. For example, in one case a court enjoined a termination for convenience because the termination would violate a federal law requiring an environmental impact statement for a federal project.[8]

The right to terminate for convenience is also limited by the rules of contract law. The following case established this principle.

---

[8]*National Helium Corp. v. Morton*, 455 F.2d 650 (10th Cir. 1971).

■ **Case 19.3**
Torncello v.
United States
United States Court of Claims, 1982
681 F.2d 756

Background and Facts *Plaintiff was the president of Soledad Enterprises which received a government contract for grounds maintenance and refusal removal at Navy facilities near San Diego. The pest control portion of the contract specified a price of $500 per call. After the contract was entered, the Navy decided that this price was too high and did not use Soledad for pest control. Instead, the Navy used a competing bidder, who offered a lower price, but who had been rejected in favor of Soledad in the original bidding.*

Soledad filed suit in the Armed Services Board of Contract Appeals. The Board found that the Navy may have committed a breach, but the availability of termination for convenience justified the government's action. Although the government did not give notice of the termination for convenience, the Board held that it was a constructive termination. Soledad appealed to the Court of Claims.

BENNETT, Judge.

* * * *

* * * the convenience termination clause developed as a wartime concept, and it was a way for the government to avoid the continuance of contracts that the rapid changes of war, or the war's end, had made useless or senseless. See *Nash & Cibinic, Federal Procurement Law* 1104-07 (3d ed. 1980) [hereinafter Nash & Cibinic]. The government could halt a contractor's performance and settle with the contractor for the progress made. As such, termination for convenience functioned to allocate to the contractor the risk of losing the benefit of its full performance if full performance became unneeded. Even when termination for convenience was imported into peacetime military and civilian procurement, only 20 or 30 years ago, and receiving its almost universal application only from 1967, Nash & Cibinic at 1107, the basic idea remained constant that convenience termination was an allocation of the risk of changed conditions. A long line of cases in this court bears this out.

* * * *

It remains only to summarize what this opinion does and what it does not do. We are not holding here that the government cannot settle with contractors on those contracts that the government needs to settle. The termination for convenience clause is a valuable and important aspect of federal procurement. It has a long history and is founded solidly on Corliss of 1876. Nor are we holding that the government cannot draft for itself some method of exculpation so long as it also binds itself to something that will support the contract. We hold in this opinion only that the government may not use the standard termination for convenience clause to dishonor, with impunity, its contractual obligations.

In the case before us, the Navy had accepted Soledad's bid and had executed a contract knowing that another bid was lower. This contract bound the Navy to give to Soledad all of its pest control needs at the six housing projects covered. The Navy could not just walk away from this promise without making a mockery of the contract. It is nothing more than basic contract law that a power to terminate must be limited in some meaningful way, as measured by the requirement of consideration. The government has argued that there are no limits on its power to invoke termination for convenience. However, since the government's convenience termination procedures (giving notice and paying for services rendered), at least as applied to this case, also put no sufficient limits on the government, its unrestricted use of the clause cannot be correct. Any contract containing the clause, in the absence of something else to furnish consideration, would fail for the lack of any binding obligation. Therefore, we must read the termination for convenience clause in Soledad's contract to require some kind of change from the circumstances of the bargain or in the expectations of the parties. These are just the historical limits on the use of the clause as they have developed from Corliss.

Decision and Remedy   *The court granted Soledad's motion for summary judgment and remanded the case for further proceedings for damages for the breach of contract.*

▬ Contractor Fraud

Contractor fraud is a major concern of the government. Scandals, such as the infamous $500 screwdriver or toilet seat, have caused government officers to attempt to crack down on overcharges. Congress has passed several laws in an attempt to halt contractor fraud.

The most prominent fraud is of a type known as **defective pricing**. Defective pricing occurs when the contractor's bid contains inaccurate and inflated estimates of its costs, thereby providing the contractor a hidden extra profit. This generally occurs in cost reimbursement contracts, though it may also exist in fixed-price contracts with adjustment. A 1988 report by the Defense Contract Audit Agency found that 47 percent of all contracts investigated contained overpricing.

Truth in Negotiations Act

The Truth in Negotiations Act, as amended in 1986, requires all prime contractors and subcontractors to provide the government with cost and pricing data that they certify to be "accurate, complete and current." Cost and pricing data includes virtually all costs relevant to performing a contract, including costs such as computer time.

Under the Act, cost and pricing data must be submitted on Standard Form 1411 or its equivalent. The contractor also must explain the significance of this data to the government whenever necessary. The contractor must execute a Certificate of Cost or Pricing Data, which formally certifies to the accuracy, completeness and currency of the data submitted.

To succeed in a claim under the Truth in Negotiations Act, the government must have relied on the defective pricing in the contract. Regulations create a presumption of government reliance on this information, and the contractor has the burden of proof to show that the government did not so rely.

The Truth in Negotiations has no requirement of fraudulent intent. A contractor can violate this act, even if the defective pricing submitted to the government was accidental or innocent in nature.

The Truth in Negotiations Act applies to all government contracts that exceed $100,000. If the winning contractor's original pricing data is later found to be inaccurate, incomplete, or noncurrent, the government is entitled to a price adjustment of the amount that the price was overstated, plus any related overhead, profit, or fee.

Some contracts are exempted from the Truth in Negotiations Act. The first important exemption exists when there is "adequate price competition" for a contract. Adequate price competition occurs when there are two or more responsible offerors for a contract, and they compete independently for a contract to be awarded to the offeror submitting the lowest price. Another exemption exists when the price submitted is established in a catalog or privately negotiated market price.

False Claims Act

Defective pricing and other forms of contractor fraud are covered by the False Claims Act (FCA). Congress amended this law in 1986 to enhance the government's ability to prosecute fraud. This Act "piggybacks" on other statutes: A false certification of pricing data under the Truth in Negotiations Act would also be a false claim prohibited by the FCA.

The False Claims Act makes it illegal to submit a false claim to any government agency. A "claim" exists any time that a contractor submits a bill for recovery on a government contract, and each invoice or voucher is a separate claim.

The False Claims Act prohibits the *knowing* submission of a false claim for payment from the government. The 1986 amendments to the act defined the term "knowing" to mean that the claimant has actual knowledge of the falsity of the information underlying the claim, acts in deliberate ignorance of the truth or falsity of the information, or acts in reckless disregard of its truth or falsity. The FCA does not extend to innocent mistakes.

The False Claims Act provides significant civil penalties for its violation. The government can recover triple its actual damages, a $5000 to $10,000 penalty per false claim, and the costs of the lawsuit. A contractor can reduce its potential damages, however, by promptly disclosing any false claims that it has made and cooperating with the government investigation.

Qui Tam Actions

Qui tam actions are suits brought by private citizens against contractor fraud under the FCA. A private person who becomes aware of fraud, often an employee of the contractor, can file a suit against the fraud. The private prosecutor in a qui tam suit can recover a percentage of the government's recovery. Successful private plaintiffs can recover up to 30 percent of the government's damage award, plus attorneys' fees and expenses of the lawsuit. This is sometimes called a "bounty-hunter" provision. Government employees cannot use the qui tam recovery authority.

After a qui tam complaint is filed, the government has sixty days in which the Attorney General can take over the private action. The government is most likely to take over an action when the stakes are high and the case is strong. Alternatively, the government can permit the private plaintiff to attempt to enforce the law and recover an award. In recent years, hundreds of qui tam suits have been filed.

Criminal Fraud

Fraud on the government is a crime, and government contractors have been convicted of filing false statements and making false claims. Both individual employees and the corporation itself may be found guilty of crimes. Some prosecutions have been under generalized criminal statutes against mail fraud, wire fraud, or conspiracy.

The Criminal False Statements Act is a specific law that penalizes any person who knowingly and willfully submits false material statements to the government or who knowingly and willfully conceals or covers up such a falsification. A conviction under the Criminal False Statements Act requires proof of the following five elements:

1. The submission of a statement.

2. The submitted statement was intended to bear a relation to some matter under the jurisdiction of a federal agency.

3. The statement was material (significant).

4. The statement was false.

5. The party submitted the statement knowing it to be false.

Government contracts necessarily involve the submission of statements relating to the jurisdiction of a federal agency. Unlike a false claim, the statute prohibits all fraudulent statements, even if they do not involve a direct claim for money from the government. If the statement affects the awarding of a contract or the amount to be paid on the contract, it is likely to be found to be material. Knowingly false statements by contractors often fall within the statute.

In a recent case, a NASA contractor had to modify contract performance under a changes clause order and submitted its increased costs to the government. The contractor certified that its costs were accurate but was aware that the costs were significantly inflated over their actual costs. The defendants were convicted under the Criminal False Statements Act.[9]

Congress also has passed the Criminal False Claims Act, that covers any claims for federal money that are false or fraudulent. The general requirements are similar to the Criminal False Statements Act and this law requires a knowing or willful violation but is limited to actual claims on the government. A violation of either the false statements or false claims act is punishable by maximum fines of up to $250,000 for individuals and $500,000 for corporations per violation. Defense contractors can be fined up to $1 million per violation. Individual violators may be sentenced to prison for up to five years.

Exhibit 19-1 on page 382 compares and contrasts the requirements and penalties of the major laws regulating contractor fraud.

Several major military contractors have been convicted of fraud within the past year. Exhibit 19-2 summarizes some of the major convictions and penalties in 1990 alone.

Suspension and Debarment

Suspension or debarment is a drastic sanction undertaken by a federal agency, which prohibits a company or individual from receiving government contracts. A **suspension** is temporary (pending an investigation) and can last no longer than eighteen months, while a **debarment** is a final judgment that can last for a time period of years, as specified by the government. Both actions essentially involve a finding that the contractor lacks the responsibility necessary for government contracting. The government now suspends hundreds of contractors every year.

Because many companies are highly dependent on government contract work, suspension or debarment can be a crushing sanction.

---

[9]*United States v. White*, 765 F.2d 1469 (11th Cir. 1985).

Exhibit 19-1

Requirements and Penalties of Contractor Fraud Laws

	Truth in Negotiations	False Claims Act	Criminal False Statement Act	Criminal False Claims Act
ACTION	Submission of inaccurate, incomplete or noncurrent data	Making of false claim	Making material false statement	Making of false claim
INTENT	None required	Knowing false submission or disregard for truth	Knowing and willful submission	Knowing submission
RELIANCE	Required	Not required	Not required	Not required
REMEDY	Refund of overstatement	Triple damages plus $5000 to $10,000 penalty per false claim	Up to $1 million penalty & 5 years imprisonment	Up to $1 million penalty & 5 years imprisonment

Exhibit 19-2

Major Fraud Convictions and Penalties of Military Contractors in 1990

Date	Company	Crime	Penalty
10/4/90	LTV/Sierra Systems	Illegally obtaining documents	$1.5 million
5/11/90	Fairchild Industries Vol-Shan Division	Test fraud	$18 million
5/11/90	Emerson Electric	Price overcharging	$14 million
3/20/90	Raytheon	Illegally obtaining documents	$1 million
3/16/90	Grumman	Illegally obtaining documents	$2.5 million
2/27/90	Northrop	Test fraud	$17 million
2/2/90	General Electric Matsco Division	Price overcharging	$18.3 million

Suspension and debarment cannot be used as "punishment" for fraud, but can be imposed when in the "public interest." This standard, though, is a vague one.

Suspension is usually triggered by a contractor's indictment for a criminal offense. An agency advises the contractor, and the suspension takes effect immediately to disqualify new contracting. The contractor has an opportunity to submit a rebuttal in response to the notice. The agency may grant the contractor a hearing, but need not always do so. If the contractor is found innocent, the suspension is lifted. If the contractor is found to lack the necessary responsibility, the agency may impose a debarment. A debarment by one federal agency precludes a company from contracting with any federal executive agency.

The federal regulations list several causes that will justify a debarment order. One such cause is a lack of business integrity, as evidenced by a conviction for fraud or other crimes. Debarments have been based on violations of civil rights laws, antitrust laws, and environmental laws. Another cause is a willful violation of the terms of existing government contracts. For example, in one case a contractor was debarred for three years for construction of a building foundation that violated minimum state building code requirements, which the contractor knew or should have known.[10]

Debarment is not inevitable, even if a company has been convicted of a crime that justifies debarment. A company can always argue that "unusual circumstances" justify a decision not to bar the company. The following case illustrates the application of this principle.

———————————

[10]*Donald Schutte*, AGBCA 77-189.

■ Case 19.4
Federal Food Service, Inc. v. Donovan
United States Court of Appeals
for the District of Columbia Circuit, 1981
658 F.2d 830

Background and Facts *Federal Food Service was in the business of furnishing mess services to military installations around the country. A Department of Labor investigation found that Federal Food Services had violated the terms of the Service Contract Act by occasionally failing to pay employees their required holiday overtime pay and back pay. The law provides that violators of this Act are debarred from all government contracts for three years, unless the Secretary of Labor finds that unusual circumstances warrant removal from the debarment list.*

After an administrative law judge found Federal Food Service guilty of violating the Service Contract Act, the company appealed the debarment order, alleging unusual circumstances. Federal Food Service appealed to the Secretary of Labor, who affirmed the debarment. The debarment had a "catastrophic impact" on the company's business, so Federal Food Service sought a court ruling that the debarment was inappropriate.

NICHOLS, Judge.

* * * *

The next issue is whether the decision to debar was arbitrary, capricious, or otherwise not in accordance with law. 5 U.S.C. @ 706. Section 5 of the Walsh-Healy Act, 41 U.S.C. @ 39, incorporated by Section 4(a) of the Service Contract Act, 41 U.S.C. @ 353 (a), provides that the Secretary's findings of fact must be supported by a preponderance of the evidence.

In *Washington Moving and Storage Co.*, No. SCA-168, March 12, 1974, the Secretary established the following guidelines by which "unusual circumstances" should be judged:

Whether "unusual circumstances" are present in a case within the meaning of the Act must be determined on the basis of the facts and circumstances of the particular case. Some of the principal factors which must be considered in making this determination are whether there is a history of repeated violations of the Act; the nature, extent, and seriousness of past or present violations; whether the violations were willful, or the circumstances show there was culpable neglect to ascertain whether certain practices were in compliance, or culpable disregard of whether they were or not, or other culpable conduct (such as deliberate falsification of records); whether the respondent's liability turned on bona fide legal issues of doubtful certainty; whether the respondent has demonstrated good faith, cooperation in the resolution of issues, and a desire and intention to comply with the requirements of the Act; and the promptness with which employees were paid the sums determined to be due them. It is clear that the mere payment of sums found due employees after an administrative proceeding, coupled with an assurance of future compliance, is not in itself sufficient to constitute "unusual circumstances" warranting relief from the ineligible list sanction. It is also clear that a history of recurrent violations of identical nature, such as repeated violations of identical minimum wage or record-keeping provisions, does not permit a finding of "unusual circumstances."

*   *   *   *

These guidelines provide a rational and lawful approach to a determination of whether "unusual circumstances" exist. The "law to apply" presents the issue whether he has applied his own guidelines correctly in this instance.

In the instant case, after finding appellants were responsible for a deficiency of $3,328.35—an amount less than one-fifth of 1 percent of the contract values and in a labor intensive business, no doubt almost as low a ratio compared to total payrolls—the ALJ ostensibly applied the *Washington Moving* guidelines. The ALJ found that there was no evidence the violations were willful or deliberate and that appellants cooperated with the extensive and complex investigation of the case except for one unexplained instance at the Norfolk location. Payments were made fully and promptly even though substantial amounts had to be estimated through no fault of appellants. Previous violations in the past were not substantial and did not result in debarment because of unusual circumstances.

The vital finding which most influenced the ALJ and the district court was that "proper management would have precluded the continuing occurrence of these widespread underpayments." This is an important finding in view of the small ratio of violations to value of contracts (and to total payrolls, presumably) and the absence of consideration—admitted at oral argument—of offsetting over-payments. Large underpayments might be res ipsa loquitur of improper management. There are no facts in the record to refute the judicial belief that no rational precautions could reduce violations to absolute zero. In the instant case there was no showing in the record to support the ALJ's findings of what proper management would have accomplished in these premises and it was bald assumption. The ALJ cited to no testimony of management experts or of prevalent business practices to establish what practices appellants should have followed and did not. Certainly, contractors could hire an army of bookkeepers, accountants, and supervisors to insure no underpayments would occur, and perhaps most needful to all, lawyers at each location. Such a practice, however, would elevate the cost of operation to a level to endanger the future of appellants' type of business as a source of employment.

Decision and Remedy   *The court reversed the Secretary of Labor's ruling and remanded the case to district court with directions to vacate the debarment.*

■ **Ethical Perspectives**

Government Contracts and Corporate Codes of Ethics

Contractor fraud involves lying to and stealing from the federal government and is rather obviously unethical. Yet such fraud is fairly widespread. Unlike some areas of the law, government agencies attempt to enforce business ethics in contracting. The federal acquisition regulations specifically require that a government contractor maintain a satisfactory record of integrity and business ethics.[11]

A 1986 Presidential Commission, known as the Packard Commission, reported on the extensiveness of defense contractor fraud and urged that contractors adopt and enforce corporate codes of ethics. The Commission also promulgated Defense Industry Initiatives on Business Ethics and Conduct. These initiatives establish six guiding principles:

1. Each company will have and adhere to a written code of business ethics and conduct.

2. The company's code establishes the high values expected of its employees . . . each company will train its employees concerning their personal responsibilities under the code.

3. Each company shall create a free and open atmosphere that allows and encourages employees to report violations of its code to the company without fear of retribution for such reporting.

4. Each company has the obligation to self-govern by monitoring compliance with federal procurement laws and adopting procedures for voluntary disclosure of violations of federal procurement laws and corrective actions taken.

5. Each company has a responsibility to each of the other companies in the industry to live by standards that preserve the integrity of the defense industry.

6. Each company must have public accountability for its commitment to these principles.

Forty-six major defense contractors agreed to adopt and enforce these initiatives.

---

[11]48 C.F.R. section 9.104-1 (1988).

The defense contracting industry has been at the forefront of the move to employ ethical codes, and a survey by the Ethics Resource Center found that 92 percent of defense contractors have adopted a corporate code of ethics. Some companies have implemented codes of ethics in response to government demands.

The defense industry certainly illustrates that the adoption of a code of ethics is insufficient to ensure ethical behavior. Contractor fraud is still appallingly frequent. Some of the ethical codes are themselves deficient, and there are shortcomings in communicating the codes to employees and enforcing the ethical precepts found in the code.

Nevertheless, the government believes that such codes are valuable. The Defense Department regulations virtually insist that a contractor adopt a written code of ethics and an ethics training program for employees. The Department of Justice has adopted guidelines that consider the existence of a corporate code and training program in the decision of whether to prosecute a company for criminal fraud. The presence of a corporate code can also help a company avoid or shorten a debarment ruling.

■ International Perspectives

International Government Contracting

Competing for government contracts in foreign nations can be extremely lucrative. Government contracts in the European Community (EC) exceed $700 billion. South Korea recently has agreed to open over $500 million of government contracts for competition by foreign firms. Many countries, however, reserve government contracts for domestic firms. U.S. companies currently have about $5 billion in contracts in Western Europe.

An international Procurement Code has been adopted in connection with the General Agreement on Tariffs and Trade (GATT). The GATT Procurement Code has been signed by twenty-three nations, including all twelve members of the European Community, Japan, and the United States. The Code covers contracting by a nation's central government but does not extend to regional, state or local contracting.

The GATT Procurement Code is intended to open government contracting to international competition. Consequently, the Procurement Code restricts "buy national" laws, such as the Buy American Act. The U.S. Buy American Act does not apply to procurements covered by the Code, with respect to companies from other countries that have signed the Code. The Procurement Code also establishes rights and procedural obligations in government procurement.

The GATT Procurement Code is still limited, however, to a relatively small amount of government contracting. The Code does not cover contracting in the sectors of telecommunications, heavy equipment, transportation, and energy utilities. The Code's application is also limited to only some government agencies. Approximately 10 percent of the European Community's procurements are covered by the GATT Code. Seventy-five percent of European government contracts are granted to domestic companies on the basis of bidding specifications tailored for the national firm.

The United States government increasingly uses our trade laws to attempt to open overseas government procurement markets. Title VII of the Omnibus Trade Act of 1988 authorizes the president to close federal procurements to suppliers in any country that discriminates against U.S. companies. Section 301 of the Trade Act of 1984 permits the president to retaliate against unfair trade practices.

Section 301 was applied when Oslo, Norway, bid a contract for electronic toll booth equipment. After an American company won the bidding, the Norwegian Transportation Minister intervened and gave the contract to a Norwegian supplier. The U.S. threatened to apply section 301, and Norway agreed to compensate the U.S. company.

The U.S. has threatened to use section 301 or Title VII against Japan. Japan has a $300 billion total construction market, and U.S. firms have about $430 million in total construction contracts and $85 million in government contracts. The U.S. claims that Japanese companies use "dango," a procedure by which they rotate winning bids among themselves and exclude foreign companies. Trade officials are still trying to negotiate a resolution to this dispute.

Questions and Case Problems

1. Bay Cities Services had a contract with the Navy to provide service that had been issued on a sole-source basis. When the Navy sought an extension of the contract it requested cost and pricing data, but the company refused to supply such information. The Navy then solicited a new contract on a competitive basis and excluded Bay Cities from even competing for the contract due to their refusal to supply the requested information. Only one company submitted a proposal, which the Navy accepted. Bay Cities sued over their exclusion from the contract. Should the General Accounting Office uphold the exclusion of Bay Cities from contracting? [*Bay Cities Services, Inc.*, B-239880 (1990)].

2. The Army Tank Division Command solicited a contract for forklifts, and its proposal stated that "cost [is] of primary importance and is worth significantly more than technical, and somewhat more than technical, logistics/MANPRINT, and production capability combined." The contracting official was directed to make an award to the offeror whose proposal was "most advantageous and offers the greatest value." Later, the Command official awarded the contract to an offeror who was not the low price offeror. The lowest price offeror claimed that the contract award violated the Request for Proposals and should be overturned and granted to the low price offeror. Should a court overturn the contract award? [*BMY, a Division of HARSCO Corp.*, 693 F. Supp. 1232 (D.D.C. 1988)].

3. Cutler-Hammer, Inc., contracted with the U.S. Air Force to design, develop, and manufacture an electronic reconnaissance system to be carried in aircraft. The contract price was over $24 million and contained a defective pricing clause. The government sought a reduction in the total contract price when it discovered that Cutler-Hammer had disclosed a subcontractor's bid of $406,445 for a component lens and had not disclosed another subcontractor bid of $91,260 for the lens. Cutler-Hammer responded that the lower subcontractor's bid was so low that it was not a plausible offer. Should the government be able to obtain a cost reduction due to Cutler-Hammer's failure to disclose the low subcontractor bid? [*Cutler-Hammer, Inc. v. United States*, 416 F.2d 1306 (Ct. Cl. 1969)].

4. An aircraft manufacturer negotiated a $10.5 million fixed price contract with the U.S. Air Force to develop and produce an electronic Malfunction Detection and Recording System to be installed in B-52 aircraft. A subsequent audit discovered that a subcontractor had overstated material and labor costs by $234,623. The Air Force demanded a refund of this amount from the general contractor aircraft manufacturer. The company defended that it was unaware of the overcharge and bore no fault. Should the company be required to refund money to the government? [*Lockheed Aircraft Corp. v. United States*, 485 F.2d 584 (Ct. Cl. 1970)].

5. The Defense Logistics Agency solicited contracts for pediatric cystourethroscope kits. The solicitation required the kits to contain three different scope devices to examine certain internal body organs. A company's proposal was for kits that contained two different scope devices. After that company was awarded the contract, a losing bidder protested that the proposal did not match the solicitation. The winning bidder then promised to supply kits with three scope devices at the same price as in its original offer. The protester persevered. Should the General Accounting Office accept the modified proposal and uphold the contract award? [*Circon Acme*, B-231108 (1988)].

CHAPTER TWENTY

Legal Representation of Business

KEY BACKGROUND

Effective use of legal representation is increasingly important to business success. Every business action is potentially subject to a plethora of common law principles or regulatory requirements. The successful businessperson must be able to maneuver through this legal web, avoiding sources of liability. Legal problems lie at the doorstep of many failed businesses.

Many businesses perceive legal representation purely in terms of liability avoidance. They see potential liability for the negligent actions of employees or from manufacturing violations of environmental laws, or from any number of similar rules. Lawyers may be used preventatively to avoid sources of liability or in defense at a trial.

Some businesses use lawyers affirmatively, even as a profit center. The owner of patents must use lawyers to protect rights in those patents and obtain possibly lucrative royalty arrangements. Other businesses use lawyers to enforce their valuable rights in contracts or to sue in tort when they have been injured.

Moreover, virtually all businesses employ lawyers even when no lawsuit is present. Lawyers are important in negotiating and drawing up contracts for companies and for advising companies on their general legal rights and responsibilities.

Law is very important to contemporary business practice. A survey of recently appointed chairmen of boards of directors found that over 70 percent of these business leaders believed that business law education was important to a career in business management. Businesses in America spend over $25 billion every year for legal services.

Given the significance of legal problems, the modern businessperson must understand how to use the law, and lawyers, wisely. Quality legal representation can save a business (or gain a business) millions of dollars. Equally important is the need to understand how to use lawyers efficiently. Legal representation is expensive and a legal victory may become an economic loss, as legal fees and expenses mount.

This chapter discusses several key issues in the legal representation of business. First, the chapter considers the relationship of a business and its lawyers, and the rights of the businessperson. This includes the nature of the attorneys' duties toward clients and the rights and responsibilities of clients. Second, the chapter discusses business approaches to legal matters, such as litigation strategies.

Attorney-Client Relationship

When a person or a business retains legal counsel, it also obtains certain defined benefits in the **attorney-client relationship**. An attorney has a responsibility of great fidelity to the interests of the client. This is true regardless of whether the attorney is advising the client or litigating in court on the client's behalf.

A critical question in many cases is whether the parties have an attorney-client relationship. When a lawyer purchases a car, for example, she would be acting simply as a regular citizen and no attorney-client relationship is created. The following recent decision illustrates the process of identifying the protected attorney-client relationship.

■ Case 20.1
Sheinkopf v. Stone
United States Court of Appeals,
First Circuit, 1991
No. 90-1838

Background and Facts   *In 1987, the Omni Group was formed as a joint venture to develop real estate. Warren Sheinkopf was invited to join the venture by David Saltiel, a partner in the Boston law firm of Nutter, McLennen & Fish. Sheinkopf invested $100,000 in Omni. Saltiel organized the venture out of his law office and told Sheinkopf that many of his other clients were participating in the venture. Omni's projects ultimately failed, and Saltiel eventually entered personal bankruptcy. As a result, Sheinkopf lost his entire investment and suffered additional liability as a guarantor on several mortgages.*

Sheinkopf then "dove toward the deepest pocket in sight" and sued John Stone and other partners in the Nutter firm. Sheinkopf claimed that he relied on Saltiel's legal advice in investing and this constituted a breach of fiduciary duty by Saltiel in the course of an attorney-client relationship as an agent of the Nutter firm. The district court held that no attorney-client relationship existed and therefore granted summary judgment to defendants. Sheinkopf appealed.

SELYA, Judge.

*   *   *   *

Human beings routinely wear a multitude of hats. The fact that a person is a lawyer, or a physician, or a plumber, or a lion-tamer, does not mean that every relationship he undertakes is, or can reasonably be perceived as being, in his professional capacity. Lawyers/physicians/plumbers/lion-tamers sometimes act as husbands, or wives, or fathers, or daughters, or sports fans, or investors, or businessmen. The list is nearly infinite. To imply an attorney-client relationship, therefore, the law requires more than an individual's subjective, unspoken belief that the person with whom he is dealing, who happens to be a lawyer, has become his lawyer. If any such belief is to form a foundation for the implication of a relationship of trust and confidence, it must be objectively reasonable under the totality of the circumstances. We agree with the court below that this threshold was not crossed in the instant case. A reasonable businessman in Sheinkopf's shoes might have assumed that Saltiel had become his real estate guru, his business partner, his investment adviser, or even his fugleman—but no reasonable businessman would have assumed, on these facts, that Saltiel had become his attorney.

Appellant's assertion that such a relationship came into being rests on little more than his subjective belief, bolstered by his recollection of a general conversation, unanchored in time or place, concerning his desire to avoid personal liability in the Omni venture and Saltiel's assurance that he would "protect" appellant. We find nothing in such an exchange, however construed, suggesting that Saltiel (himself an investor in, and organizer of, Omni) thereby became appellant's attorney or agreed to furnish legal advice. At the very most, the comment was ambiguous, consistent with the role of either a legal or an investment adviser.

* * * *

By the same token, the assistance Saltiel subsequently rendered—obtaining appellant's check and having him sign various documents—fell equally, if not more appropriately, within Saltiel's professional competence as a promoter or investment adviser. It could scarcely have been reasonable for appellant, himself a successful entrepreneur, to give Saltiel a hefty check, blindly sign the signature page of the J/V Agreement, proceed to execute a series of loan guarantees patently inconsistent with any limitation of personal liability, and assume, nonetheless, that Saltiel had tacitly agreed to act as his attorney, and was doing so. In short, appellant's assertion that he reasonably relied on Saltiel for legal advice does not flow rationally from the evidence of what he, an experienced businessman, did with regard to investing in Omni.

Decision and Remedy   *The court affirmed the grant of summary judgment against Sheinkopf.*

When an attorney-client relationship does exist, the attorney assumes certain responsibilities. The American Bar Association has developed a Code of Professional Responsibility to guide an attorney's duties to the client. Among the "canons" of conduct for lawyers are:

- A lawyer should preserve the confidences and secrets of a client.

- A lawyer should exercise independent professional judgment on behalf of a client.

- A lawyer should represent a client competently.

- A lawyer should represent a client zealously within the bounds of the law.

These canons are elaborated by more specific ethical considerations and disciplinary rules governing attorneys.

Not every lawyer lives up to his or her duties every minute of the time. A client does have a right to count on a lawyer's responsibility, and this right is legally enforceable in a variety of circumstances.

▬ Attorney-Client Privilege

The **attorney-client privilege** provides that confidential communications between a client and an attorney are protected from disclosure. The attorney-client privilege belongs to the client—the client can generally prevent disclosure regardless of the attorney's desires. If an attorney, for some reason, chose to testify in violation of the privilege, the evidence would be inadmissible in court, and the attorney would be subject to sanctions.

The attorney-client privilege exists in order to encourage frank discussions between the attorney and the client. The client is less likely to be honest with an attorney if the client believes that its communication may be turned against it. Honest attorney-client communications enable the attorney better to represent the client's interests. In contrast, the privilege denies the courts' access to relevant evidence.

The Corporate Client

The attorney-client privilege is relatively straightforward in representation of an individual, such as a criminal defendant. The privilege becomes more complex if the attorney is representing a corporation.

This issue is an important one—corporations are commonly sued and need effective legal representation. Suppose that a company is sued for violation of an environmental regulation. The corporate counsel needs to know the true facts surrounding the alleged violation (for defending the case or for settling it). A corporation needs the assurance of the privilege of confidentiality for communications with its attorney.

The Supreme Court conclusively settled the issue of whether the attorney-client privilege protected corporations. The Court emphasized the importance of the privilege, noting that "[i]n light of the vast and complicated array of regulatory legislation confronting the modern corporation, corporations, unlike most individuals, 'constantly go to lawyers to find out how to obey the law.'"[1]

Communications with Corporate Agents

Of course, a corporation cannot itself communicate with attorneys but must speak through its agents (directors, employees, etc.). There remains a question of which communications are protected by the privilege. Some courts held that the privilege was limited to communications by the "control group," high corporate officers and directors.

The Supreme Court rejected the control-group limitation on attorney-client privilege and extended it more broadly, writing:

> Middle-level—and indeed lower-level—employees can, by actions within the scope of their employment, embroil the corporation in serious legal difficulties, and it is only natural that these employees would have the relevant information needed by corporate counsel if he is adequately to advise the client with respect to such actual or potential difficulties.[2]

The Supreme Court adopted a "subject matter" test that applies the privilege to the communications of any employee, so long as the communication relates to the employee's corporate duties and the communication is made at the direction of a higher level corporate officer. This decision applied only in federal courts, however, and some states continue to use the control group test.

Even communications with former corporate employees may fall within the attorney-client privilege. Several courts have held that a privilege applies to communications between a corporation's attorney and the corporation's former employees, if the discussion relates to matters taken in the course of the past employment relationship.

Suppose that Lance Bihalik was a vice president of Techtron in 1987 but subsequently moved on to another corporation. While working for Techtron, Bihalik helped prepare documents for the company's issuance of stock. Techtron shareholders sue the company for false and misleading statements in connection with the stock issuance. Techtron's defense attorney may discuss the issue with Bihalik, and the contents of this discussion may be privileged. The plaintiff shareholders may, however, themselves question Bihalik and obtain evidence for their case.

Courts also have suggested that a corporation's attorney-client privilege can apply to communications with nonemployee insiders. Techtron may have brought in an outside accounting firm to prepare materials for its share offering. Communications between Techtron's attorneys and its accountants may also be covered by the privilege, though this issue is not conclusively settled.

Officers' Right to Privilege

If a corporation has a privilege when its officers communicate with its attorneys, do the officers have a privilege in these communications? This issue is also an important one, because the government is increasingly seeking *individual* liability of corporate officers, as well as of the corporation itself.

A key case involved a Securities and Exchange Commission investigation into the actions of a corporation and its employees. The court held that employees theoretically could claim the attorney-client privilege but only in limited circumstances. The court ruled that the individual employees would be required to show:

1. That they made clear to the lawyer that they were seeking advice in their individual personal interest.

2. That the lawyer communicated to them in their personal capacity.

3. The substance of the communication did not involve the employees' official duties.[3]

Seldom will individual employees be able to meet this test and take advantage of the privilege themselves. Most employees remain dependent on their corporation to invoke the attorney-client privilege.

---

[1] *Upjohn Co. v. United States*, 449 U.S. 383, 392 (1981).
[2] *Id.* at 391.

[3] *In re Grand Jury Investigation*, 575 F.Supp. 777 (N.D. Ga. 1983).

Exceptions to Privilege

There are exceptions to the attorney-client privilege for both corporations and individuals. In some cases, a client may have the protection of the privilege and then lose it.

The attorney-client privilege is limited to confidential communications. If a client fails to keep the communications confidential, there is no privilege. If a corporate director discusses a case with an attorney and then describes this discussion at a large luncheon meeting, the privilege may be lost. In addition, a client may always waive the privilege and permit disclosure of the communications.

Another significant exception to the privilege exists where the communication does not involve legal advice. Corporate attorneys are often business counselors, and some attorneys have independent positions in a business. If a corporate president discusses a matter with his attorney and seeks business advice, rather than legal advice, the communication is not covered by the privilege.

Another problem with the attorney-client privilege exists when the attorney's duty of confidentiality would force him or her to engage in fraud. Model Rule 8.4(c) of professional responsibility creates in lawyers an obligation not to engage in dishonesty, fraud, deceit, or misrepresentation. In such circumstances, a lawyer should withdraw from representing the client.

The following recent decision details the requirements that must be proved for a party to take advantage of the attorney-client privilege.

■■ Case 20.2
Helman v. Murry's Steaks, Inc.
United States District Court for the
District of Delaware, 1990
728 F. Supp. 1099

Background and Facts   *Gloria Helman and her mother were shareholders in Murry's Steaks, Inc. ("MSI"). MSI subsequently merged with another company, and Helman and her mother were paid cash for their shares in MSI. Helman brought this suit complaining that MSI and individual officers of the company withheld material information regarding MSI's business in order to get Helman and her (now deceased) mother to sell their MSI shares for less than their true value.*

At the closing in which MSI purchased the shares, John Cogar attended in representation of Ms. Helman and her mother. The price was renegotiated and the parties later undertook a second and final closing. MSI sought to depose Cogar and question him about his discussions with Helman. The six discussions in question all occurred after the first closing, and Cogar did not bill Helman for this advice. Helman and Cogar resisted this testimony as protected by the attorney-client privilege. MSI moved the court to compel this testimony, arguing that no attorney-client relationship existed.

LONGOBARDI, Chief Judge.

*   *   *   *

The attorney/client privilege exists to encourage full and frank communications between attorneys and their clients. *Upjohn Co. v. United States*, 449 U.S. 383, 389, 101 S.Ct. 677, 682, 66 L.Ed.2d 584 (1981). The ability of clients to confer confidentially with attorneys enhances the caliber of legal representation an attorney can offer a client. *Valente v. Pepsico Inc.*, 68 F.R.D. 361, 367 (D.Del.1975). Yet not all communications between an attorney and an individual qualify for the protection of the attorney/client privilege "simply because [they are] made by or to a person who happens to be a lawyer." *Diversified Industries, Inc. v. Meredith*, 572 F.2d 596, 602 (8th Cir.1977), quoted in *United States v.*

Costanzo, 625 F.2d 465, 468 (3rd Cir.1980), cert. denied, 472 U.S. 1017, 105 S.Ct. 3477, 87 L.Ed.2d 613 (1985). In order to qualify for the protection, the Third Circuit requires that a communication adhere to the requirements annunciated in *United States v. United Shoe Machinery Corp.*, 89 F.Supp. 357, 358-59 (D.Mass.1950):

The privilege applies only if (1) the asserted holder of the privilege is or sought to become a client; (2) the person to whom the communication was made (a) is member of the bar of a court, or his subordinate and (b) in connection with this communication is acting as a lawyer; (3) the communication relates to a fact of which the attorney was informed (a) by his client (b) without the presence of strangers (c) for the purpose of securing primarily either (i) an opinion on law or (ii) legal services or (iii) assistance in some legal proceeding, and not (d) for the purpose of committing a crime or tort; and (4) the privilege had been (a) claimed and (b) not waived by the client.

* * * *

Defendants rely on *United States v. Wilson*, 798 F.2d 509 (1st Cir.1986) for the proposition that the Plaintiff was not a client of Coger's. In *Wilson*, the court held that where the defendant had not stated his desire to obtain legal services from the attorney, and the attorney testified that he did not give any legal advice to the defendant, and the defendant was not billed by the attorney, a memo written by the defendant to the attorney was not protected by the attorney/client privilege because the defendant was not, nor sought to become a client. *Id.* at 513. Although in the present case the Plaintiff was not billed for the services rendered by Cogar, it is evident from the deposition testimony of both the Plaintiff and Cogar that the Plaintiff was seeking legal advice. Thus, the present case is distinguishable from *Wilson*. Further, the Third Circuit has stated that unless the communication is in furtherance of some crime or fraud or the privilege has been waived, "communications with an attorney are privileged when they concern 'legal advice of any kind . . . sought . . . from a professional legal advisor in his capacity as such.' " Matter of Grand Jury Empanelled Feb. 14, 1978, 603 F.2d 469, 474 (3rd Cir.1979) (quoting J. Wigmore, Evidence s 2292 at 554 (1961), quoted in *United States v. Costanzo*, 625 F.2d at 468. The essence of whether one communicating with an attorney is a "client" depends upon whether that person is seeking legal advice not whether there is a payment of a fee or an execution of a formal contract.

Decision and Remedy   *The court ruled that MSI was not entitled to depose Cogar regarding the discussions in question.*

The privilege also does not apply when the communications are for the purpose of committing a crime or a fraud, when the attorney has an ethical obligation to disclose the communication (e.g., in order to prevent a client's perjury in court), and when the attorney acquired the information through his or her own research from outside third parties or even from business records.

▬ Work Product Privilege

A separate protection is found in the **work product privilege**. This privilege means that lawyers need not disclose the contents of materials that they prepare in the course of pursuing a case or defending a client.

When an attorney is preparing a defense, he or she typically will do extensive analyses of both the facts and the law of the case. A good attorney will prepare honest analyses, but these may be embarrassing to a client, as the attorney may find potential liability for the client. The work product privilege protects against disclosures of these analyses.

Unlike the attorney-client privilege, the work product privilege historically was for the benefit of the attorney, who theoretically could waive the privilege and incriminate the client. Courts now may permit the client to claim the benefit of the work product privilege as well.

The work product privilege was also historically limited to litigation and applied only to trial preparation activities of lawyers. Standard corporate counseling was excluded from the privilege. The lawsuit need not have been filed, however, and the privilege applies to documents prepared for possible future litigation. Some states, such as California, have extended the work product privilege to counseling in the course of contract litigations, even if litigation is not imminent.

▬ Legal Representation of the Corporation

As noted above, attorneys have ethical duties to represent the interests of their clients zealously and competently. If a lawyer fails to do so, the client may sue the lawyer for malpractice. When a lawyer is representing a corporation, however, the obligations of loyalty may become unclear.

Conflict of Interest

Attorneys who represent corporations may be put into difficult positions. The interests of the corporation as an entity are difficult to separate from the interests of its constituent parts. Nevertheless, the attorneys' Code of Professional Responsibility states:

> A lawyer employed or retained by a corporation or similar entity owes his allegiance to the entity and not to a stockholder, director, officer, employee, representative, or other person connected with the entity. In advising the entity, a lawyer should keep paramount its interests and his professional judgment should

not be influenced by the personal desires of any person or organization.[4]

The interests of the corporate entity are not easy to find, however. There is a natural tendency for corporate attorneys to identify themselves with the officers and directors who hired the attorneys.

A lawyer may violate duties, however, by identifying too closely with a corporate officer. The officer may have a conflict of interest with the corporation as a whole. In this case, the lawyer may have a duty to side with the corporation, even to blow the whistle on the director and seek his or her ouster. If a lawyer fails to do so, the corporation may sue the lawyer for breach of ethical duties.

The Securities and Exchange Commission ("SEC") has sought to require lawyers to play a greater role in supervising corporate governance and to be more aggressive in exposing and fighting self-interested actions of officers and directors. The SEC has sued lawyers for failing to go over the heads of the directors and inform shareholders of false and misleading information issued by the corporation.

Officers and directors may also seek to retain the corporation's lawyer to represent them in their individual capacities. In such cases, the lawyer must be careful that the individual interests of the officers and directors do not conflict with the interests of the corporation. If a lawyer is representing both the corporation and individual officers and if a conflict arises, the lawyer may be disqualified from representing *either* side in the dispute.

Even if the lawyer is scrupulous in representing the corporate entity, the representation may become controversial. A lawyer working with individual corporate officers may become so intertwined in both personal and corporate matters that a conflict arises. The following case involves such a claim.

---

[4]Ethical Consideration 5-18.

■ Case 20.3
**Professional Service
Industries, Inc. v. Kimbrell**
United States District Court for the
District of Kansas, 1991
No. 90-1326-C

Background and Facts *The attorneys John Thomason and Jerry Mitchell of the law firm of Harvey, Johnson, Mitchell, Blanchard & Adams represent Hall-Kimbrell Environmental Services, Inc. The company founders and president, David and Janet Kimbrell, sold their majority interest in the company to Professional Service Industries (PSI), Inc., in 1990. Shortly before the sale, the Environmental Protection Agency (EPA) served formal complaints against Hall-Kimbrell regarding the company's work in removing asbestos-containing materials from buildings. David Kimbrell met with Thomason and Mitchell, who were representing PSI. At the meeting he discussed the company's historic relationship with the EPA and the strong and weak points in the EPA's case.*

After investigating the EPA complaints further, PSI, as new owners of Hall-Kimbrell, locked David Kimbrell out of his corporate office. They also served a summons on Kimbrell, suing him personally for damages in the EPA matters. Kimbrell sought to disqualify PSI's lawyers from the case, claiming that they had a conflict of interest in the suit against him. He argued that because he was still an officer at the time of the meeting with the attorneys, he was a client of theirs and the attorneys should be barred from bringing an action against him.

CROW, Judge.

*   *   *   *

10.   David Kimbrell next contends the plaintiff's counsel violated Model Rule 1.13(d), which provides:

In dealing with an organization's directors, officers, employees, members, shareholders or other constituents, a lawyer shall explain the identity of the client when it is apparent that the organization's interests are adverse to those of the constituents with whom the lawyer is dealing. This Model Rule establishes a guideline of fairness for functioning with a legal fiction. When it becomes apparent that the interests of the corporate client and some of its constituents are no longer aligned and may even become adverse, the attorney must fairly inform the constituent that his only client is the corporation. Leading commentators on the Model Rules explain:

In such situations it might be said that the lawyer's duty of diligent representation requires him to discover as much information as he can from a co-worker with interests potentially adverse to those of the entity, even if that person is severely disadvantaged. However, although the lawyer's co-workers are not entitled to the full loyalty that a client deserves, they may have grown accustomed to treating the lawyer as if he owed full loyalty to them, and may not understand that he has served them only because they were serving the common master. Fairness therefore dictates that they not be lulled into confiding in someone who might become an adversary's lawyer. To learn confidences under false pretenses would be taking unfair advantage of non-clients, and must be avoided even if the information might be useful to the client.

*   *   *   *

There are times when the organizations' interest may be or become adverse to those of one or more of its constituents. In such circumstances the lawyer should advise any constituent, whose interest the lawyer finds adverse to that of the organization of the conflict or potential conflict of interest, that the lawyer cannot represent such constituent, and that such person may wish to obtain independent representation. Care must be taken to assure that the individual understands that, when there is such adversity or (sic) interest, the lawyer for the organization cannot provide legal representation for that constituent individual, and that discussions between the lawyer for the organization and the individual may not be privileged.

Whether such a warning should be given by the lawyer for the organization to any constituent individual may turn on the facts of each case. Rule 1.13(d) was intended to require a Miranda-type warning when it was likely a corporate officer could be confused over whether the corporate counsel was likewise representing his interests.

12. The very same facts in this case which defeat an implied attorney-client relationship also preclude the notion of any "dealing." There was no personal or direct contact between David Kimbrell and the attorneys. Interaction was strictly confined to group functions. There was no setting in which David Kimbrell could reasonably believe he was confiding in attorneys for his own personal benefit. Mere presence at a single corporate business meeting hardly constitutes "dealing."

Decision and Remedy   *The court held that plaintiff's counsel had not represented Kimbrell personally and could continue to prosecute the action against him.*

Malpractice

Clients may sue their attorneys for legal malpractice. Malpractice is a distinct tort, but this action may also take the form of a breach of contract action, assuming that the client and the attorney have a contract.

To maintain a malpractice action, the client first must show that there was an attorney-client relationship. Payment of fees to an attorney is generally sufficient to establish such a relationship, unless evidence indicates that the services rendered by the attorney were not legal in nature. In general, a client can sue only his or her own attorney for malpractice and cannot sue an opposing party's attorney.

The second requirement of a malpractice action is proof that the attorney failed to exercise ordinary legal skill and knowledge. Some courts use a "locality" standard and hold the attorney to the ordinary standard of skill found in the lawyer's community. A New York attorney therefore might be held to a different standard than that for a Nebraska attorney.

The third and most difficult requirement of a malpractice action is proof of damages. Suppose that Cole Corporation hires a lawyer to sue its competitor Hanom Corporation for unlawful monopolization. Cole's attorney fails to use ordinary skill, and the case is dismissed. If Cole sues its attorney, it must prove that it would have won the antitrust case against Hanom, had it had proper representation. Otherwise, Cole suffered no damages from the malpractice. It may be difficult for a plaintiff to show that it would have prevailed in the initial action.

Various legal errors may produce malpractice actions. Some of the traditional sources of malpractice are: (i) failure to file a claim before the statute of limitations runs out; (ii) failure to sue all the proper defendants; and (iii) failure to raise a legal defense. All these represent fairly clear-cut circumstances of malpractice.

An increasingly important area of malpractice litigation involves the settlement of lawsuits. As discussed in the following section, lawyers are being sued for negligently conducting settlement negotiations.

Settlements

Over 90 percent of lawsuits are settled without going to trial. Settlement saves legal costs and avoids risks. Many parties leave the substance of settlement negotiations to their attorneys, who understand the law and the client's relative prospects.

Although the lawyers often conduct the settlement negotiations, the client retains ultimate control over the decision to settle (unless the client has expressly delegated this control to the attorney). An attorney-client relationship does not give the lawyer the power to settle the case.

A lawyer has specific duties when conducting settlement negotiations. First, the lawyer must exercise ordinary skill and knowledge in the conduct of settlement negotiations. This includes the investigation of the details of any settlement offers. Second, the lawyer must communicate settlement offers to the client, to enable the client to make a choice of whether to accept the offer. This generally should be done in writing.

A number of lawyers have been held liable for negligently settling or failing to settle cases. The following decision provides an example of such a case.

■■ Case 20.4
Smiley v. Manchester Insurance & Indemnity Company of St. Louis
Supreme Court of Illinois, 1978
375 N.E.2d 118

Background and Facts *The underlying lawsuit arose when Charles Toney's car crossed the center line of the road and struck a vehicle in which Roy Smiley, Byron Emanuel, and the Arnolds were riding. Smiley was seriously injured and Emanuel was killed, as was Toney. The Arnolds suffered relatively minor injuries. Toney had been poor, having only assets of an insurance policy with Manchester Insurance & Indemnity Company for $20,000 per accident. Plaintiff's attorney, Bernard Reese, sought to settle for this amount, but the insurance company refused. Reese then sued Toney's estate for $50,000 for Smiley and $100,000 in wrongful death damages for Emanuel. The Arnolds threatened suit for their minor injuries.*

Manchester assigned the case to William Knight and encouraged him to seek a settlement. The company authorized Knight to settle all claims arising from the accident for $20,000: $17,000 for the Smiley and Emanuel claims and $3000 for the possible claims of the Arnolds. Reese sought $10,000 each for Smiley and Emanuel. Knight refused and made no counteroffer.

After a trial, a jury returned an award of $25,000 for Smiley and $50,000 for Emanuel's estate. The insurance company paid $10,000 to each, the maximum policy limits. Reese then sued Manchester for the remaining $55,000 on a claim of bad faith refusal to settle. A court declared that Manchester was liable for $35,000. Manchester then sued Knight for negligently failing to settle the initial claim for $20,000. A jury returned a verdict for Knight, but an appellate court overturned this holding and found Knight liable for negligence. Knight appealed.

RYAN, Justice.

* * * *

It is clear that an attorney is liable to his client only when he fails to exercise a reasonable degree of care and skill; he is not liable for mere errors of judgment. (*Brown v. Gitlin* (1974), 19 Ill.App.3d 1018, 313 N.E.2d 180; *Dorf v. Relles* (7th Cir. 1966), 355 F.2d 488.) In viewing the evidence in this case most favorably to Knight, we must affirm the decision of the appellate court that as a matter of law he failed to act as a reasonable and skillful attorney in the area. The uncontroverted evidence at trial shows that as early as November 1967 he was instructed to attempt settlement with all of the claimants. He never contacted the Arnolds, nor did he ever discuss settlement with their attorney, Clifford Stoner, testifying that he had not been hired to handle their claims. The undisputed evidence also shows that on June 18, 1968, Knight was expressly authorized to settle the Smiley and Emanuel claims for $17,000 and to reserve $3,000 for the Arnolds. In spite of this authority, he never offered any amount to settle the claims, nor did he disclose his authority to Reese or to the trial judge. On June 24, 1968, at the start of the trial when Reese asked if there was any offer and renewed his demand to settle the cases for policy limits, Knight replied "no comment." Even if we accept Knight's testimony that he only had $17,000 authority, his complete inaction when he had knowledge of the seriousness and probable liability of the claims clearly did not comport with the actions of a reasonable attorney. In addition, the evidence shows that Knight had the complete file, including the adjuster's report of Reese's plan to sue in an attempt to collect any judgment in excess of policy limits. His failure to make even a token offer on the record constituted strong proof of bad faith in support of the claim for recovery of the excess. Even if Reese would not have accepted $17,000 in settlement, such an offer would at least support a claim by Manchester of a good faith attempt at settlement. Attorney Ohlson also testified that even if Knight only had $17,000 authority, he had not acted reasonably in failing to offer it.

* * * *

Knight also contends that even if he were found to be negligent as a matter of law, the appellate court erred in reversing the jury verdict in his favor. He argues that even if the jury had found him to be negligent, it could have decided that Manchester had been contributorially negligent or that his negligence was not the proximate cause of damage. The evidence adduced at trial showed that Manchester was aware that the case may have been one of liability as early as March 1967. Blackwell testified that he had determined, as early as March 1967, that the possible value of Smiley's and Emanuel's claims was probably in excess of the policy limits, although he did not conclude that the insured was liable until December 1967. The vice president and general counsel of Manchester wrote a letter to a reinsurer on August 4, 1967, which indicated he was aware of the extent of injuries, the likelihood of liability and the probability that liability would exceed the policy limits. Apparently it is Knight's theory that the jury could have concluded from these facts that Manchester was contributorially negligent in failing to settle the claims at an early stage. Such a conclusion would be erroneous. The mere fact that an insurer makes a preliminary evaluation of liability based on an adjuster's investigation does not mandate immediate settlement of the claims. The evidence shows that one eyewitness was not located until December 1967. In fact, depositions were not taken of the two claimants until June 1968. Under Knight's theory, an insurer would have a duty to immediately settle a case as soon as it became aware of facts indicating fault. This theory ignores the realities of the settlement and litigation process. In addition to investigating the factual occurrence, both parties must research the applicable legal principles, ascertain the possibility of success at trial, and determine the nature and extent of damages to a reasonable certainty.

> Thus, we hold that Manchester's failure to settle at an early stage did not constitute contributory negligence.
>
> **Decision and Remedy** *The court affirmed the finding that Knight was negligent and remanded the case for a trial on damages.*

▆ Document Retention and Destruction

Corporate documents are an enormously significant part of most litigation. After a plaintiff files an action, the plaintiff makes **discovery requests** to go through the defendant's document files. Attorneys may scour many file cabinets' worth of files including millions of documents, in hopes of finding a single key document that will support their action. Sometimes, the plaintiff's attorney may find a "smoking gun" document, in which some employee of the defendant virtually confesses that the defendant engaged in illegal activity.

Companies also must be concerned about the documents retained in private files. A company settled a case for hundreds of millions of dollars, after the plaintiff found a "smoking gun" document in the possession of a retired employee that he kept at home in his personal files.

A company's policy on *retention of documents* can thus have a significant bearing on its ultimate liability. Obviously, companies have reasons to keep documents on hand to preserve a record of past decisions and inform future decisions. In most cases, however, it is lawful for companies to destroy most of their documents. Companies today are far more likely to have a formal program to destroy documents systematically.

A systematic program is important to a lawful document destruction program. It is important that document destruction be a matter of a company's ordinary course of business and not a selective destruction of potentially incriminating documents.

It is also unlawful to destroy documents even in a systematic program if those documents are potential evidence in a lawsuit. Once a company is sued, document destruction related to the suit must halt. Indeed, a company must cease document destruction as soon as it is placed on notice of a potential lawsuit against it. Failure to abide by these rules can result in substantial sanctions against a corporation.

When a company has documents in its possession, it must provide them to an opposing party who makes a relevant request for the documents. In a 1991 case, a company promised to turn over relevant documents but then intentionally failed to do so. A judge found that the company had obstructed justice and ordered the company to pay $2.98 million in sanctions. The company's attorneys were fined $300,000 for their participation in the obstruction of justice.

▆ Management of Legal Affairs

Legal issues are so important to companies that most major businesses have separate legal departments. The management of legal issues involves many of the same business decision-making principles as do more traditional business decisions. Wise decision making involves an understanding of the legal context, however.

In-House vs. Outside Counsel

Traditionally, when a company ran into legal trouble the company called upon an outside law firm to help resolve the difficulty. Most companies thereby developed long-standing relationships with particular law firms that handled the companies' business.

Using law firms is rather expensive, however, as many attorneys bill at high hourly rates. Companies discovered that many routine legal tasks could be handled more cheaply "in-house." The company would hire full-time lawyers as employees of the company in order to handle these tasks.

Companies are making increased use of in-house counsel to cut costs. The number of in-house counsel is growing at a rate twice as fast as for outside counsel. Over 90 percent of business consumer affairs legal problems are handled by in-house counsel. Two-thirds of litigation practice, however, is handled by outside counsel, and a much higher percentage of complex litigation is handled by outside counsel.

A business must decide how much of its legal work will be sent to more expensive (but perhaps more expert) outside counsel and how much legal work will be done in-house. The company also must decide how many resources to devote to in-house legal departments. Better pay will attract better in-house lawyers, which will reduce the need to use outside counsel.

There are some significant advantages to developing a large in-house legal department. These lawyers will be particularly familiar with the firm and its needs. In-house counsel also help the company efficiently use outside counsel, when necessary. In-house counsel is always on hand to respond quickly to crises.

One of the greatest advantages to in-house counsel is its close involvement with management and ability to engage in *preventive* legal analysis. The firm's general counsel is a member of senior management near the top of the corporate hierarchy. In this position, a general counsel can insist on early legal involvement in business actions to prevent future legal problems. In-house counsel can educate employees to avoid sources of liability. The in-house counsel of Digital Equipment Corporation, for example, devotes 50 percent of its time to preventive actions.[5]

There are some disadvantages to in-house counsel, though. Some suggest that they actually increase the total legal costs of a corporation because its desire "to provide the company with maximum legal protection" actually produces more work for outside counsel.[6] In-house counsel may also have more difficulty giving independent legal advice, divorced from business considerations.

The decision of whether to employ in-house or outside counsel is closely analogous to ordinary production decisions made by companies. Manufacturing companies typically must decide whether to buy raw material inputs for their products or to invest capital resources and make their own raw material inputs. Capital budgeting models are available to make this type of decision.

The legal services area presents unique factors that must be considered in the choice between in-house and outside counsel. For example, outside counsel may better protect the attorney-client privilege between a corporation and its lawyer. The privilege exists for communications between a corporation and its in-house counsel. A court may be more likely, however, to find that a discussion with in-house counsel was a business discussion rather than a protected legal discussion.

In-house counsel may have other disadvantages in litigation. Many trials require one side to disclose trade secrets or other sensitive business information. When this material is disclosed, it is often subject to a protective order. The protective order might limit disclosure of the trade secret to the attorneys and require that the attorneys keep the information secret.

Some courts have been reluctant to permit in-house counsel to see such sensitive materials. The fear is that in-house counsel may be so closely connected with a company's management that maintaining secrecy is difficult or impossible.

As noted above, there is a trend toward making greater use of in-house counsel. There will remain some need for outside counsel, however, and companies should apply sound business principles in determining the size and responsibilities of their own legal departments.

Litigation Strategy

When a company is involved in litigation, as either a plaintiff or a defendant, the company may take a combative posture. The opposing litigant becomes defined as the enemy, who must be vanquished at all costs. This attitude is an inefficient one, however, and companies should consider litigation strategy as simply another business decision, to be guided by concern for the financial success of the enterprise.

This means that companies should seriously consider settling claims and take a rigorous approach to settlements. In fact, over 90 percent of lawsuits brought in the United States end in settlements. How can a company decide whether to settle a claim and for how much?

---

[5]Chayes & Chayes, "Corporate Counsel and the Elite Law Firm," *37 Stanford L. Rev.* 277, 287 (1985).

[6]Samuelson, "The Changing Relationship Between Managers and their Lawyers," *33 Business Horizons* 21, 25 (1990).

A company's litigation strategy should consider three key factors. First, the company should consider its prospects or probabilities of success in the action. Second, the company should consider the financial consequences if it does succeed or if it fails in the litigation. Third, the company should consider the costs involved in pursuing the litigation to a conclusion.

A standard way for considering these factors is through the use of a decision tree. This is a mechanism for evaluating the consequences of various choices and ascribing a present value to each of these choices.

Exhibit 20-1 presents a decision tree analysis of the following hypothetical case. ChemCorp purchases raw materials from LedCorp and turns them into final products that are sold to AmCorp. LedCorp breaches its contract with ChemCorp by failure to provide raw materials, which costs ChemCorp $1 million in profits on its AmCorp contract. Then AmCorp considers ChemCorp an undependable supplier and exercises its right to cancel other contracts, costing ChemCorp another $4 million in profits.

ChemCorp sues LedCorp for breach of contract, and claims $5 million in damages. LedCorp's attorneys and ChemCorp's attorneys get together to discuss settlement. LedCorp's attorneys state: "We think we have a defense to the breach of contract count, and we don't have any liability for the $4 million lost profits, because this was unforeseeable and therefore cannot be recovered." The LedCorp attorneys go on to say that they will be "nice guys" and agree to settle the whole case for $1 million payment to ChemCorp. Should ChemCorp accept this settlement offer?

The offer obviously has some appeal. Accepting the settlement eliminates any risk of losing at trial and also avoids the need to spend litigation costs. Plus, ChemCorp will be covered for its immediate losses. But look at the problem more rigorously.

The ChemCorp attorneys decide that they have an 80 percent probability of winning the case at trial but only a 50 percent probability of winning the full $5 million in damages as foreseeable. In addition, a full trial of the case will cost the company $500,000. These calculations are then plugged into the decision tree found in Exhibit 20-1.

This decision tree considers the probability of each consequence. If ChemCorp wins at trial, it has a 50 percent chance of making $4.5 million ($5 million minus $500,000 in costs) and a 50 percent chance of making $500,000 ($1 million minus $500,000 in costs). The expected value of a win at trial is therefore $2.5 million (50 percent of $4.5 million plus 50 percent of $500,000).

Of course, there is a 20 percent possibility that ChemCorp will lose at trial. The consequences of this outcome are a net loss of $500,000 in litigation costs with no counterbalancing recovery. When this risk is factored in, the expected value of going to trial is $1.9 million.

Based on this assessment, assuming that ChemCorp's probabilities are reasonably accurate, ChemCorp might decide to reject the settlement offer. ChemCorp would demand a settlement of at least $1.9 million to forego litigation.

The decision tree presents a financial analysis of litigation. But legal issues present other issues that must be factored into a decision, even if they cannot be so readily quantified.

A business might have strong reasons to settle the case. Litigation might expose trade secrets or facts that could embarrass the business and injure its position in the marketplace. Defendants often want to settle personal injury cases, because settlements are not officially reported. If a defendant tries a case and loses, that case becomes a precedent that both alerts and assists other plaintiffs in similar circumstances.

In contrast, a business might want to litigate in order to set a precedent for future circumstances. If a company faces a recurring legal problem, the company may benefit significantly from settling the problem conclusively. If the business wins, it may avoid future litigation and associated expenses. If the business loses, at least it has more certainty to plan for the future.

Alternative Dispute Resolution

The above discussion assumed that the only choice in resolving a dispute was litigating or settling. Businesses are increasingly turning to a third alternative, that has become known as **alternative dispute resolution**, or ADR. ADR involves a variety of nontrial procedures, with the most common being arbitration and mediation. ADR is discussed in some detail in Chapter 3 of *West's Business Law, Fifth Edition* and in Chapter 3 of *West's Legal Environment of Business*.

ADR is typically less expensive than litigation because it is less formal. In a dramatic example, Texaco and Borden had been litigating a $200 million antitrust and contract case for several years and then tried ADR. They were able to settle the case within three weeks.[7]

Arbitration is the most common form of ADR. Arbitration is also much like a trial, though somewhat less formal. The system is adversarial in nature, as both sides present witnesses and often are represented by attorneys. An arbitrator or a panel of arbitrators substitute for a judge or jury, however, and the rules of evidence are typically relaxed in arbitration.

---

[7]Allison, "Five Ways to Keep Disputes Out of Court," *Harvard Business Review*, January-February 1990, at 11.

Arbitration has advantages and disadvantages as opposed to litigation. Arbitrators are not bound by legal precedents and have great discretion in structuring a remedy. This means that they have flexibility to do justice, but it also means that they may ignore the law and reach unpredictable results. Arbitration decisions generally cannot be appealed.

Arbitration does not create a binding precedent and generally permits less discovery, which may be good or bad depending upon the circumstances of the parties. Arbitration gives parties some ability to select a decision maker with business experience who understands the industry, rather than a less informed judge or jury.

One of the greatest advantages of arbitration is secrecy. In the course of a trial, documents will be publicly unearthed that may prove embarrassing or that may reveal business secrets. The law provides for protection of trade secrets, but this protection may be insufficient. In arbitration,

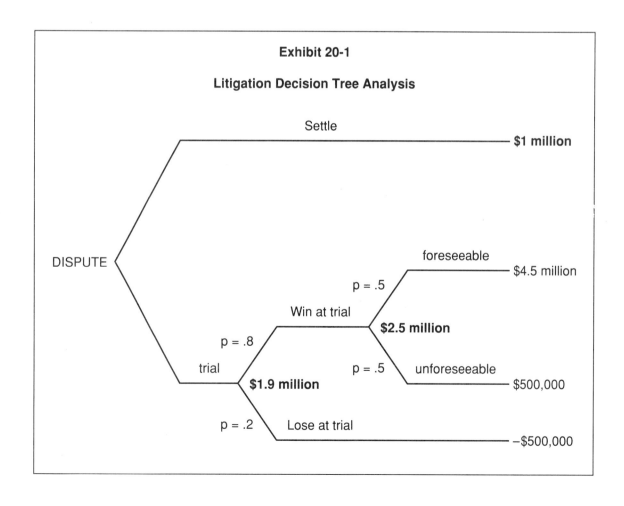

Exhibit 20-1

Litigation Decision Tree Analysis

it is much easier to preserve confidentiality. The arbitrator's code of ethics requires total confidentiality.

A party, even a plaintiff, may not simply choose arbitration, however. Most arbitration requires the consent of both parties. This consent may be expressed in advance. Thus, many business contracts provide that any disputes arising out of the contract must be arbitrated and not taken to court.

The law is very supportive of these arbitration agreements and enforces them. If there is an agreement to arbitrate and one side ignores the agreement and sues in court, the other side may halt the trial and compel arbitration. The winner in an arbitration can go to court if necessary and get a judgment compelling the loser to pay the damages found in arbitration.

Mediation is another important form of ADR. In mediation, like arbitration, an outside party is called in to help settle a dispute. Unlike an arbitrator, the mediator cannot decide the case but can only help the parties reach their own settlement. Mediation may therefore fail, and a lawsuit could still result.

Mediation often succeeds, however, as a neutral outsider can assist parties in resolving their differences. The mediator can set an agenda of issues and help each side understand the other's position, as well as suggesting compromise solutions. Businesses have significantly increased their use of mediated dispute resolution in recent years.

In addition to arbitration's advantages of speed, confidentiality and cost savings, mediation offers even greater advantages in preserving business relationships. Even those companies with long-standing and profitable business relationships may have disputes. Litigating the disputes may poison the relationship and cost everyone business. Mediation and other forms of ADR help preserve ongoing goodwill even among disputants.

▬ Ethical Perspectives

Whistle-Blowing and the Corporate Counsel

As previously discussed, employee whistle-blowing presents several ethical dilemmas. The ethical problems of whistle-blowing are complicated when the individual is an in-house lawyer of a corporation. The ethical code of lawyers holds them to an especially high standard of loyalty to their clients, which whistle-blowing may violate.

In-house counsel typically has a broad mandate to audit the corporation and investigate potential legal problems. Thus, these lawyers are especially likely to discover unethical or illegal actions taken by the company. If the lawyer discovers such actions and tries to correct them, higher corporate officers may refuse to cease the unethical or illegal behavior. Should the lawyer then report the action to a government agency or to the press?

In addition to the duty of loyalty to the client, the lawyer's problem is further complicated by the attorney-client privilege. Attorneys are bound to preserve the confidences told them by clients. whistle-blowing also seems to violate this duty.

There are countervailing ethical concerns as well. Suppose that a lawyer for Western Automobile Corporation discovers that the company is installing defective seat belts in order to save costs in its new convertible model. If the lawyer informs government agencies, he or she may be violating ethical duties of loyalty and the attorney-client privilege. But if the lawyer fails to disclose the defective seat belts, he or she may be contributing to the deaths of innocent persons.

Because the attorney-client privilege is a legal matter, the courts have had to deal with lawyer whistle-blowing. In one case, an in-house attorney for a corporation was told to destroy documents to protect the company in litigation. This would violate another ethical duty of lawyers, so the attorney refused, and the corporation fired the counsel. After the counsel sued the corporation, an Illinois court held that the firing was lawful.[8]

Another recent Illinois decision reached a somewhat different result. An in-house lawyer was fired after he informed the Food and Drug Administration that his employer was selling defective dialysis machines. The court held that this firing violated public policy and permitted the attorney to sue the corporation.[9] That court emphasized the societal harm that would result from a failure to blow the whistle.

In yet another case, an attorney for IBM believed that a Colorado facility was discriminating against minority employees and was fired for complaining. He released to the press confidential internal IBM documents even after IBM had obtained a court order prohibiting their disclosure. The lawyer currently faces criminal contempt of court charges for disclosing the information.

Becoming an attorney does not answer all ethical problems in favor of the client, and the in-house counsel may have an ethical responsibility to blow the whistle on especially wrongful corporate practices. The special situation of the attorney should affect the whistle-blowing decision, however. The attorney should exhaust all opportunities to correct the problem in-house. If this fails, the attorney might blow the whistle to correct the problem, but should do so in a manner that protects client confidences as much as possible.

---

[8]*Herbster v. North American Co. for Life and Health Insurance*, 501 N.E.2d 343 (Ill. App. 1986).

[9]*Balla v. Gambro, Inc.*, 560 N.E.2d 1043 (Ill. App. 1990).

▬ **International Perspectives**

International Practice for U.S. Attorneys

An increasingly important issue, from both legal and business perspectives, is the international legal representation of American companies. To what extent can United States lawyers practice law in foreign nations? This issue arises in many important contexts, including international finance law, international tax law, international antitrust law, international trade and contracts, and international litigation and arbitration.

As U.S. companies extend their global reach, foreign representation becomes more significant. Most companies have an established relationship in the United States with a lawyer or a law firm that has served the company as a trusted counselor and advocate. The U.S. company understandably believes that its longstanding American lawyer can best represent it, and is reluctant to rely upon unknown foreign attorneys, even for foreign legal problems.

Many law firms are attempting to expand overseas to provide legal services. Differences in legal systems and language complicate the ability to practice law in foreign countries, however. In addition, foreign nations may have rules restricting the practice of nonnationals as attorneys.

In Japan, an American attorney cannot become a "lawyer" (bengoshi) but may serve as a legal consultant. The legal consultant, though, may not give advice on Japanese law and may not litigate in the courtroom. The European Community ("EC") is relatively open to American lawyers. The EC directive on lawyers' freedom to provide services prohibits certain forms of discrimination against foreign lawyers.

Lawyers practicing in foreign nations must be careful to follow local ethical codes. For example, a number of nations prohibit attorney advertising and contingency fees, which are accepted in the United States.

Clients also must be aware of transnational differences in the attorney-client relationship. For example, a 1982 opinion of the European Court of Justice addressed the attorney-client privilege in Europe. The court held that the privilege did not apply to communications with in-house counsel and was limited with respect to foreign lawyers not licensed under the laws of the European nation.

Questions and Case Problems

1. MiraCo is negotiating a merger with Simple, Inc. The negotiations are far along and the merger agreement is nearly complete. MiraCo consults its attorney regarding whether the company should disclose the imminent merger agreement in documents sent to shareholders. The attorney advises that the company should disclose the merger under federal securities law, but the company decides not to do so. Should the lawyer disclose this violation or withdraw from representation of MiraCo?

2. The water pollution control laws require that a company report any accidental discharge of chemicals into a river. ChemCo suffers such an accidental discharge, but the company's president directs its in-house counsel not to report the discharge as required by law. In-house counsel agrees with the president that disclosure will lead to many unjustified lawsuits against the company, because the discharge was small and harmless. Should the in-house counsel go along with the admonition not to report the discharge?

3. Jill Apsit is an outside attorney representing the Growth company. At an emergency meeting of Growth, with Jill present, an engineer reports that Growth is emitting a chemical that causes cancer into the community. Jill advises that Growth take steps to halt these emissions. The Growth chief executive officer then discharges Jill, saying that she doesn't understand how business works. Jill fears that the emissions may cause multiple deaths in the community, which is wholly unaware of this risk. May Jill disclose this information to the public?

4. Four major officers of Sandro Corporation were considering conducting a management-led takeover of Sandro. The Sandro chief executive officer, Susan Becker, approached an outside attorney, John Lamar, about the takeover. He suggested that they form an acquisition company, which they did, naming it SA Acquisition. After the takeover was completed, a creditor of Sandro claimed that Susan and the other officers had engaged in fraud and acquired the company at an unfairly low price. The creditor demands that Lamar testify about his discussions with Susan. He claims that these discussions are confidential, but the creditor claims that he was representing SA and not Susan. Should Lamar be compelled to testify concerning his discussions with Susan?

5. An attorney represented a corporation in connection with a share issuance. Subsequently, individuals who purchased shares in the corporation sued the company for violation of securities laws in a shareholders' derivative action. This is where shareholders sue on behalf of the company itself to protect the company's assets. The shareholders sought to obtain the testimony of the attorney regarding the advice that he gave the corporation, but he defended with the attorney-client privilege. The shareholders claimed that they *were* the client and that their derivative action was on behalf of the client, so the privilege did not apply against them. How should the court rule on this matter? [*Garner v. Wilfinbarger*, 430 F.2d 1093 (5th Cir. 1970)].

Glossary

A

Actually foreseen test A principle holding accountants liable in negligence to non-client third parties that the accountants know will rely on the accountants' work.

Affirmative action A policy that gives some special preference to minority groups or women in order to overcome present effects of past discrimination.

Alternative dispute resolution The use of non-judicial procedures, such as arbitration or mediation, in order to resolve disputes, including legal disputes.

Ambiguity doctrine A principle of law that states that unclear insurance policy provisions will be construed in favor of the policy holder and against the insurance company.

Antidilution statutes State laws that restrict the use of new trademarks that may diminish the value of established trademarks.

Antidumping duties Tariffs charged importers who sell goods in the U.S. at unfairly low prices.

Appraisal The right of shareholders to reject the price offered for their shares in a merger and invoke a special proceeding to set a fair value for those shares.

Arbitration A method for resolving legal disputes through agreed-upon submission to a disinterested third party, rather than to a court.

Assumption of risk A doctrine that bars a plaintiff's recovery in tort when the plaintiff has knowledge of a danger and its nature and voluntarily accepts that danger.

At-will contracts An employment agreement that permits employer or employee to cancel the agreement at any time.

Attorney-client privilege A rule of law providing that confidential communications between a client and an attorney are generally protected from disclosure at law.

Attorney-client relationship The special affiliation created when a person retains a lawyer for legal representation, creating special duties for the attorney.

Average worker test Rule permitting workers' compensation recovery for stress so severe that the ordinary employee would be harmed.

B

Bailment An agreement in which goods or personal property of one person (the bailor) are entrusted to another (the bailee), who is obligated to return the property to the bailor or dispose of it as directed.

Bank holding companies Umbrella corporations that control a number of banks in different states, but which are regulated by federal law in order to preserve competiton in banking.

Bank mergers The acquisition of one bank by another, regulated by both banking and antitrust laws.

Bill of lading A document serving as evidence of the receipt of goods for shipment and as documentary evidence of title to the goods.

Branch banking The ability of a bank to establish divisions in other geographic areas, which remains limited by state laws.

Break-up fee A provision in which a company seeking a merger partner agrees to pay that company's costs in the event that the merger fails to succeed.

Bridging the gap The probability that a trademark user may expand its use of the mark into new product lines.

Burden of proof The presumption that a party must overcome in order to establish its case; the burden of proof on most issues lies with the complainant.

Business judgment rule A rule that immunizes corporate management from liability for actions taken in good faith, so long as such actions are within the power of the corporation and the authority of management.

C

Changes clause A provision in government contracts that gives the government the unilateral right to insist upon necessary changes in the original contract during the course of its performance.

Charitable immunity A doctrine that charities cannot be found liable for certain torts; now largely abandoned.

Charter The federal authorization from the Comptroller of the Currency required for entry into banking.

Chinese Wall An office procedure that isolates groups of workers in an attempt to avoid a conflict of interest.

Churning A prohibited practice in which stock brokers trade excessively in a client's account in order to accumulate greater commissions.

Collateral Property that is used as security for a loan.

Community ascertainment A requirement of communications licensing that a broadcaster research the needs of the local community.

Comparable worth compensation A policy intended to equalize the pay between jobs traditionally held by women (such as nursing) and those traditionally held by men (such as plumbing).

Comparative advertising The practice whereby the advertiser for one company compares its product with those of its competitors.

Comparative negligence A theory of tort law under which the liability for injuries resulting from negligent actions is shared by all persons who were negligent (including the injured party), on the basis of proportional negligence.

Constructive fraud Fraud that results from a party's failure to disclose material facts, notwithstanding a duty to disclose.

Contracts of adhesion An agreement in which one party has a stronger bargaining position and requires acceptance of its contract language without negotiation, such as in an insurance contract.

Control-share acquisition statutes State laws that limit the voting rights of corporate acquirers once they obtain some "control share" of stock, such as 33% or 50% ownership.

Cost justification The principle that permits price discrimination among buyers if the price differential is reflective of different costs.

Cost plus incentive fee contract A cost reimbursement contract in which the contractor is pro-

vided financial incentives to cut costs and accomplish the contract more efficiently.

Cost reimbursement contract A government contract in which reimbursement is based upon the actual costs of completing the contract.

Countervailing duties Authorization of U.S. law that requires additional tariffs be paid on imports to offset effects of foreign subsidization of an industry.

Covenant A promise in a contract to undertake or not to undertake certain actions.

Coverage In insurance law, when an occurrence is within the scope of the policy, requiring the insurer to pay.

Crown jewels A corporation's most profitable asset.

D

Debarment A prohibition on contracting with the government for an extended time.

Defalcations by a corporation's employees Illegal actions by workers that steal from or defraud an employer.

Defamation A tort providing damages when a spoken or written statement causes injury to another's good name, reputation or character.

Defamatory statement A remark that injures the reputation of another person.

Defective pricing A bid by a party seeking a government contract that contains inaccurate or inflated estimates of its true costs of contracting.

Deficiency judgment A judgment against a debtor for the amount of a debt remaining unpaid after collateral has been repossessed and sold or after foreclosure proceedings.

Deposition A generic term referring to any evidence verified by oath and generally applied to the pretrial testimony of a witness taken under oath.

Diagnosis-Related Groups Organizations administering the federal health care reimbursement system that set schedules of payments for specific categories of medical procedures.

Discovery requests A pretrial procedure in which a party to litigation seeks information in the possession of the opposing party.

Disparagement Economically injurious falsehoods referring to the product or property of another.

Disparate impact discrimination A rule of civil rights law that prohibits certain employment practices or procedures that, while neutral on their face, have a significant discriminatory effect against members of a certain protected class.

Disparate treatment discrimination A rule of civil rights law that prohibits intentional employment discrimination against members of a certain protected class.

Distribution License A special permit facilitating the export of even sensitive groups to certain approved countries.

Doctrine of compelled self-publication A principle that permits a person to sue for defamation if he or she is required to repeat the defamatory statement of another.

Doctrine of increased risk A rule permitting employee recovery in workers' compensation when the job created an enhanced risk of the type of injury suffered by a worker.

Doctrine of positional risk A rule permitting employee recovery in workers' compensation when the job placed the worker in the position that caused an injury.

Draft Any instrument drawn on a drawee (such as a bank) that orders the drawee to pay a certain sum of money.

Dram shop laws Statutes that make alcohol servers liable for harm caused by patrons who become drunk.

Due-on-sale A clause in mortgages that accelerates the date of full payment whenever the mortgaged property is sold to another.

Dumping Selling goods in a foreign country at a price below that charged for the same goods in the domestic market.

Duty of fidelity An ethical and legal responsibility of loyalty in certain circumstances, such as an agent's duty to a principal.

E

80 percent rule A guideline suggesting the presence of discrimination when an employment selection procedure chooses members of one protected class at a rate less than 80% of that for choosing members of another protected class.

Employee stock option plan A corporate program that enables employees to acquire stock in the corporation.

Escape clause A provision enabling U.S. companies to obtain financial relief from imports that seriously injure domestic producers.

F

Failing company defense A legal doctrine permitting even those mergers that significantly increase market concentration when the acquired company is on the brink of failure.

Fair competition A defense to business torts that permits certain accepted market activities, such as advertising a low price.

Fairness opinion A statement by a financial adviser that makes conclusions regarding the financial fairness of an offer such as a tender offer.

Faltering company exception A circumstance in which a company need not provide 60-day advance warning for a plant closing, because the company was seeking capital to keep the plant open.

Fixed price contract A government contract in which the private contractor will receive a set payment determined in advance.

Fixed price contract with economic price adjustment A fixed price contract that allows for modification during the contract to account for increased cost or other changed circumstances.

Flip-in poison pill A corporate program that grants shareholders some special benefit (such as stock options) whenever an outsider purchases a large stake in their corporation.

Flip-over poison pill A corporate program that permits shareholders to acquire discount shares of stock in any corporation that seeks to acquire the company.

Foreclosure A procedure in which a lender takes possession of real property after the borrower has failed to make mortgage payments.

Fraudulent concealment Doctrine permitting employee to sue employer in tort if employer covers up the presence of a harm to the employee.

Free agency The ability of professional athletes to switch teams in order to obtain a better contract.

G

General duty clause A requirement of the Occupational Safety and Health Act that businesses be maintained free of known hazards that could cause serious injury to workers.

General License A permit required for the export of goods other than especially sensitive goods.

Generally Accepted Accounting Principles The conventions, rules and procedures necessary to define accepted accounting practices at a particular time.

Generally Accepted Auditing Standards A set of professional qualities and judgments for accountants set by the American Institute of Certified Public Accountants.

Generic trademark A mark that merely states what the product is (such as aspirin) and is unprotected by trademark law.

Going private merger A combination of companies that has the effect of eliminating public shareholders by purchasing their shares.

Going-private transaction A corporate restructuring action of purchasing all public shares of the company, leaving the corporation owned by a single entity or small group.

Golden parachutes Provisions that provide large severance payments to corporate officers who lose their jobs as a consequence of a takeover.

Good cause defense A response to wrongful discharge actions that permits the firing of employees who have taken certain actions deemed to justify discharge.

Good character A standard for obtaining a government communications license that considers the past behavior of the party seeking the license.

Goodbye fee A payment made by a company to an acquirer who seeks but fails to take over the company.

Greenmail A procedure in which a party purchases shares and threatens a takeover of a corporation in order to get its management to repurchase their shares at a premium price.

Guest-innkeeper relationship A special affiliation between a hotelkeeper and a guest that imposes specific duties on the hotelkeeper.

H

Hazard communication standard An OSHA rule that requires that employees be informed of certain hazardous substances in the workplace.

Hello fee A payment made to a party in order to induce them to make a takeover offer for a company.

Hostile environment harassment A prohibited practice in which continual sexual slurs or comments makes it difficult for an employee to work.

I

Implied contract of employment A legally enforceable employment agreement in addition to a written contract arising out of the conduct of the parties.

Implied warranty of suitability An unstated promise in a contract for lease of real estate to the effect that the property will suit the needs of the party leasing the property.

Implied-in-fact contract A contract formed in whole or in part from the conduct of the parties (as opposed to express language)

In the course of Rule that limits workers' compensation recovery to injuries that resulted while an employee was on the job.

Independent contractor One who works for, and receives payment from, an employer, but whose working conditions and methods are not controlled by the employer (and therefore is not an employee).

Innocent purchaser defense A rule of Superfund liability that permits certain acquirers of property to escape damages for cleanup costs on that property, if the acquirer meets certain conditions of innocence.

Insider lending A practice whereby a bank makes loans to its officers, directors or leading shareholders, which are permitted but restricted by federal law.

Intentional infliction of emotional distress A claim of action in tort when one party's outrageous action purposefully causes severe emotional distress in another.

Intentional tort exception Rule that permits employee to sue employer in court if employer intentionally causes harm to worker.

Interstate commerce Business that crosses state lines or affects enterprise in other states; defined very broadly.

Investment banker A financial professional who performs services such as valuation of stock in connection with mergers and acquisitions.

J

Joint bidding A procedure that creates an exception to antitrust laws in order to promote exports.

Junk bonds Debt securities that carry a high risk of default, such as those issued in connection with a leveraged buyout.

K-L

Lending limits A legal restriction on banking that sets a ceiling on loans to a single person or entity.

Leveraged buyout A corporate takeover financed by loans secured by the assets of the corporation to be acquired, resulting in a high level of debt financed with junk bonds.

Licensing standards Rules by which the government grants a limited authority to enter into a service, such as a radio or television station.

Limited liability company A business structure in Hungary that roughly parallels U.S. corporations.

Liquidated damages A provision in a contract that establishes an amount of damages owed in the event of a breach of the contract.

Liquidation A final government determination of tariff duties owed in international trade.

Lock-up An agreement where a corporation conditionally agrees to sell some asset to a third party at a specified and usually discounted price.

M

Malice A requirement that a public figure may not succeed in a defamation claim unless the defendant's statement was knowingly or recklessly false.

Management buyout A procedure in which the executive officers of a corporation obtain ownership of the corporation by purchasing the shares of public shareholders.

Manager's privilege A principle that allows corporate officers to interfere with the contracts of their employer, so long as the interference is in the employer's interest.

Material safety data sheets Documents that set forth the risks of hazardous chemicals found in the workplace.

Mechanics' lien security interest A doctrine that gives builders a security interest in a building until they are paid for their services in erecting or repairing the building.

Mediation A method of dispute resolution employing a neutral third party, who acts as a communicating agent between the parties in order to promote a voluntary settlement of the dispute.

Minority ownership A standard for granting communications licenses that encourages the participation of minority groups, such as African Americans or Hispanics.

Misappropriation A tort creating liability for a party that uses the likeness or other attributes of a person without permission.

Mortgage A written instrument giving a creditor (the mortgagee) an interest in the debtor's property as security for a debt.

N

Negligence A source of tort liability for failure to exercise reasonable care.

Negligence per se A doctrine that holds that a party who violates a law is therefore automatically considered negligent.

Negotiated procurement A government contracting procedure where the government negotiates contract terms with specific contractors.

Newsworthiness The right to publish private information about another due to the legitimate public interest in the information.

No-shop clause An agreement between an acquirer and the company to be acquired in which the latter's management promises not to seek out competing offers.

O

Opinion A non-verifiable statement of a subjective view, as distinguished from a fact.

Opinion shopping A practice in which a client retains a series of accountants in order to find one that produces results favorable to the client.

Ostensible agency liability A doctrine holding hospitals potentially liable for torts of non-employee doctors who use the hospitals' facilities.

P

Paramour liability A form of sexual discrimination in which a supervisor favors one employee because of their private relationship.

Parody A comment (such as a political cartoon) that makes light of a person or event and is largely protected by freedom of speech.

Participation agreement A contract in which two or more banks combine to extend credit and which has become a common source of lender liability litigation.

Peer review organization A group of physicians that review the health care decisions of other physicians to determine if they are reasonably and medically necessary.

Penalty clause A provision in a contract that appears to provide for damages in the event of breach but that is unenforceable because it is intended as a penalty and not an estimate of damages.

Per se negligence See negligence per se.

Personal animosity exception Exception to workers' compensation recovery when an injury results from personal relationship of worker and not the workplace context.

Personal injury by accident Rule of workers' compensation that limits employee recovery to harms that resulted in injury by accident (as opposed to intentional action).

Poison pill A corporate program that makes the company unattractive to a hostile acquirer, such as a shareholder rights plan.

Pollution exclusion A provision of insurance contracts that eliminates coverage for damages resulting from gradual pollution by the policyholder.

Possessory liability A doctrine that provides that the possessor of property is liable for certain harms produced by the condition of the property.

Posting A requirement that certain warnings or notices be placed prominently, such as hotel disclaimers of liability for personal property.

Predatory pricing A prohibited practice of selling goods at a very low price in order to destroy the competition and monopolize a market.

Prehearing discovery An opportunity for disputants to obtain information about the other's case in advance of the hearing on their dispute.

Prepayment prohibitions A provision in a loan such as a mortgage that precludes the borrower from paying off the loan before the end of its term.

Price discrimination A practice in which the same good is sold at different prices to different customers and which is sometimes illegal under the Robinson-Patman Act.

Primary line competition Harm to competition from price discrimination, where the practice reduces competition among sellers of goods.

Privilege In tort law, a defense providing the ability to act contrary to another person's right without liability.

Privity The relationship that exists between the two or more parties to a contract.

Programming A standard for communications licensing that considers the type of shows offered by broadcasters.

Proximate cause The "substantial" or legal cause in tort law used to determine whether a defendant should bear the burden for a plaintiff's injuries.

Proxy card A card sent to shareholders in order to authorize a specific person to vote their shares at a shareholders' meeting.

Public policy A rule that prohibits firing employees for certain highly objectionable reasons, such as refusal to violate the law.

Purchase and assumption transaction A method in which the federal government seeks to salvage a failed bank by getting a solvent bank to take over its assets and liabilities.

Q

Quasi contract An obligation or agreement imposed by law in the absence of an actual agreement, in order to prevent unjust enrichment.

Qui tam actions The authority for private citizens to bring suits for fraud in government contracting and obtain part of the government's recovery.

Quid pro quo harassment A prohibited employment action in which an employee is forced to grant sexual favors in order to obtain an employment opportunity.

R

Real estate Property in the form of land and buildings fixed to the land that is immovable, as opposed to personal property that can be moved (also real property).

Reasonable expectations doctrine A legal principle that states that insurance policies cover claims that are within the reasonable expectations of the policyholder.

Redemption right The opportunity for a borrower to pay off a mortgage loan even after the lender has declared a default and begun foreclosure proceedings.

Related products rule A principle that permits a trademark holder to sue producers of similar products that use an infringing trademark.

Renewal expectancy A presumption in favor of the incumbent holder of a broadcast license in an ownership challenge in a government relicensing proceeding.

Reserve clause A provision in professional sports contracts that binds an athlete to a given team.

Restructuring A corporate program that usually provides shareholders with a substantial dividend that is financed by taking on additional corporate debt.

S

Scalping A prohibited practice in which brokers purchase shares and then promptly resell them to their clients at a profit.

Sealed bid procedures A government contracting procedure in which private contractors submit secret offers and the government selects a winner without negotiations.

Secondary line competition Harm to competition from price discrimination, where the practice reduces competition among purchasers of goods.

Secondary meaning The association of a trademark with a particular maker's product, required for protection of descriptive or unregistered trademarks.

Section 1981 A statutory provision prohibiting race discrimination in private contracts.

Self tender A procedure in which a company makes a tender offer to purchase its own stock.

Setoff A rule permitting banks to take money from one account of a debtor to pay off an overdue obligation in another account with the same institution.

Sex plus discrimination A rule that discriminates based on a person's sex plus another characteristic, such as prohibiting males from wearing long hair.

Shareholder rights plan A program in which shareholders of a corporation receive some valuable right (such as purchase of additional shares) that usually vests in the event of a takeover.

Shark repellants Provisions in a corporate charter or bylaws that make a takeover more difficult or unattractive.

Sole source contracting A government contracting procedure when a single contractor can perform the required work.

Special duty clause The requirement that employers comply with the specific regulations promulgated by OSHA.

Stakeholders Employees, bondholders and others who have a financial interest in the continued operation of a corporation.

Standing The requirement that an individual must have a sufficient stake in a controversy (actual injury or threat of future injury) before he or she can maintain a lawsuit.

Substantial privity test A rule that holds accountants liable in negligence to certain parties, not their client, but who are in a close connection with the accountants.

Successor liability The rule that holds the surviving corporation in a merger liable for the debts of the company that was merged out of existence.

Suggestive trademarks Product marks that suggest the attributes of the product but do not directly describe them.

Superlien A provision in environmental law that gives a priority security interest to ensure that resources are available to clean up hazardous wastes.

Supermajority vote A requirement that the approval of more than a majority of shareholders (e.g., 75%) is required for certain significant corporate actions.

Suspension A temporary prohibition on an individual's ability to contract with the government.

T

Tender offer A procedure for taking over a company by making a public offer to all shareholders to purchase their shares for a set price.

Termination for convenience The authority of the government in contracts enabling it to cancel a contract at any time, if the contract becomes unnecessary.

Trademark A word or symbol that has become sufficiently associated with a good or registered with the government such that others may not use the trademark without illegal infringement.

Transactions with affiliated banks A regulation of banking that restricts loans to associated banks.

Treasury shares Stock in a corporation that is owned by the corporation itself.

Truth-in-menu laws Statutes requiring an accurate description of the food served in restaurants.

Two-tier tender offer A tender offer that offers different prices for the shares of a target corporation, depending on the timing of acceptance of the offer.

U

Unpreventable employee misconduct defense An employer's defense to a job injury arising where the harm resulted from the fault of the employee and the employer could not reasonably have prevented this action.

V

Valid trademark A product mark that is defensible at law against infringers.

Validated License A permit required for the export of certain products that the government considers sensitive or to certain countries.

Vicarious liability A doctrine whereby one party, such as an employer, may be liable for the torts of another party, such as an employee.

W-Z

White knight An ally of management enlisted to purchase a company in order to avert a hostile takeover.

White squire An ally of management who purchases shares in a company with a promise not to tender those shares to a hostile acquirer.

Work product privilege The right of attorneys and their clients to keep documents prepared for litigation secret.

Wrongful constructive eviction claim A tenant's allegation that the landlord has rendered the leased property uninhabitable.

Wrongful discharge tort A claim of action in tort enabling an employee to sue an employer for a firing that is conducted unfairly.

Wrongful eviction A tort in which a guest can sue a hotel for improperly removing the guest from a room without justification.

Table of Cases

The principal cases are in bold type. Cases cited or discussed are in roman type.

A

A. P. Smith Manufacturing Company v. Barlow, 13-14

Abkco Music, Inc. v. Harrisongs Music, Ltd., 314

AC Acquisition Corp. v. Anderson Clayton & Co., 166

Ackerman v. Western Electric Company, 76

Adames, United States v., 26-28

Algonac Manufacturing Co. v. United States, 370

ALPO Petfoods, Inc. v. Ralston Purina Company, 253-255

Amanda Acquisition Corp. v. Universal Foods Corp., 166-167

American Home Products v. Johnson & Johnson, 252

American Home Products Corp., *In re,* 251

American Medical Association v. Bowen, 285

Aromin v. State Farm Fire & Casualty Company, 170-172

Arthur Young & Co., United States v., 116

Avondale Industries, Incorporated v. Travelers Indemnity Company, 174-175

B

Baker v. F & F Investment, 356

Bakers Franchise Corp. v. Federal Trade Commission, 248

Balla v. Gambro, Inc., 405

Bank of Shaw, The v. Posey, 214-215

Banks v. National Collegiate Athletic Association, 302-304

Barber v. Time, Inc., 361

Barrera v. State Farm Mutual Automobile Insurance Co., 182

Basic, Incorporated v. Levinson, 133-134

Bay Cities Services, Inc., 387

Bayless v. Philadelphia National League Club, 309

Beauford v. Helmsley, 140-142

Berger v. State, 343

Bhattal v. Grand Hyatt-New York, 334-336

Bick v. Peat Marwick and Main, 108

Billings Clinic, The v. Peat Marwick Main & Co., 116

Bily v. Arthur Young & Company, 104-106

Blue Bell, Inc. v. Peat, Marwick, Mitchell & Co., 111-112

BMY, a Division of HARSCO Corp., 387

Boles v. La Quinta Motor Inns, 330-331

Bose Corp. v. Consumers Union of U.S., Inc., 234

Boykin v. Hermitage Realty, 198

Bradler v. Craig, 217

Braesch v. Union Insurance Company, 177-178

Bratt v. International Business Machines Corp., 54

Brewer v. Roosevelt Motor Lodge, 343

Brickner v. FDIC, 208

Broderick v. Ruder, 71

Brown & Williamson Tobacco Corporation v. Jacobson, 358-360

C

C&J Fertilizer, Inc. v. Allied Mutual Insurance Co., 170

Camel Manufacturing Co. v. United States, 29

Cardinal Consulting Co. v. Circo Resorts, Inc., 338

Carl M. Loeb, Rhoades & Co., 125

Carpenters Southern California Administrative Corporation v. Manufacturers National Bank of Detroit, 218-219

Carr, United States v., 277

Carson v. Here's Johnny Portable Toilets, Inc., 258

Castleglen, Inc. v. Commonwealth Savings Association, 222

Charles of the Ritz Dist. Corp. v. FTC, 247

Cher v. Forum International, Ltd., 317

Chiarella v. United States, 131

Chiari v. City of League City, 76-77

Circon Acme, 388

City Capital Associates Limited Partnership v. Interco Incorporated, 153-155

City of Los Angeles v. Preferred Communications, Inc., 366-367

Cleland v. Bronson Health Care Group, Inc., 293-294

Clifford V. Hollander, 363

CMI South, Inc. v. Occupational Safety and Health Review Commission, 84-85

Coca-Cola, Inc. v. Tropicana Products, Inc., 252

Coca-Cola Co. v. Gemini Rising, Inc., 231

Coleman v. Gulf Insurance Group, 186

Community for Creative Non-Violence v. Reid, 314

Con-Tech Sales Defined Benefit Trust v. Cockerham, 266

Connecticut v. Teal, 66

Conner v. Fort Gordon Bus Co., 80

Connor v. Great Western Savings & Loan Association, 217

Cooper v. Amster, 300

Cooper v. Jevne, 200

County of Broome v. Aetna Casualty & Surety Co., 172

Crain v. Burroughs Corp., 47

Credit Alliance v. Arthur Andersen & Co., 110

Crinkley v. Holiday Inns, Inc., 326-328

Cruz v. Ortho Pharmaceutical Corp., 282

Cutler-Hammer, Inc. v. United States, 388

D

DAR Construction, Inc., United States v., 278

Datapoint Corp. v. Plaza Securities Co., 156

Daugherty v. Kessler, 197

Davidow v. Inwood North Professional Group—Phase I, 193-195

Dawn Associates v. Links, 317

DC Comics, Inc. v. Filmation Associates, 317

DeCintio v. Westchester County Medical Center, 71

DeFillippo v. National Broadcasting Co., 324

DeMatteo Construction Co. v. United States, 370

Detroit Lions, The v. Argovitz, 306-307

Doe v. Sarasota-Bradenton Television Co., 364

Dold v. Outrigger Hotel, 337-338

Dominguez v. Brackey Enterprises, Inc., 116

Donald Schutte, 383

Drotzmann's, Inc. v. McGraw-Hill, Inc., 357

Duane Jones Co. v. Burke, 21

E

EEOC. *See* Equal Employment Opportunity Commission

Eldridge v. Downtowner Hotel, 329

Elkins, United States v., 26

Emergency Devices, Inc., *In re,* 247

Emily v. Bayne, 203

Entrepreneur, Ltd. v. Yasuna, 195

Equal Employment Opportunity Commission v. Arabian American Oil Co., 79

Equal Employment Opportunity Commission v. Carolina Freight, 67

Equal Employment Opportunity Commission v. Townley Engineering & Manufacturing Co., 80

Ernst & Ernst v. Hochfelder, 145

Eversharp, Inc., *In re,* 251

F

Falls v. Sporting News Publishing Co., 54

Fargo Women's Health Organization, Inc. v. FM Women's Help and Caring Connection, 260

Federal Communications Commission v. Midwest Video Corporation, 351, 352-353

Federal Communications Commission v. Sanders Bros. Radio Station, 349

Federal Food Service, Inc. v. Donovan, 383-385

Federal Trade Commission v. Borden, Co., 241

Fera v. Village Plaza, Inc., 197

57 E. 54 Realty Corp. v. Gay Nineties Realty Corp., 196

First Federal Savings and Loan Association v. Twin City Savings Bank, FSB, 4-5

First Overseas Inv. Corp. v. Cotton, 329

Fish v. Los Angeles Dodgers Baseball Club, 308

Five Platters, Inc., The v. Purdie, 317

Flanigan v. Prudential Federal Savings & Loan Ass'n, 62

Fleet Factors Corp., United States v., 282

Flynn v. Bass Brothers Enterprises, 133

Foley v. Interactive Data Corp., 50

Fossett v. Davis, 197

Foxx v. Williams, 313

Fragrante v. City and County of Honolulu, 80-81

Francis College v. Al-Khazraji, 63
FTC. *See* Federal Trade Commission

G

Gargiulo v. Gargiulo, 92
Garner v. Wilfinbarger, 407
Garrett v. Coast & Southern Federal Savings
 and Loan Ass'n, 203
Garzilli v. Howard Johnson's Motor Lodges,
 Inc., 326
Gershunoff v. Panov, 310-311
Gilliam v. American Broadcasting Companies,
 Inc., 318-320
Globe Newspaper Co. v. Superior Court, 357
Goncalves v. Regent International Hotels,
 Ltd., 333
Gordinier v. Aetna Casualty and Surety
 Co., 170
Grand Jury Investigation, *In re,* 392
Grand Metropolitan PLC v. Pillsbury Co., 166
Greenstein, Logan & Co. v. Burgess Marketing,
 Inc., 107

H

Haagen-Dazs, Inc. v. Frusen Gladje, Ltd., 255
Hackbart v. Cincinnati Bengals, 309
Halla Nursery, Inc. v. Baumann-Firrie &
 Co., 107
Hancock v. American Steel & Wire Co., 229
Hansen Brothers Logging, 89
Hardy v. Procter & Gamble Mfg. Co., 260
Harmonica Man, Inc., The v. Godfrey, 234
Hartford Life Ins. Co. v. Randall, 203
Hayes Int'l Corp., United States v., 277
Heen & Flint Associates v. Travelers Indem.
 Co., 179
Helle v. Landmark, Inc., 47
Helman v. Murry's Steaks, Inc., 393-394
Henderson v. Heyer-Schulte Corp., 288
Herbster v. North American Co. for Life and
 Health Insurance, 405
Hoffman v. Federal Deposit Insurance
 Corporation, 209-210
Hoffman v. Red Owl Stores, Inc., 7
Hoflin, United States v., 276-277
Holloman v. Life Insurance Co., 183
Home Box Office, Inc. v. Wilkinson, 366
Houchins v. KQED, 357
Hustler Magazine, Inc. v. Falwell, 367
Hutchinson v. Proxmire, 367

I

Idaho v. Bunker Hill Co., 268
In re _____ (see name of party)
Internal Revenue Service (IRS), 107
International Boxing Club, Inc. v. United
 States, 305
International Business Machines Corp., 375
International Mortgage Co. v. John P. Butler
 Accountancy Corp., 112
Ipsco, Inc. v. United States, 32-34
Ives Laboratories, Inc. v. Darby Drug Co.,
 Inc., 240

J

Jackson v. Fontenot Building, Inc., 199
Jakco Painting Contractors v. Industrial
 Commission of the State of Colorado, 95
Japan Line, Ltd. v. County of Los Angeles, 41
Jevic v. The Coca-Cola Bottling Company of
 New York, Inc., 56-57
Johns Manville Products v. Contra County
 Superior Court, 98
Jones v. NCAA, 302
Jordache Enterprises, Inc. v. Hogg Wyld, Ltd.,
 229-230

K

Kayser-Roth Corp., United States v., 282
Kelley v. Schlumberger Technology Corp., 62
King v. Palmer, 71
King-Seeley Thermos Co. v. Aladdin Industries,
 Inc., 227
Kingsmen v. K-Tel International, Ltd., 324
Kirchoffner v. Quam, 308
Korr v. Thomas Emery's Sons, Inc., 325
Kraft v. Metromedia, Inc., 51
Kumpf v. Steinhaus, 62

L

L. L. Bean, Inc. v. Drake Publishers,
 Inc., 232-234
Landon v. Twentieth Century-Fox Film
 Corp., 324
Larimore v. Comptroller of the Currency, 208
Larsen v. United Federal Savings & Loan
 Association, 217
Las Vegas Television, Inc., 347
Lazar v. Thermal Equipment Corp., 101
Lee v. Beauchene, 309
Lee v. National League Baseball Club, 308

Leigh Furniture & Carpet Co. v. Isom, 225-227
Letter to Lonnie King, 351
Levy v. Bendetson, 198
Lewis v. United Airlines, 54
Life Insurance Co. v. Lopez, 183
Lincoln Grain, Inc. v. Coopers & Lybrand, 106,
    120-121
**Lincoln Savings and Loan Association v.
    Wall, 19-20**
Lindner v. Barlow, Davis & Wood, 104
Lititz Mutual Insurance Co. v.
    Commonwealth, 179
Lockheed Aircraft Corp. v. United States, 388
Los Angeles Memorial Coliseum v. National
    Football League, 304

M

**Mansfield v. American Telephone &
    Telegraph Corporation, 52-53**
Maybelline Co. v. Noxell Corp., 252
Medico-Dental Bldg. Co. v. Horton &
    Converse, 203
Mele v. Sherman Hospital, 290-291
Memorex Corp., 377
Memphis Publishing Co. v. Nichols, 358
Mennen Co. v. Gillette Co., 255
Merritt v. Colonial Foods, Inc., 163
Messina V. Sheraton Corporation of
    America, 326
Midler v. Ford Motor Company, 258-259
Miller Brewing Co. v. G. Heileman Brewing
    Co., Inc., 227
Milliron v. Francke, 289
Mobile Drilling Co., 371
**Monroe Communications Corporation v.
    Federal Communications Commission,
    347-348**
Montandon v. Triangle Publications, Inc., 357
Mosley v. Perpetual Savings & Loan
    Association, 217
Motown Record Corporation v. Brockert, 313
Mottolo, United States v., 273

N

National Collegiate Athletic Association v.
    Board of Regents of the University of
    Oklahoma, 302
National Collegiate Athletic Association v.
    Tarkanian, 304
**National Funeral Services, Inc. v.
    Rockefeller, 244-246**

National Helium Corp. v. Morton, 378
National Realty and Construction Co., Inc. v.
    OSHRC, 84
National Refining Co. v. Benzo Gas Motor Fuel
    Co., 240-241
NCAA. *See* National Collegiate Athletic
    Association
**New York Life Insurance Company v.
    Johnson, 180-182**
999 v. CIT Corporation, 213
Normand v. Research Institute of America,
    Inc., 81
Northeastern Pharmaceutical and Chemical
    Co., Inc., United States v., 275
Norton v. Argonaut Insurance Company, 300
Novosel v. Nationwide Insurance Co., 48

O

O'Brien v. Pabst Sales Co., 259
O'Connor v. CertainTeed Corporation, 16-17
Ocean Spray Cranberries, Inc., United States v.,
    278
Ocean State Physicians Health Plan, Inc. v. Blue
    Cross & Blue Shield of Rhode Island, 300
**Oki America, Inc. v. Microtech International,
    Inc., 3-4**
**Oliver Productions, Inc., *In re* Request of,
    350-351**
Olivia N. v. National Broadcasting Co., 320

P

Paolillo v. Dresser Industries, Inc., 75
Paramount Communications, Inc. v. Time,
    Inc., 157
Patrick v. Burget, 284
Patterson v. McLean Credit Union, 72
Pedroza v. Bryant, 300
People v. Thorpe, 343
Pfizer, Inc., *In re*, 262-263
Pierce v. Ortho Pharmaceutical Corp., 48-50
Pine River State Bank v. Mettille, 44
Pinter v. Dahl, 128-129
Platner v. Cash & Thomas Contractors, Inc., 80
Poling v. Wisconsin Physicians Service, 186
Polk v. Good, 160
Porter v. Dallas Independent School District, 92
Posadas de Puerto Rico Associates v. Tourism
    Company of Puerto Rico, 244
Presto v. Sequoia Systems, 224
**Professional Service Industries, Inc. v.
    Kimbrell, 396-397**

Protest of DALFI, Inc., 376-377
Protex Industries, Inc., United States v., 275
Prudential Insurance Co. v. Executive Estates, Inc., 216
Purcell v. Zimbalman, 290

Q

Quincy Cable TV, Inc. v. FCC, 355

R

R. H. Bishop Co., 89
Raritan River Steel Co. v. Cherry, Beckaert & Holland, 113
Red Lion Broadcasting Co. v. FCC, 355
Reed v. Classified Parking System, 193
Reed v. King, 198-199
Removatron International Corporation v. Federal Trade Commission, 248-250
Revlon, Inc. v. MacAndrews & Forbes Holdings, Inc., 157
Rewe-Zentral, AG Bundesmomopol ver Waltung fur Branntwein, 41
Richards Medical Company v. United States, 29-31
Riverside Market Development Corp. v. International Building Products, 273-274
Robert Wooler Company v. The Fidelity Bank, 108-109
Robinson v. Jacksonville Shipyards, Inc., 69-70
Robinson v. McAllen State Bank, 213
Rose v. Giammati, 305
RSO Records, Inc. v. Peri, 314
Rulon-Miller v. International Business Machines Corp., 45-46

S

Sahadi v. Continental Illinois National Bank and Trust Company of Chicago, 213
St. Louis S.F.R. Co. v. Wade, 224
Salisbury v. St. Regis-Sheraton Hotel, 333
Samjens Partners I v. Burlington Industries, Inc., 158-159
Savers Federal Savings & Loan Association v. Reetz, 191-192
Schatz v. York Steak House, 98
Scher v. Liberty Travel Service, 338
Schoenbaum v. Firstbrook, 36
Schreiber v. Burlington Northern, Inc., 145
Seattle Stevedoring Co., 101

Securities and Exchange Commission v. Ridenour, 138-139
Securities and Exchange Commission v. Texas Gulf Sulfur, 130
Security Insurance Co. v. Nasser, 93-94
Seelbach, Inc. v. Cadick, 328
Sentry Insurance v. Brown, 179
Severn Companies, Inc., 375
Shamrock Holding, Inc. v. Polaroid Corp., 156
Sheinkopf v. Stone, 390-391
Sheppard v. Maxwell, 364
Silberg v. California Life Insurance Co., 176
Silver Hills Country Club v. Sobieski, 124
Sipple v. Chronicle Publishing Company, 361-363
Siskind v. Newton-John, 315-316
Sletteland v. Federal Deposit Insurance Corporation, 207-208
Smiley v. Manchester Insurance & Indemnity Company of St. Louis, 398-400
Smith v. Van Gorkom, 149-151
Smith-Corona Group v. United States, 41
Social Security Administration Baltimore Federal Credit Union v. United States, 107
Spancrete Northeast, Inc. v. Occupational Safety and Health Review Commission, 87-88
Spargnapani v. Wright, 203
Spiller v. Barclay Hotel, 326
Sportsmen's Boating Corporation v. Hensley, 227
State Accident Insurance Fund Corporation v. McCabe, 95-97
Stephens Industries, Inc. v. Haskins & Sells, 113
Steuer v. National Medical Enterprises, 295
Sunshine State Bank v. FDIC, 222
Swerdloff v. Miami National Bank, 216
Swiss Colony v. Dep't of ILHR, 97
Sztorc v. Northwest Hospital, 288

T

Taggart v. Time Incorporated, 72-74
Tanglewood East Homeowners v. Charles-Thomas, Inc., 267-268
Teca-Print A.G. v. Amacoil Machinery, Inc., 41
Technical Tape Corp. v. Industrial Commission, 94
Tenants' Corp. v. Max Rothenburg & Co., 121
Tennant v. Lawton, 200
Texaco Inc. v. Hasbrouck, 235-236
Thomas v. Bourdette, 62

Todorov v. DCH Health Care Authority, **295-297**
Torncello v. United States, 378-379
Toussaint v. Blue Cross & Blue Shield of Michigan, 62
Trident Center v. Connecticut General Life Insurance Company, 189-190
Turner Broadcasting System, Inc. v. CBS, Inc., 155
TW Services, Inc. v. SWT Acquisition Corp., 167

U

U-Haul, Int'l v. Jartran, Inc., 253
Union Planters Corporation v. Peat, Marwick, Mitchell & Co., 117-118
United States v. _____ (see name of party)
United States Aviex Co. v. Travelers Insurance Co., 173
Unocal Corp. v. Mesa Petroleum Co., 152, 160
Upjohn Co. v. United States, 392

V

Variety Children's Hospital v. Osle, 300
Vaughn v. Edel, 64-66
Verway v. Blincoe Packing Co., 51
Vidal Sassoon, Inc. v. Bristol Myers Co., 262
Video Ventures, Inc., 372
Virgil v. Sports Illustrated, Inc., 361
Virginia State Board of Pharmacy v. Virginia Citizens Consumer Council, 243

W

Wagenheim v. Alexander Grant & Co., 114
Walker v. IRS, 63

Walt Disney Productions v. Air Pirates, 316
Walters v. Fullwood, 308
Ward, United States v., 266
Wards Cove v. Atonio, 66, 67
Warner Brothers, Inc. v. Gay Toys, Inc., 240
Washington v. Time Oil Co., 270-271
Weinberger v. UOP, Inc., 161-163
Wetherbee v. United Insurance Co. of America, 176
Whaley Engineering Corp., 88
White, United States v., 381
Wickline v. State, 285-286
Wilk v. AMA, 297
William R. Davis & Son, Co., 84
Willis, United States v., 131-132
Wisconsin Ave. Associates, Inc. v. 2720 Wisconsin Ave. Co-Operative Association, 190

X

Xerox Corporation v. United States, 372-373

Y

Yale Electric Corp. v. Robertson, 230
Young v. Caribbean Associates, Inc., 328

Z

Zamora v. Columbia Broadcasting System, 320
Zenith Radio Corporation v. United States, 32

Index

A

Abandonment:
  of leased premises, 196-197
  of trademark, 231
Acceleration clauses, 188-189
Access channels, 354
Accidents:
  on-the-job, 92-97. *See also*
    Workers' compensation
  press coverage of, 357
Accountants:
  confidentiality and, 113-114
  conflicting interests and, 118-119
  duty of, to clients, 103-106
  ethics and, 118-119
  independence of, 16
  international standards for,
    119-120
  management consulting by,
    115-118
  professional principles and
    standards for, 103-106, 119-120
  regulation of, 114-115
Accountants' liability:
  accountants' disclaimers and, 113
  for bad business advice, 116-118
  balancing test of, 112-113
  to clients, 103-109
  defenses to, 107-109
  for fraud or gross negligence, 113
  to non-clients, 110-113
  reasonable foreseeability test of,
    112
  Restatement (actually foreseen)
    test of, 110-112
  under RICO, 115
  under securities laws, 115
  sources of, 106-107
  substantial privity test of, 110
Acquired immune deficiency
  syndrome (AIDS):
  disclosure of, in sale of real
    property, 201-202
  in employment context, 58, 75
  insurance coverage and, 183-184
  international health care and, 299
Acquisitions. *See* Mergers and
  acquisitions; Takeovers
Act on Economic Associations
  (Hungary, 1989), 37

Act on Investment of Foreigners in
  Hungary (Hungary, 1989), 37-38
Actual malice, 358-361
Actually foreseen test, 110-112
Ad valorem duties, 29
Adequate price competition, for
  government contract, 380
Adhesion contract, 169
Administrative law judge (ALJ), 247
Advertising, 243-263
  alcohol and tobacco, 257
  on cable television, 352
  children's, 256-257
  comparative, 262
  deceptive, 247-251. *See also*
    Deceptive advertising
  First Amendment rights and,
    243-246
  food and drug, 257
  government regulation of,
    244-251, 256-257
  international perspective on,
    261-262
  misappropriation and, 258-259
  negligent claims in, 259-260
  private regulation of, 255-256,
    261-262
  social responsibility in, 260-261
  sweepstakes, 248, 256
Advertorials, 244
Affirmative action, 71-72
  government contract awards and,
    375
Age discrimination, 72-75
Age Discrimination in Employment
  Act (ADEA), 72, 78
Agents:
  corporate, attorney-client privilege
    and, 392
  entertainment, 309-311
  ostensible, 288-289
  sports, 305-308
Agricultural Foreign Investment
  Disclosure Act, 202
AIDS. *See* Acquired immune
  deficiency syndrome (AIDS)
Alcohol:
  advertisements of, 257
  servers of, dram shop laws
    protecting, 340
  testing employees for use of, 55

"All holders rule," 136
Alternative dispute resolution,
  402-404
"Alternatives analysis," 11
Amateur sports, 301-304. *See also*
  Sports
Ambiguity doctrine, 170
American Association of Advertising
  Agencies, 6
American Bar Association, Code of
  Professional Responsibility of,
  391, 395
American Federation of Television
  and Radio Artists (AFTRA),
  311-312
American Institute of Certified Public
  Accountants (AICPA), 103, 104,
  113-114, 116, 119
  Code of Professional Conduct of,
    20, 116
American Law Institute, Principles of
  Corporate Governance of, 14-15
American Medical Association
  (AMA), 287, 297, 299
American Stock Exchange, 36
Americans with Disabilities Act
  (ADA) of 1990, 58, 75-79
Andean Common Market
  (ANCOM), 38
Andean nations, direct investment
  in, 37-38
Antidilution statutes, 231-234
Antidumping Act of 1921, 32
Anti-takeover statutes, 160
Antitrust law, 163
  athletic associations and, 302-305
  health care industry and, 294-297
  imported goods and, 35
  labor exemption from, 305
Appraisal, shareholders' right of, 163
Arbitration, 403-404
Arms Export Control Act, 24-25, 28
Articles of Incorporation (Japan), 37
Artists:
  "moral rights" of, in France,
    317-318
  rights of, in creative products,
    317-320. *See also*
    Entertainment law
  unions of, 311

Association of Representatives of Professional Athletes (ARPA), 321
Assumption of risk, 329
Assurances, oral, 47
Athletes, 301-309. *See also* Sports liability of, for injuries, 308-309
Athletic associations, 301-305. *See also* Sports Attorney(s):
  conflicting interests and, 395-397
  document retention and destruction and, 400
  malpractice by, 397
  international practice by, 405-406
  settlements and, 398-400
  work product privilege of, 394-395
Attorney-client privilege, 391-394
  corporate clients and, 391-394
  exceptions to, 393-394
  individual clients and, 391, 393-394
  "subject matter" test for, 392
Attorney-client relationship, 389-391
Auction duties, 157-159
Auditors. *See* Accountants
Automobiles, hotel guests', 333-334
Average workers test, 97

B

Bailment, of hotel guest's automobile, 333-334
Balancing test, 112-113
Bank(s):
  branch, 212
  charters of, 206
  closures of, 211
  commercial, as sources for mortgages, 187
  failing, 210-211
  directors of, 208-210
  liability of, for loans. *See* Lender liability
  mergers of, 212
  minimum capital ratios for, 206
  regulation of, 205-212
  setoffs and, 217-219
  transactions with affiliated, 206
  U.S., in Europe, 220-221
Bank holding company, 212
Bank Holding Company Act of 1956, 212
  amendments to, of 1970, 216
Bank Merger Act of 1960, 212
Bank of America, 18
Bank of Japan, 37
Bank of North America, 205
Berne Convention (Universal Copyright Convention), 322-323
Better Business Bureau, 255
Bids:
  for government contracts, 371-374
  joint, 28
Bill of lading, 29

Bill of Rights, 9
Blue Cross/Blue Shield, "Medical Necessity Guidelines" of, 287
"Boiler room operations," 138
"Bounty-hunter" provision, 381
Branch banking, 212
Break-up fee, 155
Bridging the gap, 231
British Code of Advertising Practice, 261
Broadcasting:
  cross-border, 365-366
  equal time rule in, 349-351
  FCC regulations on, 349-351. *See also* Federal Communications Commission (FCC)
  licenses for, 345-349
Broker, real estate, 200-201
Burden of proof:
  in deceptive advertising cases, 247
  in employment discrimination cases, 64, 66-67
Business, legal representation of. *See* Attorney(s); Legal representation
Business beneficence, 12-15
Business ethics:
  "alternatives analysis" and, 11
  application of, to business context, 9-10. *See also* Ethical perspectives
  business beneficience and, 12-15
  codes of, 15-17. *See also* Ethical codes
  corporate ethical culture and, 18-19
  decision making and, 9-11
  government contract requirements and, 371
  "gut instincts" and, 9
  legal compliance and, 2-5
  prima facie duties and, 6
  profit maximization and, 1-2
  profitability of good, 11-12
  requirements of, 6-11
  sources of, 5
  tools for implementing, 15-19
Business judgment rule, 151-152
Buy American Act, 374-375, 386

C

Cable Communications Policy Act, 353-354
Cable television:
  public access channels for, 354
  regulation of, 352-354
California Athlete Agent Statute, 307
Canada–U.S. free trade pact, 119
Capital markets, foreign, 35-36
Care, duty of:
  of accountants, to clients, 103-106
  of corporate directors, 149-151

of health-care providers, 292
Cartagena Agreement, 38
Cause:
  good, as defense to wrongful discharge, 44, 51
  proximate, 260
Cease-and-desist orders, 248-250
Certificate of Cost or Pricing Data, 380
Change in Bank Control Act (CBCA) of 1978, 207-208
Changes clause, 378
Charitable immunity, 288
Charter, bank, 206
Checkrooms, hotel, 334
Children's advertising, 256-257
Children's Television Act of 1990, 257
Chinese Wall, 119
Churning, 137
Citations, by OSHA, 89
Civil Rights Act of 1964, Title VII of, 63-68, 71-72, 78-80
Clayton Act, 163, 297
Clean Air Act, 265, 266, 271, 272, 278, 279
Clean Water Act (Federal Water Pollution Control Act), 265, 266, 271, 278, 279
Code of ethics. *See* Ethical codes
Code on Takeovers and Mergers (United Kingdom), 166
Collateral:
  corporate assets as, in leveraged buyout, 148
  for mortgage, 187
Colorization, 318
Commercial banks, as sources for mortgages, 187
Commercial leasing, 193-197. *See also* Leases
Commercial speech, 243-246. *See also* Freedom of speech
Commission of the European Communities, 185
  Directive 73/239 of, 185
Commission on Freedom of the Press, 364
Commissioner of Customs, 31
Commodity Control List (CCL), 25
Common areas, of hotel, 328-329
Common (communications) carriers, 345, 351-352, 355
Common disease, 95
Communication requirement, for defamation, 54
Communications law, 345-367
  ethical perspective on, 363-365
  Federal Communications Commission and, 345-352
  First Amendment and, 355-357
  international perspective on, 365-366

mass media liability under,
357-363
new technologies and, 352-355
Community ascertainment, by
media, 347
Comparable worth, 78-79
Comparative advertising, 251
European regulation of, 262
NBC guidelines for, 255-256
Comparative negligence, 107-108
as defense, 329
Competition:
fair, as defense, 224
for government contracts, 371-374
primary line, 235
secondary line, 235
unfair. *See* Unfair competition
Competition in Contracting Act,
371, 372
Comprehensive Environmental
Response, Compensation, and
Liability Act of 1980 (CERCLA,
Superfund), 173, 265-270,
272-274
application of, 265-266
criminal liability under, 277
defenses to liability under, 268-269
European Community Directive
compared to, 281
individual liability under, 273-274
lender liability under, 215-216
liability standards under, 268
penalties imposed by, 279
responsible parties under, 266-268
retroactive liability under, 268
type of transaction and liability
under, 269-271
Comprehensive Omnibus Budget
Reconciliation Act (COBRA) of
1986, 292-294
Comptroller General, of General
Accounting Office, 375
Comptroller of the Currency, 206,
211, 212
Confidentiality:
accountants and, 113-114
attorneys and. *See* Attorney-client
privilege; Attorney-client
relationship
Conflict of interests:
accountants and, 118-119
attorneys and, 395-397
Confusion, of trademarks, 228-231
Constitution, U.S.:
amendments to. *See* specific
amendments
Bill of Rights of, 9
drug testing constrained by, 55
privacy rights and, 54
procedural fairness guaranteed
by, 304
supremacy clause of, 160

Constructive fraud, 198-199, 200
Continental Congress, 205
Contract(s):
adhesion, 169
at-will, 43. *See also* Employment
contracts
cost reimbursement, 369-370
discrimination in, 72. *See also*
Employment discrimination
employment. *See* Employment
contracts
entertainment, 311
fixed price, 369
government, 369-388
implied-in-fact, 370
international, 24-25
quasi-contracts, 370-371
remedies for breach of. *See*
Remedies
sales, 23-24
Contractors:
government. *See* Government
contractors
independent, 28
Contributory negligence, 107-108
Control-share acquisition statutes, 160
Conversion, by hotel, 334-336
Copyright:
creative works and, 313-316
fair use doctrine and, 316
international protection for,
322-323
substantially similar test for
infringement of, 314
Copyright Act, 316
Corporate ethical culture, 18-19
Corporations:
agents of, 392
contributions by, 12-15
ethics and. *See* Business ethics;
Ethical codes; Ethical
perspectives
Japanese (*kabushiki kaisha*), 37
legal representation of, 395-400.
See also Attorney(s); Legal
representation
Cost justification, as defense, 237
Cost plus incentive fee, 370
Cost reimbursement contracts,
369-370
Countervailing duties, 32-35
Court of International Trade, 29, 31
Criminal False Claims Act, 381, 382
Criminal False Statements Act,
381, 382
Criminal procedure, 9
Crown jewels, 156
Customs, 29-35. *See also* U.S.
Customs Service

D

Damages:

for deceptive advertising, 252-253
liquidated, 190
proof of, in malpractice action, 397
punitive, 200, 337-338
special, 234
Dango (Japanese bid rotation), 387
Death benefits, under workers' compensation laws, 97
Debarment, 381, 383-385
Deceptive advertising. *See also*
Advertising
comparative advertising and, 251
damages for, 252-253
private remedies for, under
Lanham Act, 251-255
prohibited by Federal Trade
Commission, 244, 246-251
remedies for, 248-255
Deceptive Trade Practices Act, 307
Deceptive trade practices acts (state),
237-238
Decision tree analysis of litigation,
403
Deed of association, 38
Defalcations, 106
Defamation:
communication (publication)
requirement for, 54
defenses to, 358-361
mass media liability for, 357-361
privilege against, 361
requirements for, 357-358
tortious wrongful discharge and,
51, 54
Defamatory statement, 357
Default, on mortgage, 191-193
Defective pricing, 380
Defense Contract Audit Agency, 380
Defense contractors. *See* Government
contractors
Defense Industry Initiatives on
Business Ethics and Conduct, 385
Defenses:
to anticompetitive merger, 297
to defamation, 358-361
to employment discrimination, 64,
66-67
to environmental liability, 268-269
of insurance company, 179-183
to negligence, 329
to occupational safety violations,
84-85
to price discrimination, 237
to takeover attempts, 148, 152-159
to wrongful interference with
business, 224-225
Deficiency judgment, 191
Department of. *See* U.S. Department
of
Diagnosis-Related Groups (DRGs),
285, 287
Direct broadcast satellite (DBS), 355

international controversies over, 365-366

Directives, European Community, 185, 281-282

Directors:
  bank, 208-210
  business judgment rule and, 151-152
  duties of, 148-152
  "inside," 148
  liability of, 208-210
  staggered terms for, as takeover defense, 156

Directors Guild of America, 318

Disability, covered by workers' compensation, 97

Disclaimers:
  by accountants, 113
  "limited quantity," 251

Discovery, 375, 400

Discrimination:
  age, 72-75
  employment. *See* Employment discrimination
  price, 234-237
  under Section 1981, 72

Diseases:
  covered by American Disabilities Act, 75
  covered by workers' compensation, 95

Disparagement, 234

Disparate impact discrimination, 66-67

Disparate treatment discrimination, 64-67

Distribution license, 25

Diversity of media ownership, 347

Doctrine of compelled self-publication, 54

Doctrine of increased risk, 92

Doctrine of positional risk, 92

Documents:
  retention and destruction of, 400
  "smoking gun," 400

Domestic preference, in government contracting, 374-375

Double-leasing, 198

Draft Convention on the Hotelkeeper's Contract, 342

Dram shop laws, 340

Drug testing, 55-57

Drug-Free Workplace Act of 1988, 55

Due diligence, environmental, 269

Due-on-sale clause, 188

Due process, 9

Dumping, 32

Duties:
  of accountants, to clients, 103-106
  of care. *See* Care, duty of
  of directors, 148-159
  of loyalty, 7-8, 148-149

of rescue, hotel's, 329-331

Duties (customs), 29-32
  ad valorem, 29, 35
  antidumping, 32
  countervailing, 32-35

E

EEOC. *See* Equal Employment Opportunity Commission
  80 percent rule, 67

Electronic Communications Privacy Act of 1986, 58

Electronic monitoring of employees, 58

Emergency medical situation, 292

Emergency Planning and Community Right-to-Know Act (EPCRA), 277

Emotional distress, 51-53, 178

Employee(s):
  AIDS testing of, 58
  discrimination against. *See* Employment discrimination
  drug testing of, 55-57
  illegal activities required of, 48-50
  lie detector testing of, 54-55
  monitoring of, 58
  plant closing legislation protecting, 58-59
  privacy rights of, 54-58
  workers' compensation for, 91-98
  wrongful discharge of, 43-54. *See also* Wrongful discharge

Employee Polygraph Protection Act of 1988, 54-55

Employee stock option plan (ESOP), 156

Employers:
  discrimination by. *See* Employment discrimination
  liability, under *respondeat superior*, 68
  sexual harassment of employees and, 68-70
  responsibility of, for occupational safety, 88-89
  wrongful discharge by. *See* Wrongful discharge

Employment:
  at-will, 43-54. *See also* Wrongful discharge
  comparable worth issue and, 78-79
  discrimination in. *See* Employment discrimination
  "in the course of," 94-95
  occupational safety and. *See* Occupational safety

Employment contracts:
  at-will, 43-44
  employment manuals and, 44-47
  implied, 44-47

Employment discrimination, 63-81
  affirmative action and, 71-72
  on basis of age, 72-75
  on basis of handicap, 75-79
  "bottom-line" defense against, 66
  cable television companies and, 354
  damages for, under Section 1981 vs. Title VII, 72
  defenses against, 64, 66-67
  disparate impact, 66-67
  disparate treatment, 64-67
  international prohibitions on, 79-80
  prima facie case of, 64
  prohibited by Section 1981, 72
  prohibited by Title VII, 63-68, 71-72, 78-80
  racial, 63-67
  sex plus, 66
  sexual harassment as, 67-71

Endangered Species Act, 272, 278

Entertainment law, 309-321, 322-323
  artists' rights and, 317-320
  compensation of entertainers and, 313
  compulsory licensing under, 316-317
  copyrights protected under, 313-314
  entertainment agents and, 309-311
  entertainment contracts and, 309-313
  international perspective on, 322-323
  misappropriation and, 317
  refusal to perform and, 312-313
  tort of incitement and, 320
  trademarks protected under, 317
  unfair competition and, 317

Environmental due diligence, 269

Environmental law, 173, 265-282. *See also* Comprehensive Environmental Response, Compensation, and Liability Act of 1980 (CERCLA, Superfund)
  ethical perspective on, 280-281
  individual liability under, 273-274
  international perspective on, 281-282
  lender liability under, 215-216
  penalties imposed under, 279
  seller's liability under, 272-273
  state, 279-280
  successor liability under, 272

Environmental pollution:
  ethics and, 8
  insurance coverage and, 173

Environmental Protection Agency (EPA), 275, 278, 280

Equal employment opportunity, 354.

See also Employment discrimination
Equal Employment Opportunity Commission (EEOC), 66-67, 72-73, 78-80
80 percent rule of, 67
Equal time rule, 349-351
Escape clause, 32, 35
Ethical codes, 15-17
corporate, and government contracts, 385-386
government contracts and, 385-386
professional, 20, 391, 395
topics covered in, 16
Ethical perspectives:
on accountant's conflicts of interest, 118-119
on AIDS disclosure in sale of real estate, 201-202
on behavior of sports agents, 321-322
on comparable worth, 78-79
on environmental law, 280-281
on government contracts and business transactions, 385-386
on insider trading, 142-143
on insurance and the AIDS crisis, 183-184
on life-extending technologies and health care, 298
on media coverage of criminal proceedings, 353-365
on opportunistic behavior, 238-239
on overbooking, 341
on social responsibility in advertising, 260-261
on stakeholder rights in takeovers, 164
on whistle-blowing, 59-60, 404-405
on workers' compensation, 98-99
Ethics, business. *See* Business ethics
Ethics Resource Center, 386
Europe 1992, 24, 40-41
insurance markets and, 185
European Community (EC), 40, 120
advertising regulation in, 262
American lawyers in, 406
employment discrimination prohibited in, 80
future insurance markets in, 185
government contracts in, 386-387
hazardous waste disposal rules in, 281-282
insider trading banned in, 144
mergers and acquisitions in, 165
new banking rules in, 220-221
protection of broadcasting services in, 366
European Court of Justice, 406
European Economic Community. *See* European Community (EC)

European Human Rights Convention, 366
Eviction, 196
wrongful, of hotel guest, 336-337
Export Administration Act of 1979, 24-26
Export Administration Regulations, 28
Export Commodity Control Number (ECCN), 26
Export-Import Bank (Eximbank), 28
Export licensing, 25-28
Export Trading Company Act of 1982, 28
Exports, 24-28

F

Failing banks, 210-211
Failing company defense, 297
Failure of notice, as insurer's defense, 182-183
Fair competition, as defense, 224
Fair Credit Reporting Act of 1970, 212
Fair use doctrine, 316
Fairness, as ethical requirement, 8-9
Fairness doctrine, 351
Fairness opinion, 161
False Claims Act (FCA), 380, 382
False or misleading advertising. *See* Deceptive advertising
False representation. *See* Misrepresentation
Faltering company exception, 59
Federal Bureau of Investigation, 50
Federal Communications Act of 1934, 345, 352
Federal Communications Commission (FCC), 345-352
broadcasting regulated by, 349-351
cable television regulated by, 352-354
common carriers regulated by, 351-352
direct broadcast satellites and, 355
fairness doctrine of, 351
hearings by, 347-349
licensing by, 346-349
multipoint distribution service allowed by, 354
spectrum allocation by, 345-346
teletext rules of, 355
Federal Deposit Insurance Corp. (FDIC), 20, 205-208, 210-212
Federal Insecticide, Fungicide and Rodenticide Act, 278
Federal Reserve, 205, 211
Federal Trade Commission (FTC):
cease-and-desist orders by, 248-250

children's advertising and, 256-257
comparative advertising and, 250
enforcement procedures of, 247
mergers and, 163
regulation of advertising by, 244, 246-251, 256-257, 261
sweepstakes advertising and, 256
Federal Trade Commission Act, 257, 260
Federal Water Pollution Control Act (Clean Water Act), 265, 266, 271, 278, 279
Fifth Amendment, 9
Financial Accounting Standards Board (FASB), 103, 104, 114
Financial Institutions Reform, Recovery and Enforcement Act (FIRREA) of 1989, 211-212
First Amendment:
advertising and, 243-246
communications law and, 355-357
disparagement and, 234
fairness doctrine and, 351
trademark infringement and, 231-234
Fixed price contract, 369
with economic price adjustment, 369
Flip-in poison pill, 153
Flip-over poison pill, 153
Food and Drug Administration (FDA), 257, 405
Food and drug advertising, 257
Foreclosures, 191-193
Foreign capital markets, 35-36
Foreign direct investments, 36-40
Foreign Exchange and Foreign Trade Control Law (Japan), 37
Foreign investment, in U.S. real estate, 201-202
Foreign Investment Code (ANCOM), 38
Foreign Investment in Real Property Tax Act of 1980, 202
Foreign trade zones, 31
Franchises, 7, 353-354
Fraud:
constructive, 200
criminal, 381
government contracts and, 379-386
on innkeepers, 339-340
"on the market," theory of, 134
real estate, 197-201
remedies for, 200
securities, 132-134, 138, 142
silence as, 199-200
Fraudulent concealment, 98
Free trade pact, 119
Freedom of speech:
advertising and, 243-246

communications law and, 355-357
disparagement and, 234
fairness doctrine and, 351
trademark parody and, 231-234
Freedom of the press, 355-365. *See also* Communications law
fair trial vs., 363-365
French National Council of the Association of Physicians, 299

G

General Accounting Office (GAO), 120, 375, 377
General Agreement on Tariffs and Trade (GATT), Procurement Code of, 386-387
General license, 25
General Medical Council of the United Kingdom, 299
General Services Board of Contract Appeals (GSBCA), 375-377
Generalized System of Preferences (GSP), 31, 100
Generally Accepted Accounting Principles (GAAP), 103-105, 115
Generally Accepted Auditing Standards (GAAS), 103, 115
Generic trademark, 227
Geography, and trademark confusion, 231
Going-private merger plan, 132, 148, 163
Golden parachutes, 156
Good cause, as defense to wrongful discharge, 44, 51
Good character, FCC licensing and, 346-347
Good faith, 8
Good samaritan statute, 288
Goodbye fee, 155
Government contract(s), 369-388
affirmative action preference in awarding, 375
challenges of, 375-377
collateral policies and, 374-375
competition for, 371-374
contractor qualifications for, 371
corporate codes of ethics and, 385-386
cost reimbursement, 369-370
domestic preference in awarding, 374-375
fixed price, 369
formation of, 370-371
fraud and, 379-382, 385-386
international perspective on, 386-387
modification or termination of, 378-379
performance of, 377-378

requirements for, 371-374
small business "set asides" for, 374
suspension and debarment from, 381-385
types of, 369-370
Government contractors:
ethical initiatives adopted by, 385-386
fraud by, 379-386
qualifications of, for government contracts, 371
requirements and penalties for, 382
suspension and debarment of, 381, 383-385
Government regulation:
of advertising, 244, 246-251, 256-257
of banking, 205-212
of communications, 345-352
of employment, 64-81, 83-101
of environmental pollution, 265-282
of exports, 24-25
of health care, 283-287, 292-294
of hotels and restaurants, 340
of imports 29-35
of mortgage process, 188
of occupational safety, 83-101
of securities transactions, 123-145
of takeovers (tender offers), 135-137, 160, 163
Great Depression, 205
Greenmail, 160-161
Grey market, 239-240

H

Handicapped persons, 75
Harassment, sexual, 67-71
Hart-Scott-Rodino Antitrust Improvements Act of 1976, 163
Hazard communication standard, 90-91
Hazardous substances, 266. *See also* Environmental law
Hazardous wastes, export of, 280-281
Health and Safety at Work Act of 1974 (Great Britain), 100
Health and safety laws, 340. *See also* Health care; Occupational safety
Health care:
antitrust liability and, 294-297
chiropractors and, 297
common law duty of care and, 292
ethical perspective on, 298
government regulation of, 283-287, 292-294
hospital liability for, 288-291

international perspective on, 299
malpractice liability for, 287-288
patient "dumping" and, 291-292
private regulation of, 287
provided for athletes, 309
Health Care Quality Improvement Act (HCQIA) of 1986, 284, 289, 297
Hello fee, 155
"Honest error in judgment" rule, 288
Honesty, as ethical requirement, 6-7
Hospitality management law, 325-343
guest-innkeeper relationship and, 325-326
guests' rights under, 339
innkeepers' rights under, 339-340
international perspective on, 342
liability for refusing or evicting guests under, 336-337
licensing and other regulations, 340
reservations and, 337-339
responsibility for guests' property under, 331-336
responsibility for guests' safety under, 326-331
Hospitals:
direct liability of, for negligence, 289-291
liability of, for refusing emergency medical treatment, 292-294
mergers of, 297
staff privileges of, and antitrust violations, 295-297
vicarious liability of, for malpractice, 288-289
Hostile environment, 67-68
Hostile takeover. *See* Takeovers
Hotel(s):
checkrooms of, 334
common areas of, 328-329
duty of rescue and, 329-331
guests of. *See* Hotel guests
guests' reservations and, 337-339
intentional torts by, 334-336
liability of, state limits on, 331-332
licensing and regulation of, 340
negligence of, 326-336
overbooking by, 337, 341
posting by, of liability limitations, 331-332
provision of safe by, 332-333
refusal or eviction of guests by, 336-337
relationship of, with guests, 325-326
responsibility for guests' property in, 331-336
rights of, 339-340
rooms of, guests' safety in, 326-328

Hotel guests:
    property of, responsibility for,
      331-336
    refusing or evicting, 336-337
    relationship of, with innkeeper,
      325-326
    reservations by, 337-339
    rights of, 339
    safety of, 326-331
Human immunodeficiency virus
    (HIV), 183-184. *See also* Acquired
    immune deficiency syndrome
    (AIDS)
Hungarian National Bank, 38
Hungary, direct investment in, 37-38

I

Implied employment contract, 44-47.
    See also Wrongful discharge
Implied-in-fact contract, 370
Implied warranty of suitability, 193
Imports, 29-35
Impossibility of performance, 7
"In and out trading," 138
"In the course of employment," 94-95
In-house vs. outside legal counsel,
    400-401
Incitement, tort of, 320
Increased risk, doctrine of, 92
Indecency, cable television and, 354
Independence, of accountant, 116
Independent contractors, 28
Infliction of emotional distress, 51-53
Injuries:
    on-the-job, 92-97. *See also*
      Workers' compensation
    personal, by accident, 95
Innkeeper. *See also* Hospitality man-
    agement law; Hotel(s)
    defrauding, as crime, 339-340
    lien by, 339
    relationship of, with guest,
      325-326
    rights of, 339-340
Innocent purchaser defense, 269
"Inside directors," 148
Insider lending, 206
Insider trading, 129-134, 138, 142-143
    ethics and, 142-143
    international law of, 144
Insider Trading and Securities Fraud
    Enforcement Act of 1988, 139, 144
Inspections, by OSHA, 89
Insurance, 169-186
    as adhesion contract, 169
    AIDS crisis and, 183-184
    coverage issues and, 169-172
    deposit. *See* Federal Deposit
      Insurance Corp. (FDIC)
    ethical perspective on, 183-184
    international perspective on, 185
    malpractice, 287

    misrepresentation on application
      for, 179-182
    policy exclusions and, 172-173
    workers' compensation. *See*
      Workers' compensation
    Insurance company:
    defenses of, 179-183
    duty of, to defend claims, 173-175
    wrongful issuance of life
      insurance by, 183
    wrongful nonrenewal of policy
      by, 178-179
    wrongful treatment of claimants
      by, 175-178
Insurance contract:
    ambiguity of, 170-172
    environmental coverage and, 173
    expected or intended clause of,
      172
    loss-in-progress clause of, 172
Intent:
    fraudulent, 380, 382
    implied employment contracts
      and, 47
    interpretation of insurance
      contract and, 170-172
    in wrongful interference with
      lease, 197
Intentional infliction of emotional
    distress, 51-53
Intentional torts, 224, 334-336
    by employer, workers' compensa-
      tion and, 98
International Accounting Standards
    Committee (IASC), 120
International business law, 24-41. *See*
    also International perspectives
    contract performance and reme-
      dies under, 24-25
    customs and, 29-32
    Europe 1992 and, 40-41
    exports regulated and supported
      by, 24-28
    foreign capital markets and, 35-36
    foreign direct investments and,
      36-40
    imports regulated by, 29-35
    investment risk and, 39-40
International Centre for Settlement of
    Investment Disputes (ICSID),
    39-40
International Institute for the
    Unification of Private Law
    (UNIDROIT), Draft Convention
    on the Hotelkeeper's Contract of,
    342
International Investment Survey Act
    of 1976, 202
International Labour Organization
    (ILO) of United Nations, 100
    Employment Policy Convention
      of, 79-80

International perspectives. *See also*
    International business law
    on accounting standards, 119-120
    on advertising, 261-262
    on attorneys' rights to practice,
      405-406
    on copyright protection, 322-323
    on cross-border broadcasting,
      365-366
    on employment discrimination,
      79-80
    on government contracting,
      386-387
    on health care and AIDS problem,
      299
    on insider trading, 144
    on marketing of motion pictures,
      322
    on occupational safety protection,
      100-101
    on real estate investments, 202
    on takeovers, 165-166
    on trademark protection and grey
      market goods, 239-240
    on waste disposal, 281-282
    on wrongful discharge, 60-61
International Trade Administration
    (ITC), 28, 35
Interstate commerce, 234
Invasion of privacy:
    in employment context, 54
    by press, 361-363
Investment banker, 148
Investment, foreign. *See* Foreign
    investment

J

Japan:
    Bank of, 37
    Commercial Code of, 37
    Constitution of, 61
    corporate acquisitions in, 165
    direct investment in, 36-37
    employment relationships in,
      60-61
    Foreign Exchange and Foreign
      Trade Control Law of, 37
    government contracting practices
      in, 387
    Labor Standards Law of, 61
    loyalty of employees to employers
      in, 8
    Ministry of Finance of, 37, 144
    Securities Exchange Law
      (*Shokentorihikiho*) of, 35, 144
    securities regulation in, 35-36
    U.S. attorneys in, 406
    wrongful discharge in, 60-61
Jockeys, 309
Joint bidding, 28
Joint Commission on Accreditation of
    Hospitals (JCAH), 289-291

Joint venture, 37
Judgment:
    business. *See* Business judgment
        rule
    honest error in, 288
    deficiency, 191
Junk bonds, 148
"Just say no" defense, 157

K

Kabushiki kaisha (Japanese
    corporation), 37

L

Labor Standards Law (Japan), 61
Lanham Act, 231, 234
    private suits under, for deceptive
        advertising, 251-255
Law(s):
    accounting and, 103-121
    advertising, 243-263
    communications, 345-367
    compliance with, and ethics, 2-5
    dram shop, 340
    entertainment, 309-321, 322-323
    environmental, 173, 215-216,
        265-282
    extraterritorial application of, 36
    health care, 283-300
    hospitality management, 325-343
    insurance, 169-186
    international, 24-41
    occupational safety, 83-101
    securities, 123-145
    shield, 356
    sports, 301-309, 321-322
    workers' compensation, 91-99
Leases:
    commercial, 193-197
    covenants in, 195
    implied warranty of suitability
        and, 193-195
    material breach of contract and,
        195-196
    residential, AIDS disclosure and,
        201-202
    tenant's abandonment of premises
        and, 196-197
    wrongful interference with, 197
Legal representation, 389-407
    attorney-client privilege and,
        391-394
    attorney-client relationship and,
        389-391
    of the corporation, 395-400
    cost of, 390
    document retention and destruc-
        tion and, 400
    in-house vs. outside, 400-401
    international perspective on,
        405-406

    settlements and, 398-400
    whistle-blowing and, 404-405
    work product privilege and,
        394-395
Lender liability, 212-217
    common law sources of, 212-213,
        216-217
    contexts of, 213-215
    under environmental law, 215-216
    indirect, 217
    for mortgages, 216-217
    statutory sources of, 215-216
Lending limits, 206
Leveraged buyout (LBO), 148,
    161-163
Liability:
    of accountants. *See* Accountants'
        liability
    antitrust, in health care industry,
        294-297
    in employment context, 43-58,
        68-70
    environmental. *See*
        Environmental law
    of health care providers, 287-294
    of hotels, 326-337
    lender, 212-217
    of mass media, 357-365
    ostensible agency, 288-289
    retroactive, 268
    successor, 272
    vicarious, 288
License:
    broadcast, criteria for, 346-349
    distribution, 25
    general, 25
    validated, 25
Licensing:
    compulsory, for distributed music
        recordings, 316-317
    export, 25-28
    of hotels, 340
    of restaurants, 340
Lie detector tests, 54-55
Lien:
    innkeeper's, 339
    mechanic's, 216
Life-extending technologies, 298
Life insurance, wrongful issuance of,
    183
Likelihood of trademark confusion,
    228-231
Limited liability company (Hungary),
    38
"Limited quantity disclaimer," 251
Liquidated damages, 190
Liquidation, issued by Customs
    Service, 31
Litigation strategies, 401-402
    decision tree analysis and, 403
Lloyds of London, 40

Loans:
    ethical perspective on, 219-220
    lender liability for. *See* Lender
        liability
Lock-up of assets, 148, 155-156
Loyalty, duty of, 7-8, 148-149

M

Malpractice liability:
    of accountants, 103-110
    of attorneys, 397
    of hospitals, 288-289
    of media, 363
    of nurses', 289
    of physicians, 287-288
Management buyout (MBO), 157,
    161-163
Management consulting, 115-118
Management of legal affairs, 400-404.
    See also Legal representation
Manager's privilege, as defense, 224
Marine Mammal Protection Act, 278
Mass media, 345, 363. *See also* Media
Material safety data sheets (MSDS),
    90
Mechanics' lien security interest, 216
Media. *See also* Communications law
    malpractice by, 363
    mass, 345, 363
    ownership of, and licensing, 347
Mediation, 404
Medicaid, 283-284, 287, 292
Medicare, 283-284, 287, 292, 294, 297
Mergers and acquisitions, 147-167.
    See also Takeovers
    by banks, 212
    directors' duties and, 148-159
    going-private, 163
    by hospitals, 297
    second-step, 135, 148, 160-163
    successor liability and, 272
Mexico, direct investment in, 38-39
Migratory Bird Treaty Act, 278
Minimum capital ratios, 206
Minimum compensation law
    (California), 313
Ministry of Finance (Japan), 37, 144
Minority ownership, of media, 347
Misappropriation, advertising and,
    258-259
Misappropriation theory of insider
    trading, 130
Misrepresentation. *See also* Fraud
    by accountant, of financial
        condition, 106
    on insurance application, 179-182
    lender liability for, 217
Monitoring:
    of employment performance, 58
    of government contract
        performance, 377

"Moral minima," 6
Mortgages, 187-190
    collateral for, 187
    default and foreclosure on,
        191-193
    due-on-sale clauses in, 188-189
    lender liability and, 216-217
    liquidated damages for breach of,
        190
    penalty clauses in, 190
    prepayment prohibitions in,
        189-190
Motion pictures, international
    marketing of, 322-323
Multilateral Investment Guarantee
    Agency, 39-40
Multipoint Distribution Service
    (MDS), 354-355
Musical recordings, compulsory
    licensing of, 316-317

N

National Advertising Division
    (NAD), 255
National Advertising Review Board
    (NARB), 255
National Association of Broadcasters,
    257
National Association of
    Intercollegiate Athletics (NAIA),
    301
National Association of Securities
    Dealers (NASD), 137
National Basketball Association
    (NBA), 304
National Broadcast Company,
    255-256
National Collegiate Athletic Associa-
    tion (NCAA), 301-304, 307
    Committee on Infractions of, 304
    "death penalty" rule of, 301
National Football League (NFL),
    304, 307
National Labor Relations Act, 59
National·Machine Tool Builders'
    Association, 28
Negligence:
    in advertising, 259-260
    comparative, 107-108, 329
    contributory, 107-108
    of hospital, 289-291
    of hotel, 326-336
    per se, 260, 329
    requirements for, 260, 326
    wrongful discharge and, 51, 53-54
Negligent misrepresentation, lender
    liability for, 217
Negotiated procurement, 371-374
New Jersey Environmental Clean-Up
    Responsibility Act (ECRA), 279
New York Stock Exchange, 35, 147

Newsgathering rights, 356-357
Newsworthiness, 361
No-shop clause, 155
Notice to insurer, 182-183
Nurses, malpractice by, 289
Nutrition Labeling and Education Act
    of 1990, 257

O

Obscenity, cable television and, 354
Occupational disease, 95
Occupational safety, 83-101
    costs of, 98-99
    employer responsibility for, 88-89,
        98-99
    in international context, 100-101
    OSHA standards for, 83-88, 90-91
Occupational Safety and Health Act
    of 1970:
    general duty clause of, 83-85
    penalties under, 89-90
    special duty clause of, 85-88
Occupational Safety and Health
    Administration (OSHA), 98-99
    hazard communication standard
        of, 90-91
    inspections and citations by, 89
    record-keeping requirements
        imposed by, 91
    safety standards adopted by,
        83-88
Occupational Safety and Health
    Review Commission (OSHRC),
    89, 91
Occupational stress, 95-97
Office of Criminal Enforcement, 275
Office of Export Administration, 24
Office of Technology Assessment, 266
Office of the Comptroller of the
    Currency, 206, 211, 212
Office of the Inspector General (OIG),
    284
Office of the United States Trade
    Representative (USTR), 100
Officers, attorney-client privilege and,
    392-393
Officers, duties of, 7-8
Omnibus Trade Act of 1988, 387
Opinion, defamation vs., 361
Opinion shopping, 115
Opportunistic behavior, 237-239
Oral assurances, and implied employ-
    ment contract, 47
Ostensible agency liability, 288-289
"Outsiders," insider trading by, 130
Overbooking, 337
    ethical perspective on, 341
Overseas Private Investment Corp.
    (OPIC), 40, 100

P

Packard Commission, 385
Paramour liability, 71
Parody, defamation vs., 361
Participation agreements, 213
Patent violations, imported goods
    and, 35
Patient "dumping," 291-292
Peer review organization (PRO)
    system, 284
Penalty clauses, in mortgages, 190
Per se negligence, 260, 329
Performance:
    of government contracts, 377-378
    impossibility of, 7
    of international contracts, 24-25
    monitoring employees', 58
Performers. *See* Entertainment law
Personal injury by accident, 95
Photographs, defamatory, 357
Physicians. *See also* Health care
    AIDS treatment and, 299
    malpractice liability of, 287-288
    Medicare reimbursements for,
        284-287
Plant closing legislation, 58-59
Poison pill, 148, 153-155
    flip-in, 153
    flip-over, 153
Pollution exclusion, 173
Polygraphs, 54-55
Positional risk, doctrine of, 92
Posting, by hotel, 331-332
Predatory pricing, 235
Prehearing discovery, 375
Prepayment prohibitions, 189-190
Presidential Commission of 1986
    (Packard Commission), 385
Price competition, for government
    contracts, 371-374
Price discrimination, 234-237
Pricing:
    defective, by government
        contractors, 380
    predatory, 235
Primary line competition, 235
Privacy rights:
    of cable television subscribers, 354
    of employees, 54-58
    of hotel guests, 339
    invasion of, 54, 361-363
Privilege:
    attorney-client, 391-394
    defamation and, 361
    manager's, 224
    reporter's, 356
    work product, 394-395
Privity of contract, 110
Professional ethics, 19-20. *See also*
    Business ethics; Ethical codes
Professional sports, 304-305

Profit maximization, as ethical duty,
    1-2
Programming, by broadcast media,
    347, 351
Prohibition, repeal of, 257
Promises, 7
Proof:
    burden of. *See* Burden of proof
    of damages, required for malprac-
        tice action, 397
Property of hotel guests, 331-336
Proposition 65 (California), 279
Proximate cause, 260
Proxy, 135
Proxy card, 135
Proxy regulation, 134
Public figures, defamation of, 358-361
Publication requirement, for
    defamation, 54, 358
Punitive damages, 200, 337-338
Purchase and assumption (P&A)
    transaction, 211

Q

Quasi-contract, 370-371
Qui tam actions, 380
Quid pro quo harassment, 67-68
Quito Protocol of 1987, 38

R

Racial discrimination, 63-67
Racketeer Influenced and Corrupt
    Organizations (RICO) Act:
    accountants' liability under, 115
    securities violations and, 124,
        139-142
Radio broadcasting:
    cross-border, 365-366
    regulation of. *See* Federal
        Communications Commission
        (FCC)
    spectrum allocation for, 346
Radio Free Europe, 365
Real estate:
    defined, 187
    foreign investment in U.S., 202
    leasing of. *See* Leases
    residential, AIDS disclosure and,
        201-202
Real estate finance, 187-193
    default and foreclosure and,
        191-193
    government regulation of, 188
    late payment fees and, 190-191
    mortgage for, 187-190. *See also*
        Mortgages
Real estate fraud, 197-201
    broker liability for, 200-201
    constructive, 198-199
    remedies for, 200
    by silence, 199-200

Real Estate Investment Trusts, 187
Real Estate Settlement Procedures Act
    (RESPA) of 1974, 188
Real property. *See* Real estate
Reasonable accommodation, 77-78
Reasonable and prudent physician
    standard, 288
Reasonable expectations doctrine,
    169-172
Reasonable foreseeability test, 112
Record-keeping requirements of
    OSHA, 91
Redemption right, 191
Registration of securities, 123-126. *See
    also* Securities Act of 1933
Regulation S-K, 115
Rehabilitation Act of 1973, 58, 75, 76
Related products rule, 230
Remedies, 24-25
    for deceptive advertising, 248-255
    for fraud, 200
Renewal expectancy, broadcast
    licenses and, 347
Reporter's privilege, 356
Reports, unaudited, 108-109
Rescue, duty of, 329-331
Reservations, for hotel room, 337-339
Reserve clause, 304
Resource Conservation and Recovery
    Act (RCRA), 271, 275-277, 280
Respondeat superior, 68
Restatement (Second) of Contracts,
    195
Restatement (Second) of Torts,
    110-112
Restaurants, licensing and regulation
    of, 340
Restructuring, as takeover defense,
    155
Retirement, voluntary, 74-75
Right-to-die issue, 298
Risk:
    assumption of, 329
    doctrine of increased, 92
Robinson-Patman Act, 234-237
Rule 10b-5, 129, 131-132, 137

S

Safe, provided by hotel, 332-333
Safe Drinking Water Act, 279
Safety:
    of hotel guests, 326-331, 340
    occupational. *See* Occupational
        safety
Sales contracts, international, 23-24
Saving and loan associations, 205
    as sources for mortgages, 187
Scalping, 138
Sealed bid procedures, 371
Second-step merger, 135, 148, 160-163
Secondary line competition, 235

Secondary meaning, of trademark,
    228
Section 1981, 72
Securities Act of 1933, 123-129, 134
    accountants' liability under, 115
    definition of securities and,
        123-125
    Japanese securities law modeled
        on, 35
    registration requirements of,
        125-126
    section 8 of (stop orders), 126
    section 11 of (private actions), 126
    section 12 of (private actions),
        127-129
Securities and Exchange Commission
    (SEC), 36, 71, 114-115, 139, 163
    accountants regulated by, 104,
        114-116
    actions against attorneys by, 395
    broker-dealers regulated by,
        137-138
    corporate governance and, 135
    disclosure of greenmail payments
        required by, 160-161
    important rules and schedules of,
        listed, 137
    insider trading regulated by, 129,
        131-132, 137
    proxy solicitation regulated by,
        135, 137
    review of registration statement
        by, 125-126
    Rule 10b-5 of, 129, 131-132, 137
    stop orders by, 126
    tender offers regulated by, 135-137
    tombstone ads and, 125
Securities Exchange Act of 1934,
    129-140
    accountants' liability under, 115
    amendment to, in 1968 (Williams
        Act), 135-136, 160, 163, 164, 165
    Japanese securities law modeled
        on, 35
    liability under RICO and, 139-142
    section 10(b) of (insider trading,
        fraud), 129-134, 138, 142
    section 14 of (proxy regulation),
        135
    section 15 of (broker-dealer regu-
        lation), 137, 139
Securities Exchange Law (Japan), 35,
    144
Securities fraud, 132-134, 138, 142
Securities laws, 123-145. *See also*
    Securities Act of 1933; Securities
        and Exchange Commission;
        Securities Exchange Act of
        1934
    extraterritorial application of, 36
    in Japan, 35-36, 144
    lender liability under, 215

successor liability under, 272
Self tender, 157
Seller, environmental liability of, 272-273
Setoffs, 217-219
Settlements, 397-400
Sex plus discrimination, 66
Sexual harassment, 67-71
    employer liability for, 68-70
    paramour liability for, 71
Shareholder rights plan, 153-155. *See also* Poison pill
Shareholders:
    appraisal rights of, 163
    auction duties and, 157-159
    supermajority vote of, for merger or takeover, 156
Shark repellant, 156
Sherman Act, 294-295, 297, 302-305
Shield laws, 356
Shipper's Export Declaration, 28
Shokentorihikiho (Japanese Securities Exchange Law), 35, 144
Silence, fraud and, 199-200
Single European Act, 40, 366
Sixth Amendment, 9
Small Business Administration, 374, 375
Small business preference, in government contracting, 374
"Smoking gun" document, 400
Social audits, 18
Social responsibility, in advertising, 260-261
Society of Professional Journalists, 365
Sole source contracting, 374
Solid Waste Disposal Act (Texas), 279
Special damages, 234
Special duty clause, 85-88
Spectators, liability of team owners to, 308
Spectrum allocation, 345-346
Speech. *See* First Amendment; Freedom of speech
Sports, 301-324, 321-322
    amateur, 301-304
    annual player draft in, 305
    antitrust law and, 301-305
    contracts involving, 304
    ethical perspective on, 321-322
    free agency issue in, 304
    private bodies regulating, 301-305
    professional, 304-307
    sports agents and, 305-308, 321-322
    torts, 308-309
Staff, hospital. *See* Hospitals, staff privileges of
Stakeholder rights, in corporate takeover, 164-165

State deceptive trade practices acts, 237-238
State environmental laws, 279-280
Statute(s):
    anti-takeover, 160
    antidilution, 231-234
    control-share acquisition, 160
    of Frauds, 47, 224
    good samaritan, 288
    limiting liability of hotels, 331-332
    on overbooking, 337
Stop orders, by SEC, 126
Stress, occupational, 95-97
Strict liability of innkeeprs, 331
"Subject matter" test, 392
Substantial privity test, 110
Substantially similar test, 314
Suggestive trademark, 227
Suitability, implied warranty of, 193-195
Super-lien, 279
Supermajority vote, 156
Supremacy clause, 160
Suspension, 381, 383
Sweepstakes, 248, 256

T

Takeovers, 147-167. *See also* Mergers and acquisitions
    anti-takeover statutes and, 160
    defenses to, 148, 152-159
    ethical perspective on, 164-165
    factual scenario for, 147-148
    greenmail and, 160-161
    in international context, 165-166
    regulation of, 135-137, 160, 163
Tariff(s):
    common-carrier, 352
    on imported goods. *See* Duties (customs); Imports
Tariff Act of 1930, 31, 35, 239-240
Tax preparation, accountants' liability for, 107
Technology, communications law and, 352-355
Teletext, 355
Television. *See also* Communications law
    cable, 352-354
    "intoxication" by, 320
    spectrum allocation for, 346
"Temporary insiders," 130
Tender offers, 148
    regulation of, 135-137, 160, 163
    two-tier, 152
Termination for convenience, 378-379
Texas Solid Waste Disposal Act, 279
Texas Water Code, 280
Threat/proportionality test, 152, 160
Tipper/tippee theory of insider trading, 130

Title VII of Civil Rights Act of 1964, 63-68, 71-72, 78-80
Tobacco ads, 257
Tokyo Stock Exchange, 35-36
Tombstone ad, 125
Toronto Stock Exchange, 36
Tort(s):
    accountants' liability for, 116-118
    employer's liability for, 68
    intentional, 224, 334-336
    sports, 308-309
    wrongful discharge as, 51-54
Toxic Substances Control Act, 279
Trade Act of 1974, 35
Trade dress, 227
Trademark:
    antidilution statutes protecting, 231-234
    entertainment works protected by, 317
    generic, 227
    infringement of, 227-234
    international protection for, 239-240
    likelihood of confusion of, 228-231
    secondary meaning acquired by, 228
    suggestive, 227
    valid, 227
Trademark Law Revision Act of 1988, 251
Trading:
    cross, 138
    in-and-out, 138
    insider. *See* Insider trading
Transactions with affiliated banks, 206
Treasury shares, 155
Trial, media coverage of, 356-357, 363-365
Truth, as defense to defamation, 358
Truth-in-Lending Act, 188, 340
Truth-in-menu laws, 340
Truth in Negotiations Act, 380, 382
Twenty-First Amendment, 257
Two-tier tender offer, 152

U

Unaudited reports, of accountant, 108-109
Unfair competition, 223-241
    deceptive advertising as. *See* Deceptive advertising
    disparagement as, 234
    ethical perspective on, 238-239
    international perspective on, 239-240
    opportunistic behavior and, 237-239
    price discrimination and, 234-237

under state deceptive trade practices acts, 237-238
trademark infringement as, 227-234, 239-240
wrongful interference with business as, 223-227
Unfair Insurance Practices Act, 179
Unfair Settlement Practices Act, 179
Uniform Commercial Code, compared to Convention on the International Sale of Goods, 24
Unions of performing artists, 311
United Kingdom, mergers and takeovers in, 165-166
United Nations:
Convention for the International Sale of Goods of, 23-24
General Assembly of, 366
International Labour Organization (ILO) of, 100
World Health Organization of, 299
U.S.–Canada free trade pact, 119
U.S. Court of Claims, 377
U.S. Customs Court, 32
U.S. Customs Service, 29-32, 239-240
U.S. Department of Commerce, 24-25, 202
Commodity Control List of, 25
International Trade Administration in, 28
Office of Export Administration in, 24
U.S. Department of Defense, 50, 369, 386
U.S. Department of Health and Human Services, 284
U.S. Department of Housing and Urban Development, 188

U.S. Department of Justice, 163, 275, 386
U.S. Department of State, 25, 28
U.S. Department of the Treasury, 29, 206
U.S. Department of Transportation, 55
U.S. Football League (USFL), 305
U.S. Patent and Trademark Office, 228
Universal Copyright Convention (Berne Convention), 322-323
Unocal test, 152, 160
Unpreventable employee misconduct defense, 84

V

Valid trademark, 227
Validated license, 25
Valuables, of hotel guest, 333
Variance, from OSHA standard, 86
Vicarious liability, 288
Videotext, 355
Voluntary retirement, 74-75

W

"Walkaround rights," 89
Warranties, 24-25
Whistle-blowing, 18, 50
corporate legal counsel and, 404-405
ethical perspective on, 59-60
White knight, 148, 155
White squire, 155
Williams Act of 1968, 135-136, 160, 163, 164, 165
Work product privilege, 394-395

Worker Adjustment and Retraining Notification Act (WARNA) of 1988, 58-59
Workers' compensation, 91-99
administration of, 92
benefits of, 97
costs of, 98-99
employees covered by, 91-92
ethical perspective on, 98-99
exclusivity of, 97-98
injuries covered by, 92-97
"Workers' right-to-know rule," 90
Workplace, safety in. *See* Occupational safety
Works for hire, copyright in, 313-317
World Health Organization (WHO), 299
World Sports & Entertainment, Inc., 307
Wrongful construction eviction claim, 196
Wrongful discharge:
based on breach of implied employment contract, 44
based on public policy, 48-50
in Japan, 60-61
tortious, 44, 54
for whistle-blowing, 50
Wrongful eviction, 336-337
Wrongful interference:
with business, 223-227
with lease, 197